NELSON EDUCATION SERIES
IN HUMAN RESOURCE MANAGEMENT

SECOND EDITION

Industrial Relations in Canada

NELSON EDUCATION SERIES
IN HUMAN RESOURCE MANAGEMENT

SECOND EDITION

Industrial Relations in Canada

Robert Hebdon
McGILL UNIVERSITY

Travor C. Brown
MEMORIAL UNIVERSITY

Series Editor:
Monica Belcourt
YORK UNIVERSITY

NELSON EDUCATION

NELSON / EDUCATION

Industrial Relations in Canada, Second Edition

by Robert Hebdon and Travor C. Brown

Vice President, Editorial Higher Education:
Anne Williams

Senior Acquisitions Editor:
Alwynn Pinard

Marketing Manager:
Dave Stratton

Senior Developmental Editor:
Elke Price

Permissions Coordinator:
Natalie Barrington

Content Production Manager:
Claire Horsnell

Production Service:
MPS Limited, a Macmillan Company

Copy Editor:
Rodney Rawlings

Proofreader:
Susan Fitzgerald

Indexer:
Edwin Durbin

Senior Manufacturing Coordinator:
Joanne McNeil

Design Director:
Ken Phipps

Managing Designer:
Franca Amore

Interior Design:
Katherine Strain

Cover Design:
Martyn Schmoll

Cover Image:
René Mansi/iStock photo

Compositor:
MPS Limited, a Macmillan Company

Printer:
Edwards Brothers

Library and Archives Canada Cataloguing in Publication Data

Hebdon, Robert, 1943-

Industrial relations in Canada/ Robert Hebdon, Travor C. Brown.—2nd ed.

Includes bibliographical references and index.
ISBN 978-0-17-650249-2

1. Industrial relations—Canada—Textbooks. I. Brown, Travor, 1968– II. Title.

HD8104.H43 2011   331.0971
C2011-902429-2

ISBN-13: 978-0-17-650249-2
ISBN-10: 0-17-650249-1

To my wife, Mariana, and children, Tal, Ronen, and Sheri, and their wonderful families.

—Robert Hebdon

To my wife, Andrea, and our three children, Davin, Alexandrea, and Maddison. On a regular basis you prove to me the power of collective bargaining!

—Travor C. Brown

Brief Contents

April 3rd week — 6 chapter

April 4th week — 5 chapters

May 1st week —

Contents

About the Series

The management of human resources has become one of the most important sources of innovation, competitive advantage, and productivity. More than ever, human resources management (HRM) professionals need the knowledge and skills to design HRM policies and practices that not only meet legal requirements but also are effective in supporting organizational strategy. Increasingly, these professionals turn to published research and books on best practices for assistance in the development of effective HR strategies. The books in the *Nelson Series in Human Resources Management* are the best source in Canada for reliable, valid, and current knowledge about practices in HRM.

The texts in this series include

- *Managing Performance Through Training and Development*
- *Management of Occupational Health and Safety*
- *Recruitment and Selection in Canada*
- *Strategic Compensation in Canada*
- *Strategic Human Resources Planning*
- *An Introduction to the Canadian Labour Market*
- *Research, Measurement, and Evaluation of Human Resources*
- *Industrial Relations in Canada*
- *International Human Resource Management: A Canadian Perspective*

The *Nelson Series in Human Resources Management* represents a significant development in the field of HRM for many reasons. Each book in the series is the first, and now best-selling, text in the functional area. Furthermore, HR professionals in Canada must work with Canadian laws, statistics, policies, and values. This series serves their needs. It is the only set of HRM books, standardized in presentation, that provides students and practitioners with complete access to information across many HRM disciplines. The books are essential sources of information that meet the requirements for the CCHRA (Canadian Council of Human Resources Associations) National Knowledge Exam for the academic portion of the HR certification process. This one-stop resource will prove useful to anyone looking for solutions for the effective management of people.

The publication of this series signals that the field of human resources management has advanced to the stage where theory and applied research guide practice. The books in the series present the best and most current research in the functional areas of HRM. Research is supplemented with examples of the best practices used by Canadian companies that are leaders in HRM. Each text begins with a general model of the discipline and then describes the implementation of effective strategies. Thus, the books serve as an introduction to the functional area for the new student of HR and as a validation source for the more experienced HRM practitioner. Cases, exercises, and endnotes provide opportunities for further discussion and analysis.

As you read and consult the books in this series, I hope you share my excitement in being involved and knowledgeable about a profession that has such a significant impact on organizational goals and employees' lives.

Monica Belcourt, Ph.D., CHRP
Series Editor
May 2011

About the Authors

Robert Hebdon

Professor Bob Hebdon joined McGill University's Faculty of Management in 2000. After graduating from the University of Toronto with an M.A. in economics in 1968, he worked for the Ontario Public Service Employees Union for 24 years. He completed his Ph.D. in industrial relations at the Centre for Industrial Relations at the University of Toronto in 1992. His academic career began at Cornell University, where he taught collective bargaining for seven years at the School of Industrial Relations. In 1999, he taught at the University of Manitoba in the Faculty of Management. Professor Hebdon also has experience as a neutral in labour–management relations, acting as an arbitrator in Ontario. He won the 2007 Morley Gunderson Prize in Industrial Relations in recognition of his outstanding professional achievement and his significant service to the Centre for Industrial Relations and Human Resources at the University of Toronto.

His research interests include public-sector labour relations and restructuring, collective bargaining, dispute resolution, and industrial conflict. He has published in a wide variety of major journals including *American Economic Review, Industrial and Labor Relations Review, Berkeley Journal of Industrial Relations, Journal of Policy Analysis and Management, Relations industrielles, Journal of Collective Negotiations in the Public Sector, Labor Studies Journal*, and *Arbitration Yearbook*.
http://people.mcgill.ca/robert.hebdon

Travor C. Brown

Dr. Travor C. Brown is the Director of the Master of Employment Relations (MER) Program and a Professor, Labour Relations & Human Resources Management, at Memorial University. Since joining Memorial University, he has received several teaching and research awards. He has also taught at the University of Toronto and University of Ulster (Northern Ireland). He holds a B.A. (Memorial University), a Master of Industrial Relations (University of Toronto), and a Ph.D. in Industrial Relations (University of Toronto).

Prior to taking academic appointments, Dr. Brown worked with Nortel Networks and Abitibi-Price. With these firms, he gained extensive real-world labour relations and human resources experience in Canada and the United States. This industry experience continues today, as Dr. Brown regularly provides consulting services to a number of private, public, and nonprofit organizations.

Dr. Brown's research tends to focus on areas related to diversity/equity, training and development, and performance appraisal. Many of his studies have taken place in unionized workplaces. His work has been published in several journals including *Personnel Psychology, Journal of Management Education, Relations industrielles, Canadian Journal of Administrative Sciences, Human Resources Development Quarterly, Applied Psychology: An International Review*, and *Small Group Research*.
http://www.busi.mun.ca/travorb

Preface

The field of industrial relations is both complex and fascinating. At its heart, it examines the relationship between three actors: labour (employees and their associations), management (employers and their associations), and government and associated agencies. Over the past few years, shifts in the makeup of the Canadian economy, changes in the demographics of the work force, and ongoing difficulties related to technological and legal frameworks have proven challenging to all three actors.

It is indeed an interesting time to study the field of industrial relations, and the authors are delighted to launch the second edition of *Industrial Relations in Canada* during this period of change. Before completing Ph.D.s at the University of Toronto and joining academia, the authors of this textbook were practitioners in the field and therefore offer a unique perspective. Robert Hebdon worked for several years with the Ontario Public Service Employees Union (OPSEU), while Travor Brown worked in a variety of human resources and labour relations roles with Abitibi-Price and Nortel Networks. Moreover, their collective experience includes public-, private-, and nonprofit-sector as well as U.S. and Canadian work experience. This combination of academic and "real world" experience is apparent throughout the chapters of this textbook:

1. Introduction
2. The Legal Environment
3. Economic, Social, and Political Environments
4. Labour History
5. The Union Perspective
6. The Management Perspective
7. Negotiations
8. Collective Agreement Administration
9. Strikes and Dispute Resolution
10. Impacts of Unionization
11. Public-Sector Issues
12. Globalization of Labour Markets

Given the authors' combination of practical and academic experience, this text is grounded in leading research and examines true-to-life issues. Each chapter starts with an opening vignette, contains a minimum of two inserts (labelled "IR Today" and "IR Notebook") concerning authentic IR issues, and includes examples, many from real Canadian organizations. In addition, each chapter ends with a case, discussion questions, and Internet exercises. All these elements are designed to bridge the academic content of the text and the real-world issues in the field. Additionally, since many students may pursue a career in human resources, each chapter includes RPC (Required Professional Capabilities) icons, which represent the learning objectives for the Certified Human Resources Professional (CHRP) designation. Also, a Weblink icon appears in the margin of the text and the web addresses can be found at the end of each chapter. Given the vast quantity of material readily available on the popular website YouTube, we have also included numerous YouTube references in this edition. These too are marked with a Weblink icon.

As former students, we appreciate the need for key points and hands-on activities. Therefore, we have included learning objectives at the beginning of every chapter, key terms in bold in the text and in the margins (and at the end of each chapter), and end-of-chapter summaries. We have also included two collective bargaining simulations and several arbitration cases. These activities can be assigned by the instructor to give students a taste of the topic at hand from a practitioner's perspective.

We hope that students and instructors will find the second edition of this textbook helpful as they seek to understand this dynamic area. We look forward to their feedback and suggestions for future editions.

Additional Resources

Ancillaries for Instructors

 The **Nelson Education Teaching Advantage (NETA)** program delivers research-based resources that promote student engagement and higher-order thinking and enable the success of Canadian students and educators.

Recognizing the importance of multiple-choice testing in today's classroom and in response to instructors' concerns, Nelson Education has created the *NETA Assessment* program, a research-based program that improves the quality of our test banks by ensuring that they measure not just recall (as is typical with test banks) but also *higher-level thinking* skills.

The program was created in partnership with David DiBattista, a 3M National Teaching Fellow, professor of psychology at Brock University, and researcher in the area of multiple-choice testing.

All NETA test banks include David DiBattista's guide for instructors, *Multiple Choice Tests: Getting Beyond Remembering.* This guide has been designed to assist you in using Nelson test banks to achieve the desired outcomes in your course.

Instructor's Resource CD (0-17-661743-4)

Key instructor ancillaries are provided on the *Instructor's Resource CD,* giving instructors the ultimate tool for customizing lectures and presentations. The IRCD includes:

- **Instructor's Manual.** The Instructor's Manual to accompany Industrial Relations in Canada, Second Edition has been prepared by the text's authors, Robert Hebdon and Travor Brown. This manual contains learning objectives, chapter summaries, suggested classroom activities, and suggested answers to all end-of-chapter Discussion Questions, Using the Internet features, Exercises, and Cases, and teaching notes for the end-of-book Simulations to give you the support you need to engage your students within the classroom.
- **NETA Assessment.** The Test Bank was written by Shelagh Campbell, Saint Mary's University. It includes over 420 multiple-choice questions written according to NETA guidelines for effective construction and

development of higher-order questions. Also included are true/false and short answer questions.

Test Bank files are provided in Word format for easy editing and in PDF format for convenient printing whatever your system.

The Computerized Test Bank by ExamView® includes all the questions from the Test Bank. The easy-to-use ExamView software is compatible with Microsoft Windows and Mac platforms. Create tests by selecting questions from the question bank, modifying these questions as desired, and adding new questions you write yourself. You can administer quizzes online and export tests to WebCT, Blackboard, and other formats.

- **Microsoft® PowerPoint®.** Key concepts from *Industrial Relations in Canada, Second Edition* are presented in PowerPoint format, with generous use of figures and short tables from the text. The PowerPoint presentation was created by Shelagh Campbell, Saint Mary's University.

- **Image Library.** This resource consists of digital copies of figures and short tables used in the book. Instructors may use these jpegs to create their own PowerPoint presentations.

- **DayOne.** Day One—Prof InClass is a PowerPoint presentation that you can customize to orient your students to the class and their text at the beginning of the course.

Website (http://www.hrm.nelson.com)

- All instructor's resources can be downloaded directly from the book's companion site.

Ancillaries for Students

Website (http://www.hrm.nelson.com)

- The second edition is supported by our student companion website. The site contains chapter quiz questions allowing students to self-test their understanding of chapter concepts.

Acknowledgments

As we move to the second edition of this textbook, we need to acknowledge and thank the many people who aided us in the process. While our names may appear on the cover, this text would have never come to life without the assistance of the following people.

First are the reviewers who took the time to read (and provide feedback on) early versions of the chapters. Their helpful suggestions resulted in a number of improvements to the text, and we thank each of them: Shelagh Campbell (Saint Mary's University), Gordon Cooke (Memorial University), Joseph B. Rose (McMaster University), and Scott Walsworth (University of Saskatchewan). We would also like to acknowledge many others who assisted in reviewing the first edition of this text book: Gordon Cooke (Memorial University), Randy Joseph (University of Lethbridge), Lori Buchart (Mount Royal College), Ted Mock (Seneca College), and Tim Bartkiw (Ryerson University).

Second, we thank the research assistants who spent many hours online, at the library, or editing chapters: Adrian Beaton and Vipul Khatter. We also thank research assistants who assisted us with the previous edition: Kimberly Chaulk, Tara-Lynn Hillier, Krista Stringer, David Parsons, Christian Keen, and Elliot Siemiatycki. Your efforts greatly enhanced the manuscript.

Third, we thank our colleagues, students (past and present), as well as our friends currently working in the field for their ideas, their feedback, and their "sympathetic ears" as we went through this process. In particular, we thank Scott Walsworth and Andrew Luchak, who allowed us to incorporate material from them into our bargaining and arbitration exercises.

Fourth, in many cases the examples we used in this textbook came from friends and contacts currently working in the field of industrial relations. Our thanks to you for providing us with ideas we could incorporate into the text as we tried to "make the content real."

Fifth, we cannot thank enough the team at Nelson—Elke Price, Developmental Editor; Alwynn Pinard, Acquisitions Editor; Claire Horsnell, Content Production Manager; Dave Stratton, Marketing Manager; Natalie Barrington, Permissions Researcher; Monica Belcourt, Series Editor; and Rodney Rawlings, Copy Editor—for their assistance and support. We are lucky to have had such a dedicated team of supporters guiding us each step of the way.

Finally, we thank our families, for their ongoing support and love.

CHAPTER 1

Introduction

Learning Objectives

By the end of this chapter, you will be able to discuss

- the similarities and differences between such terms as *labour relations, human resources, employment relations,* and *industrial relations;*
- a systems framework that can be used to assess and understand industrial relations issues;
- the differing views in the field of industrial relations; and
- how this textbook is structured to follow the industrial relations system framework.

The subway stops, the chime sounds, the doors open, and Rajeev Verma and Ashley Cooke enter the train to look for seats. They have about a 30-minute ride before they reach the stop for Ryerson, where they are both taking classes. Ashley looks at Rajeev and says, "Have you seen the news today? York is still on strike. My roommate, Robyn, is really worried."

Rajeev nods, "I know. Remember my brother Sudhir is going to York as well. He told me that they may lose the entire term if this does not end soon. What a mess."

Ashley opens a newspaper and sees several stories related to the strike. "Hey, Rajeev, guess what? Sudhir's right. According to this article, there is a risk that classes will extend into May, or worse yet, that the entire semester will be lost, if the strike does not end soon."

Rajeev looks at her in disbelief. "Are you serious? Sudhir will not be impressed." Leaning over to read the article, he asks, "What else does it say?"

"Let's see. . . . It says that the government may bring in special legislation to end the strike . . . that a mediator was brought in to try and settle the strike, and that a ratification vote was supervised by a representative from the Ontario Ministry of Labour."

Rajeev says, "I really wish I better understood the issues concerning industrial relations. I have no idea what a ratification vote is? Do you?"

Ashley laughs. "Studying engineering. I can tell you about how the subway operates, but I have absolutely no idea about unions or industrial relations."

Sources: L. Brown, "School year at risk as strike drags on," *The Star*, 15 December 2008, retrieved 22 December 2010 from http://www.thestar.com/News/GTA/article/553759; Canwest News Service, "McGuinty to introduce back-to-work legislation to end York strike," *The Calgary Herald*, 24 January 2009, retrieved 22 December 2010 from http://www.calgaryherald.com/Business/Ontario+legislate+York+strike/1214791/story.html.

Important Terms Related to Industrial Relations

Shakespeare is often credited with the expression "What's in a name? that which we call a rose/By any other name would smell as sweet." The issue of names is certainly important to this text and the field we are studying. Employment relationships between employers (and their management groups) and employees (unionized or not) can be characterized in a number of ways. In this section of the book, we will review and discuss several of the common names (or terms) relevant to the field of industrial relations. As you will see, there is considerable diversity in the terms used in this field:

- industrial relations
- labour relations
- human resources management (human resources)
- employee relations
- employment relations

Industrial Relations

The term *industrial relations* has often been used by academics to examine all employment issues and relationships between employees (and their **union** if they are unionized), employers (and managers who act on their behalf), and governmental agencies (as well as their associated legislation and policies). As a result, the field of industrial relations has been argued to include the study of both union and nonunion employment relationships.

However, in industry, the term **industrial relations** has become synonymous with issues concerning unionized employment relationships. Perhaps because of the association of *industrial relations* with unionized work relationships, many people would argue that *industrial relations* focuses almost exclusively on issues related to unionized employment relationships. In fact, perhaps because of the narrowing view of the term, some academic programs have changed names in recent years. For example, the Master of Industrial Relations (MIR) degree at the University of Toronto has become the Master of Industrial Relations and Human Resources (MIRHR), and the Centre for Industrial Relations has become the Centre for Industrial Relations and Human Resources. In contrast, a similar program offered at Queen's University continues to use the MIR designation. (See the Weblinks section at the end of this chapter.)

Labour Relations

The term **labour relations** refers to the examination of the relationship between groups of employees (usually labour unions) and their employers (including management groups). Consequently, the term is often considered interchangeable with *union–management relations* and has often focused on issues concerning collective employment relationships (e.g., **collective agreements, collective bargaining, strikes**).

Noah Meltz, an influential scholar in Canadian industrial relations, often used Barbash's (1987) equity–efficiency theory to define employment relationships. Barbash argued that employers usually focus on efficiency (e.g., production/service levels, costs, productivity) while unions and employees most often concentrate on equity (e.g., fair workplace practices). Therefore, it can be argued that *labour relations* refers to the balance between equity and efficiency (Meltz, 1997).

union

a group of workers recognized by law who collectively bargain terms and conditions of employment with their employer

industrial relations

the study of employment relationships and issues, often in unionized workplaces

labour relations

the study of employment relationships and issues between groups of employees (usually in unions) and management; also known as *union–management relations*

collective agreement

a written document outlining the terms and conditions of employment in a unionized workplace

Human Resources Management

Whereas *labour relations* examines collective employment relationships between groups of employees (usually in labour unions) and their employer, **human resources** focuses on the employment relationship between the individual employee and his or her manager or employer. In brief, the field of human resources typically examines issues related to selection, training, performance appraisal, and compensation. More details about human resources can be found in Chapter 6.

Given the focus on the individual employee–employer relationship in the human resources field, Meltz (1997) argued that human resources is mostly efficiency-focused but that it also considers issues associated with equity and fairness. This may be a result of how human resources management scholars and practitioners are trained and educated. For example, human resources courses are often taught in business schools, where the concentration is arguably on the efficient running of the business. However, as we point out in Chapter 6, fairness is certainly a key element in current human resources thinking and practices.

Employee Relations

Like *human resources*, the phrase **employee relations** has also been used to describe the employment relationship between individual employees and their employers, particularly in the United States. In fact, in the labour movement, it has often been considered a strong anti-union term. In Canada, we see the term used in differing contexts, including unionized workplaces. For instance, Alberta's *Public Service Employee Relations Act* relates to unionized, public-sector employees, and there are unions who use the term *employee relations* in some of their staff's titles. Likewise, the Nova Scotia Government and General Employees Union (NSGEU) website uses the term *employee relations officers* for some of its staff's roles. Given the diversity in perspectives concerning the term *employee relations*, it will not be used in this text.

Employment Relations

Employment relations is a relatively new term. It was proposed by Meltz (1997), in essence, to be the new phrase to represent the comprehensive study of all employment relations (i.e., union and nonunion). The term has started to be used more frequently in the field and Memorial University now offers a graduate designation with the title Master of Employment Relations (MER) degree.

Industrial Relations and This Textbook

Because there are a variety of terms representing different forms of employment relationships, it is important that we map out the focus of this text. Both authors of this text have been schooled in the field of industrial relations and, more specifically, completed graduate education centred on the broader definition of *industrial relations* as the comprehensive study of all employment relationships (both union and nonunion). As a result, we use industrial relations frameworks to examine issues relevant to this text. In addition, the focus of much of this text will be on issues related to union–management or labour relations. For example, you will see chapters examining contract administration, collective bargaining, strikes, etc. To better understand some of the core industrial frameworks used to examine employment relationships, we now turn to a discussion of the industrial relations system framework that grounds this text.

The Industrial Relations System

Unlike other courses you may have taken, the field of industrial relations is relatively new. It is an interdisciplinary field that encompasses knowledge and scholars from areas such as economics, law, history, sociology, psychology, and political science in an effort to examine employment relationships and issues. For example, economic scholars may examine the impact of unions

legal aids.
4 certificate
1800-668-8258
Bail conditions.

IR Today 1.1

Relevant Journals

As we discuss in this chapter, the field of industrial relations is studied in many social science disciplines. Since you may be assigned term papers concerning matters related to employment relationships or wish to further your study of certain topics, the following list of journals may be helpful. Articles from many of these journals were referenced in the creation of this textbook. Journals with a Canadian focus are marked with an asterisk.

- Academy of Management Journal
- Administrative Science Quarterly
- American Sociological Review
- British Journal of Industrial Relations
- Canadian Journal of Administrative Sciences*
- Canadian Public Policy*
- Employee Relations
- Employee Relations Law Journal
- European Journal of Industrial Relations
- Human Relations
- Human Resource Management
- Industrial and Labor Relations Review

- Industrial Relations (Berkeley)
- Industrial Relations Journal
- Journal of Applied Psychology
- Journal of Industrial Relations
- Journal of Management
- Journal of Management Studies
- Journal of Occupational and Organizational Psychology
- Journal of Organizational Behavior
- Journal of Social Psychology
- Journal of Vocational Behavior
- Labor Law Journal
- Labour/Le Travail*
- Organization Studies
- Organizational Behavior and Human Decision Processes
- Personnel Psychology
- Relations industrielles/Industrial Relations*
- Sociology
- Work & Stress
- Work, Employment, and Society

on wages; law scholars may examine the impact of legislation on access to unionization; history scholars may examine the evolving and historical nature of employment relationships; sociology scholars may examine the dynamics and processes involved in workgroups; psychology scholars may look at issues related to employee satisfaction and motivation; and political science scholars may examine issues related to the roles of unions in the political process. Given the broad scope of the topic, attempts to build unifying frameworks and theories are relatively new, dating back only to the 1950s. In this section, we will present the two most commonly used system frameworks in North America, namely, that of American John Dunlop and that of Canadian Alton Craig.

Dunlop's Industrial Relations System Model

John Dunlop was one of the first scholars to develop a systematic method to analyze employment relationships in North America. This model consists of actors, a shared ideology, and contexts, as well as a web of rules.

Actors

When Dunlop studied employment relationships and issues, he described three distinct actors:

SPECIALIZED GOVERNMENTAL AGENCIES The role of this actor is to develop, implement, and administer legislation and policies pertinent to the employment relationship.

A HIERARCHY OF MANAGERS AND THEIR REPRESENTATIVES This actor represents the business owners and the management staff hired to run the business. The role of this actor is to manage the workers and workplace in question. As we usually consider employment issues on a firm-by-firm basis, we often look at a single management actor when examining an employment relationship (e.g., see the opening vignette in which the employer is York University). Yet there are also a number of associations that represent groups of employers. A current example would be the Newfoundland & Labrador Employers' Council (NLEC), whose website sees its role as providing "advocacy, communication and training for its members in matters that affect the employment relationship."

When examining this actor, it is important to focus on the employment relationship at hand. Remember, both unions and governments employ staff and can thus represent the actor of management.

A HIERARCHY OF WORKERS (NONMANAGEMENT) AND ANY SPOKESPERSONS This actor represents the nonmanagement workers in the employment relationship and any relevant associations. In most cases, these associations consist of labour unions representing the workers.

Shared Ideology

As we will discuss in Chapter 4, the North American employment relationship might be described as "bread-and-butter-focused." Unlike more radical approaches in Europe, where labour leaders sought to overthrow employers and have workers own and run workplaces, in North America unions have traditionally sought to get "the best deal" for their members. In so doing, they have been seen to accept the business-oriented and capital-based economy in which business owners manage their firms with the goal of earning profit.

Thus, Dunlop's (1958, p. 16) system discussed the concept of shared ideology, or "a set of ideas and beliefs commonly held by the actors that helps to bind or integrate the system together as an entity." This shared ideology was seen to define the role and function of each of the actors and required that all three actors respect and value the roles of the other two. Dunlop further stresses that industrial stability depends on the three actors sharing this ideology. In this way, the shared ideology legitimatized the role of each actor in the eyes of the other two.

Contexts

Dunlop envisioned that the three actors might be influenced by any of several environmental contexts:

MARKET AND BUDGETARY CONSTRAINTS   While Dunlop focused mostly on the product market, he saw two key areas as critical to the employment relationship: product and labour. As we will discuss in Chapter 5, unions seek to influence both the supply and the demand of labour—labour that employers require for production of goods and services. In so doing, unions can impact the wages employees earn, as well as the final cost of the product/service that is produced by the organization. As such, the issue of budgetary constraints becomes key, particularly for the actor of management.

TECHNICAL CHARACTERISTICS OF THE WORKPLACE AND WORK COMMUNITY   This context focuses on how work is structured and performed, including such factors as the processes used to produce goods and services, the stability of the work force and operations, the size of the workgroup, job tasks, hours of work, and the technology/machinery used.

DISTRIBUTION OF POWER IN THE LARGER SOCIETY   This context examines the power relationship among the actors within a particular employment relationship in the broader society. In particular, Dunlop (1958, p. 11) noted that the distribution of power among the actors reflects "their prestige, position, and access to authority figures within the larger society [that] shapes and constrains an industrial relations system." While the power distribution within the larger society is not seen to determine the relative power of the actors in the system, it does play an important role. For example, a more business-friendly government may pass legislation that better empowers the employer.

This is important because the actor with the most power will have the greatest ability to influence both the dynamics of the employment relationship and the terms and conditions of employment.

Web of Rules

Perhaps the most complicated and contested element of Dunlop's system is the web of rules. Dunlop discussed that the employment relationship consisted of a web of rules that outlined the rights and responsibilities of the actors in question. More specifically, he presented three key elements concerning rules.

PROCEDURES FOR ESTABLISHING RULES   This element focuses on the processes used for making the rules and who has the authority to make and administer the rules that govern the workplace.

distributive

SUBSTANTIVE RULES   These rules pertain to outcomes of the employment relationship—for example, for the employee, compensation, job and performance expectations, and worker rights and duties.

PROCEDURAL RULES   Dunlop envisioned procedural rules as those rules that could determine and/or apply substantive rules—for example, rules concerning how wages are determined, rules concerning work schedules, and rules concerning how an employee is able to use or earn vacation time.

Criticisms of Dunlop's Industrial Relations System

There is no doubt that both Dunlop and his systems model have made significant impacts on the field of industrial relations, some scholars arguing that "no one has put together as long and as distinguished a record" as he (Kaufman, 2002, p. 324). As outlined by several authors, there has been considerable debate concerning the merits of Dunlop's systems approach over the past 30 years (Craig, 1988; Hyman, 1989; Kochan, Katz & McKersie, 1986; Meltz & Adams, 1993; Wood, Wagner, Armstrong, Goodman & Davis, 1975). A number of criticisms of Dunlop's systems approach follow.

First, the model is descriptive in nature, as it essentially consists of a classification system. Thus, while it allows us to examine an industrial relations issue, it lacks the ability to predict outcomes and/or relationships.

Second, the model underestimates the importance of power and conflict in the employment relationship. For example, the model assumes the concept of shared ideology—that all actors see a legitimate role for each of the three actors. As we will see in greater detail in Chapter 6, many scholars are questioning this concept of shared ideology, particularly as it relates to the importance and role of labour unions.

Third, the model is static in nature. At no point does it examine how events from one employment relationship can impact other employment relationships, or even the same relationship at a later time.

Fourth, the model cannot provide an explanation for the rapid decrease in unionization, particularly in the United States. Rather, the framework is often assumed to ground itself in the premise of unionized workplaces being the norm.

In summary, Dunlop's model is a classic work in the field of industrial relations that will continue to be studied for years to come. However, as is often the case with the first model in any discipline, it has been, and will continue to be, expanded upon by subsequent work. In the Canadian context, one of the most studied expansions of Dunlop's model is that of Craig (1967, 1988; see also revision in Craig & Solomon, 1996). Readers familiar with the sciences will note that Craig's model is similar to the systems models used in biology. In biology, we see that a plant takes air from the environment and, through a series of internal conversion systems, takes the carbon dioxide it needs and then releases oxygen back into the environment. Similarly, in Craig's model, we see that the industrial relations actors take elements from the external environment and convert these inputs into outputs through a series of conversion mechanisms. These outputs then flow back into the environment through a **feedback loop**. Figure 1.1 shows our adaptation of Craig's model. As this expanded systems framework will form the basis of this textbook, we will now take time to walk through it.

feedback loop
the mechanism by which outputs of the industrial relations system flow back to the external environment

FIGURE 1.1

Industrial Relations System Model[1]

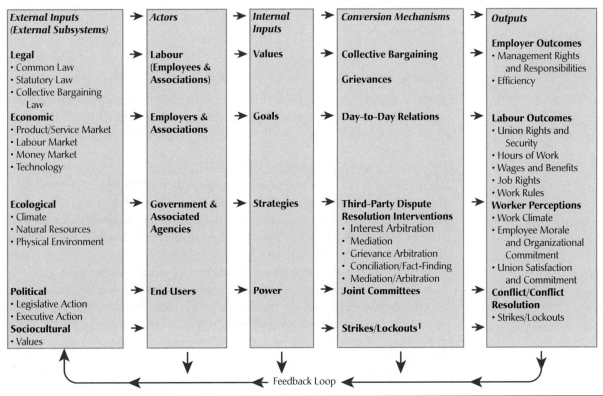

External Inputs (External Subsystems)	Actors	Internal Inputs	Conversion Mechanisms	Outputs
Legal • Common Law • Statutory Law • Collective Bargaining Law	**Labour (Employees & Associations)**	**Values**	**Collective Bargaining** **Grievances**	**Employer Outcomes** • Management Rights and Responsibilities • Efficiency
Economic • Product/Service Market • Labour Market • Money Market • Technology	**Employers & Associations**	**Goals**	**Day-to-Day Relations**	**Labour Outcomes** • Union Rights and Security • Hours of Work • Wages and Benefits • Job Rights • Work Rules
Ecological • Climate • Natural Resources • Physical Environment	**Government & Associated Agencies**	**Strategies**	**Third-Party Dispute Resolution Interventions** • Interest Arbitration • Mediation • Grievance Arbitration • Conciliation/Fact-Finding • Mediation/Arbitration	**Worker Perceptions** • Work Climate • Employee Morale and Organizational Commitment • Union Satisfaction and Commitment
Political • Legislative Action • Executive Action	**End Users**	**Power**	**Joint Committees**	**Conflict/Conflict Resolution** • Strikes/Lockouts
Sociocultural • Values			**Strikes/Lockouts**[1]	

← Feedback Loop ←

[1]Adapted from: Craig, A.W.J., and Solomon, N.A. (1996). *The System of Industrial Relations in Canada*, 5th edition, pg. 4. Toronto, Ontario: Prentice Hall Canada Inc. Reprinted with permission by Pearson Canada, Inc.

1.1

External Inputs

The left-hand side of the model shows that several external inputs (or environmental subsystems) are important elements of the industrial relations system. These inputs can be legal, economic, ecological, political, or sociocultural in nature.

Legal Subsystem

In Chapter 2, we more fully discuss the importance of the legal subsystem in industrial relations. In brief, three areas of law are key to the study of industrial relations: (1) common law, which is the earliest form of employment law and applies to nonunion employment relationships; (2) statutory law, or laws concerning minimum employment standards and employment discrimination, covering issues such as minimum wage, overtime payment, and employers' discrimination based on factors not linked to job performance (e.g., race, gender, age)—note that these laws apply to union and nonunion employment relationships; and (3) collective bargaining law, or legislation pertaining to unionized employment relationships.

It is also important to note that Canada has a decentralized legal framework, with most provinces having their own provincial laws. In fact, with the exception of industries key to national safety and security (e.g., communication, interprovincial transportation, railways, airlines, banks), most workplaces fall under provincial legislation. The York case discussed in the opening vignette is an example, and would be subject to Ontario legislation.

Economics Subsystem

Since Chapter 3 provides a full overview of the economics subsystem, this section will just briefly introduce four key elements to this subsystem: product/service markets, labour markets, money markets, and technology.

One can think of product/service markets in terms of the availability of products or services from competitors as well as an organization's relative competitive position in its market (e.g., Does it have a large market share? Does it face considerable competition from other service/product suppliers?). This being so, the product/service market can play a large role in industrial relations. For example, the movement to Internet-based shopping means that Canadian retailers face competition from firms in numerous countries. In many cases, employers' collective bargaining proposals will be based on factors related to the product/service market (e.g., the impact of the union's suggested wage increase on the total product/service cost, how wage increases and associated costs compare to competitors' costs, etc.).

Labour markets can be thought of in terms of the supply of, and demand for, workers with the skills needed for the workplace in question. As we will discuss in Chapter 4, issues related to labour markets have been important to the history of industrial relations and can play a significant role in any employment relationship. Often, actors of the system will examine issues related to the number of employees available (or labour supply) and the number of employees needed (or demand for labour). For example, unions will often encourage employment practices that limit the employer's ability to use contact labour; management will often seek flexibility to use alternative sources of labour (contractors, temporary employees, etc.).

Money markets also play a key role in the industrial relations system. As outlined by the Bank of Canada (2010; also Côté, 2011), the Canadian economy is impacted by global issues, in particular those of its largest trading partner, the United States. Consequently, issues concerning the money market are very important. If, for example, the Canadian dollar increases in value by 5 percent, relative to American currency, a Canadian product then costs 5 percent more in the United States, based only on money market factors. Conversely, if the **exchange rate** drops 5 percent relative to the U.S. dollar, Canadian products are then 5 percent cheaper in the States. It is also important to remember that the Bank of Canada can also adjust **interest rates** on the basis of exchange rates and that interest rates can impact **inflation** (Bank of Canada, 2006, 2010). For these reasons, actors of the industrial relations system, whether or not they are involved in exporting or importing products and services, can be impacted by the money market.

exchange rate
the value of one country's currency relative to another country's currency

interest rate
the rate a bank charges for borrowing money

inflation
the increase in prices over time

Technology can impact the industrial relations system in a number of ways. It can result in new work methods, job redesign, and, in some cases, layoffs or lower levels of employment as fewer employees may be needed. For example, technology allows work to be performed almost anywhere in the world, particularly in the technology and call-centre industries. In fact, we even see companies in emerging markets such as India marketing their "cost-efficient" services (Call Center India, 2011).

Ecological Subsystem

The ecological subsystem includes the physical environment, climate, and natural resources that influence actors and the industrial relations system. For example, the large concentration of petroleum-based companies in Alberta is largely due to the availability of natural resources (i.e., oil) in that province, the physical environment (i.e., access to the Pacific Ocean) explains the importance of shipping employment in British Columbia, and the presence of iron ore explains the prevalence of mining in Labrador. In addition, the climate, in terms of seasons and weather, can influence when unions would likely strike (e.g., snowplow operators in Winnipeg would gain little from an August strike).

Political Subsystem

Canada's political subsystem is founded on a form of democracy in which citizens elect politicians to represent them in various forms of government (i.e., municipal, provincial, federal). These governments have the ability to

mandatory retirement

a requirement that employees retire at age 65

pass legislation. In the industrial relations field, governments use legislative action to create and amend legislation relative to employment issues. For example, over the past decade, we have seen a number of governments amend legislation related to ending **mandatory retirement**—forcing workers into retirement at age 65 (Warren & Kelloway, 2010).

Governments can also use executive action (e.g., passing emergency legislation to end a strike). The first usage of such legislation in the federal jurisdiction was in the railway sector in 1950 (Library of Parliament, 2011). However, as suggested by the opening York University strike vignette, the practice continues today.

Sociocultural

values

a set of standards or principles

The **values** and beliefs of the society in which the actors operate can also influence the actors, providing a sense of what is perceived as being fair and appropriate in terms of the employment relationship. In fact, we often see public opinion survey results reported in the media during large strikes (McLintock, 2004). Turning to the York strike example that opened this chapter, we even see the use of a blog geared toward undergraduate students (YorkStrike2008, 2008). Information from such sources can be used by both sides to gauge the extent to which the public supports the positions of labour and/or management.

Actors

The actors of the industrial relations system are influenced by the previously discussed external inputs. The actors shown in Figure 1.1 mirror those of Dunlop (1958) and include

- labour (employees and their associations);
- employers and their associations; and
- government and associated agencies.

In subsequent chapters, we will provide more details on each of these actors and their roles in the industrial relations system. Note that we have added a fourth actor, the end user of the services/products generated from the employment relationship in question. We have added this fourth actor because scholars now note the importance of the end user in the industrial relations system (Bellemare, 2000).

Internal Inputs

goal

that which a person seeks to obtain or achieve

While the actors of the system are influenced by the external inputs, they, too, provide inputs to the system in terms of their values, goals, strategies, and power. Each actor of the system will have values that guide their actions. Using Barbash's (1987) equity–efficiency theory, we could argue that employers may hold the values of profitability and competitive advantage and that these values will influence their actions; in contrast, labour may hold values relative to fair treatment of workers, and these equity values may guide their actions. These differing values would cause employers to develop **goals** that maximize efficiency, while labour would seek to maximize equity.

Industrial Relations in Canada

Strategies would then be developed by both actors to achieve their desired goals. The relative **power** of the actors would help determine which parties' goals were achieved.

Conversion Mechanisms

The processes that the actors use to convert internal and external inputs into outputs of the industrial relations system are known as **conversion mechanisms**. Note that many of these conversion mechanisms are akin to what Dunlop called procedural rules, as they can be methods for determining how workplace outcomes are determined. In Chapters 7 to 9, we will discuss many of the following conversion mechanisms in more detail:

- Collective bargaining, by which the parties negotiate a collective agreement.
- Grievances, by which employees (and/or their union) can submit a written complaint that the collective agreement has not been followed.
- Day-to-day relations. The day-to-day activities in the organization represent conversion mechanisms; for example, prior to launching a formal grievance, a worker may meet directly with his or her manager to resolve an issue).

- Various third-party interventions:

  - Interest arbitration. A third-party process used when parties cannot reach a collective agreement on their own. The decision of the arbitrator(s) becomes a binding collective agreement. This process is most often used by actors who are unable to legally strike (i.e., police, firefighters, etc.).
  - Mediation. A process whereby a third party attempts to facilitate a resolution between labour and management. Note that mediators do not have the power to enforce a resolution.
  - Grievance arbitration. A third-party resolution process used when employers and labour cannot resolve a grievance in a mutually acceptable manner. In such cases, the arbitrator(s) makes a final and binding resolution to the conflict at hand.
  - Conciliation. In many Canadian labour relations laws, a conciliator must assess the proposals of both employers and labour and submit a report to the appropriate federal or provincial minister of labour prior to a strike/lockout taking place.
  - Fact-finding. A process mostly used in British Columbia that is similar to conciliation.
  - Mediation/arbitration. A process that starts off with a third party acting as a mediator. If, however, the parties fail to reach an agreement on their own, the third party becomes an arbitrator and makes a binding decision.

- Joint committees. Many organizations have joint labour–management committees to examine issues of common concern, particularly health

Can enforce

Resolution cannot be enforced

Resolution can be enforced

Unions, Industrial Relations, and Youth

W W W

Given the demographic shifts in Canada, many unions are purposely examining issues important to youth. For example, we see YouTube entries that discuss "why to join a union" by the United Food and Commercial Workers (UFCW Canada, 2009). Take a look at the text from a presentation by Ken Georgetti, President of the Canadian Labour Congress, which highlights the youth agenda:

The Canadian Labour Congress is the largest trade union central in Canada, representing 3.2 million workers in 53 affiliated unions from coast-to-coast-to-coast.

We are also represented at the provincial and municipal levels in Canada by provincial and territorial federations of labour and local labour councils. And we all recognize some very important needs: the need to make space for young workers in our union structures, and the need to reach out to non-union young workers and spread the word about the union advantage so that they might become interested in joining, or even forming a union in their workplace.

A few years ago we did some research that showed the union advantage in Canada was on average $5 more an hour. That same research showed by joining a union, the pay gap for women was significantly reduced. And for young women in Canada, where the pay gap is around 32 cents an hour, joining a union is simply the best pay equity plan around.

To help us in our work to attract young workers to the labour movement, the Canadian Labour Congress has a full-time staff person dedicated to that work—Erin Harrison-Taylor is our current young workers national representative.

The CLC also has youth representation on our governing Executive Council, a position elected by the youth caucus at our national conventions every three years. Every provincial and territorial federation of labour has young worker representation in their governing structures or committees. Also, most local labour councils have young worker member-at-large positions on their governing structures. The CLC has a young workers' working group that meets regularly. The group is made up of young worker representatives of our affiliates and they help us bring our campaigns to their members.

I recall a particularly great campaign the CLC ran a couple of years ago—the women's economic equality campaign to highlight the wage gap in Canada between women and men. Working with the Canadian Federation of Students on university and college campuses across the country, our young worker representative and the committee organized bake sales where the baked goods were sold for $1 to the male students and 68 cents for the women students—an innovative way to highlight the wage gap between young men and women workers. The CLC's working group is currently involved in bringing our retirement security campaign to young workers—a pretty big challenge in itself!

I don't mind telling you—I first became active in my union, the United Steelworkers as a 22 year old apprentice in Trail, British Columbia, because I was angry my union was negotiating pensions. I thought they should be negotiating higher wages and should drop pensions! I've learned a lot since then of course. But the lesson for me was how tough it is to bring a pension message to workers just starting out, who have their whole lives ahead of them, with such promise and optimism for the future.

The working group also helps us with bringing our campaign messages to young workers in ways they can relate to—through Facebook, Twitter, and text messaging. These are the ways of the future for communicating with individuals. People under 30 these days only use cell phones. They text more often than they make a phone call.

So, of course unions have to adjust to these new realities to get our messages out, and to mobilize young workers around our issues. I am also pleased with the work our young workers committee is doing around mobilizing support to press Canada to ratify ILO Convention 138 on minimum age. This is a great campaign that really engages young people. The committee members have lobbied our federal politicians to get their support on this important convention. They have received media coverage on the issue as well.

I know you are going to be discussing the minimum age campaign later in your meeting, so I won't take up more time on that. But this is what happens in unions when we give young workers the space they need to develop and run with ideas.

Source: Georgetti, G. (19 June 2010). Speech to the ITUC Youth Committee Meeting. Reprinted with permission of Canadian Labour Congress. Retrieved on 14 December 2010 from http://www.canadianlabour.ca/news-room/speeches/speech-ituc-youth-committee-meeting.

and safety. Other workplaces use committees for broader issues, and some jurisdictions, such as Newfoundland and Labrador and British Columbia, even promote their usage, and provide assistance in establishing such committees (Labour Relations Agency, 2010; Labour Relations Board British Columbia, 2011).

- Strikes and lockouts. Work stoppages can be both a conversion mechanism and an outcome. When used as a conversion mechanism, strikes and lockouts are used to bring closure to the negotiation process and produce a collective agreement.

Outputs

The outputs may be thought of as the results, or outcomes, of the conversion mechanisms. As such, they are similar to what Dunlop called substantive rules. Often, such outputs may be captured in a collective agreement between labour and management (Craig, 1988). The collective agreement (which will be discussed more fully in Chapter 8) outlines key agreements and procedures reflecting the employment relationship in question. Elements that can be considered outputs of the industrial relations system include, but are not limited to, the following (as you read through the textbook, many of these outcomes will be discussed in more detail):

- Employer outcomes. For example, the rights and responsibilities of management in the employment relationship, as well as efficiency elements (productivity, profitability, etc.).
- Labour outcomes. Equity issues or ways to instill fairness in the workplace, including
    - the rights of, and security for, the union;
    - hours of work, including schedules, overtime, etc.;
    - wages and benefits;
    - job rights (e.g., job assignment and selection, layoff provisions, **seniority**); and

seniority

the length of time a person has been a member of the union

- Work rules, or rules that employees and employers are expected to follow.
- Worker perceptions. Workers' reactions in terms of
  - work climate, or workers' sense of the overall work environment in the organization at hand;
  - employee morale and organizational commitment, or the extent that employees are satisfied with and committed to their organization and workplace; and
  - union satisfaction and commitment, or the extent that employees are satisfied with and committed to their union.

- Conflict (or conflict resolution). An output of the system can be conflict (e.g., strikes and lockouts) or conflict resolution.

Views of Industrial Relations

As one examines the industrial relations system outlined in Figure 1.1, it is clear that industrial relations can be seen as an interdisciplinary field, involving scholars from various social science disciplines including economics, psychology, sociology, history, law, and political science. Thus, it should not be surprising that several different viewpoints have been used within the field. For an in-depth, historical look at how these social disciplines have shaped the teaching and research of Canadian industrial relations, see Hébert, Jain, and Meltz (1988). In the present section, we will briefly summarize several of the more prevalent views.

Neoclassical Economics View

neoclassical economics view

a view of industrial relations grounded in economics that sees unions as an artificial barrier to the free market

As outlined by Gunderson (1988, p. 50), the **neoclassical economics view** examines "the application of basic principles of neoclassical economics to . . . the market for labour services." In particular, we see an emphasis on factors that influence the supply and demand of labour, or workers. As we will define in more detail in Chapter 3, the "free market" assumption governing this economics view is that the number of people willing to work at a given wage rate (i.e., labour supply) is equal to the number of workers needed by organizations (i.e., labour demand). As a result, collective bargaining and unions can be seen as an artificial barrier to the free market in that they can artificially influence the supply and demand of labour. Researchers with this view often examine issues concerning the impact of unions on wages, productivity, etc.

Pluralist and Institutional View

pluralist and institutional view

a view of industrial relations stressing the importance of institutions and multiple actors (including labour) in the employment relationship

Led by scholars such as John R. Commons (1918) and Selig Perlman (1928), this view largely grew out of what is known as the "Wisconsin School." While the pluralist view began in economic circles, it is in direct contrast to that of neoclassical economics. Rather than considering unions an artificial barrier to the free market, the **pluralist and institutional view** believes that labour unions act as a countervailing force that attempts to balance the interests of employers and employees. As the name implies, this view emphasizes the need for strong institutions as well as multiple (i.e., plural) actors in the employment relationship. Perhaps American scholar Kaufman (2003, p. 25) best summarizes this view when he states,

> the Wisconsin strategy [which founded the institutional view] looks to use institutions such as trade unions, government, and corporations to establish a set of "working rules" that lead to stable, full employment conditions in labor markets, a level playing field in wage determination, and democratic mechanisms for due process and voice in the firm.

As this quote suggests, the systems framework is pluralist in nature. It is worth noting that the systems framework, and the pluralist view in which it is grounded, is considered the predominant mainstream view of industrial relations in Canada (Craig, 1988).

Human Resources/Strategic Choice

As we will discuss in more detail in Chapter 6, a seminal work by Kochan, Katz, and McKersie (1986) suggested that the American industrial relations climate had shifted significantly in the 1970s and 1980s. In brief, the evidence collected by these scholars suggested that Dunlop's shared ideology no longer existed and that there was a movement away from unionization toward non-unionized employment relationships. Moreover, Kochan, Katz, and McKersie argued that employers were implementing deliberate strategies designed to minimize unionization and the role of collective bargaining. Hence, their model is often referred to as the *strategic choice perspective*.

A key element of this perspective is the importance of human resources strategies and practices linked to the firm's overall business strategy. While human resources strategies and practices are not anti-union per se, they are often designed to foster cooperation between employees and employers. As such, this view tends to pay very little attention to the role of unions in the employment relationship (Kervin, 1988). Thus, the human resources view may minimize the inherent conflict between the employer (who seeks to maximize efficiency and owner/shareholder gain) and the employee (who seeks to maximize equity and worker gain). In fact, some scholars have argued that the human resources perspective minimizes the elements of democracy in the workplace (since it does not focus on collective representation) and the inherent conflict between management and worker as they attempt to achieve their competing needs (Godard & Delaney, 2000).

Political Economy

Unlike many of the industrial relations views discussed previously, political economy is heavily grounded in the fields of sociology and political science rather than economics. While the pluralist and human resources perspectives are viewed as minimizing (if not ignoring) the inherent con-

political economy

a view of industrial relations grounded in socialism and Marxism that stresses the role of inherent conflict between labour and management

flict between employers and employees, the political economy perspective does the reverse—it sees inherent conflict between employer and employee. This view has been more prevalent in Europe, where it is often associated with the University of Warwick Industrial Relations Research Unit (Ackers & Wilkinson, 2005) and scholars such as Richard Hyman (1989). The view largely took root in the United Kingdom in the 1970s, following a period of extensive strikes, the breakdown of national-level collective bargaining, and high levels of unemployment. During this time, there was a focus away from the institutional view, with an emphasis on stability and shared ideology, toward a more radical view that focused on "class struggle and workers' self-activity" (Ackers & Wilkinson, 2005, p. 449). This view stresses the need to look more fully at societal and political factors. In fact, Hyman (1994, p. 171) argues that the actions of management, labour and governments

> cannot sensibly be studied in isolation from their environing social relations. . . . Only if we understand how labour power is transformed . . . and the social and economics forces that structure this transformation, can we make sense of the rules that apply to the employment relationship. . . .

In brief, a goal of Marxism was to overthrow management and allow employees to have more control of their workplace.

Outline of the Text

As discussed earlier in this chapter, we will largely focus on issues concerning union–management relations, but we will use industrial relations frameworks and a pluralist view to guide us. Accordingly, the industrial relations system shown in Figure 1.1 will provide the foundation of this text and will be used to guide us through the chapters.

First, we will examine the external inputs important to employment relationships. In particular, we will pay particular attention to the legal subsystem in Chapter 2, while the economics subsystem and other environmental inputs will be presented in Chapter 3.

Second, we move to an examination of the actors, including a discussion of internal inputs (e.g., values, goals, strategies, and power) as well as the history between them. Accordingly, we will focus on the labour history in Chapter 4 and on the actors of labour and management in Chapters 5 and 6, respectively.

Third, we shift to a discussion of the conversion mechanisms. Specifically, we discuss contract negotiations (Chapter 7) and collective agreement administration (Chapter 8), as well as strikes and dispute resolution processes (Chapter 9).

Fourth, we discuss the outputs of the system. In particular, Chapter 10 examines the impacts of unionization, with particular focus on the elements of equity and efficiency.

Fifth, we look at the industrial relations system and the role of the feedback loop in terms of the dynamics of employment relationships. Thus, we end our text with a discussion of several special cases and issues in the

field of industrial relations. More specifically, we discuss industrial relations issues related to the public sector in Chapter 11, the role of unions in today's economy, and the importance of the increasing internationalization/globalization of labour markets in Chapter 12.

Summary

While scholars argue that "industrial relations is one of the oldest and most established . . . social science disciplines that feed into business and management studies" (Ackers & Wilkinson, 2005, p. 444), there is considerable debate concerning what is and is not industrial relations. No single theory can be said to ground the field, and several terms can be used to describe various issues germane to it (e.g., industrial relations, employment relations, labour relations, etc.).

Given the diversity of perspectives in the study of employment relationships, several key views related to this text and the field of industrial relations must be kept in mind: neoclassical economics, pluralist/ institutional, strategic choice/human resources, and political economy. In particular, it is important to note that the pluralist/institutional view, and specifically the systems approach, will provide the foundation for this textbook. As we move from chapter to chapter, we will focus on several key elements of the systems model presented in Figure 1.1. More specifically, we will (1) start with a review of the external inputs (or environmental subsystems), such as law and economics, (2) move to a discussion of the actors and their associated internal inputs (e.g., values, power, strategies, and goals), (3) present various conversion mechanisms (e.g., collective bargaining and strikes), (4) discuss outputs (e.g., terms and conditions for the employment relationship), and (5) finish with an overview of emerging trends in Canada.

Key Terms

collective agreement 3
collective bargaining 4
conversion mechanisms 13
employee relations 4
employment relations 4
exchange rate 11
feedback loop 9
goal 12
human resources 4
industrial relations 3
inflation 11
interest rate 11

labour relations 3
mandatory retirement 12
neoclassical economics view 16
pluralist and institutional view 16
political economy 17
power 13
seniority 15
strategies 13
strike 4
union 3
values 12

Weblinks

University of Toronto's Centre for Industrial Relations and Human Resources:

http://www.chass.utoronto.ca/cir
http://www.chass.utoronto.ca/cir/aboutcir/cirhr_director.html

Queen's MIR designation:

http://www.queensu.ca/sps/future_students/MIR/program_features.php

Nova Scotia Government & General Employees Union (NSGEU):

http://www.nsgeu.ca/Contact/index.cfm

Memorial University's MER designation:

http://www.business.mun.ca/programs/graduate/mer.php

Newfoundland & Labrador Employers' Council:

http://www.nsgeu.ca/Contact/index.cfm

UFCW Canada's Why Join a Union YouTube entry:

http://www.youtube.com/watch?v=wKBjqLOgo0I

RPC Icons

1.1 Provides advice to clients on the establishment, continuation, and termination of bargaining rights

- labour legislation
- institutions and processes (both regulatory and nonregulatory) that govern the relationship between employers and employees

1.2 Collects and develops information required for good decision making throughout the bargaining process

- institutions and processes (both regulatory and nonregulatory) that govern the relationship between employers and employees
- the effects of collective bargaining on corporate issues (e.g., wages, productivity, and management processes)
- possible outcomes of contract negotiation (e.g., impasse, conciliation, and legal strike)
- the legal context of labour relations

1.3 Contributes to communication plan during work disruptions

- applicable dispute resolution mechanisms for work stoppages
- relevant legislation and regulations and third-party procedures
- internal and external organizational environments and working procedures

- common and statutory law (e.g., employment standards, labour relations)
- government labour relationship acts
- institutions and processes (both regulatory and nonregulatory) that govern the relationship between employers and employees
- the effects of collective bargaining on corporate issues (e.g., wages, productivity, and management processes)

Discussion Questions

1. IR courses can be taught in business schools, departments of economics, and even interdisciplinary centres devoted to IR. Which department best presents the "owner" of the course you are now taking? Given this "ownership," to what extent do you think each of the perspectives covered on pages 16–18 will be used to ground your course?
2. Many of your peers may argue that the field of industrial relations is dead and that it has no relevance to today's youth. What do you think?
3. Unions are increasing their focus on youth workers. In your opinion, what should unions do to make them more appealing to youth?
4. Many students will take this course in a business school. From your perspective, should industrial relations courses be required in business schools?

Using the Internet

Part of the university experience is self-exploration and determining potential career interests. Since you will be studying the field of industrial relations this term, it's a good time to explore different programs and career options in the field. There are several English and French graduate programs dedicated to the study of employment relationships, some of which are listed below. Take a look at a few of these weblinks and answer the questions that follow.

English Programs

Cornell University IRL School

http://www.ilr.cornell.edu

Memorial University's MER program

http://www.business.mun.ca/programs/graduate/mer.php

Queen's MIR program

http://www.queensu.ca/sps/future_students/MIR/MIR_brochure.pdf

University of Toronto's MIRHR program

http://www.chass.utoronto.ca/cir/mirphd/index.html

Warwick University IR master's programs

http://www2.warwick.ac.uk/fac/soc/wbs/research/irru/masters_programmes

French Programs

L'Université Laval—Maîtrise en relations industrielles program

https://capsuleweb.ulaval.ca/pls/etprod7/y_bwckprog.p_afficher_fiche?
p_session=200909&p_code_prog=M-RLT&p_code_majr=RLT&p_code_
camp=#obje

L'Université de Montréal—M.Sc. (relations industrielles)

http://www.eri.umontreal.ca/cycles_2_3/index.html

1. To what extent does the structure of these graduate programs reflect the industrial relations system shown in Figure 1.1? (For example, are there courses in economics, law, sociology, etc.?)
2. Which of the industrial relations views discussed in this chapter do you feel is prevalent in each school?
3. Judging from the information provided on these websites, what types of careers are available in the IR field?

Exercises

1. Go to the hard copy or the online edition of a large, national newspaper. Using the IR system presented in this chapter, can you see elements of external inputs and conversation mechanisms in the quote? How many of the actors are covered in the article?
2. Most university faculties are unionized. Examining the university you are currently attending,

   a. name and identify the main actors of the industrial relations system;
   b. discuss the relevant internal inputs of these actors; and
   c. identify the external inputs that you feel have the greatest impact on the actors at this time.

3. University calendars are available in a variety of places (e.g., libraries, registrars' offices, and university web pages). Take a look at your university's calendar and examine where courses relevant to this textbook are being taught. (*Hint:* Look at faculties and departments of business, economics, history, sociology, psychology, industrial relations, and political science.) Reading these course descriptions, do you see differing views of industrial relations?

4. Professors who teach industrial relations come from a broad range of backgrounds, and most schools have websites listing professors' education, teaching experience, and research areas. Take a look at the web pages of the faculty who teach topics related to industrial relations. On the basis of the website data provided, which of the industrial relations views do you expect to see emphasized in their courses? Explain.
5. Watch the national or local evening news. Examine the stories that cover issues related to employment relationships and then group them into three themes: (a) collective bargaining, (b) strikes, and (c) other areas. Is there a predominant theme? If so, why do you think it exists?

Case

Metrobus Strike

The Amalgamated Transit Union (ATU) represents about 100 workers (e.g., drivers, mechanics, administrative staff) employed with Metrobus, a city-wide transit authority. On November 3, after the parties failed to negotiate a settlement, the union conducted a vote. In an overwhelming majority, 97 percent voted to reject the contract offer and go on strike. On November 4, picket lines were assembled at the worksite and all bus services were suspended.

The main reason for the strike appears to centre on the cost of benefits. While the employer has offered to increase wages by 15.5 percent over four years, management is asking that all newly hired workers pay for 50 percent of their benefit plan costs. The employer feels that this 50/50 cost sharing of benefits is reasonable and consistent with other collective agreements. For example, numerous public-sector employees such as city employees, firefighters, and regional water employees all pay 50 percent of their benefit costs. The union, on the other hand, feels that this benefit sharing is unacceptable and unfair.

As a result of the strike, many potentially vulnerable citizens, such as students, seniors, and lower-income earners who cannot afford their own vehicles, are left with few transportation options during the winter. They now have to rely on getting rides with others, paying the high cost of cabs, or even not showing up to work or school. Students of the university even set up a ride-sharing website where they could attempt to coordinate rides during the strike.

Six weeks into the strike, the level of frustration has mounted. The mayor of the city, Dennis O'Keefe, has publicly urged both sides to settle the dispute and other councillors seem hopeful that the government-appointed mediator will help resolve the issue. There have even been public protests and petitions asking the provincial government to legislate an end to the strike. Despite the frustration, the strike remains in full force with no foreseeable end.

Sources: CBC News, 2010a, 2010b, 2010c; Metrobus, 2011; *The Telegram*, 2011.

Chapter 1: Introduction

Questions

1. Using the industrial relations model presented in this chapter (Figure 1.1),

   a. identify and name the actors in this case;
   b. discuss what external inputs you feel are most relevant in this case; and
   c. name and identify the conversion mechanisms and outputs presented in the case.

2. To what extent are Barbash's concepts of equity and efficiency echoed in the arguments of labour and management in this case?

Endnote

1. A preliminary version of this model was presented at the 2007 Annual Meeting of the Canadian Industrial Relations Association of Canada (see Brown, 2007).

References

Ackers, P., & Wilkinson, A. (2005). British industrial relations paradigm: A critical outline history and prognosis. *The Journal of Industrial Relations, 47*, pp. 443–456.

Bank of Canada. (April 2006). Fact sheets: The exchange rate. *The Bank in Brief.* Retrieved 29 June 2006 from http://www.bankofcanada.ca/en/backgrounders/bg-e1.html

Bank of Canada. (December 2010). *Financial system review.* Retrieved 11 January 2011 from http://www.bankofcanada.ca/en/fsr/2010/highlights_1210.pdf

Barbash, J. (1987). Like nature, industrial relations abhors a vacuum. *Relations industrielles, 42,* pp. 168–179.

Bellemare, G. (2000). End users: Actors in the industrial relations system? *British Journal of Industrial Relations, 38,* pp. 383–405.

Brown, T. C. (2007). What happened to the "I" in IR? The role of individual measures in IR theory and research. Paper presented at the annual meeting of the Canadian Association of Industrial Relations, Montreal, 5–7 June.

Call Centre India. (2011). Retrieved 2 January 2011 from www.callcentreindia.com

CBC News. (4 November 2010a). Metrobus workers vote to strike. Retrieved 11 January 2011 from http://www.cbc.ca/canada/newfoundland-labrador/story/2010/11/03/metrobus-strike-vote-113.html

CBC News. (4 November 2010b). St. John's transit strike strands riders: Students start program to share rides; union decries Metrobus demands. Retrieved 14 January 2011 from http://www.cbc.ca/canada/newfoundland-labrador/story/2010/11/04/nl-metrobus-picket-1104.html

CBC News. (14 December 2010c). End Metro bus strike by Christmas: Mayor. Retrieved 11 January 2011 from http://www.cbc.ca/canada/newfoundland-labrador/story/2010/12/14/metrobus-strike-okeefe-114.html

Commons, J. R. (1918). *History of labor in the United States.* (Vols. 1–2). New York: Macmillan.

Côté, A. (10 January 2011). Household finances and economic growth. Remarks by Agathe Côté, Deputy Governor of the Bank of Canada to Canadian Club of Kingston. Retrieved 13 January 2011 from http://www.bankofcanada.ca/en/speeches/2011/sp100111.pdf

Craig, A. W. J. (1967). A model for the analysis of industrial relations systems. Paper presented to the annual meeting of the Canadian Political Science Association.

Craig, A. W. J. (1988). Mainstream industrial relations. In G. Hébert, C. J. Jain & N. M. Meltz (Eds.), *The state of the art in industrial relations* (pp. 9–43). Kingston, ON: Industrial Relations Centre, Queen's University, and Centre for Industrial Relations, University of Toronto.

Craig, A. W. J., & Solomon, N. A. (1996). *The system of industrial relations in Canada* (5th edition). Toronto: Prentice Hall Canada Inc.

Dunlop, J. T. (1958, 1993). *Industrial relations system*. New York: Henry Holt and Company.

Dunlop, J. T. (1993). *Industrial relations system.* (Revised edition). Boston, MA: Harvard Business School Press.

Georgetti, G. (19 June 2010). Speech to the ITUC Youth Committee Meeting. Retrieved 14 December 2010 from http://www.canadianlabour.ca/news-room/speeches/speech-ituc-youth-committee-meeting

Godard, J., & Delaney, J. (2000). Reflections on the "high performance" paradigm's implications for industrial relations as a field. *Industrial and Labor Relations Review, 53,* pp. 482–502.

Gunderson, M. (1988). Labour economics and industrial relations. In G. Hébert, C. J. Jain & N. M. Meltz (Eds.), *The state of the art in industrial relations* (pp. 45–71). Kingston, ON: Industrial Relations Centre, Queen's University, and Centre for Industrial Relations, University of Toronto.

Hébert, G., Jain, C. J., & Meltz, N. M. (Eds.). (1988). *The state of the art in industrial relations.* Kingston, ON: Industrial Relations Centre, Queen's University, and Centre for Industrial Relations, University of Toronto.

Hyman, R. (1989). *The political economy of industrial relations: Theory and practice in a cold climate.* Basingstoke: Macmillan.

Hyman, R. (1994). Theory and industrial relations. *British Journal of Industrial Relations, 32,* pp. 165–180.

Kaufman, B. E. (2002). Reflections on six decades in industrial relations: An interview with John Dunlop. *Industrial and Labor Relations Review, 55,* pp. 324–348.

Kaufman, B. E. (2003). John R. Commons and the Wisconsin School on industrial relations strategy and policy. *Industrial and Labor Relations Review, 57,* pp. 3–30.

Kervin, J. B. (1988). Sociology, psychology and industrial relations. In G. Hébert, C. J. Jain & N. M. Meltz (Eds.), *The state of the art in industrial relations* (pp. 187–234). Kingston, ON: Industrial Relations Centre, Queen's University, and Centre for Industrial Relations, University of Toronto.

Kochan, T., Katz, H., & McKersie, R. (1986). *The transformation of American industrial relations.* New York: Basic Books.

Labour Relations Board British Columbia. (2011). *Towards better labour management relations.* Retrieved 11 January 2011 from http://www.lrb.bc.ca/mediation

Library of Parliament (2011). *Federal back to work legislation 1950 to date.* Retrieved July 18, 2011 from http://www.parl.gc.ca/Parlinfo/Compilations/HouseOfCommons/Legislation/LegislationBackToWork.aspx?

Library of Parliament. (20 November 2009). *Federal back to work legislation 1950 to date.* Retrieved 11 January 2011 from http://www2.parl.gc.ca/Parlinfo/compilations/houseofcommons/legislation/LegislationBackToWork.aspx

McLintock, B. (10 May 2004). How did Premier lose public on strike? *The Tyee: A Feisty One Online.* Retrieved 28 June 2006 from http://thetyee.ca/News/2004/05/10/How_Did_Premier_Lose_Public_on_Strike

Meltz, N. M. (1997). Introduction to employment relations. Paper presented to the Conference on Teaching in Human Resources and Industrial Relations, Atlanta, GA.

Meltz, N. M., & Adams, R. J. (1993). *Industrial relations theory: Its nature, scope, and pedagogy.* Rutgers University: Scarecrow Press.

Metrobus (2011). Communications bulletin #8: Council fully supports Transportation Commission. Retrieved 15 January 2011 from http://www.metrobus.com/content/commbull8_.html

Perlman, S. (1928). *A theory of the labor movement*. New York: Macmillan.

The Telegram. (12 January 2011). Protesters want government to legislate end to Metrobus strike. Retrieved 14 January 2011 from http://www.thetelegram.com/News/Local/2011-01-12/article-2110705/Protesters-want-government-to-legislate-end-to-Metrobus-strike-/1

UFCW Canada. (2 November 2009). Why join a union? Retrieved 13 December 2010 from http://www.youtube.com/watch?v=wKBjqLOgo0I

Warren, A. M., & Kelloway, E. K. (2010). Retirement decisions in the context of the abolishment of mandatory retirement. *International Journal of Manpower, 31*, 286–305.

Wood, S. J., Wagner, A., Armstrong, E. G. A., Goodman, J. F. B., & Davis, J. E. (1975). The "industrial relations system" concept as a basis for theory in industrial relations. *British Journal of Industrial Relations, 13*, pp. 291–308.

YorkStrike2008. (2008). *About YorkStrike2008*. Retrieved 11 January 2011 from http://yorkstrike2008.wordpress.com/about-yorkstrike2008

CHAPTER 2

The Legal Environment

Learning Objectives

By the end of this chapter, you will be able to discuss

- the basic elements of the Canadian model of union recognition and collective bargaining;
- collective agreement administration;
- the role of the *Charter* in industrial relations;
- the impact of international law on labour relations policy; and
- the impact of employment law on employee rights and conditions.

CONTRACT SETS NEW PRECEDENT FOR RIGHTS OF MIGRANT WORKERS

A breakthrough collective agreement was reached September 21 between UFCW [United Food & Commercial Workers] Canada and Floralia Growers of Abbotsford, B.C.

The new UFCW Canada Local 1518 contract provides wage improvements, but is particularly noteworthy for the protections it establishes for the rights of seasonal migrant agriculture workers to return to Canada under the federal government's Seasonal Agricultural Workers Program (SAWP).

"We have had a lot interest from migrant farm workers in joining the union," said Ivan Limpright, President of UFCW Canada Local 1518, "and this contract is a huge step forward in providing the kinds of basic protections and recall rights that migrant farm workers in Canada deserve."

"These are among the most vulnerable workers in Canada, because too often when workers would dare complain, let alone join a union, the farm employers would make sure they didn't call those workers back for the next season's work, or just send them straight back to their home country," said Limpright.

"This contract establishes a real measure of justice and dignity for the Floralia workers."

The new contract establishes recall rights for migrant agriculture workers, and the union and employer have agreed to a process for recalling SAWP workers that will enhance workers' opportunities to return year after year.

In addition, when the growing season slows down and a smaller workforce is needed, a process is now established whereby those volunteering to return home would be the first to go, and if necessary, other workers would then return to their home based on seniority.

"Previously, the workers would be 'repatriated', as the employers like to call it, and strictly at the employer's whim," said Limpright. "For example, we have had cases where there was a slowdown in the growing season and a worker volunteered to go home because his wife was pregnant or there was another family emergency, but the employer would refuse and send someone else home instead. Now, under this contract, the workers at least have some control over their own fates, and this is a huge and important breakthrough."

The migrant agriculture workers at Floralia are from Mexico, and make up approximately 90 percent of the Floralia workforce.

In addition to recall rights, the crucial topic of overtime was also addressed in the new contract. It had been apparent that when workers developed an interest in joining UFCW, those workers were punished by having their overtime eliminated or minimized.

The new contract has a process by which overtime will be balanced among all workers, and monitored so that it is not awarded by favouritism nor used as a form of punishment against workers interested in the union. . . .

Source: UFCW Canada, Historic Victory for Migrant Farm Workers. Reprinted with permission. Retrieved from http://www.ufcw.ca/index.php?option=com_content&view=article&id=661&catid=5&Itemid=99&lang=en.

The preceding vignette highlights why understanding the regulatory framework is so important in industrial relations. Migrant workers have tended to be excluded from Canadian collective bargaining laws. In this chapter, we will uncover the origins of the current industrial relations legislation in Canada; examine the principles upon which the law is based; canvass the current state of employment law in Canada; and identify legislative trends. Since the origin of Canadian labour law can be traced to the American *Wagner Act* of 1935, we will employ a comparative approach to illuminate the key aspects of labour legislation.

Wagner Act History

Prior to the passage of the **Wagner Act** in the United States, unions were seldom recognized without a violent power struggle between management and labour. In Canada, while unions had achieved legal recognition in the *Trade Union Act* of 1872, they encountered the same hostile employers in the Canadian context. Unions in both countries struggled to attain recognition or any degree of democracy in the workplace (Panitch & Swartz, 1993). The state tried to contain labour conflict in the 1907 *Industrial Dispute Investigations Act* (IDIA) in Canada but again failed to provide an orderly mechanism for union recognition. In the second decade of the twentieth century, a number of broader social and economic factors would contribute to the decline of organized craft labour in both countries: the influence of **scientific management** and mass production; the increasing use of company unions as a method of union substitution; and a generally hostile legal environment. It would take a new model of unionism—industrial

Wagner Act

named after the bill's sponsor, Senator Robert F. Wagner of New York, and more formally known as the *National Labor Relations Act* of the United States

scientific management

the application of engineering principles to define specific tasks in the production process thereby removing the autonomy of skilled craft workers (associated with Frederick Taylor)

unionism—for workers in Canada and the United States to achieve industrial democracy.

The Great Depression of the early 1930s gave rise to a new wave of unionism. As the paternalist model of company unions declined and unemployment surged, workers increasingly distrusted companies to provide basic rights and benefits. Industrial unions, who sought to organize all workers in an industry regardless of skill or occupational status, emerged as a more active and socially oriented movement to protect workers. In the United States, the cause of industrial unionism was advanced by the 1932 election of President Franklin D. Roosevelt. A major feature of Roosevelt's New Deal was the 1935 *National Labor Relations (Wagner) Act*, which protected—under federal law—the right to organize unions for the purpose of collective bargaining and the right to strike. While the *Wagner Act* model might have been enacted principally to reduce conflict and aid in the rebuilding of the American economy, it had the effect of legitimizing industrial unionization. As such, union density increased from 12.9 percent in 1930 to 22.5 percent in 1940 (Troy & Sheflin, 1985).

The *Snider* Case

The case of *Toronto Electric Power Commissioners v. Snider et al.* grew out of a labour dispute between the commission and its employees in 1923. The established protocol of the day provided that a conciliation board would be appointed under the *Industrial Dispute Investigations Act*. This federal statute called for the conciliation board to analyze the circumstances of the dispute and the probable impact on the public before a strike could be taken. However, in this case, Toronto Electric Power refused to acknowledge the conciliation board, arguing that the federal statute did not apply to a labour dispute in Toronto. This line of argument derived from the *British North America (BNA) Act*, the statute that effectively served as Canada's constitution until 1982. In the *BNA Act*, civil and property matters were the responsibility of the provinces. Thus, the underlying issue was whether labour relations legislation would be a provincial or federal responsibility.

Snider Case

a landmark court case in 1925 that determined that labour matters fell under the purview of the provinces under the *British North America Act*

The **Snider Case** went to the British Privy Council, the highest court in Canada at that time. The Privy Council found that the federal government had exceeded its jurisdiction in applying the 1907 IDIA to a province and that in the absence of a national emergency, the provincial responsibility over civil matters must be respected. As a result of this decision, the distinctive Canadian system of shared jurisdiction was given legal authority. The federal government was given responsibility over such interprovincial industries as communication and transportation, while the provinces were given responsibility for all other areas of commerce. But not every province had labour legislation in 1925. The next twenty years would see each province and the federal government design separate labour policies to govern industrial relations within their jurisdiction.

Canada's P.C. 1003

It would be nine years before Canada passed its own version of the *Wagner Act* model in 1944. The outbreak of World War II in 1939 and employer resistance delayed the introduction of labour legislation. The dissatisfaction of Canadian workers with their employment conditions resulted in increased conflict—especially in the all-important steel industry. It was this unrest that gave rise to a new political movement. When the strength of the Canadian labour movement appeared to threaten the survival of the Liberal Party in 1944, Prime Minister William Lyon Mackenzie King enacted **P.C. 1003**. This legislation was almost a copy of the American *Wagner Act* except that P.C. 1003 was not intended to be a permanent measure. Only with sustained pressure from organized labour was the 1948 *Industrial Relations and Dispute Investigation Act* (IRDIA) introduced to replace P.C. 1003 at the federal level. Soon thereafter, because of the *Snider* case and the provincial jurisdiction over labour policy (discussed next), each province either extended the IRDIA or enacted a comparable act of its own. By 1948, union density had grown to 30 percent in Canada from 16 percent in 1940 (Lipset & Meltz, 2004). Thus, the *Wagner Act* model would prove to be the underlying framework for the postwar system of industrial relations, which saw increasing unionization and economic growth in both Canada and the United States.

P.C. 1003
the Canadian government imported the *Wagner Act* model in 1944; under the *War Measures Act*, it was introduced by the Privy Council as P.C. 1003

According to the *Constitution Act* and its interpretations, the Parliament of Canada has jurisdiction for labour relations in a number of key industries. For the purposes of the *Canada Labour Code*, Part I, these include

- broadcasting (radio and television);
- chartered banks;
- postal service;
- airports and air transportation;
- shipping and navigation (including loading and unloading of vessels);
- interprovincial or international transportation by road, railway, ferry, or pipeline;
- telecommunications; and
- industries declared to be for the general advantage of Canada, such as grain handling and uranium mining and processing.

Thus, each province has its own version of the *Wagner Act* model. Summaries of private-sector collective bargaining legislation for each province are available at the Human Resources and Social Development Canada website in PDF format.

Union Recognition Under the *Wagner Act* Model

Recall that the *Wagner Act* was passed in a period of intense conflict between labour and management. The conflict, however, was not restricted to labour and management. Because the employees of a given firm could belong to more than one union, interunion conflict over representation rights was not uncommon.

To deal with this conflict, the *Wagner Act* provided the following:

1. Recognition strikes and lockouts were declared illegal.
2. As a substitute for industrial conflict over union recognition, labour boards were established to provide a process where employees could obtain union recognition by a free expression of support.
3. The union that obtained recognition was granted exclusive jurisdiction to represent all employees in a given bargaining unit. This is known as the **exclusivity principle**.

exclusivity principle
the idea that a union is granted the sole right to represent all employees in the defined bargaining unit

Labour Boards

Neutral labour relations boards serve a vital function in the North American model of industrial relations. Their purpose is to provide an alternative to the courts that is faster, cheaper, and has greater expertise in matter pertaining to industrial relations. Their structure is **tripartite**, where cases are heard by a panel consisting of union- and management-appointed representatives and a neutral chairperson. Quebec employs a labour court model but the functions of the board are very similar to those in the rest of Canada. In broad terms, the main function of a labour board is to enforce the *Labour Relations Act*. Boards may hear several kinds of cases:

tripartite
a tripartite board has three stakeholders: management, labour, and government

1. certification and decertification;
2. unfair labour practices; and
3. declarations of illegal strikes or lockouts.

certification
recognition of a union by a labour board after completion of the procedures under the labour act

Certification is the process of gaining recognition under the appropriate labour act. The variations in procedure by provincial and federal jurisdictions are set out in Table 2.1. A key element that defines the Canadian version of the *Wagner Act* model is the possibility of automatic certification—that is, certification based on the number of signed cards without a formal vote. A union can obtain certification without a vote under private-sector law in the federal sector and in those of Manitoba, New Brunswick, Prince Edward Island, and Quebec (see second column in Table 2.1). Not shown in Table 2.1 is an amendment to the *Ontario Labour Relations Act* to provide for automatic certification but only in the construction sector (section 128.1 of the OLRA). In several provinces, however, the board may certify without a vote if a firm has been found guilty of an unfair labour practice and if the true wishes of the employees would likely not be expressed through a vote (see third column of Table 2.1).

TABLE 2.1

Trade Union Application for Certification: General Private Sector Collective Bargaining Legislation

Jurisdiction	Proof of Support for Trade Union in Bargaining Unit	Minimum Support Required to Hold a Representation Vote[1] or for Certification Without a Vote	Power to Certify If Unfair Labour Practice by Employer
Federal	Signing an application for membership and paying at least $5 to the union for or within the 6 months preceding the application.	Representation vote: 35%. A representation vote is void if less than 35% of eligible employees actually vote. Certification without a vote: more than 50%.	The Board[2] may certify if it considers that, in the absence of the unfair labour practice, the union could reasonably have been expected to have had the support of a majority of employees in the bargaining unit.
Alberta	Maintaining membership and/or applying for it, and paying on one's own behalf at least $2 within 90 days preceding the application, or signing a petition supporting the union within that same period.	Representation vote: 40%. No certification without a vote.	
British Columbia	Signing and dating a membership card (effective January 18, 1993, the card must contain a specific statement) or maintaining active membership by paying dues, within 90 days preceding the application.	Representation vote: 45% (a majority in the case of an application to displace another union). No certification without a vote (also see last column). The Board may order another vote if fewer than 55% of the employees in the unit cast ballots.	The Board may certify if it believes that it is likely the union would otherwise have obtained the required support. The union may be required to fulfill certain conditions to remain certified.
Manitoba	Being a member of the union 6 months before the application for certification or joining the union during those 6 months, and maintaining membership prior to the date of application.	Representation vote: 40% (45% in the case of an application to displace another union). Certification without a vote: 65% or more.	The Board may certify if it believes that the employees' true wishes are not likely to be ascertained and the union has adequate membership support.
New Brunswick	Paying to the trade union on the employee's own behalf an amount of at least $1 in respect of initiation fees or periodic dues.	Representation vote: 40%. Certification without a vote: the Board may certify if more than 50%, and must certify if more than 60%.	The Board may certify if it believes that the employees' true wishes are not likely to be ascertained and the union has adequate membership support.

TABLE 2.1

Trade Union Application for Certification: General Private Sector Collective Bargaining Legislation (continued)

Jurisdiction	Proof of Support for Trade Union in Bargaining Unit	Minimum Support Required to Hold a Representation Vote[1] or for Certification Without a Vote	Power to Certify If Unfair Labour Practice by Employer
Newfoundland and Labrador	Signing an application for membership in the union within 90 days before the application for certification.	Representation vote: 40%. No certification without a vote, unless the parties jointly request the Board not to proceed with the vote (if so, it may certify if satisfied that the trade union has the support of a majority of employees).	
Nova Scotia	Joining the union or signing an application for membership, and paying on the employee's own behalf at least $2 in union dues during the 3 months before the month in which the application is made, up to the date of application.	Representation vote: 40%. No certification without a vote (also see last column).	The Board may certify if it believes that the vote does not reflect the true wishes of the employees and the union represents at least 40% of those in the unit.
Ontario	Employees in the unit who are members of the union on the application date.	Representation vote: 40%. No certification without a vote.	When a trade union was not able to demonstrate support from at least 40% of the employees in the proposed bargaining unit, or a representation vote did not likely reflect the employees' true wishes, the Board may order that another certification vote be taken. It can also certify the union if no other remedy would be sufficient to counter the effects of an unfair labour practice.
Prince Edward Island	Being a member of the union or signing a document stating support for certification, and paying at least $2 in union dues within the 3 months preceding the application.	Representation vote: at discretion of Board (no percentage specified). Certification without a vote: at discretion of Board (but majority support must be demonstrated).	
Quebec	Signing an application for membership, duly dated and not revoked, and personally paying at least $2 in union dues within the 12 months preceding the application.	Representation vote: 35%. Certification without a vote: more than 50%.	

TABLE 2.1

Trade Union Application for Certification: General Private Sector Collective Bargaining Legislation (Continued)

Jurisdiction	Proof of Support for Trade Union in Bargaining Unit	Minimum Support Required to Hold a Representation Vote[1] or for Certification Without a Vote	Power to Certify If Unfair Labour Practice by Employer
Saskatchewan	Signing a card stating that the employee wishes to be represented by the union.	Representation vote: 45%. No certification without a vote.	Despite lack of evidence of support from at least 45% of employees, the Board must order a representation vote if it considers that sufficient evidence of such support would otherwise have been obtained.

[1]The result of a representation vote is determined by a majority of the employees in a bargaining unit who exercise their right to vote. In Newfoundland and Labrador, if at least 70% of eligible employees have voted, the union will be certified if a majority of those who cast ballots support it; if less than 70% of the eligible employees have voted, the union will be certified if it has the support of a majority of those included in the bargaining unit. In Saskatchewan, a majority of employees entitled to vote must cast a ballot for the results to be considered valid. In New Brunswick and Quebec, the result of a representation vote is determined by a majority of those who are eligible to vote (i.e., the employees comprised in the bargaining unit). In New Brunswick, employees who are absent from work during voting hours and who do not cast their ballots are not counted.

[2]"Board" means the Labour Relations Board, except in Manitoba (Labour Board), in New Brunswick (Labour and Employment Board), and in the federal jurisdiction (Canada Industrial Relations Board).

Source: Labour Law Analysis, Strategic Policy, Analysis and Workplace Information Labour Program, July 2009. Retrieved from http://www.hrsdc .gc.ca/eng/labour/labour_law/ind_rel/tuac.shtml. Human Resources and Skills Development Canada, 2009. Reproduced with the permission of the Minister of Public Works and Government Services Canada, 2011.

Two important elements of the recognition process require explanation: the **bargaining unit** and **unfair labour practices**.

Bargaining Unit

Unless the parties agree, the labour board will be called upon to make a critical determination of which employees are eligible to be covered by the union. This is an important question, because the percentage of employees needed by the union to win a vote or get an automatic certification is expressed as a proportion of the defined bargaining unit. Labour boards typically apply several criteria to decide which employees are eligible to be included in the bargaining unit.

bargaining unit
the group of employees in an organization that are eligible to be represented by a union

unfair labour practice
an alleged violation of the labour relations act

MANAGEMENT EMPLOYEES Management employees are excluded from union representation. They are defined as those employees who have supervisory responsibility over bargaining-unit employees, including the ability to effectively recommend the hiring, firing, or discipline of employees. Management employees may also be defined as those having confidential information with respect to labour relations.

The rationales for excluding managers are

1. access to confidential labour relations information might compromise management's position in bargaining; and
2. the union would be in a conflict of interest if a union member was disciplined by another union member.

On the other hand, persons are not excluded simply because they have a job title that may indicate management responsibilities or if they have access to confidential information not related to labour relations. The labour board will examine the actual duties of the job in question.

COMMUNITY OF INTERESTS The fundamental criterion to form a bargaining unit is that a community of interests should exist among employees. The board must settle disputes, for example, over the inclusion of part-time employees into a unit of full-timers or to combine office and plant employees. Too many bargaining units in a company may lead to labour instability and threaten labour peace. Also, if bargaining units are too small, they may not be viable entities—that is, they may lack the bargaining power to effectively represent their members.

WISHES OF EMPLOYEES Boards will take into account the desires of employees to be separate from or part of a defined group. For example, stationary engineers have a history of craft unionism and organize on the basis of a single occupational unit. The result has been that in hospital settings, stationary engineers responsible for a steam plant have been allowed by labour boards to have their own bargaining units. The history of the craft or profession also matters in these cases.

EMPLOYER STRUCTURE The labour board must consider the employer's structure in determining appropriate bargaining units for collective bargaining. Suppose, for example, a firm has two plants in a city producing similar products with the same management, pay structure, and array of jobs. A board might determine that the employees of these two plants constitute a single bargaining unit for purposes of collective bargaining. The union would then have to organize both plants if it wished to represent the employees. The selection of a bargaining unit can be a major source of conflict between management and labour.

RPC 2.1

Unfair Labour Practices

Unfair labour practices are alleged violations of the *Labour Relations Act* by employers, unions, or employees. To ensure that workers are free to choose a union, companies and unions are prevented from using intimidation or coercion. Other prohibited actions include the calling or counselling of illegal strikes or lockouts and the failure or refusal to bargain collectively (see IR Notebook 2.1). Criticism of the current Canadian system of processing unfair labour practices has recently surfaced in the academic literature. Scholars argue that employer penalties are insufficient (Slinn, 2008) and forced speeches by management (captive-audience meetings) may violate the *Canadian Charter of Rights and Freedoms* (Doorey, 2008).

To redress these violations, labour board remedies include cease-and-desist orders for coercion or intimidation; reinstatements if fired for union activities; and orders to resume bargaining if a party refuses to bargain in good faith.

IR Notebook 2.1

Unfair Labour Practices Under the *P.E.I. Labour Act*

Employer Unfair Labour Practices

10. (1) No employer, employers' organization or an agent or any other person acting on behalf of an employer or employers' organization shall

(a) interfere with, restrain or coerce an employee in the exercise of any right conferred by this Act;

(b) participate or interfere with the formation, selection or administration of a trade union or other labour organization or the representation of employees by a trade union or other labour organization; or contribute financial or other support to such trade union or labour organization;

(c) suspend, transfer, refuse to transfer, lay-off, discharge, or change the status of an employee or alter any term or condition of employment, or use coercion, intimidation, threats or undue influence, or otherwise discriminate against any employee in regard to employment or any term or condition of employment, because the employee is a member or officer of a trade union or has applied for membership in a trade union;

(d) refuse to employ any person because such person is a member or officer of a trade union or has applied for membership in a trade union or require as a condition of employment that any person shall abstain from joining or assisting or being active in any trade union or from exercising any right provided by this Part;

(e) fail or refuse to bargain collectively in accordance with this Act;

(f) call, authorize, counsel, procure, support, encourage or engage in a lockout except as permitted by section 41.

Prohibitions re Employees, Trade Unions Etc.

(2) No employee, trade union or person acting on behalf of a trade union shall

(a) interfere with the formation, selection or administration of an employers' organization or the representation of employers by an employers' organization, or by intimidation or any other kind of threat or action, seek to compel an employer to refrain from becoming or to cease to be a member or officer or representative of an employers' organization;

(b) except with the consent of the employer, attempt at the employers' place of employment during working hours to persuade an employee of the employer to join a trade union;

(c) fail or refuse to bargain collectively in accordance with this Act;

(d) call, authorize, counsel, procure, support, encourage or engage in a strike except as permitted by section 41;

(e) use coercion or intimidation of any kind with a view to encouraging or discouraging membership in or activity in of for a trade union or labour organization.

Source: Government of Prince Edward Island, *P.E.I. Labour Act, Unfair Labour Practices*, p. 10, retrieved from http://www.gov.pe.ca/law/statutes.

Duty of Fair Representation

Finally, a union has a **duty of fair representation**. Under this duty, a union must not discriminate or act in an arbitrary manner in the representation of all employees. An example of a breach of this duty might be a union that fails to support a grievance by an employee because she is in a faction of the union

duty of fair representation
a legal obligation on the union's part to represent all employees equally and in a nondiscriminatory manner

that is in opposition to the current union leadership. McQuarrie (2010) examined 138 duty-of-fair-representation cases over the period 2000–2006 before the British Columbia Labour Relations Board. She found that complaints against the union were upheld in only 8 or 5.8 percent of the cases.

Collective Bargaining

Good Faith Bargaining

good faith bargaining

an obligation on union and management to make a serious attempt to reach a settlement

Labour laws in North America all require the parties to bargain in good faith. The idea of **good faith bargaining** is that union and management must make a serious attempt to negotiate a collective agreement. The concept of good faith bargaining is not easy to define, because it has been rarely tested, and boards have displayed a reluctance to interfere in private negotiations between the parties. One of the reasons that good faith bargaining rarely goes before labour boards is that between 75 and 90 percent of all cases are settled by mediation (Davenport, 2003). In general, unless there is a clear demonstration of anti-union bargaining behaviour, labour boards will not interfere. Boards will not hear bad faith bargaining charges based on the reasonableness of offers and counteroffers. An exception might be a first agreement, in which a firm deliberately makes offers that it knows the union will not or cannot accept.

Dispute Resolution

voluntarism

the notion that collective bargaining is a private matter between the parties and that government intervention should be kept to a minimum

mediation

a dispute-resolution process in which a neutral third party acts as a facilitator

conciliation

see *mediation*

Canadian labour laws have always differed from their *Wagner Act* parent in several respects. Generally, the *Wagner Act* is crafted on the principle of **voluntarism**, which involves minimal government intervention in collective bargaining. Under the *Wagner Act*, for example, **mediation** of disputes is used only if either party requests it. Canadian laws generally provide for greater government intervention especially on the question of industrial conflict. Thus, distinguishing features of Canadian labour law include the ban on strikes during the term of a collective agreement (Haiven, 1990) and mandatory government **conciliation**, or mediation, in the collective bargaining process before a legal strike can take place.

The latter feature has been a controversial intrusion in the negotiation process. Described as a cooling-off period before a strike, unions complain that it gives management time to prepare for a strike by stockpiling or building up inventories and simply delays serious bargaining. Policymakers, on the other hand, argue that conciliation gives third parties a chance to avoid costly strikes. They also claim that Canada's greater dependence on the exports of raw materials and the need for stability of supply requires a stronger government role in dispute resolution to avoid strikes. We will return to this topic in Chapter 9.

In several Canadian jurisdictions—federal, Alberta, British Columbia, Manitoba, Quebec, and Saskatchewan (see Table 2.2)—the requirement to complete the conciliation/mediation procedure before a strike has been removed, but the procedure is still required in New Brunswick, Newfoundland, Nova Scotia, Quebec, Ontario, and Prince Edward Island. Despite this move toward *Wagner Act* voluntarism by removing conciliation/mediation as a required step before a strike, Canadian governments have gradually expanded the role

TABLE 2.2

General Private-Sector Collective Bargaining Legislation: Third-Party Intervention in Collective Bargaining Disputes

JURISDICTIONS	THIRD-PARTY ASSISTANCE BEFORE STRIKE/ LOCKOUT	STANDARD THIRD-PARTY INTERVENTION	OTHER TYPES OF INTERVENTION	SPECIAL DISPUTE RESOLUTION MECHANISMS
Federal	Notification of failure to settle dispute required before a strike or lockout, except if the Minister[1] has already taken action to assist the parties.	*Conciliation* At the discretion of the Minister.[2] *Mediation* The Minister[2] may appoint a mediator upon request or on his/her own initiative.	*Industrial Inquiry Commission* The Minister[2] may appoint a commission upon request or on his/her own initiative. *Arbitration* The parties may agree to refer a dispute to a person or body for binding settlement.	*First Agreement Arbitration* At the discretion of the Minister after the acquisition of the right to strike/lock out; settlement at the discretion of the CIRB.[3] *Vote on Last Offer* At the discretion of the Minister, if it is in the public interest to order a vote.
Alberta	No strike or lockout may be declared unless a mediator has been formally appointed.	*Mediation* At the discretion of the Director of Mediation Services upon request, unless required by the Minister;[1] a party who accepts a mediator's recommendations may request a vote on them by the other party.	*Informal Mediation* On the request of either or both parties to the Director of Mediation Services after notice to bargain. *Disputes Inquiry Board* At the discretion of the Minister; vote on Board's recommendations unless they have been accepted. *Arbitration* The parties may agree to refer a dispute to an arbitration board whose decision is binding.	*Emergency Settlement Procedures* The Government may order these procedures in certain circumstances before or after a work stoppage. *Vote on Last Offer* Only one request by either party for a vote after the exchange of bargaining proposals; the Board[4] will conduct a vote when it is satisfied that, if accepted, the offer could form a collective agreement.

TABLE 2.2

General Private-Sector Collective Bargaining Legislation: Third-Party Intervention in Collective Bargaining Disputes (continued)

Jurisdictions	Third-Party Assistance Before Strike/ Lockout	Standard Third-Party Intervention	Other Types of Intervention	Special Dispute Resolution Mechanisms
British Columbia	Not required. However, unless the parties agree otherwise, no strike or lockout until at least 72 hours' notice to the Board.[4]	*Mediation* At the discretion of the associate chair of the Board's Mediation Division, upon request; or a mediation officer may be appointed by the Minister.[1] *Special Mediation* At the discretion of the Minister.	*Fact Finder* At the discretion of the associate chair of the Board's Mediation Division before or after a work stoppage. *Industrial Inquiry Commission* The Minister may appoint a commission upon request or on his/her own initiative.	*First Agreement Arbitration or Mediation/Arbitration* On the request of either party to the Board's Mediation Division after bargaining and a vote authorizing a strike; settlement at the discretion of the Division. *Vote on Last Offer* Before a strike or lockout, a single ballot is held upon the request of either party to the Mediation Division; while it is in progress, the Minister may order a vote if this is in the public interest.
Manitoba	Not required.	*Conciliation* The Minister[1] makes an appointment on the request of either party or on his/her own initiative. *Mediation* The Minister makes an appointment on the joint request of the parties, or may do so on the request of either party or on his/her own initiative.	*Industrial Inquiry Commission* The Minister may appoint a commission upon request or on his/her own initiative.	*Arbitration of First Agreement (FA) or Subsequent Agreement (SA)* On the request of either party to the Board,[4] for FA after a specified period following certification and conciliation; or for SA at least 60 days after the start of a strike or lockout during which conciliation or mediation took place for at least 30 days. If no agreement is reached, settlement by the Board or an arbitrator within certain time limits. *Vote on Last Offer* At the discretion of the Minister, if it is in the public interest to order a vote.

TABLE 2.2

General Private-Sector Collective Bargaining Legislation: Third-Party Intervention in Collective Bargaining Disputes (continued)

JURISDICTIONS	THIRD-PARTY ASSISTANCE BEFORE STRIKE/ LOCKOUT	STANDARD THIRD-PARTY INTERVENTION	OTHER TYPES OF INTERVENTION	SPECIAL DISPUTE RESOLUTION MECHANISMS
New Brunswick	No strike or lockout may be declared unless a party has requested the appointment of a conciliator.	*Conciliation and Mediation* The Minister[1] may make an appointment on the request of either party or on his/her own initiative.	*Industrial Inquiry Commission* The Minister may appoint a commission upon request or on his/her own initiative. *Arbitration* The parties may agree to refer a dispute to binding arbitration. Such an agreement is effective when filed with the Minister.	*Vote on Last Offer* On the request of either party to the Board,[4] upon acquisition of the right to strike/lock out (only one request per dispute).
Newfoundland and Labrador	No strike or lockout may be declared unless a party has requested a conciliation board.	*Conciliation* The Minister[1] may appoint a conciliator or conciliation board at the request of either party or on his/her own initiative. *Mediation* The Minister may appoint a mediator when he/she receives a request for a conciliation board or on his/her own initiative.	*Industrial Inquiry Commission* The Minister may appoint a commission upon request or on his/her own initiative.	*First Agreement Arbitration* On the request of either party, the Minister may ask the Board[4] to inquire into the dispute; settlement at the discretion of the Board. *Vote on Resumption of Work* The Government may order a secret vote when a strike or lockout poses a threat to an industry or region in the province.

General Private-Sector Collective Bargaining Legislation: Third-Party Intervention in Collective Bargaining Disputes (continued)

JURISDICTIONS	THIRD-PARTY ASSISTANCE BEFORE STRIKE/ LOCKOUT	STANDARD THIRD-PARTY INTERVENTION	OTHER TYPES OF INTERVENTION	SPECIAL DISPUTE RESOLUTION MECHANISMS
Nova Scotia	No strike or lockout may be declared unless a conciliator or conciliation board has been appointed and the Minister[1] has received a 48 hours' strike/ lockout notice.	*Conciliation* The Minister may appoint a conciliator at the request of either party or on his/her own initiative. After a conciliation report, the Minister must appoint a conciliation board if requested by both parties. *Mediation* At the discretion of the Minister.	*Industrial Inquiry Commission* The Minister may appoint a commission upon request or on his/her own initiative.	
Ontario	No strike or lockout may be declared unless a conciliator or mediator was appointed.	*Conciliation* When requested by either party, the Minister[1] must appoint a conciliator after notice to bargain, or may do so when no notice was given. If a conciliator is unsuccessful, the Minister may appoint a conciliation board. *Mediation* On request of both parties, the Minister may appoint a mediator selected by them. Either party may apply to the Ministry of Labour for mediation services after the conciliation procedures have been exhausted.	*Disputes Advisory Committee* The Minister may appoint a disputes advisory committee and request it to assist the parties at any time during bargaining when he/she considers that normal conciliation and mediation procedures have been exhausted. *Industrial Inquiry Commission* The Minister may establish a commission and refer an industrial matter or dispute to it. *Arbitration* The parties may agree to refer all matters in dispute to an arbitrator or arbitration board for binding settlement.	*First Agreement Arbitration* On the request of either party to the Board[4] after conciliation (the decision on the request to settle is based on whether certain positions of either party have caused an impasse). *Vote on Last Offer* When requested by the employer before or after the beginning of a strike or lockout, the Minister will order a vote (only one request per dispute). The Minister may order a vote at any time after the beginning of a strike or lockout if he/she believes it is in the public interest to do so.

Table 2.2

General Private-Sector Collective Bargaining Legislation: Third-Party Intervention in Collective Bargaining Disputes (continued)

Jurisdictions	Third-Party Assistance Before Strike/Lockout	Standard Third-Party Intervention	Other Types of Intervention	Special Dispute Resolution Mechanisms
Prince Edward Island	No strike or lockout may be declared unless a conciliator, or a conciliation board or mediator, has been appointed.	*Conciliation/Mediation* The Minister[1] may appoint a conciliator on the request of either party or on his/her own initiative. If a conciliator is unsuccessful, the Minister may appoint a conciliation board or a mediator.	*Industrial Inquiry Commission* The Minister may establish a commission to inquire into matters referred to it and attempt to effect a settlement.	*First Agreement Arbitration (not yet in force)* At the discretion of the Minister when requested by either party after the right to strike/lock out has been obtained. If he/she refers the matter to the Board[4] and the parties cannot reach an agreement, it settles the dispute.
Quebec	Not required.	*Conciliation* The Minister[2] must appoint a conciliator on the request of either party or may do so on his/her own initiative. *Special Mediation* The Minister[2] may appoint a special mediator at any time.	*Arbitration* A dispute is referred to arbitration by the Minister[2] upon application by the parties.	*First Agreement Arbitration* At the discretion of the Minister when requested by either party after conciliation. If he/she[2] refers the matter to an arbitrator, the content of the agreement is determined when a settlement is unlikely within a reasonable time. *Vote on Last Offer* At the discretion of the Commission[5] when requested by the employer, (only one such vote per dispute).

TABLE 2.2

General Private-Sector Collective Bargaining Legislation: Third-Party Intervention in Collective Bargaining Disputes (continued)

JURISDICTIONS	THIRD-PARTY ASSISTANCE BEFORE STRIKE/LOCKOUT	STANDARD THIRD-PARTY INTERVENTION	OTHER TYPES OF INTERVENTION	SPECIAL DISPUTE RESOLUTION MECHANISMS
Saskatchewan	Not required. However, the Minister[1] must be notified of the beginning of a strike or lockout (the notification must be sent promptly after the minimum 48 hours' strike or lockout notice has been given to the employer or trade union).	*Conciliation and Special Mediation* Upon request by either party or on his/her own initiative, the Minister may establish a conciliation board and/or appoint a special mediator.	*Arbitration* The parties may agree to refer a dispute to the Board[4] for binding settlement.	*First Agreement Arbitration* At the discretion of the Board when requested by either party after they have bargained without reaching an agreement, and a majority of employees have voted in favour of a strike, a lockout has commenced, there has been a failure or refusal to bargain collectively, or 90 days or more have elapsed since the certification. *Vote on Last Offer* At the discretion of a special mediator when a strike has continued for 30 days (only one such vote per dispute).

[1]*Minister* means the Minister responsible for labour.
[2]The Minister of Labour may delegate his/her powers of appointment to a designated official in his/her Department.
[3]*CIRB* means the Canada Industrial Relations Board.
[4]*Board* means the Labour Relations Board, Labour Board in Manitoba, or Labour and Employment Board in New Brunswick.
[5]*Commission* means the Quebec Labour Relations Commission (Commission des relations du travail).

Source: Labour Law Analysis, Labour Program, International and Intergovernmental Labour Affairs, 1 January 2006. Retrieved from http://www.hrsdc.gc.ca/eng/labour/labour_law/ind_rel/int.shtml. Human Resources and Skills Development Canada, 2009. Reproduced with the permission of the Minister of Public Works and Government Services Canada, 2011.

of government in collective bargaining. Three examples of this trend are the ability of the minister of labour (or in some jurisdictions, the parties) to create an industrial inquiry commission, order a vote on the last offer in bargaining, or settle a dispute over the first collective agreement by **arbitration**.

arbitration
a quasi-judicial process whereby a neutral third party makes a final and binding determination on all out-standing issues in dispute

Examples of the Expanded Government Role in Collective Bargaining

Industrial Inquiry Commission

Inquiry commissions are employed, though rarely, by governments to investigate the causes and consequences of industrial actions and strikes. After a confrontation with its teachers that involved a province-wide strike, the British Columbia government established an inquiry commission in October 2005.

 2.2

> The provincial government has appointed respected mediator Vince Ready as an Industrial Inquiry Commission to recommend a new collective bargaining structure for teachers and school employers, Labour Minister Michael de Jong announced today. "Over the past 15 years we've seen this bargaining system fail students and teachers time and time again," de Jong said. "We need a system where the parties can sit down and negotiate an agreement without having to resort to legislative intervention." Ready will be looking for ways to improve the collective bargaining system for teacher contracts. (Government of British Columbia, 2005)

W W W

Last-Offer Vote

Employers have complained that unions call strikes without putting the last offer to their members. To accommodate these employer concerns, labour laws have been amended to permit forced votes. There are several variants of this process across Canada (see Table 2.2, fourth column). In Newfoundland the right is restricted to cases in which the strike or lockout poses a threat to an industry or region. In Ontario the request by an employer for a last-offer vote must be granted when a strike is in progress (one vote per dispute). Also, the Ontario minister may order a vote if it is deemed in the public interest to do so. In several other jurisdictions, including the federal one, a vote is at the discretion of the minister.

First Contract Arbitration

The U.S. *National Labor Relations Act (Wagner Act)* has been amended only twice since 1935. The Taft-Hartley amendments in 1947 were designed to strengthen management in bargaining, and the Landrum-Griffin changes in 1959 promoted internal union democracy. In contrast, because of the *Snider* decision and pressure from labour-friendly political parties, Canadian labour laws have changed on a regular basis (Bruce, 1989), generally becoming more supportive of collective bargaining and unions. The law on first contract arbitration is a good illustration of this point.

In the United States, winning a free election does not necessarily guarantee the security of a union. One study, for example, found that unions were able to obtain a collective agreement in the first round of bargaining in fewer than 60 percent of the cases (Department of Labor study, reported in Abraham, 1997). To correct this problem in Canada, eight of eleven jurisdictions have adopted one of three models of first contract arbitration. Only Alberta, Nova Scotia, and New Brunswick have no provision for first contract arbitration.

The three models according to Abraham (1997) are (1) a bad faith bargaining remedy; (2) a complete breakdown in bargaining; and (3) a no-fault approach.

In the federal, British Columbia, and Newfoundland jurisdictions, a union must establish that the employer has been bargaining in bad faith in order to obtain first contract arbitration. According to Abraham (1997), "there has been a trend away from this concept because of the difficulty of defining and establishing 'bad faith bargaining.'" In Ontario, and more recently in British Columbia, first contract arbitration is available only when the labour board determines that a complete breakdown in negotiations has occurred. Finally, the no-fault approach of Quebec, Prince Edward Island, and Manitoba does not require the union to establish either bargaining in bad faith or a complete breakdown in negotiations.

Replacement Worker Laws

Finally, we canvass the wide variation in policies with respect to replacement employees during a strike or lockout. Quebec and British Columbia have outright bans on strikebreakers during a strike. Ontario, Manitoba, and Alberta prohibit the use of professional strikebreakers. Manitoba, Prince Edward Island, and Saskatchewan prevent replacement workers from permanently replacing employees but only after a strike. The federal *Canada Labour Code* prevents the use of replacement workers but only when their purpose is to undermine the union rather than pursue legitimate collective bargaining objectives. New Brunswick, Newfoundland, and Nova Scotia have no significant policies with respect to the use of replacement workers. For the source of replacement laws see the Human Resources and Social Development Canada (HRSDC) website.

RPC 2.3   Collective Agreement Administration

The law in Canada dealing with collective agreement administration again differs significantly from its American parent. In all Canadian jurisdictions, strikes are illegal during the term of a collective agreement. The *Wagner Act* contains no such prohibition. In Canada, all laws substitute arbitration for the right to strike during the contract term. However, this restriction on strikes is known as the "labour peace" provision of the law. Not all scholars agree that restricting strikes produces labour peace, since Canada has a relatively high number of illegal strikes during the term of the agreement (Haiven, 1990).

The labour peace provision is also known as the "deemed provision" of the labour law, because the law deems it be included in every collective agreement. The Nova Scotia law provides a typical example of how this provision works (see IR Today 2.1). Note that even if labour and management choose not to include an arbitration provision in the collective agreement,

Excerpt from Nova Scotia *Trade Union Act*

Final Settlement Provision

42(1) Every collective agreement shall contain a provision for final settlement without stoppage of work, by arbitration or otherwise, of all differences between the parties to or persons bound by the agreement or on whose behalf it was entered into, concerning its meaning or violation.

(2) Where a collective agreement does not contain a provision as required by this Section, it shall be deemed to contain the following provision:

> Where a difference arises between the parties relating to the interpretation, application or administration of this agreement, including any question as to whether a matter is arbitrable, or where an allegation is made that this agreement has been violated, either of the parties may, after exhausting any grievance procedure established by this agreement, notify the other party in writing of its desire to submit the difference or allegation to arbitration. If the parties fail to agree upon an arbitrator, the appointment shall be made by the Minister of Labour for Nova Scotia upon the request of either party. The arbitrator shall hear and determine the difference or allegation and shall issue a decision, and the decision is final and binding upon the parties and upon any employee or employer affected by it.

(3) Every party to and every person bound by the agreement, and every person on whose behalf the agreement was entered into, shall comply with the provision for final settlement contained in the agreement. *R.S., c. 475, s. 42.*

Powers and Duty of Arbitrator or Arbitration Board

43(1) An arbitrator or an arbitration board appointed pursuant to this Act or to a collective agreement . . .

> (e) has power to treat as part of the collective agreement the provisions of any statute of the Province governing relations between the parties to the collective agreement.

Source: Nova Scotia House of Assembly, retrieved from http://www.gov.ns.ca/legislature/legc/statutes/tradeun.htm.

---

the law puts it in the agreement as if the parties had agreed to it (see 42(2) above).

Because the law provides "labour peace" by banning strikes during the collective agreement term, there is an implicit role for the arbitrator not found in the United States. Under Canadian law, both the collective agreement and the law give arbitrators the jurisdiction to settle disputes, defining a public policy role for arbitration that does not exist in U.S. law. More significantly, the public policy role of Canadian arbitrators has expanded in the decades since World War II. With the passage of employment law governing such matters as human rights, health and safety, employment equity, pensions, and plant closures, arbitrators have been increasingly called upon to apply these laws in arbitration decisions.

We have chosen two examples where Canadian laws explicitly mandate arbitrators to interpret employment law. The first is found in section 43(1) of the Nova Scotia law (see IR Today 2.1). The Nova Scotia law gives the power to the arbitrator to treat relevant employment laws as part of the collective agreement. In the second case, Ontario, arbitrators are more explicitly given the power to interpret employment law (see excerpt in IR Today 2.2).

In summary, Canadian laws define a greater public policy role for arbitrators in two respects. First, arbitration, as a strike substitute procedure, gives arbitrators a public policy role in settling all disputes during the contract term—hence the term "labour peace." Second, labour legislation and arbitrational jurisprudence have given arbitrators an increasingly important role in interpreting relevant employment law (human rights, employment equity, health and safety, plant closure, pension, termination, etc.).

RPC 2.4

Role of the *Charter*

In the process of repatriating the Constitution in 1982, Canada preserved labour as a provincial responsibility and created a *Charter of Rights and Freedoms* (see IR Today 2.3). The important question raised by the *Charter* was its effect on existing Canadian labour laws. Since the Canadian constitution requires that all laws be consistent with the *Charter* (section 52), it was an open question whether the *Charter* would negatively or positively affect existing law. Note that the rights set out in the *Charter* (e.g., freedom of association) are subject to s. 1: "reasonable limits prescribed by law as can be demonstrably justified in a free and democratic society." In addition, governments could invoke the "notwithstanding clause," which provided a legislative override of the freedom or right for five years (s. 33).

Review of Supreme Court *Charter* Decisions

In this section, we canvass some of the important decisions affecting labour and management.

Right to Strike

The most significant early interpretation of freedom of association was found in three cases that have together become known as the Labour Trilogy: restrictions on the right to strike in Alberta, the federal government wage controls, and back-to-work laws in Saskatchewan and various unions (reference *Public Service Employee Relations Act (Alta.)*, [1987] 1 S.C.R. 313 (*"Alberta Reference"*); *PSAC v. Canada*, [1987] 1 S.C.R. 424; *RWDSU v. Saskatchewan*, [1987] 1 S.C.R. 460). In these three 1987 cases, the court found that freedom of association did not include a right to strike and bargain collectively (Swinton, 1995).

Charter of Rights and Freedoms

The Charter of Rights of Freedoms Constitution Act, 1982

Enacted as Schedule B to the *Canada Act* 1982 (U.K.) 1982, c. 11,

which came into force on April 17, 1982

PART I

CANADIAN CHARTER OF RIGHTS AND FREEDOMS

Whereas Canada is founded upon principles that recognize the supremacy of God and the rule of law:

Guarantee of Rights and Freedoms

Rights and Freedoms in Canada

1. The *Canadian Charter of Rights and Freedoms* guarantees the rights and freedoms set out in it subject only to such reasonable limits prescribed by law as can be demonstrably justified in a free and democratic society.

Fundamental Freedoms

Fundamental Freedoms

2. Everyone has the following fundamental freedoms:
   a) freedom of conscience and religion;
   b) freedom of thought, belief, opinion and expression, including freedom of the press and other media of communication;
   c) freedom of peaceful assembly; and
   d) freedom of association.

Source: Department of Justice Canada, *Charter of Rights and Freedoms*, retrieved from http://laws.justice.gc.ca/en/charter/index.html.

For organized labour in Canada, the early trilogy losses resulted in some negative views about the *Charter*'s ability to protect workers' right to freedom of association. More recently, however, four cases have produced more positive outcomes and indicated a more labour-friendly direction (Cameron, 2002). We will discuss these cases more fully below.

Union Dues

The *Lavigne* decision in 1991 was interesting because an earlier case in the United States very similar to this one was heard by the Supreme Court of Canada (SCC). Both the Abood case (*Abood v. Detroit Board of Education*, 431 U.S. 209 1977) and the Lavigne case (*Lavigne v. Ontario Public Service Employees Union*, [1991] 2 S.C.R. 211) involved teachers who objected to their union dues going to political causes that they did not support. These decisions provide an example of a major difference between U.S. and Canadian views of freedom of association and collective bargaining. In the U.S. decision, the court upheld Abood's complaint and ordered the union to rebate that portion of his dues that was for purposes other than collective bargaining. In the *Lavigne* case, on the other hand, the Canadian court justified the restriction on his freedom of association by a view of unionism that includes legitimate social and political goals that go beyond collective bargaining. Whereas the U.S. constitution has emphasized individual rights, the Canadian *Charter* has respected both individual and collective rights (Sack, 2010).

Here is an excerpt from *Lavigne v. OPSEU*:

> The limitation on appellant's freedom of association is justified under s. 1 of the Charter. The state objectives in compelling the payment of union dues which can be used to assist causes unrelated to collective bargaining are to enable unions to participate in the broader political, economic and social debates in society, and to contribute to democracy in the workplace. . . .

Picketing

The court has decided that secondary picketing is part of freedom of expression. In the *Pepsi-Cola* case (*R.W.D.S.U., Local 558 v. Pepsi-Cola Canada Beverages (West) Ltd.*, [2002] 1 S.C.R. 156, 2002 SCC 8), the court held that it was legal to picket at locations other than the firm's premises as long as the picketing is peaceful. Here is an excerpt from the decision:

> The union engaged in a variety of protest and picketing activities during a lawful strike and lockout at one of the appellant's plants. These activities eventually spread to "secondary" locations, where union members and supporters picketed retail outlets to prevent the delivery of the appellant's products and dissuade the store staff from accepting delivery; carried placards in front of a hotel where members of the substitute labour force were staying; and engaged in intimidating conduct outside the homes of appellant's management personnel. An interlocutory injunction was granted which effectively prohibited the union from engaging in picketing activities at secondary locations. A majority of the Court of Appeal upheld the order against congregating at the residences of the appellant's employees, as these activities constituted tortious conduct. However, the section restraining the union from picketing at any location other than the appellant's premises was quashed, thus allowing the union to engage in peaceful picketing at secondary locations. (Supreme Court of Canada, 2002)

Union Recognition

In 1994, during the term of the New Democratic Party (NDP) government, the Ontario legislature enacted the *Agricultural Labour Relations Act*, 1994 (ALRA), which extended trade union and collective bargaining rights to agricultural workers. Prior to the adoption of this legislation, agricultural workers had always been excluded from Ontario's labour relations regime. A year later, under the Harris Conservative government, the legislature repealed the ALRA in its entirety, in effect subjecting agricultural workers to section 3(b) of the *Labour Relations Act*, 1995 (LRA), which excluded them from the labour relations regime set out in the LRA. Section 80 also terminated any certification rights of trade unions, and any collective agreements certified, under the ALRA.

The United Food & Commercial Workers (UFCW), on behalf of Tom Dunmore and other farm workers, brought an application challenging the repeal of the ALRA and the union's exclusion from the LRA, on the basis that it infringed its workers' rights under sections (d) and 15(1) of the *Canadian Charter of Rights and Freedoms* (*Dunmore v. Ontario (Attorney General)*, [2001] 3 S.C.R. 1016, 2001 SCC 94). While both the Ontario Court (General Division) and the Ontario Court of Appeal upheld the challenged legislation, the Supreme Court struck it down as follows:

> Here, the appellants do not claim a constitutional right to general inclusion in the LRA, but simply a constitutional freedom to organize a trade association. This freedom to organize exists independently of any statutory enactment, although its effective exercise may require legislative protection in some cases. The appellants have met the evidentiary burden of showing that they are substantially incapable of exercising their fundamental freedom to organize without the LRA's protective regime. While the mere fact of exclusion from protective legislation is not conclusive evidence of a Charter violation, the evidence indicates that, but for the brief period covered by the ALRA, there has never been an agricultural workers' union in Ontario and agricultural workers have suffered repeated attacks on their efforts to unionize. The inability of agricultural workers to organize can be linked to state action. The exclusion of agricultural workers from the LRA functions not simply to permit private interferences with their fundamental freedoms, but to substantially reinforce such interferences. The inherent difficulties of organizing farm workers, combined with the threat of economic reprisal from employers, form only part of the reason why association is all but impossible in the agricultural sector in Ontario. Equally important is the message sent by the exclusion of agricultural workers from the LRA, which delegitimizes their associational activity and thereby contributes to its ultimate failure. The most palpable effect of the LRESLAA and the LRA is, therefore, to place a chilling effect on non-statutory union activity. (Supreme Court of Canada, 2001)

In an 8–1 vote, the Supreme Court of Canada (SCC) granted the appeal and declared the impugned legislation unconstitutional. The Harris government was given eighteen months to comply with section 2(d) of the *Charter* and to provide a statutory framework that would be consistent with the principles established in the case.

The *Dunmore* decision may be important for several reasons (Adams, 2003; Fudge, 2008). For a more critical view of the court's interpretation of freedom of association see Langille (2009):

1. Until *Dunmore*, the SCC had tended to defer to elected legislatures.
2. All Canadian workers have the right to organize to advance employment interests without fear of reprisals.
3. Canadian governments have legal responsibility to proactively intervene to ensure freedom of association.
4. The *Charter* extends rights to both individuals and collectivities.

5. Finally, the SCC acknowledged the importance of the core labour standards established through the International Labour Organization (ILO), in which freedom of association is viewed as a fundamental human right:

> 27. The notion that underinclusion can infringe freedom of association is not only implied by Canadian Charter jurisprudence, but is also consistent with international human rights law. Article 2 of Convention (No. 87) concerning freedom of association and protection of the right to organize, 67 U.N.T.S. 17, provides that "[w]orkers and employers, *without distinction whatsoever*, shall have the right to establish and . . . to join organisations of their own choosing" (emphasis added), and that only members of the armed forces and the police may be excluded (Article 9). In addition, Article 10 of Convention No. 87 defines an "organisation" as "*any* organisation of workers or of employers for furthering and defending the interests of workers or of employers" (emphasis added). Canada ratified Convention No. 87 in 1972. The Convention's broadly worded provisions confirm precisely what I have discussed above, which is that discriminatory treatment implicates not only an excluded group's dignity interest, but also its basic freedom of association. (Supreme Court of Canada, 2001)

Political Activity

In 1991 the Supreme Court upheld a challenge to restrictions on the political activities of civil servants (*Osborne v. Canada (Treasury Board)*, [1991] 2 S.C.R. 69). Under section 33 of the *Public Service Employment Act*, it was illegal on threat of dismissal to engage in work for or on behalf of a political party or candidate. The court found that the restrictions violated freedom of expression under 2(b). Here is an excerpt from the decision:

> Section 33 of the Act, which prohibits partisan political expression and activity by public servants under threat of disciplinary action including dismissal from employment, infringes the right to freedom of expression in s. 2(b) of the Charter. Where opposing values call for a restriction on the freedom of speech, and, apart from exceptional cases, the limits on that freedom are to be dealt with under the balancing test in s. 1, rather than circumscribing the scope of the guarantee at the outset. In this case, by prohibiting public servants from speaking out in favour of a political party or candidate, s. 33 of the Act expressly has for its purpose the restriction of expressive activity and is accordingly inconsistent with s. 2(b) of the Charter. (Supreme Court of Canada, 1991)

A New Direction for the Supreme Court

It has been argued that the *Pepsi-Cola* and *Dunmore* cases, together with the *Advanced Cutting* decision (*R. v. Advanced Cutting and Coring Ltd.*, [2001]

S.C.R. 70), in which collective rights trumped individual rights, have resulted in a new Labour Trilogy being defined by Canada's highest court (Cameron, 2002). Contrary to the earlier trilogy of cases (discussed above), these more recent decisions provide more positive outcomes for labour. While the former trilogy limited labour's ability to strike, the later cases strengthened collective rights, expanded picketing and freedom of expression, and gave new meaning to union recognition and freedom of association.

The case for a new direction was made even stronger by a landmark decision of the Supreme Court of Canada on June 8, 2007. In a dramatic reversal of past decisions, the Court declared collective bargaining a constitutional right under the freedom of association guarantee. Once again, the Court relied on international labour standards as established by the ILO in its reasoning. The preamble and decision excerpt in IR Today 2.4 explain the context of the case. For a more recent Supreme Court of Canada case that represents a follow-up to *Dunmore*, see IR Today 2.5.

IR Today 2.4

Supreme Court Relies on ILO Standards

Preamble

The *Health and Social Services Delivery Improvement Act* was adopted as a response to challenges facing British Columbia's healthcare system. The *Act* was quickly passed and there was no meaningful consultation with unions before it became law. Part 2 of the *Act* introduced changes to transfers and multi-worksite assignment rights (sections 4 and 5), contracting out (section 6), the status of contracted-out employees (s. 6), job security programs (ss. 7 and 8), and layoffs and bumping rights (s. 9). It gave healthcare employers greater flexibility to organize their relations with their employees as they see fit, and in some cases to do so in ways that would not have been permissible under existing collective agreements and without adhering to requirements of consultation and notice that would otherwise obtain. It invalidated important provisions of collective agreements then in force, and effectively precluded meaningful collective bargaining on a number of specific issues. Furthermore, s. 10 voided any part of a collective agreement, past or future, that was inconsistent with Part 2, and any collective agreement purporting to modify these restrictions. The appellants, who are unions and members of the unions representing the nurses, facilities, or community subsectors, challenged the constitutional validity of Part 2 of the Act as violative of the guarantees of freedom of association and equality protected by the *Canadian Charter of Rights and Freedoms*. Both the trial judge and the Court of Appeal found that Part 2 of the *Act* did not violate ss. 2(d) or 15 of the Charter.

Decision Excerpt

Freedom of association guaranteed by s. 2(d) of the Charter includes a procedural right to collective bargaining. The grounds advanced in the earlier decisions of this Court for the exclusion of collective bargaining from the s. 2(d)'s protection do not withstand principled scrutiny and should be rejected. The general purpose of the Charter guarantees and the broad language of s. 2(d) are consistent with a measure of protection for collective bargaining. Further, the right to collective bargaining is neither of recent origin nor merely a creature of statute. The history of collective bargaining in Canada reveals that long before the present statutory labour regimes were put in place, collective bargaining was recognized as a fundamental aspect of Canadian society, emerging as the most significant collective activity through which freedom of association is expressed in the labour context. Association for purposes of collective bargaining has long been recognized as a fundamental Canadian

IR Today 2.4 (continued)

right which predated the Charter. The protection enshrined in s. 2(d) of the Charter may properly be seen as the culmination of a historical movement towards the recognition of a procedural right to collective bargaining. Canada's adherence to international documents recognizing a right to collective bargaining also supports recognition of that right in s. 2(d). The Charter should be presumed to provide at least as great a level of protection as is found in the international human rights documents that Canada

has ratified. Lastly, the protection of collective bargaining under s. 2(d) is consistent with and supportive of the values underlying the Charter and the purposes of the Charter as a whole. Recognizing that workers have the right to bargain collectively as part of their freedom to associate reaffirms the values of dignity, personal autonomy, equality and democracy that are inherent in the Charter. (Health Services and Support–Facilities Subsector Bargaining Assn. v. British Columbia, 2007 S.C.C. 27)

IR Today 2.5

Supreme Court Rules on Collective Bargaining for Agricultural Workers

There is a difference between winning the battle and winning the war. In the April 29, 2011, Supreme Court of Canada decision in *Ontario (Attorney General) v. Fraser*, the UFCW (United Food & Commercial Workers) and Ontario's agricultural workers lost in their argument that the *Agricultural Employees Protection Act* (AEPA) was insufficient to protect their *Charter* freedom of association. That was the battle.

But what was really at stake in this case was whether the Supreme Court's earlier *B.C. Health Services* decision, which established limited *Charter* protection for collective bargaining, was going to be overturned or substantially weakened—and it wasn't. That was the real danger for Canadian workers—the war, if you will—and Canadian workers did not lose this war today.

Summary

This case dealt with the question of whether collective representation legislation applying to agricultural workers in Ontario, the AEPA, lacks sufficient protections for collective representation and bargaining such as to violate the workers' section 2(d) *Charter*-protected freedom of association. The Ontario Court of Appeal had held that it was an unjustifiable violation of this freedom, and held that the *B.C. Health Services* decision effectively constitutionalized the Wagner Model of collective bargaining. The Court of

Appeal had held that because the AEPA did not include key features of the Wagner Model, it violated these workers' freedom of association, and this breach was not saved under section 1 of the *Charter*. The Ontario government appealed this decision to the Supreme Court of Canada.

A majority of the Supreme Court of Canada held that the AEPA does not violate either section 2(d) or 15 (equality rights) of the *Charter*. However, the majority opinion of five justices, drafted by Chief Justice McLachlin and Justice LeBel, affirmed the *B.C. Health Services* decision, noting that it was "consistent with previous cases on the issue of individual and collective rights" and that the "unworkability of *Health Services* has not been established. There is no concrete evidence that the principles enunciated in *Dunmore* and *Health Services* are unworkable or have led to intolerable results. It is premature to argue that the holding in *Health Services*, rendered four years ago, is unworkable in practice."

Emphasizing that the *Health Services* decision does not guarantee any particular model of collective bargaining, the majority concluded that because the AEPA does not make association by these workers in pursuit of workplace goals impossible, it does not meet the necessary threshold of substantially impairing the workers' section 2(d) rights. In coming to this conclusion, the majority ruled that, by implication, the collective bargaining provisions of the AEPA must impose a duty on employers to consider employee representations in good faith.

Addressing the UFCW's argument that the AEPA has not been sufficient to permit effective collective bargaining, the majority concluded that this was a premature argument, that "the union has not made a significant attempt to make it work," and that "the process has not been fully explored and tested."

The decision is a disappointment to the UFCW and Ontario's agricultural workers, as it makes clear that the *Charter* and *B.C. Health Services* does not constitutionalize or entrench the Wagner Model—or any particular system—of collective bargaining. However, the decision does offer strong support for the *B.C. Health Services* decision and inclusion of limited protection of the process of collective bargaining in the *Charter*'s freedom of association. It also offers some guidance on the content and extent of this protection of collective bargaining and good-faith negotiations.

Source: Report by Prof. Sara Slinn, Osgoode Hall Law School, York University, and the Centre for Industrial Relations and Human Resources, University of Toronto. Reprinted with permission.

Employment Law

Some scholars argue that private-sector union decline has led to the emergence of a new regime defined by individual employment rights (Piore & Safford, 2006). The argument is more compelling in the United States than in Canada, since union decline is much greater south of the border. Nonetheless, employment law has also expanded in Canada. The essence of the argument is that collective bargaining under the *Wagner Act* model has been replaced by a system of rights and obligations that apply to all firms and employees whether unionized or not. This trend has created a tension between individual and collective rights. In this section, we summarize the conditions of employment and the rights that apply to both union and nonunion firms and to all employees.

Employment Conditions

We make a distinction between employment conditions—commonly known as *employment standards*—and employment rights. However, it should be born in mind that these two categories cannot be easily separated; in the case of health and safety regulation, for example, we will find both conditions and rights.

Generally, conditions are established in legislation by minimums (e.g., hours of work, overtime, minimum wages, vacation, meal breaks). Unionized employees may typically build on these minimum conditions. Like most employment conditions, there is wide variation across Canada. This section draws on the summary provided by Human Resources and Social Development Canada (HRSDC).

Hours of Work

According to Human Resources and Social Development Canada, there are two models for the regulation of hours of work provisions. In one model, the law provides for a standard workday or workweek and overtime pay if the standard is exceeded; in the other, there are standard hours of work and a legal maximum number of hours per day or per week.

Overtime

This excerpt from HRSDC provides a summary of the law with regard to overtime in Canada:

> The overtime rate is payable to the employees for each hour or part of an hour they work in excess of the standard hours. Most jurisdictions have established an overtime rate equivalent to one and a half times the employee's regular rate of pay. British Columbia further provides that hours in excess of 12 in a day must be remunerated at twice the regular rate. New Brunswick and Newfoundland and Labrador have established the overtime rate as being one and a half times the minimum wage. In many jurisdictions, subject to certain conditions, an employer and an employee may agree to replace the payment of overtime by paid leave equivalent to one and a half times the overtime hours worked. (HRSDC, n.d.)

Scheduling of Hours

Some employers may be required to give notice to employees in advance of changes in scheduled hours. For example, where there is a change in shift, some employers depending on jurisdiction might need to give twenty-four hours' notice to affected employees. In addition, companies might have to provide a minimum period between shifts (at least eight hours) and a rest day wherever practicable.

Coffee and Meal Breaks

British Columbia, Manitoba, New Brunswick, Ontario, Prince Edward Island, Quebec, and Saskatchewan provide an employee entitlement to a meal break of at least half an hour after each period of five consecutive hours of work. This meal break is normally unpaid unless an employee is required to remain at their workstation or to be available for work during the meal break. There is no legislation that requires an employer to provide a coffee break. However, if a coffee break is provided in Ontario, Quebec, or Saskatchewan, employers have to consider it time worked.

Exclusions

The long list of exclusions usually includes students, members of designated professions, ambulance drivers and attendants, domestics, fishermen, farm workers, construction workers, and managerial staff. Additionally, more flexible arrangement of work hours for certain jobs may be permitted by the statutes as explained below:

> The modification of the standard work week or the averaging of hours over a period of two or more weeks, for example, can be authorized under the terms of the *Canada Labour Code*, the *Labour Standards Act* in Saskatchewan and in all three territories. Similarly, Quebec allows the staggering of hours of work on a basis other than a weekly basis with the authorization of the Labour Standards

Commission (Commission des normes du travail). These provisions are especially useful to employers because they provide flexibility while allowing to economize on overtime premiums. (HRSDC, n.d.)

Employee Rights

Rights have been granted to all employees in the following areas: human rights and discrimination, health and safety, plant closure, pension, maternity, pay equity, employment equity, and dismissal. In this section, we provide examples of how the laws vary across Canada.

Human Rights

Human rights are protected in each of the eleven jurisdictions by means of a human rights commission. There is some variation in the human rights codes with respect to the protected groups, but the administration of the law is quite uniform across Canada. We have chosen the federal jurisdiction as representative. Under the *Canadian Human Rights Act*, it is against the law for any employer or provider of a service that falls within federal jurisdiction to discriminate on the basis of

- race;
- national or ethic origin;
- colour;
- religion;
- age;
- sex (including pregnancy and childbearing);
- sexual orientation;
- marital status;
- family status;
- physical or mental disability (including dependence on alcohol or drugs); or
- pardoned criminal conviction.

Enforcement of human rights is by means of an employee (or group of employees) complaint. Complaints are heard by tribunals of the respective provincial or federal commission that are composed of neutral adjudicators.

The *Human Rights Act* also protects employees against harassment by other employees. According to the Canadian Human Rights Commission, "harassment, whether by a supervisor or co-worker, creates a barrier to equality by demeaning its victims, interfering with their ability to work effectively and, in some instances, even forcing them to resign. Despite the publicity surrounding this issue, studies consistently show that employees continue to face harassment in the workplace."

Health and Safety

In the United States, the *Occupational Safety and Health Act*'s (OSHA) administrative model attempts to encourage and enforce improved health and safety practices through the development of regulations, inspections, fines, and, in some instances, criminal prosecutions. An alternative is the Canadian internal responsibility model (IRM), which places greater emphasis on establishing the framework within which the workplace parties mutually address health and safety concerns (Hebdon & Hyatt, 1998). The IRM mandates employee involvement by conferring three basic rights and responsibilities upon workers:

- the right to know about the hazards to which they are exposed;
- the right to participate in mandatory joint worker–management health and safety committees; and
- the right to refuse unsafe work without fear of reprisal.

Research indicates that IRM has a significant effect on reducing lost-time injury rates, especially where labour and management have co-managed health and safety issues through the joint committee (Lewchuk, Robb & Walters, 1996).

Pay and Employment Equity

Pay equity is parity in wages and salaries between men and women. **Employment equity** is a broader term that involves the removal of barriers that have an adverse impact on certain designated groups. The federal employment equity legislation, for example, targets employment levels of visible minorities, women, Aboriginals, and the disabled (Mentzer, 2002).

It is important to make a distinction between direct and systemic discrimination:

- *Direct discrimination* occurs when, for example, an employee discriminates against a fellow employee.
- *Systemic discrimination* occurs when the organizational rules are followed but protected groups are disadvantaged.

Direct discrimination may be dealt with through a complaint under a human rights code or under a union's grievance procedure. Systemic discrimination is much harder to prove and to remedy. It might be built into human resources functions such as recruitment, selection, training, staff development, compensation, performance evaluation, and discipline (Weiner, 1995).

The federal government has the only employment equity legislation in Canada. The coverage of the act was defined in the HRSDC *Employment Equity Act* annual report 2004:

> Four types of employers are covered by the *Employment Equity Act*: federally regulated private sector employers, the Federal Public Service, Separate Employers, and employers under the Federal Contractors Program (FCP). In 2003, these employers accounted for 13 percent of the Canadian workforce or over 2.2 million employees, compared to 2 million in 2002. (HRSDC, 2004)

From 2002 to 2003, there were employment gains in the combined totals of all reporting employers as follows:

- Women went from 95.9 to 97.9 percent.
- Aboriginal peoples went from 80.7 to 84.6 percent.

pay equity

women and men being paid relatively equally for work of equal value

employment equity

equity in employment levels and opportunities between targeted community groups (women, visible minorities, Aboriginals, and disabled employees) and major employers

- Persons with disabilities went from 46.9 to 58.5 percent.
- Members of visible minorities went from 77.5 to 90.5 percent (HRSDC, 2004).

Pay equity and employment equity have proven to be difficult goals to achieve despite the apparent success shown in employment equity above. For a comprehensive analysis of the Canadian experience, see Jain, Lawler, Bai, and Lee (2010). IR Today 2.6 documents the saga of a pay equity case involving the federal government and the Public Service Alliance of Canada (PSAC). It seems that getting a favourable pay equity award is not enough—the question of the appropriate taxable rate on the pay equity amounts is an issue for the courts to decide. Table 2.3 provides a comprehensive review of pay equity legislation in Canada. Note that all provinces have a version of pay equity legislation that covers both the public and the private sector.

IR Today 2.6

Pay Equity Payment Interest Case to Get Judicial Review

The question of how to tax pay equity settlement payments will go before a court after the Canadian Human Rights Tribunal ruled against PSAC. The story begins in 1985 and 1990 when PSAC filed two wage discrimination complaints against Treasury Board under the *Canadian Human Rights Act*, section 11. These complaints were settled in 1999. In 2000, many PSAC members past and present received settlement cheques to cover the wages they would have earned if the federal government's wage structure didn't discriminate against women. But the cheques had income tax deducted as if the money was income earned in 2000. This put pay equity recipients into higher tax brackets.

PSAC argued that since the lump sum payments were retroactive wage adjustments, they should be taxed as if they were income earned in the years covered by the complaint.

Example Pay Equity Tax Calculation	
In 2000, a CR received her lump sum pay equity payment.	
Pay Equity Settlement:	$25,548
Total income for 2000:	$93,452
Basic federal tax:	$15,433
Basic federal tax under QRLSP:	$18,494

In Feb. 1999, the government introduced the Qualifying Retroactive Lump-Sum Payment (QRLSP) mechanism which allowed pay equity settlement payments of $3000 or more to be taxed as income earned in the years covered by the settlement.

While that felt like victory, the QRLSP also resulted [in] interest charges on tax owing on lump sum payments as if the person had been in arrears.

That wiped out any savings from avoiding being taxed on the whole lump sum in one year. In some most cases [sic] it made the situation worse.

In 2002, PSAC filed a complaint with the Human Rights Commission over this practice. The Commission rejected the complaint, but the union went to federal court to have the decision reviewed.

The court sent the complaint back to the Canadian Human Rights Commission in 2004. The Commission later accepted PSAC's position, and referred the complaint to the Canadian Human Rights Tribunal.

The tribunal dismissed the union's complaint April 23, 2010. But PSAC has sent the tribunal decision to Federal Court for review. The union expects the Federal Court to hear the case some time in 2011.

Source: Public Service Alliance of Canada, retrieved 14 April 2011 from http://psac.com/news/2010/issues/20100614-e.shtml.

TABLE 2.3

Equal Pay Legislation in Canada by Jurisdiction

Note: To save space, the footnotes have been omitted. They may be found on the HRSDC website.

JURISDICTION	APPLICATION	TYPE OF PROHIBITION	BASIS FOR MEASURING EQUAL PAY	BASIS FOR THE COMPARISON OF WORK	FACTORS THAT JUSTIFY A DIFFERENCE IN PAY	TIME LIMIT TO FILE COMPLAINT	RESTRICTIONS ON RECOVERY
Federal Jurisdiction (*Canadian Human Rights Act* Equal Wages Guidelines, 1986)	Federal public service and federally regulated undertakings	Male–female pay differential	Wages (*Act*, s. 11(1))	Work of equal value performed in the same establishment, assessed by the composite of the skill, effort and responsibility required and the working conditions under which work is performed. (*Act*, s. 11(1), (2))	Different performance ratings; seniority; a re-evaluation and downgrading of an employee's position; a rehabilitation assignment; a demotion procedure or a procedure of gradually reducing an employee's wages on the same grounds that justify a demotion procedure; a temporary training position; the existence of an internal labour shortage in a particular job classification; a reclassification of a position to a lower level; or regional rates of wages. Gender is not a reasonable factor justifying a difference in pay. (*Act*, ss. 11(4), (5); Guidelines, s. 16)	1 year (an extension of time is possible) (s. 41(1)(e))	No
Alberta (*Human Rights, Citizenship and Multiculturalism Act*)	Private and public sectors	Male–female pay differential	Rate of pay s. 6(1)	The same or substantially the same work for an employer in an establishment. s. 6(1)	The contravention of the *Act* was reasonable and justifiable in the circumstances. (s. 11)	1 year (s. 20(1)(b))	Recovery is limited to wages, income lost and/or expenses incurred during the 2 years preceding the complaint. A limit also applies for civil proceedings. (s. 34)

Equal Pay Legislation in Canada by Jurisdiction (continued)

Note: To save space, the footnotes have been omitted. They may be found on the HRSDC website.

Jurisdiction	Application	Type of Prohibition	Basis for Measuring Equal Pay	Basis for the Comparison of Work	Factors That Justify a Difference in Pay	Time Limit to File Complaint	Restrictions on Recovery
British Columbia *(Human Rights Code)*	Private and public sectors	Male–female pay differential	Rate of pay (s. 12(1))	Similar or substantially similar work. This must be assessed by the concepts of skill, effort and responsibility, subject to factors in respect of pay rates, such as seniority systems, merit systems and systems that measure earnings by the quantity or quality of production. (ss. 12(1), (2))	A factor that would reasonably justify the difference, other than sex. (s. 12(3))	6 months (an extension of time is possible) (s. 22)	No (a limit does apply for civil proceedings)
Manitoba *(Human Rights Code)*	Private and public sectors	Male–female pay differential	Scale of wages (s. 82(1))	The kind or quality of work and the amount of work required of, and done by, the employees, is the same or substantially the same. (s. 82(1))	No provisions	6 months (s. 82(2))	Recovery is limited to wages due and payable in the 6 months before the date the complaint was filed or, if employment was terminated, in the last 6 months of employment. (s. 96(2))

TABLE 2.3

Equal Pay Legislation in Canada by Jurisdiction (continued)

Note: To save space, the footnotes have been omitted. They may be found on the HRSDC website.

Jurisdiction	Application	Type of Prohibition	Basis for Measuring Equal Pay	Basis for the Comparison of Work	Factors That Justify a Difference in Pay	Time Limit to File Complaint	Restrictions on Recovery
New Brunswick (*Employment Standards Act*)	Private and public sectors	Male–female pay differential	Rate of pay (s. 37.1(1))	Work that is substantially the same in nature, performed under similar working conditions in the same establishment and requiring substantially the same skill, effort and responsibility. (s. 37.1(1))	A seniority system; a merit system; a system that measures earnings by quantity or quality of production; or any other system or practice that is not unlawful. (s. 37.1(1))	12 months (s. 61(1))	No
Newfoundland and Labrador (*Human Rights Code*)	Private and public sectors	Male–female pay differential	Wages, pension rights, insurance benefits and opportunities for training and advancement. (ss. 11(1), (2))	The same or similar work on jobs requiring the same or similar skill, effort and responsibility, performed under the same or similar working conditions in the same establishment. (s. 11(1))	A seniority system or a merit system. (s. 11(1)) These factors apply only in respect of wages (i.e. not for insurance benefits or opportunities for training and advancement).	6 months (s. 20(1))	No

TABLE 2.3

Equal Pay Legislation in Canada by Jurisdiction (continued)

Note: To save space, the footnotes have been omitted. They may be found on the HRSDC website.

Jurisdiction	Application	Type of Prohibition	Basis for Measuring Equal Pay	Basis for the Comparison of Work	Factors That Justify a Difference in Pay	Time Limit to File Complaint	Restrictions on Recovery
Northwest Territories *(Human Rights Act)*	Private and public sectors	General anti-discrimination	Rate of pay (s. 9(1))	The same or substantially similar work performed by employees in the same establishment. Work is deemed to be similar or substantially similar if it involves the same or substantially similar skill, effort and responsibility and is performed under the same or substantially similar working conditions. (ss. 9(1), (5))	A seniority system; a merit system; a system that measures earnings by quantity or quality of production or performance; a compensation or hiring system that recognizes the existence of a labour shortage in respect of the field of work or of regional differences in the cost of living; a downgrading, reclassification or demotion process or system; the existence of a temporary rehabilitation or training program; or any other system or factor. These cannot be based on a prohibited ground of discrimination. (s. 9(2))	2 years (an extension of time is possible) (ss. 29(2), (3))	No
Nova Scotia *(Labour Standards Code)*	Private and public sectors	Male-female pay differential	Rate of wages (s. 57(1))	Substantially the same work performed in the same establishment, the performance of which requires substantially equal skill, effort and responsibility and that is performed under similar working conditions. (s. 57(1))	A seniority system; a merit system; a system that measures wages by quantity or quality of production; or another differential based on a factor other than sex. (s. 57(2))	6 months (s. 21(3A))	No

TABLE 2.3

Equal Pay Legislation in Canada by Jurisdiction (continued)

Note: To save space, the footnotes have been omitted. They may be found on the HRSDC website.

JURISDICTION	APPLICATION	TYPE OF PROHIBITION	BASIS FOR MEASURING EQUAL PAY	BASIS FOR THE COMPARISON OF WORK	FACTORS THAT JUSTIFY A DIFFERENCE IN PAY	TIME LIMIT TO FILE COMPLAINT	RESTRICTIONS ON RECOVERY
Ontario (*Employment Standards Act, 2000*)	Private and public sectors	Male–female pay differential	Rate of pay (s. 42(1))	Substantially the same kind of work performed in the same establishment under similar working conditions and that requires substantially the same skill, effort and responsibility. (s. 42(1))	A seniority system; a merit system; a system that measures earnings by quantity or quality of production; or any factor other than sex. (s. 42(2))	2 years (s. 96(3))	An order to pay unpaid wages made by an employment standards officer cannot exceed $10,000 per employee. (ss. 42(5), 103(4)) Furthermore, an officer cannot make an order to pay unpaid wages if the wages became due more than 6 months before the complaint was filed. (s. 111)
Prince Edward Island (*Human Rights Act*)	Private and public sectors	General anti-discrimination	Rate of pay (s. 7)	Substantially the same work, requiring equal education, skill, experience, effort and responsibility and which is performed under similar working conditions. (s. 7)	A seniority system; a merit system; or a system that measures earnings by quantity or quality of production. The factor cannot be based on discrimination. (s. 7)	1 year (s. 22(1)(b))	No (a limit does apply for civil proceedings)

TABLE 2.3

Equal Pay Legislation in Canada by Jurisdiction (continued)

Note: To save space, the footnotes have been omitted. They may be found on the HRSDC website.

JURISDICTION	APPLICATION	TYPE OF PROHIBITION	BASIS FOR MEASURING EQUAL PAY	BASIS FOR THE COMPARISON OF WORK	FACTORS THAT JUSTIFY A DIFFERENCE IN PAY	TIME LIMIT TO FILE COMPLAINT	RESTRICTIONS ON RECOVERY
Quebec (*Charter of Human Rights and Freedoms*)	Private and public sectors	General anti-discrimination	Salary or wages (s. 19)	Equivalent work performed at the same place. (s. 19)	Experience; seniority; years of service; merit; productivity; or overtime. These criteria must be common to all members of the personnel in order to justify a difference in pay. (s. 19)	Not specified	No
Saskatchewan (*Labour Standards Act*)	Private and public sectors	Male–female pay differential	Rate of pay (s. 17(1))	Similar work performed in the same establishment under similar working conditions, requiring similar skill, effort and responsibility. (s. 17(1))	A seniority system or a merit system. (s. 17(1))	Not specified	No
Yukon Territory (*Employment Standards Act*)	Private sector	Male–female pay differential	Rate of pay (s. 44)	Similar work performed in the same establishment under similar working conditions, requiring similar skill, effort and responsibility. (s. 44)	A seniority system; a merit system; a system that measures earnings by quantity or quality of production; or a differential based on any factor other than sex. (s. 44)	6 months (s. 73(3))	No

TABLE 2.3

Equal Pay Legislation in Canada by Jurisdiction (continued)

Note: To save space, the footnotes have been omitted. They may be found on the HRSDC website.

JURISDICTION	APPLICATION	TYPE OF PROHIBITION	BASIS FOR MEASURING EQUAL PAY	BASIS FOR THE COMPARISON OF WORK	FACTORS THAT JUSTIFY A DIFFERENCE IN PAY	TIME LIMIT TO FILE COMPLAINT	RESTRICTIONS ON RECOVERY
Yukon Territory *(continued)* *(Human Rights Act)*	Public sector, including municipalities and their corporations, boards and commissions.	Male-female pay differential	Wages (s. 15(1))	Work of equal value, assessed by the criterion of the composite of skill, effort, and responsibility required and the working conditions. (s. 15(1), (3))	No provisions	6 months (s. 20(2))	No

Source: Labour Law Analysis, International and Intergovernmental Labour Affairs Labour Program. Retrieved from http://www.hrsdc.gc.ca/eng/labour/labour_law/esl/equal_pay_tb.shtml. Human Resources and Social Development Canada, 2008. Reproduced with the permission of the Minister of Public Works and Government Services Canada, 2011.

The reader will note that several conditions and rights are not discussed in this section. There are laws that provide employee rights and conditions, for example, in the areas of pensions, statutory holidays, vacation, plant closures, workers' compensation, and more.

International Law

The globalization of trade and the increased mobility of capital have resulted in new challenges and opportunities for labour. Labour policy is shifting from a state-centred model to one in which international considerations must be taken into account. Globalization is creating some new international rules that apply to the labour market. The International Labour Organization (ILO), a tripartite agency of the United Nations, is playing a key role in this process. Labour rights such as freedom of association and expression are seen as fundamental human rights not subject to the whims of politicians.

We have already seen the references made to ILO standards in the *Dunmore* and *B.C. Health Care* decisions of the Supreme Court. The ILO governing body has established international labour standards. To give effect to these standards, it passed three key conventions that nation states are encouraged to ratify through their political processes. They are

- *Convention 87*, freedom of association and protection of right to organize (1948). Ratified by Canada in 1972.
- *Convention 98*, right to organize and collective bargaining (1949). Not ratified by Canada.
- *Declaration on Fundamental Principles and Rights at Work* (1998). Canada voted for it.

The *Declaration* states:

all Members, even if they have not ratified the Conventions in question, have an obligation arising from the very fact of membership in the Organization to respect, to promote and to realize, in good faith and in accordance with the Constitution, the principles concerning the fundamental rights which are the subject of those Conventions, namely:

(a) freedom of association and the effective recognition of the right to collective bargaining;
(b) the elimination of all forms of forced or compulsory labour;
(c) the effective abolition of child labour; and
(d) the elimination of discrimination in respect of employment and occupation. (ILO, 1998)

Summary

Earlier we introduced the debate about a shift from an emphasis on collective rights under labour legislation to a greater role for individual rights under various employment laws. We wish to revisit this debate and ask the question "Is there a new individual-rights regime in Canada?"

There is no doubt that Canadian employment laws have significantly expanded both union and nonunion employee rights and conditions, as the chapter illustrates. There are two problems, however, with the argument that a new individual-rights regime has replaced the old one based on collective rights.

1. The argument advanced by Piore and Safford (2006) is more relevant in the U.S. case, because union decline is so much more pervasive there. Moreover, the idea that employment laws are a substitute for unionization has less resonance when placed in international comparative perspective. As the Canadian case shows, stronger employment laws are associated with more powerful labour movements, not vice versa.
2. The Supreme Court of Canada strengthened collective rights in the more recent decisions affecting labour discussed above.

Key Terms

arbitration 45
bargaining unit 35
certification 32
conciliation 38
duty of fair representation 37
employment equity 58
exclusivity principle 32
good faith bargaining 38
mediation 38

pay equity 58
P.C. 1003 31
scientific management 29
Snider Case 30
tripartite 32
unfair labour practice 35
voluntarism 38
Wagner Act 29

Weblinks

Amendment to the *Ontario Labour Relations Act*:

http://www.e-laws.gov.on.ca/html/statutes/english/elaws_statutes_95l01_e.htm

The *P.E.I. Labour Act*:

http://www.gov.pe.ca/law/statutes/pdf/l-01.pdf

B.C. Industrial Inquiry Commission appointment:

http://www2.news.gov.bc.ca/news_releases_2005-2009/2005LCS0016-000902.htm

Dunmore v. Ontario:

http://csc.lexum.org/en/2001/2001scc94/2001scc94.html

Employment conditions, hours of work, etc.:

http://www.hrsdc.gc.ca/en/labour/employment_standards/index.shtml

Canadian Human Rights Commission:

http://www.chrc-ccdp.ca/discrimination/default-en.asp

International Labour Organization:

http://www.ilo.org/global/lang—en/index.htm

Private-sector industrial relations legislation in Canada:

http://www.hrsdc.gc.ca/eng/labour/labour_law/ind_rel/index.shtml

Part I of the *Canada Labour Code*:

http://www.hrsdc.gc.ca/en/lp/lo/fll/part1/index-fll.shtml

Provincial labour relations boards, mediation/conciliation information, and collective agreements:

http://www.hrmanagement.gc.ca/gol/hrmanagement/site.nsf/en/hr05195.html

Overview of the *Canada Labour Code*:

http://www.hrsdc.gc.ca/eng/labour/health_safety/overview.shtml

RPC Icons

2.1 Provides advice to clients on the establishment, continuation, and termination of bargaining rights

- labour legislation
- the rights and responsibilities of management and labour during the processes of organizing and negotiation
- union practices, organization, and certification

2.2 Collects and develops information required for good decision making throughout the bargaining process

- possible outcomes of contract negotiation (e.g., impasse, conciliation, and the legal strike)
- the legal context of labour relations

2.3 Contributes to communication plan during work disruptions

- relevant legislation and regulations and third-party procedures
- common and statutory law (e.g., employment standard: labour relations)

2.4 Advises clients of signatories' rights, including those with respect to grievance procedures

- context and content of collective agreement
- common and statutory law (e.g., employment standard: labour relations)
- concepts and processes of politics and conflict

Discussion Questions

1. Using Table 2.1, determine which provinces provide for certification without a formal vote and under which circumstances.

2. What has been the impact of the *Snider* decision on the development of Canadian labour legislation?
3. How do labour boards determine which persons should be eligible for inclusion in a bargaining unit? Which employees are not eligible?
4. What are the steps in a typical organizing drive?
5. What is an unfair labour practice? Give examples. What is the duty of fair representation? Give examples.
6. How does public policy play a role in arbitration during the term of a collective agreement?
7. What is evidence of a new pro-labour direction of the Supreme Court?
8. Discuss how any three laws covering conditions of employment vary across Canada.
9. Discuss the proposition that there is a new individual-rights regime in Canada.

Using the Internet

Blogs on labour law:

- Dr. David Doorey's Workplace Law Blog: **http://www.yorku.ca/ddoorey/lawblog**
- Freedom of Association discussion blog: **http://foa2010.blogspot.com**
- List of labour and employment law blogs: **http://www.lawblogs.ca/category/labour-employment**

There are several websites containing information about the principles upon which the law is based, the current state of employment law in Canada, and legislative trends. A few of these are listed below.

- Department of Justice Canada: **http://www.justice.gc.ca/eng/index.html**
- Government of Canada: Industrial Relations Legislation in Canada: **http://www.hrsdc.gc.ca/eng/labour/labour_law/ind_rel/index.shtml**
- Canadian Human Rights Commission: Pay Equity: **http://www.chrc-ccdp.ca/DisputeResolution_ReglementDifferends/payequity_paritesalariale-eng.aspx**
- Canadian Human Rights Tribunal: **http://www.chrt-tcdp.gc.ca/index_e.asp**
- Understanding pay equity: **http://www.hrsdc.gc.ca/eng/labour/equality/pay_equity/index.shtml**
- International Labour Organization: **http://www.ilo.org/global/lang--en/index.htm#3**
- **http://www.ilo.org/global/standards/subjects-covered-by-international-labour-standards/freedom-of-association/lang—en/index.htm**

For industrial relations journals and cases, have a look in a law library such as one of the following:

- Nahum Gelber Law Library, McGill University: **http://www.mcgill.ca/library/library-using/branches/law-library**

- Bora Laskin Law Library, University of Toronto Faculty of Law: **http://www.law-lib.utoronto.ca**
- Bibliothèque de droit, Université de Montréal: **http://www.bib. umontreal.ca/DR**

For links to provincial labour relations boards, mediation/conciliation information, and collective agreements, go to **http://www.hrmanagement.gc.ca/ gol/hrmanagement/site.nsf/en/hr05195.html**.

1. Why does each province have its own human rights commission?
2. Use the links here to find a typical human rights commission or tribunal. What are the functions of the tribunal?
3. Find a website that provides links to labour legislation in Canada. Find the *Manitoba Labour Relations Act*. Have you found a current version of the legislation?

See also YouTube videos on labour law, history, legislation, etc.

Exercises

1. Using the weblinks provided in this chapter, find the labour relations act of any of the provinces. Summarize the sections of the act that define the jurisdiction of the labour board and its duties.
2. Select any two provinces and obtain the minimum wage law and human rights code.

Case 1

Recognition Under the *Canada Labour Code*

Collective bargaining under the *Canada Labour Code* begins when a group of employees decides to organize in order to negotiate a collective agreement with their employer. The employees must first form their own trade union or join an existing one. Recognition of the union as their bargaining agent may be acquired by the employer voluntarily agreeing to enter into a collective agreement or by the union applying for certification. When this occurs, the following general framework for collective bargaining, as set out in Part I of the *Canada Labour Code*, applies:

General Principles

Role of the Canada Industrial Relations Board:

- The Canada Industrial Relations Board decides the certification of bargaining agents and determines questions of membership support.
- The board also decides matters such as the appropriateness and structure of the negotiating unit and polling constituency, and questions of employee status or exclusion.

- Management may voluntarily recognize a union, thereby bypassing the formal certification procedures.

Management and union obligations:

- Bargaining agents and employers have a duty to meet and negotiate in good faith and to make every reasonable effort to conclude a collective agreement.
- The Canada Industrial Relations Board adjudicates allegations of failure to bargain in good faith and other unfair labour practices.

How bargaining starts and what may be negotiated:

- Notice to bargain for renewal and revision of an existing collective agreement may be given by either party within three months of the expiry date. The parties are required to notify the Minister of Labour of any dispute that they cannot resolve before they may acquire the right to strike or to lock out.
- The scope of collective bargaining is not limited by the *Code*; all subjects are potentially negotiable and, subject to the agreement of the parties, may be included in a collective agreement.

How strikes are restricted:

- Conciliation procedures may be imposed at the discretion of the Minister of Labour, and no strike or lockout may legally take place unless the dispute notification and settlement procedures have been completed or dispensed with by authority of the Minister.
- Strikes and lockouts are not permitted during the term of an agreement. The agreement must contain a provision for the settlement by arbitration or otherwise of disputes concerning the interpretation of the agreement that arise during its term, without resort to a work stoppage.

Term of agreements:

- Collective agreements must be for a fixed term of at least one year.

Questions

1. If union or management fails to bargain in good faith, what recourse does an affected party have under the *Code*?
2. What restrictions are there on the right to strike? Why do you think these restrictions exist?
3. What are the functions of the Canada Industrial Relations Board?
4. What action may I take under the *Code* if I want to become unionized?

Case 2

An USWA Organizing Drive at Canada Metals, Winnipeg

To help you understand how the law works to provide an orderly process of union recognition, we have constructed a representative case based on the

Manitoba law. The steps in a typical organizing campaign between the United Steelworkers of America and Canada Metals are set out below:

1. Employees of Canada Metals contact USWA.
2. An internal committee is established and an organizing drive to sign cards in the union begins.
3. An application is made to the labour board, and signed cards are submitted.
4. (i) If the union has more than 40 percent of the bargaining unit but less than 65 percent of the employees signed up, there will be a vote (see second column in Table 2.1); if a vote is ordered, the union must win 50 percent plus one of the ballots cast.
   (ii) If the union has more than 65 percent of the cards signed, there is automatic certification without a vote.
5. If the union is certified, the company and union must bargain in good faith and conclude a collective agreement.

Question

1. How would the procedure differ if the province was Ontario, British Columbia, or your province? (*Hint:* See Table 2.1.)

References

Abraham, S. E. (1997). Relevance of Canadian labour law to US firms operating in Canada. *International Journal of Manpower, 18*(8), pp. 662–674.

Adams, R. (2003). The revolutionary potential of Dunmore. *Canadian Labour and Employment Law Journal, 10,* pp. 83–116.

Bruce, P. G. (1989). Political parties and labour legislation in Canada and the U.S. *Industrial Relations, 28,* pp. 115–141.

Cameron, B. J. (2002). The "second labour trilogy": A comment on *R. v. Advance Cutting, Dunmore v. Ontario,* and *R.W.D.S.U. v. Pepsi-Cola. Supreme Court Review, 16*(2d), pp. 67–102.

Davenport, G. (2003). Approach to good faith negotiations in Canada: What could be the lesson for us? *New Zealand Journal of Industrial Relations, 28,* pp. 150–156.

Doorey, David. (2008). The medium and the "anti-union" message: "Forced listening" and captive audience meetings in Canadian labor law. *Comparative Labor Law and Policy Journal, 29,* pp. 79–118.

Fudge, Judy. (2008). The Supreme Court of Canada and the right to bargain collectively: The implications of the *Health Services and Support* case in Canada and beyond. *Industrial Law Journal, 37*(1), pp. 25–48.

Government of British Columbia. (6 October 2005). Commission appointed to improve teacher bargaining. News release. Retrieved 11 Jan. 2011 from http://www2.news.gov.bc.ca/news_releases_2005-2009/2005LCS0016-000902.htm

Haiven, L. (1990). Industrial conflict and resolution in Canada and Britain. *Employee Relations, 12*(2), pp. 12–19.

Hebdon, R., & Hyatt, D. (1998). The impact of industrial relations factors on health and safety conflict. *Industrial and Labor Relations Review, 51*(4)(July), pp. 579–593.

Human Resources and Social Development Canada. (2004). Annual report: *Employment Equity Act 2004.* Retrieved 15 Jan. 2011 from http://www.hrsdc.gc.ca/en/lp/lo/lswe/we/ee_tools/reports/annual/2004/2004AnnualReport.pdf

Human Resources and Social Development Canada (HRSDC). 2006. Hours of Work, Overtime, Meal and Other Breaks. Retrieved July 31, 2011 from http://www.hrsdc.gc.ca/eng/lp/spila/clli/eslc/21Hours_Work_Overtime_Meal.shtml Human Resources and Skills Development Canada. Reproduced with the permission of the Minister of Public Works and Government Services Canada, 2011.

Jain, Harish C., Lawler, John J., Bai, Bing, & Lee, Eun Kyung. (2010). Effectiveness of Canada's employment equity legislation for women (1997–2004). *Relations industrielles, 65*(2), pp. 304–329.

Langille, Brian. (2009). The freedom of association mess: How we got into it and how we can get out of it. *McGill Law Journal, 54*, pp. 177–212.

Lewchuk, W., Robb, L. A., & Walters, V. (1996). The effectiveness of Bill 70 and joint health and safety committees in reducing injuries in the workplace: The case of Ontario. *Canadian Public Policy, 22*(3), pp. 225–244.

Lipset, M., & Meltz, N. M. (2004). *The paradox of American unionism*. Ithaca, NY: ILR Press.

McQuarrie, Fiona. (2010). In good faith? An analysis of the features and outcomes of duty of representation cases. *Relations industrielles, 65*(1), pp. 118–133.

Mentzer, M. S. (2002). The Canadian experience with employment equity legislation. *International Journal of Value-Based Management, 15*(1), pp. 35–50.

Panitch, L., & Swartz, D. (1993). *The assault on trade union freedoms*. Toronto: Garamond Press.

Piore, M. J., & Safford, S. (2006). Changing regimes of workplace governance, shifting axes of social mobilization, and the challenge to industrial relations theory. *Industrial Relations, 45*(3), pp. 299–325.

Sack, Jeffrey. (2010). U.S. and Canadian labour law: Significant distinctions. *American Bar Association Journal of Labor and Employment Law* (Chicago), *25*(2), pp. 241–258.

Slinn, Sara. (2008). No right (to organize) without a remedy: Evidence and consequences of the failure to provide compensatory remedies for unfair labour practices in British Columbia. *McGill Law Journal, 53*, pp. 687–737.

Supreme Court of Canada. (1991). *Osborne v. Canada (Treasury Board)*, [1991] 2 S.C.R. 69. *Judgments of the Supreme Court of Canada*. Retrieved from http://scc.lexum.umontreal.ca/en/1991/1991rcs2-69/1991rcs2-69.html

Supreme Court of Canada. (2001). *Dunmore v. Ontario (Attorney General)*, [2001] 3 S.C.R. 1016, 2001 SCC 94. *Judgments of the Supreme Court of Canada*. Retrieved 1 Aug. 2010 from http://csc.lexum.org/en/2001/2001scc94/2001scc94.html

Supreme Court of Canada. (2002). *R.W.D.S.U., Local 558 v. Pepsi-Cola Canada Beverages (West) Ltd.*, [2002] 1 S.C.R. 156, 2002 SCC 8. *Judgments of the Supreme Court of Canada*. Retrieved 15 Jan. 2011 from http://scc.lexum.umontreal.ca/en/2002/2002scc8/2002scc8.html

Swinton, C. (1995). The *Charter of Rights and Freedoms*. In G. Swimmer & M. Thompson (Eds.), *Public sector collective bargaining in Canada*. Kingston, ON: IRC Press pp 53–77.

Troy, L., & Sheflin, N. (1985). *Union sourcebook: Membership structure, finance, and directory* (1st edition). West Orange, NJ: Industrial Relations Data Information Services.

Weiner, N. (1995). Workplace equity. In G. Swimmer & M. Thompson (Eds.), *Public sector collective bargaining in Canada*. Kingston, ON: IRC Press pp. 78–100.

CHAPTER 3

Economic, Social, and Political Environments

Learning Objectives

By the end of this chapter, you will be able to discuss

- the supply of and demand for labour;
- the elasticity of supply and demand and its impact on labour power;
- the impact of free trade, deregulation, and privatization on unions;
- the importance of work–leisure decisions;
- the institutional and noncompetitive factors that affect labour supply;
- recent demographic changes in the labour force;
- the social conditions of the labour market;
- public attitude toward unions in North America;
- current trends in income distribution and poverty;
- the impact of compositional shifts in the labour market on labour;
- the importance of achieving a work–life balance;
- the structural elements of the political system that help labour; and
- globalization and politics.

CANADA'S TOP PROBLEM IS FILLING LABOUR SHORTAGE

OTTAWA—When Prime Minister Stephen Harper gathered the country's premiers at 24 Sussex Drive last fall, he wanted them to focus on what he saw as the country's No. 1 economic problem: within a decade or two, there simply will not be enough workers in the country.

Although recent headlines about thousands of layoffs in Canada's struggling manufacturing sector may suggest otherwise, Harper and his cabinet are struggling to find ways to boost training programs and increase immigration to find more workers to avoid what some Conservative strategists say is an "economic time bomb."

That Canada is heading for a problem seems unavoidable. In the last 50 years, Canada's workforce grew by 200 per cent. That growth was responsible for raising standards of living and creating the public and private wealth the country now enjoys. But government forecasters say that, without some radical changes, the workforce will only grow by 11 per cent in the next 50 years—and that figure includes the effects of current levels of immigration.

"Our demographics are working against us," Human Resources Minister Monte Solberg said in a speech Monday to the Canadian Building and Construction Trades' Legislative Conference. "Baby boomers are set to retire and our low birth rate means demand for workers will soon outstrip supply."

Already, more than 80 per cent of working-age Canadians have a job—an all-time high.

Solberg marshalled the following data to back up his claim:

- British Columbia will be short 350,000 workers over the next 12 years.
- Alberta will require 100,000 workers over the next 10 years.
- Ontario will need 560,000 more workers by 2030.
- Quebec will have 1.3 million job openings by 2016.

"We have a significant shortfall of workers in every region across Canada," said Solberg.

The environment of industrial relations helps shape the labour–management relationship and such system outcomes as wages, benefits, work rules, and conflict. We saw in Chapter 2 how labour legislation influences the industrial relations system. In this chapter, we examine how the labour market, social conditions, and the political environment affect industrial relations.

The Economic Context

Macroeconomic Policy

The Canadian economy sank into a deep recession in late 2008. Growth has been negligible and unemployment has been high. Canadian unemployed increased from 6.3 percent in 2008 to 8.3 percent in 2009 (see Table 3.1). This rate of 8.3 percent was only marginally higher than the Organisation for Economic Co-operation and Development's (OECD) average of 8.1 percent (Table 3.1). The recession meant than about 1.5 million workers were out of work in Canada. We fared considerably better than our leading trading partner, the United States, who saw unemployment increase steeply from

TABLE 3.1

Annual Rate of Unemployment as Percentage of Civilian Labour Force, 2004–2009						
	2004	2005	2006	2007	2008	2009
Spain	11.0	9.2	8.5	8.3	11.4	18.1
Turkey	10.8	10.6	10.2	10.3	11.0	14.0
Ireland	4.5	4.7	4.6	4.7	5.7	12.0
Hungary	6.2	7.3	7.5	7.4	7.9	10.1
Portugal	6.7	7.7	7.7	8.0	7.6	9.5
United States	5.5	5.1	4.6	4.6	5.8	9.3
France	8.8	8.8	8.8	8.0	7.4	9.2
Greece	10.2	9.6	8.8	8.1	7.2	8.9
Sweden	6.6	7.8	7.1	6.2	6.2	8.3
Finland	8.8	8.4	7.7	6.9	6.4	8.3
Canada	7.2	6.8	6.3	6.0	6.1	8.3
OECD–total	6.8	6.6	6.1	5.6	5.9	8.1
Belgium	8.4	8.4	8.2	7.5	7.0	7.9
Italy	8.1	7.8	6.9	6.2	6.8	7.9
Germany	10.3	11.2	10.3	8.7	7.6	7.8
United Kingdom	4.7	4.7	5.4	5.3	5.3	7.7
New Zealand	4.0	3.8	3.8	3.7	4.2	6.2
Denmark	5.7	5.0	4.1	4.0	3.4	6.1
Australia	5.4	5.0	4.8	4.4	4.2	5.6
Mexico	3.7	3.5	3.2	3.4	3.5	5.2
Japan	4.7	4.4	4.1	3.9	4.0	5.1
Austria	5.0	5.2	4.8	4.4	3.8	4.8
Switzerland	4.2	4.3	3.9	3.5	3.3	4.1
Korea	3.7	3.7	3.5	3.2	3.2	3.6
Netherlands	4.6	4.7	3.9	3.2	2.8	3.4
Norway	4.5	4.6	3.5	2.5	2.6	3.2

Source: OECD, "Annual labour force statistics," Labour (database), OECD. Stat Extracts http://stats.oecd. org (Accessed on 21 April 2011)

Chapter 3: Economic, Social, and Political Environments

5.8 percent to 9.3 percent. In this so-called **great recession**, governments of all political stripes offered various forms of action packages designed to stimulate demand. The Canadian government 2009 Action Plan had five elements:

- *Action to Help Canadians and Stimulate Spending:* Providing $8.3 billion for the Canada Skills and Transition Strategy to help Canadians weather today's economic storm and to provide them with the necessary training to prosper in tomorrow's economy. In addition, $20 billion will be provided in personal income tax relief over 2008–09 and the next five fiscal years.
- *Action to Stimulate Housing Construction:* Providing $7.8 billion to build quality housing, stimulate construction, encourage home ownership and enhance energy efficiency.
- *Immediate Action to Build Infrastructure:* Accelerating and expanding the recent historic federal investment in infrastructure with almost $12 billion in new infrastructure stimulus funding over two years, so that Canada emerges from this economic crisis with more modern and greener infrastructure.
- *Action to Support Businesses and Communities:* Protecting jobs and supporting sectoral adjustment during this extraordinary crisis with $7.5 billion in extra support for sectors, regions and communities.
- *Action to Improve Access to Financing and Strengthening Canada's Financial System:* Providing up to $200 billion through the Extraordinary Financing Framework to improve access to financing for Canadian households and businesses. (Government of Canada, 2011)

Arguably the most important single influence on industrial relations has been the federal government **macroeconomic policy** with respect to the liberalization of markets. Almost all industries have been affected either directly through **deregulation** or **privatization** (or both) (e.g., trucking, airlines, and communications) or indirectly through policies that promote free trade in goods and services (e.g., the **North American Free Trade Agreement** between Canada, the United States, and Mexico). The net effect of these liberalization policies on workers is in dispute but there can be little doubt that firms are under greater competitive pressure due to tariff reductions or deregulation policies.

Globalization has resulted in greater mobility of capital and increases in the flow of goods and services. It has also meant increased worldwide competition between firms and between nation states over attracting foreign investment. But global competition is not the only pressure on labour markets, as Gunderson and Verma (1992) point out:

. . . the labor market is subject to the forces of continual technological change, industrial restructuring, just-in-time delivery systems, deregulation, privatization, public sector retrenchment, and the ever-present threat of recession.

Research shows that deregulation policies, at least as they were applied in Australia, may have negative consequences for the economy by increasing equality in the labour market (Neville & Kriesler, 2008).

The Labour Market[1]

For nonunion firms, labour market forces will largely determine employee compensation and conditions. The vignette at the start of this chapter shows what can happen when growth of the supply of labour through population growth and immigration is forecasted to insufficient to meet the future labour demand. The main implication of this is that our current high standard of living will be difficult to maintain unless the demand for labour is matched by supply.

Supply and Demand Framework

The purpose of this section is to provide the reader with the tools to analyze the impact of economic conditions on industrial relations (Gunderson & Riddell, 1988). To do this, we need to employ some of the basic supply and demand analysis of economics. In Figure 3.1, we portray a typical labour market equilibrium in which supply (SS) and demand (DD) curves for labour determine the quantity of labour supplied at the competitive wage (Wc) and employment level (Nc). If the demand for labour shifts to D1D1 due to external factors such as the oil sands boom, we can predict some outcomes. The new equilibrium shows higher wages (Wc1) and a higher employment level (Nc1).

Elasticity of Supply and Demand

The reader will note that the effect of the demand shift will depend on the slope of the supply curve (SS). The steeper the supply curve, the greater is the

FIGURE 3.1

Labour Market Equilibrium

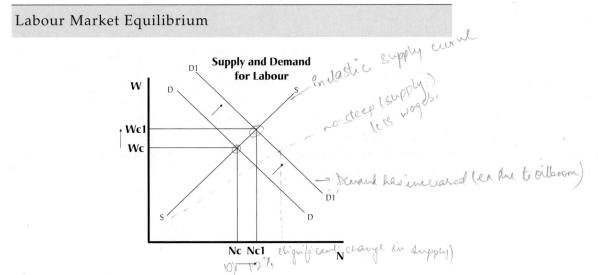

increase in wages by 2$ will due the supply enormously

increase in wages, caused by a shift in demand. A steep supply curve is what economists call an inelastic supply of labour. Conversely, a flat supply curve indicates an **elasticity of supply** for labour, because a small increase in the wage rate will significantly increase labour supply. Thus, the wage elasticity of supply is measured by the proportionate (or percentage) change in labour supplied, caused by a proportionate (or percentage) change in the wage rate. Proportions or percentages of elasticity are used because wages and labour are measured in different units.

The same reasoning applies to **elasticity of demand** for labour. The steeper the demand curve, the greater the inelasticity of demand, since a relatively small increase in the quantity demanded will cause a relatively large increase in wages. Conversely, a flat demand curve indicates an elastic demand, because a large increase in the demand for labour will have a relatively small effect on the wage rate.

increase in demand for labour

Labour Power and Marshall's Conditions

The shape of the demand curve is important, because it influences a union's ability to raise wages without significantly affecting employment levels. This effect is known as the wage–employment tradeoff.

What factors determine the shape of the demand curve for labour? How does the shape of the demand curve affect labour power? We know from economic theory that the demand for labour is a "derived" demand, because it is determined solely by supply and demand forces in the market for the firm's product. Marshall (1920) describes four theoretical conditions that determine the wage elasticity of labour as we have defined it (i.e., the employment responsiveness to an increase in wages).

Small inc. in wages causes a large increase in demand of labour

PRODUCT MARKET   The more competitive the product market, the greater the employment impact of a wage increase and the elasticity of demand for labour. This is known as the *wage–employment tradeoff* in the sense that when a union increases wages, the higher costs may be reflected in reduced sales. Reduced sales cause reduced demand for labour. Hence, unions will tend to have more power when there is less competition in the firm's product market. Industries where firms have some degree of monopoly power can more easily absorb a wage increase without affecting employment levels. They can do this because their monopoly power gives them room to raise prices without suffering lower sales (and thus employment levels). Thus, to the extent that free trade increases market competition, union power will be reduced. In terms of elasticity, the more inelastic the demand for labour, the lower the employment tradeoff from a wage increase and the greater, therefore, union power.

The case of Canada Post's planned outsourcing of 300 call-centre jobs across Canada illustrates the effect of the wage–employment tradeoff in a highly competitive environment (see IR Today 3.1).

SUBSTITUTION EFFECT   The easier it is to substitute capital (machines, new technology, etc.) for labour, the less power labour will have to raise wages. The firm

walmart

elasticity of supply (demand)

the labour responsiveness of supply (demand) caused by a change in the wage rate; for example, if a small increase in wages causes a large increase in the supply of labour, the supply curve is said to be *elastic*

IR Today 3.1

Canada Post to Outsource Call Centre Jobs

Canada Post is planning to outsource call centre jobs in a move that will impact about 300 employees across the country. Part of a plan to reduce costs in an era of declining mail volumes and revenue, the cuts are expected to begin by the first quarter of 2011. "Our current in-house approach to call centres is costly, significantly more than the industry standard," spokesman John Caines said.

Management met with staff at its five call centres in Fredericton, Antigonish, Ottawa, Winnipeg and Edmonton Tuesday to break the news. "Obviously we were very respectful of what we had to announce to them and to many, I'm sure it came as a shock," Mr. Caines said. "But we're giving them a year's notice that this is coming." Mr. Caines said contract staff won't have their terms renewed beyond 2011. But full and part time staff, about two-thirds of call centre employees, will be able to hang on to their jobs for a while. "We don't know how long it's going to take to move everything over to an outsourced service provider, so what were looking at doing is keeping these people in their positions," he said. "As they move out of their position or retire, those calls will then be moved over to the new service provider."

By mid 2011, Canada Post hopes to have half its calls handled by an outside service provider. While a growing number of call centre jobs are being outsourced to places like India, Caines said Canada Post will be looking to keep the jobs in Canada.

Source: Shereen Dindar, "Canada Post to outsource call centre jobs," 31 March 2010, retrieved 21 April 2011 from http://network.nationalpost.com/NP/blogs/posted/archive/2010/03/31/canada-post-to-outsource-call-centre-jobs.aspx. Material reprinted with the express permission of POSTMEDIA NEWS, a division of Postmedia Network, Inc.

---

that can easily substitute other factors of production for labour will possess more bargaining power. This substitution effect may be a longer-term phenomenon, since technological change may take years to implement. Certain jobs are more essential to the production process than others and hence harder to substitute. For example, airlines cannot function without pilots, and buildings cannot be constructed without electricians.

LABOUR INTENSITY   Labour intensity is the degree to which labour costs account for production costs. Thus, an industry is labour-intensive if labour costs are a high proportion of totals costs. The smaller the proportion of total costs labour is, the lower the employment impact of a wage increase will be, thus giving labour more power. In firms that are highly capital-intensive (e.g., high tech, printing, aerospace), labour will have more bargaining power according to this theory, because firms can absorb a wage increase without a serious impact on total costs and employment. On the other hand, many highly labour-intensive public services, such as police and teachers, will have less bargaining power.

MARKET FOR SUBSTITUTES   _land, labor, capital_ Finally, the more competitive the market for substitute factors of production is, the greater the bargaining power firms will have. The cheaper and more available these substitutes, the greater the impact on employment, and hence the greater the employer's bargaining power.

A clear implication flowing from the economic theory discussed above is that the more competitive the economy, the greater the bargaining power of

Chapter 3: Economic, Social, and Political Environments

employers. Thus, given our earlier discussion of globalization and the shift to freer markets, we can infer a parallel shift to greater bargaining power on the part of management.

To summarize, demand is more inelastic and unions will have more power when

- product markets are less competitive;
- it is harder to substitute labour for capital;
- labour costs are a small proportion of total costs; and
- the market for substitutes is less competitive.

Noneconomic Sources of Union Power

Unions also derive power from sources other than labour markets. They are more powerful when they build strong links with their local communities. Evidence reveals, for example, that unions have successfully forged alliances with community groups to

- assist in organizing new members;
- strengthen positions in bargaining;
- support political lobbying campaigns;
- oppose plant closures; and
- support strikes and other industrial actions (Craft, 1998).

Supply of Labour

What factors in society determine labour supply? The number of workers is a function of such elements as population growth, immigration, retirement choices, work–family decisions, career patterns, leisure choices, and labour mobility.

Population and Immigration

Labour-force growth is fuelled by population growth and immigration. Population growth is determined by births less deaths plus net immigration (immigration less migration). Female fertility rates have an important effect on future labour-force growth. Canada has lower rates than the United States, but about the average of other developed countries (see IR Notebook 3.1).

National and international migration patterns are important determinants of fertility rates. In Alberta, forty-nine out of every one hundred births in 2004 were to women who had immigrated to Alberta—twenty-nine from other provinces, twenty from other countries. Ontario's population growth, on the other hand, relied more on international migration, with thirty-six out of every one hundred births attributed to women born outside Canada; only eight percent of Ontario babies were born to Canadian women who hailed from another province.

The other important trend revealed by Statistics Canada is the continued pattern of births by older women. In 2004, women thirty-five years and older had babies at a rate almost four times greater than in 1979 (see IR Notebook 3.1).

Canadian Fertility Rates

Fertility Rate Unchanged

The total fertility rate is an estimate of the average number of children that women will have during the years they are aged 15 to 49, based on current age-specific birth rates. The statistics show that the rate in 2004 was unchanged from the 2003 rate of 1.53 children per woman. The record-low fertility rate for Canada was set in 2000, at 1.49 children per woman.

At 1.53, the total fertility rate in Canada is very close to the 2003 average rate of other industrialized countries: 1.56 children per woman (Organisation for Economic Co-operation and Development). The Canadian rate is much lower, however, than the rate in the United States. In 2004, the total fertility rate in the United States edged up to 2.05, compared with 2.04 in 2003, as a result of increases in birth rates for women in their thirties.

National, International Migration Driving Trends

Trends in migration from province-to-province, as well as inflows of international migrants, have a major impact on the number of births in various provinces. On the receiving end of migration trends, about 29 births in every 100 in Alberta were to women who were born elsewhere in Canada, while about 20 were to international immigrants. Only 51 in every 100 were to women born in Alberta.

In contrast, Ontario relied much more on international immigrants for births. A total of 56 births out of every 100 in Ontario were to women born in Ontario, while 36 out of every 100 were to international immigrants. Only 8 in 100 were to women born elsewhere in Canada. Studies have shown that immigrants have higher fertility rates compared with Canadian-born women, but those rates decline to Canadian levels with the second-generation.

Moms Keep Getting Older

The average age of women giving birth in Canada was 29.7 years in 2004, a slight increase from 29.6 in 2003. This continues a long-established upward trend. The bulk of the births now occur to women aged 25 to 34, who accounted for 62.1% of all births in 2004 compared with 54.7% in 1979. Births to older mothers, those aged 35 and older, were almost four times as frequent as a generation earlier.

Source: Statistics Canada, "Canadian fertility rates," *The Daily*, 31 July 2006, Catalogue 11-001, retrieved 21 April 2011 from http://www.statcan.ca/Daily/English/060731/d060731b.htm.

Work–Leisure Decisions

Economists see a tradeoff choice between leisure and work. In this decision-making framework, leisure is treated as an ordinary commodity. The impact of a wage increase on leisure is analyzed in terms of substitution and income effects. On the one hand, as our incomes rise, we may substitute leisure for work because more goods and services per hour of work can be purchased. But higher incomes make both leisure and work more desirable. That is, we can afford more leisure, but we may also find work more attractive because of the higher pay rate or salary. Thus, in theory, there are two opposing effects on the leisure–work tradeoff when our wages rise.

Economics texts typically discuss the dominance of the income effect over the substitution effect in terms of the long-term decline in hours worked. In Canada, for example, hours declined from an average of 58.6 hours per week in 1901 to 39.2 hours in 1981 (Gunderson & Riddell, 1988). But more recently, from 1979 to 2000, average annual hours worked decreased only 1.7 percent (OECD, 2001). This relative stability in hours in Canada is in contrast to double-digit decreases in hours in France, Germany, Japan, and Norway over the same period. In the United States and Sweden, average hours have actually increased over the period (Hayden, 2003). If we apply the work–leisure framework to the pattern of stability in hours worked in Canada, it indicates that the long-term substitution and income effects are offsetting each other. The slight decrease in average annual hours indicates that the income effect is only slightly greater than the substitution effect.

Noncompetitive and Institutional Factors

We have analyzed the labour market assuming that markets are competitive, that labour is always mobile (meaning workers can always relocate), and that there are no institutional barriers to competition. In practice, markets are not always competitive, workers are not mobile, and there may be substantial institutional barriers to competition.

monopsony

occurs when a firm is the sole market buyer of a good, service, or labour

NONCOMPETITIVE FACTORS   In economic theory, **monopsony** exists when a firm is not a wage-taker but a wage-setter. This situation is somewhat analogous to monopoly in the product market. The firm is so dominant in the labour market that it has some control over the wages offered. Theory predicts lower wages and employment levels in monopsonistic markets. For example, researchers have found the market for teachers and nurses to be monopsonistic (Currie, Farsi & Macleod, 2005; Luizer & Thornton, 1986). In the market for nurses in California, private hospitals exercised their monopsonistic power through an increase in workload (patients per nurse) and not wages (Currie, Farsi & Macleod, 2005). Some important research on this topic has revealed significant new evidence of very high levels of monopsony power particularly in markets for nurses and teaches (Ashenfelter, Farber & Ransom, 2010). Their policy remedies for these market imperfections are unionization or minimum wage laws.

A key economic assumption is that labour is perfectly mobile, but if this is not the case, less than optimal outcomes may result. In a recent analysis of interprovincial movement of labour in Canada, several barriers to mobility were identified (Finnie, 2004). It was found that the probability that an individual changed his or her province of residence from one year to the next over the 1982–1995 period was lower if

- the person's home province had a large population;
- language was a factor;
- the person lived in a larger city versus a smaller city, town, or rural area;
- the person was older, married, or had a family;
- the provincial unemployment rate was low or there were low levels of individual unemployment insurance or social assistance; and
- the person was a prime-age male with low income.

Finally, labour mobility as measured by the propensity to move to another province was relatively stable over time. However, there were gender differences, with men's rates declining slightly and women's holding steady or rising a little over the fourteen-year period (Finnie, 2004).

The lack of labour mobility has also been shown to negatively affect wage inequality in international trade agreements (Devillanova, Di Maio & Vertova, 2010).

INSTITUTIONAL BARRIERS TO SUPPLY   Other barriers to the supply of labour are institutional in nature. Labour supply may be inhibited by governments through a lack of resources to training or higher education, resulting in a restriction on the supply of graduates to a given occupation or profession. Applying Weber's (1922) theory of social closure, research has shown that various occupations erect barriers to entry to restrict supply and thereby affect earnings (Weeden, 2002). Professional associations and craft unions use licensing and certification requirements, association memberships, and educational credentialling to restrict entry into the occupation.

The case described in IR Notebook 3.2 is indicative of the negative role that the lack of uniform licensing, inadequate training, and funding problems can play in restricting labour supply.

IR Notebook 3.2

Licensing Problems Cause Shortages in the Trucking Industry

OTTAWA, Ont.—A cross-section of Canada's trucking industry, government agencies and training institutions are joining forces to address a critical shortage of qualified truck drivers, the Canadian Trucking Human Resources Council (CTHRC) has announced.

Representatives from these groups recently participated in a Toronto summit to discuss challenges including licensing standards that vary from one province to the next, training programs that don't meet industry needs, and a lack of funding options for future drivers who want to be effectively trained. Focus groups across the country are now being scheduled to help identify related solutions.

"We are entering a time in the transportation industry where we are looking at the potential loss of 3,000 drivers per month," explains Roy Craigen, chairman of the CTHRC, which hosted the Toronto summit. "The cost of doing nothing is that Canada will be less competitive in the world marketplace. We will end up with more dangerous highways."

The impact of the loss is heightened by the fact that the industry is losing its most experienced workers.

"We are losing drivers with 30 and 40 years of driving experience and replacing them with individuals with one and two years of experience, who may not have been trained to professional standards," Mr. Craigen says, referring to the aging workforce. . . .

Licensing Standards Seen as Inadequate

One of the immediate challenges identified during the Toronto summit was the gap that exists between the entry-level skills required to earn a licence, and those required to be effective in a career at the wheel.

Licensing standards vary from one province to the next, and rarely meet the needs of the industry, CTHRC studies have found. Training programs are often developed to meet these minimum licensing requirements rather than identified National Occupational Standards. And half of Canada's entry-level drivers do not attend formal training schools before earning a license.

The summit also identified several funding-related challenges to training would-be truck drivers.

Source: Steven Macleod, "Groups join forces to address driver shortage," *Truck News*, 23 February 2006, retrieved 21 April 2011 from http://www.trucknews.com/issues/story.aspx?aid=1000049084&issue=02232006.

hiring hall

a union-run centre that refers union labour to job sites as requested by firms

UNIONS AND LABOUR SUPPLY   Research reveals that craft unions' control of labour supply through access to apprentice programs and **hiring halls** has positive and negative effects. On the one hand, European experience shows that without proactive government regulation, minorities and women will tend to be excluded from unionized construction work (Byrne, Clarke & Van Der Meer, 2005). But in the United States, evidence shows that unions have positive effects in terms of higher graduation rates for women involved in joint union–management apprentice programs (Berik & Bilginsoy, 2000). Research also shows that apprenticeship training and hiring halls tend to increase union productivity, while jurisdictional disagreements and restrictive work rules lower it (Allen, 1984). Jurisdictional disputes are found in the construction industry and involve interunion rivalries between craft unions (e.g., labourers and carpenters) over the appropriate trade to perform a particular task. Research on the union impact on training in Germany indicates that by imposing minimum wages and wage compression, unions increase on-the-job training (Dustmann & Shonberg, 2009).

Demographic Factors

Demographic factors are important determinants of labour force patterns. Like most industrialized countries, Canada experienced a postwar baby boom between 1947 and 1966 (Foot & Soffman, 1996). This large baby-boom cohort created challenges for organizations. The traditional hierarchical management structure and conventional career patterns were disrupted by the higher numbers of boomers in the middle ranks. Thus, a substantial mismatch emerged in the 1980s between labour force structure and organizational needs (Foot & Venne, 1990). Organizations found solutions in "flattening organization hierarchies and adopting and rewarding spiral career paths" (Foot & Venne, 1990).

Social Conditions

In this section, we examine some of the social conditions that exist in Canada that, to some extent, provide a test of the effects of globalization and are part of the environment of industrial relations. We look at support for unions and worker satisfaction, and then discuss some evidence on trends in income distribution and poverty in a North American context. Finally, employing the concept of a work–life balance, we will look at societal changes that have disturbed this delicate balance.

Public Attitudes to Unions

It has been argued by some that unions have outlived their usefulness as organizations. Union decline, so goes the argument, is an inevitable consequence of several factors:

- globalization and the greater pressures on firms to be competitive;
- more individual protection under employment laws;
- changes in the nature of work, with employees exercising greater control over scheduling (e.g., telework, self-employment); and
- improved human resources practices geared toward individual needs.

If this argument is valid, surely the demand for unionization should be falling over time. The demand for unionization is rarely measured by researchers or opinion seekers. A less direct question about support for unions, however, has been surveyed in the population. Of course, the desire to be a union member and showing general support for unions are distinct things. But the support question is probably correlated with the desire to unionize and thus a useful indicator.

Opinion polls are random samples of the population that provide only snapshots of population preferences. Their reliability as indicators of preferences, therefore, increases as results are repeated over time. We will first look at the longest repeated sample on the question of support for unions provided by the Gallup Organization in the United States.

The Gallup Organization has asked the same question to Americans for almost seventy years: Do you approve of unions? As is shown in Figure 3.2, there is no long-term decline in the support of the American population for unions. There was, however, a dramatic drop in support in 2009 to 48 percent, the lowest since 1936. It bounced back a little in 2009 to 53 percent. This sharp drop was undoubtedly due to the unpopular government bailout of General Motors and Chrysler (in Canada and the U.S.). It seems that unions took their share of the blame for the near-collapse of these automotive giants. Nonetheless, during the long period of union decline from the mid-1950s until today there was stability in union support (to be discussed further in Chapter 5).

FIGURE 3.2

U.S. Union Approval: Gallup Polls 1936–2010

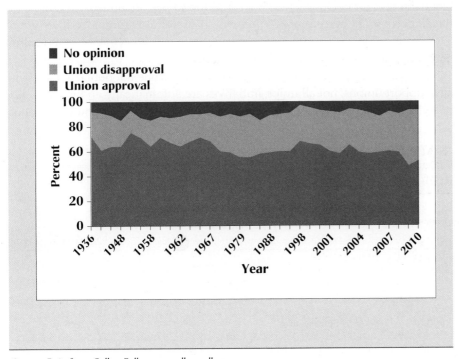

Source: Data from Gallup Polls. www.galluppoll.com

Chapter 3: Economic, Social, and Political Environments

TABLE 3.2

General Support for Unions: Leger Poll

		POPULATION	YOUTH <25 YEARS
2001	Unions always necessary	72%	84%
1998	Unions always necessary	67%	80%

Source: Leger Poll, Quebec, March 24, 2001.

In Canada, similar questions have been asked at various times about union support and desire for unionization. Quebec is one of the most heavily unionized provinces, so we might expect strong union support. Leger Marketing polled Quebeckers in 1998 and in 2001 (see Tables 3.2 and 3.3). The approval question was translated as "Are unions necessary?" A follow-up question asked about the respondents' desire to be in a union. Answers for some years provided a breakdown for women and youth (the latter defined as less than 25 years of age).

On the question of the necessity of unions, the results show that a high percentage of persons (72 percent) in 2001 supported unions; this was an increase from 67 percent in 1998. The hopeful sign for unions was the high support from Quebec's youth at 84 percent in 2001, up from 80 percent in 1998.

On the second question of unionization, 37 percent of nonunion employees said they'd like to be in a union. Again, the positive side for unions is that a higher number of nonunion women (55 percent) and youth (57 percent) indicated a desire to be in a union. Also, 37 percent is not an unexpected result when we remember that this percentage was of the nonunion work force (about 60 percent in Quebec). So if we add the 40 percent already in unions to the 22 percent (37 percent of 60) that would prefer to be unionized, we get a 62 percent unionization rate. In any event, there is little evidence of a decline in demand for unionization in North America.

One caveat must be added to this discussion. While the public may generally support unions, not all union initiatives are automatically endorsed. Leger polled Quebeckers about their support for the demands of the common front of

TABLE 3.3

Unionization Preference: Leger Poll

YEAR	SURVEY QUESTION	YES—NONUNION EMPLOYEE REPLY	YES—UNION EMPLOYEE REPLY
2001	Prefer to be unionized	Overall 37% Women 55% Youth 57%	81%
1998	Prefer to be unionized	27%	70%

Source: Leger Poll, Quebec, March 24, 2001.

TABLE 3.4

View of Work, 1996 (% of employed workers)		
	CANADA	UNITED STATES
Workers who are somewhat or very satisfied with their jobs	86%	85%
Workers who think they were paid fairly in the past year	73%	74%
Workers taking some or a great deal of pride in their work	97%	99%
Workers who agree that they would do their best regardless of pay	77%	75%

Source: Reprinted from *The Paradox of American Unionism: Why Americans Like Unions More Than Canadians Do but Join Much Less,* edited by Seymour Martin Lipset, Noah M. Meltz, Rafael Gomez, and Ivan Katchanovski. © 2004 by Cornell University. Used by permission of the publisher, Cornell University Press.

public-sector unions in March of 2010. Only 10 percent of the population supported these union demands (Institut économique de Montréal [IEDM], 2010).

Work Attitudes

Demand for unionization may stem from worker dissatisfaction with their jobs (Barling, Kelloway & Bremermann, 1991). To examine this question, we have drawn from a joint Canada–U.S. population survey conducted in 1996 (Lipset, Meltz, Gomez & Katchanovski, 2004). Despite the general support for unions indicated above, workers displayed very positive attitudes toward work and conditions (see Table 3.4). Attitudes were very similar between Canadian and American workers, with 86 percent and 85 percent, respectively, indicating satisfaction with their jobs. High proportions of those surveyed also thought they were fairly paid and took pride in their work.

We can only conclude from these apparently contradictory results that the majority of Canadian and American workers want unions for reasons other than economics or job dissatisfaction. Employee demand for a collective and independent voice in the workplace in Canada and the United States appears to be strong despite some profound changes over the past three decades in work organization, labour force composition, and the individualization of human resources.

 3.1

TRENDS IN INCOME DISTRIBUTION AND POVERTY   Critics of globalization and free trade policies argue that a consequence of these trends is a widening income gap between the rich and poor. Restructuring policies, so the argument goes, have disproportionate negative effects on workers who lack the necessary skills and training to compete in the new economy. This is an important factor for those who have concerns about the human condition, for in the United States, high rates of income inequality have been associated with low rates of economic growth (Hsing, 2005). It has also been argued that the replacement of relatively-high-paying unionized manufacturing jobs with lower-paying service-sector jobs will result in a smaller middle class and a widening gap between high- and low-income groups.

We begin by looking at child and family poverty rates in Canada. In 1989, coincidently the same year that Canada signed the Free Trade Agreement with the United States, the Canadian House of Commons unanimously adopted a resolution to achieve the goal of eliminating poverty by the year 2000. Campaign 2000, a nonpartisan network of over ninety national, provincial, and community partner organizations committed to working together to end child and family poverty in Canada, issued a report card on the subject in 2005. Here is what the Conference Board of Canada concluded about child poverty:

> Canada's high rate of child poverty is shocking for a country ranked among the wealthiest in the world. Canada ranks bronze on childhood poverty, with a rate almost six times that of Denmark! (Conference Board of Canada, 2005, p. 61)

Here are some of the more noteworthy findings from the report card:

- More than 1.2 million children—one child out of every six in Canada—were still living in poverty.
- The child poverty rate had stayed at around 18 percent since 2000, despite economic growth.
- The number of children living in poverty had risen by 20 percent since 1989.
- The poverty rate had remained virtually unchanged at 12 percent.
- The child poverty rate for female lone-parent families had dropped slightly to 52.5 percent.
- Despite economic growth, no progress had been made to bridge the gap between rich and poor.
- Forty-one percent, approximately 325,390, of food bank users in 2004 were children.
- Social exclusion had worsened, with child poverty rates for Aboriginals, immigrants, and visible-minority groups more than double the average for all children; child poverty rates among children with disabilities was also disturbingly high at 27.7 percent.

Publications of both advocacy groups and academics (i.e., literature critically examined by peers) have cited evidence that poverty has increased in the United States and Canada. One study found a large increase in poverty intensity in the United States in the 1980s, causing U.S. poverty rates to exceed those of Canada (Osberg & Kuan, 2000; see Figure 3.3). Another study revealed that earning inequality increased for both union and non-union workers in the U.S. from 1982 to 1990 (Chaykowski & Slotsve, 1996). The inequality found in the latter study, however, was significantly less for unionized workers. Evidence also showed a decline in earnings of the middle-income earners and increased polarization for male workers in the U.S. from 1968 to 1990 (Beach, Chaykowski & Slotsve, 1997). Another study could not rule out deindustrialization as a significant cause of increased earnings inequality (Chevan & Stokes, 2000). More recent data revealed a direct link between union decline and wage inequality in U.S. labour markets (Kim & Sakamoto, 2010).

FIGURE 3.3

Poverty Rates for Selected OECD Countries, Mid-2000s*

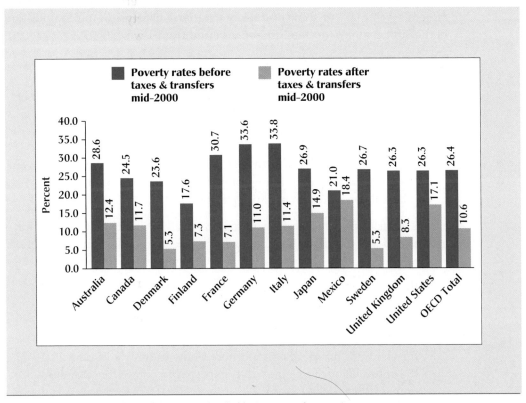

*Before and after taxes and transfers. Poverty threshold 50 percent of current income.

Source: Data extracted from "Income distribution," OECD iLibrary, retrieved 16 January 2011 from http://www.oecd-ilibrary.org/social-issues-migration-health/data/income-distribution_els-indi-data-en.

Poverty rates, defined as the proportion of the labour force below 50 percent of current median income, are shown in Figure 3.3 for selected OECD countries in the mid-2000s. Poverty rates are shown before the effect of taxes and transfer payments and after. Income after taxes and transfers is often labelled **disposable income**. It captures the impact of such factors as the progressive tax structure and the social safety net. Looking at poverty rates before taxes and transfers, we see that the U.S. and Canada rates of 24.5 and 26.3 percent, respectively, are slightly below the OECD average of 26.4 percent and well below those of such European countries as France (30.7), Germany (33.6), Italy (33.8), and even Sweden (26.7). But when disposable income is examined—that is, after taxes and transfers have been factored in—the story dramatically changes. Only Mexico (18.4) had a higher relative poverty rate than the United States (17.1). Canada (11.7), Australia (12.4), and Japan (14.9) all had higher poverty rates than the OECD average of 10.6 percent. The Scandinavian nations had the lowest poverty rates, undoubtedly reflecting their superior safety nets and more progressive taxation policies.

disposable income

income after taxes and benefits from social programs (e.g., unemployment insurance payments)

CHANGING WORK FORCE COMPOSITION   In 1965, Canada's work force was almost 70 percent male, but by 2005, almost half of the work force (46 percent) was female. The change was due to a doubling of the female labour participation rate (Human Resources and Skills Development Canada [HRSDC], 2004). Here is a summary of some of the key long-term changes in the composition of the labour force over the forty-year period from 1965 to 2005:

- In 1965, only three out of every ten Canadian workers were female, as against close to half (46 percent) of the work force in 2005.
- In 1965, only one-quarter of mothers with children under the age of six were in the labour force; that proportion was 70 percent in 2005.
- From 1970 to 2000, the fertility rate in Canada dropped 2.3 to a record low of 1.5 (live births per woman).
- The Canadian labour force continues to experience less than 1 percent annual growth, with immigration expected to account for all net labour force growth by 2011 (HRSDC, 2004).

In order to prevent labour shortages caused by inadequate labour force growth and low fertility rates, Canada has increasingly relied on immigration. According to Human Resources and Social Development Canada,

> the country of origin for immigrants has significantly shifted from Europe to Asia over the past 30 years, leading to greater cultural diversity in the workplaces. Whereas in the 1960s over 75% of the immigrant population in Canada consisted of immigrants from the U.S. and Europe, the proportion is now roughly a fifth. In 2011, the entire labour force growth is expected to come from immigration. (HRSDC, 2004)

These immigration shifts present challenges in terms of integrating newcomers into the Canadian work force.

An Aging Population

According to HRSDC, the percentage of the population 65 and over will grow from 12.7 percent in 2001, to 14.4 percent in 2011, and to 17.9 percent in 2021 (see Figure 3.4; HRSDC, 2002).

A consequence of the aging population is an increase in poverty for persons above the age of 55. Research indicates that poverty for elderly families is on the increase in Canada (Milligan, 2008); that Canadian social programs for the elderly are woefully inadequate (Audet & Makdissi, 2009; MacDonald, Andrews & Brown, 2010); and that the recession has made matters worse (OECD, 2009).

Employer Challenges to Workforce Aging

The Department of Human Resources and Skills Development has produced some tangible recommendations for employers to consider. It is contemplated that policies and/or collective agreements (if unionized) might permit, enable, and legitimize the following:

FIGURE 3.4

Projected Age and Gender Profile of the Labour Force, 2021

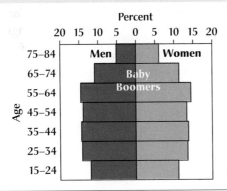

Source: Human Resources and Development Canada, found at Statistics Canada, "Overview of the aging workforce challenges: Diagnostic." Retrieved from http://www.rhdcc-hrsdc.gc.ca/eng/lp/spila/wlb/aw/08overview_diagnostic.shtml. Human Resources and Development Canada. Reproduced with the permission of the Minister of Public Works and Government Services Canada, 2011.

- elimination of age discrimination; adoption of proactive measures in the workplace, in human resources practices
- safer workplaces, healthier environments, holistic approach to wellness
- flexible work arrangements, job redesign
- appropriate training opportunities
- flexible retirement options (HRSDC, 2005)

Impact of Compositional Changes on Unions

More Women

There was a substantial shift in the proportion of women in unions from just 12 percent in 1977 to 48 percent in 2004 (Statistics Canada, 2004). This shift reflected, in part, the significant growth of the services sector and the corresponding decline in manufacturing over the period.

Occupational Shifts

Over the past ten years, unions have made significant gains among women, youth, and workers in public administration and in the fast-growing childcare and home-support sectors. On the other hand, unions lost members in manufacturing and technical health fields (medical, dental, veterinary, and therapeutic).

Union density has also declined because unions have failed to make inroads in the fast-growing information-technology industries or occupations. However, the labour movement has managed to "maintain its overall presence by offsetting losses in the goods sector with successes among employees in small workplaces and among part-time and non-permanent employees. These last two groups have large concentrations of youth and women" (Statistics Canada, 2004).

Contingent Workers

What is contingent work? Armstrong-Stassen (1998) defines five types of alternative work arrangements: part-time work, temporary or contingent work, flextime, compressed work weeks, and teleworking.

1. *Part-time.* According to Statistics Canada (1995), a person is considered to be employed part-time when the number of hours worked at the main job is usually less than thirty hours per week.
2. *Contingent.* There is no accepted definition of contingent work. It falls into two broad categories of workers: (1) those who have traditionally worked on a temporary or casual basis and (2) a smaller but growing group of professional and technical contingent workers who desire the freedom and flexibility provided by contingent work (see Koen, Mitchell & Crow, 2010).
3. *Flextime.* Flextime, as the name indicates, permits employees to start earlier or later as long as the required number of hours are worked per week (Christensen, 1990). The advantage for employees is that they can travel outside of morning and/or afternoon rush hours and may be better able to juggle family commitments (e.g., day care, school, etc.) (see Zeytinoglu, Cooke & Mann, 2009).
4. *Compressed work weeks.* The compressed work week involves reallocating the work time by condensing the total hours in the traditional work week into fewer days (Duxbury & Haines, 1991). A typical example is the four-day, forty-hour work week (4/40) in which employees work four ten-hour days. While the longer work day can create more pressure, some employees prefer this schedule because of the increased number of days off.
5. *Teleworking.* Teleworking may involve working at home, a satellite work centre, or other nontraditional workplace, either full-time or part-time, and using telecommunications and the electronic processing of information (Gray, Hodson & Gordon, 1993; Long, 1987; Morganson, Major, Oburn, Verive & Heelan, 2010).

Unions have had less success organizing contingent workers. In 2004, for example, 23.6 percent of part-time employees were in unions, compared to 32 percent full-time (Statistics Canada, 2004).

Work in Canada is undergoing significant structural change. Part-time employment (less than thirty hours per week) represented only 4 percent of the work force in the 1950s. It has been estimated that contingent workers have grown over the past twenty years to 30 percent of the labour force. It is predicted that the "nonstandard" job of today will become the standard job of the future (Armstrong-Stassen, 1998). In the next section, we examine and define various emerging forms of work.

Labour and Employment Relations Challenges

One result of these new forms of work is that the typical firm today has a significant part of its work force made up of part-time and contingent employees. This new structure poses major challenges for labour and employment relations. Collective bargaining was designed for workers in a stable year-round employment relationship. The new work forms represent a significant change in the balance of power between labour and management in favour of management. Even if unions were able to organize the new groups, it is not clear that labour boards would find that a sufficient community of interests exists to warrant a single bargaining unit. Another difficulty, at least for the affected employees, is the inapplicability of existing law to many of the categories of employees outside of the core work force. Most employment laws were designed to cover the core work force and therefore may have minimum (hourly, weekly, or yearly) thresholds to qualify for benefits.

Work–Life Balance

The economic and social changes discussed above have put substantial pressure on individuals in the workplace. Work–life balance (WLB), defined as the desire on the part of both employees and employers to achieve a balance between workplace obligations and personal responsibilities, offers a useful framework for analyzing the effects of environmental changes.

> Work–Life Conflict (WLC) occurs when the cumulative demands of work and non-work roles are incompatible in some respect so that participation in one role is made more difficult by participation in the other. Sometimes described as having too much to do and too little time to do it, role overload is a term that is sometimes used as a means of examining the conditions that give rise to WLC. WLC has three components . . .
>
> 1. role overload;
> 2. work to family interference (i.e., long work hours limit an employee's ability to participate in family roles); and
> 3. family interferes with work (i.e., family demands prevent attendance at work). (HRSDC, 2004; see also Lero, Richardson & Korabik, 2009).

Having introduced the concept of work–life balance, we want to provide an analysis of how the changing environment of industrial relations has placed pressures on workers and managers. To do this, we construct a systems framework with three categories of the environment: economic, social, and demographic (see Figure 3.5). To some extent, this framework provides a summary of the environmental changes described above.

Economic

As we discussed earlier, the Canadian economy has been undergoing a fundamental restructuring from a manufacturing- to a service-based economy. This is a consequence of free trade and represents a shift that is found in all industrialized countries. Contingent work has grown as part of this restructuring process. A stress point for industrial relations is the pressure on firms for more flexibility. This pressure has, in turn, eliminated plant work rules and reduced economic rewards. Recall that we have discussed above how deregulation, outsourcing, and labour shortages have affected industrial relations.

FIGURE 3.5

A Framework for Analysis of Work–Life Balance

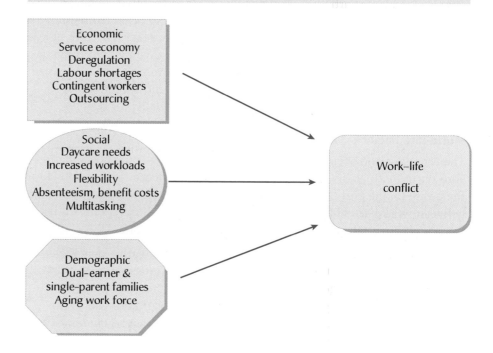

Social

Summarizing the previously identified factors, work–life balance will be affected by such issues as daycare needs; increases in workload, including multitasking; job insecurity; and employers' pressure for more flexibility. Firms are concerned about work–life issues because they affect the bottom line through increased absenteeism, benefit costs, and reduced productivity.

Demographic

Recall the demographic changes of dual-earner and single-parent families, an aging work force, and baby-boomer effects. According to the HRSDC (2005), the most significant labour market changes "include greater labour market participation of women, the increase in dual-wage earner families, the rise in numbers of lone-parent families, the aging of the population, changing immigration patterns, the growth of non-standard work, and new working arrangements."

The Political Environment

In contrast to its American counterpart, the Canadian labour movement has managed to organize new members and avoid the steep decline in union density found in the United States. One of the reasons for this divergence is the more labour-friendly laws in Canada (discussed in Chapter 2). A major factor in the development of Canadian law has been the political support that labour has received from political parties. In Canada, labour has tended to be supported by the New Democratic Party (NDP) in English Canada and the Parti Québécois (PQ) in Quebec.

Two structural elements of the Canadian political system have made it possible for labour parties to translate their pro-labour policies into legislation (Bruce, 1989):

1. *Not all eggs are in one basket.* In the United States, there is only one labour law for the entire private sector. The ability to produce legislative change is lacking in the American system, where only two amendments (Taft-Hartley in 1947 and Landrum-Griffin in 1959) have been made to the *Wagner Act* since its passage in 1935. Since under the Canadian constitution, labour is a provincial matter, we have eleven labour laws, including that of the federal jurisdiction (more if we include the territories'). This fact alone increases the probability of legislative change. The NDP has been in power in four provinces at various times and has held the balance of power in minority governments. This leads to the second enabling element:

2. *The parliamentary system of government.* Unlike the American two-party system, in which it is nearly impossible for parties other than the governing and official opposition parties to have any power and in which minority governments are not possible, the Canadian system favours multiple parties. Moreover, minority governments are possible, meaning that even if no party wins a majority of seats, the party with the largest number may govern with the support of smaller parties. Needless to say, in any minority government, the smaller coalition partners will have a list of demands that must be met for the coalition to exist and the arrangement to survive.

   The parliamentary system and constitutional fragmentation mean that labour has been able to use its political association with the NDP, and in Quebec with the PQ, to win significant legislative gains. In Saskatchewan, for example, the NDP labour association produced the first collective bargaining legislation in Canada for public employees (see Sass, 1985). Canada, unlike the United States, has a card system of certification in five out of eleven jurisdictions: federal, Manitoba, Quebec, Prince Edward Island, and New Brunswick. The card system has been associated with success in union-organizing campaigns (Johnson, 2002).

According to Taras (1997), there have been three important social and historic experiences that have caused Canada to reject U.S. opposition to collective bargaining:

- The 1982 *Canadian Charter* protected individual rights but facilitated collective bargaining.
- Even with similar legislation in the United States, American firms in Canada are more restricted in anti-union activities.
- Canada has rejected the U.S. right-to-work approach that prevents unions from forcing nonmembers to join or pay dues despite enjoying the benefits of unionization.

Globalization and Politics

The pressure globalization puts on governments to conform to international policy norms means there is less policy space for provincial governments to experiment with reforms. In fact, some theories predict that trade liberalization policies will force a convergence of labour policies. If governments stray too far from international policy norms, they will lose investment (both foreign and domestic), with negative consequences for economic growth.

There is evidence in support of this convergence theory. As more conservative governments took power in such provinces as Saskatchewan, Ontario, and British Columbia, Canadian labour law drifted toward the U.S. model. Saskatchewan, Ontario and British Columbia, for example, have scrapped the card system of certification in favour of the U.S. *Wagner Act* mandatory voting system.

Whatever the effect of globalization, there is also evidence that the election of an NDP provincial government has not been a guarantee of progressive change in labour legislation. For example, amending labour law proved to be controversial in a case involving the NDP government in Manitoba.

The Manitoba Case

With labour support, the NDP was elected in Manitoba in 1981 on a promise to amend the *Labour Relations Act* and to bring in new legislation on plant closures. As the outcome is described by Black (1985),

> In 1983, the NDP finally moved to address these issues, but in contrast to policies elsewhere, sought solutions through an arrangement involving business, unions, and government. Trade union leaders participated in the process but failed to make their influence felt. Business strongly opposed the proposed legislation, and the NDP bowed to their influence, changing Bill 22 before its passage in June 1984. The NDP has tentatively promised to address labor's concerns in 1985 legislation, but labor must mobilize its members if it is to prevent another retreat by the NDP.

Summary

Together with the discussion of the legal environment in Chapter 2, this chapter examines the context or environment within which industrial relations take place. We have seen how the economic, social, and political environments affect industrial relations. Also discussed were some of the developments in these environments, brought about by such factors as changing demographics, the forces of globalization and free trade, and labour force composition. There is another important part of the industrial relations context to be studied: the history of labour in Canada. It is not possible to comprehend where organized labour is headed in Canada without understanding its origins. It is to this task that we turn next.

Key Terms

deregulation 78

disposable income 91

elasticity of supply (demand) 80

"great recession" 78

hiring hall 86

macroeconomic policy 78

monopsony 84

North American Free Trade Agreement
  (NAFTA) 78

privatization 78

Weblinks

Campaign 2000's 2009 Report Card on Child and Family Poverty in Canada: 1989–2009:

http://www.campaign2000.ca/reportCards/national/2009EnglishC2000NationalReportCard.pdf

The Changing Face of Canadian Workplaces:

http://www.rhdcc-hrsdc.gc.ca/eng/labour/employment_standards/fls/resources/resource01.shtml

Research on work–life balance:

http://www.hrsdc.gc.ca/en/lp/spila/wlb/13research_documents.shtml

RPC Icons

3.1 Provides advice to clients on the establishment, continuation, and termination of bargaining rights

- structure of unions
- institutions and processes (both regulatory and nonregulatory) that govern the relationship between employers and employees

3.2 Provides advice to clients on the establishment, continuation, and termination of bargaining rights

- unions and the labour movement

Discussion Questions

1. Describe two ways in which labour markets have been liberalized in Canada in the past twenty years.

2. What are Marshall's four conditions? How do they affect labour power?
3. What are the barriers to labour supply? Provide examples.
4. Explain how a wage increase affects leisure in terms of the income and substitution effects.
5. What do economists mean by the term *monopsony*? Give two examples of occupations that may be in monopsonistic markets.
6. What positive and negative effects may craft unions have on productivity?
7. According to the Gallup Organization, what evidence has there been of a long-term decline in support for unions? Have union disapproval numbers increased?
8. Does North American polling data show widespread worker dissatisfaction with their jobs?
9. Using relative poverty rates before and after taxes and transfers, how do Canadian poverty rates compare to those of other industrialized countries? Why does it matter whether taxes and transfers are taken into account?
10. What is contingent work? Define five types.
11. What is meant by the term *work–life balance*? Give two examples of factors that may have upset this balance in the past five years.
12. How have the parliamentary system and constitutional fragmentation helped Canadian unions organize new members compared to their U.S. counterparts?

Using the Internet

1. Using the Internet or another source, find an example of the substitution effect as it affects either the elasticity of demand or the supply of labour.
2. Using the Internet or another source, find an example of a highly labour-intensive organization and an example of a highly capital-intensive organization.

Exercises

1. Using Marshall's conditions, analyze the effect on union power of the North American Free Trade Agreement (NAFTA) between Canada, Mexico, and the United States.
2. Compare public attitudes toward unions between Canada and the United States. How do you account for the divergence between union density rates between the two countries?
3. How do poverty rates in Canada compare with those of other industrialized countries? Explain your findings.
4. Describe the factors that account for changes in the balance between work and life in Canada.

Case

Outsourcing and Canada—A Good Place to Outsource To!

"Offshore outsourcing" is the practice of hiring an external organization to perform business functions in another country. This can be contrasted with "offshoring," in which the functions are typically performed by a foreign division or subsidiary of the parent company.

"Nearshore outsourcing" is a form of outsourcing in which functions are relocated to cheaper yet geographically close locations. In the case of the United States, the most obvious nearshore jurisdictions are Canada and Mexico.

Canada: A Unique Outsourcing Jurisdiction

Canada is uniquely situated in the world of offshore outsourcing of Information Technology and Business Process functions. It is a significant importer and exporter of outsourcing activities, is a primary nearshore outsourcing destination for U.S. business, and is emerging as a broker jurisdiction in global outsourcing arrangements.

The statistics are impressive:

- According to the McKinsey Global Institute, in 2002, Canada generated US$3.7 billion in offshore BTO revenue behind only Ireland (US$8.3 billion) and India (US$7.7 billion).[1]

- Canada is the 8th most attractive offshore location overall and places 2nd of all jurisdictions when it comes to quality of people skills and availability of skilled workers (behind India), and quality of business environment (behind Singapore).[2]

- Canada ranks among the top five places in the world for communications providers to offshore call center and IT operations.[3]

- Canada is a main beneficiary of outsourcing from the United States, which represents approximately 70% of the total global outsourcing market.[4]

- Outsourcing within North America is projected to grow at an average of 10–15% annually.[5]

[1] McKinsey Global Institute, "Offshoring: Is it a win-win game?," August 2003. See http://www.mckinsey.com/knowledge/mgi/rp/offshoring/perspective.
[2] A. T. Kearney, "Making offshore decisions: 2004 offshore location attractiveness index," 2004. See http://www.atkearney.com/shared_res/pdf/Making_Offshore_S.pdf.
[3] Deloitte, "Making the off-shore call: The road map for communication operators," 2004. See http://www.deloitte.com/dtt/cda/doc/content/ca_tmt_offshoreoutlook.pdf.
[4] McKinsey Global Institute.
[5] PWC, "A fine balance: The impact of offshore IT services on Canada's IT landscape," 2004. See http://www.pwc.com/ca/afinebalance.

Source: Theodore Ling, "Outsourcing to Canada: Legal and tax considerations," Technology Executives Club website, retrieved 22 April 2011 from http://www.technologyexecutivesclub.com/Articles/outsourcing/artGlobalOutsourcing.php.

Questions and Assignments

1. Using the information provided in this article, ask students to write a short essay on the scope, limitations (if any), and benefits of outsourcing.
2. Using the Internet, find a current example of outsourcing in your province, and ask students to do a cost–benefit analysis of the example.
3. Divide the class into pro- and con-outsourcing. Let each side select a spokesperson (or spokespersons), provide time for preparation, and supervise a debate.

Endnote

1. For a more in-depth study of the labour market see Drost and Hird (2005).

References

Allen, S. G. (1984). Unionized construction workers are more productive. *The Quarterly Journal of Economics, 99*(2), pp. 251–275.

Armstrong-Stassen, M. (1998). Alternative work arrangements: Meeting the challenges. *Canadian Psychology, 39*(1/2).

Ashenfelter, Orley, Farber, Henry, & Ransom, Michael. (2010). Labor market monopsony. *Journal of Labor Economics, 28*(2), pp. 203–210.

Audet, Mathieu, & Makdissi, Paul. (2009). Assessing the impact of historical changes in social protection on poverty in Canada. *Applied Economic Letters, 16*, pp. 523–526.

Barling, J., Kelloway, E. K., & Bremermann, E. H. (1991). Preemployment predictors of union attitudes: The role of family socialization and work beliefs. *Journal of Applied Psychology, 76*(5), pp. 725–31.

Beach, C. M., Chaykowski, R. P., & Slotsve, G. A. (1997). Inequality and polarization of male earnings in the United States, 1968–1990. *North American Journal of Economics and Finance, 8*(2), pp. 135–151.

Berik, G., & Bilginsoy, C. (2000). Do unions help or hinder women in training? Apprenticeship programs in the United States. *Industrial Relations, 39*(4), pp. 600–625.

Black, E. (1985). In search of "industrial harmony": The process of labour law reform in Manitoba 1984. *Relations industrielles, 40*(1), pp. 140–161.

Bruce, P. G. (1989). Political parties and labour legislation in Canada and the U.S. *Industrial Relations, 28*, pp. 115–141.

Byrne, J., Clarke, L., & Van Der Meer, M. (2005). Gender and ethnic minority exclusion from skilled occupations in construction: A Western European comparison. *Construction Management and Economics, 23*(10), pp. 1025–34.

Chaykowski, R. P., & Slotsve, G. A. (1996). A distributional analysis of changes in earnings inequality among unionized and nonunionized male workers in the United States: 1982–1990. *The Canadian Journal of Economics, 29*(1), pp. 109–128.

Chevan, A., & Stokes, R. (2000). Growth in family income inequality, 1970–1990: Industrial restructuring and demographic change. *Demography, 37*(3), pp. 365–381.

Christensen, K. (1990). Here we go into the "high-flex" era. *Across the Board*, July–August, pp. 22–23.

Conference Board of Canada. (2005). Performance and potential 2005–06. *The World and Canada, Special Edition*.

Craft, J. A. (1998). The community as a source of union power. *Journal of Labor Research, 11*(2), pp. 145–160.

Currie, J., & Farsi, M., & Macleod, W. B. (2005). Cut to the bone? Hospital takeovers and nurse employment contracts. *Industrial and Labor Relations Review, 58*(3), pp. 471–493.

Devillanova, Carlo, Di Maio, Michele, & Vertova, Pietro. (2010). Labour mobility and the redistributive effects of trade integration, *Journal of Economics, 100*(2), pp. 95–116.

Drost, H., & Hird, R. (2005). *Introduction to the canadian labour market* (1st Canadian edition). Toronto: Thomson Nelson.

Dustmann, Christian, & Shonberg, Uta. (2009). Training and union wages. *The Review of Economics and Statistics, 91*(2), pp. 363–376.

Duxbury, L., & Haines, G. (1991). Predicting alternative work arrangements from salient attitudes: A study of decision makers in the public sector. *Journal of Business Research, 23* (August), pp. 83–97.

Finnie, R. (2004). Who moves? A logit model analysis of inter-provincial migration in Canada. *Applied Economics, 36*(16), p. 1759–1779.

Foot, D. K., & Soffman, D. (1996). *Boom, bust, and echo: How to profit from the coming demographic shift.* Toronto: Macfarlane Walter & Ross.

Foot, D. K., & Venne, R. A. (1990). Population, pyramids and promotional prospects. *Canadian Public Policy, 16*(4), pp. 387–399.

Government of Canada. (2011). Canada's Economic Action Plan comprises five main elements. Canada's Economic Action Plan website, retrieved 22 April 2011 from http://www.actionplan. gc.ca/eng/feature.asp?pageId=90. Reproduced with the permission of the Minister of Public Works and Government Services Canada, 2011.

Gray, M., Hodson, N., & Gordon, G. (1993). *Teleworking explained.* New York: John Wiley & Sons.

Gunderson, M., & Riddell, W. C. (1988). *Labour economics* (2nd edition). Toronto: McGraw-Hill, p. 616.

Gunderson, M., & Verma, A. (1992). Canadian labour policies and global competition. *The Canadian Business Law Journal, 20*(1), pp. 63–90.

Hayden, A. (2003). International work-time trends: The emerging gap in hours. *Just Labour, 2* (Spring), pp. 23–35.

Hsing, Y. (2005). Economic growth and income inequality: The case of the U.S. *International Journal of Social Economics, 32*(7), pp. 639–648.

Human Resources and Skills Development Canada (HRSDC). (2002). Summary: Adaptive measures accommodating an aging workforce—recommendations. Published in Overview of the Aging Workforce Challenges. http://www.rhdcc-hrsdc.gc.ca/eng/lp/spila/wlb/aw/10overview_ recommendations.shtml#5. Human Resources and Skills Development Canada, 2002. Reproduced with the permission of the Minister of Public Works and Government Services Canada 2011.

Human Resources and Skills Development Canada (HRSDC). (2004). The changing face of Canadian work-places. Retrieved 15 Jan. 2011 from http://www.rhdcc-hrsdc.gc.ca/eng/ labour/employment_standards/fls/resources/resource01.shtml. Human Resources and Skills Development Canada. Reproduced with the permission of the Minister of Public Works and Government Services Canada, 2011.

Human Resources and Skills Development Canada (HRSDC). (2005). Overview of the aging work-force challenges: Recommendations. Retrieved 22 April 2011 from http://www.rhdcc-hrsdc. gc.ca/eng/lp/spila/wlb/aw/10overview_recommendations.shtml#50. Reproduced with the permission of the Minister of Public Works and Government Services Canada, 2011.

Institut économique de Montréal (IEDM). (19 March 2010). Léger Marketing poll on negotiations with public sector unions. Retrieved 22 April 2011 from http://www.iedm.org/3411-leger-marketing-poll-on-negotiations-with-public-sector-unions-only-10-of-quebecers-support-the-union-demands

Johnson, S. (2002). Mandatory votes or automatic certification: How the choice of union recognition procedure affects certification success. *The Economic Journal, 112*, pp. 334–361.

Kim, ChangHwan, & Sakamoto, Arthur. (2010). Assessing the consequences of declining unionization and public-sector employment: A density-function decomposition of rising inequality from 1983–2005. *Work and Occupations, 37*(2), pp. 119–136.

Koen, Clifford, Mitchell, Michael, & Crow, Stephen. (2010). Your workers may be contingent but your liability for them is certain: Part III: Other employment issues. *The Health Care Manager, 29*(3), pp. 213–222.

Lero, Donna, Richardson, Julia, & Korabik, Karen. (2009). Cost–benefit review of work–life practices. Report for the Canadian Association of Administrators of Labour Legislation. 115 pp.

Lipset, Seymour Martin, Meltz, Noah M., Gomez, Rafael, & Katchanovski, Ivan. (2004). *The paradox of American unionism: Why Americans like unions more than canadians do but join much less.* Ithaca, NY: ILR Press.

Long, R. J. (1987). New office information technology: Human and managerial implications. London: Croom Helm.

Luizer, J., & Thornton, R. (1986). Concentration in the labor market for public school teachers. *Industrial and Labor Relations Review, 39*(4), pp. 573–85.

MacDonald, Bonnie-Jean, Andrews, Doug, & Brown, Robert. (2010). The Canadian elder standard: Pricing the cost of basic needs for the Canadian elderly. *Canadian Journal on Aging, 29*(1), pp. 39–56.

Marshall, A. (1920). *Principles of economics* (8th edition). London: Macmillan and Co., Ltd.

Milligan, Kevin. (2008). The evolution of elderly poverty in Canada. *Canadian Public Policy, 34*, Supplement, pp. 79–94.

Morganson, Valerie, Major, Debra, Oburn, Kurt, Verive, Jennifer, & Heelan, Michelle. (2010). Comparing telework locations and traditional work arrangements; Differences in work–life balance support, job satisfaction, and inclusion. *Journal of Managerial Psychology, 25*(6), pp. 578–595.

Neville, John, & Kriesler, Peter. (2008). Minimum wages, unions, the economy and society. *The Economic and Labour Relations Review, 19*(1), pp. 25–38.

Organisation for Economic Co-operation and Development. (2001). *Employment outlook.* Paris: OECD.

Organisation for Economic Co-operation and Development. (2009). Economy: Thoughts on the crisis, tipping back the balance. *OECD Observer, 270/271* (December 2008–January 2009).

Osberg, L., & Kuan, X. (2000). International comparisons of poverty intensity: Index decomposition and bootstrap inference. *The Journal of Human Resources, 35*(1), p. 51.

Sass, R. (1985). *Union Amendment Act, 1983*: The public battle. *Relations industrielles, 40*(3), pp. 591–623.

Statistics Canada. (1995). *Labour force annual averages 1995.* Ottawa: Statistics Canada.

Statistics Canada. (2004). *Perspectives on labour and income.* Ottawa: Statistics Canada.

Taras, D. G. (1997). Collective bargaining regulation in Canada and the United States: Divergent cultures, divergent outcomes. In B. Kaufman (Ed.), *Government regulation of the employment relationship* (pp. 295–341). Madison, WI: Industrial Relations Research Association.

Weber, M. (1922; 1978 ed.). *Economy and society: An outline of interpretive sociology.* Berkeley & Los Angeles: UCLA Press.

Weeden, K. A. (2002). Why do some occupations pay more than others? Social closure and earnings in the United States. *The American Journal of Sociology, 108*(1), pp. 55–101.

Zeytinoglu, Isik U., Cooke, Gordon B., & Mann, Sara L. (2009). Flexibility: Whose choice is it anyway? *Relations industrielles, 64*(4), pp. 555–574.

CHAPTER 4

Labour History

Learning Objectives

By the end of this chapter, you will be able to discuss

- the preunionization work environment and the movement toward unionized relationships;
- the relationship between the Canadian and American labour movements;
- how exclusive jurisdiction, business unionism, and political nonpartisanship have divided the labour movement over time; and
- how significant events from the 1850s to the present day have shaped the history of workplace relations.

THE WINNIPEG GENERAL STRIKE

On the morning of May 15, 1919, a group of female telephone operators took actions that started one of the more memorable events in Canadian labour history. While they ended their shifts as normal, no one came in to replace them. The operators were holding a sympathy strike in support of the metalworkers. By 7:00 a.m., the phone system was no longer functioning. A few hours later, at 11:00 a.m., Alex Sheppard (a union leader with the metalworkers) placed a One Big Union (OBU) hat on his head and marched to the intersection of Portage and Main. Workers from various establishments followed. The general strike was now in full gear.

Within twenty-four hours, between 20,000 and 35,000 mostly nonunion workers had left their workplaces. Winnipeg, Canada's third-largest city was at a standstill. Workers from public services (e.g., postal workers, waterworks, police, firefighters), the private sector (e.g., cooks, waiters, retail staff), manufacturing, and building trades were on strike.

Employer and government concern over the strike led to several key events. Employers organized a group called the Citizens Committee of One Thousand, which declared the strike a revolutionary conspiracy. On June 6, the federal government amended the *Immigration Act*. Any non-Canadian-born person deemed to be a revolutionary could now be immediately deported. In addition, the government amended the *Criminal Act*. As a result of these legislative changes, several strike leaders were arrested and jailed on June 17. From 1919 to 1920, the federal government would pay over $196,000 for the prosecution of these labour leaders.

Saturday, June 21 marked a dark day in the strike. Thousands of strikers gathered in front of city hall in defiance of the mayor's ban on parades. The mayor called in the North West Mounted Police, who, along with federal troops, charged the crowd. By the end of the afternoon, downtown Winnipeg was empty, one person was dead, and another thirty were injured. The day became known as Bloody Saturday. Concerned that more violence would occur, the strike leaders declared an end to the strike on June 26. The two groups key to the start of the strike (metalworkers and phone operators) made no gains.

Metalworkers did not receive any wage increases; phone operators were rehired only if they promised to never again go on a sympathy strike.

Sources: D. J. Bercuson, *Confrontation at Winnipeg: Labour, industrial relations and the general strike* (Montreal and Kingston: McGill–Queen's University Press, 1990); Canadian Museum of Civilization, 2002; J. Chaboyer and E. Black, "Conspiracy in Winnipeg: How the 1919 general strike leaders were railroaded into prison and what we must do now to make amends," 2006, retrieved 27 November 2006 from http://www.policyalternatives.ca/documents/Manitoba_Pubs/2006/Conspiracy_in_Winnipeg.pdf; Government of Canada, 2006b; M. Horodyski, Women and the Winnipeg General Strike of 1919, *Manitoba History, 11*(Spring) (1986), retrieved 28 November 2006 from http://www.mhs.mb.ca/docs/mb_history/11/women1919strike.shtml; T. Mitchell, "Legal gentlemen appointed by the federal government: The Canadian state, the Citizens' Committee of 1000, and Winnipeg's seditious conspiracy trials of 1919–1920," *Labour/Le Travail, 53* (2004), pp. 9–46; Mitchell and Naylor, 1998.

Preunionization

In today's workplace, employees have many rights. For example, they have access to break times, are paid overtime, are protected from unsafe work environments, have the right to refuse unsafe work, etc. Many of these workplace practices that we now take as givens were the result of victories won by the labour movement over the past hundred years. To understand just how far we have come, let's review the type of workplace practices that existed prior to the rise of the labour movement.

Master–Servant Relationship

Prior to unionization, the employment relationship was best described as **master–servant** in nature. The employer, as the master, made all the rules. The employee, as a servant, was required to follow these rules. As such, employees had limited protection or rights. This was because the basis of the relationship was common law. Under common law, the employment contract required that employees perform the work and employers pay workers' wages (Kahn-Freund, 1967). There was such a power imbalance between workers and employers that employees were often coerced into agreeing to employment terms and conditions (Fox, 1974). It was illegal for workers to quit; for them to bargain collectively or to form a union was deemed a conspiracy; and management controlled virtually all aspects of the employment relationship (Labour Law Casebook Group, 2004).

master–servant relationship
employment relationships in which employees have few rights

While employees of today can look to unions or governmental agencies for protection from abusive workplace practices, this was not always the

1935 - Robert Wagner → National Labor Relation Act
- created labour board
1. to enforce rights of employee's to bargain collectively
2. define ~~labo~~ unfair labour practices by management
3. remedied ev violation of the act → work re-instatement
4. only one union can represent one bargaining union.

case. Unions at that time were illegal, and the laws of the day did little to protect employees. In essence, there were only two actors in the industrial relations system: employers and employees. There were no "associations" (e.g., unions), and the third actor (i.e., government) was largely absent. In fact, as outlined by the Labour Law Casebook Group (2004), the laws and courts did little to protect employees; rather, they provided additional power to the employer. For example, the *Master and Servant Act* stated that workers who refused to report to work or failed to follow lawful orders were guilty of a criminal offence. This act even provided special penalties for workers who attempted to bargain collectively to seek wage increases. Even the rights to choose your employer or leave your employer were restricted. England's *Statute of Artificers* (1563), from which Canada's common law originated, required workers to accept jobs when they were offered and allowed employers to punish people who left a job before the work was completed (Fox, 1985).

As you can see, preunionization workplaces and work practices looked very different from those of today. There was little consideration of workers and their rights, and only marginal court protection. It was this very environment, and the large power imbalance between workers and employers, that led to the rise of a labour movement. In the sections that follow, we will present some of the more significant milestones in that history.

The Movement to Unionization

In this section, we will walk through the significant events related to unionization and workplace relationships. (See also Table 4.1.) We will start with pre-1900 Canada and then move mostly decade by decade to present-day events.

The Early Years (Pre-1900)

R P C 4.1

The early years in the labour movement were marked by a number of important developments including the introductions of new model unionism, the *Trades Union Act*, the American Federation of Labour, the Trades and Labour Congress of Canada, and the Knights of Labor.

New Model Unionism

new model unionism
the movement to trade (or craft) unions

In the 1800s, in their study of British unions, sociologists Beatrice and Sidney Webb (1898) described an event they called **new model unionism**. A key element of these new world unions was that they were craft-based—all members performed the same trade or specialty.

apprenticeship
a process in which trainees learn a trade under the supervision of a senior tradesperson

Generally composed of specialist employees performing a common trade, new model unions often restricted access to the trade through the use of **apprenticeships**. In so doing, unions minimized wage competition by influencing the supply of labour in terms of the number of craftsmen available to perform the work. As a monopoly supplier of labour, these unions usually sought to negotiate solutions to any workplace issues versus going on strike.

TABLE 4.1

Some Key Dates in Canadian Labour History

Year	Events
1872	Nine-Hour Movement
	Trade Union Act
1886	Trade and Labour Congress (TLC) founded
1902	Berlin Convention results in foundation of National Trades and Labour Congress (NTLC)
1907	*Industrial Disputes Investigation Act* (IDIA)
1919	The Winnipeg General Strike
1944	Wartime Labour Relations Regulation (P.C. 1003)
1945	Rand Formula
1956	Canadian Labour Congress (CLC) formed
1961	New Democratic Party (NDP) formed
1967	Public Service Staff Relations Act (PSSRA)
1975–78	Anti-Inflation Board (AIB)
1985	Canadian United Auto Workers formed

While the Webbs focused on British unions, we will see that Canada had similar issues concerning trade unions in the late 1800s. Arguably, it is new model unionism's focus on trades that may have led to the use of the term **trade union**.

The Nine-Hour Movement and *Trade Union Act* of 1872

The 1870s were marked by several key events in Canadian labour history. The Nine-Hour Movement of 1872 (see IR Today 4.1) was sparked by a group of about 1,500 Hamilton workers who sought a reduction in the length of the workday, defying the legislation of the day (CBC, 2006b; Kealey, 1995). That same year, Toronto printers went on strike against the *Globe* founder, George Brown. While the movement became widespread, it did not result in significant gains. However, the movement is believed to have influenced the prime minister of the day (Sir John A. Macdonald) to create the *Trade Union Act*. Declaring himself "the working man's friend," Macdonald had his government introduce legislation that permitted employees to join unions (Government of Canada, 2006a). That same year, an amendment to the *Criminal Law Amendment Act* (1872) stated that it was no longer a conspiracy or a crime for a person to join a union. That being said, the *Criminal Law Amendment Act* did allow jail penalties for striking. Nevertheless, the passage of these two legislations provided the foundation for the birth of a formalized Canadian labour movement.

trade union

unions that organize all workers of a trade regardless of their industry or workplace

The Nine-Hour Movement

The late 1800s were marked by numerous events resulting from employee discontent with the working conditions and practices of the time. Perhaps one of the best known was the Nine-Hour Movement, which occurred between January and June of 1872. The following passage from **http://www.thecanadianencyclopedia.com** provides an excellent summary of those events:

> *Beginning in Hamilton, the demand for the 9-hour day (some workers were expected to labour as long as 12 hours) spread quickly to Toronto and Montréal, gathering support in Ontario towns from Sarnia to Perth. Echoes were heard as far east as Halifax. For the first time Canadian labour organized a unified protest movement, developed tactics of resistance, and cultivated articulate working-class leaders. Nine-Hour leagues united union and non-union workers, and in May labour representatives formed the Canadian Labor Protective and Mutual Improvement Association.*
>
> *Some newspapers popularized labour's causes. In March–April an unsuccessful Toronto printers' strike reminded labour that employers were strongly antagonistic to workers' initiatives and that trade unions were actually illegal in Canada. On May 15 Hamilton's "nine-hour pioneers" defied opposition with a procession of 1500 workers. Skilled, respectable craftsmen emerged as labour leaders. James Ryan, a Great Western Railway machinist–engineer, recently arrived in Canada, was Hamilton's central figure. In Toronto his counterpart was cooper John Hewitt, and in Montréal, James Black.*
>
> *Although some groups won concessions, the movement was unsuccessful. Employer hostility helped its defeat, as did the waning of post-Confederation prosperity. Equally significant were divisions within the working class. Women and the unskilled figured peripherally at best, ensuring that the struggle touched certain sectors more fully than others. All this, in conjunction with the apparent failure of militant strikes and workplace action to win decisive victories for workers, fed the attempt to secure rights politically through labour law.*
>
> *The Nine-Hour Movement was not an utter failure. Its struggle in 1872 indicated that labour had a public presence and that its interests, institutions and political stance reflected its unique social position and economic needs. It represented a necessary, if ambiguous, beginning in labour's capacity for self-government.*
>
> *The right to associate in trade unions was obtained. Working-class activists won major concessions immediately after 1872: repeal of repressive legislation, passage of laws strengthening workers' hands against employers, and franchise extension. The nine-hour pioneers gave way to the Canadian Labor Union.*

The nine-hour movement laid the foundation for many of the elements in current labour and employment standards acts. For example, many now require that overtime be paid for an employee working more than eight hours per day. To this day, some of the issues we face (e.g., what is deemed to be a "normal" workday) have been traditional topics on the labour agenda.

Source: B.D. Palmer (2006). *The Nine Hour Movement*. Used with permission of The Historica-Dominon Institute. Retrieved November 8 from http://www.thecanadianencyclopedia.com/index.cfm?PgNm=TCE&Params=A1ARTA0005757

American Federation of Labor and the Trades and Labour Congress of Canada

Cigar maker Samuel Gompers was the first and longest-serving president of the American Federation of Labor (AFL). In 1886, he founded the AFL as a federation of trade unions built upon three key principles. As this chapter will show, these three principles both united and divided the labour movement in

Canada and the United States for more than half a century. These principles were as follows (AFL, 2006):

EXCLUSIVE JURISDICTION   Gompers believed that unions should be craft- or trade-based. This meant that only wage earners could be union members and that each union would be responsible for a single occupation or trade: "one union per craft; one craft per union." Thus, only one union could represent each of bricklayers, blacksmiths, etc. As we will see later in this chapter, this **exclusive jurisdiction** view conflicted with that of groups like the Knights of Labor, which were open to skilled and unskilled labour.

exclusive jurisdiction
what exists when a single union represents all workers of a trade or occupational grouping

BUSINESS UNIONISM (OR PURE-AND-SIMPLE UNIONISM)   Gompers believed that the primary focus of unions should be the economic well-being of their members rather than political reform. He felt that the best way to ensure workers' rights was to ensure they had economic security. In fact, he is often quoted as saying, "more, more, and more"—referring to more economic gains being needed for workers. Because of this view, North American unionism is often referred to as "bread and butter" unionism or **business (or pure-and-simple) unionism**—its focus being to make certain there was bread and butter on the tables of workers. Accordingly, the AFL did not seek to overthrow capitalism or business owners, as was the case of **socialist unionism**. Rather, Gompers advocated that unions needed to operate in the capitalistic economy with the goal of getting the best deal possible their members.

business unionism (or pure-and-simple unionism)
unionism that focuses on improving wages and the working conditions of its members

socialist unionism
unionism that challenges capitalism and seeks equity for union and nonunion members

POLITICAL NONPARTISANSHIP   Gompers believed that labour should practise **political nonpartisanship**—that is, it should not align itself with any one political party or group. Rather, he asserted that labour should create its own priorities, clearly articulate these priorities, seek the endorsement of existing political parties for these priorities, and mobilize members to vote for those politicians or parties that supported labour's priorities. In IR circles this became known as "rewarding friends (those that supported labour's priorities) and punishing enemies (those that did not support labour's priorities)."

political nonpartisanship
a belief that unions should not be aligned with any political party

As will be shown later in this chapter, the guiding principles that grounded the formation of the AFL, summarized in Table 4.2, have both divided and united the labour movement in Canada.

TABLE 4.2

Guiding Principles or "Divide and Conquer"?

Exclusive jurisdiction	The concept that each union would be responsible for a single trade; often referred to as "one union per craft; one craft per union"
Business unionism (or pure-and-simple unionism)	The view that the focus of labour unions is to improve the economic well-being of its members rather than to seek to overthrow capitalism or business owners.
Political nonpartisanship	The view that labour should not align itself with any one political party or group

The same year that the AFL was formed in Ohio, the Trades and Labour Congress (TLC) was formed in Canada. It was largely composed of trade groups similar to those in the AFL; however, it also included groups such as the Knights of Labor, which included unskilled workers.

We should point out that the AFL was not the first trade federation in Canada. Its lineage can be traced to the 1873 Canadian Labour Union (CLU) (Kealey & Palmer, 1995; Palmer, 1983).

The CLU was made up of about thirty-five unions. Its mandate was "to agitate such questions as may be for the benefit of the working classes, in order that we may obtain the enactment of such measures by the Dominion and local legislatures as will be beneficial to us, and the repeal of all oppressive laws which now exist" (Ottawa & District Labour Council, 2005). Accordingly, the CLU's priorities went beyond those of Gompers's AFL and included mandating shorter working hours, ending private employers' use of convict labour, restricting the use of child labour (particularly for children under ten years of age), setting minimum standards for the sanitation and ventilation of factories, creating a government statistics bureau to track information related to wages and working conditions, and instituting resolutions related to public education (Ottawa & District Labour Council, 2005).

An Irish printer named Daniel O'Donoghue, considered by many the "father of the Canadian labour movement," was key to the formation of the CLU (O'Donoghue, 1942–1943). Unfortunately, due to economic downturns of the 1870s, the CLU was short-lived. However, as the economy improved, so did the cause of labour. In the 1880s, O'Donoghue was involved in organizing the initial meeting of the Trades and Labour Congress, which replaced the defunct CLU (Ottawa & District Labour Council, 2005). As you will see IR Notebook 4.1, O'Donoghue's involvement in politics and the Knights of Labor contradicted the three core values of Gompers's AFL. This early linkage between politics and labour may also explain why, even today, Canadian labour organizations are seen as more socialist than their American equivalents.

The Knights of Labor

The Knights of Labor was first formed in 1869 in Philadelphia. Based in the United States, it was originally a secret society, similar to the Freemasons, but it removed the cloak of secrecy in 1881. It was more radical in nature, an three factors differentiated it from other labour organizations of the day (Knights of Labor, 2009):

1. It believed in the creation of a single large union for skilled and unskilled workers; thus, it did not follow the doctrine of "one union per craft; one craft per union."
2. It was opposed to strikes. The Knights leadership felt that strikes led to hardship for workers. However, while the leadership may have opposed strike action, its membership did not. Members of the Knights were actively involved in many large strikes (Kealey & Palmer, 1995).
3. The Knights sought to establish cooperative businesses, which would be owned and operated by members of the union rather than employers per se. This was in direct contrast to the idea of "bread and butter" or business unionism espoused by Gompers.

Daniel O'Donoghue: The Father of the Canadian Labour Movement

Daniel O'Donoghue is considered by many to be the founding father of the Canadian labour movement. Born in Ireland in 1844, he immigrated to Canada at the age of six. When he turned fourteen, he became a printing apprentice. Given the shortage of jobs, he moved to New York, where he was exposed to the printers' union. After returning to Canada to work with the *Ottawa Times*, he, at the age of 21, organized the first printers' union in Ottawa. Union members saw their wages increase to $8 a week in 1869 and $10 in 1873.

Given his success with the printers' union, O'Donoghue was a natural for a leadership role in Ottawa's new trades council, which was formed in 1872. In fact, O'Donoghue held a role as a founding member, secretary, and president of the Ottawa Trades Council. He also participated in the formation of the first national labour federation, the CLU, and became its first vice-president in 1873.

His influence in the labour movement resulted in his being nominated in, and winning, a provincial byelection in Ottawa. He held the position of an independent "working man's representative" from 1874 to 1879. During that time, he focused on a labour agenda by pressing the government of the day to act on trade union issues related to workplace conditions, unemployment, and immigration.

Upon losing his seat in 1879, he returned to his labour movement roots. He moved to Toronto, where he was involved in the revival of the Toronto and District Labour Council. He was a member of this council as a representative of both the Typographical Union and the Knights of Labor. Moreover, O'Donoghue became secretary of the legislative committee in 1883 and was involved in organizing the first meeting of the Trades and Labour Congress in 1886.

During the 1880s and 1890s, O'Donoghue held several positions within the provincial government. Three years after it created a Bureau of Industries (1882), he was named the bureau clerk. In this role, he often wrote on issues important to labour (e.g., poor working conditions, the work of trade unions, etc.). In 1900, O'Donoghue left this position because he was assigned to the federal government's first Department of Labour. There, he worked as a fair wages officer, ensuring people employed under government contracts had fair pay and working conditions.

O'Donoghue died in 1907. During his years in the labour movement, he clearly played a key role in both the transformation and documentation of Canadian labour history.

Sources: O'Donoghue, 1942–1943; Ottawa & District Labour Council, 2005.

Because of the initial secrecy of the Knights of Labor, it is difficult to completely track its history. We do know that the membership was very diverse. Some estimates from the Knights (2009) suggest that it grew from 10,000 workers in 1881 to more than a million by 1886 (note that the 1886 membership included 50,000 African-American workers and 10,000 female workers at a time when these groups had very few rights in society at large). Kealey and Palmer (1981, 1995) have documented the Knights' history in Canada, in particular in Ontario. It is estimated that the Knights organized a minimum of 21,800 workers nationally, more than 18 percent of whom were employed in the manufacturing sector in 1881 (Kealey & Palmer, 1995). While the Knights may be considered a defunct group, you will note that it does still have a present, as is evidenced by its website. Its current focus is on shortening the standard workday to six hours (Knights of Labor, 2009).

1900–1920: The Years of Struggle

The years between 1900 and 1914 marked one of the most accelerated phases of economic development in Canadian history (Palmer, 1992). During the same period (1901–1913), there were fourteen large strikes in which some form of violence occurred; in eleven of these, the militia or military were called in (Canadian Labour Congress, n.d.). This period also marked the beginning of World War I. Thus, this early part of the twentieth century laid a foundation in the Canadian labour movement as well as created a rift between the skilled (i.e., trades) and unskilled workers that would last almost half a century. Some of the important events of this period included the Berlin Convention, the introduction of the *Industrial Disputes Investigation Act* (IDIA), the Winnipeg General Strike, and One Big Union. We will now discuss each in more detail.

The Berlin Convention, 1902

Following the lead of the American Federation of Labor, the Trade and Labour Congress's 1902 convention created a large divide in the Canadian labour movement—one that would remain for fifty years. Held in Berlin (now Kitchener), Ontario, this convention resulted in the TLC becoming composed solely of unions affiliated with the AFL and the unions that did not share the three core philosophies of Gompers's AFL (i.e., exclusive jurisdiction, business unionism, and political nonpartisanship) being ejected from the TLC. Only unions that espoused the views of exclusive jurisdiction, and perhaps those without jurisdictional conflicts with AFL-affiliated unions, remained part of the TLC. In essence, the industrial-based unions of less-skilled workers were expelled (including the Knights of Labor), while the craft-based unions remained. Given the connection between the "new" TLC and the AFL, unions that did not meet these three core philosophies of Gompers's AFL split off to form the National Trades and Labour Congress (NTLC) in 1902, which later became the Canadian Federation of Labour (CFL) in 1908 and the All-Canadian Congress of Labour (CCL) in 1927 (Canadian Labour Congress, n.d.; MacDowell, 2006).

Industrial Disputes Investigation Act (IDIA), 1907

Conciliation services had been offered by the federal Department of Labour starting in 1900 with the passage of the *Conciliation Act* (Kealey, 1995). William Lyon Mackenzie King, who would later become a prime minister, had firsthand experience with it, given his role as the chief conciliator of the department. King had attended Harvard and the University of Chicago, where he examined issues relevant to labour relations. In 1907, when he held the position of deputy minister of labour, he created the *Industrial Disputes Investigation Act* (IDIA). The act, which would become a cornerstone of Canadian law, marked an ongoing trend in Canadian legislation, namely the need for third-party intervention prior to a strike (Heron, 1989). Many of the key elements of the IDIA still hold true, some historians arguing that "the IDIA laid the foundation for the particular industrial relations system that exists in Canada" (Kealey, 1995, p. 417).

RPC 4.2

The act required that all workers and employers in certain industries (i.e., resources, utilities, transportation) submit their disputes to a three-person conciliation board prior to a strike or lockout. Parties would present evidence to the panel, and the panel would issue a report. However, there was a required "cooling-off" period once the board completed its report, during which the parties were not permitted to proceed to work stoppage (Heron, 1989).

The Winnipeg General Strike

This chapter's opening vignette presented an overview of the strike itself. Now we need to set the context of that historic event. In the early days of May 1919, the building trades were on strike. The metalworkers joined them, as both sought to have their unions recognized as well as their working conditions and wages improved. They took their cases to the Winnipeg Trades and Labour Council (WTLC). The WTLC held a vote for a general strike of all unions to support the metal and building workers. Support was impressive: over 11,000 voted in favour of the strike as against about 500 who opposed it (Mitchell & Naylor, 1998). Estimates suggest that the votes cast in favour of it cut across occupations, 149 police staff supporting the strike (11 did not), all 278 waiters and cooks supporting it, and 250 postal workers supporting it (19 did not) (Canadian Museum of Civilization, 2002). The Collections Canada website hosts a silent film of the strike that you might find interesting (Collections Canada, n.d.). —— to be watched.

While the vignette suggests that the strikers did not achieve their goals, the strike did result in a number of positive changes in relation to one actor of the IR system—the government (Government of Canada, 2006b). In the 1920 Manitoba election, labour candidates won eleven seats, four of which were won by strike leaders. The next year, James Woodsworth (a Methodist minister who was involved in the strike) was elected as the first independent labour member of Parliament (MP). Woodsworth would later form the Co-operative Commonwealth Federation, the precursor to the present-day New Democratic Party (NDP).

One Big Union and Other Socialist Movements

As suggested by the vignette's account of strike leader Alex Sheppard wearing an OBU hat, OBU has often been associated with the Winnipeg General Strike. OBU was radical in nature with a social unionism orientation. One of its key demands was the introduction of a six-hour workday to minimize unemployment. OBU's Canadian roots date back to the March 1919 Western Labour Conference in Calgary (Heron, 1989; Palmer, 1983). During this conference, a referendum was held to separate from the TLC and create a new militant labour organization, OBU (Mitchell & Naylor, 1998).

OBU differed from the TLC in several important ways. It focused on organizing all workers (not just craft/trade workers), identified closely with the revolutions taking place in Germany and Russia (greetings were even sent from the Calgary conference to the Bolsheviks and Spartakists), and had a strong link to the Socialist Party of Canada (SPC), given that several OBU leaders were members of the SPC (Mitchell & Naylor, 1998). OBU is estimated to have had a total membership of 50,000 in 1919 and about 1,800 some eight years later (Palmer, 1983). While relatively short-lived, OBU is considered by some historians to have been the most influential socialist labour organization in Canada (Palmer, 1983).

It is interesting to note that OBU's lineage can be traced to two other labour groups: the Knights of Labour and the Industrial Workers of the World (IWW). As argued by Kealey and Palmer (1995, pp. 239–240), "it was the fires of the Knights of Labor it (OBU) chose to rekindle. . . . The Knights were regarded as 'a mass organization grouped into geographic units' that prefigured the industrial unionism of One Big Union."

The IWW, or Wobblies, were socialist in nature. They argued that workers received low wages, toiled hard, and had limited security; however, they, as the producers of goods, had the ability to shut down the economy if they worked in a single, united force (Palmer, 1983). Like the Knights, the Wobblies were open to various ethnic groups as well as unskilled labour. The Wobblies' presence in Canada was largely contained to the 1910s. At their high point, 40 percent of the railway construction workers who built the Canadian National Railway (CNR) and the Grand Truck Pacific were Wobblies. By the end of 1918, the IWW membership of Canada was, in essence, nonexistent (Palmer, 1983). Nevertheless, the group still exists, continues to advocate the concept of one big union, and is actively seeking to unionize Starbucks in the United States (IWW, 2011a, 2011b). There are even YouTube postings concerning the IWW and Starbucks.

The 1930s and 1940s: Decline and Resurrection

Great Depression

a period of significant economic downturn resulting from the stock market crash of 1929

The stock market crash of 1929 created a period called the **Great Depression**. In what are considered to be the worst years of the Depression (the mid-1930s), the statistics tell a sad tale of the plight of the working class. In 1933, 32 percent of workers were unemployed; in 1935, about 20 percent of the entire country was receiving some form of social assistance (Palmer, 1983). The economy was in a tailspin. Yet it was during these turbulent times that important changes

> transformed the Canadian industrial relations system from one that combined *ad hoc* coercion and conciliation in an unpredictable nature to one that endorsed compulsory bargaining . . . through an extraordinary complex of administrative boards and a mystifying maze of what soon . . . would become "labour law." (Kealey, 1995, pp. 433–434)

Two elements critical to this transition were the *Wagner Act* of the United States and the removal of the Congress of Industrial Organizations from the AFL.

The *Wagner Act*

In Chapter 2, we discussed the basis of the law; now we will present an overview of the history of this seminal act. Like Canada, the United States had introduced legislation concerning compulsory conciliation. However, in 1935,

Senator Robert Wagner introduced a bill to create the *National Labor Relations Act* with the statement that

> [d]emocracy cannot work unless it is honored in the factory as well as the polling booth; men cannot be truly free in body and spirit unless their freedom extends into the places where they earn their daily bread. (National Labor Relations Board 60th Anniversary Committee, 1995, p. viii)

The *Wagner Act* (also called the NLRA) set forth several key elements that remain core to current labour relations law (National Labor Relations Board 60th Anniversary Committee, 1995):

1. It created an independent agency (the National Labor Relations Board—NLRB) to enforce the rights of employees to bargain collectively rather than to mediate disputes.
2. It required that employers bargain collectively with certified unions (e.g., when the majority of workers in an appropriate bargaining unit seek collective representation).
3. It defined unfair labour practices on the part of employers (e.g., bargaining directly with employees, disciplining employees for union activity).
4. It gave the NLRB the ability to order remedies for employer violations of the NLRA, including back pay and reinstatement of employees.
5. It adhered to the doctrine of exclusivity. Only one union, the one that the majority of workers selected, would represent the entire bargaining unit.
6. Perhaps most important to both workers and employers of the day, it encouraged collective bargaining.

Clearly this act contrasted with the common law, or master–servant, work relationships of the time—and as is shown in a historical piece on the *Wagner Act*, reaction from employers was not positive. While the *Act* certainly changed the face of employment relations from the 1930s to the present day, not all scholars agree that it was a positive move. For example, Adams (1999, 2002) argues that it created a culture of animosity between the actors of labour and management.

Committee of Industrial Organization, 1935

While many of the early unions were focusing on organizing all the workers of a craft or trade, the economy was in transition. Prior to the 1930s, some unions had organized all workers (regardless of trade) in sectors such as mining, but the 1930s saw a rapid increase in industrial (i.e., factory-based) workplaces and **industrial unions** (Palmer, 1983). While the traditional wisdom of the union movement was to divide the employees of each factory into the appropriate craft unions, the 1935 AFL meeting called this practice into question. In fact, the leader of the United Mine Workers, John Lewis, is said to have punched the leader of the carpenters' union while announcing the need for (and creation of) an industrial-focused organization within the AFL.

industrial unions

unions that organize all workers of an industry/ workplace regardless of trade

Chapter 4: Labour History

This group, called the Committee for Industrial Organization (CIO), sought to organize the nonunion workers in industrial settings. The CIO became a large social movement as workers in various industries (e.g., auto, electrical parts, steel) hosted "sit-ins" to improve their workplaces. As in the past, the craft-based values of the TLC proved to be solid. In 1937, the CIO was expelled from the AFL. The committee became an independent congress, namely, the Congress of Industrial Organizations (Heron, 1989). The split received considerable public reaction, as is shown by a YouTube posting.

Canadian Implications

A trend of this period was that actions in the United States were often transplanted to Canada. For example, in 1937, Nova Scotia became the first Canadian jurisdiction to pass a Wagner-type law requiring that employers bargain collectively with recognized unions (Kealey, 1995). Similarly in 1939, the TLC followed the AFL's lead and expelled CIO-affiliated unions. These CIO affiliates formed the Canadian Congress of Labour (CCL), together with the All-Canadian Congress of Labour (Palmer, 1983). However, it was the outbreak of World War II and the creation of the *Wartime Labour Relation Regulation*, also known as "P.C. 1003," that were perhaps the most significant events of this period.

P.C. 1003, 1944

After the outbreak of the war, the federal government's use of wartime emergency measures meant that it had jurisdiction over most labour relations issues. The conciliation procedures of the day (the IDIA) were unable to address the labour issues. Thus, the *Wartime Labour Relation Regulation* (P.C. 1003) was tabled by the government of Mackenzie King in February 1944. In essence, it copied the key elements of the *Wagner Act* (i.e., certification procedures, employer duty to bargain in good faith, unfair labour practices, etc.). However, it also put in place requirements in terms of

- mechanisms to handle workplace disputes during the term of the collective agreement (i.e., a grievance procedure); and
- conciliation procedures prior to strike (Kealey, 1995).

The Rand Formula, 1945

With the growing number of industrial unions, the implementation of formal procedures for union certification, and the introduction of compulsory collective bargaining among certified bargaining units, the 1940s saw a large increase in the number of unionized workers. However, in industrial workplaces, unions were lacking financial security. In a landmark decision to settle a Ford strike in Windsor, Justice Ivan Rand decided that all union dues would be paid directly to the union (i.e., deducted from the workers' pay through a **dues check-off**), regardless of whether or not the person chose to be a union member. Workers in a bargaining unit certified under the *Labour Relations Act* would not be required to join the union but would nevertheless have to pay union dues. This became known as the Rand Formula (Heron, 1989). Ontario's

dues check-off
a process whereby union dues are deducted automatically from pay

minister of labour declared it a "resounding blow for the advancement of labour's rights . . . [and] a great milestone in the development of labour–management relations" (Palmer, 1983, p. 242).

The 1950s and 1960s: Reconciliation and Expansion into the Public Sector

While the 1940s marked large increases in the number of industrial unions and the legal entrenchment of labour rights, it had left a labour movement divided largely along skilled (i.e., trade) versus unskilled (i.e., industrial) lines. However, the 1950s and 1960s provided an environment of reconciliation between these two groups, the formation of a union-backed labour organization, and landmark legislation permitting the unionization of public-sector employees.

ALF–CIO Merger, 1955

In 1952 George Meany was elected president of the AFL. His priority was to reunite the labour movement. In 1955 he succeeded in bringing the AFL and CIO together. After a fifty-year divorce, skilled and unskilled workers were reunited. The newly formed AFL–CIO then elected Meany as its first president. More details on Meany and the merger can be found on the AFL-CIO website (American Federation of Labor—Congress of Industrial Organizations, 2007) and historical footage can be found on YouTube.

Canadian Labour Congress (CLC), 1956

Following the lead of the United States, Canadian labour groups also reunited. The industrial-based CCL and the trade-based TLC formed the Canadian Labour Congress (CLC) in a convention held in Toronto in April 1956. Some fifty years later, it remains the largest federation of Canadian labour (CLC, n.d.). As stated by the current president of the CLC, Ken Georgetti,

> Delegates to the Founding Convention in 1956 called for the establishment of a national health care scheme, a bill of rights, improvements to unemployment insurance, elimination of discrimination against women, equal pay, a national pension scheme, and increases to federal and provincial minimum wages. (CLC, 2006)

The terms of the merger required compromise on both sides. You will note that we see elements of social and business unionism in the previous quote. The TLC had traditionally adhered to principles of political nonpartisanship; the CIO had traditionally supported the reform-oriented Co-operative Commonwealth Federation (CCF). The compromise became the creation of a political education department that would be tasked with aiding in the formation of a new political party encompassing unions, farmer organizations, cooperatives, and other progressive organizations. This compromise position is believed to have been brokered as the CCF was largely defunct and "even the 'old guard' within the TLC recognized that Liberal and Conservative parties offered labour no real voice and even worked against labour in moments of crisis" (Palmer, 1983, p. 254). In 1961, the NDP was formed, with the support of labour. Even today, the bond remains strong. At the 2008 CLC convention, Jack Layton, leader of the NDP, made a presentation (*Canadian Business*, 2008).

Public Service Staff Relations Act (PSSRA), 1967

As will be discussed in detail in Chapter 11, employees in the public sector had limited rights in terms of appealing, or influencing, their employers' decisions. However, in 1961, the government introduced a new *Civil Service Act* that allowed workers to appeal certain employment decisions (i.e., promotions, transfers, demotions, suspensions, and terminations). Moreover, what was perhaps the second-most-important piece of labour legislation in Canadian history (the first being P.C. 1003) was passed on March 31, 1967. That day, government passed the *Public Service Staff Relations Act* (PSSRA), which enabled federal government employees to bargain collectively with their employer (Felice, 1998).

The PSSRA marked an important turn in Canadian labour relations for two reasons. First, its passage, combined with the passage of similar laws in provincial jurisdictions, resulted in the public sector representing a large percentage of the unionized work force in Canada. Second, it marked an important departure from the United States, where civil servants are largely prohibited from bargaining collectively.

The 1970s and 1980s: Changing Relationships with Governments and the United States

The 1970s and 1980s marked turbulent times in the Canadian economy. Concerns over the fluctuation of oil prices, skyrocketing inflation, and the movement to freer trade made for challenging years in the labour movement. In the United States, it marked a time of attack on the labour movement in terms of both legislation and employers' actions. As we will discuss in detail in Chapter 6, it was a period of management and governments taking action to move the American work force toward being union-free and/or reducing the power of unions. However, in Canada, it showed our increasing independence from the American labour movement. In particular, it marked the removal of Canadian auto workers away from the United Auto Workers (UAW) union to form an independent Canadian union. Now let's look at a few of these events in greater detail.

Wage and Price Controls and Legislation

This period of history included several pieces of legislation that restricted labour's ability to seek wage increases. In 1973, inflation rose to over 13 percent and showed little sign of slowing down (Bank of Canada, 2006). In an effort to reduce inflation in the economy, in 1975 Prime Minister Pierre Trudeau went against his 1974 election platform and passed legislation designed to restrict wage increases. This was done through the Anti-Inflation Board (AIB), which monitored wage settlements from the private and public sectors for the years 1975–1978. The AIB, and its effectiveness, was subject to great inquiry during this period (Auld, Christofides, Swidinsky & Wilton, 1979; Lipsey, 1981; Reid, 1979). Thirty years later, we continue to see Bank of Canada reviews of the AIB program (Sargent, 2005).

In the early 1980s, we again saw a spike in the inflation rate, as it passed the 12 percent mark (Bank of Canada, 2006). In 1982, the federal government brought in what was known as the "6 and 5" program. In an effort to curb inflation, public-sector increases were frozen at 6 percent in the first year and 5 percent in the second (Sargent, 2005). This trend of freezing and/or restricting wage increases continued into the new millennium as we discuss in more detail in Chapter 11. For example, in April of 2004, four provinces reported that they were going to implement wage freezes, spending cuts, or layoffs in the public sector (Centre for Industrial Relations, 2004); in 2010, Ontario announced plans for additional wage freezes (Benzie, 2010).

Free Trade Agreements — reduce wages, job security, competition

As was outlined in a report by Haggart (2001), the 1980s also marked the first major trade agreement between Canada and the United States. In the fall of 1987, a free trade agreement was finalized; it became effective January 1, 1989. In the 1990s, Mexico joined the United States and Canada to form the *North American Free Trade Agreement* (NAFTA). Arguments for the agreements included a belief that reducing trade barriers would lower tariffs as well as improve Canadian productivity and standard of living (Haggart, 2001). Labour opposed the deal, fearing that it could lead to reduced wages and/or lower job security. To date, there is little evidence that Canada's productivity level has caught up with that of the U.S., nor is there any evidence that our standard of living has improved (Wise, 2009). While it is difficult to assess the exact impact of free trade on employment, many economists state that the free trade agreement was partially responsible for reducing wages and employment in the recession of the 1990s (Haggart, 2001). More recent research suggests that the removal of trade tariffs resulted in reduced wages for workers with the median worker experience in a real wage decline of 2 percent (Townsend, 2007).

Canadian Auto Workers Union

The 1980s furthered the trend toward a less U.S.-dependent labour movement. As will be discussed in more detail in Chapter 6, the 1980s in the United States were marked by concession bargaining as well as less-labour-friendly governments and employers. These changes played very strongly in the U.S. automotive industry. However, as fully outlined by Gindin (1995), the Canadian division of the union saw things differently than its American parent. In the late fall of 1984, Bob White, then director of the Canadian United Auto Workers Union, sought increased autonomy for the Canadian branch of the UAW, including allowing the Canadian division to set independent goals, have its own ability to call a strike, and access the strike fund. When these requests were denied, he set into motion a plan that would create an independent Canadian union. In the fall of 1985, the Canadian UAW was

works independently from UAW
- sets own goals
- calls its own strike
- has its own strike fund.

formally established. The next year, the union was renamed the Canadian Auto Workers. The union has since grown to become one of Canada's largest private-sector unions.

The 1990s and Beyond: Increased Resistance

[handwritten margin notes: decline of unionization — globalization/increasing competition — downsizing (outsourcing) — lots of manufacturing jobs lost 2004-2008 - 320,000 manuf. jobs lost.]

The 1990s and the new century have proven to be challenging environments for labour. As already discussed, the 1990s marked the expansion of the free trade zone to include Mexico in what became known as NAFTA (Haggart, 2001). Some other key events of this period included a severe recession (with historic levels of unemployment), significant levels of government restructuring, and increased use of legislation to replace collective bargaining in the public sector.

[margin: w(w)w symbol]

Recession, Unemployment, and Increased Focus on Global Competitiveness

The 1990s marked a dark period in Canada's economy. A speech by the governor of the Bank of Canada, Gordon Thiessen, on January 22, 2001 (Bank of Canada, 2001), presented the severity of the situation. The level of inflation was four times that of 1970; large government deficits were making investors wary of Canadian bonds (causing a "premium" in interest rates); and unemployment rates were above 10 percent. Labour costs, government cutbacks, layoffs, and global competitiveness issues all painted a rather bleak picture for labour. Excerpts from Thiessen's speech best illustrate the severity of the country's economic state at that time:

> By the early 1990s, the realities of the New World economic order were becoming clearer to Canadian companies too. Only, at that time, they were also coping with the fallout from the high-inflation years, especially the sharp drop in the prices of speculative investments and the burden of servicing large debts, as well as with declining world commodity prices.
>
> Working their way out of these difficulties was disruptive and painful for Canadian businesses. Defaults, restructurings, and downsizings became the order of the day. With all this, unemployment took a long time to recover from the 1990–91 recession and, in many instances, wages and salaries were frozen or reduced.

Perhaps no industry has been as hard-hit by either competitive pressure or job loss as the manufacturing sector—one of the traditional strongholds of labour. In fact, the CLC recently released a statement suggesting that while the economy had improved greatly since the 1990s, manufacturing was in a state of crisis. The CLC report suggested that in a four-year period from August 2002 to October 2006,

- over 250,000 jobs (over 10 percent of positions) had been lost due to layoffs, plant closures, and nonreplacement of retirees;
- job loss in unionized firms had almost doubled that of nonunion jobs (16.4 percent versus 8.7 percent); and

- the rate of job loss differed across industries, with one-third of jobs being lost in the textiles, clothing, and leather-products manufacturing groups.

Several years later, an analysis of Canadian employment by Bernard (2009) reinforced the CLC report. He concluded that over 320,000 jobs (or 14 percent of all jobs) disappeared from the manufacturing sector between the years 2004 and 2008. In particular, the textile and clothes manufacturing sector was decimated, with almost half of the jobs lost in that period. Perhaps more alarming for labour was that many of these lost jobs were unionized. While 32.2 percent of manufacturing job were unionized in 2004, only 26.4 percent were in 2008. Interestingly, for the rest of the economy unionization rates were largely stable (30.1 percent in 2004, 29.5 percent in 2008).

Similarly, the two decades have been marked by strong job loss and competitive pressures in the union strongholds of the resource sector (e.g., fishing and forestry). For example, Human Resources and Development Canada (HRDC, 2004) suggested that job loss in the B.C. salmon fishery was estimated to have been nearly 50 percent during the 1990s. Factors potentially contributing to this job loss included growth in foreign competition in terms of increased supply from other sources and the removal of trade barriers between Canada and the United States. In Newfoundland a province with a population only slightly higher than 500,000, the collapse of the cod fishery resulted in more than 25,000 people losing their jobs (Sinclair, 2003). In both cases, significant government aid was needed to ease the impact of these losses on the workers affected and to help them transition to new industries.

The forestry industry throughout Canada has been hard-hit since the start of the new millennium. In fact, it has been described by the union (the Communications, Energy & Paperworkers) and the employers (e.g., the Forest Products Association of Canada) as a "perfect storm" (CBC, 2006a). Over a five-year period, some 40,000 people have lost jobs in this sector due to economic trends (e.g., the higher Canadian dollar), competition from lower-cost regions (e.g., China, Russia), more efficient European mills, and a decrease in demand because of the movement to computers versus paper (CBC, 2006a). In fact, in British Columbia alone, it is estimated that 20,000 workers lost their jobs between 2007 and 2009 (Hamilton, 2009).

Government Restructuring

The previously discussed issues of competition and job loss in the private sector were also at play in the public sector in the 1990s and beyond. The public sector, which is also a union stronghold, faced severe restructuring. As pointed out by a Bank of Canada report by Fenton, Ip, and Wright (2001), we have seen significant changes in the public sector as a result of an increased focus on debt- and deficit-reduction. In fact, this report highlights an overall loss of about 6 percent of Canadian public-sector jobs between the years 1992 and 1998 (with an 18 percent drop in federal government jobs) in contrast to an overall increase of 11 percent in U.S. public-sector jobs.

privatization

the transfer or contracting out of services to the private sector

Crown corporations

corporations owned by the government

back-to-work legislation

legislation requiring that strike action cease and employees return to work

The decrease in public-sector jobs in Canada was attributed to several factors—specifically, an increase in contracting out, **privatization**, and an increased use of contractors and consultants rather than full-time employees (Fenton, Ip & Wright, 2001). As we will discuss in Chapter 6, this trend toward employing contractors and consultants is not unique to the public sector. Nevertheless, the aforementioned Bank of Canada report suggests that of the nearly 40,000 permanent jobs lost in the federal public sector between 1995 and 1998, about 10,000 were due to privatization or devolution. In fact, one federal government report states that between 1985 and 2005, close to thirty federal **Crown corporations**, with a value approaching $12 billion, were privatized through either sales to private firms or sales of shares on the stock market (Padova, 2005). Some of these privatized corporations included Canadair Inc., Canadian National Railways (CNR), and Petro-Canada.

Legislation Replacing Collective Bargaining

Given the significant changes taking place in the public sector in the 1990s, one would expect to have seen unions fighting hard to minimize the impacts of such changes on their members. However, public-sector unions faced a great deal of restrictions on their ability to negotiate on behalf of their members. For example, over the past decade we have seen **back-to-work legislation**, whereby striking workers are legislated to cease their strikes and return to work. In addition, we have seen wages and benefits issues, which are normally negotiated by unions, included in back-to-work legislation, as happened in the 1997 Canada Post strike (Came & DeMont, 1997), the 2004 Newfoundland provincial government strike (CBC, 2004), and the 2005 British Columbia teachers' strike (CBC, 2005). These issues will be discussed in more detail in Chapter 11.

Public-sector restructuring led to resistance from labour. For example, when Bob Rae's NDP government was in power in Ontario, it announced what it called a Social Contract. In an effort to save jobs and maintain pay levels in the public sector, Rae's government required that public-sector employees take twelve unpaid days off per year—these became known as "Rae Days" (Hebdon & Warrian, 1999). Labour was strongly opposed to such actions. Similarly, when Mike Harris's Conservative government came into power, there were severe budget cuts. In response, labour leaders called for a massive public strike against the government and a public strike/rally at Queen's Park, the Ontario legislature (CBC, 2004). This resulted in the "Days of Action," a five-day protest against the Conservative government in October of 1996. One estimate suggests that a quarter of a million people took part in the protest on October 26, 1996 (Heron, 1998), making it perhaps the largest strike since the Winnipeg General Strike.

Summary

As we have seen in this chapter, the past century has resulted in significant changes to the employment relationships between Canadian employers and their employees. The beginning of the twentieth century marked a time when employees had few rights. It was illegal for employees to form groups and bargain collectively. As the years progressed, there was a movement to permit the formation of collectives, albeit with restrictions on the actions they could take (e.g., conciliation prior to strike). The early 1900s also saw a focus on trade unions, which are formed by employees of a specific trade (or craft). The 1940s and 1950s marked significant changes in terms of a transition in the economy and the labour movement to industrial workplaces and unions rather than trade unions, as well as legislation that permitted (and even encouraged) collective bargaining. This was followed by landmark legislation of the 1960s that permitted public-sector unionization.

However, the years that followed have been less favourable to labour. The 1980s and 1990s represented times of increased government intervention on labour's ability to negotiate wages and benefits, increased competition from international sources, and a stronger employer focus on efficiency. Moreover, the new century has marked a time of significant job loss in many of the traditional strongholds of labour.

Through the years, we have also seen two important trends. First, we saw how the elements of exclusive jurisdiction, business unionism, and political nonpartisanship both united and divided the labour movement. While these guiding principles led to the formation of the AFL, they also led to a huge rift between industrial and trade unions that lasted more than fifty years. Second, we saw how the Canadian labour movement shifted from merely following the lead of the American movement in the early years to setting out on its own path.

As this chapter has clearly shown, the nature of the relationship between employers, employees, and their associations and governments is constantly shifting. If the past one hundred years are any indication, we will continue to see significant developments unfold throughout the twenty-first century.

Key Terms

apprenticeship 108
back-to-work legislation 124
business unionism (or pure-and-simple unionism) 111
Crown corporations 124
dues check-off 118
exclusive jurisdiction 111
Great Depression 116

industrial unions 117
master–servant relationship 107
new model unionism 108
political nonpartisanship 111
privatization 124
socialist unionism 111
trade union 109

Weblinks

Australian YouTube posting showing the main "mainstays" of employment gained by the labour movement:

http://www.youtube.com/watch?v=184NTV2CE_c&playnext=1&list=PL787 40D20E54D002Ad

Knights of Labor:

http://www.6hourday.org/knightsoflabor.html

Winnipeg General Strike footage:

http://www3.nfb.ca/objectifdocumentaire/index.php?mode=view&language=english&filmId=33

IWW and its campaign to organize Starbucks:

http://www.iww.org/en/culture/official/obu/index.shtml
http://www.iww.org/en/node/3044

http://www.starbucksunion.org

YouTube postings concerning the IWW and Starbucks (note language might offend some):

http://www.youtube.com/watch?v=slmv_mA2BL8&feature=related

http://www.youtube.com/watch?v=QWFybJKw7Kc

A YouTube posting concerning the Wagner Act:

http://www.youtube.com/watch?v=i2GSnBhYpvc

A YouTube video discussing the split of industrial unions from AFL:

http://www.youtube.com/watch?v=2IsJZAknuIQ

A YouTube video discussing the merger between AFL and CIO:

http://www.youtube.com/watch?v=fpmHbH522Y0

AFL–CIO:

http://www.afl-cio.org

Canadian Labour Congress:

http://canadianlabour.ca

Gordon Thiessen's 2001 speech to Canadian Club of Toronto:

http://www.bankofcanada.ca/en/press/2001/pr01-3.html

RPC Icons

4.1 Contributes to communication plan during work disruptions
- applicable dispute resolution mechanisms for work stoppages
- relevant legislation and regulations and third-party procedures
- the process of collective bargaining
- the history and environment of industrial relationships, unions, labour relations, and collective bargaining
- the rights and responsibilities of management and labour during the processes of organizing and negotiation

4.2 Collects and develops information required for good decision-making throughout the bargaining process

- institutions and processes (both regulatory and nonregulatory) that govern the relationship between employers and employees
- the history and environment of industrial relationships, unions, labour relations, and collective bargaining
- the rights and responsibilities of management and labour during the processes of organizing and negotiation
- the rights and obligations of management and labour during a certification process

Discussion Questions

1. This chapter shows that collective representation has taken many forms over the past hundred years. For example, the change from trade-based to industrial-based unions. In 2030, do you feel that we will still have forms of collective representation in Canada? If so, do you feel that they will be any different than the unions of today?
2. Why do you think North American labour has adopted more of a business unionism than a social unionism perspective?
3. Gompers clearly decided that labour should not have affiliations with any political party. In Canada, we see stronger links between labour and political parties. Do you feel that Gompers was correct in his assertion of political voluntarism? Why or why not?
4. While it is clear that the *Wagner Act* provided the blueprint for the North American industrial relations system, there is debate concerning its effectiveness. From the perspective of labour, what do you see as the advantages and disadvantages of this legislation?
5. The chapter clearly shows that union's current strongholds are in decline at present. Do you feel that this is signalling the end of the labour movement? Why or why not?
6. The economy is clearly becoming more global. How do you feel that this will impact the future of IR in general and labour more specifically?

Using the Internet

1. North American unions are often perceived as being more "bread and butter" versus socialist in nature. Yet in Canada, we see that several unions and the CLC deal with issues important to both unionized and nonunionized workers (e.g., equality, minimum wage). Have a look at the CLC website and those of two or three large unions (e.g., CAW, CEP, CUPE, provincial government unions). Do you see issues relevant to nonmembers?

2. Labour has played an important role in history. Have a look at the following sites to see how Canadian labour history is presented. Note that in some cases you may need to search using the words *labour history* or *Canadian workers* to find the information:

   - http://www.civilization.ca
   - http://www.collectionscanada.ca
   - http://canadianlabour.ca
   - http://www.pc.gc.ca
   - http://www.canadianheritage.org

3. You may be surprised to discover just how much labour history material can be found on the web. For example, YouTube has extensive coverage of issues. Go to that site and search the terms *labour, union, Wagner Act*, etc.

4. You may be asked to write a labour history paper in this course. The website of the *Journal of Canadian Labour Studies/Revue d'Études Ouvrières Canadiennes* may help you gather information for this paper: **http://www.mun.ca/cclh/llt**.

5. As we presented in the chapter, of the national parties, the NDP has always been seen as the most friendly to labour. To more closely examine the relationship between the two, go to

   a. the CLC website (**http://www.clc-ctc.ca**) and search for the term "NDP."
   b. the NDP (**http://www.ndp.ca**) website and search for the term "CLC."

Exercises

1. If you have access to grandparents or other senior citizens, why not conduct your own "labour history" interview. Sample questions might include

   - Tell me about the work practices at your first job (e.g., pay, leaves, hours of work, rights).
   - Were you ever a member of a union? If so, which one? Did you and your peers think that unionization was a good thing? Why or why not?
   - What was the most important change you saw in terms of employment rights in your work life?

2. Have a look at recent union or labour congress websites and publications. Based on what you find, what will historians state were the biggest issues of this year?

3. As this chapter demonstrates, the relationship between unions, governments, and political parties is complex and dynamic. Have a look at recent media (i.e., newspaper, television, Internet) coverage of elections, public policy, or economy issues. To what extent are the roles or the views of labour presented?

4. Many students are employed full- or part-time as they take courses. How do you think the labour movement has impacted the rights you have as an employee today versus if you had been employed in 1900?
5. Throughout history, unions have sought to improve the working conditions and wages of their members. Find recent media (i.e., newspaper, television, Internet) stories of union campaigns. To what extent are issues of working conditions and wages still prevalent in these stories?

Case

The CAW

As shown by the discussion of the 1940s Rand Formula decision, the UAW had a long history in Canada. For much of that period, the Canadian union members simply followed the directions provided by their American leaders. However, the 1980s marked a turbulent time in the auto industry. There were numerous layoffs and increased competition from non–North American manufacturers. The following events show how the CAW was created in this turmoil to become Canada's largest private-sector union.

In 1982 negotiations, the president of General Motors made a public statement that if Canadian workers did not follow the concessions of their American counterparts, there would be plant closures and relocations. GM settled with small gains for workers and without a strike. However, the Chrysler negotiations that followed resulted in a strike. As Gindin (1995) states, after a five-week strike, Chrysler agreed to accept the opening-day proposals of the union—Canadian workers even won a wage increase. In so doing, the Canadians had shown they were a force to be reckoned with.

The next round of bargaining came in 1984. GM settled in the United States with no wage gains for workers. After a thirteen-day strike, Canadian workers earned an annual increase that their American counterparts did not. This again signalled the independence, and strength, of the Canada component of the UAW. In December of that year, Bob White (then Canadian director of the UAW) called for a vote regarding the formation of a new, independent Canadian union. Only four of the 350 delegates voted against the call for the Canadian union.

In September of 1985, after nine months of negotiating the terms of separation, the legal and monetary issues were settled; the Canadian UAW was formed. In 1986, it was renamed to the Canadian Auto Workers (CAW).

In the twenty years that followed, the CAW became the largest public-sector union in Canada. Since its founding, it has merged with more than thirty other unions/locals and now represents workers in many industries outside of the auto sector (e.g., airline, fishery, retail, mining, rail). Given the diversity of its membership, the CAW has taken a leadership role in the areas of equity. In fact, since 1986, it has held an annual human rights conference. As its human rights policy states,

Unions emerged to not only collectively protect workers from the arbitrary use of power by employers and governments, but also to create a culture of equality and dignity for all members in their ranks. Achieving higher wages and better working conditions for workers is no more important in the final analysis than achieving solidarity amongst all workers. (CAW, 2006b)

The CAW fight for equity among disadvantaged workers even includes workers not represented by it. For example, the CAW website shows policy and discussion papers on issues ranging from employment insurance to protection of workers in the sex trade. It is a union that has clearly made a mark on the country.

Sources: CAW, 2005, 2006a, 2006b, 2006c; Gindin, 1995.

Questions

1. How does the CAW relationship with the UAW in the 1980s contrast with the historical relationship between the American and Canadian labour movements?
2. Discuss how the CAW can be seen to have both a "bread and butter" and "social justice" orientation.
3. The CAW is said to be a tough bargainer. Does the case provide evidence to support this claim?
4. As is shown in the chapter, the large labour federations have often had rifts and separations. If the CAW ever left the CLC, do you believe it has sufficient membership diversity to form an organization that would rival the CLC?

References

Adams, R. J. (1999). Why statutory union recognition is bad labour policy: The North American experience. *Industrial Relations, 30,* pp. 96–101.

Adams, R. J. (2002). The *Wagner-Act* model: A toxic system beyond repair. *British Journal of Industrial Relations, 40,* pp. 122–127.

American Federation of Labour–Congress of Industrial Organizations. (2006). Samuel Gompers (1850–1924). Retrieved 10 November 2006 from http://www.aflcio.org/aboutus/history/history/gompers.cfm

American Federation of Labor–Congress of Industrial Organizations. (2007). George Meany (1894–1980). Retrieved 1 July 2007 from http://www.aflcio.org/aboutus/history/history/meany.cfm

Auld, D. A. L., Christofides, L. N., Swidinsky, R., & Wilton, D. A. (1979). The impact of the Anti-Inflation Board on negotiated wage settlements. *Canadian Journal of Economics/Revue Canadienne d'Économique, 12,* pp. 195–213.

Bank of Canada. (2001). Canada's economic future: What have we learned from the 1990s? Remarks by Gordon Thiessen, Governor of the Bank of Canada to the Canadian Club of Toronto. 22 January 2001. Retrieved 1 February 2011 from http://www.bank-banque-canada.ca/en/speeches/2001/sp01-1.html

Bank of Canada. (2006). Canada's inflation performance, and why it matters. *Why Monetary Policy Matters: A Canadian Perspective.* Retrieved 1 December 2006 from http://www.bankofcanada.ca/en/ragan_paper/inflation.html

Benzie, R. (26 March 2010). Budget: Ontario vows freeze on public-sector wages. *Thestar.com*. Retrieved 10 February 2011 from http://www.thestar.com/news/ontario/ontariobudget/article/785340

Bernard, A. (2009). Trends in manufacturing employment. *Perspectives on Labour and Income, 21*(1), 27–35. Retrieved 11 February 2011 from CBCA Business (Document ID: 1680692901).

Came, B., & DeMont, J. (1997). Postal strike ends. *Maclean's,* December 15. Retrieved 19 December 2006 from http://www.thecanadianencyclopedia.com/index.cfm?PgNm=TCE&Params=M1ARTM0011454

Canadian Auto Workers. (2005). National executive board discussion paper on the sex trade. Retrieved 6 December 2006 from http://www.caw.ca/whatwedo/women/sextrade.asp

Canadian Auto Workers. (2006a). CAW mergers. Retrieved 6 December 2006 from http://www.caw.ca/whoweare/mergers/cawmergers.asp

Canadian Auto Workers. (2006b). Policy statement on human rights: Workers' rights. Retrieved 6 December 2006 from http://www.caw.ca/whoweare/CAWpoliciesandstatements/policystatements/cawrights_index.asp

Canadian Auto Workers. (2006c). Unemployment insurance and labour market deregulation. Retrieved 6 December 2006 from http://www.caw.ca/whoweare/CAWpoliciesandstatements/discussionpapers/unemployment_index.asp

Canadian Business (29 May 2008). Jack Layton national NDP leader addressed the CLC convention. *Canadian Business Online*. Retrieved 10 February 2011 from http://www.canadianbusiness.com/markets/cnw/article.jsp?content=20080529_160503_2_cnw_cnw.

Canadian Labour Congress. (2006). 50 years of making a difference. *Canadian Labour Online, 7* (November 1). Retrieved 10 November 2007 from http://canadianlabour.ca/index.php/canadianlabouronline/November_1_2006__Iss

Canadian Labour Congress. (n.d.). Canadian labour history. Retrieved 10 November 2006 from http://canadianlabour.ca/updir/labourhistory.pdf

Canadian Museum of Civilization. (2002). Labour's revolt: Winnipeg General Strike. Retrieved 27 November 2006 from http://www.civilization.ca/hist/labour/labh22e.html

CBC. (2004). Ontario's Conservatives: In transition. 17 September 2004. Retrieved 5 December 2006 from http://www.cbc.ca/news/background/provpolitics

CBC. (2005). B.C. teachers end strike. 23 October 2005. Retrieved 19 December 2006 from http://www.cbc.ca/canada/story/2005/10/23/teachers-sunday051023.html

CBC. (2006a). Forestry pulp and paper. 13 April 2006. Retrieved 5 December 2006 from http://www.cbc.ca/includes/printablestory.jsp

CBC. (2006b). Strikes: A Canadian history. 22 February 2006. Retrieved 10 November 2006 from http://www.cbc.ca/news/background/strike

Centre for Industrial Relations. (2004). Provincial budgets bring job cuts and wage freezes for government employees across Canada. *Weekly Work Report,* April 5. Retrieved 27 November 2006 from http://www.chass.utoronto.ca/cir/library/wwreport/wwr2004_04_05.html

CLC (2006). The Manufacturing Crisis: Impacts on workers and an agenda for government action. Ottawa, ON: CLC

Collections Canada. (n.d.). Winnipeg General Strike, May 15–June 25, 1919 [silent film]. Retrieved 27 November 2006 from http://www.collectionscanada.ca/05/0509/050951/05095176_e.html

Felice, M. (1998). A timeline of the public service commission of Canada. Retrieved 1 December 2006 from http://www.psc-cfp.gc.ca/research/timeline/psc_timeline_e.htm

Fenton, P., Ip, I., & Wright, G. (2001). *Employment effects of restructuring in the public sector in North America: Working paper 2001–19*. Ottawa: Bank of Canada.

Fox, A. (1974). *Beyond contract: Work, power and trust relations*. London: Faber & Faber.

Fox, A. (1985). *History and heritage: The social origins of the British industrial relations system*. London: George Allen and Unwin.

Gindin, S. (1995). *The Canadian autoworkers: The birth and transformation of a union*. Toronto: James Lorimer and Company.

Government of Canada. (2006a). 1873—The Canadian labour union: The birth of Canadian organized labour. Retrieved 9 November 2006 from http://www.canadianeconomy.gc.ca/english/economy/1873Canadian_Labour_Union.html

Government of Canada. (2006b). 1919—The Winnipeg General Strike. Retrieved 26 November 2006 from http://www.canadianeconomy.gc.ca/English/economy/1919Winnipeg_general_strike.html

Haggart, B. (2001). *Canada and the United States: Trade, investment, integration and the future*. Ottawa: Government of Canada (Economics Division). Retrieved 27 November 2006 from http://dsp-psd.communication.gc.ca/Collection-R/LoPBdP/BP/prb013-e.htm#4

Hamilton, G. (29 April 2009). B.C. forest job losses climb to more than 20,000; Workers forced to move to Alberta for retraining. *Vancouver Sun*. Retrieved 11 February 2010 from http://www2.canada.com/vancouversun/news/business/story.html?id=0d724d33-5f7b-48c2-b811-e9d706cebfdd&k=34782

Hebdon, B., & Warrian, P. (1999). Coercive bargaining: Public sector restructuring under the Ontario Social Contract, 1993–1996. *Industrial and Labor Relations Review, 52*, pp. 196–212.

Heron, C. (1989). *The Canadian labour movement: A short history*. Toronto: J. Lorimer.

Heron, C. (Ed.). (1998). *The workers' revolt in Canada, 1917–1925*. Toronto: University Press.

Human Resources and Development Canada. (2004). Summative evaluation of HRDC's component of the Pacific fisheries adjustment and restructuring program: Final report. Ottawa: Government of Canada.

Industrial Workers of the World. (2011a). One Big Union—By the Industrial Workers of the World. Retrieved 10 February 2011 from http://www.iww.org/en/culture/official/obu/index.shtml

Industrial Workers of the World. (2011b). This holiday season remember the Starbucks baristas struggling for justice. Retrieved 28 November 2006 from http://www.iww.org/en/node/3044

Kahn-Freund, O. (1967). A note on status and contract in British labour law. *Modern Law Review, 30*, p. 635.

Kealey, G. S. (1995). The Canadian state's attempt to manage class conflict. In G. S. Kealey (Ed.), *Workers and Canadian History* (pp. 419–440). Montreal and Kingston: McGill–Queen's University Press.

Kealey, G. S., & Palmer, B. D. (1981). The bonds of unity: The Knights of Labor in Ontario, 1880–1900. *Social History, 14*, p. 369–411.

Kealey, G. S., & Palmer, B. D. (1995). The bonds of unity: The Knights of Labor in Ontario, 1880–1900. In G. S. Kealey (Ed.), *Workers and Canadian History* (pp. 238–288). Montreal and Kingston: McGill–Queen's University Press.

Knights of Labor. (2009). The official website of the Knights of Labor. Retrieved 10 February 2011 from http://www.6hourday.org/knightsoflabor.html

Labour Law Casebook Group. (2004). *Labour and employment law: Cases, material and commentary* (7th edition). Toronto: Irwin.

Lipsey, R. G. (1981). The understanding and control of inflation: Is there a crisis in macro-economics? *Canadian Journal of Economics/Revue Canadienne d'Économique, 14(4)*, pp. 545–576.

MacDowell, L. S. (2006). Industrial unionism. *The Canadian encyclopedia*. Retrieved 24 November 2006 from http://www.thecanadianencyclopedia.com/index.cfm?PgNm=TCE&Params=A1ARTA0003990

Mitchell, T., & Naylor, J. (1998). The prairies: In the eye of the storm. In C. Heron (Ed.), *The workers' revolt in Canada 1917–1925* (pp. 176–231). Toronto: University of Toronto Press.

National Labor Relations Board 60th Anniversary Committee. (1995). *The first sixty years: The story of the National Labor Relations Board 1935–1995*. Chicago: American Bar Association. Retrieved 28 November 2006 from http://www.nlrb.gov/About_Us/History/thhe_first_60_years.aspx

O'Donoghue, J. G. (1942–1943). Daniel John O'Donoghue: Father of the Canadian Labor Movement. CCHA *Report, 10* (pp. 87–96). Retrieved 7 November 2006 from http://www.umanitoba.ca/colleges/st_pauls/ccha/Back%20Issues/CCHA1942-43/Donoghue.html

Ottawa & District Labour Council. (2005). Daniel O'Donoghue (1844–1907). Retrieved 7 November 2006 from http://www.ottawalabour.org/index.php?p=history_daniel

Padova, A. (2005). *Federal commercialization in Canada.* Ottawa: Government of Canada.

Palmer, B. D. (1983). *Working-class experience.* Toronto: Butterworth.

Palmer, B. D. (1992). *Working-class experience* (2nd edition). Toronto: McClelland & Stewart.

Palmer, B. D. (2006). Nine-Hour Movement. Retrieved 8 November 2006 from http://www.thecanadianencyclopedia.com/index.cfm?PgNm=TCE&Params=A1ARTA0005757

Reid, F. (1979). The effect of controls on the rate of wage change in Canada. *Canadian Journal of Economics/Revue Canadienne d'Économique, 12,* pp. 214–227.

Sargent, J. (2005). *The 1975–78 anti-inflation program in retrospect.* Bank of Canada working paper 2005-43. Ottawa: Bank of Canada.

Sinclair, P. R. (2003). "A very delicate world": Fishers and plant workers remake their lives on Newfoundland's Bonavista Peninsula after the cod moratorium. *Maritime Studies, 2*(1), pp. 89–109.

Townsend, J. (2007). Do tariff reductions affect the wages of workers in protected industries? Evidence from the Canada–U.S. Free Trade Agreement. *Canadian Journal of Economics, 40,* pp. 69–92.

Webb, S., & Webb, B. (1898). *History of trade unionism.* Printed by the authors especially for the Amalgamated Society of Engineers. ASIN: B00085AVQA.

Wise, C. (2009). The North American free trade agreement. *New Political Economy, 14,* pp. 133–148.

CHAPTER 5

The Union Perspective

Learning Objectives

By the end of this chapter, you will be able to discuss

- the function and role of unions in contemporary Canadian society;
- union purposes and philosophies;
- the organization and structure of unions;
- the differences between craft/occupational, industrial, and public-sector unionism;
- the democratic processes of unions;
- why employees join unions;
- changing union membership patterns; and
- labour and the environment.

Administrative Staff of Queen's University in Kingston, Ontario, Vote to Join the United Steelworkers (USW)

Dec. 13, 2010—"This is a great day for Queen's staff," said Kelly Smith, a 20-year Queen's employee in the Faculty of Arts and Science. "Now that we have our vote counted, we can move forward with real bargaining rights that give staff a voice in the decisions that affect us. Staff have always been proud contributors to the life of our university and that will continue."

The Ontario Labour Relations Board (OLRB) today completed the counting of ballots that were cast in a representation vote on March 31, 2010. The final count of ballots was delayed due to differences between the union and the university regarding the bargaining unit's structure.

After engaging in discussions and a formal mediation process, the USW and Queen's reached a settlement with the assistance of mediator/arbitrator Janice Johnson, paving the way for today's final count.

The new bargaining unit will number more than 1,200 employees. Queen's staff join 7,500 other university employees in Ontario who are already members of the USW—at the University of Guelph and at the University of Toronto and its affiliated colleges Victoria University and St. Michael's University College.

"Staff are a key part of Queen's successes and we have for a long time needed a stronger voice," said Mark Publicover, a 30-year Queen's employee in the geography department. "It is a time of great change in the university sector and finally staff have a place at the table.

"Throughout the campaign, we reached out and talked about real issues with our colleagues, like fairness, a genuine voice for staff, consistent policies, job security, pensions and a better way to resolve complaints. Now we can look forward to reaching out to all staff to get ready for the exciting challenges of collective bargaining."

"Our union is excited by this vote of confidence," said USW Ontario Director Wayne Fraser. "In June 2008 we were chosen by Queen's staff to assist them in forming their union. We backed this long and challenging campaign because we knew that Queen's staff were committed to a solid effort. The vote results show that Queen's staff and the union made the right choice."

"Our union is growing steadily with new members joining across the country, and this is one of the largest organizing wins in Canada in the last few years," said Ken Neumann, USW National Director for Canada.

> "We welcome the Queen's staff. They will be a great part of our union. Now it is time to get ready for the opportunities that real collective bargaining brings."
>
> Sources: United Steelworkers, "Queen's University staff join United Steelworkers" (news release), 13 December 2010, retrieved from http://www.usw.ca/media/news/releases?id=0578. Reprinted with permission.

Unions in the twenty-first century face many challenges emanating from globalization and the liberalization of markets, changes in the nature of work, and shifts in the composition of the labour force. Globalization has allowed capital to move more freely between countries and has no doubt decreased the bargaining power of unions. Many aspects of the changes in markets and work have affected union identity through a shift to a more individualistic employment relationship. Examples of structural changes that affect union identity are the increase in the participation rate of women; the decline in manufacturing and other heavily unionized industrial sectors; the increase in multiple forms of contingent employment; the increase in diversity by groups such as nonwhite and gay and lesbian minorities; the growing need for higher education; and the increasing importance of knowledge work (Lévesque, Murray & Le Queux, 2005). We will return to these themes in Chapter 12.

The purpose of this chapter is to introduce to the reader the function and role of unions in contemporary Canadian society. We will examine unions' purposes and philosophies; organization and structure, including their democratic processes; and changing membership patterns.

Union Purposes and Philosophies

Union Purposes

Why do unions exist? There are three broad approaches used to justify the existence of unions: economics, politics, and human rights. Two of these, the economic and political approaches, are derived from the early views expressed by the **institutionalists** in industrial relations (Commons, 1921; Perlman, 1928; Webb & Webb, 1902). The human rights rationale is more recent, and grew out of the internationalization of labour rights after World War II and to some extent in Canada by the adoption of the *Charter of Rights and Freedoms* after 1982.

institutionalists

those subscribing to the theory that the operation of labour markets requires a knowledge and understanding of such social organizations as unions, nongovernmental community organizations, and international institutions

Economics

The institutional economists believed that unions would improve both the efficiency and equity of markets by providing a greater balance of bargaining power between individuals and firms (Kaufman, 2000). This belief was in part a reaction to the unregulated markets of the nineteenth century that

Chapter 5: The Union Perspective

led to exploitative wages, excessive workplace injuries and deaths, and the general lack of "opportunities for personal growth and development at work" (Kaufman, 2000, p. 189).

The macroeconomic purpose of wealth redistribution could be achieved by replacing individual bargaining with collective bargaining through unions. Conditions of unfettered markets that produce such negative outcomes as substandard wages would be replaced with union protection. Thus, the institutionalists envisioned win-win outcomes for employers, workers, and the public at large (Kaufman, 2000).

Politics

Even more important than enhancing economic outcomes was the institutionalist objective for unions: promoting industrial democracy. Scholars defined industrial democracy in various ways, ranging from simple profit-sharing to government ownership of the means of production (Kaufman, 2000). For the institutionalists, there were four key elements of industrial democracy:

1. *Employee voice in determining work rules.* "Representative democracy in industry is representation of organized interests" and "it is the equilibrium of capital and labor—the class partnership of organized capital and organized labor, in the public interest" (Commons, 1919, p. 40).

2. *A written law of workplace rules.* "Whether carved on stone by an ancient monarch or written in a Magna Carta by a [sic] King John, or embodied in collective agreement between a union and employer, the intent is the same, to subject the ruler to definite laws to which subjects or citizens may hold him when he attempts to exercise arbitrary power" (Leiserson, 1922, p. 75, cited in Kaufman, 2000).

3. *A binding procedure for the enforcement of the written law.* "Like the Constitution of the United States, the agreement has become a 'government of law and not of men.' A man is not deprived of his job without 'due process of law'" (Commons, 1919, p. 108).

4. *A balance of power between management and labour.* "If one party to the employment relationship has a preponderance of power, it is likely that this power will be used in ways that are both arbitrary and onerous" (Kaufman, 2000, p. 197).

Human Rights

The **International Labour Organization** (ILO), a tripartite (management, labour, and government) agency of the United Nations, has established standards on such human rights as child labour, forced labour, freedom of association, and the right to collective bargaining. In 1998, the ILO passed the *Declaration on Fundamental Principles and Rights at Work*. In a unanimous vote (but with some abstentions), it declared a core set of labour standards to be fundamental human rights, thereby bringing them under the umbrella of international human rights law (Adams, 2002). In 2008, these fundamental principles were affirmed in the *Declaration on Social Justice for a Fair Globalization* acclaimed by the 182 member

International Labour Organization

a tripartite (government, management, and labour) agency of the United Nations with the mandate to establish and enforce global labour standards

states of the ILO including Canada. Freedom of association is also a freedom guaranteed in the *Canadian Charter of Rights and Freedoms* and has been interpreted by the Supreme Court of Canada to include collective bargaining (see Chapter 2 and the *B.C. Health* case, 2007). Thus, unions are needed to give effect to this fundamental human right. We will return to this topic in Chapter 12.

Philosophies

Unions have different world-views than managers and corporate leaders. The democratic mandate of union leaders is both a source of strength and a constraint on their behaviour. We start with the definition of a union derived from Canadian labour law. All eleven labour laws in Canada provide such a definition. The *Saskatchewan Trade Union Act*, for example, defines an employee organization as follows:

RPC 5.1

> 2 (j) "labour organization" means an organization of employees, not necessarily employees of one employer, that has bargaining collectively among its purposes;

and

> 2 (l) "trade union" means a labour organization that is not a company dominated organization. (Government of Saskatchewan, 2006)

Two elements of this legal definition are essential components of unions. First, unions must have, as one of their purposes, collective bargaining with the firm. Second, it is clear from this typical definition that unions must be independent of the employer. Thus, an organization created by the employer, a **company union**, would not qualify as a union under Canadian labour law.

company union
a union that a company helped create

As long as collective bargaining is one of the functions of a union, unions are free to pursue other goals. Non–collective bargaining activities of unions vary considerably according to such factors as

- the union's history (violent struggle or peaceful recognition);
- industry (private or public); and
- the aims of the founding members (economic, political, or religious).

As we saw in Chapter 4, there have been three great waves of unionization in Canada, each with its own defining elements. The three waves were

- craft (late 1890s to 1920s);
- industrial (1930s and 1940s); and
- public-sector (1960s).

Reflecting their historical roots, Canadian unions tend to fall into one of three broad categories of institutions: craft or occupationally based; industrial or multiple-skill based; or public-sector. The reader will note, however, that these categories are not distinct, nor do they define all unions. The International Association of Fire Fighters (IAFF), for example, is both a craft and a public-sector union. The first union of firefighters was affiliated with the American Federation of Labor (the craft union federation) in 1901 in Washington, D.C. (IAFF, 2006).

Craft/Occupational Unionism

The earliest wave of unionization was marked by the extensive craft-union organizing that took place between the end of the nineteenth century and beginning of the twentieth. To a great extent this **craft or occupational unionism** was defined by the way goods were produced in North America at the time. Production was very much a skill-based activity often involving a variety of artisans working independently of each other. A modern example is production in the residential housing sector, in which various trades are called upon to contribute toward the completion of a house.

Single occupation unions tend to focus on the non–collective bargaining activities of maintaining the skill, training, and education of the craft or profession. They may also try to control entry into the craft or profession. The singular focus on standards means that these unions are more likely to have a world-view limited to providing for the security and economic well-being of their members. The philosophy of craft unions is often referred to as business unionism that emphasizes economic gains through collective bargaining. Since the primary non–collective bargaining activities are related to promoting the craft or profession, there is often not a strong social agenda.

We are familiar with craft or occupational unionism in the construction trades (e.g., carpenters, electricians, stonemasons, bricklayers, plumbers) and firefighting. In addition, in some provinces, some professional associations such as those for teachers, nurses, and doctors also fall into this category. Professional organizations may not think of themselves as remotely related to craft unions, but if they are judged objectively by the stated aims of their constitutions, a case can be made for more similarities than differences. To illustrate the philosophy of occupational unionism, we have provided three examples from the constitutions of these organizations: the International Brotherhood of Electrical Workers (IBEW), the Ontario Nurses' Association (ONA), and a bricklayer's union. A more rigorous examination of an organization's character would require a detailed analysis of the full range of activities of each organization, which is beyond the scope of this text. Nonetheless, the aims and purposes as defined in their constitutions provide useful indicators of the nature of these organizations.

Our enquiry begins with an excerpt from the constitution of the International Brotherhood of Electrical Workers (see IR Today 5.1.) The objects of the union emphasize conditions of employment for workers in the electrical industry. What is most noteworthy about the IBEW is the absence of any focus on social issues that might affect all union and non-union employees.

The next example is a case of a typical professional union where the focus is again on a single occupation and less on the wider social conditions of society. The Ontario Nurses' Association philosophy and vision statement indicate a focus on nursing practice and care (see IR Today 5.2). Like the IBEW, the emphasis is on the social and economic status of the association's members.

craft or occupational unionism

unions that typically allow into membership only trades or occupations that are in the same family of skills

→ focus on maintain the skills/education of members

→ entry into craft union was controlled.

→ focus on achieving economic gains!

"bread + better" unionism

Craft Union: International Brotherhood of Electrical Workers

Constitution

Objects

The Objects of the International Brotherhood of Electrical Workers are:

- To organize all workers in the entire electrical industry in the United States and Canada, including all those in public utilities and electrical manufacturing, into local unions,
- To promote reasonable methods of work,
- To cultivate feelings of friendship among those of our industry,
- To settle all disputes between employers and employees by arbitration (if possible),

- To assist each other in sickness or distress,
- To secure employment,
- To reduce the hours of daily labor,
- To secure adequate pay for our work,
- To seek a higher and higher standard of living,
- To seek security for the individual,
- And by legal and proper means to elevate the moral, intellectual and social conditions of our members, their families and dependents, in the interest of a higher standard of citizenship.

Source: International Brotherhood of Electrical Workers, 2001 constitution, p. 4, retrieved from http://www.ibew213.org/site_assets/www.ibew213.org/images/dynamic/Preamble.pdf. Reprinted with permission.

Craft Union: Ontario Nurses' Association

Philosophy

Members of the Union are committed to a program, which enhances their social and economic status. As well, the organization's goals include the right to be involved in the determination of policies and legislation concerning nursing practice and the quality of care.

To achieve this goal, it is essential that the organization build positive relationships, and create and maintain harmonious environments within the Union, with employers and other groups to stimulate a free exchange of ideas and information.

Objectives

- The advancement of the social, economic and general welfare of nurses.
- The regulation of employee/employer relations and the negotiation of written contracts that implement progressively better conditions of employment.
- The promotion of effective communication with employers.

- The promotion of knowledge of nurses in all areas related to their social and economic welfare through education and research.
- The promotion of the highest standards of health care.
- The promotion of unity within the nursing profession and other allied fields through co-operation with and support of other organizations that share these objectives.
- To promote an environment where individuals have an opportunity to safely express their differing views and opinions. Conflict does occur and it should be managed constructively encouraging positive relationships, mutual respect and personal satisfaction. Ultimately, conflict management should advance the ability of the leadership to represent the membership.

Source: Ontario Nurses' Association, "Statement of beliefs 2009" retrieved 18 January 2011 from http://www.ona.org/documents/File/guides/ONAStatementofBeliefs2009.pdf. Reprinted with permission.

Our final example of a craft or occupational union is the International Union of Bricklayers and Allied Craftworkers; information on the BAC union can be found at http://www.bacweb.org/about_us/who_we_are/pdf/member_booklet-english.pdf. From the union's constitution objectives, we can see that the most important aim is to "improve members' quality of life—both on and off the job—through access to good jobs, fair wages and quality benefits, and by building solidarity and support" among all its members' interests. While raising the standard of the craft is an important goal, the International Union of Bricklayers and Allied Craftworkers also shows a concern for the wider interests of all workers.

Note the distinction here between national or international unions and local unions. Locals are subunits of the parent national or international union, and as such may have aims that diverge somewhat from the parent organization, which in this case is the International Union of Bricklayers and Allied Craftworkers.

Industrial or Multi-Skill Unionism *(1930s –1980s)*

The second great wave of union organizing began in the 1930s, after manufacturing enterprises introduced the assembly-line method of production. With this method, the typical production worker became more of a generalist lacking specific training in any particular craft or trade. Craft unions were not interested in organizing these new generalists. Thus, as a competing vision to craft unionism, **industrial unionism** welcomed both skilled and unskilled occupations into membership. Rather than organize a single occupation or craft in a firm, industrial unions sought to represent all of the production or office workers of a firm at a given location or at several locations or plants.

industrial unionism

a type of inclusive unionism that represents a broad range of skills and occupations

The vision of most industrial unions is more class-based and goes beyond collective bargaining to include societal reform. Members' interests are served by promoting a wide agenda of social issues. Within industrial unionism, there is also considerable variation in the scope of the social agenda and the radical nature of the reforms sought. The unions in this category often use the term *social unionism* to describe their philosophy.

An excerpt from Canadian Auto Workers' (CAW) constitution provides an illustration of this type:

Statement of Principles—Social Unionism

Our collective bargaining strength is based on our internal organization and mobilization, but it is also influenced by the more general climate around us: laws, policies, the economy, and social attitudes. Furthermore, our lives extend beyond collective bargaining and the workplace and we must concern ourselves with issues like housing, taxation, education, medical services, the environment, the international economy. Social unionism means unionism which is rooted in the workplace but understands the importance of participating in, and influencing, the general direction of society. (Canadian Auto Workers, 2009)

Industrial Union: United Food and Commercial Workers Canada

Article 2

Objectives and Principles

The object of this International Union shall be the elevation of the position of its members, and further:

- to conduct an International Union of persons engaged in the performance of work within its jurisdictions;
- to encourage members and all workers to register and vote;
- to support research in its industries for the benefit of its members;

- to advance and safeguard the full employment, economic security, and social welfare of its members and of workers generally;
- to protect and extend democratic institutions, civil rights and liberties, and the traditions of social and economic justice of the United States and Canada....

Source: United Food and Commercial Workers Canada, "Article 2: Objectives and principles," *UFCW Canada Constitution*, retrieved 25 April 2011 from http://www.ufcw.ca/images/constitution.pdf. Reprinted with permission.

The CAW's broad social agenda stands in stark contrast to those of the occupational unions. The CAW stands on the left of the Canadian political spectrum, but its support for the NDP and the mainstream left in Canada has waxed and waned over the years. Recently, the CAW's president, Buzz Hargrove, encouraged members to support Liberal candidates in the 2006 federal election in those ridings where the NDP had little or no chance of winning (Livingston, 2006). This practice intensified existing splits within labour between unions that support the NDP and those that do not—some from the right (e.g., craft unions) and others (e.g., CAW) from the left.

Another example of industrial unionism can be seen in the constitution of the United Food and Commercial Workers (UFCW) (IR Today 5.3). The UFCW constitution also highlights two of the key elements of a social union: namely, a wide social agenda and a desire to have this progress apply to all workers, not just the members of the UFCW.

Public-Sector or Social Justice Unionism

The third phase of unionism was the most recent to develop. Public-sector collective bargaining took off in the 1960s in Canada due to expansion in services, the passage of favourable public-sector collective bargaining laws, and the social activism brought on by the civil rights and antiwar movements (Rose, 1995). Most public-sector unions have embraced some form of **public-sector or social justice unionism**, as the example of the Canadian Union of Public Employees below aptly illustrates (see IR Today 5.4).

The CUPE constitution has some elements that warrant closer examination. There is a wide range of objectives, from promoting efficiency in the provision of public services to the elimination of discrimination in the workplace, the conservation of the environment, and the pursuit of world peace.

public-sector or social justice unionism

unions of public-sector employees at all three levels of government: local, provincial, and federal; typically advocates of a philosophy of social justice

IR Today 5.4

Public-Sector Union: Canadian Union of Public Employees Constitution

Objectives

2.1 The Union has as its objectives:

(a) The organization of workers generally, and in particular all workers in the public service of Canada.

(b) The advancement of the social, economic and general welfare of active and retired employees.

(c) The defence and extension of the civil rights and liberties of public employees and the preservation of free democratic trade unionism.

(d) The improvement of the wages, working conditions, hours of work, job security and other conditions affecting all employees including retirees' pension benefits.

(e) The promotion of efficiency in public service generally.

(f) The promotion of peace and freedom in the world, and the cooperation with free and democratic labour movements throughout the world.

(g) The utilization of our world's natural and human resources for the good of all the world's people while promoting the respect and conservation of the environment and the creation of sustainable communities and jobs.

(h) The elimination of harassment and discrimination of any sort or on any basis; for the equality of treatment regardless of class, race, colour, nationality, age, sex/gender, language, sexual orientation, place of origin, ancestry, religious beliefs, or mental and physical disability; and the active opposition to discrimination of same wherever it occurs or appears.

(i) The establishment of strong working relationships with the public we serve and the communities in which we work and live.

Source: Canadian Union of Public Employees, "Article II: Objectives," *CUPE Constitution 2009*, retrieved 18 January 2011 from http://cupe.ca/updir/Constitution_2009.pdf. Reprinted with permission.

Almost all unions engage in some form of political activity in the form of lobbying for, endorsing, and supporting candidates, or fully affiliating with a political party. With respect to the latter activity of political-party affiliation, some public-sector unions prefer to be nonpartisan organizations. The last paragraph in the objects of the British Columbia Government and Service Employees' Union (BCGEU) indicates such: "The Union shall not affiliate to any political party" (BCGEU, 2008).

Other Union Categories

There are unions that do not fit into the categories of craft or professional, industrial or social, or public-sector. One is the Christian Labour Association of Canada. IR Today 5.5 provides excerpts from the CLAC website that reveal its policies on social unionism, political affiliation, and strikes. The CLAC world-view illustrates the pluralist nature of unions in Canada.

A final union type that reinforces this pluralist portrayal of unions is the independent local union or enterprise union. It is possible to organize a union that is not affiliated with either a national or international union. Since the focus of local unions is typically on enterprise concerns, these organizations tend to have limited political and social objectives. For an example, read about the McGill University Non-Academic Certified Association (MUNACA) in IR Today 5.6.

IR Today 5.5

Christian Labour Association of Canada

What Is CLAC?

Is CLAC a Real Union?

That depends on what a real union means to you. If it means an organization that

- pits workers against employers;
- thinks effective negotiating means threatening a strike all the time;
- feels it has to "kill or be killed" to get respect; or
- thinks bullying is a sign of strength

... then it would be best for you to look elsewhere—CLAC is not that kind of union.

　　We are a real union but we take a different approach that

- builds positive work environments and creates positive results through constructive, values-based dialog;
- negotiates on your behalf while you get to keep working at full pay (that's right, union doesn't

have to mean strike, though CLAC has, and will, strike . . . but as a last resort);

- is tough when it's called for but without poisoning your work environment.

We also

- represent over 50,000 workers in just about every type of workplace, operating as both a union and a confederation of local unions;

How Are You Affiliated?

Within Canada, we're not affiliated with any provincial or national labour federation or congress, which means we're independent. At the international level, however, we're affiliated with the International Trade Union Confederation (ITUC). Most Canadian labour unions are affiliated with ITUC, which has 168 million members in 155 different countries.

Source: Christian Labour Association of Canada, "Frequently asked questions," 2011, retrieved 27 April 2011 from http://www.clac.ca/pages/faqs. Reprinted with permission.

IR Today 5.6

Association of Employees of McGill University

Constitution

Article 3—Purpose

- The purpose of this Association is as follows: to study, safeguard and develop the economic, social and educational interests of its members, including notably the negotiation and application of a collective agreement with McGill University regarding the working conditions of its members.
- To promote the general interests of its members and to provide an effective means of communication between members of this Association and other members of the University community and groups external to the University.
- To bring about improvement in the working conditions and benefits of the members through fair

wage standards, with equal pay for work of equal value for all employees, regardless of age, colour, disability, marital status, national origin, race, religion, sex or sexual orientation; and to work to improve job security, opportunities for advancement and transfer, and uniformity and consistency of job classifications and to uphold the dignity of all its members in the workplace.

- To provide a democratic form of government within the Association which allows free voice and vote to all members, and to provide members with an environment free from discrimination and harassment.

Source: McGill University Non-Academic Certified Association (MUNACA), "Article 3: Purpose," *Constitution*, retrieved 18 January 2011 from http://munaca.com/sites/data/legaldocs/constitution-eng.pdf. Reprinted with permission.

TABLE 5.1

Unions with Largest Membership, 2001 and 2009

	MEMBERSHIP (000s)		% CHANGE
	2001	2009	
Canadian Union of Public Employees (CLC)	505	570.0	0.13
National Union of Public and General Employees (CLC)	325	340.0	0.05
United Steel Workers of America (AFL-CIO/CLC)	190	280.0	0.47
National Automobile, Aerospace, Transportation and General Workers Union of Canada (CAW-Canada) (CLC)	220	245.0	0.11
United Food and Commercial Workers International Union (AFL-CIO/CLC)	220	225.0	0.02
Public Service Alliance of Canada	148.7	182.5	0.23
Communications, Energy and Paperworkers Union of Canada (CLC)	149	128.5	−0.14
International Brotherhood of Teamsters (AFL-CIO/CLC)	100.2	122.0	0.22
Fédération de la santé et des services sociaux (CSN)	102	108.5	0.06
Laborers' International Union of North America (AFL-CIO/CLC)	85	92.7	0.09
Fédération des syndicats de l'enseignement (CSQ)	55	74.0	0.35
Service Employees International Union- Canada (AFL-CIO/CLC)	65	68.7	0.06
Elementary Teachers Foundation of Ontario (CLC)	50.4	63.0	0.25
International Brotherhood of Electrical Workers (AFL-CIO/CLC)	80.1	60.0	−0.25
Canadian Union of Postal Workers (CLC)	44.1	58.1	0.32
Ontario Secondary School Teachers Federation (CLC)	55	57.0	0.04
United Brotherhood of Carpenters and Joiners of America (AFL-CIO/CLC)	46	56.0	0.22
Ontario Nurses Association (CLC)	45	54.0	0.20
Fédération des infirmières et infirmiers du Quebec (Ind.)	56	50.0	−0.11
Professional Institute of the Public Service (Ind.)	32.5	50.0	0.54
British Columbia Teachers' Federation (Ind.)	39.6	50.0	0.26
Syndicat de la fonction publique du Québec (Ind.)	40	48.0	0.20
International Association of Machinists and Aerospace Workers (AFL-CIO/CLC)	46.1	45.6	−0.01
Fédération des employées et employés de services publics inc. (CSN)	32.2	42.7	0.33
United Association of Journeymen and Apprentices of the Plumbing and Pipe Fitting Industry of the United States and Canada (AFL-CIO/CLC)	36	42.0	−0.17
International Union of Operating Engineers (AFL-CIO/CLC)	46.8	41.0	−0.12
Ontario English Catholic Teachers Association (CLC)	45.6	41.0	−0.10
Fédération du commerce inc. (CSN)	33	37.5	0.14
Alberta Teachers Association (Ind.)	35	36.2	0.03
Totals	**2,928.3**	**3,269**	**0.12**

Sources: Statistics Canada. Union perspectives, 2001; and Table 2: Unions with Largest Membership 2009, published in Union Membership in Canada 2009. http://www.rhdcc-hrsdc.gc.ca/eng/labour/labour_relations/info_analysis/union_membership/index2009.shtml. Human Resources and Skills Development Canada, 2009. Reproduced with the permission of the Minister of Public Works and Government Services Canada, 2011.

The focus of this enterprise union is almost entirely on the collective bargaining activities of negotiating terms of employment and resolving disputes. Such independent local unions may be described as embracing business unionism.

Organization and Structure

Union Size

You should by now have a sense of the purpose and objectives of unions and their diversity in Canada. We will now take a look at union democracy and the external links that give unions much of their power to influence Canadian society.

Our starting point is a simple introduction to the largest unions in Canada as measured by membership. The relative size of unions in Canada is a rough measure of their power and influence as organizations. In Table 5.1, we see Canada's 29 largest unions and associations as of 2001 and 2009. It is significant that the two largest unions both represent public-sector employees. With over half a million members, the largest union is the Canadian Union of Public Employees (CUPE). CUPE represents workers mostly at the municipal level of government. The National Union of Public and General Employees (NUPGE) is second-largest, and represents mostly employees at the provincial level of government. Both of these public-sector unions have shown modest membership increases between 2001 and 2009, reflecting, in part, the small growth in public-sector employment.

The third-largest union, the United Steelworkers of America (USWA), is an international industrial union. It shows a 47 percent increase in membership, because in 2005 it increased its membership by over 85,000 by merging with the Industrial, Wood and Allied Workers of Canada (IWA). The fourth-largest is another industrial union, the CAW National Automobile, Aerospace, Transportation and General Workers Union of Canada. The CAW has been highly active in terms of mergers and takeovers of existing unions, listing mergers with 34 unions since 1985, adding about 148,000 members. Thus like the USWA, its growth since 1985 can be mostly attributed to mergers and not new organizing. The mergers have helped to compensate for member losses resulting from the decline in manufacturing in Canada. We will have more to say about this topic later.

The average increase in membership of 12 percent over the eight years from 2001 to 2009 reflects a labour movement experiencing modest growth. On the other hand, six of these unions suffered membership losses and, as mentioned, in the case of the USWA and the CAW, member losses were offset only by mergers with other existing unions.

Union Affiliation

The list in Table 5.1 also identifies whether the union is affiliated. CUPE, for example, is affiliated with the Canadian Labour Congress (CLC), and the British Columbia Teachers' Federation is independent (i.e., unaffiliated). Table 5.2 shows union membership by affiliation. By far, the dominant

Chapter 5: The Union Perspective

TABLE 5.2

Union Membership by Congress Affiliation, 2004–2010

Congress Affiliation	2004		2010	
	Membership	%	Membership	%
CLC	3,121,010	73.2	3,234,677	69.6
CLC only	1,960,530	46.0	2,067,429	44.5
AFL–CIO/CLC	1,160,480	27.2	665,234	14.3
CtW/CLC			501,959	10.8
CSN	278,170	6.5	303,601	6.4
CSQ	126,060	3.0	122,879	2.4
CSD	63,070	1.5	66,642	1.4
CCU	8,940	0.2	7,900	0.2
AFL–CIO only	17,630	0.4	36,040	0.8
Unaffiliated national unions	488,200	11.5	618,056	13.3
Change to Win (CtW) only			68,650	1.5
Unaffiliated international unions	2,120	0.0	1,992	0.0
Independent local organizations	155,800	3.7	178,625	3.8
Total	4,261,000	100.0	4,645,095	100.0

Note: Due to rounding, sums may not always equal totals.
Legend:
CLC: Canadian Labour Congress
AFL-CIO: American Federation of Labour–Congress of Industrial Organizations
CtW: Change to Win
CSN: Confederation of National Unions (Quebec)
CSQ: Union Central (Quebec social services and education)
CSD: Democratic Central of Unions (Quebec–construction)
CCU: Confederation of Canadian Unions

Source: Table 3: Union Membership by Congress Affiliation, published in Union Membership in Canada 2010. http://www.hrsdc.gc.ca/eng/labour/labour_relations/info_analysis/union_membership/2010/unionmembership2010.shtml#results. Human Resources and Skills Development Canada, 2010. Reproduced with the permission of the Minister of Public Works and Government Services Canada, 2011.

federation is the Canadian Labour Congress, representing 69.6 percent of the 4.6 million union members in Canada. The Quebec-based federations account for another 10.2 percent. Finally, unaffiliated national and local organizations represent 17.1 percent of union members in Canada.

To better understand why unions affiliate with the CLC, study the flow chart of affiliations in Figure 5.1, which outlines the CLC's main functions and components—provincial labour federations and local labour councils. The CLC's mandate is to advance a broad social agenda to improve the lives of all workers—that includes the principles of social justice, economic security, a sustainable environment, and a peaceful world (see IR Today 5.7).

FIGURE 5.1

Union Affiliation in Canada

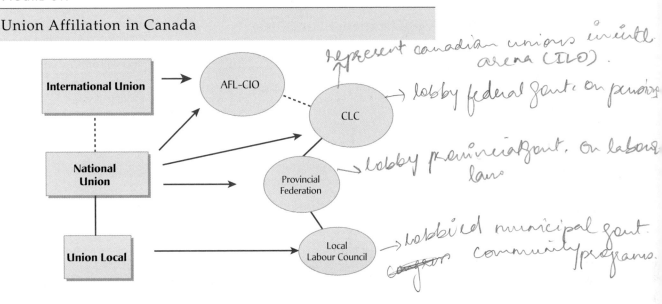

Handwritten annotations:
- represent canadian unions in intl arena (ILO).
- → lobby federal govt. on pensions
- → lobby provincial govt. on labour laws
- → lobbied municipal govt. community programs.

In the next section, we will examine the links that unions sometime forge with national and international organizations to gain strength and exert influence over Canadian governments at all levels—local, provincial, and federal.

The arrows in Figure 5.1 indicate the options that unions have in Canada to affiliate and in which organizations' activities they can participate. International unions will usually be affiliated with the AFL-CIO (the American equivalent of the CLC), and most are also affiliated with the CLC. The thick lines indicate an organic connection between organizational units; thus, Canadian unions that can affiliate with the CLC have the option of also affiliating with provincial federations and local labour councils in the provinces and cities where members are located.

IR Today 5.7

Canadian Labour Congress Constitution

Preamble

- The strength of the labour movement is built on solidarity and respect among workers.
- We commit ourselves to the goals of worker democracy, social justice, equality, and peace.
- We are dedicated to making the lives of workers and their families safe, secure, and healthy.
- We believe that every worker is entitled, without discrimination, to a job with decent wages and working conditions, union representation, free collective bargaining, a safe and healthy workplace, and the right to strike.
- We believe that we, as members of society, are entitled to basic human rights, political freedom, quality public services, good democratic government, a safe and sustainable environment, a just and equitable society, and a peaceful world.

Source: Canadian Labour Congress, *Constitution*, May 2008, Used with permission. Retrieved 25 April 2011 from http://www.canadianlabour.ca/sites/default/files/pdfs/clc-constitution-english.pdf.

FIGURE 5.2

Organizational Functions

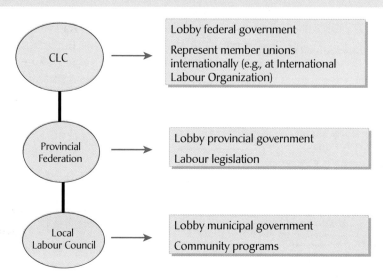

The organizational functions of the CLC and its components are set out in Figure 5.2. The CLC's primary duties are to lobby the federal government on such policy concerns as national social programs (e.g., Medicare, child care, pensions, employment insurance, trade arrangements) and to represent member unions internationally—for example, at meetings of the International Labour Organization).

The provincial federations perform similar tasks but at the provincial level of government. Since labour is a provincial responsibility under Canada's constitution, there is an important emphasis on a range of laws affecting all citizens whether union members or not. To illustrate this point, here is an excerpt from the Newfoundland and Labrador Federation of Labour:

> . . . The NLFL is dedicated to advancing the cause of working people and promoting a progressive civil society where no one gets left behind. We advocate for improved workplace rights and stronger laws including occupational, health and safety laws as well as workers' compensation and Employment Insurance programs that are fair and there when people need them.
>
> We fight for better labour laws and strong, accessible public services such as universal health care, education, worker training, elder/home care and child care and early learning.
>
> We stand up for the principles of equality, equity and social justice and we work with our affiliate unions and social partners to build a better world for all citizens. (Newfoundland and Labrador Federation of Labour, 2011)

Labour councils are an important and often critical link between unions and the wider community. Some scholars believe that forming labour–community coalitions is critical to the revitalization of the labour movement and the organizing of the service sector (Cornfield, 2005).

As a representative example of a labour council in Canada, we examine the activities of the Edmonton and District Labour Council (EDLC). The EDLC works with a number of social organizations to effect change in public policy and in the quality of life in the greater Edmonton area. See IR Notebook 5.1 to learn more about the six organizations with which the EDLC has forged a cooperative relationship.

IR Notebook 5.1

Activities of the Edmonton & District Labour Council

The Edmonton Community Foundation

The Edmonton Community Foundation exists to help the people of Edmonton and area by encouraging philanthropy and funding charitable activities. Through contributions from donors, the Foundation assembles and administers permanent pools of capital so the returns can be perpetually reinvested in our community. The foundation complements and supports other charitable agencies (Edmonton Community Foundation, 2011).

The Edmonton Social Planning Council

The ESPC is an independent, nonprofit, charitable organization, and a United Way member agency. The ESPC provides leadership to the community and its organizations in addressing social issues and effecting changes to social policy.

Friends of Medicare

This organization is "committed to preserving a single comprehensive public health care system accessible to all citizens." Friends of Medicare is a coalition of individuals, service organizations, social justice groups, unions, associations, churches, and organizations representing various sectors of our communities. As a volunteer organization receiving no funding from any government or political party, Friends of Medicare seeks to raise public awareness on concerns related to medical care (in Alberta).

Vibrant Communities Edmonton

In order to reduce poverty and enhance the quality of life in households throughout Canada, Vibrant Communities provides a process and a working environment where diverse community leaders from across the country work together to share ideas, practices, and policies that strengthen their community-based poverty reduction initiatives.

Parkland Institute

The Parkland Institute is an Alberta research network situated within the Faculty of Arts at the University of Alberta. The Parkland Institute studies economic, social, cultural, and political issues facing Albertans and Canadians, using the perspective of political economy (The Parkland Institute, 2011).

Public Interest Alberta

Public Interest Alberta (PIA) is a provincewide organization focused on education and advocacy of public interest issues. PIA exists to foster in Albertans an understanding of the importance of public services,

RPC 5.2

Union Democracy

Institutional scholars have identified the necessity for unions to practise strong internal democratic procedures (Kaufman, 2000). After all, how can unions fulfill the expectations of industrial democracy if they are autocratic themselves?

> If labor organizations also exercise autocratic powers over their members, then workers may merely be substituting dictatorial rule of union officials for the arbitrary authority of the employer or his managers. (Leiserson, 1959, p. 54)

Internal union democracy has been shown to be an important factor in winning union elections (Catano, 2010), union renewal (Ashby & Hawking, 2009), and worker perceptions of union power (Peetz & Pocock, 2009). Not only is democracy intrinsically good but it is also important for unions for the following reasons (Strauss, 2000, p. 211):

1. Unions exist not just to better workers' economic conditions but to give them a voice. Democracy gives them that voice. It is not enough to assume that union officers know what members want, for the officers are often wrong (Gallagher & Strauss, 1991). In any case, democracy to me means government by the people, not just for them.

2. Over the long run, democracy makes unions more effective: it weeds out the corrupt and incompetent. It gives the officers an incentive to perform better.

3. Decisions made by the members (such as a decision to go on strike) are more likely to be implemented by the members. Democracy helps mobilize member support.

4. Having a choice is of great symbolic value and considerably increases the members' identification with their union.

5. Democracy unearths and trains leaders, especially the unpaid, shop-level leaders who would seem to be essential for strong unions. The paid staff can't do it all.

There is no comprehensive theory of union democracy, but scholars have identified several factors that may influence their democratic practices:

- Newly organized groups of workers will be highly active in the union—control by members over leaders is highest at this stage.

- Member control and influence may decline over time as the union establishes itself.
- As product markets grow, local unions amalgamate into larger more centralized entities—unions can become large, bureaucratic, and more remote from the rank and file (Webb & Webb, 1902).
- This bureaucratization leads to a dependence on professionals and nonelected officials—rank and file inevitably lose some control.
- Internal democracy can be diminished in unions by the apathy and ignorance of the members; except in a crisis (e.g., a strike vote), members do not attend meetings.
- Elected leaders tend to stifle opposition, but bargaining requires some discipline and control in order to maintain solidarity; the challenge is to achieve a balance between these competing forces.

ex: automobile industry CAW +

not interested

conflict b/w union leaders desire for power need to represent group interest that reduces democracy

The evidence of union democracy is often anecdotal. The most infamous and well-documented story of union corruption was the case of Jimmy Hoffa, president of the International Brotherhood of Teamsters (IBT). The IBT, a union mostly of truck drivers, was America's largest union in the 1950s and 1960s. Despite the IBT's connections to organized crime, serious misuse of members' pension funds by union officials, and strong pressure against him from the AFL-CIO, Hoffa was reelected in 1957 by an overwhelming majority of IBT members (Sloane, 1991). After a major investigation led by the then attorney general, Bobby Kennedy, Hoffa was finally sent to prison in 1967 on charges of jury tampering and mail fraud (Sloane, 1991). This case highlights one of the dilemmas of union democracy. Despite the corruption, the IBT rank and file repeatedly elected Hoffa because he delivered the goods at the bargaining table.

Some research on U.S. unions shows that, measured by turnover of elected officials, union democracy is improving. The other mixed finding was that corruption among some unions persists but seems to be declining overall (Strauss, 2000).

Information technology has undoubtedly had a positive impact on democracy in unions, enabling members to participate more in the activities of the union in such areas as collective bargaining and union governance (Greer, 2002). Email has made top union officials more accessible, involvement in union politics has increased, and some union dissidents are able to use alternative websites as forums for opposition politics (Greer, 2002).

Union Democracy in Practice

All unions have democratic structures. This means that decisions about collective bargaining, grievances, policies, political affiliation, etc., are made by union members. One of the consequences of this is that the decision-making process is often slower than management's. In collective bargaining, for example, unions must be careful to seek a strong mandate. Changes to the mandate will frequently involve renewing it by holding another membership meeting and voting. Management, on the other hand, is better positioned to make faster decisions as the situation changes. To gain an understanding of what democracy means for the typical union member, we provide an example

— union democracy slows down the decision-making process / cumbersome process

of how it works in the network of political positions and connections in a national union—the CAW. (See the COPE case, discussed at the end of this chapter.) Democracy plays an important function in a union's national structure. To illustrate this, we reproduced an organizational chart of the CAW (see Figure 5.3). CAW members may be elected to bargaining committees, local union executive positions, and local committees (e.g., health and safety, grievance, trustee). The CAW organization goes further to reveal member paths for elected delegates to CAW councils, constitutional conventions, industry councils, and ultimately to the national executive council.

R P C 5.3

Why Employees Join Unions

There are three major theories in the industrial relations literature that help us understand why workers join unions: collective voice, utility, and ideology (Wheeler & McClendon, 1991).

Collective Voice

When dissatisfied or frustrated on the job, employees join unions to remedy the sources of dissatisfaction through collective representation. Existing research

FIGURE 5.3

CAW's Democratic Structure

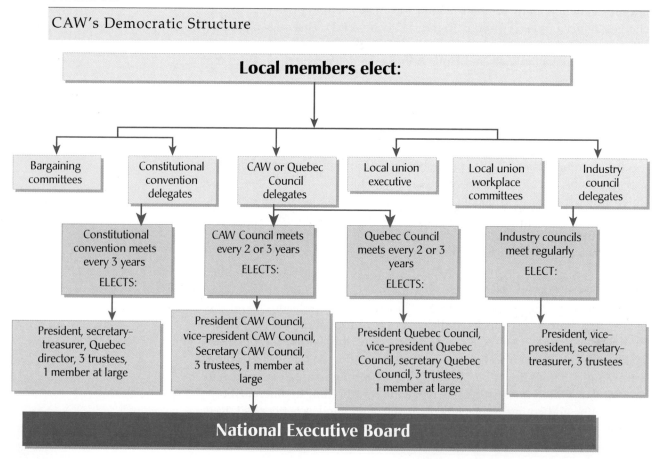

suggests that nonunion employees who are dissatisfied with their jobs and the companies for which they work want union representation more than those employees who are satisfied with their jobs and companies. Employees who perceive that their company is doing better financially or that their industry has more growth potential have a much greater desire to join a union. This desire is perhaps due to a feeling of entitlement to share in the company success. Thus, it is also important to consider a company's performance variables (Friedman, Abraham & Thomas, 2006).

[handwritten margin notes: → to remedy dissatisfaction → entitlement → we should share in profits → economic satisfaction]

Utility *[handwritten: → satisfaction → unions can deliver the goods → unions are able to satisfy needs.]*

This theory asserts that employees will join unions if the unions are able to satisfy a **utility function** consisting of such economic concerns as wages and benefits or anxiety over job security. Unions have to be seen as able to "deliver the goods."

utility function
the sum of individual preferences for such measurable items as wages and benefits

Politics or Ideology

Under this theory, employees join unions for political or ideological reasons. Employees who have more positive attitudes to unions are more likely to want to join. Reasons for supporting a union may range from purely political to familial (having a family member in a union) to communal (community attitudes are supportive of unions). One study found, for example, that pro-union youth workers had a predisposition for "collective solutions to social and economic issues" (Lowe & Rastin, 2000).

[handwritten margin notes: social justice to overthrow capitalism. familia]

A recently published work confirms earlier findings linking union support to employee dissatisfaction, but adds attitudes toward work, perceived company performance, and intention to quit as other factors for supporting unions (Friedman, Abraham & Thomas, 2006). When determining the desire for unionization among blue-collar workers, economic or extrinsic satisfaction appears to be more important than noneconomic or intrinsic satisfaction. In addition, workers who had more company tenure were more likely to want to join a union. The study also found that women and minorities were significantly more likely to want unionization than men and nonminorities. Forrest (2001) argues that women organize around "women's issues" such as pay equity, harassment, child care, and maternity. She also adds that if unions are to be successful in organizing women, they will have to find ways of accommodating their needs.

Why Employees Leave Unions

Unionized employees who work for larger companies are more likely to want to leave their unions. This might be because of the union security clauses of larger companies requiring their employees to join unions even if the employees have no desire to do so (Friedman, Abraham & Thomas, 2006). Unionized employees who are less satisfied with their compensation and benefits also have a greater desire to leave their unions. Research also identified a strong relationship between the employees' level of dissatisfaction with the company and their desire to leave both the company and the union (Friedman, Abraham & Thomas, 2006).

Generally, unionized employees will express discontent with the union if it fails to fulfill its primary function of providing distributive justice for its members. A company's performance appears to significantly influence employees' desire to join and, to a lesser extent, leave an existing union. Employees will generally seek change if they perceive that their current working environment is not in their best interests.

Membership Patterns

We have gained an understanding of the aims and purposes of unions and their structure. In this next section, we examine union membership patterns in the United States and Canada. You might wonder why we are interested in the United States when the focus of this text is Canada. There are at least three reasons. First, the United States is by far our largest trading partner (and vice versa), and our economies are inextricably linked through the North American Free Trade Agreement (NAFTA). It is therefore important for Canadians to know what is happening south of the border. Second, in many areas of society, including the economy, culture (everything from TV to fashion), and to some extent our social fabric, we tend to follow U.S. patterns. Thus, a comparative examination may reveal the future for Canada. Third, in general, a comparative approach permits a more rigorous analysis of union membership patterns, because we are able to use controls for various factors. As the reader will soon discover, Canadian and American patterns of unionization are quite divergent. Through a cross-border analysis, we are able to learn more about our own patterns and future directions.

Figure 5.4 shows a comparison between Canadian and American union membership patterns from the post–World War II period, after 1945, when Canadian jurisdictions passed their versions of the U.S. collective bargaining law (*Wagner Act*), until 2009. In both countries, union membership grew for the first twenty-five years as markets expanded in the sectors that were most heavily unionized, and unions enjoyed some measure of success in organizing new members. In the 1980s, union membership started to fall in the United States, and the rate of increase slowed down in Canada. In the past fifteen years, the rates of decline in the United States and growth in Canada levelled off as unionization bottomed out in the U.S., more highly unionized industries declined in importance in Canada, and unions encountered obstacles in organizing new members in both countries.

$$\text{Union density} = \frac{\text{Union members}}{\text{Labour force}} \times 100$$

Union membership patterns tell only half the story. To explore the reasons for union decline and to generally measure the strength of the labour movement, researchers express union members as a percentage of the nonagricultural labour force (agricultural workers have traditionally been excluded

FIGURE 5.4

U.S.–Canada Union Members, 1945–2009

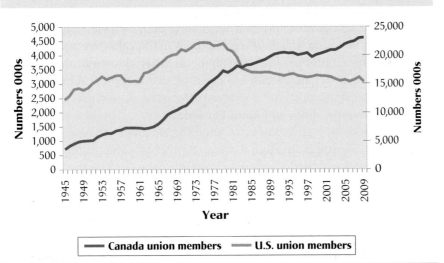

Sources: United States Bureau of Labor Statistics, "Current population survey" (press release), 2010, retrieved 20 January 2011 from http://www.bls.gov/news.release/union2.nr0.htm; Strategic Policy, Analysis, and Workplace Information Directorate, Labour Program, Human Resources and Skills Development Canada, "Union membership in Canada–2009," rev. 15 January 2010.

from labour laws in Canada and most other industrialized countries). This is known as **union density** (see Figure 5.5). Union density statistics answer the question of whether the growth in union membership has kept pace with the natural growth in the labour force.

union density

a fraction that expresses union members as a percentage of the nonagricultural labour force

FIGURE 5.5

U.S.–Canada Union Density, 1945–2009

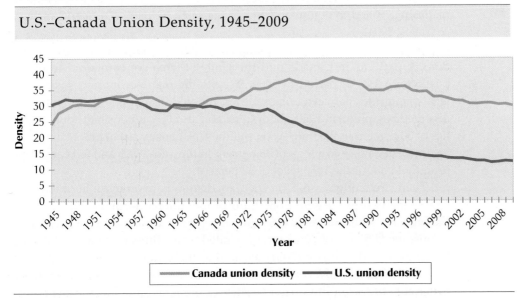

Sources: United States Bureau of Labor Statistics, "Current population survey" (press release), 2010, retrieved 20 January 2011 from http://www.bls.gov/news.release/union2.nr0.htm; Strategic Policy, Analysis, and Workplace Information Directorate, Labour Program, Human Resources and Skills Development Canada, "Union membership in Canada–2009," rev. 15 January 2010.

union coverage

a broader measure than union density; includes nonmembers covered by the collective agreement

union security

the method by which unions are able to maintain membership and dues collection in a bargaining unit

closed shop

a form of union security in which membership in the union is a condition of employment

union shop

a form of union security in which new employees must join the union but only after a probation period

Rand Formula

a union security provision in which employees do not have to join the union but all employees must pay dues

Industrial relations scholars often use another measure of unionization, called **union coverage**. To explain the difference between union density and union coverage, we need to explain the various forms of union security.

Union security refers to the ability of the union to sign up new members that are hired by the firm into their bargaining unit. Certain aspects of union security may be found in labour legislation or in the collective agreement. As a result of some bitter conflict over union security clauses in the collective agreement, the policy in Canada has been to provide for a minimum form of security in the legislation. The important categories of union security include **closed shop**, **union shop**, and **Rand Formula**.

The closed shop still exists in Canada in sectors such as construction, but it is rare. Hiring is through a union hiring hall. The union shop, more common than the closed shop, requires employees to join the union after a probation period (typically ninety days). The Rand Formula, the most common union security arrangement in Canada, requires that all bargaining unit employees pay dues and is based on the legal requirement that the union must represent all employees whether union members or not.

Thus, we can see that in most bargaining units today, employees do not have to belong to the union. This means that bargaining units have a mix of members and nonmembers—typically about 90 percent of the bargaining unit are union members, and 10 percent are dues-paying nonmembers. Union coverage is then a higher number than union density, because nonmembers are included. Union coverage is particularly important to take into account when making comparisons between North American and European industrial relations systems. France provides a good illustration of our point. Union density in France is only about 10 percent, but union coverage is close to 90 percent. This is because, in France, the outcomes of union negotiations are often automatically applied to nonunion firms in the same industry (Bamber, Lansbury & Wailes, 2004).

Now let's return to our Canada–U.S. comparison. In Figure 5.5, union density patterns in Canada and the United States are compared from the post–World War II period to 2009. Despite the many economic, social, and legal similarities between our countries, union density patterns dramatically diverged beginning in 1960s. Both Canadian and U.S. unions had equal densities of 30 percent in the mid-1960s, but the U.S. density fell to just 12.3 percent and in Canada rose to a high of 38 percent in the mid-1980s and fell back more recently to about the 1960 level of 30 percent.

There are many reasons for the Canadian–U.S. divergence in union density. In the first place, about one-third of the difference can be explained by the higher rate of public-service unionization in Canada, over 60 percent, as against the U.S. rate of 37.4 percent (United States Bureau of Labor Statistics, 2010). Rose and Chaison (2001) argue that the difference can be explained by a greater ability of Canadian unions to recruit new members. Unions are better able to recruit in Canada because of more favourable laws; the affiliation between organized labour and the New Democratic Party (NDP); and an ability to resist concession bargaining (Rose & Chaison, 2001).

In Canada, it is easier for unions to organize because labour laws provide for faster certification procedures and card systems that provide for automatic recognition without the requirement of a vote. These more favourable Canadian laws came about, in part, because the labour movement has been able to exert influence on legislation through the NDP. Godard (2003) argues that, in fact, the stronger laws in Canada are the main factor in explaining differences in union density. In addition, because labour in Canada has the strength of numbers, it has been able to resist some of the concessions made by its counterpart unions south of the border.

To attempt to explain U.S.–Canadian differences in union density, Lipset and Meltz (2004) compared various attitudes toward unions and work in Canada and the United States. They predicted that higher union density in Canada would be a result of more favourable attitudes toward unions in Canada: Canadians tend to hold positive collectivist views, while Americans are more individualistic in outlook, leading to less support for unions. (See Table 5.3.)

To their surprise, Lipset and Meltz (2004) found very little difference in public support for unions between the two countries (see Table 5.3). In fact, in the United States a slightly higher proportion of workers (70 percent) approved of unions than in Canada (67 percent). When the nonunion workers were asked the same question about whether they would vote for a union, the lower percentage (33 percent) in Canada, in contrast to 47 percent in the

TABLE 5.3

Employee Attitudes to Unions

% OF EMPLOYED WORKERS	CANADA	UNITED STATES
Workers who approve of unions	67	70
Workers who believe that, as a whole, unions are good	52	57
Nonunion employees who, if an election were held tomorrow, would vote for unionization	33	47
Nonunion employees who would personally prefer to belong to a union	21	29
Nonunion employees who think unions do not have enough power	7	20
Nonunion workers who feel that unions have too much power	40	26
Nonunion employees who, when hearing of a labour dispute and before knowing all the details, would side with the union	40	57

Source: Reprinted from *The Paradox of American Unionism: Why Americans Like Unions More Than Canadians Do but Join Much Less*, edited by Seymour Martin Lipset, Noah M. Meltz, Rafael Gomez, and Ivan Katchanovski. © 2004 by Cornell University. Used by permission of the publisher, Cornell University Press.

TABLE 5.4

Union Voting Intentions of Nonunion Employees by Gender and Age, 1996 (%)

	UNITED STATES		CANADA	
	VOTE FOR UNION	ACTUAL DENSITY	VOTE FOR UNION	ACTUAL DENSITY
Male	45.6	18.8	37.9	34.4
Female	55.7	14.3	45.7	30
Total	48.2	16	33	36
Youth (15–24)	60.5	6.6	58.5	10.7
Adult (25+)	45.2	19.8	37	35.7
Total	48.2	16	33	36

Source: Reprinted from *The Paradox of American Unionism: Why Americans Like Unions More Than Canadians Do but Join Much Less*, edited by Seymour Martin Lipset, Noah M. Meltz, Rafael Gomez, and Ivan Katchanovski. © 2004 by Cornell University. Used by permission of the publisher, Cornell University Press.

U.S., can be entirely explained by the smaller pool of nonunion employees in Canada. That is, if the "already in a union" category is added to the "would vote for a union" category in each country, the result in both the U.S. and Canada is just over 50 percent. Similarly, other cross-border differences (e.g., union preferences and power) in answers between union and nonunion employees are explained by the higher unionization rates in Canada. Thus, surprisingly, there was very little difference between U.S. and Canadian attitudes toward unions.

The Lipset and Meltz (2004) study provided a breakdown of union voting intentions of nonunion Canadian and American employees by gender and age, believing it was possible, for example, that Canada–U.S. density differences could be explained by union-preference differences for women and younger employees. Table 5.4 reveals that both women and youth (fifteen to twenty-four years old) had higher than average union propensities. It further showed that this was equally true for both countries (recognizing that Canada had higher numbers already in unions).

This result is significant for the future of unionization in both countries, because these are key cohorts for new members. The emerging service sector has a higher proportion of female employees, and the attitudes of our nations' youth are a good indicator of union growth potential. It's still an open question, of course, whether unions will be able to satisfy this apparently strong demand for unionization.

Despite the general support for unions, workers had very positive attitudes toward work and working conditions (see Table 5.5). Again, Canadian and American workers shared similar attitudes. A vast majority of employees in each country were satisfied with their jobs, thought they were paid fairly, and took pride in their work.

We can only conclude from these apparently contradictory results that the majority of Canadian and U.S. workers want unions for reasons other

TABLE 5.5

View of Work, 1996 (% of employed workers)

	CANADA	UNITED STATES
Workers who are somewhat or very satisfied with their jobs	86	85
Workers who think they were paid fairly in the past year	73	74
Workers taking some or a great deal of pride in their work	97	99
Workers who agree that they would do their best regardless of pay	77	75

Source: Reprinted from *The Paradox of American Unionism: Why Americans Like Unions More Than Canadians Do but Join Much Less*, edited by Seymour Martin Lipset, Noah M. Meltz, Rafael Gomez, and Ivan Katchanovski. © 2004 by Cornell University. Used by permission of the publisher, Cornell University Press.

than economics or job dissatisfaction. Employee demand for a collective and independent voice in the workplace in Canada and the United States appears to be strong despite some profound changes over the past three decades in work organization, labour force composition, and the individualization of human resources.

The Changing Face of Unionization

Table 5.6 shows how unionization in Canada changed over the twenty-nine years between 1981 and 2010. The decline in union density noted above in Figure 5.5 is confirmed here, as union density has declined by 8 percent, from 37.6 percent in 1981 to 29.6 percent in 2010. Table 5.6 further shows that the decline is far from uniform when gender, age, and sector differences are taken into account.

The Growing Proportion of Women

Women's unionization rates were relatively stable over the twenty-three-year period (see Table 5.6). Given the decline in the rate for men, women's union density gradually gained on men's to the point that starting in 2004 it exceeded the men's rate.

Decline in Youth Densities

The greatest density decline occurred in the fifteen-to-twenty-four age group. About one-third of this decline was a result of increasing employment in traditionally nonunion industries (e.g., consumer-services sector) and less in unionized ones (e.g., manufacturing). This decline raises questions about youth preferences for unions. We cited above a poll taken by Lipset and Meltz (2004) in 1996 that showed a higher preference for unionization among younger employees. Leger (2001) confirmed this result in a poll taken

TABLE 5.6

Unionization Rate by Sex, Age, and Sector 1981–2010

	1981	1989	2000	2001	2004	2010	1981–2010, % CHANGE
Both sexes	37.6	35.9	30.7	30.2	30.6	29.6	−8.0
Men	42.1	39.2	31.6	31.0	30.4	28.2	−13.9
Women	31.4	32.1	29.8	29.4	30.8	30.9	−0.5
Age							
15 to 24	26.4	18.4	11.9	13.2	13.6	16.5	−9.9
25 to 34	39.8	34.7	25.0	25.8	26.1	N/A	
35 to 44	42.0	42.9	35.8	32.8	32.8	N/A	
45 to 54	41.7	44.6	42.8	41.8	41.2	37.8	−3.9
55 to 64	41.9	41.6	38.4	37.4	38.2	36.3	−5.6
Sector							
Public services	61.4	61.5	60.8	61.2	61.4	71.2	9.8
Private sector	29.8	26.8	20.3	20.1	20.0	16.0	−13.8

Source: Statistics Canada: "Survey of work history," 1981; "Labour market activity survey," 1986, 1989; "Labour force survey," 1998, 2001, 2004, 2010.

in Quebec in 2001. In answer to the Leger poll question whether "unions are always necessary," 72 percent of the population answered yes and 84 percent of the under-twenty-five cohort answered yes. Also, 37 percent of the general population and 57 percent of the under-twenty-five group indicated a preference for unionization.

Researchers attribute the youth–adult difference in union density rates to variation in the costs and benefits for younger workers (Bryson, Gomez, Gunderson & Meltz, 2005).

Public–Private Sector Differences

There are also significant differences between public and private unionization rates and trends. The overall public-sector union density was more than four times that of the private sector in 2010. The public sector rate increased over the period to a union density rate of 71.2 percent, whereas the private sector rate declined by 13.8 percent.

Provincial Differences

Union density varies widely by province (see Table 5.7). In 2010 Newfoundland (37.9 percent) and Quebec (36.1 percent) had the highest overall densities. On the other hand, the lowest overall densities were recorded in Alberta (22.6 percent) and Ontario (26.5 percent). The sharpest declines over the twenty-nine-year-period were in British Columbia (−12.9 percent) and New

TABLE 5.7

Unionization Rate by Province

							% CHANGE
PROVINCE	1981	1989	1998	2001	2004	2010	1981–2010
Alberta	28.4	30.1	23.0	22.9	21.7	22.6	−5.8
British Columbia	43.3	39.1	34.8	33.7	33.1	30.4	−12.9
Manitoba	37.9	37.9	34.9	35.7	35.4	35.9	−2.0
New Brunswick	39.8	35.4	26.6	28.8	28.8	27.8	−12.0
Newfoundland and Labrador	45.2	41.7	39.7	40.6	39.1	37.9	−7.3
Nova Scotia	33.8	34.2	28.9	27.2	27.4	28.4	−5.4
Ontario	33.7	32.8	28.0	26.4	27.3	26.5	−7.2
Prince Edward Island	38.0	31.6	26.3	28.1	30.1	30.7	−7.3
Quebec	44.2	40.8	35.7	36.3	37.4	36.1	−8.1
Saskatchewan	37.9	36.8	33.6	35.5	35.2	33.8	−4.1

Source: Statistics Canada: "Survey of work history," 1981; "Labour market activity survey," 1986, 1989; "Labour force survey," 1998, 2001, 2004; *Perspectives*, October 2010.

Brunswick (−12.0 percent). The smallest declines were in two predominantly NDP-governed provinces over the period, Manitoba and Saskatchewan. A more complete analysis in the private sector revealed that the small decline here had more to do with the small manufacturing base than with a labour-friendly government.

Labour and the Environment

Unions have been slow to fully embrace environmental issues out of fear of job losses in such sectors as energy and natural resources. Coalitions between unions and environmentalists often dissolved because unions were forced to choose between job security and occupational or environmental health (Mayer, 2008; Senier, Mayer, Brown & Morello-Frosch, 2007). To respond to this problem the Canadian Labour Congress developed a program that involves allaying job loss fears by transitioning to a green economy and a more sustainable future (Burrows, 2001; see IR Today 5.8).

Blue–Green Coalitions

Mayer (2008) shows how labour and environmental groups can work together by focusing on the role health-related issues have played in creating a common ground between the two groups. His cases reveal that the same toxins that cause workplace hazards escape into surrounding communities and the environment; thus, workers and environmentalists are able to collaborate for the protection of all. The Good Jobs for All Coalition is a example of a successful coalition

Excerpt from CLC Plan for Green Jobs

Canada can create hundreds of thousands of jobs through investment into green job creation. Not only can we build an economy of good jobs, strong enough to lift people out of poverty, but we can invest in climate change solutions.

What Is a "Green Job"?

Green collar jobs will grow our economy in a greener and more sustainable direction. In general a green job is any job that greens our economy.

The solutions are simple yet multifaceted; we need to:

- Increase energy efficiency, building retrofits and green building;
- Invest in rail and mass transit infrastructure;
- Reduce the distance between producer and consumer and encourage production of everything from green vehicles to windmill blades here in Canada; and
- Develop renewable energy sources.

Source: Canadian Labour Congress, "Green jobs." Used with permission. http://www.canadianlabour.ca/issues/green-jobs.

in Canada's largest urban centre. The coalition, formed in 2008, is an alliance of community, labour, social justice, youth, and environmental organizations. Here is an excerpt from a Good Jobs for All campaign directed at Toronto Hydro that began in 2010:

The Good Jobs for All Coalition is calling on Toronto Hydro to:

- Plan for an aggressive expansion of Toronto Hydro's role in renewable energy generation in partnership with other public institutions, such as the city, school boards, colleges, universities and hospitals;
- Make local procurement of green products a priority in all activities;
- Use Toronto Hydro's buying power to attract green manufacturers to Toronto and/or assist existing manufacturers to retool; and
- Work with local training organizations and Toronto's Social Development Office to ensure equitable access and inclusion of workers of colour and youth from marginalized communities in new job opportunities in the sector (Good Jobs for All, 2011).

In addition to forming coalitions and generally working with environmental organizations, unions are also using the collective bargaining process to promote environmental issues. Below is an example from a collective agreement between DaimlerChrysler and the CAW:

Letter (15.3): Joint National Environmental Committee

During these negotiations the Company demonstrated its concern for the environment by outlining the programs and policies which are in place in the plants and offices.

As well, the CAW has become deeply involved in environmental issues, at both the National and local levels.

Therefore, it is agreed that to demonstrate this joint interest a National Environmental Committee will be established by the parties. The committee will consist of two people from the Union, the National Health & Safety Coordinator and a Representative designated by the President of the National Union for the CAW and two people, from the company, the Manager of Health & Safety and Manager of Environment representing DaimlerChrysler Canada.

The National Committee shall:

- Meet 4 times annually at mutually agreeable times and place to review and discuss issues involving the environment, recycling and energy conservation which pertain to DaimlerChrysler Canada employees.
- Develop and issue a joint statement regarding the environment, recycling and energy conservation pertaining to DaimlerChrysler Canada employees.
- Discuss and make recommendations regarding possible future programs for the plants and offices concerning the environment, recycling and energy conservation.
- Promote and support ongoing programs in the plants and offices relating to the environment [and] recycling....
- Receive and discuss appropriate issues referred to them by the plants and offices.
- Develop and issue educational materials to employees and their families concerning the environment, recycling and energy conservation.
- Discuss other duties and responsibilities of this Joint Environmental Committee at its regular meetings as jointly agreed on.
- Be agreed by the parties that this committee and its functions will not be adversarial and its clear purpose is to promote environmental awareness of all DaimlerChrysler Canada workers.
- Be agreed by the parties that environmental issues and statistics pertaining to DaimlerChrysler Canada discussed at this committee are to be held confidential if so requested by any member. (Canadian Auto Workers, 1996)

Summary

This chapter has introduced you to the function and role of unions in contemporary Canadian society. We studied the range of union purposes and philosophies found in craft or occupational, industrial, and public-sector unions. The pluralism of unions in Canada was further demonstrated by national and local independent unions. We discovered that public-sector unions are the largest unions and that most unions are affiliated with the Canadian Labour Congress. It was shown how union affiliations with federations at the local, provincial, and national levels give union members a voice in the economic and social affairs of Canada. There was a special focus on the democratic character of unions and the importance of this function to industrial democracy. Changing membership patterns and density decline were examined in an international comparative perspective. We found that women make up a larger proportion of union members, and younger workers a smaller one. Finally, we discovered that the greater decline in union density in the United States was due to public-sector, legal, and organizing differences and not public attitudes.

Key Terms

closed shop 158

company union 139

craft or occupational unionism 140

industrial unionism 142

institutionalists 137

International Labour Organization 138

public-sector or social justice unionism 143

Rand Formula 158

union coverage 158

union density 157

union security 158

union shop 158

utility function 155

Weblinks

Canadian Legal Information Institute:

http://www.canlii.org/index_en.html

International Brotherhood of Electrical Workers constitution and bylaws:

http://www.ibew213.org/site_assets/www.ibew213.org/images/dynamic/Preamble.pdf

Ontario Nurses' Association statement of beliefs:

http://www.ona.org/documents/File/guides/ONAStatementofBeliefs2009.pdf

CAW mergers:

http://www.caw.ca/en/3012.htm

Edmonton District and Labour Council:

http://www.edlc.ca

Edmonton Community Foundation:

http://www.ecfoundation.org

Edmonton Social Planning Council:

http://www.edmspc.com

Friends of Medicare:

http://www.friendsofmedicare.org/default.asp?mode=webpage&id=1

Vibrant Communities Edmonton:

http://www.vibrantedmonton.ca

Parkland Institute:

http://parklandinstitute.ca

Public Interest Alberta:

http://www.pialberta.org

Good Jobs for All:

http://goodjobsforall.ca/?p=2112

RPC Icons

5.1 Provides advice to clients on the establishment, continuation, and termination of bargaining rights

- unions and the labour movement

5.2 Provides advice to clients on the establishment, continuation, and termination of bargaining rights

- structure of unions

5.3 Collects and develops information required for good decision-making throughout the bargaining process

- union decision-making process

Discussion Questions

1. Give an economic, political, and human rights rationale for the existence of unions.
2. What were the three waves of union organizing? Give examples.
3. Describe the five largest unions in Canada by type. What are the main occupations in each union's membership?
4. What proportion of Canadian workers are not affiliated with a national labour federation?
5. What are the purposes of the Canadian Labour Congress?
6. What do local labour councils do?
7. Name four ways that union democracy makes a positive contribution to unions' well-being.
8. How has information technology positively affected unions?
9. Give three reasons that workers join unions. What three factors may cause workers to leave unions?
10. Compare Canadian and U.S. union membership patterns.

11. Define and compare three types of union security.
12. What does union density measure? Compare Canadian and American union density.
13. Compare Canadian and American public attitudes toward unions. Also compare proportions that would vote for a union. Why is the proportion lower in Canada if support for unions is the same?
14. Highlight provincial differences in union density in Canada.
15. Explain why unions and environmental organizations may have competing interests. How have unions managed to overcome this problem and form successful coalitions with environmentalists?

Using the Internet

1. On the Internet, find a union and its constitution not discussed in this chapter. From the constitution or from other information on its website, describe the union's aims, objectives, and main activities. Determine the union's type: craft/occupational, industrial, or public-sector. (You may use the list of unions found in Table 5.1.)
2. Find a local labour council in any Canadian community. Determine what its main activities on behalf of its members are. Do any of these activities include actions on behalf of nonmembers?
3. Find the Walmart campaign organized by the UFCW through e-mail. What are the goals of the campaign? Has it achieved any of them?

Exercises

1. Compare and contrast the aims and purposes of the IBEW and the CAW.
2. By finding the aims and purposes of the United Steelworkers of America, determine what type of union it is. What is the purpose of the USWA development fund? What has it achieved?

Case

Democracy and Finances in a COPE Local

This case is about a typical local of the Canadian Office and Profession Employees union (COPE). Unions are nongovernmental organizations (NGOs) run by their members. All union officers are elected by the members in their workplace. The COPE 378 president, executive board, and council members stand for election every three years (adapted from COPE Member Orientation Participant Kit. Updated December 2005, p. 20). Job stewards are also elected from their work areas. The organizational chart shown online at **http://www.cope378.ca/system/files?file=MemberOrientation%20-%20**

website.pdf, page 22, identifies the constituent parts of the union and shows the reporting relationships. The various roles of each of the elected and staff positions identified in the organizational chart are explained below.

Constitution and Bylaws

The rules governing Local 378 are its constitution and bylaws. Only members of the local can make amendments to the constitution or change the dues structure. These decisions are made by secret ballot voting at regional membership meetings held throughout the province. Job stewards have a copy of the union constitution and bylaws.

Executive Council

This is the senior policymaking body of the union. The approximately one-hundred-member executive council is responsible for policy, the annual budget, and major financial decisions. There is one executive councillor for every eighty to one hundred members, and they meet at least five times a year.

Duties of Executive Councillors

Councillors bring forward suggestions from stewards and members on ways the union can improve its policies, services to members, or financial management. These issues are debated at executive council meetings. Councillors act as chief job stewards, recruiting and advising job stewards in their constituency. Councillors also inform members in their area about union decisions.

Executive Board

The union's executive board is made up of sixteen officers, which includes the president, three vice-presidents, secretary–treasurer, and eleven directors. The board is the administrative management body of the union and meets monthly to discuss recommendations to council on policy and financial matters.

Duties of Executive Board

The executive board suggests ways the union can improve its policies, services to members, or financial management. Board members represent the interests of the members in the bargaining units they represent. They sit on the union negotiating committee when their company is bargaining.

Table Officers

Table officers are the president, the three vice-presidents elected by their respective bargaining units, and the secretary–treasurer. They represent the interests of all union members in discussions at board and council meetings on matters regarding administration, policies, and financial decisions of the union.

The President

The president assigns staff responsibilities and manages the union office, chairs executive meetings, and acts as the union's representative to all outside unions, labour and government organizations, and conventions.

Trustees

Trustees, who shall hold no other office in the union, shall examine the books and executive board and executive council minutes of the union at least once every three months and determine whether all receipts have been properly recorded and all expenditures duly authorized. They shall report in writing to the executive board and executive council every quarter.

In addition to elected positions, unions hire staff to perform such specialized functions as negotiations, research, communications, grievance handling, and administrative support. Hiring policies often restrict recruitment to existing members of the union unless the expertise cannot be found there.

Nonelected Staff—COPE Local 378

Union representatives and administrative support staff are employed in the union office. Union reps are full-time employees in the union office who provide technical advice to stewards and councillors and teach them how to handle complaints and stage-one grievances. Reps handle more complex grievances, keep members up to date on grievance statuses, take members' cases to arbitration, and act as coordinators of bargaining teams during contract negotiations.

Administrative Support Staff

Administrative support staff are responsible for ensuring membership, steward, and councillor address and phone lists are up to date; recording information on grievance files; advising members about meetings; and ensuring that union officers have appropriate forms, bulletins, and union booklets to perform their duties.

Communications

Local 378 has a communications director who handles union communications programs. This includes developing communications strategies and writing and producing member orientation participant kits, the union newspaper (*COPE 378 News*), and other publications as well as handling media relations.

Questions

After reading the job descriptions and examining the organizational chart, describe the checks and balances in COPE over

1. union democracy and
2. union finances.

Source: Adapted from COPE, "Member information package," upd. December 2005, pp. 19–21, retrieved 26 April 2011 from http://www.cope378.ca/system/files?file=MemberOrientation%20-%20website.pdf.

References

Adams, R. (2002). Implications of the International Human Rights Consensus for Canadian labour and management. *Canadian Labour and Employment Law Journal, 1,* pp. 119–139.

Ashby, Stephen, & Hawking, C. J. (2009). *Staley: The fight for a new American labor movement.* Champlain: University of Illinois Press.

Bamber, G. J., Lansbury, R. D., & Wailes, N. (2004). *International and comparative employment relations* (4th edition), chapter 7. London: Sage.

British Columbia Government and Service Employees' Union. (2008). Article 3: Objects. *Constitution 2005* (p. 7). Retrieved 26 April 2011 from http://www.bcgeu.ca/sites/default/files/BCGEUConstitandbylaws2008_0.pdf

Bryson, A., Gomez, R., Gunderson, M., & Meltz, N. (2005). Youth–adult differences in the demand for unionization: Are American, British, and Canadian workers all that different? *Journal of Labor Research, 26*(1), pp. 155–167.

Burrows, Mae. (2001). Just transition: Moving to a green economy. *Alternatives Journal, 27*(1), pp. 29–32.

Canadian Auto Workers (CAW). (15 September 1996). "Agreement between Chrysler Canada Ltd. and the CAW," retrieved 10 May 2011 from http://206.191.16.137/eng/agreement/history/0193510a.pdf. Used with permission of CAW-Canada.

Canadian Auto Workers (CAW). (2009). Statement of principles: Social unionism. *CAW constitution.* Retrieved 27 April 2011 from http://www.caw.ca/en/about-the-caw-policies-and-papers-statement-of-principles.htm

Catano, Victor. (2010). Union members' attitudes and perceptions about their union: Winning a representational election following a merger of four hospitals. *Economic and Industrial Democracy, 31*(4), pp. 579–592.

Commons, J. (1921). *Industrial government.* New York: Macmillan.

Cornfield, D. B. (2005). Tactics and the social context of social movement unionism in the service economy. *Labor History, 46*(3), p. 347.

Edmonton Community Foundation. (2011). Retrieved from www.ecfoundation.org. Used with permission of the Edmonton Community Foundation.

Forrest, A. (2001). Connecting women with unions: What are the issues? *Relations industrielles, 56*(4), pp. 647–676.

Friedman, B. A., Abraham, S. E., & Thomas, R. K. (2006). Factors related to employees' desire to join and leave unions. *Industrial Relations, 45*, pp. 102–110.

Gallagher, D., & Strauss, G. (1991). Union attitudes and participation. In G. Strauss, D. Gallagher & J. Fiorito (Eds.), *The state of the unions.* Madison, WI: Industrial Relations Research Association, pp. 139–174

Godard, J. (2003). Do labor laws matter? The density decline and convergence thesis revisited. *Industrial Relations, 42*(July), pp. 458–492.

Good Jobs for All. (2011) Retrieved from www.goodjobsforall.ca. From "Support Green Jobs in TO", Good Jobs for All website. Used with permission. http://goodjobsforall.ca/?p=2112

Government of Saskatchewan. (1978). *Saskatchewan Trade Union Act,* R.S.S. 1978, c. T-17. Retrieved 24 April 2006 from http://www.canlii.org/sk/laws/sta/t-17/20060310/whole.html

Greer, C. R. (2002). E-voice: How information technology is shaping life within unions. *Journal of Labour Research, 23*(2), pp. 215–236.

International Association of Fire Fighters. (2006). History and mission of the IAFF. Retrieved 18 May 2006 from http://www.iaff2400.org/history.html

Kaufman, Bruce. (2000). The early institutionalists on industrial democracy and union democracy. *Journal of Labor Research,* Spring 2000, pp. 189–210.

Leger Marketing–Quebec Federation of Labour. (24 March 2001). Public opinion poll.

Leiserson, W. (1922). Constitutional government in American industries. *American Economic Review, 12*, pp. 56–79.

Leiserson, W. (1959). *American trade union democracy.* New York: Columbia University Press.

Lévesque, C., Murray, G., & Le Queux, S. (2005). Union disaffection and social identity: Democracy as a source of union revitalization. *Work and Occupations, 32*(4), pp. 400–422.

Lipset, M., & Meltz, N. M. (2004). *The paradox of American unionism*. Ithaca, NY: ILR Press.

Livingston, G. (2006). New Democrats unmoved by CAW decision to end traditional support of NDP. *The Brockville Recorder and Times*, April.

Lowe, G. S., & Rastin, S. (2000). Organizing the next generation: Influences on young workers' willingness to join unions in Canada. *British Journal of Industrial Relations, 38*(2), pp. 203–222.

Mayer, Brian. (2008). *Blue–green coalitions: Fighting for safe workplaces and healthy communities*. Ithaca, NY: ILR Press, Cornell.

Newfoundland and Labrador Federation of Labour. (2011). Who we are. Used with permission. Retrieved 20 January 2011 from http://www.nlfl.nf.ca/about/who-we-area

The Parkland Institute. (2011). Retrieved from www.parklandinstitute.ca. Used with permission of the Parkland Institute.

Peetz, David, & Pocock, Barbara. (2009). An analysis of workplace representatives, union power and democracy in Australia. *British Journal of Industrial Relations, 47*(4), pp. 623–652.

Perlman, S. (1928). *The theory of the labor movement*. New York: Macmillan.

Public Interest Alberta. (2011). Retrieved from www.pialberta.org. Used with permission of Public Interest Alberta.

Rose, J. (1995). The evolution of public sector unionism. In G. Swimmer & M. Thompson (Eds.), *Public sector collective bargaining in Canada*. Kingston, ON: Queen's University IR Press, pp. 20–52.

Rose, J., & Chaison, G. (2001). Unionism in Canada and the United States in the 21st century: Prospects for revival. *Relations industrielles, 56*, pp. 34–65.

Senier, L., Mayer, B., Brown, P., & Morello-Frosch, R. (2007). School custodians and green cleaners: New approaches to labor–environment coalitions. *Organization & Environment, 20*(3), pp. 304–325.

Sloane, A. (1991). *Hoffa*. Cambridge, MA: MIT Press, p. 430.

Strauss, G. (2000). What's happening inside U.S. unions: Democracy and union politics. *Journal of Labor Research, 21*(2), pp. 211–225.

United States Bureau of Labor Statistics. (2010). Current population survey [press release]. Retrieved 20 January 2011 from http://www.bls.gov/news.release/union2.nr0.htm

Webb, S., & Webb, B. (1902). *Industrial democracy*. London: Longmans Green.

Wheeler, H. N., & McClendon, J. A. (1991). The individual decision to unionize. In G. Strauss, D. Gallagher, & J. Fiorito (Eds.), *The state of the unions* (pp. 201–236). Madison, WI: Industrial Relations Research Association.

CHAPTER 6

The Management Perspective

Learning Objectives

By the end of this chapter, you will be able to discuss

- the evolving managerial view;
- the growing role of management in the industrial relations system;
- the relationship between business and industrial relations strategies;
- the various management strategies as they relate to unionization; and
- current managerial perspectives and trends.

COMPETING IN A GLOBAL ECONOMY

Jean and Ashley are walking to their next class. On the way, they discuss their plans for mid-term break. Jean starts, "Just think, in one week's time, we will be on the gondola heading up Mont Tremblant. I just can't wait to hit the slopes this year. I checked their website and the conditions are incredible—all runs are open, lots of fresh powder . . . it's a skier's dream." He is smiling from ear to ear as he says, "Boy, do I miss living in Montreal where I could ski every weekend. Ashley, do you have all your gear for the trip?

"Almost," she replies. "You remember the place we booked through Expedia? Well, their website had a link for a ski rental place. I have already pre-booked the ski equipment online so it will be there when we arrive. So I am just taking ski clothes. Though I do need to get a helmet—I have been putting it off for years, but Mom and Dad have finally guilted me into wearing one. You've skied for years—do you any idea where to get a good one?"

Jean nods. "Do I? I just ordered one from an eBay retailer. It was about half the price of the same model in the sporting goods store across the street from campus. And they ship the same day to Canada. So you'll have it in time for skiing next week." Jean pulls out his phone. "Here, I am sending you the link now."

A few second later the familiar "bing" is heard. Ashley opens the message, hits the link, and scans through the content. Jean leans over her and taps her screen. "Ashley, there it is. The one for $29.99." Ashley quickly places the helmet in the shopping basket and then pays with PayPal. "Great," she says. "All done. Now we just need to get through this week's classes so we can hit the slopes."

While the shopping experience Jean and Ashley discuss is typical for us today, the Canadian economy has seen a huge shift in the last 30 years. It was not that long ago that shopping meant going to a local retailer to purchase whatever goods and services you needed. In many ways, the only competition retailers faced at that time was the other merchants in town. Today, we see rapid increases in technology and increased competition from around the world. With the movement to Internet shopping, increased global travel, and websites such as eBay, etc., retailers, and indeed almost all goods and service providers, face increased global competition from around the world. In this new, global economy we see that the priorities of management have changed and that these changing priorities in turn have impacted their relationships with their employees.

The Evolving Managerial View

To understand the current management perspective, it is helpful to review some of the most significant perspectives that have influenced managerial thinking. These can be labelled as

R P C 6.1

- the master–servant relationship;
- scientific management;
- human relations; and
- human resources management.

Master–Servant Relationship

As is discussed in detail in Chapter 4, the early employment relationship was marked by a significant power imbalance. While the essence of the common-law employment relationship was a contractual association in which the employee was obligated to perform work and the employer required to pay wages (Kahn-Freund, 1967), the power imbalance between the employer and employee was such that the worker was often coerced into agreeing to employment terms and conditions (Fox, 1974). Thus, the employee was akin to a servant with limited rights and privileges. For example, it was illegal for employees to quit; it was deemed a conspiracy for employees to bargain collectively or to form a union; and management controlled virtually all aspects of the employment relationship (Labour Law Casebook Group, 2004).

Under this **master–servant relationship,** the third actor of the IR system, namely the government and its legislature, did little for the employee. There was rarely interference by courts, and when there was, it was usually in the employers' favour. The inequity between employees and employers was so severe that the *Master and Servant Act* stated that an employee who refused to go to work or failed to follow lawful orders was guilty of a criminal offence—it even provided special penalties for employees collectively seeking high wages (Labour Law Casebook Group, 2004). Moreover, the *Statute of Artificers* of 1563 required that a person accept a job when it was offered and allowed employers to punish people who left a job before their work was completed (Fox, 1985). In a nutshell, this philosophy marked a time where labour was viewed as a commodity that could be bought and sold at will, with little ramification to the employer, limited consideration of the employee, and marginal court protection of the employee. You might recall that it was the very environment that spurred the onset of organized labour as a way to "balance" the power between management and labour.

master–servant relationship

the essence of the common-law employment relationship pertaining to nonunion workplaces

Scientific Management (Taylorism)

The Industrial Revolution brought forth a new form of workplace organization. We saw a movement toward large-scale industrial workplaces employing numerous workers. In these large workplaces, much of the focus was on mass production through assembly lines. As such, workers moved from performing a large number of tasks to becoming specialists in a small number of tasks, and in some cases, a single task. Much of this push for task specialization started in the early 1900s with the advent of Frederick Taylor's theory of scientific management (Taylor, 1911). Two key principles of Taylor's theory follow. First, work should be divided into simple tasks, and workers should be trained to perform a small number of these simple tasks. Second, managers should perform all planning and decision-making tasks while workers merely perform simple tasks in accordance with the plans and decisions made by management. Given the role of management in the planning and decision making, and the employees' role of following directions, we see that elements of the master–servant relationship remained in this industrial-based perspective. That is, the master made the rules, and the worker followed, having little say in work processes or the workplace as a whole.

In North America and abroad, time–motion studies became key tools for scientific management in its pursuit of improving manufacturing efficiency (Campion & Thayer, 1987). The purpose of these studies was to find the most efficient way to perform a task and the best way to divide the large, complex task into small, simple tasks. Thus, the successful adoption of scientific management required that workers become "specialists" in a small number of tasks; such specialization was believed to result in highly efficient and productive organizations. In many ways, this perspective saw the employee as an extension of the machines they ran—the goal was to reduce costs by making the production line (and those running it) as efficient as possible. Accordingly, Taylor also advocated the use of performance pay–based systems, in which people were paid according to how much they produced.

IR Today 6.1

Ray Kroc, the New Frederick Taylor?

Taylorism was based on two factors: (1) the search for the best and most efficient way to perform a task and (2) the quest for the best way to divide a large, complex task into small, simple tasks. Many people assume that the principles of scientific management are no longer used in modern organizations. Yet a trip to a local McDonald's would suggest that Ray Kroc, the founder of the chain, followed the principles of Frederick Taylor's scientific management. Next time you are at a McDonald's drive-through, take a look at the food packaging. You will notice that the drink container has a line showing how much of the container should contain ice versus soda. McDonald's also provides a complete ingredient and nutrition breakdown in a publication it calls "Food Facts," as well as on its website. You'll also notice on that web page a product disclaimer, stating that all foods are essentially identical in all locations as each restaurant must "meet McDonald's strict specifications and standards of quality."

For more information, please see "Nutrition Calculator," McDonald's Canada website, http://www.mcdonalds.ca/en/food/calculator.aspx; "Food Facts Brochure," McDonald's Canada website, http://www.mcdonalds.ca/en/food/foodFacts.aspx.

Human Relations

Whereas earlier managerial perspectives saw workers as akin to slaves or machines, a movement in the 1930s presented a more enlightened approach to management. This new approach, called **human relations**, was largely influenced by Elton Mayo and the Human Relations School that he founded (O'Connor, 1999a). It is worth noting, however, that while the majority of scholars view Mayo as the driver of this movement, some evidence suggests that followers of the scientific management perspective may have been instrumental in the development of the human relations view (Bruce, 2006). Regardless of its origins, the human relations perspective was grounded in the belief that while managers and workers have conflicting views and values, these differences could be resolved using effective policies and procedures (Godard & Delaney, 2000).

This perspective eventually evolved into the field of organizational behaviour and laid the foundation of much of the human resources management field (O'Connor, 1999a). Accordingly, this paradigm focused heavily on the role of effective leadership (i.e., improved communication, humanistic workplace designs, and participative decision-making processes) as a way to improve the workplace (Goddard & Delaney, 2000; O'Connor, 1999b).

The human relations school and Mayo are probably best known for the Hawthorne studies, conducted in the Hawthorne plant of Western Electric (Mayo, 1933). These focused on the effects of lighting, breaks, and other factors on plant workers' productivity. The results revealed that productivity increased when lighting was either increased or decreased, leading to the conclusion that management needed to pay attention to the work environment, and the social needs and satisfaction of workers, if they wished productivity to increase. This focus remains today as employee satisfaction and performance are the two most heavily studied areas in the field of organizational behaviour (Latham & Pinder, 2005).

While this perspective put more emphasis on employees than the managerial views of master–servant and scientific management, it was heavily criticized by the labour movement as anti-union. This anti-union view of human relations may well have been spawned by the funding of the human relations school. Many of the early founders of this school were CEOs of enterprises, including John Rockefeller, who sought ways to improve the relationship between workers and management without reducing managerial control (O'Connor, 1999b). However, not all scholars agree that the human relations school was anti-union, and some unionists even embraced the human relations concepts (Kaufman, 2001).

Human Resources Management (HRM)

Many of the key concepts of the HRM perspective grew out of the human relations school and the principles of organizational behaviour (O'Connor, 1999a). At the core of this view is the relationship between individual employees and their employers, often represented by management (Hébert, Jain & Meltz, 1988). As such, as you can see by examining any HRM textbook, most HRM practitioners and scholars focus on issues associated with the selection,

human relations
a managerial view that believes that effective management practices can minimize the conflict between managers and employees

performance appraisal, training, and compensation of individual employees. In this role, the HRM professional seeks to balance the need for fairness in workplace procedures with the organization's need to remain efficient and productive. It can be argued that the HRM perspective minimizes the elements of industrial democracy, or democratic processes in the workplace (since it is not focused on collective representation), as well as the inherent conflict between management and worker as they attempt to achieve their competing needs (Godard & Delaney, 2000).

While some argue that this perspective, like human relations, is a non-union view, others disagree. For example, Barbash's (1987) equity–efficiency theory has been advocated as a theoretical link between the HRM and traditional IR perspectives (Meltz, 1997). In essence, Barbash (1987) defined *efficiency* in terms of the organizational outputs such as profits, revenues, and productivity. Therefore, *efficiency* focuses on the needs of the organization. In contrast, Barbash described *equity* in terms of fair, or ethical, treatment of employees by employers. In particular, Barbash (1987) highlighted five elements of equity:

1. Employees need to have a say in the work they perform. This is often referred to as the "voice" concept.
2. Employees require due process in the handling of complaints.
3. Employees are entitled to fair treatment at work.
4. Employees are entitled to meaningful work.
5. Employees need fair compensation and secure employment.

In the pluralist view of IR, unions are seen as focusing their efforts on these five elements of equity while management is seen as focusing its efforts on elements of efficiency. The result is that collective agreement terms protect employees from exploitation, inconsistent management practices, and potentially unsafe work practices while still ensuring that the operation remains financially viable (Barbash, 1987).

Although the equity–efficiency theory had been discussed extensively in IR circles, Barbash (1987) argued that management itself could introduce equity through HRM practices. Thus, we should not be surprised that the essence of Barbash's concept of equity is very similar to the organizational justice theory that entered mainstream HRM literature in the 1980s. In fact, the topic has become so central to the field that entire sections of academic conferences such as those of the Academy of Management and even special issues of academic journals (i.e., *Journal of Vocation Behavior, 68*[2]) have been dedicated to organizational justice theory.

organizational justice
employees' perception of fair treatment at work

To get a better understanding of **organizational justice** theory, let's examine the HRM functions of compensation and performance appraisal. Greenberg (1986), a seminal researcher in the area of organizational justice, discusses the following procedural justice elements of performance appraisal: two-way communication between the manager and the employee; the consistent application of performance standards for all employees; the soliciting of employee input before performance evaluations and the use this input in the final evaluation; the employee's right to challenge and/or rebut performance evaluations; and the performance assessor's familiarity with the employee's work. He also

TABLE 6.1

Equity and Justice

INDUSTRIAL RELATIONS VIEW OF EQUITY (ADAPTED FROM GREENBERG, 1986, 1987)	HUMAN RESOURCES VIEW OF JUSTICE (ADAPTED FROM BARBASH, 1987)
Voice: Have a say in work they perform	Procedural justice: Input prior to evaluation
Due process in handling of complaints	Procedural justice: Ability to challenge evaluation
Fair treatment at work	Procedural justice: Fair treatment at work
Fair compensation/secure employment	Distributive justice: Fair pay, i.e., pay reflects performance

discusses **distributive justice** compensation elements, which focus on outcomes such as salary recommendations being based on performance ratings received and performance ratings being based on performance achieved.

In many ways Greenberg's views of **procedural justice** and distributive justice mirror Dunlop's concepts of procedural rules (i.e., rules concerning processes and procedures) and substantive rules (i.e., rules concerning the outcomes) that were discussed in Chapter 1. Given the similarities between these theories that ground the IR and HRM disciplines (see Table 6.1), it has been argued that the HRM perspective is not inherently anti-union, as both see the importance of equity and fairness (Brown, 2002).

More recently, the HRM perspective has focused on strategic HRM—that is, ways in which the organization's management of both employees and its human resources functions aids in the attainment of organizational goals and initiatives. More details on the importance of strategy follow later in this chapter.

distributive justice
employees' perception of fairness in the outcomes of workplace decisions

procedural justice
employees' perception of fairness in workplace procedures

The Growing Role of Management

As is discussed in Chapter 1, Dunlop's (1958) and Craig's (1967) system models have been the cornerstone of IR teaching and research in Canada. In these pluralist IR systems, the concept of shared ideology was key. It meant that each of the three actors (management, labour, and government) respected and saw as legitimate the roles of the other two actors. Yet these systems, and most textbooks, tend to minimize the role of management in IR.

The Strategic Choice Framework

In the 1980s, a seminal work by Kochan, Katz, and McKersie (1986) focused largely on the role of management. In fact, the authors stated that management was a driving force in transforming the IR system. In their review of the changing IR climate in the United States from the 1960s through the 1980s, they noted a number of trends in the U.S.:

- a rapid decline in the number of unionized workers (see Chapter 5);
- a large number of employers opening new locations in largely non-union areas or states;

- a large number of plant and business closures in the more heavily unionized states;
- decreased capital expenditures in nonunionized versus unionized plants;
- a shift of products from union to nonunion plants; and
- a movement toward "union-free" workplaces—for example, there was a push toward progressive HRM strategies that some saw as ways to avoid unionization (i.e., employees would not see the value in unionizing since their employer could provide the same voice mechanisms as a union).

During the 1980s, the United States also saw several anti-union trends in the National Labour Relations Board and the government:

- the appointment of "employer-friendly" and "anti-union" members to the National Labour Relations Board, and
- a pro-management/anti-union approach to labour relations by political leaders and governments of the time—for example, in what was considered a milestone event of the 1980s, former president Ronald Reagan fired striking air-traffic controllers in what some members of the labour movement saw as a "union-busting" approach.

Taken together, these trends called into question Dunlop's concept of shared ideology. In fact, the clear trend was that both the actors of management and government were questioning, if not reducing, the role of labour. Thus, it should not be surprising that Kochan, Katz, and McKersie (1986) titled their book *The Transformation of American Industrial Relations* and highlighted the role of strategic decisions (or choices) made by management. The essence of the **strategic choice framework** follows.

strategic choice framework
a view that emphasizes the role of management and strategies in the industrial relations system

It is clear that IR decisions are made at three levels:

- the business level (i.e., long-term strategic level);
- the collective bargaining level; and
- the day-to-day workplace level.

The strategic level would represent the senior management of the organization, by whom long-term strategies are developed and implemented. The collective bargaining level would represent the level of the firm where collective agreements are negotiated and implemented. The workplace level focuses on the front-line management group that deals with day-to-day workplace issues within the organization.

Effective strategies require these three levels (i.e., strategic, collective bargaining, and workplace) to work in one direction in order to achieve major goals. Thus, these strategic choices must be designed to achieve a significant goal, planned and executed from the highest level, and must have a long-term focus. As such, they can have a longer-term impact on all actors of the industrial relations system.

Let's examine a hypothetical example. If a manufacturing company had a number of unionized plants in Ontario and wanted to establish a new, non-union plant in Medicine Hat, Alberta, the following might take place. At the strategic level of the organization, there would have to be a plan to build and invest in a plant in Alberta and a conscious decision that it be union-free. This might involve an assessment of which areas of the province are least at risk for a union drive and which areas have the lowest union-density rates. At the collective bargaining level, the negotiators would need to ensure that the current collective agreements in Ontario did not provide any access to jobs, or union member rights, for the new Medicine Hat location. At the workplace level, the company would need to ensure that managers of the new plant worked in such a way that employees did not see any reason to unionize. This could be done using a number of the managerial union avoidance tactics discussed later in this chapter.

It is clear that all three actors of the IR system face a number of choices. It is important to note that while strategic choice often focuses on management choice, unions and governments also have similar choices, as shown in Table 6.2. For example, as discussed in Chapter 2, unions face choices concerning which industrial sectors to unionize, how to balance the current members' needs and new union drives, etc. For any of the union's strategic, long-term plans, they would also need to ensure that all levels of the union operated in concert to achieve major goals.

Strategic Choice and Canada

As was previously discussed, the strategic choice framework has been investigated quite heavily in the United States. A logical question is: "To what extent does it apply here in Canada?" Arguments and examples concerning the extent to which we are seeing a movement to a "nonunion" industrial relations

TABLE 6.2

Strategic Choices: Three-Level, Three-Actor Summary

	LONG-TERM STRATEGIC LEVEL	COLLECTIVE BARGAINING LEVEL	WORKPLACE LEVEL
Management	Business and investment strategies	Human resources policies and negotiation priorities	Front-line supervisor style, contract administration, employee involvement, job design
Labour	Political, representation, and organizing strategies	Negotiation priorities	Shop steward style, contract administration, employee involvement, job design
Government	Overall economic and social mandate/policies	Labour and employment law administration	Individual worker rights and protection

Source: Adapted from Kochan, T., Katz, H., & McKersie, R. (1986). *The Transformation of American Industrial Relations*. New York, NY: Basic Books, p. 17. Table 1.1.

system in Canada have been studied by Chaykowski and Verma (1992; Verma & Chaykowski, 1999) as well as demonstrated by recent media examples.

Several arguments, from the above-mentioned sources and from our interactions with industry stakeholders, might support the idea that we will see movement toward a nonunion IR system in Canada:

- Canada has historically followed the industrial relations trends of the United States (see labour history review in Chapter 4);
- the number of multinationals that are headquartered in the United States and operate in Canada will encourage a similar transition here in Canada;
- there is a low level of union density in the private sector;
- increased global competition will encourage employers to avoid the increased wage and benefit costs associated with unionization;
- progressive HRM techniques may result in employees no longer seeing significant advantages to unionization, making such workers difficult to organize;
- there has been a rise in largely nonunionized industries (e.g., retail, business services); and
- governments are taking actions that may be seen as "pro-management." For example, we have seen governments include the traditionally negotiated issues of wages and benefits in back-to-work legislation, or threaten to use such legislation to end a strike (Rose, 2008).

On the other hand, other factors support the reverse argument, that we will not see a huge shift away from unionization in Canada. For example, while the union density rate in Canada has decreased slightly, it still remains in the 30 percent range with limited evidence of a radical drop (see Chapter 5). The public sector, which, as shown in Chapter 11, employs approximately one-quarter of Canadian workers, is highly unionized with little likelihood of becoming union-free. Also, we have seen unions make inroads into new sectors of the economy. For example, the Hibernia and Terra Nova oil fields, located off the coast of Newfoundland, are the first unionized offshore workplaces in North America, and mega retailer Walmart, well known for being nonunion, has experienced successful union drives in Saskatchewan and Quebec (Canadian Press, 2010).

Finally, there is the argument that we may see a movement to a nonunion system, depending on the industry. Chaykowski and Verma (1992) suggest that in heavily unionized industries (e.g., automotive) and in the public sector, we are unlikely to see the movement to a union-free model. However, in the private sector and in largely nonunion industries (e.g., the financial sector), we may see trends toward union-free workplaces as these workplaces face more pressure from the external environment (e.g., increased competition, global trade).

Overall, our view of the evidence suggests that Canada is not going down the union-free road. More than twenty-five years after Kochan, Katz, and McKersie (1986) published their influential book, unionization rates in Canada remain near 30 percent, the public sector remains heavily unionized, there is limited evidence of a pro-management government agenda, and unions have made inroads into new industries (i.e., the offshore oilfields, Walmart). Nevertheless, it is clear that we are seeing changes in the management–union relationship. Following their review of eight industries, Verma and Chaykowski (1999) concluded that while the competitive pressures of the 1990s had not caused a negative impact on union–management relations, they did suggest that strategic alliances may be needed moving forward. At this point, we turn to a more focused discussion of the role of strategy.

Industrial Relations and Business Strategies

Given the importance of the strategic choice framework in current IR teaching and research, it is essential to understand the key elements of an overall business or organizational strategy. There is general agreement (Hitt, Ireland, Hoskisson, Rowe & Sheppard, 2006; Wheelen & Hunger, 2006) that a business/organizational strategy process includes four phases: an assessment of the external and internal environments, strategy formation, strategy implementation, and strategy evaluation.

1. *External and internal environments.* This assessment often includes a SWOT analysis, in which the firm will determine its own strengths (S) and weaknesses (W), and assess the opportunities (O) and threats (T) in the external environment.

2. *Strategy formation.* Three actions are key in this phase. First, on the basis of the SWOT analysis, the organization will develop a mission statement that maps out its overall purpose. Second, the organization will then break the mission into specific performance goals to determine a more targeted direction. A wealth of evidence shows that specific and challenging goals are very effective in bringing about high levels of performance (Brown & McCracken, 2010; Locke & Latham, 2002), so management will want to ensure that the set goals are SMART: *specific, measurable, attainable* (i.e., difficult but attainable), *relevant to the vision* and *recorded*, and *time-based* (Brown & Latham, 2000). Third, the firm will develop strategies to achieve these performance goals. More specifically, these plans should mark the path to achieve the goals developed previously.

3. *Strategy implementation.* During this step, the organization puts the strategy it formulated in step two into action.

4. *Strategy evaluation.* During this step, the organization examines the effectiveness of its strategy implementation—namely, whether it achieved its goals. Key players might also examine what factors impacted the success (or lack of success) of the industrial relations strategy. Post-evaluation, the organization will often determine next steps, resulting in a refinement of the strategy and a restart of the previous steps.

Within this organizational strategy framework, an organization has to examine the fit of its strategy with its overall people-management strategy. In other words, the goals of and plans for the broader organizational strategy should include elements related to employee and people management.

Chapter 6: The Management Perspective

As outlined by Belcourt and McBey (2004a, 2004b, 2010), strategic human resources strategies include the following:

RPC 6.2

- *Specific practices.* For example, those related to various typical human resources functions (i.e., selection, promotion, layoff, performance management, compensation, training, etc.).
- *Specific policies.* These include formal (and usually written) policies and guidelines that can outline, and even constrain, specific human resources strategies. For example, many employers have policy and procedure manuals that employees and managers are expected to follow. Human resources policies related to selection, promotion, and performance appraisal are often included in such manuals.
- *Overall human resources philosophy.* In essence, this defines the values of the organization as it relates to employees and human resources issues. For example, Betcherman, McMullen, Leckie, and Caron (1994) identified two main approaches to human resources in the 1990s and beyond. The first was participative with a focus on high levels of employee involvement and teams; the second was a compensation philosophy in which human resources direction is guided by its compensation structure (i.e., skill-based bay, variable pay, etc.). If either of these philosophies were chosen, they would form the foundation of typical human resources practice and policy decisions.

IR Today 6.2

Organizational Strategy and Human Resources Strategy at Barron & Brown Inc.

Barron & Brown Inc. (BBI)* is a computer engineering firm that has grown immensely over the past ten years. It was started by Alice Barron and Tim Brown when they finished their undergraduate degrees in 2000. They now employ more than seventy people, who move from project team to project team as required to work on specific client projects. The company's engineers are assigned to projects by one of the two senior partners (i.e., Barron or Brown). The firm has always stressed the importance of teamwork and meeting the client's needs. As Alice says, "If our employees aren't happy, our clients aren't happy. If our clients aren't happy, our employees aren't happy."

After recently conducting a SWOT analysis, BBI's senior management has identified an opportunity. BBI's mission is to provide high-quality, cost-effective software solutions throughout Canada, and the company currently lacks an office in western Canada. Brown and Barron have therefore set a goal of opening an office in Calgary by September 2014. They have already conducted the market-needs analysis to determine what services will be delivered from this new office, and they have developed a plan to design and build a new building near the airport, given the amount of travelling done by employees. They are currently implementing the plan and have set a date of September 2012 to assess the effectiveness of this plan.

In terms of people-management strategies, Tim Brown (VP, Administration) has designed specific recruitment and selection practices to fit the new market location and client needs. He has ensured that these practices are consistent with BBI's current internal policies and that they focus on the core competencies of teamwork and client satisfaction. Accordingly, candidate interviews will focus on the competency of teamwork, and feedback from both peers and clients will be used in all performance management processes.

*This case is not based on a real company; it was created by the second author for educational purposes only.

Management Strategies Related to Unions

Strategic HRM traditionally includes a discussion of how human resources functions of staffing (i.e., recruitment and selection), training and development, performance appraisal, and compensation need to be aligned to the organizational direction (Miles & Snow, 1984). However, the effectiveness of human resources management also includes an analysis of industrial relations (Huselid, Jackson & Schuler, 1997) as well as the organization's strategy vis-à-vis labour relations and unionization (Greer, 2001). Thompson (1995) discusses four specific management strategies related to unions:

RPC 6.3

- union acceptance;
- union resistance;
- union removal; and
- union substitution.

Let us review each of these four strategies, and also recent research concerning the prevalence of each in Canada today.

Union Acceptance

A strategy of **union acceptance** is grounded in the belief that unionization is somewhat inevitable. Management accepts the fact that unionization is a democratic right and part, if not all, of the company's operations will be unionized. However, this does not mean that management will relinquish control of the operation to the union. Rather, the goal is for management to obtain the best deal that it can to meet its operational needs. A good example of this would be highly unionized Southwest Airlines, an airline often highlighted for its employee base, strong customer service, and overall successful record (Miles & Mangold, 2005) as can be seen in a YouTube posting.

union acceptance
management's seeing unionization as a democratic right, and accepting that part, if not all, of its operations will be unionized

Union Resistance

A **union resistance** strategy in essence contains two, somewhat contrasting, elements. On one hand, management accepts the right of employees to organize and may follow a union-acceptance strategy in the parts of the organization currently unionized. In such unionized workplaces, management will seek to get the best deal that it can and will negotiate in good faith without any attempt to remove the union. On the other hand, management will oppose any further unionization of its work force, particularly in its nonunion operations. This attempt to stop union inroads may include active opposition to union drives and challenging certification procedures. Examples of union avoidance behaviours include illegally firing union organizers or supporters, restricting union access to the workplace, hiring consultants to assist in an anti-union campaign, training managers to oppose the drive, and threatening to close the operation if it becomes unionized (Bentham, 2002; Thomason & Pozzebon, 1998). An example of union resistance might be Delta Airlines. While the airline had unionized pilots, the union trying to organize flight attendants in 2010, the Association of Flight Attendants–CWA, claimed that management interfered in the certification vote by encouraging employees to vote against unionization and by tracking employees' computer voting—the certification

union resistance
a management policy seeking to limit the spread of unions in the firm

Chapter 6: The Management Perspective

ultimately failed (Jacobs, 2010). There is even a YouTube posting that claims to be a video given to flight attendants during a union drive, by Delta, to encourage them to remain union-free.

Union Removal

union removal

a management strategy designed to remove the union from the workplace

As the name of this strategy implies, managers using **union removal** seek to remove the union wherever it exists in the work force. This is also sometimes called "union busting." Again, it essentially has two elements. In unionized workplaces, management endeavours to ensure that unionized employees' working conditions, wages, and benefits are not superior to those of nonunion employees. In so doing, they attempt to send a message to union members that the union is not getting them a better employment package than they would receive if they were not part of a union. In nonunionized workplaces, management will try to discourage union activity by sending the message that there is little to gain from unionization and will openly resist any union certification drives. For an example, see the YouTube posting from a former union buster.

There have been recent allegations of such practices in the Canadian fast food and retail sectors. For example, in 1997, the Ontario Labour Relations Board (OLRB) ruled that Wal-Mart (now written Walmart) had engaged in unfair labour practices when, during a union certification drive of its Windsor store, it refused to answer employee questions regarding whether the store would close if it became unionized (United Steelworkers of America, 1997). As a result, the OLRB ordered automatic certification of that store. Wal-Mart subsequently decided to close its store in Jonquière, Quebec. As this was the first unionized Wal-Mart in the province, labour alleged that the company engaged in bad faith bargaining and that the closure was designed to warn other Wal-Mart employees who may consider unionizing (CBC, 2006).

Union Substitution

union substitution

a management strategy designed to give nonunion employees all the advantages of unionization

The strategy of **union substitution** applies to nonunion operations and workplaces. In essence, taken to its fullest, union substitution is designed to give employees all of the due process elements (e.g., appeal procedures, clear policies applied consistently), representation (e.g., teams), and compensation advantages of unionization. Take for example the fact that many nonunion employers have employee handbooks that contain policies concerning discipline, discrimination, hours of work, wages, benefits, appeal processes, and performance expectations (Daniel, 2003; Felsberg, 2004). In essence, these handbooks are very similar to a collective agreement with the exception that each individual employee signs the book as there is no collective agreement negotiated by a union. Therefore, it can be argued that management, through its human resources policies and practices, attempts to provide a substitute to unionization that makes employees see unionization as unnecessary.

Canadian Evidence to Date

As discussed previously, the evidence from Kochan, Katz, and McKersie (1986) suggests that union substitution and avoidance are widely used in the United States. But what about Canada? The evidence to date suggests that union removal and avoidance strategies are not as prevalent in Canada. One study (Thompson, 1995) of industrial relations executives suggests that over 70 percent of Canadian organizations have a union acceptance strategy (i.e., they seek to negotiate the best deal), while just over 9 percent have a union resistance strategy (i.e., they seek to limit spread of unions) and none have a union removal strategy. The remaining 20 percent or so used a combination of strategies. However, that same study found that in new plants, approximately 37 percent of the executives preferred to be nonunion (i.e., they accept employees' right to unionize and, thus, remain neutral) while another 34 percent actively oppose unionization.

A second Canadian study by Godard (1997) found similar results. In that study, approximately 56 percent of managers surveyed used union acceptance (i.e., tougher negotiation) policies toward unions, 17 percent used a union avoidance policy, and 9 percent used a union reduction or elimination strategy.

However, a recent study of certification applications in eight Canadian jurisdictions suggests that Canadian firms are increasingly adopting a union resistance strategy. That study (Bentham, 2002) found that 80 percent of employers stated that they had taken specific actions that opposed a union certification drive. Moreover, 12 percent of the survey respondents openly admitted to taking actions that are considered unfair labour practices (e.g., promised pay/benefit increases, threatened to fire or layoff employees, transferred employees).

Taken together, these three studies suggest that we have not seen a radical shift toward union removal policies in Canada over the past decade. However, an apparent trend toward a nonunion approach in newer operations suggests there is a movement toward union resistance—employers may well accept the legitimacy of a union in their currently unionized workplaces, but many in nonunion environments are attempting to block union inroads into them.

Current Managerial Perspectives and Trends

Given the strategies toward unionization, it is logical to question what the current trends are as they relate to the management perspective. Over the past years, we have seen a number of trends toward managerial practices that include elements of voice, due process, or alternative forms of collective relationships with the employer. In particular, the following trends will be discussed:

- high-performance workplaces and work practices;
- participative management;
- nonunion representation; and
- nonstandard work arrangements.

High-Performance Workplaces and Work Practices

Traditionally, we have seen two models of human resources practices in Canada: the salaried model and the hourly model (Betcherman, 1999). The salaried model applies to "white collar" employees (i.e., professionals, technical, office staff) and includes relatively broad job functions, compensation based on merit/performance, and job security. The hourly model applies to "blue collar" employees (i.e., usually unionized workplaces) and includes very specific job descriptions, seniority-based human resources practices (i.e., promotion, pay, etc.) outlined in collective agreements, and pay systems tightly aligned to the job. This hourly model also ties labour to production in that the labour force is adjusted to the supply and demand of the product. Accordingly, there is limited security with the exception that seniority allows more senior employees greater protection from job loss than their more junior counterparts.

Since the late 1980s, there has been an increased shift toward different models of human resources practices. In Canada, this can be attributed to external environmental factors such as increasing competition, technological change, new regulatory requirements, and the changing demographics of the work force (Betcherman et al., 1994). In these changing times, it is difficult for Canadian firms to compete solely on product price (which is heavily influenced by labour cost). Thus, many organizations are moving to a product and service differentiation strategy; namely, they seek to differentiate their products and services from others', so they are not competing solely on process. This being so, **high-performance work practices** have become important to management. Traditionally, high-performance work practices have included comprehensive staffing (i.e., recruitment and selection), incentive compensation, performance management, training and development, and employee involvement systems designed to (1) improve the knowledge, skills, and abilities of an organization's current and future employees, (2) motivate high levels of employee performance, (3) enhance retention of employees and minimize turnover, (4) reduce work avoidance and poor work quality, and (5) encourage nonperformers to leave the organization (Huselid, 1995).

More specifically, these various practices-can be clustered into several groups (Delaney & Huselid, 1996; Huselid, 1995), namely those that enhance the following:

high-performance work practices

comprehensive human resources strategies designed to improve the effectiveness of the organization

- *Employee skills and ability.* Such human resources functions seek to improve the quality of employees hired as well as provide employees with opportunities for upgrading skills through training and development. The key here is that employees have the needed skills, knowledge, and abilities to enhance organizational performance.
- *Motivation.* It is not enough to have the skills and abilities; employees must also be motivated to perform. Motivational functions can include pay incentives, performance appraisals, and due process mechanisms (e.g., grievance and appeal processes) designed to ensure fair treatment in the workplace. The idea behind this is that employees will not be motivated to perform if they are poorly paid, do not receive performance feedback, or are subject to what is perceived as unfair treatment in the workplace.
- *Work design.* Even if employees are highly skilled and motivated, a poor work design can decrease performance. As such, this area

focuses on having employees involved in both what work is performed and how such work is performed through various employee involvement systems. One can also argue that security is important in the work design as employees may be less willing to fully engage in work improvements if they fear their active involvement in such activities will result in job loss.

Within the broad area of high-performance work practices, analyses of Canadian data suggest that two high-performance models have emerged: a compensation-based model and a participation-based model, with evidence that both improve performance relative to traditional human resources models (Betcherman, 1999; Betcherman et al., 1994).

Compensation-Based Model — learn more — earn more

This model emphasizes extrinsic rewards (i.e., compensation) as a method to enhance productivity and innovation; it often includes various incentive plans that may be skill-based, in which employees earn more as they gain new skills; gain-sharing, in which workplace savings are "shared" with the employee base; and profit-sharing, in which profits are shared with the workers. Companies may also offer above-market pay rates. Many firms that use this model will also promote internally and emphasize training to enhance skills.

Participation-Based Model

This model focuses on intrinsic factors to induce productivity and innovation improvements and usually includes employee involvement through teams and committees, job enrichment, extensive communication of information, and heavy investment in training. As this is the more prevalent of the two models in Canada, it will be the focus of the next section of this chapter.

The evidence suggests that such high-performance work practices have a positive impact on firm performance (Betcherman, 1999; Delaney & Huselid, 1996; Den Hartog & Verburg, 2004; Huselid, 1995; Huselid, Jackson & Schuler, 1997) and employee satisfaction and commitment (Harley, Allen & Sargent, 2007). However, there is evidence to suggest that such high-performance models raise labour costs, potentially through increased employee compensation (Cappelli & Neumark, 2001). In fact, Godard (2007) suggests that under certain circumstances high-performance HRM practices may result in employee pay levels that equate to the union-wage level, which, as we discuss in detail in Chapter 10, is often 10 to 15 percent higher than nonunion wages in Canada.

When we examine the elements of high-performance work practice, we see that they include many of the due process elements (e.g., an appeal process), voice (e.g., input into decisions), and participation elements often cited as reasons for employees to seek unionization. Accordingly, it can be argued that they act as a union substitution strategy. In the field of industrial relations, we have seen argument suggesting that high-performance work practices are beneficial and detrimental to labour (see Godard, 2004). For example, high-performance practices can be seen as a way for unions to move away

Chapter 6: The Management Perspective

from their traditional adversarial role toward a partnership role that extends beyond the typical labour issues associated with negotiations and contract administration. In addition, they provide for improved pay, fair treatment of workers, improved work environments, and voice. However, reviews of the literature also suggest that these high-performance practices can negatively impact employees and their unions in terms of increased stress and workload (Godard & Delaney, 2000). Interestingly, while the results of past studies concerning the relationship between high-performance practices and unionized is limited and somewhat contradictory, the overall trend seems to be toward a "neutral to negative association between unionized settings" and the adoption of such practices (Liu, Guthrie, Flood & MacCurtain, 2009).

Participative Management

participative management
processes that ensure employee participation in workplace decisions

As was discussed previously, high-performance work practices often include forms of **participative management** (i.e., teams and employee involvement). However, the two concepts are not identical: high-performance workplace practices focus on gaining a competitive advantage using key HRM practices; participative management (also called *employee involvement*) focuses on HRM practices that provide front-line workers with greater decision-making ability and responsibility, in turn giving them influence over the control and coordination of work (Kaufman, 2001). Given the large focus on teams and employee involvement in practice and research, we now turn our focus to participative management.

The concepts of employee involvement and participative management are not new; some suggest "the term 'participation in management' was widely used" in the 1910s and 1920s (Kaufman, 2001, pp. 522–523). However, there was renewed interest in these issues in the 1980s, a time when Japanese management practices were believed to increase productivity, particularly in the automotive sector (Cappelli & Neumark, 2001).

While there is no single managerial approach to participative management, there are several characteristics considered essential to such plans (Lawler, Mohrman & Benson, 2001):

- Decisions are made at the lowest level possible (e.g., at the work task level).
- Jobs are best designed when individuals or teams have responsibility for a complete part of the work process (i.e., produce an entire product, provide a total service).
- Information concerning business performance, business goals, and strategies is shared.
- There is extensive investment in training and development, particularly in the areas of team and interpersonal skills such as group decision making, team building, basic business skills, and leadership skills.
- Rewards systems are in place. As rewards can influence behaviour, rewards systems must be designed to encourage individuals and teams to build on their skill sets, take on more decision-making authority, and perform in ways that foster business success. This can include both individual and team rewards systems.

In essence, participative management requires that workers (or teams) have the information, power, and knowledge to perform the task without managerial control and direction. Thus, managers play the role of coach, supporter, or mentor to facilitate work completion rather than directing work completion. In particular, we have seen a focus on two types of participative management process: teams and total quality management.

Teams

Traditionally managers assigned individual tasks to individual employees; however, many employers now assign work to teams. Research suggests that more than 50 percent of all organizations, and 80 percent of organizations with more than 100 people, use teams (Banker, Field, Schroeder & Sinha, 1996; Gordon, 1992). Often, these workplaces implement teams as a way to improve quality and group problem-solving in terms of efficiency, speed of service/production, and customer service (Saks & Haccoun, 2004).

Given these trends, it is not surprising that teams—in particular, self-managed teams—are a key component of employee involvement (Lawler, Mohrman & Benson, 2001). Broadly speaking, a team can be defined as a group of individuals who see themselves, and are seen by others, as a social entity that is mutually dependent due to the work they perform (Guzzo & Dickson, 1996). A team is composed of a group of people who are committed to achieving a common purpose and performance goals that they hold themselves accountable to achieving (Katzenbach & Smith, 1993). Because of these definitions and characteristics, much of team research has focused on long-term groups, with multiple-task responsibilities, operating within an organization (Kerr & Tindale, 2004).

Two industries have been at the forefront of team research. The first is the airline industry, largely because of the importance of airline safety. In particular, crew resource management (CRM) has been studied extensively (Kanki, Helmreich & Anca, 2010). CRM seeks to improve the performance of cockpit crews through well-tested training methods (e.g., simulators, lectures, videos) designed to improve team skills (Salas, Prince, Bowers, Stout, Oser & Cannon-Bowers, 1999). A review of CRM research (Salas, Burke, Bowers & Wilson, 2001) suggests that CRM has increased cockpit crew learning and promoted behavioural changes; however, it is not certain that it has resulted in improved performance or improved safety.

The second industry in which teams have been extensively examined is manufacturing. Research in this area has focused primarily on product quality and productivity (Banker et al., 1996; Banker, Field & Sinha, 2001). Given the high union density in manufacturing sectors, several studies have examined the influence of labour on teams. Some have argued that unions may be resistant to team processes, particularly if they reduce employment levels, attempt to reduce collective representation, or increase workload (McCabe & Black, 1997; McNabb & Whitfield, 1997), and yet may reduce the autonomy of teams (Bourque & Riffaud, 2007). Others suggest that unions can facilitate the adoption of teams (McNabb & Whitfield, 1997). Moreover, active teams can improve employee–supervisor relations, particularly when union leaders are actively involved (Cooke, 1992).

Total Quality Management (TQM) and Lean Production

Like teams, TQM has been heavily used in manufacturing environments. While you may also hear TQM called "lean production," the two terms are in essence synonyms as both practices are grounded in Japanese quality practices (Dahlgaard & Dahlgaard-Park, 2006). For simplicity, we will use the term TQM. Essentially a managerial approach, TQM has been strongly influenced by quality gurus Deming and Juran. Its basic premise is that organizations prosper if customers receive quality products and services (Preston, Sappey & Teo, 1998). To achieve this goal, TQM uses statistical process controls, cause–effect analyses, and group problem-solving techniques (Lawler, Mohrman & Benson, 2001). In terms of overall effectiveness, a survey of a sample of Fortune 1000 firms found that over 85 percent reported positive experiences with TQM programs, with over two-thirds of respondents indicating positive results for productivity, quality, and customer service (Lawler, Mohrman & Benson, 2001).

The relationship between unions and TQM has also been examined. "It is often assumed that . . . unionized facilities will resist adapting lean manufacturing techniques (such as TQM)" (Shah & Ward, 2003, p. 132), causing people to assume that such practices are less likely in unionized firms. In fact, the Canadian Auto Workers (CAW, 1993) has a formal statement on lean manufacturing, which it states includes TQM. In this statement, the union argues that the goals of TQM are to reduce jobs and work hours, increase workload and managerial control, as well as undermine the union. It asserts that "the CAW strategy is to oppose lean production (including TQM) and work to change it through negotiations." However, some studies have found that there is no relationship between unionization and the presence of TQM programs (Sadikoglu, 2004; Shah & Ward, 2003) or TQM performance (Sadikoglu, 2004); while more recent studies conclude that while unionized workplaces have different approaches to TQM, largely due to the reduced managerial flexibility in collective agreements, "unionization does not appear to have such a wide scale detrimental effect as assumed in prior studies" (Jayaram, Ahire & Dreyfuss, 2010, p. 354).

Nonunion Representation

nonunion representation occurs when a group of nonunion employees meets with management regarding employment terms and conditions

Nonunion representation can be defined as groups of employees who meet with management on matters related to the terms and conditions of their workplace (Taras, 2006). While statistics concerning nonunion representation are not as easily available as those concerning union representation, one review suggests that between 10 and 16 percent of Canadian employees have some form of nonunion representation (Taras, 2002).

It is interesting to note that despite the similarities between Canadian and American labour laws, nonunion representation is illegal in the United States. This is because such forms of nonunion representation have been considered akin to company unions, which are prohibited under the National Labor Relations Act (NLRA) (Kaufman & Taras, 1999). While legislation that would have allowed nonunion representation in the States, namely the *Teamwork for Employees and Management Act* (TEAM), was proposed, it was vetoed by former president Bill Clinton in 1996 (Chansler & Schraeder, 2003). In Canada, there has been a history of nonunion representation dating back to the 1910s, and these mechanisms are deemed lawful unless specifically designed to prevent union organizing (Taras, 1999).

As pointed out by Taras (2002), there are numerous forms of nonunion representation, including the following nonunion employee–management plans and professional organizations that represent doctors, lawyers, and engineers and represent workers often excluded from traditional collective bargaining.

Nonunion Employee–Management Plans

As far back as the 1920s, the Canadian government's labour department produced a report entitled *Joint Councils in Industry* that examined a form of nonunion employee representation. Over the years, we have seen several examples of such joint councils, and we continue to see them today: the joint council in Imperial Oil dating back to the 1910s, the former association-consultation model used in the public sector in the 1950s, and more recent plans used in both private- and public-sector organizations such as Dofasco, Husky Manufacturing, the Royal Canadian Mounted Police, and the Town of Banff (Taras, 1999; Taras & Copping, 1998).

These joint industry councils usually consist of equal numbers of management and elected employees that meet on issues related to health, safety, education, and pay and benefits (Taras & Copping, 1998). The basic philosophy of this model has been described as *quid pro quo*, or "this for that" (Taras & Kaufman, 2006). Managers hope to achieve cooperative and consultative workplace interactions with workers that minimize worker–management conflict, whereas workers seek a voice mechanism that allows them to influence managerial decision making and facilitate a respectful work environment. The primary goals of such plans therefore include the following (Taras & Kaufman, 2006):

- to improve communication between workers and management;
- to increase access to workplace dispute resolution and justice mechanisms; and
- to negotiate better terms and conditions of employment.

Given these primary functions, these plans usually have three common features (Taras, 1999):

1. They generally include workers, elected democratically, who meet with management to discuss issues of importance to the work force.
2. These worker representatives are paid by the company for these meetings.
3. Minutes (or summaries) of these meetings are often distributed to the workers, and agreements between these parties form part of the employment relationship.

There is a long history of disagreement among the industrial relations community about the role of such nonunion representation methods. Perhaps Tara and Kaufman (2006, p. 3) summarized it best when they stated that their "initial foray in [the area of nonunion representation] was greeted with reactions ranging from skepticism to hostility." A key question is whether this managerial perspective is inherently nonunion. Some argue that these nonunion systems are designed as union avoidance strategies, particularly if they are purposely designed to deny employees their lawful right to unionize (Taras, 2006). Management may argue that the purpose is to provide voice and to make the workplace better rather than to deter unionization (Taras, 2006).

Either way, research (Kaufman & Taras, 2000) suggests that the long-term success of these plans requires two managerial practices: (1) pay and benefits must meet (or exceed) what unionized workers of that industry (or comparable industries) receive, and (2) there must be considerable effort and commitment to make the plan work. One might also argue a third factor is needed: the ability to have voice and make significant changes in the workplace. While these plans may start as nonunion, they create the collective mechanisms akin to unionization. For example, as will be discussed in Chapter 11, while association-consultation was a nonunion employee-representation plan in many public-sector workplaces, employees quickly opted for the union option when it was provided to them. A potential explanation for this rapid movement to unionize in the public sector was that these associations had limited power, given that management still had final say on all matters. In addition, we have seen examples of nonunion representation models becoming unionized organizations (Taras, 1999; Taras & Copping, 1998). Clearly, this area will continue to be closely examined over the next decade.

Professional Organizations

Certification procedures often exclude professionals such as lawyers, physicians, engineers, and architects. A potential explanation for this exclusion may be that such professionals are often self-employed or employed under contract. Thus, they would not meet the definition of "employee" in most Canadian laws. However, many of these professionals are members of professional associations. These associations often set minimum standards for licensing (e.g., lawyers must pass a bar exam in each province in which they provide services); provide mechanisms for group access to (and discounts for) health benefits and retirement investment planning; and set provincial standards for fees. Therefore, we see professional associations that are "quasi-union" in status as they act as a closed shop, limiting employer ability to hire outside of the "union."

In some cases, we are seeing employers also moving to a "quasi-union" model—negotiating collectively with elected members of these associations, using joint committees, and even agreeing to arbitration processes to settle disputes. A good example of such an approach involves the Newfoundland and Labrador Medical Association.

Nonstandard Work Arrangements

While the trends of high-performance work practices, participative management, and nonunion representation have presented workplaces with ways that management can increase voice and/or due process, **nonstandard work arrangements**

nonstandard work arrangements

work arrangements that differ from the norm in terms of employment term, location, schedule, hours of work, or pay

IR Notebook 6.1

Is the NLMA a Professional Association or a Union?

The *Medical Act* of Newfoundland and Labrador requires that all physicians register with the Newfoundland and Labrador Medical Association (NLMA) in order to practise in the province. Physicians who fail to join render their medical licence "null and void"; they also face financial penalties and/or late-payment fees. Currently, the association has approximately 1,500 members. Working members are either "fee for service" (they bill the provincial government for patient visits/services) or "salaried" (they are employed by a healthcare facility and paid a salary).

In many ways, the NLMA functions similarly to a nonunion employee-representation plan. For example, representatives of the NLMA (who are elected by the NLMA membership) and representatives of the government meet at least once per month to discuss issues of mutual concern. Recently these joint committees came to an arrangement concerning vacation and job descriptions for salaried physicians. Other committees have been tasked with examining ways of recovering the current deficit in the fee-for-service budget.

The association provides its members with a number of services, including access to group insurance plans (mental, dental, accidental death, and dismemberment), professional assistance plans (referral and counselling services for a variety of personal issues), and group RRSPs (for salaried members only), to name a few. In addition to offering these services, the NLMA is the voice of physicians with the government, which acts as the employer either directly (for salaried physicians) or indirectly (most fee-for-service physicians gain the bulk of their earnings from billing the provincial health plan). In this role, the NLMA negotiates with the provincial government on issues related to salaries, provincial budget allocations for fee-for-service providers, on-call rates, retention bonuses, etc.

In the last two rounds of bargaining, the parties found it difficult to reach an agreement. In the first case, in 2003, the result was a service withdrawal, in which both fee-for-service and salaried physicians withdrew all nonessential services. Arguably, this was akin to a strike or work-to-rule initiative. Approximately sixteen days later, no agreement had yet been reached, so the parties agreed to have a third party determine the remaining issues. In fact, upon agreement of the parties, the government enacted legislation that an arbitration process mirroring that used in labour relations issues would be used.

In the fall of 2010, the parties were again deeply divided. A small group of physicians, who were salaried employees of a health board, resigned in protest. While the majority of these physicians rescinded their resignation when the parties settled, it was noteworthy that the 2010 settlement contained an "agreement in principle" that any future disputes between the parties would be resolved by a third party, an arbitration process similar to what we would see for unionized firefighters and police officers in the public sector.

Sources: Arbitration award between Newfoundland and Labrador Medical Association and Government of Newfoundland and Labrador, April 15, 2003, retrieved 11 May 2011 from http://www.gov.nl.ca/publicat/2003/NLMAArbitration.pdf; *NLMA 2005: Book of Reports for the Annual General Meeting*, June 4, 2005 (St. John's: Health Sciences Centre, 2005), retrieved 3 April 2011 from http://www.nlma.nf.ca/documents/annual_reports/annual_report_3.pdf; NLMA website, http://www.nlma.nf.ca; "NLMA board recommending acceptance of new offer from government," *The Telegram*, 16 December 2010, retrieved 15 January 2011 from http://www.thetelegram.com/News/Local/1969-12-31/article-2048073/NLMA-board-recommending-acceptance-of-new-offer-from-government/1; Memorandum of Agreement Between Newfoundland and Labrador Medical Association and Government of Newfoundland and Labrador, 15 May 2003 to 30 September 2005, retrieved 3 April 2011 from http://www.nlma.nl.ca/documents/agreements_negotiations/agreement_negotiation_1.pdf.

arguably were not designed to enhance such mechanisms. Rather, such arrangements are often implemented as a way to lower labour costs, adjust labour levels to match business production/service levels, and generally improve business performance (Belman & Golden, 2002; Lautsch, 2002). However, employers have argued that nontraditional work arrangements can offer the advantages of flexibility, work–life balance, improved ability to recruit and retain employees, lower turnover rates, less employee stress and anxiety, less commuting time, and lower childcare costs (Duffy, 2001; Emory University, 2006; Manitoba Civil Service Commission, 2011). In fact, as is argued by Zeytinoglu, Cooke, and Mann (2010), there is also a body of literature that discusses how nonstandard work arrangements, particularly those designed to provide flexibility in work schedules and hours, are driven by employees' desire to maximize work–life balance—though these scholars did conclude that business drivers, rather than employee drivers, were the main reason for such arrangements.

Broadly speaking, nonstandard work arrangements, also known as *alternative work arrangements* (Armstrong-Stassen, 1998), represent employment agreements that differ from those of typical full-time jobs in terms of (1) term of employment (e.g., nonpermanent), (2) location (e.g., telecommuting), (3) work schedule and hours of work, and (4) pay (Cooke, 2005). Regardless of how we define these practices, they are increasingly prevalent in the Canadian economy. Evidence suggests that more than two-thirds of Canadians are employed in some form of nonstandard work arrangement (Lipsett & Reesor, 1998). In fact, looking at one type of nonstandard work, 57 percent of Canadians have some form of flexibility in work schedules or hours (Zeytinoglu, Cooke & Mann, 2010). Moreover, the majority of new jobs are now considered nonstandard (Zeytinoglu & Cooke, 2006), suggesting that this work arrangement may be more common for new entrants into the labour force (immigrants, university graduates, high school graduates, etc.).

Interestingly, despite the increased use of nonstandard work, it is clear that not all employees have the same exposure to this trend. For example, Zeytinoglu, Cooke, and Mann (2010) found that (1) part-time workers had more access to flextime, variable workweeks and schedules than did full-time employees, and (2) unionized workers generally had less access to a variable workweek length or schedule. There are two potential arguments for the latter, union finding. First, details concerning work hours and schedules for unionized workers are usually contained in a collective agreement that would potentially restrict flexibility in that area. Second, building on equity–efficiency theory, these initiatives are usually linked to the firm's desire for efficiency, versus the union's focus on equity, thereby potentially reducing union acceptance of such practices.

Building on the equity argument, the evidence to date suggests that employees in nonstandard work arrangements have fewer benefits, lower wages, and less job security relative to workers in "standard" jobs (Cooke & Zeytinoglu, 2004; Kunda, Barley & Evans, 2002; Zeytinoglu & Cooke, 2005). Moreover, while some have argued that there would be fewer negative impacts in nonstandard work arrangements for those in higher-skilled occupations, research shows that managers and professionals in nonstandard contracts feel negative impacts similar to those felt by less-skilled workers (Hoque & Kirkpatrick, 2003).

Given these potentially negative impacts on workers—and the fact that unions have traditionally tried to standardize work relationships and improve job security, working conditions, and wages, as well as limit managerial discretion (see Chapter 4)—it is not surprising that labour often frowns upon these work arrangements, often calling them "precarious," as shown on a CAW web page.

Summary

As we discovered in this chapter, management has faced new challenges over the past two decades, due largely to increased global competition. Although many textbooks underestimate the role of the management actor in the industrial relations system, we have shown that management plays an important role in the current system, as it continues to respond to a more competitive product and service environment.

This chapter highlights the evolution of management perspectives from thinking of workers as akin to slaves and machines to their being a strategic resource. We have also discovered the extent to which an organization's industrial relations strategy and human resources practices must be consistent with its overall business strategy. In so doing, we have seen how the importance of managerial strategy, in particular as it relates to unions, plays a key role in current management thinking.

Moving forward, we see a number of strategic trends emerging, particularly high-performance HRM, participative management, nonunion representation, and nonstandard work practices. Some argue that these plans will reduce the influence of labour, intentionally or unintentionally, given that many of these practices produce mechanisms of due process and voice. Others argue that such trends will have a negative impact on workers and their unions. Alternatively, one can argue that if employees feel that these substitutes fail to provide the equivalent benefits of unionization, they may drive employees toward unions. Only time will tell whether these new trends will have a negative or positive impact on employees and their unions. However, the current evidence suggests that management is moving toward a union resistance strategy.

Key Terms

distributive justice 179
high-performance work practices 188
human relations 177
master–servant relationship 175
nonstandard work arrangements 194
nonunion representation 192
organizational justice 178

participative management 190
procedural justice 179
strategic choice framework 180
union acceptance 185
union removal 186
union resistance 185
union substitution 186

Weblinks

McDonald's Food Facts and Nutrition Calculator:

http://www.mcdonalds.ca/en/food/foodFacts.aspx

http://www.mcdonalds.ca/en/food/calculator.aspx

U.S. air traffic controllers:

- About NLRB and the American government being perceived as pro-management:

  http://eightiesclub.tripod.com/id296.htm

- Firing of the US air traffic controllers in 1981:

  http://www.youtube.com/watch?v=e5JSToyiyr8

Newfoundland and Labrador Medical Association:

http://www.nlma.nf.ca

Management strategies to unions:

- Southwest Airlines:

  http://www.youtube.com/watch?v=GiiOHgE8ADg

- Delta Airlines:

  http://www.youtube.com/watch?v=3eFQb0odnTA

Union busting:

http://www.youtube.com/watch?v=2qajBfEdzoE

http://www.youtube.com/watch?v=vGl3HQL-gxo&feature=related

CAW's views of lean production techniques:

http://www.caw.ca/en/services-departments-health-safety-environment-work-reorganization-responding-to-lean-production.htm

CAW's web page on precarious work:

http://www.caw.ca/en/7688.htm

RPC Icons

6.1 Collects and develops information required for good decision making throughout the bargaining process

- union decision-making process
- the history and environment of industrial relationships, unions, labour relations, and collective bargaining
- union practices, organization, and certification

6.2 Monitors applications of HR policies

- context and content of policy
- individual and organizational behaviour and ethics
- organization structure and authorities
- the identification, assessment, development, implementation, maintenance, and monitoring processes of effective systems of managing HR information

6.3 Provides advice to clients on the establishment, continuation, and termination of bargaining rights

- response of management to union organizing activity
- unions and the labour movement
- collective bargaining processes and issues
- government labour relationship acts

Discussion Questions

1. Some argue that high-performance work practices, participative management, nonunion representation, and nonstandard work practices are designed to be forms of union substitution and/or union avoidance. Do you feel this is true?
2. Do you feel that the movement toward high-performance work practices, participative management, nonunion representation, and nonstandard work practices will result in increased or decreased unionization? Why?
3. Assume you are a labour leader and that you are trying to organize a nonunion firm that has participative management and nonunion representation practices in place. What would you tell employees are the advantages of unionization even with these progressive HRM practices?
4. Given recent statistics regarding nonstandard work practices, do you feel that university graduates should expect full-time, permanent positions when they graduate?
5. In your opinion, can employers expect highly committed employees who seek to improve the performance of the firm if they continue to use nonstandard work arrangements?

Using the Internet

Many colleges and universities use part-time instructors, faculty, and teachers in addition to full-time staff. As examples, look at the websites for the Association of Part-Time Professors at the University of Ottawa **(http://www.uottawa.ca/associations/aptpuo/index.html)** and the Concordia University Part-Time Faculty Association **(http://www.cupfa.org).** Also examine an article on the Canadian Association of University Teachers, or CAUT, website written by Diane Huberman-Arnold that outlines the challenges of part-time faculty **(http://www.cautbulletin.ca/en_article. asp?articleid=2185).**

On the basis of what you have learned from this chapter, and of insights gleaned from these websites, why do you think university administrations (i.e., management) use part-timers, and would prefer that they remain nonunion?

Exercises

You will find on many universities' and colleges' websites advertisements for faculty positions, information concerning university-wide strategic plans, and collective agreements. Alternatively, you may this information in other places easily accessible by faculty, potential faculty, and students.

1. Have a look at the faculty collective agreement (or handbook if your faculty is not unionized) for your university. Does it contain language concerning any of the current managerial trends in terms of high-performance HRM, participative management, nonunion representation, and nonstandard work practices? Look for keywords such as *committees*, *work schedules*, *alternative work arrangements*, *contractual*, *part-time appointments*, *quality*, *teams*, *TQM*, etc.
2. Look at recent job postings. How many of the postings are for non-standard work versus permanent full-time work? How many are for unionized versus nonunionized positions?
3. In looking at the job postings and/or the collective agreement, would you say your university or college has a traditional (i.e., hourly or salaried human resources) model or a high-performance model? Why?
4. After having read the strategic plan, what do you feel are the industrial relations strategies needed to achieve it?
5. Of the forms of management strategies toward unions, which do you feel exists on your campus? Why?

Case

The Provincial Wine Shop

The Provincial Wine Shop (PWS) is a new agency established in April 2007. Prior to its incorporation, people could purchase wines from three places in the metro area: (1) Provincial Liquor Sales Inc. (PLSI), a provincial Crown corporation which sold wines, spirits, and beers; (2) Prestigious Wines Inc. (PWI), a private company that sold higher-end, specialty wine products not available at PLSI; or (3) small agency outlets that were not government-run and had a small inventory of lower-end wines. The newly formed PWS is a merger of PLSI and PWI. The current merger of the metro area stores has resulted in 15 PWS stores. On average, each store has one manager, one assistant manager, and twenty-five full-time and ten part-time employees. In addition, there are fifty casual workers who are called in, as needed, and can work at any of the metro stores. All non-managerial employees, whether full-time, part-time, or casual, are unionized.

Will Barnes (CEO), Janet Grayson (Vice-President Retail Sales & Operations), and Andrew Chen (Vice-President HRM) are discussing the strategic plan for PWS for the next five years. In particular, they are focusing on the environmental issues of strengths, weakness, opportunities, and threats. Will feels strongly that the key business strengths relate to the product knowledge of the staff, the product variety, and customer service. As he stresses, the province still allows the existing agency stores to offer some wine products. Hence, if PWS stores do not provide great service, products, and product knowledge, there is a huge threat—customers can simply go to one of the numerous agency outlets that still exist in the metro area.

Janet adds that from an operational perspective, employees need to be encouraged to maximize sales while also being socially responsible (i.e., not selling to underaged people, not selling to those under the influence, etc.). Janet also stresses that information sharing between staff and teamwork are key to business success, as employees often have to assist others, cover for each other, etc. However, she feels that this area needs improvement. She proposes that PWS increase training and move toward having employees work in teams to facilitate knowledge sharing.

Andrew then starts to focus on the HRM implications. The organization is in transition. Up until three years ago, all employees were covered by the provincial government's collective agreement. A new collective agreement was signed when the province spun off PWS, with the understanding that the new operation had to generate sufficient revenues to cover its own operating cost and maintain its current level of contributions to the provincial government in terms of taxes on alcohol. Failure to meet these financial goals would result in PWS being shut down. In fact, at the time of formation, there was pressure from some members of the legislature that PWS should be sold off and become a standalone, non-government-based, private company. However, the social responsibility associated with alcohol sales resulted in the organization remaining in the public sector.

Given the environment at the time of formation, the union and management realized that they needed to reach a settlement that would help ensure the long-term viability of the newly formed PWS. The union encouraged the workers to accept the 2007 deal, even though wage increases were lower than what other provincial employees received. The union argued that this was needed in order to establish the organization and enhance job security. The resulting collective agreement provided wage increases of 0, 1, and 2 percent over three years. The resulting contract also allowed PWS, for the first time, to hire more part-time and casual workers (who float from store to store as needed). However, the contract did require that when an employee had worked 2,000 hours in a two-year period, he or she would move into permanent part-time status. Similar pay and hiring practices were adopted for nonunion staff.

Three years after the initial collective agreement was signed, the restructuring has taken place, and the operation has seen many changes. While the organization lost money in year 1, it has now achieved its financial goals of covering costs and contributing tax dollars to the province; new products and new in-store wine-tasting equipment have been introduced; and there has been an increased use of temporary staff for peak periods (weekends and the holiday season). However, as they map out the strategy for the upcoming five years, they realize that their largest cost is labour but also that the success of any future quality and product improvements will require employee commitment. Therefore, the human resources strategy of Andrew's department will need to mesh with the overall business strategy.

With this as the backdrop, they start to form a plan that will continue to ensure financial stability, product quality, and a stable, committed work force.

Questions

1. What type of union strategy is PWS using?
2. Do you see evidence of the managerial trends of high-performance work practices, participative management, nonunion representation, and nonstandard work present in the case?
3. Has there been a strong linkage between the industrial relations and business strategies of the organization? To what extent?
4. Given the case at hand, what would you suggest the firm do in terms of making changes to its current strategies?

References

Armstrong-Stassen, M. (1998). Alternative work arrangements: Meeting the challenges. *Canadian Psychology, 39,* pp. 108–123.

Banker, R. D., Field, J. M., Schroeder, R. G., & Sinha, K. K. (1996). Impact of work teams on manufacturing performance: A longitudinal study. *Academy of Management Journal, 39,* pp. 867–890.

Banker, R. D., Field, J. M., & Sinha, K. K. (2001). Work-team implementation and trajectories of manufacturing quality: A longitudinal study. *Manufacturing & Service Operations Management, 3,* pp. 25–42.

Barbash, J. (1987). Like nature, industrial relations abhors a vacuum. *Relations industrielles, 42,* pp. 168–179.

Belcourt, M., & McBey, K. J. (2004a). *Strategic human resources planning* (2nd edition). Scarborough, ON: Nelson.

Belcourt, M., & McBey, K. J. (2004b). *Strategic human resources planning* (4th edition). Scarborough, ON: Nelson.

Belcourt, M & McBey, KJ (2010), *Strategic human resources planning* (4th edition). Toronto, ON: Nelson.

Belman, D., & Golden, L. (2002). Which workers are non-standard and contingent and does it pay? In I. U. Zeytinoglu (Ed.), *Flexible work arrangements: Conceptualizations and international experiences* (pp. 241–267). The Hague: Kluwer Law International.

Bentham, K. J. (2002). Employer resistance to union certification: A study of eight Canadian jurisdictions. *Industrial Relations, 57*(1), pp. 159–187.

Betcherman, G. (1999). Workplace change in Canada: The broad context. In A. Verma & R. P. Chaykowski (Eds.), *Contract & commitment: Employment relations in the new economy* (pp. 338–354). Kingston, ON: Industrial Relations Centre.

Betcherman, G., McMullen, K., Leckie, N., & Caron, C. (1994). *The Canadian workplace in transition.* Kingston, ON: IRC Press.

Bourque, R., & Riffaud, S. (2007). Présence syndicale et autonomie des équipes d'opérateurs cuvistes dans l'industrie de l'aluminium. *Relations industrielles/Industrial Relations, 6,* pp. 66–95.

Brown, T. C. (2002). Equity-efficiency theory and organizational justice theory: Two peas in a pod? Paper presented at the annual meeting of the Canadian Industrial Relations Association.

Brown, T. C., & Latham, G. P. (2000). The effects of goal setting and self-instruction training on the performance of union employees. *Relations industrielles, 55,* pp. 80–94.

Brown, T., & McCracken, M. (2010). Which goals should participants set for effective management development? *Journal of General Management, 35*, pp. 27–44.

Bruce, K. (2006). Henry S. Dennison, Elton Mayo, and human relations historiography. *Management and Organizational History, 1*, pp. 177–199.

Campion, M. A., & Thayer, P. (1987). Job design: Approaches, outcomes, and trade-offs. *Organizational Dynamics, 15*(3), pp. 66–79.

Canadian Auto Workers Union (CAW). (1993). Work reorganization: Responding to lean production. Retrieved 2 April 2011 from http://www.caw.ca/en/about-the-caw-policies-and-papers-work-reorganization-responding-to-lean-production.htm

Canadian Press. (15 October 2010). Wal-Mart union in Weyburn, Sask., upheld. Retrieved 8 February 2010 from http://www.cbc.ca/canada/saskatchewan/story/2010/10/15/sk-wal-mart-weyburn-1010.html

Cappelli, P., & Neumark, D. (2001). Do "high performance" work practices improve establishment-level outcomes? *Industrial and Labour Relations Review, 54*, pp. 737–775.

CBC. (14 February 2006). Labour rules out Wal-Mart boycott. Retrieved from http://www.cbc.ca/story/business/national/2005/02/11/ufcw-050211.html

Chansler, P., & Schraeder, M. (2003). Will the TEAM work for employees and managers: A closer look at the TEAM Act. *Journal for Quality and Participation, 26*, pp. 31–37.

Chaykowski, R., & Verma, A. (1992). Canadian industrial relations in transition. In R. P. Chaykowski & A. Verma (Eds.), *Industrial relations in Canadian industry* (pp. 448–475). Toronto: Dryden.

Cooke, G. (2005). The nature and incidence of non-standard work arrangements. Ph.D. dissertation. McMaster University. Unpublished.

Cooke, G. B., & Zeytinoglu, I. U. (2004). Temporary employment: The situation in Canada. In J. Burgess & J. Connell (Eds.), *International perspectives on temporary work* (pp. 91–111). London, UK: Routledge.

Cooke, W. N. (1992). Product quality improvement through employee participation: The effects of unionization & joint union–management administration. *Industrial and Labor Relations Review, 46*, pp. 119–134.

Craig, A. W. J. (1967). A model for the analysis of industrial relations systems. Paper presented to the annual meeting of the Canadian Political Science Association.

Dahlgaard, J. J., & Dahlgaard-Park, S. M. (2006). Lean production, six sigma quality, TQM and company culture. *The TQM Magazine, 18*, pp. 263–281.

Daniel, T. A. (2003). Tools for building a positive employee relations environment. *Employment Relations Today, 30*(2), pp. 51–64.

Delaney, J. T., & Huselid, M. A. (1996). The impact of human resource practices on perceptions of organizational performance. *Academy of Management Journal, 38*, pp. 949–968.

Den Hartog, D. N., & Verburg, R. M. (2004). High performance work systems, organisational culture and firm effectiveness. *Human Resources Management Journal, 14*, pp. 55–78.

Duffy, T. (2 July 2001). Alternative work arrangements. Retrieved 18 July 2011 from http://www.itworld.com/NWW010702work

Dunlop, J. T. (1958). *Industrial relations systems.* New York: Henry Holt and Company.

Emory University. (2006). Workplace flexibility. Retrieved 18 July 2011 from http://emory.hr.emory.edu/awa_website/awa_main.htm

Felsberg, E. J. (2004). Composing effective employee handbooks. *Employment Relations Today, 31*(2), pp. 117–122.

Fox, A. (1974). *Beyond contract: Work, power and trust relations.* London, UK: Faber & Faber.

Fox, A. (1985). *History and heritage: The social origins of the British industrial relations system.* London, UK: George Allen and Unwin.

Godard, J. (1997). Whither strategic choice: do managerial IR ideologies matter? *Industrial Relations, 36*, pp. 206–228.

Godard, J. (2004). A critical assessment of the high-performance paradigm. *British Journal of Industrial Relations, 42*, pp. 349–378.

Godard, J. (2007). Unions, work practices, and wages under different institutional environments: The case of Canada and England. *Industrial & Labor Relations Review, 60*(4), pp. 457–476.

Godard, J., & Delaney, J. (2000). Reflections on the "high performance" paradigm's implications for industrial relations as a field. *Industrial and Labor Relations Review, 53,* pp. 482–502.

Gordon, J. (1992). Work-teams: How far have they come? *Training, 29,* pp. 59–65.

Greenberg, J. (1986). Determinants of perceived fairness of performance evaluations. *Journal of Applied Psychology,71*(2), pp. 340–342.

Greenberg, J. (1987). A taxonomy of organizational justice theories. *Academy of Management Review, 22,* pp. 9–21.

Greer, C. R. (2001). *Strategic human resource management.* Upper Saddle River, NJ: Prentice Hall.

Guzzo, R. A., & Dickson, M. W. (1996). Teams in organizations: Recent research on performance and effectiveness. *Annual Review of Psychology, 47,* pp. 307–338.

Harley, B., Allen, B. C., & Sargent, L. D. (2007). High performance work systems and employee experience of work in the service sector: The case of aged care. *British Journal of Industrial Relations, 45,* pp. 607–633.

Hébert, G., Jain, C. J., & Meltz, N. M. (1988). The state of the art in IR: Some questions and concepts. In G. Hébert, C. J. Jain & N. M. Meltz (Eds.), *The state of the art in industrial relations* (pp. 1–8). Kingston, ON: Industrial Relations Centre, Queen's University, and Centre for Industrial Relations, University of Toronto.

Hitt, M. A., Ireland, R. D., Hoskisson, R. E., Rowe, W. G., & Sheppard, J. P. (2006). *Strategic management competitiveness and globalization* (2nd Canadian edition). Toronto: Thomson Nelson.

Hoque, K., & Kirkpatrick, I. (2003). Non-standard employment in the management and professional workforce: Training, consultation and gender implications. *Work, Employment and Society, 17*(4), pp. 667–689.

Huselid, M. (1995). The impact of human resource management practices on turnover, productivity, and corporate financial performance. *Academy of Management Journal, 38,* pp. 635–672.

Huselid, M. A., Jackson, S. E., & Schuler, R. S. (1997). Technical and strategic human resource management effectiveness as determinants of firm performance. *The Academy of Management Journal, 40*(1), pp. 171–188.

Kahn-Freund, O. (1967). A note on status and contract in British labour law. *Modern Law Review, 30,* pp. 635–644.

Jacobs, K. (3 November 2010). Delta flight attendants reject union. Retrieved 7 February 2011 from http://www.reuters.com/article/2010/11/03/us-delta-idUSTRE6A27M620101103

Jayaram, J., Ahire, S. L., & Dreyfuss, P. (2010). Contingency relationships of firm size, TQM duration, unionization, and industry context on TQM implementation—A focus on total effects. *Journal of Operations Management, 28,* pp. 345–356.

Katzenbach, J. R., & Smith, D. K. (1993). *The wisdom of teams.* New York: HarperCollins.

Kaufman, B. E. (2001). The theory and practice of strategic HRM and participative management: Antecedents in early industrial relations. *Human Resource Management Review, 11,* pp. 505–533.

Kaufman, B. E., & Taras, D. G. (1999). Nonunion employee representation: Introduction. *Journal of Labor Research, 20*(1), pp. 1–8.

Kaufman, B. E., & Taras, D. G. (2000). (Eds.) *Nonunion employee representation: History, contemporary practice and policy.* Armonk, NY: ME Sharepe.

Kanki, B. G., Helmreich, R. L., & Anca, J. M. (2010). *Crew resource management.* San Diego: Academic Press.

Kerr, N. L., & Tindale, R. S. (2004). Small group decision making and performance. *Annual Review of Psychology, 55,* pp. 623–656.

Kochan, T., Katz, H., & McKersie, R. (1986). *The transformation of American industrial relations.* New York: Basic Books.

Kunda, G., Barley, S. R., & Evans, J. (2002). Why do contractors contract? The experience of highly skilled technical professionals in a contingent labor market. *Industrial and Labor Relations Review, 55*(2), pp. 234–261.

Labour Law Casebook Group. (2004). *Labour and employment law: Cases, material and commentary* (7th edition). Toronto: Irwin Law.

Latham, G. P., & Pinder, C. C. (2005). Work motivation theory and research at the dawn of the twenty-first century. *Annual Review of Psychology, 56,* pp. 485–516.

Lautsch, B. A. (2002). Uncovering and explaining variance in the features and outcomes of contingent work. *Industrial and Labor Relations Review, 56*(1), pp. 23–43.

Lawler, E. E., Mohrman, S., & Benson, G. (2001). *Organizing for high performance: The CEO report on employee involvement, TQM, reengineering, and knowledge management in Fortune 1000 companies.* San Francisco: Jossey-Bass.

Lipsett, B., & Reesor, M. (1998). Alternative work arrangements in Canadian workplaces. *The changing nature of work, employment and workplace relations* (pp. 29–44). Selected papers from the 34th annual CIRA meeting. Ottawa.

Liu, W., Guthrie, J. P., Flood, P. C., & MacCurtain, S. (2009). Unions and the adoption of high performance work systems: Does employment security play a role? *Industrial & Labor Relations Review, 63,* pp. 109–127.

Locke, E. A., & Latham, G. P. (2002). Building a practically useful theory of goal setting and task motivation: A 35-year odyssey. *American Psychologist, 57,* pp. 705–717.

Manitoba Civil Service Commission. (2011). *Job sharing and/or part-time work arrangements guidelines.* Retrieved 8 February 2011 from http://www.gov.mb.ca/csc/publications/jbsharguid.html#some

Mayo, E. (1933). *The human problems of an industrial civilization.* New York: Macmillan.

McCabe, D., & Black, J. (1997). Something's gotta give: Trade unions and the road to team working. *Employee Relations, 19*(2), pp. 110–127.

McNabb, R., & Whitfield, K. (1997). Unions, flexibility, team-working and financial performance. *Organization Studies, 18*(5), pp. 821–38.

Meltz, N. M. (1997). Introduction to employment relations. Paper presented to the Conference on Teaching in Human Resources and Industrial Relations. Atlanta.

Miles, R. E., & Snow, C. C. (1984). Designing strategic human resources systems. *Organizational Dynamics, 13*(1), pp. 36–52.

Miles, S. J., & Mangold, W. G. (2005). Positioning Southwest Airlines through employee branding. *Business Horizons, 48,* 535–545.

O'Connor, E. S. (1999a). Minding the workers: The meaning of "human" and "human relations" in Elton Mayo. *Organization, 6*(2), pp. 223–246.

O'Connor, E. S. (1999b). The politics of management thought: A case study of the Harvard Business School and the human relations school. *The Academy of Management Review, 24*(1), pp. 117–131.

Preston, A., Sappey, R. B., & Teo, S. (1998). Bargaining for quality: Quality clauses in enterprise agreements in Queensland. *Employee Relations, 20*(4), pp. 333–348.

Rose, J. (2008). Regulating and resolving public sector disputes in Canada. *Journal of Industrial Relations, 50,* pp. 545–59.

Sadikoglu, E. (2004). Total quality management: Context and performance. *The Journal of American Academy of Business, 5,* pp. 364–366.

Saks, A. M., & Haccoun, R. R. (2004). *Managing performance through training and development* (3rd edition), Scarborough, ON: Nelson.

Salas E., Burke, S. C., Bowers, C. A., & Wilson, K. A. (2001). Team training in the skies: Does crew resource management (CRM) training work? *Human Factors, 43,* pp. 641–674.

Salas, E., Prince, C., Bowers, C. A., Stout, R., Oser, R. L., & Cannon-Bowers, J. A. (1999). A methodology for enhancing crew resource management training. *Human Factors, 41,* pp. 161–172.

Shah, R., & Ward, P. T. (2003). Lean manufacturing: Context, practice bundles, and performance, *Journal of Operations Management, 21*(2), pp. 129–149.

Taras, D. G. (1999). Evolution of nonunion employee representation in Canada. *Journal of Labor Research, 20,* pp. 31–51.

Taras, D. G. (2002). Alternative forms of employee representation and labour policy. *Canadian Public Policy, 28,* pp. 105–116.

Taras, D. G. (10 March 2006). Non-union representation and employer intent: How Canadian courts and labour boards determine legal status of non-union plants. *Socio-Economic Review, 4,* pp. 321–336.

Taras, D. G., & Copping, J. (1998). The transition from formal nonunion representation to unionization: A contemporary case. *Industrial and Labor Relations Review, 52*(1), pp. 22–44.

Taras, D. G., & Kaufman, B. E. (2006). Nonunion representation in North America: Diversity, controversy and uncertain future. Working paper. Andrew Young School of Policy Studies. Atlanta, GA: Georgia State University.

Taylor, F. W. (1911). *The principles of scientific management.* New York: Harper.

Thomason, T., & Pozzebon, S. (1998). Managerial opposition to union certification in Quebec and Ontario. *Industrial Relations, 53*(4), pp. 750–771.

Thompson, M. (1995). The management of industrial relations. In M. Gunderson & A. Ponak (Eds.), *Union–management relations in Canada* (3rd edition) (pp. 105–130). Toronto: Addison-Wesley.

United Steelworkers of America. (1997). *Applicant v. Wal-Mart Canada, Inc,* [1997] O.L.R.B. Rep. January/February 141 [1997] O.L.R.D. No. 207 File Nos. 0387-96-R, 0453-96-U.

Verma, A., & Chaykowski, R. P. (1999). Business strategies and employment relations. In A. Verma & R. P. Chaykowski (Eds.), *Contract & commitment: Employment relations in the new economy* (pp. 338–354). Kingston, ON: Industrial Relations Centre.

Wheelen, T. L., & Hunger, J. D. (2006). *Concepts in strategy management and business policy* (10th edition). Upper Saddle River, NJ: Pearson Prentice Hall.

Zeytinoglu, I. U., & Cooke, G. B. (2005). Non-standard work and benefits: Has anything changed since the Wallace report? *Relations industrielles, 60*(1), pp. 29–62.

Zeytinoglu, I. U., & Cooke, G. B. (2006). Who is working on weekends? Determinants of regular weekend work in Canada. In J. Boulin, M. Lallement, J. C. Messenger & F. Michon, (Eds.), *Decent working time, new trends, new issues.* Geneva: ILO Publications. pp. 395–417.

Zeytinoglu, I. U., Cooke, G. B., & Mann, S. L. (2010). Flexibility: Whose choice is it anyways? *Relations industrielles/Industrial Relations, 64,* pp. 555–574.

CHAPTER 7

Negotiations

Learning Objectives

By the end of this chapter, you will be able to discuss

- the differences between negotiations between individuals and collective bargaining;
- the four subprocesses of collective bargaining;
- examples of distributive and integrative bargaining issues;
- a collective bargaining model;
- the pressures on all of the parties to collective bargaining;
- bargaining step by step;
- the dos and don'ts of bargaining;
- the principles of adversarial negotiations;
- the principles of integrative, or win–win, negotiations;
- the elements of interest-based negotiations;
- obstacles to achieving the best bargaining outcome for management and labour
- when to use adversarial and win–win negotiations; and
- the Magna deal

VALE INCO FINALLY REACHES DEAL IN SUDBURY

Tentative deal in Vale strike in Sudbury

More than 3,100 workers at Vale operations in Sudbury and Port Colborne will vote on a tentative new contract this week that could end a strike that started almost a year ago.

The United Steelworkers and Vale reached agreement on Sunday to resolve a dispute over nine fired workers during the strike that had held up a membership vote on a five year deal last week.

"We have finally got it done and now it's up to the members," said Wayne Fraser, the union's district director.

Workers will vote on the deal at membership meetings this Wednesday and Thursday. The union won't disclose terms of the deal until the meetings.

Members of Steelworkers Local 6500 and 6200, who earn an average of about $29.50 an hour excluding benefits, walked off the job last July 13 over the issues of changes in their pension plan, a bonus formula and contracting out work.

The strike culminated deteriorating labour relations between the union and Brazilian-based Vale, which bought Canadian mining giant Inco in 2006. The workers had rejected a company offer in March.

Vale shocked the union and deepened the bitterness between both sides by resuming partial operations and hiring replacement workers during the strike. Inco had never attempted to continue operations during numerous strikes in the last 50 years.

The strike has caused growing hardships for striking workers and slowed down the Sudbury economy significantly.

The two sides had negotiated the deal after marathon talks with the assistance of mediator Kevin Burkett except for the lingering issue of a process how to handle the dismissal of nine workers for alleged infractions including damage to company property during the strike.

But Ontario Labour Minister Peter Fonseca called both sides to Toronto on Friday and instructed them to immediately resume talks. The Ontario Labour Relations Board has scheduled a hearing on Friday so both sides can present arguments on the issue of the fired workers.

The union has said Vale's decision to leave the issue at an impasse and refuse to agree to arbitration is a violation of the company's responsibility to bargain.

The strike is the longest walkout in the history of the former sprawling Inco mining operations, which trace their roots to the rich Sudbury mineral deposit more than a century ago.

> However an 8½ month strike by more than 11,000 workers at the same operations in 1978–79 is the biggest walkout in Canadian history in terms of person-lost work days.
>
> Source: "Tentative Deal in Vale Strike in Sudbury," Tony Van Alphen, *Toronto Star*, 4 July 2010. Reprinted with permission of TORSTAR SYNDICATION SERVICES. http://www.thestar.com/news/gta/article/831925--tentative-deal-in-vale-strike-in-sudbury?bn=1.

Collective bargaining is a complex, multilateral process involving the bargaining teams at the table and those in management and labour that are directly affected by the outcome. It is made difficult by the range of issues that are typically negotiated at the same time. Some issues, such as employee safety and pensions, may be best resolved using a cooperative approach. On the other hand, adversarial negotiations remain the fundamental process for most labour–management problems (see opening vignette—a bitter dispute between Vale and the United Steelworkers of America). A central question to be answered, therefore, is how to get the best outcome for both parties when there is a mix of issue types.

Conflict-of-Interest Assumption

An important assumption of the employment relationship is the existence of a conflict of interests between managers and those whom they manage. The assumption holds equally in public- and private-sector enterprises. While some conflict is inevitable, it is not all-pervasive. In fact the labour–management relationship is defined by cooperation most of the time. Cooperation may apply to little things such as agreeing to the timing and location of meetings or major issues like jointly lobbying governments over industry trade policies. A complicating factor is that cooperation and its opposite—adversarial or competitive negotiations—often take place during the same set of negotiations and sometimes between the same parties. In any successful union–management relationship, there must be a synergy between cooperation and competitiveness. This may be true because the conflict of interest does not extend to all situations, and the relationship in any union–management setting is long-term. A goal is to understand those circumstances where cooperation and competitiveness are likely to work and where they may not.

How Collective Bargaining Differs from Individual Negotiations

Individual negotiations are very different from bargaining over the terms of a collective agreement.[1] When two people bargain over the price of a car, there is a defined process. The seller inflates the price and exaggerates the positive qualities of the car. The potential buyer offers less than the seller's price and deflates the car's attributes. The seller and buyer then haggle over a price somewhere between the seller's asking price and the buyer's offer. If a deal is struck, the buyer and seller sign the necessary papers. The buyer gets the car, and the seller obtains the best acceptable price he or she can get. Typically, neither party gets everything they want out of the deal. And they go their separate ways.

In collective bargaining, the process is more complex for several reasons that we will examine. First, there are multiple parties involved, often with different interests and pressures. Second, the issues are not all the same type. Some issues have the potential for a win-win or mutual gains outcome, where both sides come out ahead. Others may be more like the adversarial bargaining described earlier over the price of a car. A third set of issues may result in a combination of elements of win-win and adversarial bargaining. Finally, unlike individual bargaining, collective bargaining involves a continuing relationship between the parties. As we will discover, a sound relationship is critical to effective union–management outcomes.

In summary, here are the main differences between individual and collective negotiations:

- Individual negotiations are bilateral in nature: there are only two parties involved in their outcome. Collective bargaining, on the other hand, is multilateral, involving employees, unions, supervisors, and higher-level managers. Each party may have distinct interests and pressures.
- Issues may be inherently adversarial, may have some potential for mutual gain, or may be a combination of both. Collective bargaining is more complex because all three types of issues are often negotiated at the same time.
- In collective bargaining, the relationship between the parties is ongoing. In individual bargaining, the parties will most likely never see each other again.

The Four Subprocesses of Collective Bargaining

Scholars have broken collective bargaining down into four subprocesses (Walton & McKersie, 1965):

- distributive bargaining;
- integrative bargaining;
- intra-team or intra-organizational bargaining; and
- building trust or attitudinal structuring.

Distributive Bargaining

distributive bargaining

a form of negotiations in which two parties compete over the distribution of some fixed resource

Distributive bargaining is a category of negotiations usually characterized by an adversarial or competitive style. Note that even though the outcome is distributive, the style is a matter of choice. In our car negotiations, for example, one or both of the parties may choose to bargain cooperatively by trying to avoid haggling. It is unlikely, however, that one party will be able to bargain cooperatively if the other party chooses to haggle. To be legitimate, distributive bargaining assumes some degree of conflict between the parties—labour and management. Thus, distributive bargaining is consistent with an industrial relations system that assumes an inherent conflict of interest between management and labour. It is distributive in the sense that the conflict is over some fixed economic reward for the work performed on the job. Conflict can also occur over the control management exerts over such issues as the pace of work, downtime, and disciplinary standards and procedures.

Distributive not only defines a process but can also be used to describe certain collective bargaining issues. For example, issues such as wages and job security are often described as inherently distributive in nature because the parties have competing interests. Economists describe distributive bargaining as a zero-sum game in which one side's gain is the other's loss. Under this characterization, for example, wage increases directly reduce profits.

Integrative Bargaining

In contrast with distributive bargaining, where the pie may be fixed, **integrative bargaining** is founded on the assumption that bargaining outcomes can expand the pie to enable both sides to win. It is assumed that the parties have shared interests in any settlement. Like the word *distributive*, *integrative* may be used to refer not just to a process but also to the bargaining issues themselves. The issue of health and safety, for example, clearly has aspects of mutual interests, but providing a safe and healthy workplace also involves costs.

integrative bargaining

a form of bargaining in which there is potential for a solution that produces a mutual gain; also called win–win bargaining, principled negotiations, and interest-based bargaining

Intra-Team Bargaining

Bargaining that takes place within each side's team is known as **intra-team or intra-organizational bargaining**. Union bargaining teams may be elected to represent an array of internal groups and their interests—shift workers, women, older workers, married employees, etc. The team consists of union members with a common interest or solidarity. But each will also have his or her own agenda with competing priorities. The reality is that in collective bargaining, often more time is spent negotiating within teams or organizations than is spent between management and labour. This usually comes as a shock to the uninitiated bargaining team member.

intra-team (or intra-organizational) bargaining

bargaining within union and management teams during the collective bargaining process; individual union team members, for example, may represent a group with particular interests, such as shift workers

Attitudinal Structuring

Attitudinal structuring is the stage in which trust is built between the parties. Typically, this is a long-term process and may not be limited to activities directly associated with collective bargaining itself. For example, many unions and managements have established a permanent joint committee that meets at regular intervals during the term of a collective agreement to discuss problems of mutual interest.

attitudinal structuring

the difficult process of building the mutual respect and trust necessary for an enduring and positive collective bargaining relationship

TABLE 7.1

Examples of Distributive, Integrative, and Hybrid Issues		
DISTRIBUTIVE	INTEGRATIVE	HYBRID
Wages	Health And Safety	Pensions
Benefits	Rest breaks	Plant closure/severance
Overtime rates		Technological change
Vacations		
Holidays		

Distributive issues generally lack the potential of a win-win mutual gains outcome. Wages or, more generally, labour cost items tend to directly affect the organization's bottom line. Profits or surpluses are proportionately reduced by a wage increase. This applies to employee benefits, overtime rates, vacations, holidays, leaves of absence, etc. (see examples in Table 7.1).

Perhaps the best example of an integrative issue with mutual gains potential is occupational health and safety. Management has a direct interest in providing safe and healthy working conditions. Workers have a similar interest in reducing occupational health and safety hazards in the workplace.

Hybrid issues combine distributive and integrative elements. Pensions, for example, are a direct cost to the employer. To the extent that providing a pension plan enhances career opportunities and reduces turnover costs, it may also produce a mutual gain for an organization and its employees.

In summary, collective bargaining may involve all three types of issues described above: distributive, integrative, and hybrid. Given this reality, a problem in achieving the optimal collective bargaining outcome is that the strategies and tactics of negotiations are quite different for each issue type. We examine these strategies and tactics next.

Strategies and Tactics of the Bargaining Subprocesses

Each of the four subprocesses has a distinct set of strategies and tactics. As we will see, the tactics of distributive and integrative bargaining are almost mirror opposites. Since in any round of collective bargaining there are likely to be distributive, integrative, and hybrid issues on the table simultaneously, employing the appropriate tactic at the right time poses a challenge to even the most experienced negotiator. This problem will become more apparent as we examine the strategies and tactics of each process.

bottom line

the minimum position necessary in negotiations to avoid a strike or lockout; it represents for the union the best possible outcome short of strike

Distributive Bargaining Tactics

As in our car sale example at the beginning of the chapter, the parties will typically inflate their positions so they have issues that can be traded off later. The notion is that to get what you want, you have to ask for more than your **bottom line**. A party will often keep secret its true position, but to withhold this information requires some control over the communication at the

Industrial Relations in Canada

bargaining table. As a rule, in distributive bargaining, the parties each have one spokesperson, which helps them avoid revealing unnecessary or even damaging information. It is important for negotiators to disguise their own bottom line while trying to discover that of the other party. Your outcome may well be affected by how well you implement these tactics.

Distributive bargaining has been criticized for unduly raising expectations since the parties will seek support from their constituencies for their inflated positions. In fact, strikes have occurred because the union executive or bargaining team has raised expectations about goals that are not possible to achieve in collective bargaining or a management team has oversold a package of concessions to their principals. Third-party intervention can help avoid these situations but fortunately they appear to be very infrequent events. As long as collective bargaining exists there will be strikes that might have been avoided by a more responsible union or management team. But collective bargaining is a manifestation of a fundamental human right—freedom of association; thus occasional excesses must be weighed against the inviolability of these rights.

Integrative Bargaining Tactics

During integrative bargaining, the parties are less likely to inflate the issues. For example, unions will probably focus more on real cases and clearly defined remedies in discussions about the health and safety of their members. A necessary component of cooperation is the sharing of information. In fact, information sharing can often be a test of commitment to a joint problem-solving approach to conflict resolution.

The form that integrative bargaining takes is different from distributive bargaining, with issues often resolved through a joint-committee structure. Unions and management typically set up joint committees on such matters as health and safety (may be required by law), pensions, and plant closures. The parties will relax the strict distributive bargaining requirement of a single spokesperson, instead involving many voices and an array of solutions rather than a single bottom line.

Intra-Team Tactics

Union and management bargaining teams represent a diversity of interests. For example, on the management team there might be line managers concerned about more flexibility, financial executives focusing on costs, human resources managers concerned about recruitment, and a chief spokesperson whose job is to produce a settlement that satisfies all of these interests. On the union team, for example, there might be a member whose priority is the pension plan, another who is stressing wages, a member who wants improvements in the maternity leave contract provisions, and one who wants better job security.

The teams within union and management groups might use the team caucus to resolve differences over which issues to drop off the table and which to keep. Negotiators must take into account the mandates that their teams have been given. In the union's caucus, the spokesperson will probably attempt to resolve by consensus but ultimately will rely on a democratic majority to decide on priorities. Special interests that lack strong constituent support will probably not make it into the final settlement package. The union spokesperson will have to represent the union on the issues that affect only the administration of the union's affairs (e.g., dues deduction).

Building Trust Tactics

Trust in the labour–management relationship cannot be achieved overnight. But clearly, parties who trust each other's word will have a higher chance of positive outcomes in collective bargaining. Unfortunately, there is no easy formula for creating trust. If there are meetings between high-level management and labour officials during the term of the agreement and if they are used creatively to bring forward issues of common concern, using a problem-solving approach, then these away-from-the-table meetings can help to build trust.

Examples of meeting discussion topics might include the following:

- management plans to introduce new technology;
- union concerns about delays in the grievance process;
- surpluses or deficits in group benefits plans; and
- firm policies on such issues as hiring and retention.

A Collective Bargaining Model

The Katz, Kochan, and Hicks (KKH) collective bargaining model provides an economic explanation of collective bargaining outcomes (Katz & Kochan, 2000). It is limited, therefore, to conflict that is derived from wages, benefits, and other monetary issues in collective bargaining. In reality, however, disputes arise over a range of nonmonetary issues, including union recognition, union security (union dues and membership requirements), outsourcing, and union roles in promotions, transfers, and layoffs. On the other hand, in the vast majority of strikes, economic issues are important issues in dispute.

In Scenario 1 below, we will assume that the parties have the same expectations about the outcome of a strike. We will also assume that all monetary issues can be aggregated into a wage-dollar-per-hour amount. In our example, both parties have the same expectations: that a strike would increase the total monetary value of the union contract to a $10 per hour wage (see Figure 7.1). At W(Es), the expected strike wage, the union expected wage outcome of W(Esu) is equal to the management expected wage of W(Esm).

In Scenario 1, employees estimate the cost of a strike per worker at $0.50 per hour (Wu). This is calculated by aggregating the total losses in pay less the costs of strike pay and other income earned during the strike and converting that to an hourly rate. Management makes a similar forecast based on losses from a strike (lost production, length of strike, etc.) converted to a wage of $0.40 per hour (Wm).

FIGURE 7.1

Scenario 1: Parties Have Same Expectations

Wage Line

$W(Es) \blacktriangleright$ $10.00

$W(Es)$ = expected strike wage $\{W(Esu) = W(Esm)\}$

For management the estimated costs of a strike are added to the expected strike wage to produce a bottom line of $10.40 (see Figure 7.2). This is the highest-cost package that management will offer to avoid a strike. For ease of presentation all costs (wages, benefits, vacation, etc.) are expressed in wage units (i.e., dollars per hour). Similarly, the union deducts its costs of striking from the expected wage to produce a bottom-line cost package of $9.50 per hour. The range between the parties' bottom lines creates a **contract zone**.

In Scenario 2, the parties have widely different expectations of what a strike outcome might be (see Figure 7.3). The union predicts that a strike would produce a package costing $10.50 per hour. Management, on the other hand, forecasts a package worth $9 per hour. Now, if union and management factor in the same costs of striking as in Scenario 1, there is a gap between the parties' bottom lines. The union will not go lower than $10 per hour and management will offer no more than $9.40 per hour to avoid a strike.

contract zone

exists if each side's bottom line overlaps; in other words, to avoid a strike or lockout, management will offer more and the union will accept less than the point where their negotiating positions intersect

FIGURE 7.2

Scenario 1: Same Expectations Showing Contract Zone

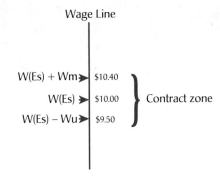

Wage Line

$W(Es) + Wm \blacktriangleright$ $10.40
$W(Es) \blacktriangleright$ $10.00 $\}$ Contract zone
$W(Es) - Wu \blacktriangleright$ $9.50

$W(Es)$ = expected strike wage $\{W(Esu) = W(Esm)\}$

FIGURE 7.3

Scenario 2: Parties Have Divergent Expectations

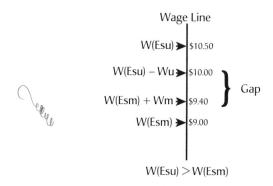

Wage Line

W(Esu) ➤	$10.50
W(Esu) – Wu ➤	$10.00
W(Esm) + Wm ➤	$9.40
W(Esm) ➤	$9.00

} Gap

$W(Esu) > W(Esm)$

The fact that the parties are able to freely negotiate a settlement about 95 percent of the time when they have a right to strike or lock out supports the existence of a contract zone most of the time. It is instructive, however, to examine the conditions that may give rise to divergent expectations as described in Scenario 2.

New Relationship or Negotiators

If the parties are negotiating a first contract or are new to the bargaining relationship, they are more likely to have unrealistic expectations about what a strike may produce. To reduce the probability of conflict in these cases, the parties may benefit from third-party intervention. Mediators and conciliators may assist by reducing the parties' expectations (see also Chapter 9). It may be that distributive bargaining would be less successful in avoiding strikes where expectations diverge. We will also learn below that more cooperative forms of negotiations such as interest-based bargaining are more common during first agreement negotiations. Finally, it is noteworthy that most jurisdictions in Canada have legislated arbitration in the special circumstances of first contract negotiations.

Changing Economic Conditions

Divergent expectations can occur because economic conditions for the organization or the economy are rapidly changing. If, for example, the organization has a number of large orders cancelled or if inflation takes a sudden upturn, the parties' expectations may diverge. Third-party intervention may also help to reduce unrealistic expectations. In extreme cases, such as the oil crisis in the 1970s that produced rapid inflation and a severe recession, incomes policies (wage and price controls) were instituted.

The Triangle of Pressures

In any negotiations, a deadline may be necessary to pressure the parties into a settlement. In collective bargaining, there is always a deadline imposed on the

FIGURE 7.4

Triangle of Pressures

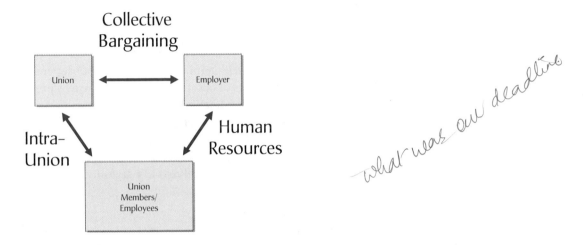

Collective Bargaining

Union ↔ Employer

Intra-Union

Human Resources

Union Members/ Employees

what was our deadline

parties by provincial or federal legislation. By serving notice to bargain and completing the conciliation or mediation steps, the union (or management) can place itself in a legal strike (or lockout) position. Just the potential of this happening creates pressure on the parties. Even when no strike mandate has been obtained or no discussion of a lockout has taken place, the parties are always aware of the potential of a strike or lockout. Their behaviour in collective bargaining will be affected by this reality. Thus, there are pressures on the parties throughout the bargaining process that affect their desire to settle. To be a more effective negotiator, it is important that the negotiator appreciate the pressures on the other party and understand the strengths and weaknesses of both parties.

We have grouped the pressures of bargaining into three broad categories of relationships that form a triangle: union–employer, employer–employee, and union–employee (see Figure 7.4). The union–employer relationship depicted in Figure 7.4 is simply the traditional collective bargaining process. Employer–employee relations are referred to today as human resources management. Finally, the relationship between the union, its members, and all employees in the bargaining unit is called the "intra-union dynamics" of collective bargaining. The next section hones in on these three categories of pressures, starting with the traditional labour–management relationship.

Union–Employer Pressures

Pressures on the Firm

In the traditional union–management collective bargaining relationship, the potential of a strike may put pressure on the firm because of the potential loss of sales, revenue, profits, and market share; decreased stock prices; bad publicity; etc.

The firm may relieve some of this pressure by *stockpiling*, or building up inventory. To the extent possible, it will have a plan to shift production to alternative sites. All this depends on the level of competition in the market for the firm's goods or services (discussed in Chapter 3). In the public sector, governments may ensure that collective agreements expire in non-election years, although governments are not above exploiting collective bargaining with their own employees as an election issue.

A firm's ability to withstand a strike may also depend on its debt load. The lower the fixed costs of operating the plant, the less pressure there will be on it during a strike. The likelihood of losing some market share also raises the spectre of uncertainty. A strike is a venture into the unknown, especially if there is no prior history. Every strike has an element of unpredictability to it. How will the bottom line be affected? How long will the strike last? What will it take to get a settlement? Buyers like stability of supply, and uncertainty is their enemy (see IR Today 7.1).

IR Today 7.1

Quebec Prosecutors, Government Lawyers on Strike

QUEBEC—Quebec's 1,400 government lawyers and Crown prosecutors walked off the job Tuesday in a bid to seek better working conditions and a 40 per cent pay hike, but the unprecedented legal strike left the government unfazed.

The Quebec government said it is willing to make some concessions but won't budge on the most contentious issue: salaries.

The lawyers and Crown prosecutors argue they are underpaid—between 30 and 40 per cent below the Canadian average—and are seeking an increase in salaries to keep up with their colleagues from other provinces.

The prosecutors also say they are overworked and have asked the government to hire some 200 new prosecutors to meet the demand.

"We are offering some catching up, but not 40 per cent—it's impossible. Nonetheless, it's a very generous offer," provincial Treasury Board President Michelle Courchesne said Tuesday.

Premier Jean Charest and Justice Minister Jean-Marc Fournier also pleaded with negotiators for the attorneys to get back to the bargaining table.

"We can't have 30 years of catching up instantly," Fournier said. "We are doing everything we can with the means we've got."

Negotiations broke down Monday night after the lawyers rejected the government's offer that included a salary catch-up of about 10 to 12 per cent and a commitment to hire 60 prosecutors.

Some 500 of the striking lawyers and Crown prosecutors marched to the national assembly Tuesday, chanting and holding up signs saying: "Least paid in the country."

Government lawyers and Crown prosecutors in Quebec top out at $102,000 a year, while the Canadian average salary for lawyers is $140,000. In Ontario, Crown prosecutors can earn as much as $196,000.

Across the province, lawyers held picket lines in front of courthouses to get their message across.

"Without the salary, we can't draw the people with experience and keep them here. We don't have the people to do the work and because of that, the system suffers, victims suffer, society suffers," said Emily Moreau, 27, a McGill University law graduate who joined the Gatineau, Que. Crown's office in August, 2009.

She noted working conditions have been deteriorating in her office for years. Crown prosecutors, she said, are paid for only 35 hours a week—there's no overtime—even though the job demands much more time.

"We're prepared to be out here as long as it takes," she said outside the Gatineau courthouse. "We have a feeling we might be here for a while."

The lawyers said they walked out reluctantly but were forced to do it because the government didn't negotiate in good faith.

"The government negotiators didn't have the mandate to discuss salaries, they didn't have any mandate to negotiate anything. That's not what I call negotiating in good faith," said Christian Leblanc, president of the Quebec Crown prosecutors association.

The government is concerned because the strike threatens to paralyze the province's legal system.

Courchesne said Tuesday it is too early to talk about a special law to force the lawyers to come back to work, but acknowledged the strike can't go on for too long.

The striking lawyers are worried their working conditions will be imposed on them.

"We are watching a play unfold as the government pretended to negotiate last fall and literally pushed us toward a strike to make it easier for them to decree our working conditions in a return to work law," Leblanc said.

Strikes by government lawyers are not common in Canada and legal ones are even less so. Quebec prosecutors were granted the right to strike in 2003 and they are using it for the first time following illegal strikes in 1986 and in 2002.

Quebec's legal system was already backlogged, a situation that will only be worsened by the strike involving some 1,000 lawyers who work for the provincial government and 450 Crown prosecutors.

According to Statistics Canada, the period it takes to settle a court case in Quebec is already one of the longest in the country, at 184 days.

The strike is expected to delay court cases and could also prevent the provincial legislature—which resumed sitting Tuesday—from making changes to laws or passing new legislation.

During the strike, criminal cases of people in custody will proceed. But in all other cases, prosecutors will be asking the court for adjournments. Many trials will also have to be rescheduled.

Source: Marianne White, "Quebec prosecutors, government lawyers on strike," *Postmedia News*, 8 February 2011; with a file from the *Ottawa Citizen*. Material reprinted with the express permission of POSTMEDIA NEWS, a division of Postmedia Network, Inc. Retrieved from http://www.globalmontreal.com/Quebec+prosecutors+government+lawyers+strike/4243067/story.html.

Management bargaining teams might be under pressure from both local managers and central or corporate management. For example, line managers will have their own agendas that they will want addressed at the table. They might want previous grievance losses reversed through collective bargaining. Corporate management, on the other hand, might choose from a range of cooperative to more aggressive strategies according to the demands of the business. In the paper industry, for example, some firms have tried a strategy of cooperating with unions, while others have taken hard-line bargaining approaches, often taking long strikes by using replacement workers (Dachis & Hebdon, 2010; Duffy & Johnson, 2009; Eaton & Kriesky, 1998). Local management teams may negotiate under rigid constraints on costs imposed from some central or corporate authority. In the public sector, financial controls over lower levels of government are typical (e.g., provinces over municipalities and school boards).

Public-sector employers will be under different kinds of pressures. The pressures on bargaining teams from line managers and central authorities will likely parallel those of private-sector firms. But since public services are very labour-intensive, payrolls will be a high proportion of total costs. Thus, public employers are likely to save money during a strike. The pressures they face will be more political than financial.

Pressures on the Union

Since unions exist to benefit their members, a strike can put this fundamental purpose on the line. There are potentially seriously damaging consequences for the union as an institution. A long strike with little or no gains may have a major impact on the strike fund, future organizing, and even the continued existence of the union.

Particularly when there are changes in economic conditions (e.g., increases in inflation), unions must deal with changing member expectations in bargaining. Unions are democracies and must listen to their members. Moreover, if a strike is to be avoided, the contract must be ratified by these same members. How should unions assist in adjusting member expectations? Critics might answer that they shouldn't—the union's role is not to dampen expectations. We believe that nearly all unions support a collective bargaining model based on realistic achievements at the table, not conflict for its own sake. Thus, there are times when union leaders and bargaining teams must explain the art of the possible to the rank and file or, alternatively, when the union members have to remind the leadership of their priorities. The tension between union leaders and members often plays out in the union negotiating team caucus meetings.

Before making its last offer, management will usually insist that the union's bargaining team unanimously recommend it to its membership. If there are dissenters, there is a higher probability that the last offer will be rejected. A rejected offer may increase the likelihood of strike and undermine the union's authority to negotiate a settlement at the bargaining table. Ideally, if expectations have to be lowered, the union leadership will try to do this at the time of setting proposals. Mediators can also play a useful role in explaining reality to a union team that has inflated expectations about what is possible when there is a disconnect between the union's leadership and its membership.

Unions also face pressures from settlements achieved by rival unions. Ross (1948) coined the phrase "orbits of coercive comparison" to describe the relative standard used by competing unions in collective bargaining. The final pressure here is derived from the active tactics and strategies of management. The inventory buildup discussed above may put pressure directly on employees (speedups, overtime, more shifts, schedule changes, etc.) and indirectly on the union by sending a signal that the firm can sustain a long strike.

Pressures on Union Members

The pressures on individual employees and union members[2] to avoid a strike are many. Union members know that strike pay usually comes after a waiting period of one or two weeks. When it finally arrives, it will normally pay only for subsistence items. The loss of income during a strike can adversely affect an employee's debt situation. Employees may have mortgage or rent payments; loan payments for cars, appliances, or schooling; or upcoming expenses for a scheduled vacation. There may be pressures from the union and other members for strike solidarity, and family pressures against striking. However, studies show that communities with a strong union presence often rally behind striking employees. Employees about to take a strike vote will be feeling psychological stress from the fear of the unknown and the insecurity a strike presents: How long will the strike last? Will the family survive financially? Will I have a job when the strike is over?

Employer–Union Member/Employee Pressures

Planning for a possible strike poses a significant challenge to the management team. Those responsible for production will do everything possible to maintain production and sales during a strike. This may include a plan to use managers and supervisors to sustain production and to hire temporary replacement employees. In British Columbia and Quebec there are laws limiting the use of replacement workers in the event of a strike or lockout.

In the pre-strike period management may attempt to stockpile inventory to keep up sales during a strike. During this buildup period, managers may face increasing discontent and resistance from employees. Employee dissatisfaction is often manifested as grievances, slowdowns, or other individual or collective actions designed to disrupt production.

Union–Union Member Pressures

Before and during a strike there are often powerful tensions between the union leadership and its members. If the leaders (national or international office, local executive, and bargaining team) can see a settlement coming, they will apply pressure on members to prepare for this eventuality. They might hold information meetings to explain the issues, use third-party procedures (discussed in Chapter 9), or work at lowering expectations—actions all designed to prepare the way for settlement and avoid a strike. Union leaders must lead, but they also have to get reelected if they wish to remain in office, so they have to be sensitive to the condition and mood of their members.

If, on the other hand, a strike is likely, a very different strategy will be adopted. The union leaders will prepare for this probability by building support in the membership for their bargaining position. They will prepare a contingency strike plan that includes a strike policy covering everything from the production of picket signs to the allocation of additional strike pay to cases of family hardship.

Bargaining Step by Step

RPC 7.2

1. *Management and the union prepare for bargaining.*

- Obtain a mandate from the constituents.
  a. Management is given its mandate from the corporate or strategic level.
  b. Union holds membership meeting to establish bargaining proposals and elect negotiating team.

- Management solicits input from line managers—this includes a grievance analysis.
- Both union and management examine comparators—for example, industry settlement patterns.

2. *The union or management serves notice to bargain.*

   - The parties prepare their proposals to amend the current collective agreement based on constituent input and research.
   - Before the current collective agreement expires, the management or union may give written notice to start negotiations for renewal agreement—the notice period is usually required by legislation.

3. *The parties meet.*

   - The parties agree to meet at a mutually acceptable location and time.
   - The purpose of this first meeting is to establish the ground rules for bargaining, including a timetable for future meetings; to introduce the teams to each other; to explain the proposed changes to the agreement; and to provide a rationale.

4. *Each party communicates its priorities.*

   - Each side provides a written list of its priority issues together with a rationale. Sometimes the priorities are indicated by the order of the list. Other guides to the importance attached to each issue are the amount of time spent on the rationale and potency of language each party uses.
   - This is the art of negotiations—skilled negotiators are able to indicate priorities with a single sentence. If, for example, the management negotiator responds to a union proposal with "We cannot do what you want; our hands are tied," this will likely be a major obstacle to a settlement.
   - On the other hand, if the management response is "We will take a look at it," the negotiator will likely test his or her committee to see if there are objections to the union proposal.

5. *Momentum builds for a settlement.*

   - The parties will often combine issues into packages. These are small groups of easily resolved issues that involve dropping union or management proposals for some modest gains.
   - A technique that is used at this stage and throughout negotiations is the caucus meeting—both management and union teams will frequently break away from the bargaining table to meet as an individual team to assess moves and countermoves.

6. *The contract zone is reached.*

   - If a settlement is possible in direct talks, then there must be an overlap in bottom lines; this is defined as a contract zone.
   - At this stage, each negotiator should have an idea of the other side's bottom line.

7. *Settlement or impasse?*

- If there is a contract zone and the parties have good negotiating skills, a settlement is reached in direct talks.
- If there is no contract zone or the parties lack the necessary negotiating skills, negotiations may reach an impasse.
- If there is an impasse, the parties may seek the services of a conciliator or mediator to assist them in bridging the remaining gaps.

8. *Ratification.*

ratification

the process by which each party approves the settlement reached at the bargaining tables by the management and union teams

- When a settlement occurs before or after an impasse, an agreement will have to undergo **ratification** by both sides. This unratified agreement between the two bargaining teams is referred to as a *tentative settlement*, because the parties must each approve it for it to take effect.

The Dos and Don'ts of Bargaining

Our first question is: What issues should be discussed first at the table and why? Students often answer this question by asserting that it would be logical that the parties start with the tough issues first. After all, if the hard ones can be successfully tackled, then the rest of the issues will fall into place. Then, assuming that economic issues are high on each party's list, it might be logical to start with the economic issues and end with the noneconomic ones.

There are at least two major problems with starting with the tough issues. The first problem is tactical. If the parties cannot generate any movement on the tough issues, talks could simply collapse, producing a premature impasse caused by the failure of the parties to fully understand each other's positions and to psychologically prepare for compromise. Starting with lesser issues can produce positive momentum, getting negotiations headed in the right direction as progress is made on the minor issues.

The second problem is more strategic. Both sides may have important nonmonetary issues that they want dealt with. The union might want improvement in job security; management, for example, might want more flexibility in scheduling weekend work via a reduction in the minimum notice period. If wages and benefits are resolved, the parties are likely to encounter difficulties in generating support for any noneconomic issues. To put it simply, neither side will want to lock out or strike over issues of lesser importance.

To illustrate the folly of settling the highest priority issues first, we present an example from a class bargaining simulation. A student bargaining team drew a line in the sand over the issue of cleaning the washrooms. It is highly unlikely that a union would get membership support for a strike over this type of issue if all other issues have been settled—especially all economic ones. A better strategy, given the minor cost nature of this issue, might be to include it in an appropriate package that includes some economic issues. Timing may be everything. By linking its resolution to more important economic issues, the union may use its leverage on wages to achieve this relatively minor issue of health and hygiene.

For a typical example of a round of negotiations in which the most important priorities were presented as the last issues, see IR Today 7.2.

At Auto Talks, Women Grabbed the Front Seats

When union leader Buzz Hargrove sauntered out of a tough bargaining session at Ford the other day, he heard a familiar voice behind him.

"Put two women in charge and they'll get it done," one of his top negotiators, Peggy Nash, said to chief Ford negotiator Stacey Allerton Firth as they walked down a Sheraton Centre hallway.

The women chuckled, and Hargrove, head of the Canadian Auto Workers, smiled. "Yes, they're right," he said later.

The two women had just found a way around a nagging money issue at the negotiating table to put another piece of the puzzle in place for a new contract.

They had also broken new ground in high-octane auto negotiations, a male bastion replete with decades of screaming, fist pounding and even the occasional scrap punctuated by a knuckle sandwich.

For the first time in Canada, two women were in the front seat of Big Three auto bargaining. They played a significant role in negotiating the tentative contract at Ford that set a pattern for the other auto giants, General Motors and DaimlerChrysler.

Both have participated in major auto bargaining before, but never with this much influence and so much at stake.

The atmosphere in this year's bargaining was noticeably different than a generation ago, according to officials familiar with talks.

On one side of the table was Nash, a former passenger agent at Air Canada who quickly took an interest in unions and women's rights, eventually rising to the CAW's inner circle. On the other side was Allerton Firth, a Ford labour relations veteran who became the first woman vice-president of human resources at Ford of Canada in 2003. The appointment meant she would automatically become the company's lead negotiator in contract talks this year.

And there they were—two married women juggling family life sitting across from each other at a bargaining table in a downtown hotel dealing with issues affecting millions of dollars and thousands of workers.

"I didn't really see gender as an issue," Nash said. "It's a different era. People now just want to see if you can do the job. That's the bottom line."

Allerton Firth added in a separate interview she also didn't give gender much thought in negotiations because both sides had to focus on resolving major issues including how to deal with pending job losses. Ford is losing money and needed to cut production because of sliding sales.

Insiders said one or two local bargaining committees still experienced heated arguments, but a lot of the macho nature of past bargaining on both sides had disappeared.

Hargrove, who has bargained contracts for more than 30 years, said he remembers occasions when chauvinism ran rampant. Some previous negotiators felt women had no place at the bargaining table or an auto plant, he said.

Although Hargrove didn't recall any CAW and Big Three negotiators resorting to fisticuffs, he remembers members of union committees trying to settle disputes physically among themselves after knock-down, drag-'em-out debates.

Nash said there are still some situations where people stereotype women as not tough or confrontational enough for contract bargaining.

"It's a Victorian notion of women as delicate flowers," added Nash, who has fought for more programs for women in the workplace.

She remembers a time when negotiators would ask her, "What's a woman doing in a job like this? . . . Don't your kids miss you? . . . How does your husband feel about you being away so much?"

It left her with the impression they felt she was abandoning her responsibilities as a mother.

Nash said bargaining was more of "a boys' club" a generation ago.

"I don't mean to be disrespectful but it was a different time and the bargaining style was different."

Nash said although there is still some occasional yelling as nerves become frayed and frustration sets in during all-night bargaining sessions, "the decibel level has gone down."

Interest-Based Bargaining (IBB)

What Is It?

Interest-based or cooperative bargaining is just one of the many labels given to integrative bargaining. In this section, we define **interest-based bargaining (IBB)**, discuss its usage by management and labour, and examine the conditions under which it might be most appropriate to use it in collective bargaining.

Economists describe distributive or competitive bargaining as a zero-sum game. One party's gain is the other party's loss. In theory, IBB is a positive-sum game, where the size of the pie may be increased. Hence IBB is often called *win-win* or *mutual gains negotiations*. Other labels for IBB include *principled, integrative, cooperative, positive-sum,* or *collaborative negotiations*. An early form of IBB, called "relations by objectives" (RBO), was developed by the U.S. Federal Mediation and Conciliation Service in 1977 (Cutcher-Gershenfeld, Kochan & Wells, 2001). Designed as a special form of preventive mediation during the term of a collective agreement to improve the union–management relationship, RBO was used in high-conflict relationships, such as those involving a strike aftermath or an unusually high rate of grievances.

Modern-day IBB is often based on four assumptions (Corry, 2000):

- both labour and management can win;
- each can assist the other to win;

interest-based bargaining (IBB)

a cooperative form of bargaining in which the parties focus more on the interests of the parties and not on the exaggerated positions; also called *principled, integrative, cooperative, positive-sum,* or *collaborative negotiations*

- open discussions expand areas of mutual interests; and
- decision making is based more on standards for evaluating options than on power.

Its main elements include (Fisher & Ury, 1981):

- a focus on issues, not personalities;
- a problem-solving approach;
- a free exchange of information;
- an emphasis on interests, not positions;
- the creation of options to satisfy mutual and separate interests; and
- an evaluation of options with objective standards.

To illustrate how IBB causes a shift in focus from positions to interests, we present the following example. Suppose the union proposes a no-contracting-out clause in the collective agreement. The intent of the proposal would be to prevent management from contracting out existing bargaining unit jobs during the life of the agreement. The position advanced by the union is apparently absolute and inflexible. Management's counterposition, on the other hand, is that it will under no circumstances give up its right to contract out work. To survive in a highly competitive environment, management needs the flexibility to outsource. The parties appear to be on a collision course on this issue alone.

Under an IBB process, the parties would be asked to shift their focus away from their extreme and seemingly intractable positions. They would be asked to reveal their real interests. What is the real interest of the union and its members? What is management's real interest on this issue? In a more open process in which both sides are willing to explore solutions, the union reveals that its real priority is job security and the protection of its members' jobs. Management reveals that its real interest is flexibility. It has no direct plans to outsource jobs, but to remain competitive in the future, it cannot rule out this possibility.

A matrix of options that shows the positions, interests, and creative solutions that are revealed using an IBB problem-solving approach is set out in Table 7.2. A simple clause that prevents layoffs but not contracting out would appear to satisfy the interests of both management and labour. Compensation may also be included. Another option is to limit the outsourcing to work not currently preformed by current union members.

TABLE 7.2

Contracting Out Matrix of Solutions

Position/Interest	Union	Management
Hard-line position	No contracting out	Contracting out is a management right
Interest	Protection of members' jobs	Flexibility
IBB solutions	There will be no layoffs as a result of contracting out.	
	Employees affected by contracting out will be compensated.	
	Contracting out will apply to new work only.	

IBB Steps

1. Identify the problem.

   - Convene frequent sessions by mutual agreement.
   - Develop agenda items that have joint problem-solving potential.
   - Formulate negotiation subjects as specific problems rather than general concerns.

2. Search for alternative solutions.

   - Give adequate notice of negotiation times.
   - Engage in informal exploratory discussion before making formal proposals.
   - Tackle easy-to-resolve issues first.

3. Systematically compare alternatives.

   - Accurately report preferences.
   - Arrange (e.g., combine) proposals to make patterns of agreement more visible.
   - Consider remedial actions that improve the relationship to be part of the general solution.

A criticism of Fisher and Ury's (1981) application of win-win negotiations in collective bargaining is that it narrowly assumes a dichotomy between integrative and distributive processes. It is our view that this is a false dichotomy and that cooperation and competition must coexist in every labour–management relationship. In fact, some scholars argue that cooperation and competition are part of the same dynamic (Kolb & Bartunek, 1992). Moreover, as we discussed above, collective bargaining often involves integrative, distributive, and hybrid issues at the same time. IBB may be inappropriate, therefore, where issues are inherently distributive. We will explore this further below.

To summarize, for integrative bargaining to be successful, there should be a free exchange of information, a problem-solving approach, an understanding of each other's needs and objectives, and a sufficient level of trust.

Why Is IBB So Difficult to Achieve?

Mixed-Issue Bargaining

Any round of collective bargaining will have a mix of inherently distributive and integrative issues. As discussed, wages are distributive while the issue of employee health and safety has integrative potential. Hybrid issues such as technological change and pensions have both distributive and integrative components. Given the complex nature of collective bargaining issues, it is sometimes difficult in the heat of battle to fully exploit integrative potential. Negotiators who prefer a highly adversarial style are most likely to ignore the integrative potential in integrative or hybrid issues. But to achieve optimal outcomes, negotiators need to adapt their tactics to meet the needs dictated by the mix of issues. This may be easier said than done.

Bargaining History

The parties may have had a long history of adversarial negotiations characterized by conflict and a lack of trust. In this climate, it is common for bargaining positions to harden. Additionally, there are unions who, for ideological reasons, oppose all forms of cooperation. For these unions, to collaborate is to be co-opted by management.

Theory

Another difficulty in achieving integrative bargaining follows from theory. Unless there is complete certainty that the other side will bargain in a cooperative manner throughout the negotiations, the risk of adopting such a strategy may be too great. This is because the party that switches to distributive bargaining during negotiations will likely obtain a much greater outcome at the expense of the other party. The cooperative style of multiple spokespersons, information sharing, etc., will not work against a disciplined hardline approach. Thus, unless there is ironclad agreement to the negotiating rules, there is a strong incentive for a party to switch from an integrative to a distributive style.

Does IBB Work?

Studies show that it works in specific sectors. It works in union–management negotiations in such diverse industries as libraries, airlines, and railways (Hargrove, 2010; Miller, Farmer & Peters, 2010). On a national basis, two scholars and a U.S. Federal Conciliation Mediation Services official conducted a national survey of union and management negotiators to determine the usage of IBB (Cutcher-Gershenfeld, Kochan & Wells, 2001). At the heart of this important research is the notion that process matters; that is, the way negotiations are conducted affects outcomes. The authors frame their research in terms of the following provocative questions:

- Is IBB an important innovation to allowing collective bargaining to keep pace with other organizational innovations (e.g., team-based work systems)?
- Alternatively, is IBB a new label for an old process called "integrative bargaining" and a well-crafted ploy to undercut the bargaining power of unions?

They argue that this important debate is fuelled by anecdotal evidence. The key element in the controversy is whether IBB can produce "mutual gains" outcomes across the full range of issues of interest to the parties. They assume that a mutual gains outcome must be viewed as a gain by both management and labour; otherwise, it is a product of the relative power of the parties. Hence, in the study, management and union negotiators are asked a series of questions about the same bargaining outcomes on a range of issues.

Some of the salient questions posed to both manager and union negotiators about IBB are shown together with some survey results in Figure 7.5.

FIGURE 7.5

IBB Survey Results: U.S., 1996

Are you familiar with IBB or win-win or mutual gains bargaining?

62.6% of management and 77.2% of union said yes

Have you employed IBB?

35.4% of management and 48.9% of union said yes

Do you prefer it?

79.8% of management and 59.6% of union said yes

As the authors indicate, these attitudes can be interpreted two ways. On the one hand, these are relatively high acceptance rates, but a significant number of negotiators did not like IBB (about 20% of managers and 40% of union). If the groups that were not aware of IBB are included, 26.2% of management and 24.8% of union negotiators prefer IBB overall.

Source: Cutcher-Gershenfeld, Kochan & Wells, 2001.

Interestingly, there were significant differences between female and male negotiators and large and small bargaining units. Female negotiators were more likely to prefer IBB, and the management–labour gap in attitude to IBB was wider in large bargaining units. Also, negotiators in first contract situations were more likely to prefer IBB.

The authors compared contract outcomes for labour and management who prefer IBB with those who do not. Labour and management who both prefer IBB were more likely to negotiate a mutual gains outcome for only one issue—increased worker input in decision making. On all other issues, the pattern reflected a power outcome rather than a mutual gains approach. For example, work-rule flexibility and benefit reductions were more likely outcomes among union negotiators who prefer IBB. The authors conclude, "Thus, adopting a more problem-solving approach by unions will make them more vulnerable to concessions or management power tactics" (Cutcher-Gershenfeld, Kochan & Wells, 2001).

Here is a summary of the key results:

- Highly distributive issues do not work in a mutual gains approach.
- A high degree of lead negotiators are familiar with IBB and have used it.
- Union negotiators rate it lower than managers do.
- On average, female and newer negotiators give IBB a higher rating.
- IBB is a relatively new innovation that is still at an experimental stage and is not fully accepted by either labour and management.

IBB appears to have taken a permanent place in the arsenal of labour–management negotiations. However, its apparent failure to produce results that are seen by both parties as mutual gains suggests that adversarial bargaining has not been replaced, nor is it likely to be in the near future. Today's negotiator needs to know both integrative and distributive negotiating styles.

Under What Conditions Does IBB Work or Not?

To help determine under which conditions IBB works and under which it doesn't, let us look at two Canadian articles, one that examined the impact of IBB (Paquet, Gaétan & Bergeron, 2000) and another that evaluated twenty-four relations by objectives (RBO) programs (Hebdon & Mazerolle, 1995). Two of the authors of the first article are academics who perform training in IBB for Quebec private- and public-sector firms and unions. In their paper, they revisit several of their own cases to evaluate the outcome of negotiations after the training was given. Results are compared with matched samples of negotiations that did not use IBB. According to the research, IBB produced a broader range of changes to the collective agreement and was more innovative than adversarial negotiations. This is consistent with a problem-solving approach. However, there were more union concessions and fewer union gains with IBB. The latter finding reinforces the results of the U.S. national survey discussed above. Today's negotiator needs to know both cooperative and adversarial negotiating styles.

RBO is a form of preventive mediation first developed by the U.S. Federal Mediation and Conciliation Service in 1977. It is referred to in the Cutcher-Gershenfeld, Kochan, and Wells (2001) article as an earlier form of IBB. The problem-solving techniques used in IBB and RBO are very similar. Research on twenty-four RBO cases in school board and teacher negotiations in Ontario in the 1990s also produced mixed results. As the authors conclude,

> RBO seemed to exhibit a "half-life" effect. For example, over a period of more than three contracts, the RBO boards returned to levels of conflict above the norm for the education sector, lending support to the view that economic (or other) differences ultimately determine the relationship. However, this conclusion does not rule out RBO as a useful tool for the reduction of conflict since even a "short-run" effect can be beneficial. In addition, our definition of the short run is three rounds of bargaining; that is, a minimum of three years and a probable average of four to six years—a substantial period of time (Hebdon and Mazerolle, 1995).

The authors also noted that a return to previous high levels of conflict after RBO was due to the difficulty of institutionalizing change in the collective agreement. Like RBO, IBB involves a considerable investment in the training of both union and management bargaining teams. An obvious problem is that with the normal turnover in these teams, the full effect of IBB may be diluted over time if no automatic process is in place to provide training for new and inexperienced negotiators.

In summary, some of the conditions where IBB may be the most beneficial to the parties include the following:

- *In a crisis.* Cooperative bargaining works under crisis conditions (we are in this together). A private-sector example is the UAW and Chrysler negotiations in the 1980s, where the survival of the company was at stake. In the public sector, cooperative bargaining occurred at the local level during Ontario's economic crisis in the early 1990s (Hebdon & Warrian, 1999).

- *In an exceptionally bad relationship.* The positive effects of IBB may be difficult to sustain in the long run unless they are institutionalized in the relationship with collective agreement language and processes. IBB can be particularly effective where a bad relationship is due to a clash of personalities. It also appears to work for grievances as long as the issues in dispute are not distributive in nature.
- *Where monetary conflicts of interest do not exist.* Research shows that interest-based bargaining has a half-life effect when the issues are economic in nature and that distributive issues seldom produced a mutual gains outcome.

Thus, in collective bargaining there is a mix of what Walton and McKersie (1965) call distributive and integrative issues. Recall that distributive issues are those where win-win outcomes are almost impossible (e.g., economic issues, job security); integrative issues, in contrast, have mutual gains possibilities (e.g., health and safety, pensions). The challenge to negotiators is to realize the full potential on both types of issue. We argue that in order to do this, it is best to separate distributive from integrative issues and to isolate the integrative components of those issues that appear to be a mix of both types.

The Magna Deal

Key assumptions of the *Wagner Act* model discussed in this chapter are a formal certification process and right to strike by the union and right to lock out by management. A new collective bargaining model has emerged that fundamentally alters these key elements. It was offered to the Canadian Autoworkers in 2007 by Frank Stronach, owner of the auto parts giant Magna International Inc.—a move referred to as the "Magna deal" (Tucker & Mucalov, 2010). In a framework agreement, the CAW has agreed to give up the right to strike in all contract negotiations with Magna. In exchange for a nonadversarial organizing process, in which Magna has agreed to be neutral, the CAW has agreed to submit all contract disputes to final offer arbitration. The CAW will have the opportunity to organize some 18,000 Magna employees in 45 plants across Canada. According to Magna and the CAW, the new paradigm reflects a reality of globalization that management and labour have a common stake in competing with foreign competition and keeping jobs in Canada. The paradigm departs from the *Wagner Act* model in three key ways:

- a nonadversarial organizing procedure;
- a cooperative method of resolving conflict at work; and
- settlement of all contract disputes by final offer arbitration and not work stoppages.

To date, the CAW has only organized four of the forty-five plants, but this may be due to the difficulty of attracting new members in a recession when union organizing typically falls.

Summary

Students should understand the difference between distributive and integrative collective bargaining processes and issues. The other bargaining processes are intra-team and building trust. Intra-team occurs because of the diversity of interests on each team, and building trust is the most difficult process because of the inherent obstacles to establishing trust in labour–management relations.

To appreciate the other side's bargaining positions, it is important for negotiators to understand the pressures that they are under. These are presented in our triangle of pressures, which shows the union–management, union–employee, and management–employee relationships. In this chapter, we also examined the bargaining steps in a typical set of negotiations, including a look at the dos and don'ts.

To facilitate an understanding of the difficulties in achieving the best outcomes of collective bargaining, we examined the principles of the two contrasting bargaining styles of adversarial and win-win negotiations. The origins and elements of interest-based bargaining were studied, including the necessary conditions that ought to apply for it to be effective.

Key Terms

attitudinal structuring 211

bottom line 212

contract zone 215

distributive bargaining 210

integrative bargaining 211

interest-based bargaining (IBB) 225

intra-team (or intra-organizational) bargaining 211

ratification 223

Weblinks

Collective bargaining and workplace information (see below for details):

http://www.rhdcc-hrsdc.gc.ca/eng/labour/labour_relations/info_analysis/index.shtml

- Collective bargaining:

    ○ Agreements and settlements
    ○ Directory of labour organizations
    ○ Collective agreement provisions
    ○ Information on Canadian legislation and client services
    ○ Federal mediation and conciliation service
    ○ Preventive mediation

- Workplace information:

    ○ Wage adjustments
    ○ Current and upcoming key negotiations
    ○ Current settlements
    ○ Negotech access to settlement summaries and full-text collective agreements

- Collective agreement expiries and reopeners
- Working conditions and benefits
- Work stoppages
- Directory of labour organizations
- Union membership
- Innovative workplace practices

Collective agreements in Canada:

http://cirhr.library.utoronto.ca/research/best-ir-hr-websites/collective-agreements

The Magna deal:

- More information supporting the deal:

  http://www.caw.ca/en/3636.htm

- An opposing view by Sam Gindin, former research director of the CAW:

  http://www.socialistproject.ca/bullet/bullet065.html

RPC Icons

7.1 Provides advice to clients on the establishment, continuation, and termination of bargaining rights

- collective bargaining processes and issues
- institutions and processes (both regulatory and nonregulatory) that govern the relationship between employers and employees
- the rights and responsibilities of management and labour during the processes of organizing and negotiation

7.2 Collects and develops information required for good decision making throughout the bargaining process

- institutions and processes (both regulatory and nonregulatory) that govern the relationship between employers and employees
- the process of collective bargaining

Discussion Questions

1. What are the key differences between individual and collective bargaining?
2. What are the differences between the four subprocesses of bargaining? Why is building trust so difficult?
3. Can strikes occur when a contract zone exists? What are the weaknesses of the KKH model?
4. Why would you begin with bargaining minor issues and save the priority ones until the end of negotiations?

5. How do adversarial tactics differ from integrative ones?
6. Give examples of distributive, integrative, and hybrid issues.
7. What is interest-based bargaining? When does it work best?
8. Describe the Magna deal. Do you think this is a better model of collective bargaining than the current one? Why?

Using the Internet

The full texts of collective agreements are increasingly available on the Internet. The Centre for Industrial Relations and Human Resources, for example, provides links to full texts: **http://cirhr.library.utoronto.ca/research/best-ir-hr-websites/collective-agreements**. Find collective bargaining wage settlement trends as reported by any provincial labour department. Compare settlements this year and last year.

1. Find a current settlement of a strike or lockout in Canada. What were the issues that caused the strike?

Exercises

1. Find the full text of a collective agreement and analyze it by separating issues by type: distributive, integrative, and hybrid.
2. Take any unionized industry in Canada and analyze the pressures on the three parties to collective bargaining: management, union, and employees.

Case

The Strike at Vale, 2009–2010
Introduction
This strike was without doubt the most important strike in Canada in past several years. It was a confrontation between Vale, a mammoth multinational corporation based in Brazil, and the strong Sudbury local of one of Canada's largest and most powerful private-sector unions—the United Steelworkers. The strike lasted almost a year from July 13, 2009, to July 7, 2010.

History
Since 1966 there have been seven strikes at this same mine involving USW local 6500 and INCO. But the 2009 strike was very different from past ones in the manner described next.

> Vale continued to run and upgrade its operations both during a shutdown prior to the strike and over the subsequent twelve months. Following the precedent set by the former Canadian mining giant Falconbridge a decade earlier, Vale used its 1,200

contract staff to do maintenance, upgrading, mining, and metal processing. It then had many of its contractors hire more workers in order to ramp up production in early 2010. After upgrading and maintenance work was completed in the plant, estimates from workers inside the operation and out estimated that the mines and facilities were functioning at near 30 per cent of capacity over the course of the year-long strike. (Peters, 2010)

Globalization of the Mining Industry

- The mining industry accounted for 19 percent of exports and 55 percent of all Canadian port traffic in 2007.
- The rapid expansion of ore extraction and processed ore and metal in nickel, aluminum, and iron figured in much of this growth, with exports more than doubling in value from $20 billion in 2000 to over $50 billion dollars in 2008.

Canada: A Low-Cost Country

- With internationally "competitive" tax and finance regimes and royalty levels that are among the lowest in the world, Canada ranks with the friendliest government regimes for mining companies. This seriously limits union political effectiveness and influence on the major political parties, as well as curtails trade union opportunities to improve wages and working conditions in the sector.

The Demand for Minerals

- Three billion tonnes of ore were mined in 1980. In 2002, 5.9 billion tonnes were extracted. By 2020, the UN predicts the annual volume of ores to exceed 11.2 billion tonnes. In recent years, such rapid extraction and consumption of structural metals (iron ore, bauxite, copper, and nickel) has risen three times faster than global GDP.
- China and India's rapid industrialization has been a chief factor in this boom.
- For mining companies, economies of scale and increasing rates of extraction are now key, as a hedge against good times turning bad, or to strengthen their hand in specific metals for economic booms in contexts of resource scarcity.

The Financial Crisis, 2008

- The credit crunch that began in late 2008 led to prices plunging as the world economy slumped and China's red-hot growth cooled off. As prices fell, steelmakers cut production, dramatically reducing demand for iron ore.
- Mining companies suffered a rapid decline in prices and returns.
- Estimates of the top companies' earnings before tax and depreciation fell by a third, though net profit margins remained above 15 percent over the course of 2008–2009.

The Parties—Management and Union

Vale

- By 2010, mining had been completely transformed. Inco and Falconbridge, along with hundreds of other small and medium sized mining operations, had completely disappeared.
- Vale expanded more than twentyfold, and climbed the ladder of globally diversified mining giants.
- It was in this context of rapid global growth and ever-expanding profits that Vale entered Canada in 2007, buying Inco Ltd. for $20 billion and establishing an independent but integrated corporate subsidiary, initially called "Vale-Inco" before it was shortened to "Vale."
- Vale adopted a more complex corporate strategy than a number of the other diversified mining giants. It set up operations around the world through direct ownership, joint ventures, and independent subsidiaries. Involved in everything from mining to railways, shipping to steelmaking, pulp and paper to reforestation and road building, the Brazilian corporation's goal was not only mining diversification but corporate diversification.

Vale Reaction to Financial Crisis

- Measures mining multinationals took to remain profitable during the recession were to cut capital expenditures, temporarily shut down operations, eliminate jobs, and in Vale's case, demand concessions from its workers.
- Vale-Inco reacted to the decline in nickel prices by

  - cutting 900 jobs at its global nickel operations, including 423 in Canada and 261 in Sudbury;
  - announcing plans to shut down the Sudbury operations in June and July in an effort to reduce supply; and
  - letting go former executives and upper managers prior to launching a much wider restructuring initiative.

Vale The United Steelworkers

- The USW is the largest private-sector union in both Canada and North America, with more than 225,000 members in Canada and more than 800,000 members continent-wide.
- Members work in nearly every industry and in every job imaginable, in all regions of the country—call centres and credit unions, mines and manufacturing plants, offices and oil refineries, restaurants and rubber plants, sawmills and steel mills, and security companies, as well as in nursing homes, legal clinics, social agencies, and universities.
- The USW goes global. Workers Uniting, representing three million members, is the international union created by Unite, the biggest union in the United Kingdom and Republic of Ireland, and the United Steelworkers, North America's largest private-sector union (**http://www.usw.ca/union/uniting**).

Union Strategy

- The USW believed that by adopting a traditional strategy of coordinating three of its Canadian collective agreements with Vale to expire in the summer of 2009, with a fourth ending in January 2010, the union would have more than enough leverage for a "wait it out" strategy against Vale.
- This would leave the union ample opportunity to bargain a common agreement for all three workplaces that would have few concessions.
- The USW believed that such a withdrawal of labour power from Vale's facilities across Canada would be more than enough to pressure the company to step back from its concessionary demands.
- The USW relied on public support and member mobilization.
- Traditional financial support from other unions, and community rallies and events, would raise the visibility of the strike and put pressure on the company to settle.

Bargaining Process Issues

A lack of trust and respect:

- The Vale strike was notable for the degree of acrimony involved.
  - The company routinely launched lawsuits and court cases proliferated.
  - Vale hired private security forces and burdened the municipality with millions of dollars in police protection and bylaw hearings.
  - Vale commonly neglected to set any dates to meet with the locals or make any promises to negotiate, let alone compromise.

- Vale demands initially included
  - a freeze in wages (though a cost-of-living clause was continued);
  - a sharp reduction in the miner nickel bonus to 15 percent of the employee's base pay; and
  - a switch in the company's pension plan from defined benefit to defined contribution.

- For workers, these concessions amounted to tens of thousands of dollars in lost income, a far less secure and far smaller pension, and the loss of jobs. The capping of the bonus was among the most contentious issues. Under the previous collective agreement, the miner's nickel bonus had no maximum limit and kicked in once nickel prices rose above $2.50 per pound.

  - As nickel prices were regularly low in the 1980s and 1990s, the bonus was often small, costing the company little.
  - But at the start of this decade, with the dramatic rise in the price of nickel from $3 to over $25 per pound, miners began to earn nearly as much in bonus as their regular pay, in some cases in excess of $60,000 per year.
  - By capping the bonus at a fixed rate of salary, the company's goal was to reduce the bonus to a fixed maximum of $15,000.

- Following wider corporate trends, Vale sought to replace its existing plan with a private defined-contribution one, in which workers carry most of the risk. Vale's third set of demands was driven by a desire to promote the retirement of older, high-paid workers and increase the flexibility of the work force that remained.

Tactics

- To win such concessions from the Steelworkers, Vale launched a wide public relations campaign prior to the strike deadline that let them and the community know that the company would not engage in any negotiations without the union first agreeing to its basic "pre-conditions":

- changing to a defined contribution pension plan for new employees, a seriously reduced nickel bonus plan, and amendments to the collective agreement which the company said were necessary for competitiveness.

- Vale then maintained an active public relations profile throughout the strike, regularly commenting in the media on "new international realities" and the need for "efficiencies," placing full-page ads about the strike in local newspapers.
- Following tactics well developed in the United States, Vale launched a comprehensive campaign to ensure its success in bargaining. Over the course of the year, Vale instructed its lawyers to use every legal option to tie up union resources in the courts and at the labour board.

  - It fired nine strikers and sued them for damages ranging from $75,000 to $120,000 because of alleged incidents on picket lines. Twice it levied lawsuits of $25 million against the union for not following picket line protocol.
  - It launched further lawsuits against the union and individuals for information posted on the USW website, and for a blockade staged by community and individual union members in May 2010.

Mediation

- Labour talks between Vale and the USW collapsed for a third time over a disagreement about eight workers who were fired during the prolonged strike at the company's Sudbury nickel operations in Ontario.
- There was common ground after ten days of mediation for all other issues, including pensions, the nickel price bonus, and transfer rights.
- The parties were deadlocked over a single issue: the legal process to determine whether Vale would rehire eight of the nine employees who were fired for alleged blockading, harassment, and intimidation on the picket line, according to Ontario provincial mediator Kevin Burkett. (*Metal Bulletin Weekly*, 2010.)

Outcomes

- The union was forced to accept major concessions on bonuses, layoffs, and pension plans, but got marginal improvements for current retirees and early retirement incentives for those with 27 years or more of experience.
- The losses to the local community over the course of the year were equally significant. Local estimates put the direct loss of wages and income due to the strike at $20 million a month and more than $250 million over the year.
- The company tactics were largely successful.
  - In the final contract offer, the bonus was capped at 25 percent of straight-time hours, effectively limiting the nickel bonus to $15,000 a year.
  - The defined contribution plan was implemented for all new hires.
  - Approximately 500 workers retired over the course of unionized work force.
  - Vale also gained new controls over the number of jobs, transfer rights, and the new grievance procedure, while having no restrictions placed on its use of contract workers throughout operations.
- The strike undoubtedly cut into Vale's profits.

More Views

http://www.workersuniting.org/our_issues/usw_miners_at_vale_inco.aspx

Videos on the Strike

Management:

http://www.youtube.com/watch?v=O0JgNtH-RLE

Union:

http://www.youtube.com/watch?v=4f59bCnkJqI&feature=related

http://www.youtube.com/watch?v=gHYAozdxaSM&feature=fvwrel

News:

http://www.youtube.com/watch?v=DPRqqVqDM48&feature=related

http://www.youtube.com/watch?v=zjA2YCMRDJ0&NR=1

http://www.youtube.com/watch?v=9m2mjZInoxA&feature=related

Important Strike Documents

The Sudbury Star:

http://www.thesudburystar.com/ArticleDisplayGenContent.aspx?e=15737

United Steelworkers:

http://www.usw.org/

Unite the Union:

http://www.unitetheunion.org/

Open letter to the Sudbury community:

http://www.usw.ca/legacy_assets/UserFiles/File/radio_ads/sudbury_star_ad.pdf

Source: This case is drawn from multiple sources, but relies primarily on John Peters, "Down in the Vale: Corporate globalization, unions on the defensive, and the Local 6500 strike in Sudbury, 2009–10," *Labour, 66* (Fall 2010), pp. 73–105.

Questions

1. Outline the legal, social, and economic context of the bargaining between Vale and the United Steelworkers.
2. Analyze the pressures on the parties before and during the strike.
3. What were the strike issues? Why did the strike last so long?
4. What were the gains and losses of Vale and the union?

Endnotes

1. For a popular work on getting the most out of individual bargaining, see *Getting to Yes* by Roger Fisher and William Ury (1981).
2. In most bargaining units, unless there exists a union shop or closed shop, not all employees are union members. In Canada, nonmembers are typically required to pay dues.

References

Corry, D. J. (2000). *Negotiation: The art of mutual gains bargaining.* Aurora, ON: Canada Law Book.

Cutcher-Gershenfeld, J., Kochan, T., & Wells, J. C. (2001). In whose interest? A first look at national survey data on interest-based bargaining in labor relations. *Industrial Relations, 40*(1), pp. 1–21.

Dachis, Benjamin, & Hebdon, Robert. (2010). *The laws of unintended consequences: The effect of labour legislation on wages and strikes.* Toronto: C. D. Howe Institute.

Duffy, Paul, & Johnson, Susan. (2009). The impact of anti-temporary replacement legislation on work stoppages: Empirical evidence from Canada. *Canadian Public Policy, 35*(1), pp. 99–120.

Eaton, A. E., & Kriesky, J. (1998). Decentralization of bargaining structure: Four cases from the U.S. paper industry. *Relations industrielles, 53*(3), pp. 486–517.

Fisher, R., & Ury, W. (1981). *Getting to yes: Negotiating an agreement without giving in.* New York: Random House Business Books.

Hargrove, Scott. (2010). Achieving improved relationships through collaboration. *Library Management, 31*(4/5), pp. 229–240.

Hebdon, R., & Mazerolle, M. (1995). Mending fences, building bridges: The effect of RBO on conflict. *Relations industrielles, 50*(1), pp. 164–183.

Hebdon, R., & Warrian, P. (1999). Coercive bargaining: Public sector restructuring under the Ontario Social Contract 1993–96. *Industrial and Labor Relations Review, 52*(2), pp. 196–212.

Katz, H., & Kochan, T. (2000). *An introduction to collective bargaining and industrial relations* (2nd edition). New York: McGraw Hill.

Kolb, D., & Bartunek, J. (1992). *Hidden conflict in organizations: Uncovering behind-the-scenes disputes.* Newbury Park, CA: Sage Publications.

Metal Bulletin Weekly. (2010). "Vale and USW fail to reach deal", *Metal Bulletin Weekly,* London: 5 July 2010, p. 9. Used with permission of *Metal Bulletin Weekly.*

Miller, Jane K., Farmer, Kevin P., & Peters, Linda M. (2010). Panacea or snake oil? Interest-based bargaining in the U.S. airline and rail industries. *Negotiation Journal, 26*(2), pp. 177–201.

Paquet, R., Gaétan, I., & Bergeron, J.-G. (2000). Does interest-based bargaining really make a difference in collective bargaining outcomes? *Negotiation Journal,* July, pp. 281–296.

Peters, John. (2010). Down in the Vale: Corporate globalization, unions on the defensive, and the Local 6500 strike in Sudbury, 2009–10, *Labour, 66* (Fall), pp. 73–105.

Ross, A. (1948). *Trade union wage policy.* Berkeley: University of California Press, p. 133.

Tucker, Sean, & Mucalov, Alex. (2010). Industrial voluntarism in Canada. *Relations industrielles, 65*(2), pp. 215–235.

Walton, R. E., & McKersie, R. B. (1965). *A behavioral theory of labor negotiation.* New York: McGraw-Hill.

CHAPTER 8

Collective Agreement Administration

Learning Objectives

By the end of this chapter, you will be able to discuss

- the role of the collective agreement in unionized workplaces;
- the common layout of a collective agreement;
- the types of clauses typically found in collective agreements;
- why management and labour may prefer certain wording in collective agreements; and
- the importance and meaning of collective agreement language.

NEWTECH SOLUTIONS INC.[1]

Tim Power, a supervisor with Newtech, was meeting with labour relations manager Marcel Simard. They were very carefully reading the collective agreement language concerning job sharing, education leaves, promotions and calculation of seniority. Both had represented management in the last round of collective bargaining, where the union and management agreed on new language concerning job sharing. This language allowed two workers to "share" a job providing that (1) the employees could agree to the division of work hours between them; (2) both workers were qualified to perform the job that they would share; (3) the proposed allocation of work between the workers ensured that one of the workers would be available to cover each of the required shifts and that each person worked a minimum of one shift a week; and (4) the department supervisor approved of the job sharing arrangement proposed by the employees. This was the first time the agreement contained such language. Both union and management teams believed that the change would facilitate work–life balance among the employees, and hopefully minimize turnover. Both parties considered it a win-win solution!

"Marcel, the language concerning calculation of seniority and promotions is very clear to me," Tim said. "Article 20.2 states that seniority calculations will include time taken for approved educational leaves. Article 10.57 states that the most senior qualified employee receives the promotion."

"Right," replied Marcel. "But the employee in question is June Peters; she is job-sharing with Andrew Hum. We also need to look at Article 26 concerning job shadowing. Clause 26.4.2 states that leaves will be provided to employees who job share on a prorated basis."

Tim replied, "That makes total sense. It basically means that as June works two of the five days a week (or 40 percent of a normal work week), she was entitled to 40 percent pay for the month she was on a course. Now, what we need to figure out is seniority. If we calculate seniority on a prorated basis, she will not be promoted, as Alex Smith is more senior; however, if we include the full month of her education leave when calculating her seniority, June gets the job."

Marcel smiled. "Ah, the joys of trying to interpret new language in a collective agreement. This is one scenario we never discussed when we negotiated the agreement in May. We should call in Melvin Lutz, the president of the union local, since he negotiated the language with us. Let's get his thoughts on the issue. I'm sure the employees will also want the union's view on this matter."

Role and Layout of a Collective Agreement

As you may recall from Chapter 2, the collective agreement is the agreement between the union—representing all workers included in the bargaining unit (i.e., union members and nonmembers)—and the employer. The role of the agreement is to establish clear rules and procedures governing both workplace practices and the relationship between the parties. While it is probably safe to say that no two collective agreements are identical, most have similar features. For example, most are printed in pocket-sized format, so workers and supervisors can carry them during the workday and refer to them as needed. Moreover, many workplaces—for example, the City of Edmonton and Concordia University—now put their collective agreements online. Union leaders have also posted YouTube videos concerning collective agreements.

In order to provide concrete examples of typical elements found in collective agreements, we will continue to use the example in IR Notebook 8.1. More specifically, it, like most agreements, includes:

- *A cover page.* The cover usually states the name of the union (including local number), the employer, and the start and end dates of the collective agreement.
- *A table of contents.* The table of contents, usually found at the front of the agreement, and sometimes called an *index*, enables the reader to quickly identify where certain terms of the agreement can be found. See IR Notebook 8.1 for an example.
- *Articles.* Collective agreements are divided into a number of **articles**, each covering a certain workplace issue. Generally, each article is numbered and has a heading. For example, Article 5 of the Medicine Hat Police agreement concerns contracting out, Article 11 covers promotion, and Article 12 focuses on layoff and recall.
- *Clauses.* Within an article, there might be a number of sub-areas, called **clauses**, also numbered. For example, in Article 26 (Leave of Absence) of the Medicine Hat Police agreement, Clause 26.1 states who can approve leave (in this case the chief of police), Clause 26.2 describes how to apply for a leave, and Clause 26.8 contains issues related to maternity, parental, and adoptive leave.
- *Appendixes/schedules.* In some collective agreements, you will find schedules or appendixes that provide specific information. These, which are located toward the end of the contract, often relate to wages and benefits, or to items usually updated during each round of collective bargaining. In the Medicine Hat Police example, Appendix I is the salary schedule and Appendix II presents the shift schedule.
- *Letters of understanding.* A **letter of understanding** usually describes a specific practice the parties have agreed to follow. In some cases, these are a result of a grievance or arbitration settlement. They too are usually put at the end of an agreement. Such a letter is not contained in the Medicine Hat Police agreement; but an example would be Letter of Understanding #2/2005-08 in the contract between Manitoba Hydro and the Communications, Energy and Paperworkers Union

article

a section of a collective agreement

clause

a specific section of an article

letter of understanding

letter between the parties, usually placed at the end of an agreement and describing a specific practice they have agreed to follow

IR Notebook 8.1

Sample Table of Contents: Medicine Hat Police

Union leaders, managers, and employees regularly refer to collective agreements for guidance concerning workplace rules and practices. The following represents a typical table of contents that can help users of the collective agreement locate the information they seek.

Source: Adapted from Medicine Hat Police Association, *2009 Collective Agreement*, retrieved 25 January 2011. http://www.medicinehat.ca/City%20Government/Departments/Human%20Resources/MHPACollectiveAgreement.pdf. Used with permission.

(2006). This one concerns job sharing, and covers many issues related to our opening vignette (e.g., how holidays, vacation, overtime, and seniority are calculated for job-sharing workers).

Types of Clauses

Not only is the layout of an agreement fairly consistent, but so are the types of clauses found in them. For several decades, the federal government has been tracking collective agreements and has clustered collective agreement language into several groupings (Human Resources and Social Development Canada, 2008). The following is adapted from HRSDC's list:

- *The rights of parties.* The rights of the union (e.g., union security clauses, restrictions on contracting out), employers, and employees.
- *The organization of work.* This includes provisions concerning how work is organized and distributed (e.g., technological change, job sharing, teams, etc.).

 8.1

- *Labour relations processes.* These clauses concern the grievance procedure, arbitration, and any language about joint committees. Collective agreement language concerning joint committees will often examine issues related to working conditions/environment, contracting out, and technological changes.

 8.2

- *Education, training, and development.* Language in this grouping can include issues concerning training leave, required/provided training, financial assistance for training, and apprenticeship programs.
- *Working conditions.* This is perhaps the broadest grouping of clauses, including issues related to hours of work/work schedules, overtime, pay and benefits, job security, termination, corrective action/progressive discipline, and part-time work.

In the following sections we provide sample contract language for each of these groupings.[2] Many of these examples come from Negotech (2009), a federal government database that allows you to access and search through collective agreement language. Negotech, and the following sample clauses, may be particularly helpful if your instructor assigns a collective bargaining simulation (such as that found in Appendix B).

Rights of Parties

Recognition of Union Security

As was discussed in Chapter 5, unions often seek collective agreement language that provides various forms of union security (e.g., dues check-off, union shop, closed shop, Rand Formula). There might also be language regarding leave for union business and restrictions on management's ability to contract out as a way to ensure union member security. Examples follow from the collective agreement between the Regional Municipality of Waterloo and the Canadian Union of Public Employees (2007). The first, from Article 5, is a general union security issue; the second, from Article 2, focuses on contracting out; the third (from Article 4) examines dues check-off.

Article 5—Membership in the Union

5.01 All employees of the Region as outlined in Article 2, shall be eligible for union membership on a voluntary basis.

5.02 The Region agrees to acquaint new employees with the fact that a Union Agreement is in effect. New employees shall be presented with a copy of this Agreement.

2.04 No Layoff Due to Contracting Out

Without restricting its right to determine the methods by which municipal services are to be provided, the Region agrees that no permanent employee shall be laid off from work as a result of contracting out present work or services of a kind presently performed by its employees.

Article 4—Check-Off Union Dues

4.01 There shall be a compulsory check-off of union dues from all persons who are employees of the Region to which this Agreement applies. The amount to be deducted shall be such sum as may from time to time be assessed by the Union on its members according to its constitution and by-laws. The Region shall be notified in writing sixty (60) calendar days prior to any required change in deductible assessments.

Management Rights

residual rights

a principle whereby management retains all rights it held before unionization except those changed by the agreement

Under the principle of **residual rights**, management retains all rights and privileges it held before unionization, with the exception of rights restricted by the agreement (and, of course, any that are now illegal under changes in legislation). Thus, not all agreements have these clauses, as some employers feel that they are not needed. Other employers will seek to negotiate such clauses to emphasize their rights. The following is an example of a management rights clause (Article 3) from Axima Services (2008).

3.01 The Union recognizes the Employer the exclusive right to:

a) maintain order, discipline and efficiency;
b) hire, classify, direct, transfer, promote, demote, lay-off or dismiss an employee for just cause;
c) operate and manage its business in all respect, in accordance with, and not incompatible with any of the provisions of this Agreement.

The foregoing statements of rights of management are not all inclusive, but indicate the type of matters which belong and are inherent to Management and shall not be construed in any way to exclude other management rights not specifically enumerated. Any of the right, power or authority the Employer had when there was no collective agreement are retained by the Company except where amended by the Agreement.

In addition, we have recently seen a number of employers seeking to include language concerning drug/alcohol testing, selection tests (e.g., medical, aptitude, and intelligence), or performance tests (i.e., electronic monitoring of performance). See the sample from the Saskatchewan Liquor and Gaming Authority (2007) that discusses drug testing of employees.

1.7 Drug and Alcohol Testing

Management may do drug testing of employees only with the prior approval of the Union

Employee Rights/Security

These clauses include language concerning antidiscrimination (employment equity, harassment, disabled workers, etc.), substance abuse, recreational and health services, and childcare/eldercare programs. In general, there are two types of equity clauses found in agreements: the first, which we call **legislative reference**, refers to legislation, and the second, which we call **explicit reference**, explicitly states inappropriate grounds for discrimination. The following are examples of each:

> *Legislative reference* The Employer and the Union acknowledge and affirm their respective obligations under the *Canadian Human Rights Act* and jointly agree that there shall be no discrimination in respect of employment by reason of any prohibited ground in the absence of any bona fide occupational requirement contemplated by the said *Act*. Accordingly, the provisions of this Agreement shall be interpreted and applied in a manner consistent with the *Act* and Regulations, as amended. (From Article 10.01 [No Discrimination], Greater Toronto Airports Authority collective agreement, 2006)

> *Explicit reference* There shall be no discrimination, interference, restriction, coercion, harassment, intimidation, or any disciplinary action exercised or practiced with respect to an employee by reason of age, race, creed, colour, national origin, religious affiliation, sex, sexual orientation, family status, mental or physical disability, membership or activity in the Council, marital status or a conviction for which a pardon has been granted. (From Clause 36.01 [No Discrimination] from the Treasury Board collective agreement, 2008)

One might wonder why the parties would choose to use a legislative reference rather than the more detailed, explicit reference clause. Our conversations with union and management leaders provide some insights. Some argue that the legislative reference is preferred as it ensures that the agreement is current with the law. Others argue that the explicit reference is better because (1) most managers, union leaders, and employees look to their collective agreement for guidance on these issues, and the lack of specifics would not meet this need; (2) explicitly referencing specific groups ensures that these groups remain protected if the law changes; and (3) the parties may feel that they wish to include a group not covered by legislation.

Take for example the issue of **same-sex benefits**. We have seen considerable debate in the media about whether legislation concerning gay marriage

legislative reference
equity clause in collective agreements that references legislation

explicit reference
equity clause in collective agreements that specifies which groups are covered

same-sex benefits
same-sex partners receiving the same benefits as opposite-sex partners

should be changed (CBC, 2005). If gay marriages were no longer considered legal, only agreements that specified same-sex partners are eligible for benefits would continue to provide such coverage. In agreements that referred to a spousal definition consistent with legislation, same-sex partners would lose such benefits, since same-sex partners would not meet the legal definition of spouse.

Organization of Work

Technological Change

There is an old saying: "The only constant is change." Since the Industrial Revolution, we have seen ongoing change in the technologies used in workplaces. It was not that long ago that employees did not have computers, the Internet, or wireless products (BlackBerrys, iPads, etc.). These are now considered staples of most organizations; so it should not be surprising that, as is discussed in Chapter 1, Dunlop included technology in his IR system, nor that many parties negotiate technological-change (often referred to as *tech-change*) language in their agreements. Included are understandings about such things as the union being notified of the change, the notification of employees who may be laid off as a result of change and the severance they will receive, any restrictions concerning layoffs, any employer requirements concerning training or retraining, and any wage protection for employees (often called **red-circling**) who might be demoted and/or moved to a lower-paying position as a direct result of tech change. The following excerpt from Article 19 (New Technology and Continuous Improvement) of the Arnprior Aerospace (2006) agreement is an example of tech-change language.

red-circling

protecting employees' pay at a level higher than the normal rate of their current job

> #### Section 19.2 Job Security
>
> Although it is not the Company's intent to reduce employees job security through the implementation of continuous improvement activities, the Company and the Union have a mutual goal to limit the impact of the implementation of technological change upon the job security of affected employees. In cases where technological change requires that employees affected by that change need specialized training to accomplish new tasks or gain new skills, those employees will be offered training, subject to the individual employee possessing the necessary skill and ability for that training and the number of positions open. In cases where there is further displacement of employees due to technological change, those employees will be offered other training or reassigned to the extent available and subject to the terms and conditions of this agreement.
>
> #### Section 19.3 Technology Planning
>
> It is understood that the implementation of technological change is, in itself, a process as well as being a part of a process of continuous

improvement. The technological changes will be introduced progressively over time, therefore the Company will discuss with the Union the planned introduction of technological change into the work place thirty (30) days prior to the implementation of such change. The discussions shall include the solicitation and consideration of recommendations of the Union as to the accomplishment of the planned changes. It is understood that cooperation between the Company and the Union is vital to the success of implementation.

As part of these discussions, the Company will provide the Union with information concerning the nature of the technological change to include:

1. A description of the changes planned,
2. The planned effective date or dates of implementation,
3. The approximate number and classifications of employees likely to be affected by the change,
4. The effect that the change is likely to have on the terms, conditions and security of employment of the affected employees,
5. The number of jobs and job classifications to be corrected or abolished by the change, to the maximum extent that such information is then available,
6. The reasons for change and/or the goals and objectives that the change is intended to fulfill.

Distribution of Work

Distribution of work clauses examine issues concerning job rotation, job sharing, teams/workgroups, and flexibility in work assignment. As is discussed in Chapter 6, many employers seek increased flexibility in work assignment and the organization of work in their workplaces. The following is from a letter of understanding (Flexible Work Practices) between Norske Canada and the Communications, Energy and Paperworkers Union of Canada (2003) that examines the issue of flexible work assignments.

1. The introduction of flexible work practices is designed to improve productivity, improve product quality, reduce down time and lower costs while ensuring that the work is completed in a safe manner. The efficiencies that result from flexible work practices are also intended to assist in fulfilling the intention of Article 25 of the Agreement.
2. The parties agree that this letter on flexible work practices recognizes that the primary responsibility for the operation of the mill will remain with operators and the primary responsibility for maintaining the mill will remain with trades persons.
3. It is understood that the intent of this letter will supersede local practices, and verbal and written agreements which would impair the implementation of flexible work practices.

Similarly, the following section from the agreement between Yukon College Board of Governors and the Public Service Alliance of Canada (2003) examines job sharing:

Article 28—Job Sharing

(a) Job sharing may be requested by an employee or the Employer. The Union will be notified of any such requests immediately after they have been made. Those employed in job sharing will continue to be members of the bargaining unit and be covered by the Collective Agreement.

(b) The terms and conditions governing job sharing will be as mutually agreed by the Union, the Employer and the participants and set out in a Memorandum of Agreement.

(c) It is agreed that job sharing will neither result in any significant additional costs nor diminish the education or support service.

(d) In the event that an employee's job share partner vacates a position, the employee remaining may choose to continue the arrangement subject to this article or assume the position on a non-job share basis.

Labour Relations

Labour relations clauses in collective agreements specifically deal with issues concerning the relationship between the parties. Typical clauses examine grievance/arbitration procedures, participatory mechanisms (e.g., joint committees), and preferred bargaining methods.

Grievance and Arbitration

You may recall that the right to a grievance procedure is not a requirement under common law. Thus, most agreements have specific language related to grievances and arbitration. Some, like the Nuna Contracting contract (2007), even define grievances (see Article 22.02):

22.02 "Grievance" will mean a complaint or claim concerning improper discipline or discharge, or a dispute with reference to the interpretation, application, administration or alleged violation of this Agreement.

A "Group Grievance" is defined as a single grievance, signed by a Steward or EI Union Representative on behalf of a group of employees who have the same complaint. Such grievance must be dealt with at successive stages of the Grievance procedure commencing with Step 1. The grievors will be listed on the grievance form.

A "Policy Grievance" is defined as one which involves a question relating to the interpretation, application or administration of this Agreement. A Policy Grievance will be signed by a Steward or a Union Representative, or in the case of an Employer's Policy Grievance, by the Employer or their representative.

The following excerpt from an agreement of Elk Valley Coal Corporation (Article 7.03, 2006) outlines a typical grievance procedure. As will be discussed in more detail in Chapter 9, notice the extent to which the parties highlight the representatives involved and the time frames.

Step 1 Within thirty (30) calendar days after the alleged grievance has arisen or within thirty (30) calendar days from the time the employee(s) should reasonably have known of the occurrence giving rise to the grievance, a Shop Steward may present the grievance in writing to the employee(s)' Foreman. At the option of the Shop Steward, the employee(s) may be in attendance. The Foreman shall record the facts as presented, investigate the grievance and provide a written answer within three (3) days. Failing a satisfactory resolution, the grievance may proceed to Step 2.

Step 2 Within five (5) days from the time a decision was made or should have been made under Step 1, the Shop Steward may present the grievance in writing to the employee(s)' General Foreman. At the option of the Shop Steward the employee(s) may be in attendance. The employee(s)' General Foreman shall investigate the grievance and provide a written answer to the grievance within three (3) days. Failing a satisfactory resolution, the grievance may proceed to Step 3.

Step 3 Within five (5) days from the time a decision was made or should have been made under Step 2, the Chief Shop Steward or his designate may present the grievance to Company Management. At the option of the Chief Shop Steward, the employee(s) may be in attendance. The Management of the Company may also require the employee(s) concerned, and members of the supervisory staff concerned in or having knowledge of the grievance, to appear before them and give evidence regarding the grievance. The Company Management will provide an answer in writing within five (5) days. Failing a satisfactory resolution, the grievance may proceed to Step 4.

Step 4 Within thirty (30) calendar days of receiving the answer at Step 3, the Union may, by written notice to the Company, refer the grievance to arbitration. Within ten (10) calendar days of receiving such notice, the Company and Union will select the arbitrator or grievance investigator and mutually set a date(s) for an arbitration.

Participatory Mechanisms and Bargaining Methods

Sometimes parties include language to "set the tone" for their relationship. A good example is Article 1 (Guiding Principles) from the Levi Strauss agreement (2001). It sets the tone for the preferred relationship and discusses both joint committees and continuous bargaining.

> The parties recognize that the employees, the Union and the Company are interdependent and are necessary for the success of the business. The parties also acknowledge that in order to meet competitive challenges and customers' needs there is a need for ongoing continuous improvement and learning skills within the workplace. This will require new skills, roles, responsibilities and relationships. Therefore, it is agreed by the parties that they will work together to develop a continually improving work environment of trust, open communications and respect which will encourage meaningful employee involvement and achieve mutually agreed upon goals. The parties agree to protect the safety and health of all employees and to provide for prompt and equitable disposition of grievances or disputes which may arise between the parties. To support their strategic alliance, they will establish joint committees of 6 members with equal representation from the Union and Company. The Union and the Company will jointly monitor and evaluate the process to assure that the values, purposes and goals of the Company are nurtured and maintained. Should any part of this Agreement be rendered or declared illegal by reason of any existing or subsequently enacted legislation or by any decree of a court of competent jurisdiction or by decision of any authorized government agency, such invalidation of such part or provisions shall not invalidate the remainder thereof. Both parties may mutually agree to amend or supplement this Agreement at any time.

Education, Training, and Employee Development

As is discussed in Chapter 10, unionized workers often have increased access to workplace training. Thus, many collective agreements contain specific language about leaves for education, repayment of educational expenses (e.g., tuition, books), access to training, the employer's ability to provide **multi-skill training**, contributions to a training fund, and apprenticeship training programs. A few examples of such clauses follow.

multi-skill training
training to provide employees with a variety of skills, some of which may not normally be part of their job

Repayment of Educational Expenses

The following is from Article 37 (Education and Training) of the Royal Canadian Mint (2005) agreement:

> 37.01 An Employee who undertakes a training course outside his normal hours of work may, at the discretion of the Employer, be reimbursed in whole or in part for the direct expense of instruction, that is, the expenses which must be paid to complete the training, and which are not primarily of a personal character.

> 37.02 To be eligible to receive reimbursement, the Employee must fulfill two conditions:

(a) obtain the Employer's approval for the proposed training before it commences; and

(b) satisfactorily complete the training, including the passing of any final examination related to the course, or if there is no final examination, establish an excellent record of attendance.

Apprenticeships

Collective agreements that employ skilled tradespersons will often have provisions for apprenticeships. These are especially prevalent in the construction industry. The following excerpt is from Appendix No. 3—Electrical–Industrial of the Nova Scotia Construction Labour Relations Association (2008) agreement:

Apprentices:

All Apprentices will be employed in accordance with the provisions of the *Nova Scotia Apprenticeship Act*, the IBEW Joint Apprenticeship Committee and the Parties hereby agree to observe all the provisions of said *Act*.

There will be one (1) Apprentice to every three (3) Journeymen. An Apprentice attending school under the terms of their indentureship will not be laid off or terminated from the job while they are attending school, and may be substituted with another Apprentice during their studies (when the employer has work available).

Apprentices shall, with the approval of "The Minister," be indentured to the Nova Scotia Joint Apprenticeship Training Committee.

Conditions of Work

RPC 8.3

North American unionism has often been described as "bread and butter" in nature given its focus on improving the wages, job security, and working conditions of its members. Thus, one could argue that conditions of work is the most referenced section of a collective agreement, because it includes issues related to work schedules, overtime, pay, health and welfare benefits (vacation, retirement, health plans, etc.), and layoff/termination of employment (including progressive discipline, probationary periods, and violations of company rules that can lead to termination). We now present several examples of collective agreement language related to such work conditions.

Hours of Work

Most collective agreements provide an overview of a typical workday (e.g., number of work hours). In workplaces with shift work, information concerning shift schedules may also be discussed. The following excerpt is from Article 7 (Hours of Work) of the Xstrata Nickel collective agreement (2007). It discusses hours of work per day and shifts.

7.01 The regular work day will be 8:00 a.m. to 4:30 p.m. with a half hour off for lunch.

However, where the efficiency of operations so requires or an employee or groups of employees so request the Company may change such hours to 8:00 a.m. to 5:00 p.m. with an hour off for lunch.

The day shift shall be considered any shift that commences at or after 5:00 a.m. and before 1:00 p.m.; the afternoon shift shall be considered any shift that commences at or after 1:00 p.m. and before 9:00 p.m.; and the night shift shall be considered any shift that commences at or after 9:00 p.m. and before 5:00 a.m.

7.02 The regular work week shall be 5 workdays, Monday to Friday, inclusive.

Overtime

Provincial labour/employment standards legislation includes provisions for overtime payment. However, most collective agreements have language concerning overtime that usually goes beyond the minimum legislative requirements. Such language often includes how overtime, which can be financially lucrative to workers, is to be assigned. The following example from Westguard Security Services (Article 15(c), 2008) shows how overtime is calculated and paid:

Overtime: Any hours worked in excess of eight (8) and up to eleven (11) hours in anyone (1) regular work day shall be paid for at the rate of time and one-half (1½). Any hours worked in excess of eleven (11) hours in any one (1) regular work day shall be paid at the rate of double time (2×).

Firms often seek to minimize what might be called *compounding*, or **pyramiding,** of payments. For example, many agreements would not allow a person to get 1½ times their base pay and 1½ times their shift premium when calculating overtime. Take a look at how Gray Line (2009), in Article 15 (Overtime), included language to avoid pyramiding:

15.04 There shall be no compounding of overtime payments or any other premium payments.

pyramiding
compounding of premiums or benefits

Holidays

As is the case with overtime, minimum requirements for paid holidays are provided in employment/labour standards legislation, and unionized workplaces often exceed these minimums. You will often find that language in this area will present the days considered to be holidays (often called "plant holidays" in manufacturing) as well as how employees who work these holidays will be paid. Let's look at a section from 8.01 (Statutory Holidays) of the EPCOR Utilities 2007 collective agreement (2008).

8.01.01. The following days shall be recognized as statutory holidays for the purpose of this agreement, and all permanent, provisional and probationary employees shall be entitled to the holidays specified, provided they meet the terms and conditions set out in this Section. New Year's Day, Good Friday, Easter Sunday, Victoria Day, Canada Day (July 1), Civic Holiday, Labour Day, Thanksgiving Day, Remembrance Day, Christmas Day, Boxing Day (December 26), Alberta Family Day and any other holiday which the Company allows employees as a whole.

8.01.03. All employees shall receive the recognized statutory holidays for which they are eligible. Such employees shall receive the recognized statutory holiday with pay, or other days with pay in lieu of the holidays, or pay in lieu. Days with pay in lieu of the holiday shall be at a time mutually agreed to between the employee and the supervisor. In the event that the mutual agreement is not reached, the employee shall be allowed a day in lieu of the holiday at a time determined by the Company. Where such a day is not provided, the employee shall receive a day's pay in lieu of the holiday.

Vacation Leave

Collective agreement language concerning vacations often states how vacation is calculated, the amount of time off an employee receives, and when an employee is eligible for vacation; it may even state how he or she will be paid. Let's look at a section of Article 22 (Vacations) of the Newfoundland and Labrador Hydro (2006) collective agreement:

22.01 The Vacation Year shall be from the first day of January to the thirty-first day of December in each year, both dates inclusive. Each employee will receive an annual vacation with pay in accordance with years of continuous employment as follows:

SERVICE	VACATION
1–9 years	15 days
10–14 years	23 days
15–19 years	26 days
20–24 years	27 days
25 and succeeding	28 days

For the purposes of this clause, one vacation day is equal to eight (8) hours. Subject to Clause 22.03, employees during their first year of employment shall receive working days of vacation with pay computed in accordance with the following formula:

Vacation Entitlement in days. 1.25 x Number of months remaining in the Vacation Year from the date of hire rounded upwards to the next whole day.

Thereafter the employee will be entitled to annual vacation each year in accordance with the service schedule. Employees will be entitled to working days of vacation based on the number of complete years of service they will have attained at the end of the current Vacation Year.

Termination, Layoff, and Discipline

One of the biggest differences between employment under common law and collective bargaining law is management's restricted ability to terminate employees. Thus, collective agreements will often contain language concerning probationary employees, just cause-based discipline and termination, layoff provisions (including recall), and progressive discipline steps, which normally take place prior to discharge. Examples of each follow.

PROBATIONARY EMPLOYEES   Language in this area usually highlights the length of the probationary period as well as the fact that the employee can be terminated (without just cause) prior to the end of the probationary period. The Hotel Saskatchewan (2007) collective agreement (Article 22: Probationary Employees) has such a clause:

> 22.1 An employee having less than three (3) months' service, will be considered as on probation, and if found unsuitable, will not be retained in the service of the Hotel.

> 22.2 An employee will not be regarded as permanently employed until after three (3) months' cumulative service.

> 22.3 Employees entering the service of the Hotel may be paid 15% per hour less than the scheduled rate for the first three (3) months' cumulative service of compensated service, after which the progressive rate schedule shall apply. This rate must be no less than fifteen (15) cents above the minimum wage.

JUST CAUSE   Such clauses state that employers require just cause for discipline and discharge. For example, the Red Deer College (2006) agreement (Article 29: Disciplinary Procedure) states:

> 29.02 No employee shall be disciplined except for just cause.

LAYOFF   Layoff language often contains information related to seniority, as seniority is a key factor in collective agreements. Generally speaking, unions will seek to protect senior workers from layoff while management will seek to ensure they can efficiently run the business. This usually means that employers seek language stating that any employees remaining after the layoff must have the skills needed to effectively perform their jobs. Take a look at the role of seniority versus efficiency in the layoff language from a section of Article 7 (Seniority) of the Allied Systems (Canada) Company (2001) agreement.

> 7.1 The purpose of seniority regulations is to provide a policy governing layoffs and rehiring. In the event of a reduction of the working

force, the Company shall apply the principle of "last on–first off" insofar as it is consistent with management's obligation to maintain an efficient working force. Following a layoff, rehiring shall be executed conversely to the outlined layoff procedure.

7.4 a) Seniority shall prevail in the event of layoffs, with the junior employee in each work classification covered by this Agreement being laid off first, providing the senior employee is qualified and capable of performing the available work.

DISCIPLINE   Most collective agreements present language related to the concept of **corrective action**. These clauses often present forms of discipline, grounds for discipline, how discipline is to be administered, what records will be kept, where these records will be kept, and how long they will be kept, as well as who will be involved in the discipline process (i.e., level of union and managerial representation). The following sections from Article 8 (Progressive Discipline, Suspension and Dismissal) of the agreement for Thompson Rivers University faculty (2004) present an example of discipline language.

> **corrective action**
> a warning process designed to improve employee performance or behaviour

8.1 Right to Have Steward Present

An employee shall have the right to have his/her steward present at any discussion with supervisory personnel that the employee believes might be the basis of disciplinary action. Where a supervisor intends to interview an employee for disciplinary purposes, the supervisor shall notify the employee and the Union of the purpose of the interview in order that the employee may contact his/her steward, providing that this does not result in an undue delay of the appropriate action being taken. This clause shall not apply to those discussions that are of an operational nature and do not involve disciplinary action. [. . .]

8.2.1 Progressive discipline steps shall be initiated for inappropriate conduct as warranted. Such discipline would normally begin with verbal warning(s), then progress to a written warning, then progress to suspension (if applicable) and finally to dismissal, as the situation may warrant.

Special Issues in Collective Agreements

In addition to the types of clauses shown above, there are a few special types of clauses and language that can found in collective agreements concerning bumping, super seniority, and the importance of language.

Bumping

Given the importance of seniority in collective agreements, there are often clauses that protect senior employees from being let go in a downsizing; this is known as **bumping**. Bumping is a process whereby a union member with

> **bumping**
> a process whereby senior employees pass on their layoff to more junior employees

greater seniority who is about to be laid off is allowed to use his or her seniority rights to remove (or bump) a more junior union member from a job that would have been otherwise unaffected by the layoff (Stringer & Brown, 2008). In essence, he or she "bumps" his or her layoff notice to the more junior employee. These clauses can be very complicated as they set out to define the conditions under which bumping can occur.

Super Seniority

Union leaders are often given special protection from layoffs. Possible reasons for this are: (1) an unscrupulous manager might declare a layoff to get rid of a challenging, but junior union rep; (2) union reps are needed to be present to represent employees' rights until the very end in the event of a massive layoff or business closing; or (3) to encourage people to become actively involved in the union.

super seniority

the status of union representatives who, while in office, have highest seniority in the bargaining unit

The following clause from Nestlé (2008) represents a typical **super seniority** clause:

> 13.06 Super Seniority. In the event of a layoff, the Plant Chairperson, Committeepersons and Stewards shall have super seniority.

The Subtleties of Language

As you read through this chapter, you will have noticed that collective agreement language can sometimes read like "legalese." However, in negotiations, both parties make serious efforts to ensure that the language is specific and clear, and that it meets their needs. They may even consult past arbitration rulings in works such as Brown and Beatty (2006) to help them decide on the language they use. In particular, pay special attention to words such as *will*, *shall*, and *must*, all of which provide no flexibility to either party—they are bound to follow the language. Words such as *will usually*, *will normally*, and *may*, on the other hand, imply a level of flexibility or discretion. You will also see parties add phrases or sentences to qualify previous statements. Some agreements even explicitly highlight the differences of these terms. For example, in clause 2.01(s), the Cambridge Bay Housing Association (2007) agreement states: "'May' shall be regarded as permissive and 'Shall' and 'Will' as imperative."

As you might imagine, employers often seek to maximize their flexibility and discretion, whereas unions often try to minimize it fearing that it could lead to management favouritism. The following two clauses about the role of seniority in layoffs will demonstrate the importance of wording. Which, in your opinion, gives the most protection to senior employees? Which provides the most flexibility to employers?

> 10.06(a). In the event that a reduction in the nursing force is required, the Employer agrees that the most junior nurse will be laid off first provided that nurses who remain are qualified to do the work available. When recalling nurses after layoff, those last to be laid off will be first to be recalled provided that in each case the nurse is qualified to do the work available. (From Victorian Order of Nurses collective agreement, Article 10 [Seniority and Job Security], 2007)

Complexity of Collective Agreement Language

Employees, managers, and union representatives regularly refer to collective agreements for guidance in workplace rules and practices; however, the language in them is often very complex. In fact, one study of thirty collective agreements suggests that many collective agreement clauses had the same reading difficulty as legal journals such as *Osgoode Hall Law Review* and the *Ottawa Law Journal* (Elliott, 1990, rev. 1998). The following represents suggestions by Elliott for ways to improve clarity in collective agreements:

- Break long text sections into short sentences.
- Divide long sections of text into paragraphs.

- Use clear headings.
- Minimize wording by using a single word (e.g., *if*) rather than a phrase (e.g., in the unlikely event that).
- Remove cumbersome language such as *aforementioned, hereinbefore, aforesaid,* etc.

Table 8.1 provides some of Elliott's examples to show how clauses can be rewritten to improve clarity. Notice how much easier it is to understand the clauses on the right.

Source: Elliott, 1990, rev. 1998. Used with permission.

31.1 Where the Board has made a decision to reduce the complement of the York Regional Police and such reduction in personnel cannot be accommodated through attrition and where such action is not in contravention of the Police Services Act, layoffs of members shall be in reverse order of seniority with the York Regional Police, and recall of members shall be in order of seniority with the York Regional Police. Members shall retain seniority rights for recall purposes for a period of eighteen (18) months.

Prior to a full-time member being laid off, all part-time, temporary members or summer students shall be laid off, provided that the full-time member who will replace them has the requisite skill and ability to perform the job in question. (From Article 4 [Lay-Off Protection] of the Regional Municipality of York Police Services Board collective agreement, 2010)

Table 8.1

Writing for Clarity

The Original	The Revised Version
The time limits expressed in the foregoing shall be exclusive of Saturdays, Sundays and statutory holidays, and normal time off.	Saturdays, Sundays, statutory holidays, and normal time off are not counted when calculating time limits in this article.
All settlements arrived at shall be final and binding upon the Company and the Union and the employee or group of employees concerned.	Settlements are final and binding on the Company, the Union, and employees concerned.

Source: Elliott, 1990, rev. 1998. Used with permission.

Summary

After reading this chapter, you should understand the role of the collective agreement in unionized workplaces, know the typical layout of a collective agreement, be familiar with the common types of clauses that are found in collective agreements, and understand the importance, and meaning, of special collective agreement language and terms.

As shown in this chapter, the role of the collective agreement is largely to define workplace practices and procedures as they relate to employees, their union, and their management. Thus, we saw that collective agreements often contain language related to five groupings: (1) the rights of parties; (2) the organization of work; (3) labour relations processes; (4) education, training, and development; and (5) working conditions. Nevertheless, it is critical to remember that every collective agreement is unique to the relationship at hand and that the specific clauses found in each were crafted to meet the needs of the two actors involved (management and labour).

The text examples also highlight the importance of language. Parties can negotiate language that provides flexibility or language that is "airtight." Regardless of the specific language chosen, it is fair to say that agreements have become increasingly legal in nature. While the original intent of collective agreements may have been to provide the actors of the IR system with plain, simple language to aid them in their daily work, the reverse is now true. The language is often very complex. Only time will tell if we will see a movement away from legalist language and back toward "everyday" wording.

Key Terms

article 245
bumping 259
clause 245
corrective action 259
explicit reference 249
legislative reference 249
letter of understanding 245

multi-skill training 254
pyramiding 256
red-circling 250
residual rights 248
same-sex benefits 249
super seniority 260

Weblinks

The collective agreements for the City of Edmonton:

http://www.edmonton.ca/city_government/jobs/
collective-agreements.aspx

The collective agreements for Concordia University:

http://hr.concordia.ca/collectiveagreements/download

YouTube postings from unions:

- Concordia Part-Time Faculty Association:

  http://www.youtube.com/watch?v=jYXDA37yrKY

- IATSE for Visual Effects Artists (VFX):

  http://www.youtube.com/watch?v=rPq2rcJa1yw

HRSDC Collective Agreement Provisions:

http://www.hrsdc.gc.ca/eng/lp/wid/07Provisions.shtml

Negotech:

http://www.hrsdc.gc.ca/cgi-bin/search/negotech/search-eng.shtml

RPC Icons

8.1 Interprets the collective agreement

- context and content of collective agreement
- institutions and processes (both regulatory and nonregulatory) that govern the relationship between employers and employees
- the process of collective bargaining
- the administration of the collective agreement

8.2 Advises clients of signatories' rights, including those with respect to grievance procedures

- context and content of collective agreements
- the atmosphere of labour relations within the organization
- organization structure and authorities

8.3 Monitors applications of HR policies

- context and content of policy
- relevant legislation (e.g., human rights, employment equity, pay equity)
- the identification, assessment, development, implementation, maintenance, and monitoring processes of effective systems of managing HR information

Discussion Questions

1. Seniority is a key issue for unions; thus, seniority is a key factor in many articles of a collective agreement. At the same time, unions are trying to increase their youth membership. How do you suggest that unions balance these competing needs in terms of their collective agreement language?

2. As is suggested by this chapter, collective agreements are often complex written documents. Unfortunately, they are often difficult for employees to understand and/or navigate when seeking answers to their workplace questions. What would you suggest that the parties can do to improve the user-friendliness of agreements?

3. We have often heard two sayings in IR circles: (1) collective agreements get longer over time; and (2) you can place a manager's name next to each clause of a collective agreement (e.g., that manager's actions resulted in the need for the clause). To what extent do you feel these sayings are true?

4. As the demographics of the labour force changes (e.g., increased ethnic and visible diversity, increased focus on attracting youth given the aging workforce, the aging workforce), do you feel we will see changes in the types of clauses contained in collective agreements or even in their format? Explain.

5. Collective agreements are often negotiated, and thus updated, every three or four years. Given the rapidly changing and complex nature of today's workplaces, do you feel that we will see changes regarding the length of time between revisions of collective agreement? If so, how do you predict this will occur?

Using the Internet

Many of the collective agreement clauses used as examples in this text were gathered using Negotech (see **http://www.hrsdc.gc.ca/cgi-bin/search/negotech/search-eng.shtml** or just google the word "Negotech"). This database is an excellent way for labour and business leaders to examine the contract language of other workplaces when they are setting out to negotiate their own collective agreements. Go to the Negotech site and conduct searches on any of the following keyword sets; feel free to restrict the sample to your province or a particular industry:

- overtime
- contracting out
- job posting and/or promotions
- layoff

1. Examine the specific language in five or so different collective agreements. In particular, pay attention to the extent to which they provide flexibility to management or provide protection to employees.

2. Of the clauses you found, which would you prefer if you were a union representative? Why?

3. Which of the clauses would you prefer as a management representative? Why?

Exercises

1. Collective agreements are often readily available in university libraries and on websites. Such agreements can also be easily found in most unionized workplaces. Find a collective agreement or two and answer the following questions:

   a. Some people say that you can sense the tone of the relationship between the parties on the basis of the first few articles of a collective agreement. Is this the case with your agreement? If so, what is the tone?

   b. Look at the wording of issues such as layoffs and promotions. Does it provide much flexibility to the parties? Is the language about these issues clear? Can you apply elements of IR Notebook 8.2 to improve the language?

2. The media often discusses issues of labour unrest and contract negotiations. Find one or two examples from a news media outlet (newspaper, TV, website, etc.).

   a. What are the main issues at hand?

   b. What type of language do you think management would aim to craft in the agreement?

   c. What type of language do you think the union seeks?

3. One could argue that a university calendar is like a collective agreement in that it governs the student's relationship with the university. Take a look at the section concerning your degree program.

   a. Is the language flexible in nature or very specific?

   b. Is the language easy to understand?

   c. Can you apply any of the suggestions from IR Notebook 8.2 to improve the clarity of the language?

Case

Automotive Sector Restructuring

Once a mainstay and stable industry in Canada, the automotive sector has been hard hit by recent global events. Over the past few years, we have seen massive layoffs and restructurings in the auto sector. For example, General Motors announced in 2005 that they would cut 25,000 or more jobs by 2008; Ford, in 2006, stated that they would cut 30,000 jobs; and in 2007, Chrysler announced plans to cut 13,000 jobs over a three-year period. These job losses were coupled with plant closures on both sides of the border, including a Ford plant in St. Thomas (scheduled for 2011) and a GM plant in Oshawa (closed in 2009). The industry also experienced extended temporary shutdowns in many plants in the summer of 2009. During that same period, industry giants received government bailouts from Canada and the

United States and sought bankruptcy protection in the United States under Chapter 11.

During this transition, the Ontario economy was particularly impacted, given that the automotive sector represents the largest industry in the province's manufacturing industry. In fact, the sector lost 50,000 jobs between 2006 and 2009. Even with these job losses, the auto industry employs over 150,000 Canadians directly, and an additional 340,000 indirectly.

Sources: CBC News, 2009; Hemeon, 2010; Krisher, 2009.

Questions

1. Assume that you are either the union representative or the human resources/labour relations manager for the St. Thomas plant scheduled for closure. What areas of the collective agreement would be relevant for you to review? (*Hint:* Look at IR Notebook 8.1 or the various clauses in the text of this chapter.)
2. Assume that you are the human resources/labour relations manager for an Ontario automotive plant not affected by the recent announcement and that you are about to enter negotiations. What would your priorities be for collective agreement language changes?
3. Assume that you are the union representative for an Ontario automotive plant not affected by the recent announcement and that you are about to enter negotiations. What would your priorities be for collective agreement language change?

Endnotes

1. The opening vignette is fictional and was created by the authors. It is not based on a real company or situation.
2. Note that all clauses were retrieved from the Negotech website rather than from hard copies. Consequently, their appearance may differ from that of the hard copy. Also note that, in places, spacing, bullets, etc., were added to improve the readability of the clauses. In no case, however, was the actual wording altered.

References

Allied Systems (Canada) Company & International Brotherhood of Teamsters. (2001). *Collective agreement.* Retrieved 11 October 2006 from http://206.191.16.137/negotech

Arnprior Aerospace & International Association of Machinists and Aerospace Workers, Local Lodge No. 1542. (2006). From Article 19, *Collective agreement.* Retrieved 25 January 2011 from http://206.191.16.137/eng/agreement/current/1370701a.pdf. Used with permission.

Axima Services S.E.C. & the International Association of Machinists and Aerospace Workers, District Lodge 140. (2008). *Collective agreement.* Retrieved 25 January 2011 from http://206.191.16.137/eng/agreement/current/1392301a.pdf

Brown, D., & Beatty, D. (2006). *Canadian labour arbitration* (4th edition). Aurora, ON: Canada Law Book.

Cambridge Bay Housing Association & Public Service Alliance of Canada. (2007). *Collective agreement.* Retrieved 25 January 2011 from http://206.191.16.137/eng/agreement/current/1054804a.pdf

CBC. (30 November 2005). Harper reopens same-sex marriage debate. Retrieved 11 October 2006 from http://www.cbc.ca/news/story/2005/11/29/harper-smaesex051129.html

CBC News. (9 February 2009). A timeline of auto sector layoffs. Retrieved 27 January 2010 from http://www.cbc.ca/canada/story/2008/10/21/f-autolayoffs.html

Elk Valley Coal Corporation: Fording River Operations & USW, Local 7884. (2006). *Collective agreement*. Retrieved 26 January 2011 from http://206.191.16.137/eng/agreement/current/0019307a.pdf. Used with permission.

Elliott, D. (1990, rev. 1998). Writing collective agreements in plain language. Paper presented to the 8th Annual Labour Arbitration Conference in 1990. Retrieved 11 October 2006 from http://www.davidelliott.ca/papers/5b3.htm

EPCOR Utilities. (2008). 2007–2010 collective agreement between EPCOR Utilities Inc. and Civic Service Union 52. Retrieved 11 May 2011 from http://www.csu52.org/publications/collective_agreements/2007-2010%20EPCOR%20CA.pdf

Gray Line of Victoria Ltd. & National Automobile, Aerospace Transportation and General Workers Union of Canada, Local 114. (2009). *Collective agreement*. Retrieved 25 January 2011 from http://206.191.16.137/eng/agreement/current/0373210a.pdf

Greater Toronto Airports Authority & Public Service Alliance of Canada, Local 0004. (2006). *Collective agreement*. Retrieved 25 January 2011 from http://206.191.16.137/eng/agreement/current/1185703a.pdf

Hemeon, J. (8 February 2010). Ontario looks beyond the struggling auto sector. *Investment Executive*. Retrieved 27 January 2011 from http://www.investmentexecutive.com/client/en/News/DetailNews.asp?id=52350&pg=1&IdSection=29&IdPub=191

Hotel Saskatchewan (1990) Ltd. (Hotel Saskatchewan Radisson Plaza) & National Automobile, Aerospace, Transportation and General Workers Union of Canada (CAW Canada). (2007). *Collective agreement*. Retrieved 25 January 2011 from http://206.191.16.137/eng/agreement/current/0920607a.pdf

Human Resources and Social Development Canada. (18 March 2008). *Negotiated benefits and working conditions*. Retrieved on 25 January 2011 from http://www.hrsdc.gc.ca/eng/lp/wid/07Provisions.shtml

Krisher, T. (9 June 2009). Oshawa GM plant closure extended. *The Star.com*. Retrieved 27 January 2011. http://www.thestar.com/wheels/article/648096

Levi Strauss & Co. (Canada) Inc. Edmonton & the United Food and Commercial Workers Union. (2001). *Collective agreement*. Retrieved 3 October 2006 from http://206.191.16.137/negotech

Manitoba Hydro & the Communications, Energy and Paperworkers Union, Local 681. (2006). *Collective agreement*. Retrieved 25 January 2011 from http://206.191.16.137/eng/agreement/current/0415610a.pdf

Negotech. (25 February 2009). Retrieved 25 January 2011 from http://www.hrsdc.gc.ca/cgi-bin/search/negotech/search-eng.shtml

Nestlé Canada Inc. & National Automobile, Aerospace, Transportation and General Workers Union of Canada. (2008). *Collective agreement*. Retrieved 26 January 2011 from http://206.191.16.137/eng/agreement/current/0057410a.pdf

Newfoundland and Labrador Hydro & the International Brotherhood of Electrical Workers, Local 1615. (2006). *Collective agreement*. Retrieved 26 January 2011 from http://206.191.16.137/eng/agreement/current/0857009a.pdf

Norske Canada, Powell River Division & the Communications, Energy and Paperworkers Union of Canada, Local 76. (2003). *Collective agreement*. Retrieved 26 January 2011 from http://206.191.16.137/eng/agreement/current/1186003a.pdf

Nova Scotia Construction Labour Relations Association Limited & the Cape Breton Island Building & Construction Trades Council & Signatory Building Trade Unions. (2008). *Collective agreement*. Retrieved 25 January 2011 from http://206.191.16.137/eng/agreement/current/0251510a.pdf

Nuna Contracting Ltd.& Construction Workers Union , Local 63. (2007). *Collective agreement.* Retrieved 26 January 2011 from http://206.191.16.137/eng/agreement/current/1287903a.pdf

Red Deer College & Support Staff Association Red Deer College. (2006). *Collective agreement.* Retrieved 27 January 2011 from http://206.191.16.137/eng/agreement/current/1273903a.pdf

Regional Municipality of Waterloo & the Canadian Union of Public Employees, Local 1656. (2007). *Collective agreement.* Retrieved 25 January 2011 from http://206.191.16.137/eng/agreement/current/0719110a.pdf

Regional Municipality of York Police Services Board & the York Regional Police Association. (2010). *Collective agreement.* Retrieved 27 January 2011 from http://206.191.16.137/eng/agreement/current/0874211a.pdf

Royal Canadian Mint & ATU: Amalgamated Transit Union. (2005). *Collective agreement.* Retrieved 25 January 2011 from http://206.191.16.137/eng/agreement/current/1291102a.pdf. Used with permission.

Saskatchewan Government Insurance & Canadian Office and Professional Employees Union. (2007). *Collective agreement.* Retrieved 25 January 2011 from http://206.191.16.137/eng/agreement/current/0459409a.pdf

Saskatchewan Liquor and Gaming Authority & Saskatchewan Government and General Employees' Union. (2007). *Collective agreement.* Retrieved 25 January 2011 from http://206.191.16.137/eng/agreement/current/0450009a.pdf

Stringer, K. G., & Brown, T. C. (2008). A special kind of downsizing: An assessment of union member reaction to bumping. *Relations industrielles Industrial Relations, 63,* pp. 648–670.

Thompson Rivers University & Thompson Rivers University Faculty Association. (2004). *Collective agreement.* Retrieved 25 January 2011 from http://206.191.16.137/eng/agreement/current/1169604a.pdf

Treasury Board & the Federal Government Dockyard Trades and Labour Council (East). (2008). *Collective agreement.* Retrieved 25 January 2011 from http://206.191.16.137/eng/agreement/current/0660410a.pdf

Victorian Order of Nurses & Ontario Nurses' Association. (2007). *Collective agreement.* Retrieved 25 January 2011 from http://206.191.16.137/eng/agreement/current/0918008a.pdf

Westguard Security Services Inc. & Teamsters, Local No. 213. (2008). *Collective agreement.* Retrieved 27 January 2011 from http://206.191.16.137/eng/agreement/current/1379801a.pdf

Xstrata Nickel & United Steelworkers, Local 2020, Unit 6855. (2007). *Collective agreement.* Retrieved 25 January 2011 from http://206.191.16.137/eng/agreement/current/0017909a.pdf

Yukon College Board of Governors and the Public Service Alliance of Canada. (2003). *Collective agreement.* Retrieved 25 January 2011 from http://206.191.16.137/eng/agreement/current/1007506a.pdf

Strikes and Dispute Resolution

Learning Objectives

By the end of this chapter, you will be able to discuss

- the different types of industrial disputes;
- the various statistics used to measures strikes;
- the theories, causes, and impacts of strikes;
- typical grievance and arbitration procedures;
- other common conversion and alternative dispute resolution procedures; and
- why nonunion employers also use grievance and alternative dispute resolution mechanisms.

STRIKE AT YORK UNIVERSITY

A strike by part-time workers has turned York University into a virtual ghost town at the height of the November mid-term crunch, with all classes cancelled, assignments postponed and pickets letting cars onto campus only every few minutes.

"To be honest, like most students I like having a couple of days to catch up on my sleep," said first-year student Krupa Shah, who commutes from Richmond Hill.

"But it'll suck if the school semester or year gets pushed into our vacation. I just got through the Viva transit strike last month (of York Region's rapid bus system). What a way to start university."

The Canadian Union of Public Employees Local 3903 walked off the job at midnight yesterday over job security, wages and benefits for its 1,850 graduate students who work as teaching assistants, 550 others who work as research and administrative assistants, plus 950 contract faculty who teach almost half the courses at York but do not have permanent status.

No new talks are scheduled. Both sides say it is up to the other to make the first move. York says it is waiting for CUPE to agree to binding arbitration, something CUPE rejects. But chief union negotiator Graham Potts says he "would go back to the table in a heartbeat if York put a serious offer on the table."

CUPE has rejected the university's latest offer, presented Tuesday, which includes a wage hike of 9.25 per cent over three years, improved dental and health benefits and paid leaves—an offer York officials have said matches other settlements across the public sector.

CUPE 3903 is seeking an 11 per cent wage hike over two years, plus stronger health benefits and more job security for long-term contract teachers.

While York's teaching assistants are believed to be the highest paid in Canada—at about $17,386 a year for roughly 10 hours of teaching a week—union officials said their wages still fall below the poverty line. "There is no percentage in being the highest paid workers in a poorly paid sector," said teaching assistant Punam Khosla.

As for contract faculty, Khosla said they are paid about $14,000 per course that they design, teach and mark—some teach as many as five courses—whereas tenured professors earn an average of about $80,000 a year yet typically teach no more than three courses.

As well, contract professors must re-apply every semester for their job, even if they have been working for 10 to 15 years. The union wants the university to restore a five-year contract for longer-term contract faculty that was scrapped in 2001.

"Yes, we know about funding cuts and the hard economic times, but the university has seen the provincial government put more money into universities, tuition fees have been rising and everyone knows when the economy falls, the number of people who enrol in university goes up," said Khosla. "The university is in a unique position to be able to count on growing revenue from increased enrolment."

York spokesperson Alex Bilyk said that when all the union's demands are factored in, the increase it is seeking amounts to a "totally unrealistic" 41 per cent hike.

The university says provincial funding shortfalls have forced it to plan cuts of 2 per cent to the operating budget for each of the next three years.

Source: "Strike brings York to standstill," Louise Brown, Toronto Star, 14 December 2010. Used with permission of Torstar Syndication Services. Retrieved 14 December 2010 from http://www.thestar.com/news/article/532380--strike-

As we have seen in several instances in this text, strikes are a mechanism unions use to achieve their bargaining goals. Thus, they are a conversion mechanism in the IR system. Considering their importance in industrial relations, in this chapter, we will review many of the conversion mechanisms presented in Chapter 1: namely, strikes, grievances, arbitrations, and alternative dispute resolution procedures. Given the number of mechanisms covered, your instructor may choose to spend several classes on this chapter.

Over the past few years, many students have witnessed faculty strikes, or near strikes, at their campuses—examples are UPEI (CBC, 2006), Ontario Colleges (Webb, 2010), Acadia (CBC News, 2007), St. Thomas (Canadian Association of University Teachers [CAUT], 2008), York (Brown, 2008), and Western (*Maclean's*, 2010). Given that strikes have often caused student reactions, including YouTube postings, we will start with a review of strikes.

Strikes

As we have seen throughout this textbook, strikes and lockouts receive considerable media attention. In this section, we will define industrial disputes (one of which is strikes), review statistics concerning strike prevalence, and discuss some of the causes of strikes.

Defining Industrial Disputes

In its simplest form, we can think of an industrial dispute as a disagreement between employers and employees. However, in industrial relations, **industrial dispute** has a more precise meaning. The *Canada Labour Code* (section 3(1), 1985) defines it as "a dispute arising in connection with the entering into, renewing, or revising of a collective agreement." Should the parties not be able to come to agreement (using any or all of the dispute resolution techniques we will present later in this chapter), they may end up in a strike or lockout position.

industrial dispute

a disagreement arising from entering into, renewing, or revising a collective agreement

In essence, the difference between a strike and a lockout depends on whether management or labour initiated the action.

Strike

strike

a work stoppage invoked by a union

A **strike** occurs when a number of workers refuse to continue working or they stop working (*Canada Labour Code*, 1985). For example, in the opening vignette, the employees "walked off the job." Thus, the York case would be considered a strike as workers initiated the action.

work to rule

the strategy of employees who perform only to the minimum standard required

wildcat strike

an illegal strike during the term of the collective agreement

Note that the *Canada Labour Code* (section 3(1), 1985) also includes work slowdowns and "other concerted activity on the part of employees in relation to their work that is designed to restrict or limit output." This would mean that worker efforts to reduce productivity would also be considered a strike. These concerted slowdowns are often referred to as **work to rule**. There are also **wildcat strikes**, which occur when employees who are not in a legal strike position walk off the job. When these happen, employers will often go to court to seek a formal injunction that requires employees to return to work on the threat of legal penalties. Some strikes are restricted, meaning that there are a limited number (or type) of employees who can go on strike. For example, there are often restrictions on the number of nurses who can go on strike at one time as hospitals must continue to operate for the public good. This will be discussed in more detail in Chapter 11.

Lockout

lockout

a work stoppage invoked by management

A **lockout** occurs when the employer suspends work (or refuses to employ a number of workers) in an effort to get workers to agree to proposed terms or employment conditions (*Canada Labour Code*, 1985). A recent example would be the St. Thomas University dispute, in which "the St. Thomas University Board of Governors pre-emptively locked out FAUST members during contract negotiations, something never before done by any other university board in Canada" (CAUT, 2008). Many hockey fans will also remember the 2004–2005 lockout involving the National Hockey League (NHL) and the National Hockey League Players' Association (NHLPA). In September of 2004, the commissioner of the NHL, Gary Bettman, publicly announced a lockout after the end of a board of governors meeting (CBC Sports Online, 2005). Let's look at a few excerpts from Bettman's statement (NHL CBA News, 2004) to see how the work stoppage was initiated:

> . . . it is my somber duty to report that at today's meeting, the Board of Governors unanimously re-confirmed that NHL teams will not play at the expiration of the CBA until we have a new system which fixes the economic problems facing our game.

> That said, we *do* apologize to our millions of fans and the thousands of people whose livelihoods depend on our game. It is truly unfortunate that we have to go through this. I assure you that no one is more unhappy about this situation than I am.

> My pledge, at this difficult moment, is that we will correct this
> untenable situation the right way—not with Band-Aids and half-
> measures, but in a way that will ensure the health and excitement
> of our game for years to come. This game's future depends upon
> getting the right economic system. In the absence of such a system,
> there is no future for our game. As difficult as today is, the reality
> is, we had no choice in the face of the Union's continued refusal to
> address economic problems that are clear to everyone but them.

As these quotes show, it was the decision of the NHL Commission (or the
employer) to cancel the games and thus suspend work. Hence, it was a
lockout, not a strike.

Strike Statistics

Having defined industrial disputes, strike, and lockouts, it is time to introduce
the statistics in this area. In particular, we will look at how strikes are tracked,
as well as at regional and industry differences in tracking. As we examine this
area, it is important to note that the statistics reported are for both strikes and
lockouts, as statistical agencies do not differentiate according to who initiated
the work stoppage.

In Canada, Human Resources and Social Development Canada (HRSDC)
compiles statistics on strikes and makes these data publicly available. Tables
9.1 to 9.3, and Figure 9.1, present data taken from the HRSDC site that show
strike trends, for strikes involving 500 or more workers, for the years 1980 to
2010. Table 9.1 presents national data for all years 1980–2010 (Figure 9.1 shows
these data as a graph); Table 9.2 presents data by industry; Table 9.3 presents
strike statistics by region.[1,2,3,4]

TABLE 9.1

Canadian Strike Statistics for All Industries, 1980–2010			
YEAR	TOTAL STRIKES	WORKERS INVOLVED	PERSON–DAYS NOT WORKED	% OF ESTIMATED WORKING TIME
2010	19	43,315	565,591	0.01
2009	19	55,178	1,402,520	0.04
2008	13	26,704	269,840	0.01
2007	27	49,172	1,243,190	0.03
2006	11	27,583	260,230	0.01
2005	41	179,482	3,645,060	0.10
2004	37	236,843	2,396,220	0.07
2003	26	56,730	1,076,560	0.03
2002	31	142,089	2,273,000	0.07
2001	44	189,240	1,296,960	0.04
2000	44	112,468	779,410	0.02
1999	55	126,822	1,408,430	0.04

TABLE 9.1

Canadian Strike Statistics for All Industries, 1980–2010 (continued)

Year	Total Strikes	Workers Involved	Person–Days Not Worked	% of Estimated Working Time
1998	63	214,847	1,631,460	0.05
1997	32	237,246	2,855,740	0.09
1996	32	250,406	2,484,250	0.08
1995	39	125,531	993,430	0.03
1994	29	55,283	736,470	0.03
1993	25	73,757	498,680	0.02
1992	44	121,831	1,145,810	0.04
1991	36	218,377	1,452,400	0.05
1990	66	226,665	3,520,150	0.12
1989	67	394,351	2,177,040	0.08
1988	54	158,888	3,393,880	0.12
1987	63	530,720	2,406,350	0.09
1986	89	431,986	5,673,310	0.21
1985	56	100,107	1,348,850	0.05
1984	67	130,852	2,331,350	0.09
1983	61	279,818	2,881,950	0.12
1982	70	410,559	3,859,810	0.16
1981	99	240,452	6,169,150	0.24
1980	137	363,470	6,901,450	0.28

Source: "Canadian Strike Statistics for All Industries," published in *Chronological perspective on work stoppages*. Retrieved 16 January 2011 from http://srv131.services.gc.ca/dimt-wid/pcat-cpws/recherche-search.aspx?lang=eng&ind=1&jurs=1. Human Resources and Skills Development Canada, 2011. Reproduced with the permission of the Minister of Public Works and Government Services Canada, 2011.

FIGURE 9.1

Estimated Lost Time Due to Work Disputes for Canada, 1980–2010

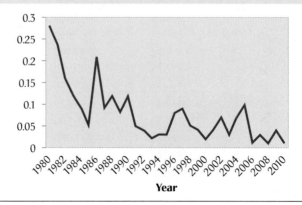

Source: Data from Human Resources and Social Development Canada, 2011.

TABLE 9.2

Canadian Strike Statistics by Selected Industries, Selected Years 1990–2010

PERIOD	TOTAL NUMBER	WORKERS INVOLVED	PERSON-DAYS NOT WORKED	% OF ESTIMATED WORKING TIME[1]
PRIMARY INDUSTRIES				
2010*	0	0	0	—
2005	4	3,273	140,260	—
2000	4	4,150	148,960	—
1995	1	985	6,890	—
1990	5	7,757	305,030	—
UTILITIES				
2010*	0	0	0	—
2005	1	850	60,260	—
2000	0	0	0	—
1995	0	0	0	—
1990	1	16,405	259,610	—
CONSTRUCTION				
2010*	2	1,450	9,380	—
2005	0	0	0	—
2000	0	0	0	—
1995	6	9,550	173,350	—
1990	8	122,300	1,136,950	—
MANUFACTURING				
2010*	3	4,507	438,970	—
2005	4	4,550	154,230	—
2000	8	20,228	138,270	—
1995	13	14,327	366,470	—
1990	22	42,654	1,407,280	—
WHOLESALE AND RETAIL TRADE				
2010*	0	0	0	—
2005	2	4,830	147,640	—
2000	2	7,815	16,080	—
1995	0	0	0	—
1990	1	609	30,380	—

TABLE 9.2

Canadian Strike Statistics by Selected Industries, Selected Years 1990–2010 (continued)

Period	Total Number	Workers Involved	Person-Days Not Worked	% of Estimated Working Time[1]
Information and Culture				
2010*	0	0	0	—
2005	3	20,600	1,533,960	—
2000	3	3,330	36,740	—
1990	0	0	0	—
Finance, Real Estate, and Management Services				
2010*	0	0	0	—
2005	1	1,100	41,640	—
2000	2	1,143	26,370	—
1995	1	580	1,740	—
1990	0	0	0	—
Education, Health, and Social Services				
2010*	11	29,905	108,979	—
2005	19	101,427	934,040	—
2000	15	36,035	190,190	—
1995	7	36,265	87,810	—
1990	24	29,240	314,960	—
Entertainment and Hospitality				
2010*	0	0	0	—
2005	1	1,071	15,000	—
2000	2	3,740	34,240	—
1995	2	2,919	70,090	—
1990	0	0	0	—
Public Administration				
2010*	2	6,623	4,112	—
2005	5	40,831	605,500	—
2000	7	34,950	184,250	—
1995	3	25,900	65,500	—
1990	3	4,400	36,030	—

*Person-days not worked as a percentage of estimated working time is only available for "All Industries" and "Canada Total."

Source: "Canadian Strike Statistics for Selected Industries," published in *Chronological perspective on work stoppages*. Retrieved 16 January 2011 from http://srv131.services.gc.ca/dimt-wid/pcat-cpws/recherche-search.aspx?lang=eng&ind=1&jurs=1search.aspx?lang=eng&ind=1&jurs=1. Human Resources and Skills Development Canada, 2011. Reproduced with the permission of the Minister of Public Works and Government Services Canada, 2011.

TABLE 9.3

Strike Statistics, Selected Years 1980–2010

YEAR	1980 PERSON-DAYS NOT WORKED	1985 PERSON-DAYS NOT WORKED	1990 PERSON-DAYS NOT WORKED	1995 PERSON-DAYS NOT WORKED	2000 PERSON-DAYS NOT WORKED	2005 PERSON-DAYS NOT WORKED	2010 PERSON-DAYS NOT WORKED
Newfoundland	753,830	35,320	100,020	0	13,950	9,960	0
P.E.I.	0	0	0	2,000	0	0	0
Nova Scotia	181,300	730	49,350	3,900	0	21,000	0
New Brunswick	215,560	3,600	211,200	0	13,920	105,600	0
Quebec	3,201,660	482,960	517,890	267,990	19,560	1,284,050	113,034
Ontario	1,047,280	561,280	2,374,390	270,500	345,350	182,180	440,907
Manitoba	24,170	0	0	19,820	2,090	0	7,500
Saskatchewan	44,650	25,090	15,510	0	0	31,370	0
Alberta	385,740	12,150	71,020	0	17,000	73,130	0
B.C.	203,010	24,740	120,970	213,770	287,350	498,840	0
Territories	0	0	0	0	0	0	0
Total federal	844,250	202,980	59,800	215,460	80,190	1,438,930	4,150

Source: Data from Human Resources and Social Development Canada, 2011.

As these tables suggest, strike statistics can be calculated in a number of ways. You will note that HRSDC provides several measures of strikes:

- total number, or frequency, of strikes;
- number of workers involved in the strike;
- person-days not worked (or the estimated number of days lost due to the strike calculated as number of workers multiplied by number of days on strike); and
- percentage of working time lost due to strike.

It is important to remember that a single statistic can be misleading. For example, as shown in Table 9.1, there were 19 strikes in both 2010 and 2009, suggesting that strikes were relatively equivalent those two years. However, the statistics for the number of workers involved, the person-days not worked, and percentage of estimated working time lost all suggest that 2009 was a worse year for strikes. As this comparison reveals, it is important to be aware of which statistic you are examining. For us, person-days not worked is the better of the statistics to use for comparison purposes. The overall economic impact of lost work days can be significant in terms of workers' losing take-home pay and firms' losing profits. "These two effects might reduce the productivity of both labour and capital, the two main components of economic productivity" (Dachis & Hebdon, 2010, p. 5).

National Statistical Trends

A review of Tables 9.1 through 9.3 and Figure 9.1 reveals a number of trends in terms of strikes over time, by industry, and by region. You will note that, historically, the general trend has been a reduction in lost time since 1980, with a sharp decrease after 1990. You will also note that certain industries (e.g., manufacturing, public administration) seem more strike-prone, particularly when we look at the number of workers involved and the person-days not worked relative to other industries (e.g., finance, real estate, management services). Similarly, we see that some regions of the country have low levels of strikes (e.g., Prince Edward Island, the Territories) compared to others (e.g., Quebec, Ontario, and British Columbia). However, we need to be careful in interpreting these trends. For example, we would expect a large province such as Ontario, which has a high concentration of manufacturing and public-sector jobs (a heavily unionized industry that Table 9.2 shows is prone to strikes) to have higher strike rates than a relatively small province such as Prince Edward Island, which is known for its hospitality/tourism industry (an industry which Table 9.2 shows has fewer strikes).

International Trends

Given the increased focus on global markets and international competition, it is also important to examine Canada's strike rates relative to those of other countries. A recent report by Hale (2008) presents the strike statistics for the Organisation for Economic Co-operation and Development (OECD) countries. The report examines the number of working days lost per 1,000 employees in all sectors and services of the economy. As is suggested by our review of Canadian strike statistics, in the OECD sample, the average rate of strikes dropped by 37 percent when the five-year period of 1997–2001 is compared to that of 2002–2006. A summary is presented in Table 9.4.

A review of Table 9.4 suggests that Canada's average number of working days not worked (or lost) due to strike (per 1,000 employees) dropped by 6 percent between the two five-year periods of 1997–2001 and 2002–2006. However, with an average of 186 working days lost per 1,000 workers over 1997–2006, only Iceland had more lost time due to strikes, at 486 days. Moreover, this rate was almost six times that of our largest trading partner, the United States (34 days).

As was the case with our review of the Canadian strike trends, we must be careful to ensure that we "compare apples to apples" when examining international strike data. In particular, the technical notes from Hale (2008) discuss the subtleties of how strikes are measured and tracked in one country versus another. Take a look at differences in the minimum criteria used by some countries for inclusion in strike statistics:

- Belgium has no size restrictions but excludes public-sector disputes.
- Denmark requires 100 workdays not worked.
- Finland statistics include all strikes of greater than one hour's duration.
- United States statistics include strikes of one day (or one shift) involving at least 1,000 employees.
- United Kingdom statistics include strikes of ten or more workers for a minimum of one day's duration, unless 1,000 workers were involved.

As these examples clearly point up, there is no simple and universal way to measure strikes internationally. Moreover they point to how statistics, taken

TABLE 9.4

Strike Data from Selected Countries: Working Days Not Worked per 1,000 Employees

Country/Region	Average 1997–2001	Average 2002–2006	Average 1997–2006	Percentage Change 1997–2001 to 2002–2006
Australia	65	30	46	−54%
Austria	1	80	41	7900%
Belgium	41*	−	10*	−
Canada	192	180	186	−6%
Denmark	292	38	164	−87%
Finland	58	91	75	57%
France	20	10*	15*	−50%
Germany	1	6	4	500%
Iceland	571	353*	486*	−38%
Ireland	86	15	47	83%
Italy	62	111	88	79%
Japan	1	0*	1*	−100%
Mexico	−**	24*	24*	−
Netherlands	5	11	8	120%
New Zealand	17	15	16	−12%
Norway	78	43	60	−45%
Portugal	19	15	17	−21%
Spain	178	164	170	−8%
Sweden	6	34	20	467%
Switzerland	3	4	3	33%
Turkey	27	11	18	−59%
United Kingdom	14	28	21	100%
United States	54	15	34	−72%
OECD average†	43*	31*	37*	−23%

*Averages were calculated using incomplete data.
**Dash indicates that data was not available for that country for that period.
†Excludes Hungary, Poland, and Slovakia after the year 2000.
Source: Hale, 2008.

at face value, may not tell the full story. For example, the number of days lost for the period 1997–2006 for Denmark and Canada were very similar; yet Denmark requires a strike to be 100 or more days to be included relative to the half-day duration plus 10 workdays lost for Canada.

Theories, Causes, and Impacts of Strikes

Having defined the various types of industrial disputes and examined the statistics and trends of strikes, it is time to turn to the theories, causes, and impacts of strikes.

Strike Theories

A recent paper by Kramer and Hyclak (2002) outlines the three common theories of strikes, namely, the accident theory (i.e., the Hicks theory), total joint costs, and asymmetric information. While these researchers focused on unions striking, we believe that managers may lock out employees for many of the same theoretical reasons.

Accident (or Hicks) Theory

The accident theory, often referred to as the Hicks theory because Hicks first proposed it, is based on the assumption that strikes represent accidents. The assumption is that "rational" negotiators would seek to avoid strikes and lockouts in order to avoid their high costs (lost wages, lost productivity, etc.). Thus, the theory states that strikes should be unexpected and that when they do occur, they are the result of errors made at the bargaining table, misunderstandings of bargaining goals, or mismatches between the expectations of the bargaining team and the group they represent.

The Total Joint Costs Theory

As stated previously, both the management team and the union membership face potential costs associated with a strike. In its simplest form, this theory argues that strikes are more likely when the cost of the strike is relatively low for both parties. Note that we must look at the total and joint costs to both the union and management groups to fully understand the model. If the cost of a strike is low to one party but high to another, a strike may not be likely given the clear power imbalance. In essence, the difference in the cost of the strike to one party, relative to the other, results in a difference in bargaining power (Maki, 1986). For example, the cost of snowplow operators in Winnipeg going on strike in July may be high to the workers (e.g., lost wages) but low to the city, as there is little need for snow clearing in July. The power dynamic is such that the workers may settle because of the high cost to them. The city, however, may readily accept a strike since citizens would not be in need of snow-clearing services at that time.

In contrast, if a company created a great deal of inventory anticipating a strike, and workers were paid overtime to create the inventory, the costs of the strike would be relatively low to both parties. The firm could continue to receive revenue in selling the product in inventory, and workers could use savings from their overtime pay to compensate for the loss in earnings. In essence, the total joint costs theory predicts that parties go on strike only when the cost of the strike is low or, in contrast, when the cost of settling is very high in comparison to the cost of striking.

Asymmetric Information Theory

Remember that during collective bargaining, parties may not candidly share goals and priorities. In fact, they might use deceptive tactics to shade the truth about their true priorities. The asymmetric information theory is grounded in the assumption that parties may strike or lock out as a way to see if the other side is bluffing. In so doing, the parties gather more information about the claims of the other party—information that would not be easily accessible in other ways. As a concrete example, we can look at strikes in professional sports. One analysis of pro sport strikes in hockey, basketball, baseball, and football found that many disputes were long and centred on issues concerning player salaries (Fisher, 2007). In many of these cases, the employer argued that players' salaries would negatively impact the long-term viability of the teams and the sport. We might surmise that the unions representing these players went on strike in an effort to see whether management was bluffing about the effect of the union's desired pay levels on team viability. The longer the employer accepted the strike, the more likely it was being honest about the potential impact. On the other hand, a quick settlement at (or near) the desired pay level might signal that the management groups were bluffing. Interestingly, Fisher (2007) concluded that management often gained concessions when the sports unions settled, suggesting they were not bluffing.

Strike Causes

While these previous theories provide us with the tools to understand potential causes of strikes, they tend to assume that strikes are rational and that their causes can be easily explained. However, there are other possible causes of strikes. In this section, we present several, many of which have been argued to have sparked strikes for over forty years.

Catalysts

More than thirty years ago, the idea that one event or action could act as a catalyst for a strike was examined in a study of the New Zealand meat industry (Geare, 1972). That study argued that strikes may have been sparked by a single trigger event. For example, in the 1960s, GM suspended seventeen union members, which resulted in the plant chairperson calling for a wildcat strike; this snowballed into 240,000 workers from twenty-two of GM's twenty-three assembly plants going on strike (Zetka, 1995). Clearly, the suspensions were a catalyst in that strike.

Isolated and Homogeneous Groups

Researchers have argued that intact groups of similar workers—particularly if they are in unpleasant jobs—may be more prone to strikes. For example, Geare's (1972) study discusses how factors such as monotonous jobs, unpleasant conditions, and geographic isolation from others (i.e., company hostels/camps) may explain some strike experiences. Similarly, "the solidarity work group thesis" (Zetka, 1995) argues that collective action, including strikes, is more likely to occur when workers form strong bonds between them (which can happen, for example, when working together to try to beat a production quota). These bonds place workers in a collective struggle that can then be mobilized for strike action (Zetka, 1995).

Chapter 9: Strikes and Dispute Resolution

Management Indifference or Unresolved Grievances

You may recall that one of the potential outcomes of the industrial relations system is employee satisfaction and commitment. Thus, it should not be surprising that management (particularly lower-level management) indifference to worker complaints has been identified as a potential catalyst for strikes (Geare, 1972). Likewise, grievances that are allowed to fester or left unresolved may become a catalyst for strike action.

Frustration–Aggression

Some scholars have presented a frustration–aggression hypothesis. This hypothesis argues that workers with feelings of work-related frustration, alienation, or dissatisfaction will naturally seek to improve the situation through their involvement in union activities and strikes (see review in Blackwood, Lafferty, Duck & Terry, 2003).

Economic Factors

Workers and management do not exist in isolation from the external labour market. Thus, research dating back to at least the 1960s has examined the relationship between the unemployment rate and the overall state of the business cycle (see reviews in Ashenfelter & Johnson, 1969; Maki, 1986). The general trend shows that strikes are more common when the economy is doing well and unemployment is low. This may be because in "good times," business is better and employers are able to pay better wages—workers may strike in an effort to make economic gains from employers. Alternatively, it may be because when the market is in an upswing, striking workers have other sources of income to turn to (i.e., a part-time job).

Intraorganizational Factors

Just as intraorganizational misalignment can reduce power at the bargaining table, so too can it result in strike activity. For example, if a union membership's expectations for wage gains are higher than the negotiation team can deliver, members have the option of either signing an agreement that may be difficult to ratify or incurring a strike. In such a case, the strike may serve to readjust the expectations of the membership toward a more realistic settlement (Ashenfelter & Johnson, 1969).

Strike Impacts

Economic

Research into the impacts of strikes has often focused on economic factors such as the relationship between strikes and market value of the affected firm (Hanrahan, Kushner, Martinello & Masse, 1997), decreased production that can result in decreased revenues and market share in the longer term (Barton & Weernink, 2003), and the fact that any negotiated wage and benefit increases can represent substantial increases in organizational expenditures (Burns, 2000). Striking workers themselves face economic impacts as they are not receiving a paycheque and have only limited access to funds via strike pay. Thus, it is not surprising that long strikes can result in significant (and negative) financial impacts on striking employees, their families, and even the communities in which they live.

Worker Well-Being

However, the consequences of a strike on affected workers stretch beyond economics. A strike can have an impact on workers in terms of their employment experience and psychological well-being. For example, Giesbrecht, Markle, and Macdonald (1982) have examined the impact of a long strike on alcohol consumption. From a workplace perspective, Nicholson and Kelly (1980) suggest that a strike can result in several organizational changes that may significantly affect the employment relationship and impact the rapport between employer and employees once workers return to their jobs. As has been pointed out in a practitioners' journal, actions taken by employers or employees during the strike (e.g., verbal abuse or other regrettable actions) can result in the employment relationship never being fully restored (Herald, 2002).

To date there has been limited examination of worker perception outputs of the industrial system (employee satisfaction, commitment, union satisfaction, union commitment, etc.). One study measured several of these variables following a three-week strike (Barling, Wade & Fullagar, 1990). Its goal was to assess the relationships between strikes and predictors of organizational and union commitment; it did not, however, assess the extent that the strike affected these variables. Similarly, Barling, Fullagar, McElvie, and Kelloway (1992) examined the relationship between organizational commitment, union loyalty, and how likely it would be for union members to strike. However, we know of only one Canadian study that examined the impact of strikes on employee perception variables of organizational commitment, job satisfaction, work environment, management satisfaction, and union commitment (Chaulk & Brown, 2008). It found that strikes had a significantly negative impact across all of these measures.

Grievances

Having discussed the conversion mechanism of strikes, we turn our attention to grievances. You may recall that a formal grievance procedure is a requirement of Canadian labour relations legislation. Arguably, the grievance procedures given by lawmakers were in exchange for Canada's "no strike" requirement. Remember, Canadian unionized workers cannot legally strike when a collective agreement is in place. Instead, unionized workers have the right to have their complaints resolved through another mechanism, namely the grievance procedure. Accordingly, grievance procedures are one of the employment practices that formally differentiate employment under common law versus employment under collective bargaining law. Only unionized Canadian workers have the legal right to file a formal grievance and have management formally respond to it. Consistent with exit voice theory, unionized employees also have the ability to "voice" their complaints using the grievance procedure as an alternative to exiting the organization. This view was supported by Rees's (1991) study of schoolteachers. He found that teachers with the strongest grievance procedures had a lower probability of quitting than those with weaker grievance procedures.

 **9.1**

In this section, we will define grievances, present a typical grievance procedure, and discuss research findings concerning the determinants of grievance initiation.

Grievances Defined

grievance

a formal complaint that a specific clause in the collective agreement has been violated

In its simplest form, a grievance may be considered a complaint. However, the meaning is more precise in the field of industrial relations. In industrial relations, a **grievance** is a formal complaint that a specific (and identified) clause contained in the collective agreement was not properly followed (Bemmels & Foley, 1996). An actual copy of a grievance is presented in Figure 9.2. (Note that the names of the people involved, the company, and the union have been blacked out.)

In addition, there are three key types of grievances in work environments: individual, group, and union. An example of each follows.

Individual Grievance

Perhaps the most common grievance filed at the workplace is the individual grievance. Examples of this type of grievance include an employee who grieves that she was not paid overtime in accordance with the collective agreement or a worker who grieves that he was inappropriately denied his vacation.

Group Grievance

Here, a group of employees grieve that the collective agreement has been violated. We could see, for example, a group of workers alleging that overtime is not being allocated per the process outlined in the collective agreement or a group of employees grieving that morning breaks are not being provided in accordance with the collective agreement.

Union or Policy Grievance

With a union or policy grievance, the union leadership, rather than members, initiates the complaint. For example, the union might grieve that a new attendance policy developed by management violates the collective agreement, or that work has been inappropriately contracted out in violation of the collective agreement.

The Grievance Procedure

A review of the literature suggests that there are several key parties and steps to the grievance procedure (see Bemmels, 1994; Bemmels & Foley, 1996; Bemmels, Reshef & Stratton-Devine, 1991; Brown & Beatty, 2006; Peterson & Lewin, 2000), which we outline below.

FIGURE 9.2

Grievance

GRIEVANCE FORM AND RECORD OF PROCEEDINGS

Employee ▮▮▮▮▮▮▮▮▮▮▮▮▮▮▮ Date grievance occurred *June 12, 2006*
If space in any step is inadequate
attach separate sheets.

The aggrieved employee(s) should follow carefully each step of the grievance procedure, answer all questions and pay close attention to the specified time limits.

STEP 1

Have you attempted to resolve your grievance with your immediate supervisor? YES ✔ NO ____

Have you had disciplinary action taken against you? YES ✔ NO ____

Have you consulted with your shop steward? YES ✔ NO ____

Describe your grievance, pointing out the article(s) of the agreement which is alleged to have been violated and the corrective action you request. This must be presented to your area superintendent/plant manager within 15 days of the occurrence of the grievance. _____

Article 6 – Managment Rights, Article 9.05 – discrimination
Article 37 – Subjugation, when grievor was wrongfully disciplined.
Settlement Requested: letter of written reprimand be removed
from personnel file, and replaced with written apology.

Signed ▮▮▮▮▮▮▮▮▮▮▮ Signed ▮▮▮▮▮▮▮▮▮▮▮
      Aggrieved employee   Steward

Parties

The three key parties in the grievance process are

- the employee, who often is the initial initiator of the grievance;
- the union, who is usually first represented by the shop steward; and
- management, who at the start of the process is usually represented by the immediate supervisor.

However, we should note that if the grievance is not settled through the "normal" grievance process, external third parties may become involved (grievance mediators, arbitrators, etc.). We will discuss this in more detail later in this chapter.

Process

We can think of the grievance process in terms of a formal (i.e., usually a paper-based process outlined in the collective agreement) as well as an informal (what some call pre-grievance) process. Given that these steps are specified in collective agreements, they differ between employment relationships. Nevertheless, while there is no standard process, most agreements have an informal stage followed by three or four formal stages. An example of a grievance procedure (up to but not including arbitration) can be found in Table 9.5 and IR Today 9.1. A typical process follows:

1. *Informal stage.* While not a requirement, and often not outlined in the collective agreement, an employee (with or without the assistance of the shop steward) may bring a complaint to his or her immediate supervisor in an attempt to settle the issue (Bemmels, Reshef & Stratton-Devine, 1991). If the complaint is resolved (either because the supervisor changes the employee's mind or because the employee is satisfied with the supervisor's answer), the process stops here. If not, the employee can take it through the formal grievance process.

2. *Formal step 1.* In a formal grievance, the employee will, usually with his or her shop steward, present a written grievance to the supervisor. The supervisor will have a specified period of time (as dictated by the collective agreement) to investigate the situation and respond. If the grievance is resolved, either because the supervisor changes the employee's mind or because the employee or union is satisfied with the answer, the process stops here. If not, it moves to step 2.

3. *Formal step 2.* The grievance is reviewed by the next level of management and union hierarchy (i.e., the department manager and a member of the union grievance committee). As in step 1, management will have a set period of time to respond to the grievance. If the grievance is not resolved to the satisfaction of the grievor or union, the process can proceed to the next step.

TABLE 9.5

An Internal Grievance Procedure

Step	Union Representative	Management Representative	Time for Management to Respond
1	Employee and, if the employee chooses, his/her shop steward	Foreman (or other supervisory employee)	4 days
2	One or more members of the union	Department manager (and/or designate)	9 days
3	The union, with or without assistance of a national union representative	General manager of the company	7 days

Source: Irving Pulp & Paper Ltd. & Communication, Energy and Paperworkers Union, *Collective Agreement*, retrieved 22 January 2010 from Negotech http://206.191.16.137/eng/agreement/current/0107107a.pdf.

Excerpt from the Irving Pulp & Paper Ltd. Collective Agreement

Article 9—Grievance Procedure

9.01 The parties recognize the prompt disposition of any difference or grievance is of the utmost importance, and they will co-operate in expediting the handling of any matter submitted for disposition under the procedure set out in this Article.

9.02 Any difference or grievance arising between the company and the Union or between the company and any employee, concerning the meaning or violation of any matter that this Agreement specifically provides may be dealt with as a Grievance and such Grievance shall be disposed of in accordance with the procedure in this Article contained, without any suspension of work or interference with the business of the Company.

9.03 (A) Grievance by Employee:

Should an employee wish to raise a grievance, the following procedure shall apply:

Step 1—Within seven (7) days from the day the alleged grievance has arisen, the employee or two (2) of a group of employees affected, accompanied by his or their Shop Steward if they desire, shall present the grievance, either orally or in writing, to their Foreman or other Supervisory employee directly concerned who shall communicate his decision within four (4) days.

Step 2—Failing settlement under Step 1 and within six (6) days from the expiration of the four (4) days delay referred to in Step 1, one (1) or more members of the Union may present the Grievance in writing to the Department Manager concerned. The Department Manager shall meet with the Union committee within three (3) days from the receipt of the written Grievance and communicate his decision to the Union within nine (9) days of the meeting.

Step 3—Failing settlement under Step 2 and within seven (7) days from the expiration of the nine (9) day delay referred to in Step 2, the Union, with or without the assistance of its National Representative, shall meet with the General Manager of the Company, who shall communicate his decision within seven (7) days of the meeting.

Step 4—Failing settlement under Step 3, the Union may within the next twenty (20) days after receiving the notice of decision under Step 3, refer the Grievance to Arbitration as provided for in Article 10 thereof.

(B) Any Grievance not appealed by the Union or Management within the time limits shall be deemed settled on the basis of Management's or the Local Union's last answer.

Source: Excerpt from Collective Agreement between Irving Pulp & Paper Ltd and Communications, Energy and Paperworkers Union of Canada. Used with permission. Found at http://206.191.16.137/eng/agreement/current/0107107a.pdf

4. *Formal step 3*. This repeats the previous step but with an even higher level of management and union hierarchy present (i.e., the plant manager or HR manager and a senior member of the union, such as an executive member or union local president). Note that it is not uncommon for several members of both management and the union to be present at this stage. If the grievance is resolved, either because the supervisor changes the employee's mind because or the employee or union is satisfied with the answer, the process stops here. If not, it moves to third-party intervention (e.g., arbitration).

5. *Formal step 4*. Here the parties turn to third-party intervention.

There are a few key points to remember about the grievance process. First, management has a specific time frame to investigate the grievance, and the union has a specific time frame to file a grievance or move it to the next step. These time frames are usually strictly enforced. Arbitrators will often refuse to hear grievances if the union filed after the time limit specified in the collective agreement, and unions can move to the next step when management fails to respond within the time frame permitted in the agreement (Brown & Beatty, 2006).

Second, note that at each stage of the grievance, the parties can agree to settle. Very few grievances go all the way to arbitration.

Third, at each stage of the process, higher levels of both the union and management hierarchy are involved. These higher levels will usually consult with the lower levels to understand the issues at hand. In fact, as is shown in Table 9.5, it is not uncommon for several levels of union and management to be present during the later steps of the procedure.

Fourth, the union is said to formally carry the grievance for the employee in question. Thus, you will note that the titles of labour arbitration cases refer to the union and organization involved—the grievor will be named in the text of the case but not the case title. However, as is also shown in the table, the employee is often present at all levels of the process.

Fifth, while the industrial relations department (whether called *human resources*, *labour relations*, *employment relations*, or *industrial relations*) may not be formally named in the collective agreement until the later steps of the process, it is often involved earlier. This is because (1) most members of the management team will consult with their industrial relations representative for guidance on how to handle the grievance; (2) given the importance of consistent interpretation of the agreement, IR staff members often have access to information concerning how the collective agreement language in question has been interpreted in the past; and (3) IR staff members have specialized training and expertise in the industrial relations field that may not exist in the rest of the organization.

Grievance Initiation

Considerable research has examined factors that can be linked to grievance initiation (Bamberger, Kohn & Nahum-Shani, 2008; Bemmels, 1994; Bemmels & Foley, 1996; Bemmels, Reshef & Stratton-Devine, 1991; Peterson & Lewin, 2000). A summary of some of the key findings from various fields (economics, industrial relations, and psychology) follows.

Grievor Characteristics

From a demographic perspective, past research found that grievors (as against non-grievors) were more likely to be young, male, well educated, and highly skilled (Peterson & Lewin, 2000). Interestingly, a newer study by Bamberger, Kohn, and Nahum-Shani (2008) suggests that there is no difference between the filing rate of men versus women and ethnic minorities versus whites per se; however, their findings did suggest that women and minorities may be less likely than their male and whites colleagues to file grievances in positive environments (non-abusive supervisors, few workplace hazards, etc.). Overall, these findings lead us to conclude that demographics alone probably play a small role in whether a person files a grievance. In addition to demographics, grievors, relative to non-grievors, are also found to be less satisfied with their jobs, have stronger views that employees should participate in workplace decisions, feel less commitment to their employers, and have less positive views of management (Bemmels & Foley, 1996).

Management Characteristics

A general trend is that the stricter the management practices in terms of enforcement of performance and disciplinary standards (what some call a structure focus), the higher the level of grievances. In contrast, supervisors having a good knowledge of the collective agreement, as well as supervisors who are considerate of employees and have friendly relations with them, experience lower levels of grievances (Bemmels & Foley, 1996; Peterson & Lewin, 2000).

Union Characteristics

Unions encouraging employees to file grievances, union leadership advocating "putting complaints in writing" (i.e., making formalized complaints), and shop stewards receiving a large number of complaints from employees result in more grievances, but unions that have stewards who attempt to informally resolve grievances see fewer grievances (Bemmels, 1994; Bemmels & Foley, 1996; Bemmels, Reshef & Stratton-Devine, 1991). In addition, when stewards have completed union steward training and received years of formal education, there tends to be an increased use of informal grievance resolution (Bemmels, Reshef & Stratton-Devine, 1991).

Regardless of factors that may be associated with the initiation of grievances, a review by Peterson and Lewin (2000) concluded that the presence of a grievance procedure is associated with increased productivity, lower turnover, and longer job tenure. Regression analyses found that the current status of a grievance had the greatest impact on employees' perceptions of the process. However, use of the procedure is associated with lower company performance. As such, this review presented several recommendations for human resources and labour relations executives (Peterson & Lewin, 2000):

- View the grievance system as a high-performance human resources practice, given its positive relationship with organizational performance. In fact, research has shown that perceptions of fairness in a unionized grievance system are positively correlated with organizational commitment (Mandville & Brown, 2009). Similarly, Fiorito, Bozeman, Young, and Meurs (2007), in a study of a HRM practices in union and nonunion firms, found that organizational commitment was positively related to grievance processes, defined by them as any formal procedure for resolving disputes.
- Understand the relationship between the presence of and usage of grievance procedures. The presence of the procedure is an important method to instill voice and fairness in the workplace; however, overly high usage rates may suggest that there is an ineffective use of informal conflict resolution. High usage of the formal process can result in employees (i.e., those filing grievances and their union representatives) and the management team directing their time away from work and toward the administration of grievance activities, thus reducing organizational performance.

- Assess the extent to which supervisors are treating workers democratically (i.e., with consideration) as opposed to focusing on issues of performance and productivity (i.e., structure), and whether any "rebalancing" between the two is needed, given that consideration reduces grievance filing.
- Ensure that front-line supervisors have a good knowledge of the collective agreement, as lack of such knowledge increases grievance rates.

In a similar vein, Nurse and Devonish's (2007) work provides guidance to practitioners. They suggest that effective grievance management systems should give workers (1) a well-defined process that is easily understood and ensures their issue is addressed in a timely manner; (2) the opportunity to be heard, without fear of management repercussions; (3) the right to union representation; and (4) the ability to shape workplace decisions that affect them.

Arbitration

As discussed above, parties can turn to arbitration when they are unable to resolve a grievance themselves. At times, because of the union's duty of fair representation, a union member may want to take an issue to arbitration even if the union does not agree that it is warranted. Regardless of how the parties get there, arbitration is a final and binding process where a third party resolves the dispute. Remember, there are two forms of arbitration processes: rights and interest.

RPC 9.2

rights (or grievance) arbitration
arbitration concerning alleged violations of the collective agreement

Rights Arbitration

Rights (or grievance) arbitration addresses alleged violations of the collective agreement. When the parties cannot resolve a grievance through the internal grievance process, it can be taken to arbitration. It is for this reason that this type of arbitration is also referred to as grievance arbitration. While we present this as the next logical step in the grievance process, we should be clear that very few grievances go as far as arbitration. Remember that the industrial systems framework that grounds this textbook includes the concept of a feedback loop. Before any arbitration, and during various steps of the grievance procedure, both union and management representatives will seek guidance from past grievance resolutions. For example, both union and management representatives may look internally to see how similar issues in the past were handled. This is because consistent application and interpretation of the collective agreement is critical. The parties may also look to external resources. One often used external resource is commonly referred to as *Brown and Beatty*. This source presents trends in arbitration and references specific arbitration rulings (known as labour arbitration cases, or LACs) by topic, so that parties can see how other parties have interpreted similar issues and collective agreement language.

The Process

The rights arbitration process has many of the same characteristics of a legal proceeding in that witnesses are sworn in, give evidence, and can be cross-examined, and evidence is formally presented and reviewed. However, it differs from a legal court proceeding in several ways: there is never a jury present; there is no true judge as the arbitrator may not be a lawyer or judge; and the proceeding does not take place in a courthouse (they often take place in hotel meeting rooms).

The process also differs on some of the key legal principles grounding the process. For example, take the issue of proof. In a criminal proceeding, the judge must be convinced beyond a reasonable doubt that the charged person committed the crime. In arbitrations, the decision is based on probable cause (i.e., is it most probable that the grievor did what management alleges?). It also differs in that arbitrators are not bound to follow **jurisprudence**, the past decisions of other arbitrators, and that arbitration decisions are considered final and binding. Only under very rare and exceptional circumstances will a court examine an arbitration ruling. However, we should stress that most arbitrators (even if not formally required to) will consult and follow past decisions. Remember, an arbitrator is deemed to be a neutral third party; it can be tough to be seen as a neutral third party if one creates rulings that contradict current arbitration trends.

jurisprudence
past decisions (usually in a legal context)

Given this backdrop, let's walk through a typical arbitration process. Since a number of arbitration cases involve discipline and discharge, we will examine a typical discharge arbitration using guidance from Brown and Beatty (2006). A summary of the key events for a discharge case on the grounds of excessive absenteeism follows and a summary of key arbitration issues is presented in Table 9.6.

First, the union will need to establish a **prima facie case**. In other words they must show that (1) the collective agreement was in place, (2) the grievor in question was covered by that agreement, (3) the grievor was employed, and (4) the grievor was disciplined. In essence, it will establish that the employee has a right to have his or her grievance heard.

prima facie case
union establishes, at arbitration, that the collective agreement was in place and that the grievor was employed, covered by that agreement, and disciplined.

Second, the management group will need to present evidence to answer the following questions in order to show that there was just cause for its disciplinary actions:

- *Did the alleged events take place?* Management would need to present evidence of excessive absenteeism (e.g., attendance records, payroll records).
- *Was it reasonable for the employer to provide some form of discipline?* Management would most likely present evidence on the basis of its interpretation of the discipline clause (and perhaps other language) of the collective agreement to justify its disciplinary actions. Similarly, it would likely present evidence (using LACs likely found in Brown and Beatty) to show how arbitrators have ruled that similar employee conduct has warranted some level of discipline.

TABLE 9.6

Key Arbitration Issues

THREE ELEMENTS OF CULPABLE BEHAVIOUR

1. The grievor was aware of what was required of him or her.
2. The grievor was capable of performing what was required of him or her.
3. The grievor chose to do otherwise.

THREE QUESTIONS EXAMINED FOR DISCHARGE CASES

1. Did management have reasonable grounds to impose some form of discipline?
2. Was the level of discipline imposed reasonable given the circumstances?
3. If the level of discipline imposed was excessive, what level of discipline (if any) is appropriate?

COMMON MITIGATING FACTORS

The grievor's work record	Isolation
Inconsistent application of rules	Grievor's length of service
Premeditation	Economic hardship
Remorse/likelihood to repeat	Seriousness of the offence
Provocation	Lack of understanding

culpable
at fault, guilty

Management will need to prove that the grievor is **culpable**—that he or she is blameworthy for his or her actions—and that the conduct warrants discipline. For the grievor's conduct to be considered the management representative will need to show that

1. the grievor was aware of what was required of him or her;
2. the grievor was capable of performing what was required of him or her; and
3. the grievor chose to do otherwise.

If management cannot demonstrate all three elements of culpability, the employee is considered nonculpable.

Let's consider two examples. Let's say that a grievor was aware of the attendance policy stating that he was to call in sick if he could not report to work; that he was able to follow the policy (i.e., nothing impeded his ability to phone in sick); and that he failed to call in sick. In this case, the grievor would be culpable, and some form of discipline would be appropriate. Now let's say that a second grievor who was also absent was aware of the attendance policy but that she was unable to phone in because the phone lines were down due to an ice storm. In that case, her conduct would not make her culpable. It is also important to stress that if management cannot provide evidence to support all three culpability elements, then the employee is nonculpable.

- *Was the level of discipline imposed by management reasonable?* In discipline cases, management has several sanctions available. These include a verbal warning, a written warning, a suspension, and a discharge. In the hearing, management would again argue (using data from collective agreement language) that the level choice of the discipline imposed (e.g., discharge) was appropriate. Remember that discharge is the most serious sanction available—it is akin to capital punishment in a criminal trial. To have the grievance denied (i.e., a ruling in favour of management), management will have to provide considerable evidence to support its decision to discharge. Given the long-standing doctrine of progressive discipline discussed in Chapter 8, you would expect management to present evidence either that it followed the concept of progressive discipline or that the alleged conduct was such that immediate discharge was warranted.

- Note that as discussed in chapter 6, non-union workplaces often use the doctrine of progressive discipline. See the example in IR Today 9.2.

Third, remember that the union representative will have an opportunity to question the management witness and provide counterevidence. Often, the union will present what is known as **mitigation factors** during arbitration (particularly with regard to the issue of whether the level of discipline imposed was appropriate). These factors are used as a way to reduce or remove the sanction (in our example, discharge) imposed by management. A review of Brown and Beatty (2006; see section 7:440) show several mitigation factors that the union may argue:

mitigation factors
factors argued by the union for a reduction in a sanction

- *The grievor's work record.* If the grievor has had few or no warnings, a good level of performance, etc., the union will often ask that this be used to lessen the sanction.
- *The grievor's length of service.* Similar to the previous factor, a long record of service (particularly if it is unblemished) may be used by the union as a reason to reduce the sanction.
- *Isolated event.* As with the previous two factors, an isolated event can be used as a mitigating factor. For example, the union could argue that a single failure to call in sick was an isolated incident unworthy of discipline (or of the level of discipline imposed).
- *Inconsistent application of rules or treatment.* If the union can find examples in which other employees conducted themselves in a similar manner and a less severe sanction or no sanction was imposed, it will argue that the management group acted inconsistently. For example, if in our case the union could find evidence that other employees with similar records of absenteeism received written warnings, not discharges, this mitigating factor might be used to argue for a reduction in the sanction imposed.
- *Premeditation.* If there is evidence that the grievor's actions were "spur of the moment" and not premeditated (i.e., planned in advance), the union may use this to argue for a reduction in sanction.
- *Remorse/likelihood to repeat.* When grievors are remorseful for their actions, their unions will often assert that there is little likelihood that the same conduct will occur again. Thus, they will argue that this

Cygnus Gymnastics

The concept of progressive discipline (or corrective action) is a cornerstone of unionized workplaces and is becoming increasingly common among nonunion firms. In essence, it is grounded in the beliefs that the punishment should fit the crime, that employees should be given the chance to improve their conduct, and that workers should be aware that failure to improve can result in discharge (Brown & Beatty, 2006). Thus, employees will normally receive lower levels of sanctions (i.e., verbal and written warnings) prior to more serious sanctions (i.e., a suspension or discharge). For example, the first time an employee failed to follow the company's dress code, he or she might receive a verbal warning. If he or she continued to ignore the dress code, a more severe sanction (i.e., a written warning) might be issued. This would continue until the behaviour improved or the employee was discharged.

The following is a (verbatim) example of a corrective action policy from a nonunionized, nonprofit gymnastics club.

Corrective Action Policy for Cygnus Gymnastics

1. Cygnus believes in the concept of progressive discipline for all of its employees. In situations where discipline is required, such actions should, wherever possible, be corrective rather than punitive in nature. The normal progression of corrective action will be as follows:

   Step 1: Verbal counseling

   Step 2: Written warning

   Step 3: Suspension without pay (equivalent to 20% of normal workweek)

   Step 4: Suspension without pay (equivalent to 100% of normal workweek)

   Step 5: Termination

2. It is understood that certain offences are sufficiently serious to warrant immediate termination and/or a faster progression through the process outlined in section 1 of this policy. While not inclusive, the following are examples of grounds for immediate termination.

   a. Using or being under the influence of alcohol and/or narcotics and/or illicit prescription drugs in the workplace or during work time.

   b. Failure to comply with a direct order from a person of authority, unless compliance would be in violation of a law or statute.

   c. Endangering the safety or well-being of athletes, staff, or parents.

   d. Fighting or committing assault in the workplace or during work time.

   e. Theft or misappropriation of Cygnus funds, equipment, materials, or property, or of the property of others that is positioned on Cygnus-owned or -operated premises or equipment.

   f. Illegal activities conducted at the workplace or during work time.

3. Wherever possible, all corrective action must be approved by the Director of Human Resources (or delegate) prior to implementation.

4. Wherever possible (a) the Director of Human Resources (or delegate) will be present when any form of discipline is presented to an employee, and (b) all forms of corrective action will be presented and discussed in a meeting between the employee, his/her immediate supervisor, and the Director of Human Resources (or delegate).

5. The primary purpose of a verbal counseling is to (a) make the employee aware of the issue at hand; (b) discuss expectations going forward; and (c) inform the employee that repeated performance/behavioural issues can result in further correction action. Given the counselling nature of this form of corrective action, the only documentation placed in the employee's human resources file will relate to the date of the counselling and the issue at hand.

6. With the exception of verbal counselling, all corrective action must be documented with a hard copy placed in the employee's human resources file and a copy provided to the employee. The Director of Human Resources (or delegate) and the employee in question will be asked to sign both copies. Provided that no subsequent corrective action steps have occurred, documentation referring to corrective action will be removed from the employee's human resources file after twenty-four (24) calendar months.

Source: Courtesy of Cygnus Gymnastics Training Centre.

factor should be used to give the grievor another chance (i.e., reduce the sanction).

- *Economic hardship.* A union can argue that the sanction imposed presents severe economic hardship, and thus should be reduced. For example, if the employee in our attendance example was one year away from qualifying for his pension, the union might argue that discharge poses extreme hardship.
- *Provocation.* If the grievor's actions were provoked by a management action, the union will often request reduction or removal of the sanction. For example, if the employee is being disciplined for swearing at his supervisor and it turns out that the supervisor swore at him first, the union might argue provocation.
- *Seriousness of the offence.* For example, the impact of an employee who stole a blank USB drive would be minimal for the organization relative to an employee who downloaded the entire customer list and sold it to a competitor.
- *Lack of understanding.* A union can argue that an employee did not truly disobey a work order as she did not fully understand it.

While we have presented mitigation factors in terms of how the union might argue them, management can argue the reverse (poor work record, consistent application of rules, etc.). Also note that while we have presented them as separate factors, either party might use multiple mitigating factors in its argument (e.g., twenty-year employee, clean work record with no performance issues, isolated event provoked by management).

Fourth, after hearing all of the evidence, a decision will be written. In the case of discharge, the arbitrator will examine three key questions:

1. Did management have reasonable grounds to impose some form of discipline?
2. Was the level of discipline imposed reasonable given the circumstances?
3. If the level of discipline imposed was excessive, what level of discipline (if any) is appropriate?

Thus, the ruling will be either "Grievance denied," meaning that management's position is supported and no changes are awarded, or "Grievance upheld," meaning that management's decision was not supported. In some cases, the ruling grievance is "partially upheld," meaning that part, but not all, of the union's argument is accepted. In many cases, when the grievance is upheld or partially upheld, the ruling will include a substitution of the sanction. For example, the discharged employee may be reinstated and the discharge replaced by a lesser penalty (e.g., suspension). Key elements in any sanction substitution or reinstatement will be seniority provisions and pay. Remember that it can be months (or even years) from the time an employee is discharged to the time he or she is reinstated. The ruling will also need to determine whether the reinstated employee accumulates seniority for any portion of the period between discharge and reinstatement and whether he or she is paid for any of that period.

Students have often asked us, "What does it take for management to win an arbitration concerning discharge?" A review of Brown and Beatty (2006) provides guidance here. Generally speaking, management's actions are most likely to be supported when management shows that (1) progressive discipline was used; (2) its treatment of the grievor was consistent with that of other employees in similar situations; (3) there is little likelihood of the grievor's conduct being reformed given his or her current employment record; and (4) past corrective action steps have failed. Of course, when management cannot prove such issues, the union is likely to win the arbitration. Thus, we see that documentation of events and progressive action steps are key. For this reason, one of the authors of this text has often reminded managers of the need to watch their *ABCD*s in discipline steps: "Always Be Consistent and Document."

The Forms of Arbitration

As we discussed in Chapter 2, Canadian labour relations laws are largely similar in content but have subtle differences between them. When it comes to grievance arbitration, the forms of arbitration differ slightly from jurisdiction to jurisdiction. Some of the following may not be available in your province.

Conventional Tripartite Arbitration

This three-person arbitration panel is the most common method used for rights arbitration. Both management and the union each choose a representative and mutually agree to a third chairperson, who is registered with the appropriate labour relations board. The chair is sometimes called the *neutral chair* as the person must be mutually agreed upon by union and management; thus, it is unlikely that the chair is seen as being either pro-management or pro-union. While it is not a requirement, common wisdom states that each side's representative be present to ensure that its side's view is heard, so the union nominee will argue for the union's position and the management nominee will argue for the management's position. Therefore, split decisions (2–1) are not uncommon in tripartite arbitration rulings.

Under this model, management will pay for the expenses of the management nominee, and the union will pay for its nominee. The two parties split the cost of the neutral chair.

Sole Arbitration

The primary difference between this form of arbitration and the previous is that there is just a neutral chair. No nominees (i.e., people on the side of management or the union) are present to represent the union or management. This form is often used in conjunction with expedited arbitration.

Expedited Arbitration

Given the long time frame that parties can wait before an arbitration hearing, some jurisdictions allow expedited arbitration. Under this form of arbitration, the labour relations board guarantees a hearing within a specified time frame, but the parties have no choice on the arbitrator.

The Problems with Current Grievance Arbitration Processes

Our conversations with labour leaders and industrial relations practitioners suggest there are several problems with the current system. First is the long delay between the actions that prompted the grievance and the arbitration ruling. As outlined by Williams and Taras (2000), even if the employee is reinstated, the extended time delay can make reintegration into the workplace difficult for all parties involved. In fact, it can result in some employees who are reinstated opting to financially settle with the employer and not return to work. As rightly pointed out by Zerbe (2009), there is an emotional element to arbitration processes, and we can imagine that significant time delays would enhance any emotional responses.

Second, arbitrations are costly. A typical arbitration requires each side to pay for its respective nominees and share the cost of the chair, the room where the hearings take place, etc. Moreover, many unions and management teams will hire lawyers to represent them, adding to the cost. Finally, there are the hidden costs of the staff time spent preparing for the arbitration.

Third, there is what can be called the "outsider" factor. Remember that the collective agreement represents a mutual understanding of the terms and conditions of the work negotiated by representatives of the union and management groups. As such, these parties have firsthand knowledge of the workplace and the implications of any language they create. On the other hand, the arbitrators who will make the final decision often lack such firsthand experience with the workplace and work relationship in question. This lack of personal understanding of the relationship can be problematic considering that the final arbitration decision is final and binding.

Fourth, the process is becoming increasingly legalistic, as is the case with collective agreement language in general. Many unions and employers hire lawyers to represent them in arbitration while others hire legal counsel as full-time employees. Thus, it is rare that management would send a manager or the union would send a front-line representative to argue the merits of the grievance. Yet, we must remember that the grievance process was conceived as a simple process to resolve workplace issues.

For these reasons, we are seeing a number of alternative dispute resolution techniques being used as potential precursors (or substitutes) to arbitration. These will be discussed in more detail later this chapter.

Interest Arbitration

R P C 9.3

Designed to resolve a disagreement during collective agreement negotiations, **interest arbitration** is a used as an alternative to strikes when parties are not permitted to strike or lock out. When they fail to reach a collective agreement on their own, they must turn to arbitration. While private-sector parties can mutually agree to such forms of arbitration, interest arbitration is most commonly used in public-sector employment relationships. Interestingly, recent evidence suggests that in places were legislation requires interest arbitration to settle public-sector disputes, compensation costs are about 1.2 percent per

interest arbitration
an arbitration that determines terms and conditions of the collective agreement while it's being negotiated

settlement (Dachis & Hebdon, 2010). In Canada, there are two common forms of interest arbitration: conventional and final-offer selection (Hebdon & Stern, 2003).

Conventional Interest Arbitration

conventional interest arbitration

interest arbitration where the arbitrator can choose among the proposals or fashion one of his or her own

In **conventional interest arbitration**, the parties submit separate potential solutions to the outstanding issues. The arbitrator can then choose among the options or craft his or her own to settle the outstanding issues.

Final-Offer Arbitration

final–offer arbitration

interest arbitration in which the arbitrator must choose one of the parties' proposals

In **final-offer arbitration**, parties submit a final offer to the arbitrator. The arbitrator must then choose the full final offer (i.e., without making any changes) of either management or the union. The rationale for the final-offer method is that the parties would be likely to submit reasonable alternatives given that the arbitrator would have to choose *all* of one of the two packages placed before him or her.

First Agreement Arbitration

first agreement (or first contract) arbitration

arbitration that determines the first collective agreement

Some jurisdictions require that when the parties cannot come to a mutually agreeable collective agreement during the very first round of negotiations, they must submit to interest arbitration. This is known as **first agreement (or first contract) arbitration**. Interestingly, recent evidence suggests that this form of arbitration is effective, reducing first agreement work stoppages by at least 50 percent (Johnson, 2010).

The Pros and Cons of Interest Arbitration

The principal strength of interest arbitration is its ability to reduce the incidences of strikes, especially for employees performing essential tasks (Currie & McConnell, 1991; Ichniowski, 1982; Olson, 1986; Rose, 1994). While interest arbitration laws may reduce the number of formal strikes, there is evidence that they have the unintended effect of increasing grievance arbitrations, unfair labour practices, absenteeism, and job actions (Hebdon, 2005; Hebdon & Stern, 1998, 2003). A job action could be any collective action designed to disrupt or slow down work (e.g., booking off sick, working to rule) or simply a button-wearing action to inform the public of union grievances.

The weaknesses of interest arbitration have been widely canvassed. Many (but not all) studies show that interest arbitration has a negative impact on the parties' ability to freely negotiate settlements.

Other Conversion Mechanisms

Conciliation and Mediation

In addition to grievances and arbitrations, conciliation and mediation represent important conversion mechanisms in the Canadian industrial relations system. As is pointed out by Auld, Christofides, Swidinsky, and Wilton (1981), any discussion of third-party interventions in Canada is complicated by the fact that we have a different set of labour relations acts for each province and another set at the federal level. Nevertheless, Auld et al. point up several similarities that cut across all jurisdictions in terms of third-party resolution procedures prior to legal work stoppages.

For example, while the specifics of the legislation vary from jurisdiction to jurisdiction there has been a long-standing requirement that private-sector disputes pass through a two-step compulsory conciliation process prior to legal work stoppages. In the first step, known as mediation, conciliation officers use their influence to try to bring the parties to a settlement. In this role, conciliators can neither judge the appropriateness of the parties' positions nor force the settlement.

If mediation fails to bring closure to the agreement, the second stage, conciliation, occurs. In this stage, a conciliation board is appointed with the power to make judgments concerning the bargaining positions as well as make recommendations for settlement. However, these recommendations are not binding, and the parties can proceed to strike/lock out if the conciliation board fails to resolve the outstanding issues.

Alternative Dispute Resolution (ADR) Options

Practitioners' journals discuss **alternative dispute resolution (ADR)**, a term commonly used in Canada. A keyword Internet search of this phrase will result in numerous hits about the previously discussed conversion processes of arbitration, mediation, and conciliation—mechanisms akin to ADRs (Carver & Vondra, 1994). The Canadian Human Rights Commission (2007) provides a good definition of ADR: "resolving disputes in ways other than going to court, including arbitration, mediation, negotiation, conciliation, etc."

In addition to the conversion mechanisms already discussed, some jurisdictions provide grievance mediation services as a form of ADR. **Grievance mediation** is a voluntary process whereby the parties can have a neutral third party examine the grievance. The mediator works with the parties to attempt to have them broker the resolution; yet it still leaves open the option for a formal arbitration hearing. IR Notebook 9.1 provides more details on this form of ADR.

alternative dispute resolution (ADR)

resolving disputes without going to court

grievance mediation

a voluntary nonbinding process whereby a neutral third party examines the grievance

Alternative Dispute Resolution in Nonunion Firms

While ADR is core to the unionized employment relationship, it also exists in nonunion workplaces. For example, mediation and conciliation interventions are available to all workers who bring forward complaints to the Canadian Human Rights Commission (Canadian Human Rights Commission, 2007).

In addition, as is discussed in Chapter 6, many nonunion firms have due process and voice mechanisms such as grievance/complaint processes and third-party review of grievances/complaints (i.e., akin to arbitration). As Colvin (2003) points out, there are three possible reasons for the adoption of ADR in nonunion firms. First, ADR can be seen as part of a high-performance work system; that is, it is seen as a way to emphasize fair treatment of employees in an effort to increase employee commitment, retention, and performance. Second, under common law, litigation was the only way employees could attempt to resolve disputes with employers; ADR provides an alternative to litigation. Third, the implementation of ADR is a form of union substitution. By having access to dispute resolution mechanisms that mirror those of the union movement, employees may be less likely to seek unionization.

Regardless of the reason, the trend is clear. Many nonunion workplaces, as well as agencies such as the Canadian Human Rights Commission, are moving to forms of ADR in an effort to provide alternatives to legal action.

IR Notebook 9.1

Grievance Mediation: An Alternative to Costly Arbitration

Given the high cost and the long time frame of dealing with grievances, many jurisdictions offer grievance mediation services. Here is an example from Saskatchewan.

Our Labour Relations and Mediation Branch offers grievance mediation, one of the more important tools used to strengthen collective bargaining relationships.

Grievance mediation is a less formal process than arbitration, and the outcome is decided by the two parties directly affected by the dispute, unlike arbitration where a decision is handed down by a third party.

Grievance mediation is a process by which the parties to a collective agreement, with the assistance of a mediator, work towards the resolution of a grievance arising from the interpretation, application, administration or alleged contravention of a collective agreement.

The mediator is a neutral third party who works constructively with the parties, in a flexible and creative manner, to assist the parties in resolving their dispute(s).

Here's How It Works:

- The program is voluntary; both parties must agree to participate.
- The mediation is informal in nature and the mediator will not produce any formal report. If an agreement is reached, the terms of settlement will be recorded.
- Arbitration remains an option if the grievance is unresolved after grievance mediation.

- Issues in industrial relations can be both unique and complex. Our mediators have extensive experience in dispute resolution in labour relations.
- All grievance mediation proceedings are without prejudice and are confidential between the parties, unless otherwise agreed.

Why Consider Grievance Mediation?

There are several reasons why employers and unions may want to consider grievance mediation:

- Attitudes—grievance mediation is designed to alleviate the build-up of negative attitudes which can develop when conflict goes unresolved.
- Control—grievance mediation allows the parties to shape a settlement. If the grievance goes to arbitration, a settlement will be imposed.
- Cost—arbitration can be an expensive process. A grievance mediator is assigned without cost for their services.
- Time—grievance mediation is designed for resolving disputes as quickly as possible. Time delays can lead to serious morale and personnel problems.

Grievance mediation works!

Source: Ministry of Labour Relations and Workplace Safety. Government of Saskatchewan (2007). Used with permission. Retrieved 23 January 2011 from http://www.aeei.gov.sk.ca/grievance-mediation.

Summary

As is shown in this chapter, there are a variety of conversion mechanisms in the current industrial relations system including strikes, grievances, arbitrations, and alternative dispute resolution mechanisms (ADRs) such as mediation and conciliation.

In terms of strikes, we examined three theories—the Hicks or accident theory, asymmetrical information, and total joint costs—as well as several factors known to potentially cause strikes (e.g., management indifference, unresolved grievances). We also discovered that Canada has one of the higher strike rates globally but that our strike rates are generally declining over time.

Given the potential high cost of grievances and strikes to employers, employees, and the Canadian economy as a whole, various alternative mechanisms designed to address workplace conflict and disagreements have been widely instituted. In terms of resolving impasses at collective bargaining, we reviewed first contract arbitration, conciliation, mediation, interest arbitration and limited, or restricted, strikes. These last two mechanisms are often used in the public sector.

We also looked at various mechanisms that can be used to address conflicts during the term of the collective agreement, and often regarding the interpretation of the collective agreement. Here, we studied the important mechanisms of grievances and rights arbitration—two mechanisms that are legally required only under collective bargaining law. However, we saw that given the movement toward more progressive human resources management policies in nonunion firms, these mechanisms are becoming increasingly more common in all workplaces—unionized and nonunionized.

In our discussion of rights arbitration, we examined how legalistic it has become in terms of language and process. The process is not without its problems, however, causing many jurisdictions to provide alternative dispute resolution mechanisms.

Overall, this chapter has shown the diversity and indeed sometimes the complexity of strike and dispute resolution procedures. As time unfolds it will be most interesting to see the extent to which these mechanisms become embedded in nonunion firms as well as the extent to which these processes becoming increasingly—or decreasingly—legalistic.

Key Terms

alternative dispute resolution (ADR) 299

conventional interest arbitration 298

culpable 292

final-offer arbitration 298

first agreement (or first contract) arbitration 298

grievance 284

grievance mediation 299

industrial dispute 271

interest arbitration 297

jurisprudence 291

lockout 272

mitigation factors 293

prima facie case 291

rights (or grievance) arbitration 290

strike 272

wildcat strikes 272

work to rule 272

Weblinks

YouTube Videos for strike reactions for Acadia:

http://www.youtube.com/watch?v=K7suWerflYw

YouTube Videos for CUPE strike at York:

http://www.youtube.com/watch?v=rUDKKLPfge4&playnext=1&list=PL2B F93E97168C1C70&index=7

HRSDC requirements for a legal strike in different Canadian jurisdictions:

http://www.hrsdc.gc.ca/en/lp/spila/clli/irlc/votes(e).pdf

HRSDC strike data:

http://srv131.services.gc.ca/dimt-wid/pcat-cpws/recherche-search. aspx?lang=eng&ind=1&jurs=1

Canadian Human Rights Commission and ADR:

http://www.chrc-ccdp.ca/disputeresolution_reglementdifferends/adr_ rdd-eng.aspx

Saskatchewan Federation of Labour grievance mediation process:

http://www.aeei.gov.sk.ca/grievance-mediation

RPC Icons

9.1 Advises clients of signatories' rights, including those with respect to grievance procedures

- context and content of collective agreements
- organization structure and authorities
- arbitration jurisprudence
- concepts and processes of politics and conflict

9.2 Provides consultation and risk assessment in issues involving arbitration

- arbitration jurisprudence
- arbitration process
- government labour relationship acts
- institutions and processes (both regulatory and nonregulatory) that govern the relationship between employers and employees

9.3 Advises client on matters related to interest arbitration

- arbitration process
- government labour relationship acts
- institutions that govern the relationship between employers and employees

- the process of collective bargaining and processes (both regulatory and nonregulatory) that govern the relationship between employers and employees
- the rights and responsibilities of management and labour during the processes of organizing and negotiation

Discussion Questions

1. Think of a current strike/lockout that is receiving media coverage in your community. Can you apply the strike theories to explain why this strike/lockout occurred? What do you feel was the primary cause of this strike/lockout?
2. Canadian legislation has perhaps the greatest restrictions on strikes. Yet we have one of the highest strike incidents on a global basis. Why do you think this is so?
3. A review of the strike data suggests that as we have moved to a more global economy our strike rates have dropped. Do you feel that the globalization of the marketplace has impacted our strike rates?
4. Look at Table 9.2. Pick two or three industries that are key players in your local economy. Are the levels of strikes in your local economy consistent with what the table suggests? If not, why not?
5. With more nonunion firms providing dispute resolutions that are akin to those of the labour movement, will unions become obsolete in the future?
6. Given the limitations of traditional rights arbitration, do you believe that we will see an increase in alternative dispute resolution processes?
7. Some unions state that all discharge cases can be taken to arbitration; others look at the issue of arbitration on a case-by-case basis. What do you see as the pros and cons of each of these options?
8. Given the problems of traditional rights arbitration, why, in your opinion, does it remain more popular than sole arbitration and expedited arbitration?

Using the Internet

1. Go to a local or national news website and look for information concerning a strike or lockout. Can you apply the strike theories to explain why this strike/lockout occurred? What do you feel was the primary cause of this strike/lockout?
2. Many universities, colleges, and other public institutions put their collective agreements online. Have a look at one or more of these collective agreements. To what extent

   a. is the grievance procedure similar to that presented in the text?
   b. does it discuss arbitration procedures?
   c. does it contain (or refer to) alternative dispute resolution processes?

3. Many provincial labour relations boards provide third-party dispute resolution procedures in addition to arbitration. Go to your province's website.

   a. What forms of third-party assistance are offered to help parties resolve grievances?
   b. What forms of third-party assistance are offered to help parties conclude a collective agreement?
   c. Which of these third-party mechanisms are compulsory versus voluntary?

4. Go to an Internet search engine and search using keywords such as *grievance*, *dispute*, and *alternative dispute resolution*. What do you find? Are there union and nonunion examples? If so, what are some key differences between these union and nonunion examples?

5. In this chapter, we discussed that management training can reduce the number of grievances filed. Conduct a search for industrial relations or labour relations training for managers/supervisors. Do you believe that the training you have found can better inform managers and thus reduce grievances?

6. Unions often provide training for shop stewards. Search the websites of three to five large unions in your area. To what extent do you see training programs for union leaders? Is there evidence that they are trained on matters related to grievances, arbitrations, and other forms of dispute resolution?

Exercises

1. Reread the opening vignette. To what extent are the theories and causes of strikes represented?

2. Look at any recent media stories about strikes and choose one such strike. To what extent can the three theories of strikes be used to explain the strike in question?

3. Many students work while they attend school. As a group or class project, check for a progressive discipline policy in your organization. If it has one, bring a copy into class.

   a. Does the policy you found contain the elements discussed in IR Notebook 9.1?
   b. Are there significant differences between the policies of unionized and nonunionized workplaces? If so, what are these differences?

4. Many university and college libraries have access to LACs and Brown and Beatty either electronically or in hard copy. Using Brown and Beatty, find an LAC that deals with discipline and discharge.

   a. Was the employee culpable or not? Why?
   b. What mitigating factors, if any, did the union raise?
   c. To what extent did these mitigating factors impact the final decision?

d. What is the time frame between the date of the disciplinary action in question and the final decision?

5. Most universities are unionized and have collective agreements readily available in hard copy or on their websites. Have a look at the grievance procedure contained in one collective agreement from your university.

   a. Is there an informal (pre-grievance) step mentioned?
   b. How many steps are in the formal process?
   c. Which levels of management and the union are present at each step?

6. Interview a parent, sibling, friend, or someone else who has been on strike. Ask what he or she feels was the cause of the strike as well as what impact it had on the workplace, workers, and management. To what extent does his or her personal experience mirror the findings discussed in this chapter?

Case 1

Island Air[5]

On January 29, Island Air Flight 101 departed from Vancouver Island Airport en route to Montreal. Upon landing in Montreal, Flight 101 skidded off the runway and crashed. No passengers or crew were injured. There was light snow and a temperature of –4 degrees Celsius. A safety board conducted an investigation. The case facts are as follows: (1) The pilot, James Brown, was forty years old, had fifteen years of service, and had no prior incidents or warnings on his employment record; (2) Captain Brown was later discharged by Island Air; (3) as a unionized Canadian employee, he filed a grievance that went to arbitration; and (4) at the arbitration, the facts were not in dispute.

Questions

1. What questions must the arbitrator examine to determine whether the employer had just cause for discharging the pilot?
2. Assume that the safety board investigation determined that the plane crashed for two reasons: (a) due to a mechanical failure, the engines were not producing maximum power; and (b) the ground crew did not de-ice the plane. As a result, once the plane was airborne, ice formed on the wings and this extra weight contributed to the crash. Hence, the crash was not caused by pilot error. Given these facts, walk through the questions raised in question 1 above and discuss how you would rule if you were the arbitrator. Justify your ruling.
3. Now, assume that the safety board determined the following: (a) The plane was landing at a speed of 600 kilometres per hour, above the recommended landing speed of 400 kilometres per hour; (b) the pilot was aware of the recommended speed; (c) the pilot had landed the plane on many occasions at the recommended speed of 400 kilometres

per hour; and (d) there was no evidence that the excessive speed was justified or caused by a mechanical failure (i.e., the safety board found that the crash was caused by pilot error). Again walk through the questions you presented in question 1 above and present how you would rule if you were the arbitrator. Justify your ruling.

Case 2

Ottawa Transit Dispute

Amalgamated Transit Union (ATU Local 279) went on strike just prior to the holiday season on 10 December 2008. As a result, 21,000 transit workers set up picket lines and the entire public transit system of the Ottawa area came to a standstill. Thousands of riders, many of whom were seniors, students, and low-income earners, now faced the challenge of carrying on their daily routines.

This was not the first time the union had gone on strike, having walked off the job in 1996. That strike lasted over 20 days and only ended when both parties agreed to an arbitrator-proposed settlement. That settlement resulted in employee benefits being cut by 1.25 million. As a direct result of the 1996 strike, estimates suggest that each worker lost about $2,500 in wages and the local economy lost $1 million in lower productivity and sales given the holiday season. Following the 1996 strike, the parties attempted to improve their working relationship through the use of Federal Conciliation and Mediation services. In 1999, the current shift schedule, which appears to be a key area of dispute in the current strike, was negotiated and placed in the collective agreement. In order to offset management's concerns regarding the inefficiencies of that schedule, the union agreed to a 2 percent wage cut.

At the time of the current strike, the final wage offer from the city included increases of 3 percent, 2 percent, and 2 percent over three years. The union sought 3.5 percent each year and reminded management that other city unions were given 3 percent a year in their last contracts. The union remained firm that they would not accept a wage and benefit package lower than that received by other city unions. In their words, issues related to wages, contracting out of maintenance work, better sick leave, and driver schedules would need to be addressed prior to any settlement.

Three weeks into the strike, the federal minister Federal Minister of Labour, Rona Ambrose, stated that he would overrule the union's leadership and force a union member vote concerning the last offer from the city. There was speculation that this move was caused by a perception that the union was divided, and that some members wished to accept the city's offer and return to work. Union leadership remained firm that the union was not divided given their strong strike mandate. They emphasized that 98 percent of union members rejected the last, very similar, offer from the city. As they also pointed out, their union members felt so strongly about the scheduling issue that they had taken a pay cut in the past to make it part of the agreement. When the vote, supervised by the Canada Industrial Relations Board, was held, 75 percent of union members rejected the offer.

As the strike continued, there was widespread speculation that binding arbitration might be used to settle the dispute. While opinions on the effectiveness of such arbitration-based settlements varied, at least one union spokesperson claimed that arbitration was not the best mechanism for resolving issues as complex as schedules. He further stressed that many arbitrators would encourage the parties to resolve such issues themselves rather than have an arbitrator make the final decision.

Almost 40 days into the strike, the parties were focused largely on what items could be settled by arbitration. The union stated that they would return to work if the city agreed to send the more contentious issues such as scheduling, hours of work, etc., to a mediation-style process and the simpler issues, such as wages, to arbitration. The city's position was that three conditions had to be met before they would agree to the union's proposal: (1) All contentious issues, including scheduling, should go to arbitration; (2) the final settlement could not be greater than the total cash value of the last offer presented by the city; and (3) any agreements concerning work hours for drivers should be consistent with federal safety rules. The union rejected this offer. However, 53 days into the strike, the parties suddenly agreed to binding arbitration as a way to resolve all remaining issues. There is wide speculation that the fact that the Minister of Transportation had drafted back-to-work legislation, and that all federal parties were prepared to debate the legislation, prompted the settlement.

Sources: Adam, 2009; Canwest News Service, 2009; CBC News, 2009; Czekaj, 2008; Rupert, 2008; Ward, 2008.

Questions

1. Media reports tend to call all work stoppages "strikes." Please justify if this case represents a strike or a lockout.
2. Please discuss the extent to which the three theories of strikes can be used to analyze this work stoppage.
3. On the basis of the list of potential causes of strikes presented in this chapter, what do you feel caused this strike?
4. It is arguably society's more vulnerable members (low-income earners, students, seniors, etc.) who are most impacted by labour disputes involving public transportation. Do you feel that transit workers should be able to strike or do you feel that other dispute resolution procedures should be used as strike replacements?
5. What forms of alternative dispute resolution procedures do you feel could have been used to avoid the work stoppage?

Endnotes

1. These data report work stoppages involving more than 500 workers. However, the HRSDC website also allows you to restrict the strike statistics to include smaller strikes.
2. Data for 2010 reflect the period of January to November only.
3. Note that percent of estimated working time lost is only by industry and province.
4. All data reported were downloaded in the period January 16–21, 2011.
5. This case is not based on any real person, company, or event.

References

Adam, M. (30 January 2009). Ottawa settles 7-week bus strike. *Ottawa Citizen*. Retrieved 15 January 2011 from http://www.canada.com/business/Ottawa+settles+week+strike/1232419/story.html

Ashenfelter, O., & Johnson, G. E. (1969). Bargaining theory, trade unions and industrial activity. *The American Economic Review, 59*, pp. 35–49.

Auld, D. A. L., Christofides, L. N., Swidinsky, R., & Wilton, D. A. (1981). The effect of settlement stage on negotiated wage settlements. *Canada Industrial and Labour Relations Review, 34*, pp. 234–244.

Bamberger, P., Kohn, E., & Nahum-Shani, I. (2008). Aversive workplace conditions and employee grievance filing: The moderating effects of gender and ethnicity. *Industrial Relations: A Journal of Economy and Society, 47*, pp. 229–259.

Barling, J., Fullagar, C., McElvie, L., & Kelloway, E. K. (1992). Union loyalty and strike propensity. *Journal of Social Psychology, 132*, pp. 581–590.

Barling, J., Wade, W. C., & Fullagar, C. (1990). Predicting employee commitment to company and union: Divergent models. *Journal of Occupational Psychology, 63*, pp. 49–61.

Barton, G., & Weernink, W. O. (30 June 2003). Strikes interrupt German output. *Automotive News, 8*(13), p. 3.

Bemmels, B. (1994). Determinants of grievance initiation. *Industrial and Labor Relations Review, 47*, pp. 285–301.

Bemmels, B., & Foley, J. R. (1996). Grievance procedure research: A review and theoretical recommendations. *Journal of Management, 22*, pp. 359–384.

Bemmels, B., Reshef, Y., & Stratton-Devine, K. (1991). The roles of supervisors, employees, and stewards in grievance initiation. *Industrial and Labor Relations Review, 45*, pp. 15–30.

Blackwood, L., Lafferty, G., Duck, J., & Terry, D. (2003). Putting the group back into unions: A social psychological contribution to understanding union support. *The Journal of Industrial Relations, 45*, pp. 485–504.

Brown, D. J. M., & Beatty, D. M. (2006). *Canadian labour arbitration* (4th edition). Aurora, ON: Canada Law Book Inc.

Brown, Louise. (2008). Strike brings York to standstill. *TheStar.com*, 7 November 2008. Retrieved 8 April 2011 from http://www.thestar.com/news/article/532380--strike-

Burns, M. (2000). Nurses strike prompts increased health spending. *Europe, 393* (February), pp. 45–47.

Canada Labour Code. R.S., 1985, c. L-2.

Canadian Association of University Teachers (CAUT). (16 January 2008). External mediator appointed in St. Thomas University lockout. Retrieved 17 January 2011 from http://www.caut.ca/news_details.asp?page=490&lang=1&txtSearch=&nid=1077

Canadian Human Rights Commission. (2007). Alternative dispute resolution. Retrieved 29 January 2007 from http://www.chrc-ccdp.ca/adr/default-en.asp

Canwest News Service. (18 January 2009). Ottawa transit union rejects arbitration offer, strike continues. *Ottawa Citizen*. Retrieved 15 January 2011 from http://www.financialpost.com/related/topics/Ottawa+transit+union+rejects+arbitration+offer+strike+continues/1189369/story.html

Carver, T. B., & Vondra, A. A. (1994). Alternative dispute resolution: Why it doesn't work and why it does. *Harvard Business Review*, May–June, pp. 120–130.

CBC. (21 March 2006). *P.E.I. university hit by faculty strike*. Retrieved 20 December 2006 from http://www.cbc.ca/canada/story/2006/03/21/upei-strike.html

CBC News. (15 October 2007). Classes cancelled as strike hits Acadia. Retrieved 17 January 2011 from http://www.cbc.ca/canada/nova-scotia/story/2007/10/15/acadia-strike.html#ixzz1BV9k4lOh

CBC News. (9 January 2009). "No one has won," Ottawa mayor says after vote extends transit strike. Retrieved 15 January 2011 from http://www.cbc.ca/canada/ottawa/story/2009/01/09/ot-091209-vote-result.html

CBC Sports Online. (13 July 2005). Lockout chronology: Some of the highlights from the longest lockout in professional sports history. Retrieved 20 December 2006 from http://www.cbc.ca/sports/indepth/cba/features/chronology.html

Chaulk, K., & Brown, T. C. (2008). An assessment of worker reaction to their union and employer post-strike: A Canadian experience. *Relations industrielles/Industrial Relations, 63,* pp. 223–245.

Colvin, A. J. S. (2003). Institutional pressures, human resource strategies, and the rise of nonunion dispute resolution procedures. *Industrial and Labor Relations Review, 56,* pp. 375–392.

Currie, J., & McConnell, S. (1991). Collective bargaining in the public sector: The effect of legal structure on dispute costs and wages. *American Economic Review, 81*(4), pp. 693–718.

Czekaj, L. (30 December 2008). Force-fed solution in Ottawa transit strike: Report says government set to wade in on OC Transpo dispute in bid to end strike. *Ottawa Sun.* Retrieved 15 January 2011 from http://cnews.canoe.ca/CNEWS/Canada/2008/12/30/7879791-sun.html

Dachis, B., & Hebdon, R. (2010). *The laws of unintended consequences: The effect of labour legislation on wages and strikes.* Toronto: C. D. Howe Institute.

Fiorito, J., Bozeman, D. P., Young, A., & Meurs, J. A. (2007). Organizational commitment, human resource practices and organizational characteristics. *Journal of Managerial Issues, 6*(2), pp. 186–207.

Fisher, G. H. (2007). Can strikes pay for management? Pro sports' major turnarounds. *Relations industrielles/Industrial Relations, 62,* pp. 3–30.

Geare, A. J. (1972). The problem of industrial unrest: Theories into the causes of local strikes in a New Zealand meat freezing works. *Journal of Industrial Relations, 14,* pp. 13–22.

Giesbrecht, N., Markle, G., & Macdonald, S. (1982). The 1978–79 INCO workers' strike in the Sudbury basin and its impact on alcohol consumption and drinking patterns. *Journal of Public Health Policy, 3*(1), pp. 22–38.

Government of Saskatchewan. (2007). Grievance mediation: An alternative to costly arbitration. Retrieved 8 April 2011 from http://www.aeei.gov.sk.ca/grievance-mediation

Hale, D. (2008). International comparisons of labour disputes in 2006. *Economic & Labour Market Review, 2*(4), pp. 32–39.

Hanrahan, R., Kushner, J., Martinello, F., & Masse, I. (1997). The effect of work stoppages on the value of firms in Canada. *Review of Financial Economics, 6*(2), pp. 151–167.

Hebdon, R. (2005). Toward a theory of workplace conflict: The case of U.S. municipal collective bargaining. *Advances in Industrial and Labor Relations, 14,* pp. 35–67.

Hebdon, R., & Stern, R. (1998). Tradeoffs among expressions of industrial conflict: Public sector strike bans and grievance arbitrations. *Industrial and Labor Relations Review, 51*(2), pp. 204–221.

Hebdon, R., & Stern, R. (2003). Do public-sector strike bans really prevent conflict? *Industrial Relations, 42,* pp. 493–512.

Herald, D. (2002). Back to work doesn't mean back to normal. *Canadian HR Reporter.* Retrieved 13 July 2007 from http://www.fgiworld.com/eng/articles/back_to_work.pdf

Human Resources and Social Development Canada. (2011). Chronological perspective on work stoppages. Retrieved 16 January 2011 from http://srv131.services.gc.ca/dimt-wid/pcat-cpws/recherche-search.aspx?lang=eng&ind=1&jurs=1

Ichniowski, C. (1982). Arbitration and police bargaining: Prescriptions for the blue flu. *Industrial Relations, 21*(2), pp. 149–166.

Johnson, S. J. T. (2010). First contract arbitration: Effects on bargaining on work stoppages. *Industrial & Labour Relations Review, 63,* pp. 585–605.

Kramer, J., & Hyclak, T. (2002). Why strikes occur: Evidence from their capital markets. *Industrial Relations, 41,* pp. 80–93.

Maclean's. (3 November 2010). No faculty strike at Western. Retrieved 16 January 2010 from http://oncampus.macleans.ca/education/2010/11/03/no-strike-at-western

Maki, D. (1986). The effect of the cost of strikes on the volume of strike activity. *Industrial and Labour Relations Review, 39,* pp. 552–563.

Mandville, S., & Brown, T. C. (2009). How do employees view their grievance system? A survey of unionized healthcare workers. Paper presented at the Annual Meeting of the Administrative Sciences Association of Canada. Niagara Falls, ON.

NHL CBA News. (14 September 2004). NHL teams will not play without a new collective bargaining agreement. Reprinted with permission. Found at: http://www.nhlcbanews.com/news/bog_meeting091504.html. Retrieved December 20, 2006.

Nicholson, N., & Kelly, J. (1980). The psychology of strikes. *Journal of Occupational Behaviour, 1*, pp. 275–284.

Nurse, L., & Devonish, D. (2007). Grievance management and its links to workplace justice. *Employee Relations, 29*, pp. 89–109.

Olson, C. (1986). Strikes, strike penalties, and arbitration in six states. *Industrial and Labor Relations Review, 39*(4), pp. 539–551.

Peterson, R. B., & Lewin, D. (2000). Research on unionized grievance procedures: Management issues and recommendations. *Human Resource Management, 39*, pp. 395–406.

Rees, D. (1991). Grievance procedure strength and teacher quits. *Industrial and Labor Relations Review, 45*, pp. 31–43.

Rose, J. B. (1994). The complaining game: How effective is compulsory interest arbitration? *Journal of Collective Negotiations in the Public Sector, 23*(3), pp. 187–202.

Rupert, J. (10 December 2008). Ottawa commuters stranded by transit strike. *Ottawa Citizen.* Retrieved 15 January 2011 from http://www.nationalpost.com/news/canada/Ottawa+commuters+stranded+transit+strike/1056668/story.html

Ward, B. (9 December 2008). Ottawa transit talks break off, strike looms. Retrieved 15 January 2011 from http://www.nationalpost.com/news/canada/story.html?id=1052073

Webb, D. (25 February 2010). Ontario colleges strike averted. *Nexus Newspaper.com.* Retrieved 16 January 2011 from http://nexusnewspaper.com/articles/27358

Williams, K., & Taras, D. (2000). Reinstatement in arbitration: The grievors' perspective. *Relations industrielles, 55*, pp. 227–249.

Zekta, J. R. (1995). Union homogenization and the organizational foundations of plant-wide militancy in the US automobile industry, 1957–1975. *Social Forces, 73*, pp. 789–810.

Zerbe, W. (2009). Chapter 6: Emotional deviance and organizational discipline: A study of emotions in grievance arbitration. In Neal M. Ashkanasy, Wilfred J. Zerbe & Charmine E. J. Härtel (Eds.), *Emotions in groups, organizations and cultures (Research on emotion in organizations,* Volume 5) (pp. 123–149). Bingley, UK: Emerald Group Publishing Limited.

CHAPTER 10

Impacts of Unionization

Learning Objectives

By the end of this chapter, you will be able to discuss

- the impacts of unions on management practices, in particular those related to human resources management (HRM) practices;
- the relationship between unions and firm efficiency; and
- the impact of unionization on employee measures.

ARE UNIONIZED FIRMS LESS PRODUCTIVE?

James Kowalski and Tammy Price both attend university part-time in the evening and work full-time during the day. They often grab a quick bite to eat before their evening industrial relations class. As they sit down, James says, "I wonder what Professor Brown's lecture on the impact of unionization will be like tonight. It might be an interesting one."

Tammy replies, "I'm not sure, but it is certainly a topic of conversation in my workplace. We often talk about how unions increase the costs of the construction projects, protect poor employees, and, through unnecessary bureaucracy, slow down construction projects. In fact, we have even seen a YouTube presentation from the Michigan Associated Builders and Contractors. Here, let me show you." Tammy then pulls it up and they have a look as they enjoy their coffee.

"Wow!" says James. "It's a good thing my dad is not here. From the time he immigrated to Canada until he retired last year, he worked as a unionized construction worker. He argued for years, as did his union, that unions increase productivity due to improved access to training, lower turnover, and higher tenure. He raved about how his union made sure that he was well treated and protected from unsafe work. He would always remind me that it was the protection he felt from his union and employer working together that made him want to come to work—and word hard. I guess he wouldn't be very popular with the Michigan Associated Builders and Contractors. Their perspective is pretty clear that unions hurt the construction industry. Let's see what else we can find."

As they continue to explore they come across a post from the Association of Union Constructors. James says, "This might be a good one to look at, Tammy. Let's have a look." Once the presentation is over, Tammy laughs. "Well, it's pretty clear that this person is saying the exact opposite. He says that unionized construction is more productive than nonunion. Could we get two more different answers to the question concerning the impact of unionization? How can two groups see this issue so differently? I am curious to see how Professor Brown handles this one tonight. We could see a great debate in class."

Sources: Michigan Associated Builders and Contractors, "The impact of forced-union agreements in Michigan" (video), retrieved 9 April 2011 from http://www.youtube.com/watch?v=k3vBA3Hm5Mk; Association of Union Constructors, "Who is more productive? Union vs. nonunion" (video), retrieved 9 April 2011 from http://www.youtube.com/watch?v=tw610qHGyM8.

Impact of Unions on Management Practices

As you may recall from previous chapters, nonunion workplaces operate under what legal experts call the master–servant relationship. The employer is free to determine workplace policies and practices, and employees are dutifully required to follow their employer's requests. About the only restrictions on employers in common law are statutory legislation covering minimum wage, overtime, grounds of discrimination, etc. However, in a unionized workplace, the numerous conversion mechanisms we discussed in Chapter 9 mean that the employer no longer has unilateral ability to determine all terms and conditions of employment. In many unionized workplaces, the collective agreement will spell out both processes and requirements related to such issues.

In Freeman and Medoff's (1984) seminal book *What Do Unions Do?*, the issue of the impact of unionization on management practices was examined in considerable detail. In this section, we will focus on how unions impact management practices, in particular those related to human resources management (HRM). Traditional HRM functions include staffing, training and development, performance appraisal, job evaluation, and compensation. Numerous reasons have been proposed for why such HRM practices would differ between union and nonunion firms (Brown & Warren, 2010; Freeman & Medoff, 1984; Ng & Maki, 1994; Verma, 2005; Wagar, 1997):

1. The **shock effect** (Slichter, Healy & Livernash, 1960), which states that the increased protection and costs associated with unionization shock management into adopting both stricter HRM practices and methods of improving production/service efficiency.

2. Differing preferences of union versus nonunion workers. Because unionized employees are often older, and remain with a firm for a longer period of time because of the advantages associated with seniority, their preferences for HRM practices may differ from those of nonunion employees.

3. Exit-voice theory (Hirschmen, 1970) states that dissatisfied employees have two choices: leave the firm (i.e., exit) or voice their dissatisfaction. Unions represent a **collective voice**, enabling workers to express their discontent. As a collective, they have greater power to convince employers to adopt HRM practices that reflect worker preferences relative to a single employee under common law.

Thus, it should not be surprising that HRM practices often differ between union and nonunion firms. Let's now examine several HRM functions in more detail to see the key differences between union and nonunion firms.

shock effect

occurs when increased costs and protection shock management into stricter management practices

collective voice

the ability of a group or union to express concerns

Staffing

There are two staffing processes, selection, in which a person is hired, and deselection, in which an employee is let go. Recall from earlier chapters that the union security clauses can play a role in hiring employees. For example, in a closed shop, where new hires must be members of the union before an employer can hire them, management plays a small role in hiring; the union itself may even decide which employees are hired. In addition, we need to remember that the concept of *layoff*, whereby an employee can be released from work and **recalled** (rehired later), applies only to unionized workplaces. In nonunionized workplaces, termination for any reason, including downsizing, does not imply the right of recall; rather, it signals the end of the employment relationship.

Recruitment

Research suggests that there are significant differences in the recruitment processes of union and nonunion organizations. For example, one study of almost 500 American firms suggests that unionized employers use fewer **recruitment** techniques (e.g., newspaper ads, private and government agencies, employee referrals, direct applicants). A potential reason for this is that unionized jobs, with the higher security and voice provisions, "make a job more attractive to applicants . . . [thus reducing the need for] more costly recruitment methods" (Koch & Hundley, 1997, p. 368). A second explanation may be the use of recruitment processes outlined in the collective agreement, such as closed-shop clauses. Such clauses, for all intents and purposes, limit the employer's ability to recruit.

In contrast, a Canadian study by Ng and Maki (1994) did not find differences in the external recruitment practices (e.g., employee referrals, walk-ins) between union and nonunion firms. However, there was an increased use of formal job posting methods (i.e., internal recruitment) in unionized companies.

Selection

Canadian evidence suggests that unionized firms are more likely to hire from within, versus externally; have probationary periods; institute formal promotion criteria; and promote workers on the basis of seniority (Ng & Maki, 1994). Similarly, unionized firms in the United States are more likely to have formalized selection practices. For example, compared to nonunion firms, they are more likely to use drug tests and physicals but not skills and aptitude tests (Koch & Hundley, 1997). One possible reason for the use of more formal selection processes is the fact that a poor hiring decision represents a larger challenge to employers in unionized firms. In nonunion firms, even after a **probationary period** (often three months), employers can terminate without cause; however, this is not possible in unionized firms given the just-cause provisions of collective agreements.

Perhaps Verma (2005, p. 423) best sums up the impact of unions on staffing:

> Unions appear to insist on promotion-from-within and the related use of internal posting-and-bidding. This, in turn, causes management to limit its channels of external recruiting and, to some extent, use only physical tests in selection.

Deselection/Termination

As discussed in other chapters, collective agreements often contain detailed layoff and bumping procedures. Union employees also have the right of recall. In contrast, in nonunion workplaces, employees are usually terminated without recall rights.

Staffing Flexibility

As we discussed in Chapter 6, many employers have introduced alternative work schedules and have increased their use of temporary and casual employees. A review of the literature (Verma, 2005) clearly shows that unionized firms are much less likely to have numerical flexibility (the ability to contract out work, to use temporary and part-time workers, etc.) and are often prohibited from assigning a worker job tasks that fall into another worker's job description. Hence, you will often hear managers of unionized firms discussing that employees (and their union) will grieve if they assign work outside an employee's job description.

Training and Development

One review concluded that unionized firms, particularly those in manufacturing, provide more training than nonunion firms (Verma, 2005). This finding is consistent with past, global work. British research has found that unionized employees have both increased access to training and increased actual training days relative to nonunion employees (Boheim & Booth, 2004; Booth, Francesconi & Zoega, 2003). Similarly, German evidence shows that unionized workplaces are twice more likely to both train employees and provide apprenticeships than nonunion firms (Dustmann & Schönberg, 2009).

Canadian evidence too has generally found increased training in unionized firms. For example, studies show a positive relationship between unionization and training and education in Canada (Betcherman, Leckie, McMullen & Caron, 1994; Livingstone & Raykov, 2005, 2008). Interestingly, a statistical analysis involving a sample of over 18,000 people (Green & Lemieux, 2001) also found a positive effect for unionized workers (i.e., 4 percent). However, when the researchers statistically took into account (i.e., controlled for) factors such as age, industry, education level, public or private sector, and province, the impact of unions on training and development was negative. As discussed in other chapters, this is because unionized firms tend to differ from nonunion firms in terms of having older employees, being clustered in certain industries (e.g., manufacturing), etc.

The research as a whole suggests that unionized employees have increased access to training relative to their nonunion peers. However, the results point to the fact that since many Canadian unionized firms are large and based in the public sector, it can be difficult to separate these other factors (i.e., size and being in the public sector) from the state of being unionized on access to training.

Performance Appraisal

Performance appraisal has two purposes. First, it has a developmental purpose—namely to develop and motivate staff. Second, it has an administrative function—namely, to determine pay, promotion, termination, and disciplinary decisions (Rynes, Gerhart & Parks, 2005). Research from Britain (Brown & Heywood, 2005) shows a negative relationship between union density and the use of a performance appraisal. A Canadian study by Ng and Maki (1994) also found that unionized firms were much less likely than nonunion firms to have a formal appraisal system. Moreover, they found that unionized firms were less likely to use performance appraisals for making pay, promotion, or layoff decisions but that they were just as likely to use them for disciplinary and training purposes. This led the researchers to conclude that unions may resist the use of performance appraisals for evaluative (e.g., pay and promotion) purposes but permit them for worker developmental purposes (e.g., training). Canadian studies involving newly introduced performance appraisal processes in unionized mining (Pieroway & Brown, 2006) and telecommunications companies (Brown & Latham, 2000) have also found that unions appear supportive of performance appraisals when they focus on developmental purposes as against evaluative purposes, particularly discipline. These studies also suggested that union involvement in the design of the system is beneficial. Interestingly, Wagar's (1997) survey study of unionized Atlantic Canadian firms did not find that the use of performance appraisals differed between union and nonunion firms.

Overall, we concur with a recent review of the performance appraisal literature conducted by Brown and Warren (2010). They concluded that in unionized workplaces (1) performance appraisals are less common; (2) in cases where such processes exist, the union appears to have no preference regarding the format of the instrument but does prefer that the process be developmentally focused; (3) unions are more supportive of performance appraisal processes in which they have been involved in the process design and in which the primary goals are not geared toward discipline and/or individual pay; and (4) goal setting has been used to introduce, or improve upon, performance appraisal systems. We believe that two factors support these conclusions. First, as unions represent a voice process, it seems natural that they would seek involvement in these issues. Second, the bulk of the typical administrative functions of performance appraisal in unionized firms (promotion, pay, layoff, etc.) are covered by specific language and procedures found in collective agreements. Thus, unions would most likely prefer that these administrative functions not be the primary goal of the process.

Job Evaluation and Job Analysis

A key element in HRM is to ensure that HRM practices (e.g., selection, promotion, pay, performance appraisal) reflect the skills needed to effectively perform the job at hand (Long, 2006). In fact, as is discussed in Chapter 2, it is a legal requirement that such decisions be based on the worker's ability to perform the key functions of a job. If firms do otherwise, they risk discrimination charges. Thus, most organizations use some form of **job evaluation** or **job analysis** to gather such data. Evidence suggests that unionized firms are as likely as nonunion firms to use what can be seen as objective methods (e.g., point-factor methods, in which key job duties are assessed and given points according to a classification system, or classification methods, in which jobs are placed into groups or grades. With each group representing jobs requiring certain skills or knowledge, and each job description is then compared to the group description). However, unionized firms are much less likely to use a subjective ranking of jobs in which jobs are ranked in terms of overall worth to the organization (Ng & Maki, 1994; Verma, 2005).

Compensation

Of all the possible impacts of unionization on human resources practices, it is fair to say that the area of compensation has received the most focus. Freeman and Medoff (1984) argued that unions have two significant impacts on compensation: first, the **monopoly effect**, namely that unions raise wages above the rate of nonunion employees. In so doing, unions are argued to reduce employment levels as employers choose to hire fewer employees given the high wage rate. Second is the collective voice impact. While much of the research has focused on wages and wage rates, it is important to remember that **total compensation** contains three elements: base pay, performance pay, and indirect pay (also known as *benefits*) (Long, 2006):

- **Base pay** represents the portion of a worker's pay that is based on time worked and not based on performance or output. For example, many students work in jobs in which their base pay is an hourly rate (e.g., $13 per hour).
- **Performance pay** represents the portion of an employee's pay provided only if certain specific performance targets are achieved. These can be both individual and group targets. For example, salespeople often make a commission for each item they sell.
- **Indirect pay** includes anything that the employer pays for that is not part of an employee's base or performance pay. This often includes various forms of benefits such as paid leaves of absence (e.g., vacation), retirement/pension plans, and health and life insurance plans. Accordingly, we will refer to indirect pay as benefits throughout this chapter.

job evaluation

a process whereby the firm determines the value of a job

job analysis

a process whereby the key competencies for a job are identified

monopoly effect

the union's ability to raise wages above nonunion rates

total compensation

the total base pay, performance pay, and indirect pay that an employee receives

base pay

the part of pay that is solely based on time worked

performance pay

the part of pay that is based on output or performance

indirect pay (or benefits)

anything that an employer pays for, to the benefit of the employee, that is not part of base or performance pay

IR Notebook 10.1

Should Unions Focus on Jobs or Wages and Benefits?

As is shown in this chapter, unions have a significant impact on wages. Yet you may recall from Chapter 3 that there has frequently been concern that these increased union wage rates negatively impact employment. A recent study even suggests that private unionized firms reduce employment by a small amount (about 2 percent a year; Walsworth, 2010a).

As a result, unions can be faced with a tough decision. Do they focus on getting wage and benefit gains for members—which, remember, is a key reason why employees join unions—or on increasing/maintaining employment? Perhaps no industry has faced this challenge more directly than manufacturing, in particular auto manufacturing.

Over the past few years, unions in this sector have been asked to give concessions, accept wage freezes (or wage cuts), increase employee co-payment of benefits, and reduce benefit plans in an effort to maintain jobs.

Chapter 10: Impacts of Unionization

IR Notebook 10.1 (continued)

Clearly this is a tough call for unions. Do they accept the concessions and lose wages and benefits in order to try and save jobs, or do they fight to retain the gains they have made and risk job losses?

The following quote from *Financial Post* journalists Nicolas Van Praet and Paul Vieira certainly shows this dilemma and the potential tension such difficult decisions can cause among the labour movement.

> *Tony Clement, Canada's industry minister, told the House of Commons Industry Committee Tuesday that current job levels in Ontario's auto industry are not sustainable. "There will be some pain. We don't know when or where."*
>
> *The CAW's [Canadian Auto Workers] top leadership has said repeatedly that wage cuts will not save jobs in the auto industry. "It's our effort as a union to try to set a higher standard than who's the most desperate and who will do it for cheapest," union economist Jim Stanford has said.*

But workers have a different perspective, highlighting what may be a growing disconnect between the CAW leadership and the rank and file, Mr. Chaison said. Many workers are putting fear of losing their jobs in a waning employment market ahead of longer term or higher union principles, he said. "The membership reflects the economy as it is now. And the leadership reflects the economy as they'd like to see it."

Sources: CBC News, "Chrysler, CAW reach deal to save company $240M a year," 24 April 2009, retrieved 31 January 2011 from http://www.cbc.ca/money/story/2009/04/24/chrysler-caw-union-concessions.html; T. Van Alphen, "CAW vows disruptions if parts makers don't stop concession demands," TheStar.com, 13 October 2010, retrieved 31 January 2011 from http://www.thestar.com/business/article/874988--caw-vows-disruptions-if-parts-makers-don-t-stop-concession-demands; N. Van Praet and P. Vieira, "Gun put to the heads of auto workers," *Financial Post*, 10 February 2009, retrieved 31 January 2011 from http://www2.canada.com/theprovince/news/story.html?id=1274476.

RPC 10.2

Base Pay

A wealth of research, largely based on U.S. data, has shown that unionized employees earn about 15 percent more than their nonunion counterparts (Blanchflower & Bryson, 2004; Freeman & Medoff, 1984; Lewis, 1986). More recent evidence suggests the American union premium may even be over 20 percent, particularly for private-sector employees (Bahrami, Bitzan & Leitch, 2009; Eren, 2007).

Turning to Canadian data, we see similar trends. Union members, on average, have had a 10–15 percent range premium since the 1970s [i.e., a 13 to 16 percent differential in the early 1970s (Grant, Swidinsky & Vanderkamp, 1987); 10.4 percent in the late 1980s (Renaud, 1998); 15 percent based on a review of North American data (Kuhn, 1998); and approximately 8 percent (Verma & Fang, 2002) and in the 9–13 percent range in the first decade of 2000 (Godard, 2007)]. While much of this data has examined traditional industries (manufacturing, construction, private sector, public sector), the same 10–15 percent premium has been found in low-wage service jobs, such as those of childcare workers (Cleveland, Gunderson & Hyatt, 2003). Thus, the evidence concerning a Canadian union premium in the 10–15 percent range is very robust.

However, this does not mean that every unionized worker receives a 10–15 percent premium. For example, Canadian evidence suggests that women, private-sector, blue-collar, and less skilled employees, as well as workers in smaller firms, receive a larger wage premium (Renaud, 1998). Other evidence from Australia suggests that the union differential is larger in smaller firms

(Waddoups, 2008), while U.S. data show that the union premium in the private sector is almost 23 percent as against 11 percent for public sector (Bahrami, Bitzan & Leitch 2009), and other data (Blanchflower & Bryson, 2004) suggest that the union premiums are countercyclical to the economy (i.e., highest when the economy is not performing well and lowest when it is). Interestingly, in a study of Ontario professors (Martinello, 2009) in the highly unionized university sector, unionization did not impact wages. Godard (2007, p. 469) even concluded that higher performance HRM practices can play a role in Canada, and that these practices "may even yield payoffs comparable to those yielded by union representation, but only where there are relatively high levels of adoption, and only when more optimistic 'upper-bound' estimates are used."

Table 10.1 shows how much higher the wages of union workers are than nonunion workers', by specific factors.

TABLE 10.1

Union versus Nonunion Wage Differentials in Canada

FACTOR	GROUPINGS	% DIFFERENCE
Gender	Male	7.8
	Female	14.6
Age	15–24	11.9
	25–34	13.6
	35–44	12.6
	45–54	4.6
	55+	4.5
Education	Less than high school	13.6
	High school graduate	8.2
	College diploma	10.7
	Undergraduate degree	6.2
	Graduate degree	18.6
Skill level	Low	19.9
	Medium	11.4
	High	6.4
Occupation	White collar	8.9
	Blue collar	12.5
Sector	Public	3.6
	Private	11.5
Firm size	Fewer than 20 employees	28.4
	20–99 employees	12.1
	100–499 employees	14.7
	500+ employees	3.9
	West Coast	8.7
	Prairies	16.6
	Ontario	7.5
	Quebec	14.4
	Atlantic Canada	10.3

Source: Adapted from Renaud, S. (1998). Unions, wages and total compensation in Canada: An empirical study. Industrial Relations, 53, 710–729. Reprinted with permission.

spillover effect

a belief that increases in union wages result in decreases in nonunion wages

threat effect

a belief that nonunion employers increase wages to avoid unionization

wage differential

the difference in wages earned by two groups of workers

A natural question is whether the 10–15 percent wage increase for unions results in a wage decrease in the nonunion sector. As pointed out by Kuhn (1998), two arguments are key here:

1. The **spillover effect** argument states that the increased wages in the union sector would cause a decrease in demand for labour in that sector, which would in turn increase supply for labour in the nonunion sector and thus reduce wages in the nonunion sector.

2. The **threat effect** argument states that nonunion employers will increase nonunion wages in an attempt to make unionization of their workplace less likely.

Note that the evidence to date suggests that the threat effect is more common and that unions "appear to *raise*, rather than lower, the wages of nonunion workers . . . in the same industry" (Kuhn, 1998, p. 1038).

Not only do unions impact wage levels; they also impact wage structures in terms of wage differentials among workers. Considerable evidence shows that the **wage differential** between the highest- and lowest-paid workers is smaller in unionized workplaces than in nonunionized workplaces (Kuhn, 1998). However, it is interesting to note that a study across three countries—Britain, Canada, and the United States—suggests that this reduction in wage differentials is more prevalent among male versus female employees (Card, Lemieux & Riddell, 2004). A potential reason for this gender impact, provided by the authors, is that unionized women are often concentrated in the upper end of the wage distribution and that the union wage gap is often larger for women, potentially because unionized women often work in health care and education. Jobs in those sectors of the economy tend to pay more than nonunion jobs in sectors such as retail and banking.

As this evidence concerning wages and wage structures shows, unions generally have what can be called an inequity-reducing effect in that they often lessen wage inequality. Thus, it is interesting to note that two of the countries with the largest declines in unionization—the United States and the United Kingdom—also experienced the biggest increases in wage inequality. While we cannot conclude that these changes were a direct result of decreased union density, the result "raises the question of whether these two phenomena are linked" (Card, Lemieux & Riddell, 2004, p. 519).

Performance Pay

As is shown in our discussion of wage structures, unions have tried to minimize pay differences between individual employees. Unions often see performance pay, particularly performance pay at the individual level, as pitting one employee against another and allowing management to play favourites by rewarding friends and punishing enemies. Moreover, it has been argued that unions prefer the security and predictability of base pay, in which pay varies by hours worked, to the uncertain nature of performance pay (Long & Shields, 2009). Thus, there is general consensus that performance pay is less common in unionized organizations (Betcherman et al., 1994; Ng & Maki,

1994; Verma, 2005; Wagar, 1997). In fact, one study found that unionized firms in Canada were 50 percent less likely to have performance pay plans (Betcherman et al., 1994).

These preceding results do not mean that performance pay plans do not exist in unionized firms. Conference Board of Canada (2002) data suggest that 30 percent of Canadian unionized firms have some form of performance pay, up from approximately 14 percent of firms a decade earlier (Ng & Maki, 1994). Additional research has shown that union and nonunion firms were equally as likely to have group-level performance plans such as **gain sharing** (Ng & Maki, 1994), with the exception of **profit sharing**. In fact, a recent study confirms no differences in group-level performance plans between union and nonunion firms (Long & Shields, 2009).

In conclusion, the current state of the literature suggests that use of performance pay in unionized firms may be increasing. That said, there is clear evidence that unionized firms are more likely to have group-level performance pay plans than individual pay plans.

gain sharing

a group performance pay that is based on firm productivity gains

profit sharing

a group performance pay that is based on firm profits

Indirect Pay/Benefits

Given that benefits account for approximately 30 percent of the total payroll of many organizations (Long, 2006), and that benefit costs are increasing, indirect pay structures have come under increasing scrutiny over the past few years. There is a wealth of research indicating that unionized workers receive greater indirect pay (i.e., benefits) than their nonunion counterparts (Betcherman et al., 1994; Long, 2006; Long & Shields, 2009). In fact, the Canadian Labour Congress (CLC) (2011) highlights increased benefit plans (e.g., vacation, pension, health) as a result of unionization. American research suggests that unionized workers have 20 to 30 percent better benefit access (Freeman & Medoff, 1984), while Canadian research suggests that the union difference may be even higher at 45.5 percent (Renaud, 1998). Moreover, we see evidence that unions have increased access to particular benefits such as **Employee Assistance Programs (EAPs)** (Betcherman et al., 1994; Wagar, 1997), pension plans (Wagar, 1997), and vacation (Altonji & Usui, 2007).

Employee Assistance Program (EAP)

a counselling service available to employees

Several reasons might explain why unionized firms have better benefits. First, given the importance of seniority in unions, unionized workers tend to be older, and thus issues such as health benefits, pensions, and EAPs may be more important to them than to younger workers. Second, as unions provide a voice mechanism, they may provide a mechanism to enable improved benefits. Third, as discussed during our review of grievances and arbitrations, many arbitrators look for good-faith efforts on the part of the employer when trying to address performance issues of employees. We would therefore expect to see more use of EAPs in unionized firms than in nonunion firms, where arbitration is not an issue, since the former must demonstrate such good-faith efforts.

As we turn specifically to the issue of pensions, the CLC website (2011) highlights that only 27 percent of nonunion workers have a pension plan versus about 80 percent of unionized workers. Luchak and Gunderson (2000)

defined benefit

a type of pension plan that guarantees a specific payout

provide several reasons why unionized organizations would be more likely to have pension plans, particularly those that are of the **defined benefit** type, in which employees are essentially guaranteed a certain pension value upon retirement. For example, the median union member may be older, with less mobility (meaning that employers may be hesitant to hire an older worker), and thus may have more to gain from a pension plan. In addition, the union can provide employee voice. Thus, union members may be more comfortable relying on the union to (1) protect them from a "bad" plan, (2) maintain knowledge concerning the complex technical issues concerning pension investments, and (3) ensure that their retirement needs are protected.

Equality and Safety

 10.3

In addition to influencing traditional human resources functions, unions can also affect other factors that come under the umbrella of HRM in many organizations, namely workplace equality and health and safety. As you may recall from earlier chapters, unions have often focused on bringing equitable processes into the workplace as well as providing the mechanism for voicing employees' concerns. That said, unions in Britain, Canada, and the United States have historically been criticized for their lack of focus on equity issues, particularly those of women (Hart, 2002b). However, over the past 30 years, we have seen labour make great strides in the equality arena (Hart, 2002b; Hunt & Rayside, 2000; Parker & Foley, 2010) and there is evidence that women's committees within the labour movement are change agents for broader equity issues. Thus, as is shown in Chapter 8, many collective agreements now contain specific clauses on employment equity, equal pay, disability, and sexual harassment, as well as special committees dedicated to such issues (Brown, 2003; Hunt & Rayside, 2000). In addition, we see that CLC and union websites often contain sections dedicated to equity issues, where issues of relevance to visible minorities and women are presented (e.g., Canadian Auto Workers, 2006; Canadian Labour Congress, 2006).

Encouraging health and safety has become an important role of unions. Historically, Canadian unions have sought to bring in safer working conditions for their members and have lobbied the government for increased legislation to protect workers (Hart, 2010). This theme still holds a special place in the labour movement. At a recent speech on the National Day of Mourning, an annual event to remember people injured or killed at work, a CLC representative told attendees that, on average, 20 Canadians die every week on the job—over 1,000 a year. Note that these statistics do not include injuries (Byers, 2010). For example, approximately 10 percent of Canadians have suffered repetitive strain injuries sufficiently serious to restrict their normal activities (Statistics Canada, 2003). The prevalence of such injuries is such that the last day of February is known, internationally, as International Repetitive Strain Injury (RSI) Awareness Day (Khan, 2007). Moreover, several workplace factors may increase an employee's risk for the development of repetitive strain injuries: repetitive movements of the fingers, hand, wrist, arm, and shoulders; awkward hand/arm positions; exposure to vibration; incorrect workstation configuration; cold temperatures;

and insufficient rest time (Barron, 2006; MFL Occupational Health Centre, 2003). Given these factors, it should not be surprising that labour organizations often devote considerable space on their websites to issues concerning workplace health and safety as well as cite the improved safety records of unionized workplaces as a key benefit of joining a union (e.g., UFCW, 2011; Canadian Labour Congress, 2011).

While all workplaces are subject to the same equality and safety legislation, unions, with collective voice, have more power than an individual employee. In recent years, equality and safety issues have been closely examined in IR literature. This literature suggests that unions play an important role in the successful implementation of such programs (Hart, 2002a, 2002b, 2010), and that unions, in particular strong ones, are effective in both addressing longer-term health hazards and improving safety outcomes (Bornstein & Hart, 2010). Moreover, several studies have highlighted the effectiveness of unions in improving workplace safety practices, through training programs offered by labour organizations as well as the use of joint committees (Hart, 2002a, 2010; Hilyer, Leviton, Overman & Mukherjee, 2000; James & Walters, 2002; Walters, 2004). In particular, one Australian historical analysis (covering a 70-year period) found that the effectiveness of these committees depended upon the relationship with unions, the degree of management commitment, and the overall industrial relations climate (Markey & Patmore, 2011). Overall, given that equality and health and safety issues are often discussed in joint committees, it should not be surprising that research finds there is more use of employee–management committees in unionized firms than in nonunionized ones (Wagar, 1997).

Unions as Employers

As we close out this section, it is important to remember that unions are also employers and manage employees. While research on the HRM practices of unions has been limited, Clark and Gray (2008) concluded that unions are increasingly moving toward formalized HRM practices similar to those found in private-sector, governmental, and nonprofit organizations. They found that over 60 percent of unions had a HRM director of department; more than 50 percent had formalized, written policies concerning affirmative action, discipline/discharge, and performance appraisal for their headquarters and professional staff; and over 45 percent had similar policies for training and hiring.

Overall Impact

After reviewing the impact of unions on human resources practices (see Table 10.2), several conclusions can be drawn. First, there is no question that unionized organizations differ significantly in the types of HRM practices put in place. Second, nonunionized workplaces are more likely to have HRM practices that focus on individual rewards and recognition (e.g., performance pay and performance appraisal). Third, unionized firms often have more formal HRM practices that limit managerial flexibility and/or

TABLE 10.2

Overall Union Impact on HRM Practices

HRM Practice	Union Impact
Recruitment	Some evidence that unionized firms use fewer recruitment techniques; more likely to use internal job postings.
Selection	Union firms more likely to hire from within, have formal promotion criteria, and have probationary periods.
Deselection/ termination	Unionized workplaces usually have more formal rules, bumping processes, recall rights, and just-cause termination requirements.
Staffing flexibility	Unionized workplaces have more restrictions concerning contracting out, task assignment, and use of part-time or casual workers.
Training and development	More training and development opportunities in unionized firms.
Performance appraisal	Unionized firms are less likely to have formal performance appraisal systems. When they do exist, they usually focus on developmental as oppose to administrative purposes. Union involvement is likely to bolster plan acceptance.
Job evaluation/ job analysis	Unionized firms are as likely as nonunion firms to use objective (e.g., point factor) job evaluation methods versus subjective ranking of jobs.
Base pay	On average, union pay in Canada is 10–15% higher than nonunion; wage differentials are lower in unionized firms.
Performance pay	Less use of performance pay in union firms; where it exists, it tends to be group- rather than individual-based.
Indirect pay (benefits)	Unionized workers have greater access to benefits in the range of 20–40% and have more elements included in their benefit plans.

management's ability to make unilateral decisions. Fourth, in unionized firms, the element of seniority plays an important role in many HRM practices. Fifth, the increased formality in processes may explain why unionized firms are more likely than nonunionized firms to have dedicated HRM departments and staff (Wagar, 1997). Sixth, unions themselves are moving to more formalized HRM practices.

Unions and Firm Efficiency

A primary concern of the employer in the IR system is efficiency (e.g., productivity, profitability) (Barbash, 1987). In their landmark book, Freeman and Medoff (1984) concluded that unions increase firm efficiency due to the shock effect. Since the publication of this report, there has been considerable research about the relationship between unionization and firm effectiveness. In this section, we will examine the research evidence concerning the impact of unionization on productivity and profitability.

Productivity

The relationship between a company's productivity and unionization is a controversial one. Doucouliagos, Laroche, and Stanley (2005) outline two competing arguments on the topic:

1. *Economic theory.* This theory would argue that unions reduce productivity by constraining management flexibility through restrictive collective agreement language, loss of labour due to strikes, encouraging an adversarial relationship between managers and employees, and increasing wages above competitive levels. Moreover, one often hears the argument that unions "protect the lazy and the incompetent," given that it is much more difficult to terminate employees in unionized workplaces (Kuhn, 1998, p. 1047).

2. *Collective voice.* Voice may increase productivity by improving communication between employees and managers, enabling methods of voicing discontent (and thus reducing quit rates and absenteeism), providing formal grievance procedures to address workplace conflicts, and shocking management into improved people- and production-management practices (Doucouliagos, Laroche, and Stanley, 2005).

From their analyses, Freeman and Medoff (1984) concluded that the voice argument held true. That is, they found that the productivity of unionized firms was higher than that of their nonunion counterparts. As the authors readily admit, their conclusion that unions are associated with increased productivity is "the most controversial and least widely accepted" finding of their research study (Freeman & Medoff, 1984, p. 180).

Evidence since that time, while somewhat mixed, suggests that there is a small yet positive relationship between unions and productivity. One review states that studies reveal "that most estimates are positive, with the negative effects largely confined to industries and periods known for conflictual union–management relations and the public sector" (Kuhn, 1988, p. 1048). A **meta-analysis** (Doucouliagos & Laroche, 2003) found both positive and negative results. Specifically, Doucouliagos and Laroche's sample of 73 studies resulted in 45 determining there was a positive relationship between unions and productivity and 28 determining there was a negative relationship. They also found that the total productivity gain of unionized firms over nonunionized firms was 4 percent (unweighted) and 1 percent when sample size was considered. Overall, they concluded that there is a slightly negative relationship between unionization and productivity in the United Kingdom and a slightly positive one in the United States—in particular, in American manufacturing.

A potential explanation for these mixed results is the workplace climate. For example, one Australian study of approximately 300 bank branches found that a more collaborative relationship between labour and management resulted in higher productivity and customer service (Deery & Iverson, 2005). Similarly, an American study of over 600 firms found that more traditional labour–management relations, with limited participative decision making and pay not linked to performance, were associated with lower productivity than

meta-analysis
a statistical technique that looks for trends across many studies

cooperative labour–management relations, where employees had increased participation in decision making as well as part of their compensation tied to firm performance (Black & Lynch, 2001). As Turnbull (1991, pp. 144–145) argued some 20 years ago,

> What matters is not so much that the workers exercise their collective voice through the union, but how the employer then responds to that discourse . . . why is the GM–Toyota joint venture (NUMMI) so much more productive than the identical plant under the sole control of GM, especially when the majority of the labor force are the very same workers employed under the old GM regime?

As this quote suggests, the relationship between the parties, and the power of the union to move from voice to results, can play a key role in the relationship between unions and productivity.

Overall, the evidence (see Table 10.3) to date produces several conclusions. First, the impact of unions on productivity is usually positive. Second, the relationship is not always positive and can vary by context (e.g., industry, country). Third, a positive labour relations climate can improve the union–productivity relationship. Fourth, as with most measures in this section, we have to watch for the "which came first—the chicken or the egg" debate. We cannot conclude that unions cause increased productivity. Rather, the evidence states that unionization *is associated with* an increase in productivity. The causes for such productivity increases could be a number of factors, such as increased health and safety focus, management being shocked into improved practices, less turnover, and so on.

IR Today 10.1

Balancing Fairness and Efficiency

Canadian retailers have faced two significant challenges in recent years. First, they have seen the movement to Internet shopping resulting in increased competition from both national and global sources. For example, Statistics Canada reports that in 2007, 70 million Internet shopping orders were made compared to 13.4 million in 2001. Showing the increased globalization of the retail sector, that same report stated that for every $100 spent online in 2007, only $56 went to a Canadian retailer.

Second, the industry has witnessed an increased concentration of retailers through mergers and acquisitions. Perhaps the most noteworthy for Canadians were the selling of Canadian Woolco and Zellers locations to American giants Walmart and Target. For example, Walmart bought 122 Woolco stores in 1994. By 2005 its

Canadian operations included 256 retail stores, six Sam's Club stores, and an employment base of 70,000 workers. Similarly in early 2011, Target announced that it would become a significant player in the Canadian retail sector, acquiring over 220 Zellers stores from Canadian icon Hudson's Bay Company.

In this increasingly competitive market, retailers are looking for ways to improve efficiencies. For example, look at the movement to self-checkouts or scanners that can be used by customers to check the price of items and/or tally their shopping cart. While we can imagine that these self-serve options may be designed to decrease customer wait times in checkout lines, unions argue that they will be used to minimize the labour costs and/or cut cashier jobs.

IR Today 10.1 (continued)

In this environment, we can imagine two competing needs. Employees, whether unionized or not, will be seeking fair wages and working conditions. Employers, given the increasingly competitive retail market, will be seeking to maximize efficiencies. These two competing views were apparent in a recent dispute involving 30,000 Ontario employees, who were represented by the United Food and Commercial Workers. The employees voted over 95 percent in favour of a strike as the employer was seeking concessions in terms of reduced wages, fewer full-time jobs, and increase waiting times for employees to be eligible for benefits. While the union felt that the management's proposal was unacceptable, management stated that these concessions were needed to enhance efficiency, flexibility, and competitiveness, as summed up by the following quote from the Canadian Press:

> "We are striving to reach an agreement that would enable the company to continue to meet the demands of today's highly competitive retail landscape," Julia Hunter, the company's vice-president of public relations, said in an emailed statement.

> "In many contracts we pay 10 per cent more than competitors and have 15 per cent less flexibility. That's a real competitive disadvantage. That's not sustainable," Hunter said.

Source: S. Berberich, "Grocers turn to hand-held scanners for shoppers: Unions decry new technology," *The Business Gazette*, 16 August 2007, retrieved 11 February 2011 from http://www.gazette.net/stories/081607/busiplo140957_32357.shtml (article also appears in full on UFCW website, http://www.ufcw.org/your_industry/retail/industry_news/grocers.cfm; CBC News Online, "Timeline of world's largest retailer," 30 June 2005, retrieved 11 February 2011 from http://www.cbc.ca/news/background/walmart; Canadian Press, "Ontario Loblaw workers give union strike mandate after negotiations stall," 12 July 2010, retrieved 14 December 2010 from http://www.cp24.com/servlet/an/local/CTVNews/20100712/100712_loblaws_vote/20100712/?hub=CP24Home; S. Freeman, "Ontario Loblaw workers approve strike mandate" (n.d.), retrieved 11 February 2011 from http://www.ctv.ca/generic/generated/static/business/article1637560.html; L. McKeown and J. Brocca, *Internet shopping in Canada: An examination of data, trends, and patterns* (Ottawa: Statistics Canada, 2009), retrieved 11 February 2011 from http://www.statcan.gc.ca/pub/88f0006x/88f0006x2009005-eng.pdf; J. Ratner, "Zellers sells 220 stores to Target," *Financial Post*, 13 January 2011, retrieved 11 February 2011 from http://www.financialpost.com/news/retail/Zellers+sells+stores+Target/4102587/story.html.

Profitability and Innovation

Several studies and reviews of the literature have found a negative relationship between unionization and firm profits (Freeman & Medoff, 1984; Kuhn, 1998), a typical estimate of the impact being in the 10–20 percent range (Hirsch, 2004). However, a recent study that examined data from 45 union-profit

TABLE 10.3

Union Impact on Organizational Measures

ORGANIZATIONAL MEASURE	UNION IMPACT
Productivity	Small, positive association between unionization and productivity (current estimates <5%).
Profitability	While results suggest profits drop by 10–20%, there is a country effect, with U.S. seeing a 20% drop as against 1% for other countries.
Innovation	Limited data and inconsistent results. Canadian evidence suggests that unions *may* have a small, positive effect (between 0–4%).

studies found a country effect: in the United States, union decreased profits by about 23 percent; whereas the impact in non-U.S. countries was relatively insignificant, at 1 percent (Doucouliagos & Laroche, 2008). Note, however, that some argue union-profit estimates may be on the low side given that (1) we would expect unions to seek to organize more profitable firms where the gains for members could be higher and (2) firms that became bankrupt due to unionization would not appear in studies as studies have looked at the profitability of existing firms (Hirsch, 2004). That said, there is no evidence to support the argument that unionized firms are more likely to go out of business (Kuhn, 1998).

In addition, the issue of innovation has become an important area to the Canadian economy. As is pointed out by Walsworth (2010b), the few studies that have examined the impact of unions on innovation found a negative impact in the United States. In Canada, one study did not find any significant relationships between unions and innovation (Verma & Fang, 2003), while Walsworth (2010b) found a positive relationship. Specifically, he found that the presence of a union increased a firm's propensity to innovate, over the seven years examined, by almost 4 percent, and that workplaces in which the majority of employees were unionized were about 7 percent more likely to innovate.

The Impact of Unionization on Employee Measures

Thus far in this chapter, we have focused on the impact of unionization on the employer, in terms of both management practices and efficiency outcomes. Now we turn to the impact of unionization on employee measures (see Table 10.4). Employee measures are becoming more important to organizations for several

TABLE 10.4

Union Impact on Traditional HRM Employee Measures	
EMPLOYEE MEASURE	UNION IMPACT
Satisfaction	Results vary. Unionized workers generally have lower overall job satisfaction; are equally satisfied with wages, benefits, and job security; and are less satisfied with their supervisor and supervision, job content, promotional opportunities, and resources available to perform the job. Satisfaction may depend on experience with the union, as newly unionized employees may experience increases in satisfaction while employees with longer union experience may experience satisfaction decreases.
Intention to quit	Results vary but generally lower in unionized workplaces.
Organizational commitment	Few studies to date. Commitment to the employing organization may facilitate union commitment, particularly if the work climate is positive.

reasons. First, the **employee value chain** essentially argues that the success of the organization is dependent upon the employees (Wilson, 1996). Employees who are treated fairly will have increased satisfaction and commitment to the organization and be more likely to put more effort into their work. This increased effort can improve work performance, resulting in customers' perceiving that they are getting good value from the organization. Higher customer satisfaction can lead to loyal customers who will refer others to the company. The overall impact is increased organizational success.

Second, there is growing consensus that firms cannot use financial measures alone to assess organizational performance. In fact, many organizations are now using a **balanced scorecard** (Kaplan & Norton, 1996) that assesses firm effectiveness using multiple measures (e.g., employee measures, customer measures, financial measures, and quality/continuous improvement measures).

Given the increasing focus on employee measures, we now review several that are influencing today's workplace. Interestingly, the IR literature has largely focused on economic versus employee measures, particularly those that are attitudinal in nature. A potential explanation for the lack of attitudinal research in IR was provided over 20 years ago by Craig (1988), who argued that concepts from organizational psychology/behaviour, an area in which employee attitudinal measures are often researched, have largely been overlooked in IR. That same year, Barling (1988), a prominent researcher in organizational psychology/behaviour, concurred, stating that his field had largely ignored issues relevant to IR. Since that time, we seen works that integrate these fields. For example, studies have looked at employee reactions to strikes (Chaulk & Brown, 2008) and bumping (Stringer & Brown, 2008). Building on such works, we will now examine the employee measures of job satisfaction, intention to quit, organizational commitment, union satisfaction, union commitment, work climate, and desire to leave a union.

Job Satisfaction and Intention to Quit

Job satisfaction represents an employee's assessment of his or her job experience (Locke, 1976) and is one of the most frequently studied issues in the organizational psychology/behaviour field (Brief & Weiss, 2002; Latham & Pinder, 2005). **Intention to quit**, which is closely related, measures the likelihood of an employee leaving the organization (Freeman & Medoff, 1984). Job dissatisfaction is known to be one of the determinants of turnover rates (Hammer & Avgar, 2005) and recent evidence from a sample of unionized nurses found that both pay and job satisfaction were negatively associated with turnover intentions (i.e., the lower the levels of pay and job satisfaction the higher the intention to quit; Singh & Loncar, 2010).

Research further suggests that several factors—namely, work climate, supervisor, job responsibilities, and coworker relationships—contribute to an employee's level of job satisfaction (Saari & Judge, 2004; Smith, Kendall & Hulin, 1969). Since collective agreements and unionization can impact many of these factors, it would be reasonable to assume that job satisfaction might differ between union and nonunion workers. In fact, evidence from Freeman

employee value chain
a belief that organizational effectiveness is based on employee effectiveness

balanced scorecard
using multiple measures to assess a firm's effectiveness

job satisfaction
an employee's assessment of his or her job experience

intention to quit
a survey measure that assesses the likelihood that an employee will quit

and Medoff (1984) suggests that unionized employees have lower levels of job satisfaction than nonunionized employees. Specifically, they found that unionized workers were more satisfied with their level of total compensation (wages plus benefits) and less satisfied with (1) their supervisors, (2) their relationships with their supervisors, (3) physical conditions of work, and (4) job safety level. Yet their intention to quit and actual quit rates were lower than those of nonunion employees. This seems contradictory, as one would expect that if the unionized workers were truly dissatisfied, they would be more likely to seek jobs elsewhere—but the reverse is true. A potential explanation to this contradiction, offered by Freeman and Medoff (1984), is the collective voice mechanism of the union. They argue that true dissatisfaction would result in turnover or intention to quit, while "voiced" dissatisfaction results from negative attitudes toward the workplace and a willingness to complain about problems. We can well imagine that the increased protection of just-cause termination and grievance procedures would increase the willingness of unionized employees to voice their dissatisfaction relative to nonunion employees, who have little or no protection.

Hammer and Avgar (2005) also offer several possible explanations for lower levels of satisfaction among unionized workers. First, unions may choose to organize workers with poor working conditions, low pay, and/or unsafe tasks in order to increase the likelihood of a positive certification vote. Second, unions may create unrealistic expectations, thus, raising worker dissatisfaction when these expectations are not met. Third, unionized and nonunionized workers may have different job outcome preferences. Unions may socialize members to value the areas that the union can improve (pay, benefits, safety, etc.) rather than job content. Fourth, unions and collective agreements may restrict job tasks and narrowly define jobs, resulting in workers not being able to fully use all of their skills and abilities. This can result in lower autonomy, challenge, and sense of achievement—all of which are associated with higher job satisfaction.

Regardless of the explanation, numerous studies (see Hammer & Avgar, 2005) have shown that unionized workers, when compared with nonunionized workers, are at least as satisfied with wages, benefits, and job security, and are less likely to quit their jobs. They are less satisfied with

- their supervisor and supervision;
- job content (job tasks, skills required to perform the job, freedom to make decisions, etc.);
- promotional opportunities; and
- resources available to perform the job.

We stress, however, that evidence from both the United States and Canada suggests that the union–nonunion difference in satisfaction levels may be more complex than it first appears. For example, one American study of public-sector employees and university professors found that when working conditions were held constant, there were no differences between satisfaction and intention to quit measures of unionized and nonunionized employees (Gordon & Denisi, 1995). They argued (p. 234) that the previously found results of higher dissatisfaction in unionized workers may have been due to "relying on data that, in essence, compare unionized work environments to nonunionized work environments." Similarly, Renaud's (2002) study of over 3,000 Canadians found that unionized workers were less satisfied with their jobs than nonunionized workers. However, when he factored out the work environment (e.g., opportunities for promotion, physical surroundings, freedom at work, and routine), there was no longer a significant difference between union and nonunion employee job satisfaction. Finally, Artz (2010) examined over 20 years of data and argued that results can be misleading if one examines only union status. He argued that one must also consider union experience, as many nonunion workers have worked previously in union jobs and vice versa. Taking these factors into account, he found that job satisfaction (1) increases for people who are in the union for the first time; (2) decreases the longer a person is a union member; (3) increases with tenure when tenure is known to be higher for unionized workers, and (4) increases for formerly unionized workers the longer they have been in their new nonunion jobs. Artz offers several explanations for these findings. First, first-time union members may experience an increase in satisfaction due to the benefits of unionization, but the voice mechanism experienced through their union experience subsequently causes a reduction in satisfaction. Second, the longer an employee works in a unionized firm, the more they can find workplace dissatisfiers that can be used as leverage during subsequent collective bargaining. Third, unions enable a workplace culture of discontent that stays with the employees even after they leave a unionized firm.

Organizational Commitment

Organizational commitment can be defined in terms of an employee's acceptance of the organization's goals and values, exertion of a substantial amount of effort on behalf of the organization, and aspiration to remain a member of the organization (Mowday, Steers & Porter, 1979; Vakola & Nikolaou, 2005). There is a long history of research concerning organizational commitment in organizational psychology/behaviour literature. In fact, a meta-analysis by Cooper-Hakim and Viswesvaran (2005) cited almost 1,000 studies on the issue. That study found a positive relationship between organizational commitment and both job satisfaction and performance, and a negative relationship between organizational commitment and turnover. Overall, these results suggest that organizations in which employees have high levels of organizational commitment will see positive employee reactions and performance.

organizational commitment

an employee's commitment to the organization

Unfortunately, few studies have examined the relationship between union status and organizational commitment (Hammer & Avgar, 2005). Those that have often examined union-member commitment to both employer (i.e., organizational commitment) and union (i.e., union commitment). For example, Snape, Redman, and Chan (2000) concluded from their review of the studies that commitment to the employing organization facilitates union commitment. Stringer and Brown (2008) also found a positive relationship between these variables, even in an environment of downsizing. On the other hand, another study that examined employees' reactions toward their employer and union following a strike (Chaulk & Brown, 2008) found a negative relationship between organizational commitment and both union commitment and

Chapter 10: Impacts of Unionization

job satisfaction. To us, this reinforces the need for a positive work environment to facilitate joint commitment.

Union Satisfaction and Commitment

Scholars have argued that **union satisfaction** is akin to job satisfaction while **union commitment** is akin to organizational commitment (Kuruvilla, Gallagher & Wetzel, 1993). Kuruvilla, Gallagher, and Wetzel (1993) suggest that union satisfaction is a reflection of, and reaction to, the immediate actions taken by the union, whereas union commitment is less specific and focuses less on the performance and actions of the union. The authors indicate that the primary distinction between these measures is that union commitment is developed over a longer period of time and is more stable than union satisfaction.

Kuruvilla, Gallagher, and Wetzel's (1993) survey study of Canadian and Swedish employees indicates that contact with the union is a key determinant of union commitment. Their study concluded that members who read union newsletters and who actively take part in union activities demonstrate more union commitment than those members who do not. They also found that friends of union members influence commitment toward unions. For example, when friends of union members have positive attitudes toward unions, the members will also develop positive attitudes and therefore will become committed to the union.

As we discussed previously, researchers (Kuruvilla, Gallagher, and Wetzel, 1993; Snape, Redman & Chan, 2000) often associate union commitment with organizational commitment. These researchers indicate several antecedents to union commitment by using the "parallels model," which suggests that commitment to the union can be studied and based on previous organizational commitment research. The model highlights personal characteristics, job characteristics, work experience, and industrial relations climate as antecedents to union commitment. Thus, scholars have concluded that commitment to the employing organization also facilitates positive union commitment (Snape, Redman & Chan, 2000), and research has found a positive relationship between these measures (Stringer & Brown, 2008). Moreover, when the industrial relations climate is perceived to be positive, commitment to the union and the employer are both positive. What can be concluded from these results is that employers and unions do not essentially compete for commitment and that a favourable work climate has positive implications for both of these actors of the industrial relations system. Interestingly though, it appears that IR events, such as strikes, may impact this relationship, as following a lengthy strike, union commitment was seen to drop and the relationship between union and organization commitment, when controlling for work environment, was also negative (Chaulk & Brown, 2008).

Work Climate

Patterson et al. (2005), reflecting upon a study conducted by Brown and Leigh (1996), concluded that a positive work environment had a positive impact on employee performance. As we have seen throughout this chapter, a positive union–management relationship is key to effective organizational and employee outcomes.

Employees' Desire to Leave a Union

Recall that in Chapter 5 we discussed how low job satisfaction and perceptions of poor work environments can encourage unionization. As was the case with the organizational measure of intention to quit, studies have also examined the concept of desire to leave a union. Remember that, as we discussed in Chapter 2, unions can face decertification, in which union members ask the labour relations board to rescind the certification order. Thus, unions too are concerned with issues of "quitting." In a U.S. study involving over 3,000 workers, Friedman, Abraham, and Thomas (2006) found that desire to leave a union increased with firm size, possibly due to larger firms having collective agreement clauses requiring that employees be union members as a condition of employment. They also found that employees less satisfied with their compensation and benefits were more likely to desire leaving the union. Given the "bread and butter" focus of unions in North America, this finding should not be surprising. If a union cannot "deliver the goods" in terms of economic gains, members are more likely to want out. Interestingly, that study, along with a second of Polish workers (Zientara & Kuczynsk, 2009), found a positive relationship between one's intention to leave a firm and one's desire to leave the union. Zientara and Kuczynsk (2009) argue that this relationship is likely explained by the fact that employees who plan to leave a firm likely have no interest in remaining with the union associated with it.

Summary

As we have seen throughout this chapter, unionization has several impacts on the employment relationship and the outcomes of the IR system. In particular, we see that unionization impacts management practices (especially those of HRM), firm efficiency, and employee measures.

Generally speaking, unionization results in more formalized HRM practices, less managerial discretion, fewer individualized practices, and HRM practices heavily influenced by seniority. We also see increased total compensation levels and increased focus on equality and health and safety in unionized firms. This difference can be explained in three ways. First, the addition of the union greatly restricts management flexibility and unilateral decision making relative to nonunion employers operating under common law. Second, the collective voice of the union allows employees to express their needs and serves as an alternative to quitting. Third, unionized workers have increased wages and benefits—probably due to the fact that North Americans often seek economic returns from unionization.

Turning to efficiency measures, the research suggests that unions are associated with a modest but positive impact on productivity and a large, negative impact on profitability in the United States. Clearly, the increased total compensation package of unionized workers is not offset by improved productivity. However, there is no evidence that this reduced profitability results in more unionized firms going out of business, and there is evidence that Canadian unionized firms are more innovative their nonunion counterparts.

But what about the worker him- or herself? The evidence suggests that unionized workers are often less satisfied with their jobs than their nonunion counterparts. However, this reduced job satisfaction does not lead to increased intention to quit or actual quitting of jobs. Other studies concerning organizational commitment and union commitment suggest these employers and unions do not "fight" for employee affect—rather, union commitment and organizational commitment tend to go hand in hand.

Perhaps the most significant lesson from this chapter is the importance of an effective labour–management relationship and a positive work climate. Considering both productivity and commitment, a positive climate plays an important role in unionization having a positive impact.

Perhaps Freeman and Medoff (1984, p. 190) best summarize the impact of unions:

> Beneficial to organized workers, almost always; beneficial to the economy, in many ways; but harmful to the bottom line of company balance sheets; this is the paradox of American trade unionism, which underlies some of the ambivalences of our national policies toward the institution.

Key Terms

balanced scorecard 329
base pay 317
collective voice 313
defined benefit 322
Employee Assistance Plan (EAP) 321
employee value chain 329
gain sharing 321
indirect pay (or benefits) 317
intention to quit 329
job analysis 317
job evaluation 317
job satisfaction 329
meta-analysis 325
monopoly effect 317

organizational commitment 331
performance pay 317
probationary period 314
profit sharing 321
recall 314
recruitment 314
shock effect 313
spillover effect 320
threat effect 320
total compensation 317
union commitment 332
union satisfaction 332
wage differential 320

Weblinks

YouTube postings concerning the union impact in the construction industry:

- Michigan Associated Builders and Contractors:

  http://www.youtube.com/watch?v=k3vBA3Hm5Mk

- Association of Union Constructors:

    http://www.youtube.com/watch?v=tw610qHGyM8

Canadian Labour Congress discussion of unions improved benefits:

http://www.canadianlabour.ca/about-clc/union-advantage

Canadian Labour Congress' Day of Mourning:

http://www.canadianlabour.ca/issues/day-mourning

Alberta Federation of Labour health and safety activities of unions:

http://www.afl.org/index.php/Unions/why-join-a-union.html

Health and safety section of UFCW's website:

http://www.ufcw.ca/index.php?option=com_content&view=article&id=32&Itemid=112&lang=en

Canadian Federation of Labour on equality activities of unions:

http://www.canadianlabour.ca/human-rights-equality

CAW on equality activities of unions:

http://www.caw.ca/en/services-departments-human-rights.htm

RPC Icons

10.1 Interprets the collective agreement

- context and content of collective agreement
- institutions and processes (both regulatory and nonregulatory) that govern the relationship between employers and employees
- the process of collective bargaining

10.2 Collects and develops information required for good decision making throughout the bargaining process

- union decision-making process
- the effects of collective bargaining on corporate issues (e.g., wages, productivity, and management processes)
- potential productivity and profitability outcomes under changing labour circumstances

10.3 Provides advice to clients on the establishment, continuation, and termination of bargaining rights

- organizing tactics of unions
- collective bargaining processes and issues
- union practices, organization, and certification

Discussion Questions

1. Given the information in this chapter, why do you believe that many employers prefer union-free status?
2. The evidence in this chapter shows that unions can have positive effects on the firm. Why then are employers generally not supportive of unionization?
3. As is shown by data in this chapter, unionization has a number of positive impacts for workers. If you were a union organizer, what would you tell employees are the greatest advantages of becoming unionized?
4. On the basis of the data in this chapter, what do you feel are the biggest impacts of a union for the management team of a firm?
5. As is mentioned in the chapter, we are seeing an increase in the earnings gap between the rich and the poor. At the same time, union density is dropping in many countries. Do you believe the two are related? If so, why?
6. Let's assume that you move from a nonunionized workplace to a unionized workplace. What do you expect will be the biggest changes you would notice in HRM practices?

Using the Internet

Health and safety has always been a key concern of unions. Have a look at several union web pages and/or web pages of your provincial federation of labour. (*Hint:* Look for health and safety committees.)

1. To what extent do you see references made to employee health and safety?
2. What health and safety activities is the union involved in?
3. Do these activities have an impact on the employer?
4. If there is a committee, what is its role?
5. Does the union use improved health and safety as a "recruiting" method to attract new union members?

Exercises

1. Take a look at recent media stories related to industrial relations. To what extent do you see issues related to unions' impact on firm efficiency, management practices, and/or employee measures?
2. In most universities, employees are unionized, many placing their collective agreements online. Take a look at a collective agreement from your university (or any other workplace you choose) and examine the following human resources functions:

   - staffing (look for language on job postings, selection, promotions, and layoffs);
   - performance appraisal;
   - training and development; and
   - compensation.

Then answer the following questions:

    a. To what extent does seniority play a role in these practices?

    b. To what extent is management flexibility restricted?

    c. To what extent are rules and processes clearly documented?

3. Many students work as they attend school. If your company is unionized (or not unionized), what do you think would be different in terms of management practices, efficiency, or employee measures if it were not unionized (or unionized)?

Case

Walmart Unionizes in Saskatchewan

Neither the Canadian retail sector nor industry giant Walmart are known for being highly unionized. Yet in December 2010, after a six-year dispute between the retailer and the United Food and Commercial Workers union (UFCW), the Saskatchewan Court of Appeal reaffirmed that the Walmart store in Weyburn, Saskatchewan, was unionized. The store is the only unionized Walmart location in western Canada. However, the union has other union certification applications in process for two other Saskatchewan locations, North Battleford and Moose Jaw.

The process to gain union recognition was a long one for the UFCW and the Walmart employees. While the Saskatchewan Labour Relations Board received the certification application in 2004, the retailer had challenged the application at several venues, including the Labour Relations Board, the court system, and even two Supreme Court of Canada bids. In December of 2008, the Saskatchewan Labour Relations Board released its decision and certified the union. Still, the certification remained unsettled.

In June 2009, following an appeal from the firm, a judge ordered that the certification order be sent back to the Saskatchewan Labour Relations Board. The rationale for this ruling was that the 2008 amendment to the province's *Trade Union Act* required a mandatory vote (as opposed to a card-based, automatic certification) for all union certification applications. For this reason, the judge felt that Walmart employees had to vote on the issue of union representation, and meet the thresholds set by the revised labour legislation, before a certification could be ordered. Simply put, the card evidence used when the union applied for certification, prior to the revised legislation requiring a vote, was deemed insufficient to grant certification. This decision was overturned by the Saskatchewan Court of Appeal in October of 2010. The store is now officially unionized and the union hopes to start negotiations shortly.

Sources: CBC News, "Union certified at Wal-Mart store in Saskatchewan," 9 December 2008, retrieved 29 January 2011 from http://www.cbc.ca/canada/saskatchewan/story/2008/12/09/wal-mart.html; CBC News, "Sask. judge overturns Wal-Mart union certification," 24 June 2009, retrieved 29 January 2011 from http://www.cbc.ca/canada/saskatchewan/story/2009/06/24/wal-mart.html; "Saskatchewan Court of Appeal upholds union bid at Weyburn Walmart," *Regina Leader-Post*, 15 October 2010, retrieved 29 January 2011 from http://www.leaderpost.com/business/Saskatchewan+Court+Appeal+upholds+union+Weyburn+Walmart/3679321/story.html.

Questions

1. Let's assume that you are the HRM manager of the Walmart store in Weyburn that just unionized. You need to brief the management team on the changes they will face as a result of unionization.

   a. What would you inform them are the key changes they can expect to see in terms of management and HRM practices?
   b. The managers will likely be concerned about efficiency. How would you advise that they best ensure that productivity remains the same or improves?
   c. If you were asked to predict levels of turnover in the newly unionized store relative to the other nonunion retailers in the area, what would you predict?

2. Employees, some of whom supported the union and some of whom did not, may have many questions. Let's assume that you and a UFCW representative hold a joint meeting with the staff. What three or four changes would you highlight as they move to a collective employment relationship?

References

Altonji, J. G., & Usui, E. (2007). Work hours, wages, and vacation leave. *Industrial & Labor Relations Review, 60*(3), pp. 408–428.

Artz, B. (2010). The impact of union experience on job satisfaction. *Industrial Relations, 49,* pp. 387–405.

Bahrami, B., Bitzan, J., & Leitch, J. (2009). Union worker wage effect in the public sector. *Journal of Labor Research, 30*(1), pp. 35–51.

Barbash, J. (1987). Like nature, industrial relations abhors a vacuum. *Relations industrielles, 42,* pp. 168–179.

Barling, J. (1988). Industrial relations: A blind spot in the teaching, research and practice of I/O psychology. *Canadian Psychology, 29,* pp. 103–108.

Barron, A. (2006). *Work-related musculoskeletal disorders.* Unpublished master's thesis. St. John's, NL: Memorial University.

Betcherman, G., Leckie, N., McMullen, K., & Caron, C. (1994). *The Canadian workplace in transition.* Kingston, ON: IRC Press, Industrial Relations Centre, Queen's University.

Black, S. E., & Lynch, L. M. (2001). How to compete: The impact of workplace practices and information technology on productivity. *Review of Economics and Statistics, 83,* pp. 434–445.

Blanchflower, D. G., & Bryson, A. (2004). What effect do unions have on wages now and would Freeman and Medoff be surprised? *Journal of Labor Research, 25,* pp. 383–414.

Boheim, R., & Booth, A. L. (2004). Trade union presence and employer-provided training in Great Britain. *Industrial Relations, 43,* pp. 520–545.

Booth, A. L., Francesconi, M., & Zoega, G. (2003). Unions, work-related training, and wages: Evidence for British men. *Industrial and Labor Relations Review, 57,* pp. 68–91.

Bornstein, S., & Hart, S. (2010). Evaluating occupational health and safety management systems: A collaborative approach. *Policy and Practice in Health and Safety, 08*(1), pp. 61–76.

Brief, A. P., & Weiss, H. M. (2002). Organizational behavior: Affect in the workplace. *Annual Review of Psychology, 53,* pp. 279–307.

Brown, M., & Heywood, J. S. (2005). Performance appraisal systems: Determinants and change. *British Journal of Industrial Relations, 43*, pp. 659–679.

Brown, S. P., & Leigh, T. W. (1996). A new look at psychological climate and its relationship to job involvement, effort, and performance. *Journal of Applied Psychology, 81*, pp. 358–368.

Brown, T. C. (2003). Sexual orientation provisions in Canadian collective agreements. *Relations Industrielles/Industrial Relations, 58*, pp. 644–666.

Brown, T. C., & Latham, G. P. (2000). The effects of goal setting and self-instruction training on the performance of union employees. *Industrial Relations, 55*, pp. 80–94.

Brown, T. C., & Warren, M. A. (2010). Performance management in unionized settings, *Human Resource Management Review*, corrected proof. ISSN 1053-4822, DOI: 10.1016/j. hrmr.2010.09.005. Retrieved 11 April 2011 from http://www.sciencedirect.com/science/article/ B6W4J-513XWY1-1/2/ccc70689fc58ed3f2e0c099a38e702a4

Byers, B. (28 April 2010). Speech at the National Day of Mourning Ceremony in Halifax. Retrieved 31 January 2011 from http://www.canadianlabour.ca/news-room/speeches/speech-national-day-mourning-ceremony-halifax

Canadian Auto Workers. (CAW). (2006). *What we do: Human rights*. Retrieved 26 July 2006 from http://www.caw.ca/whatwedo/humanrights/index.asp

Canadian Labour Congress. (CLC). (2006). *Human rights & equality*. Retrieved 27 July 2006 from http://canadianlabour.ca/index.php/equality

Canadian Labour Congress (CLC). (2011). *The union advantage*. Retrieved January 11 2011 from http://www.canadianlabour.ca/about-clc/union-advantage

Card, D., Lemieux, T., & Riddell, W. C. (2004). Unions and wage inequality. *Journal of Labor Research, 25*, pp. 519–562.

Chaulk, K., & Brown, T. C. (2008). An assessment of worker reaction to their union and employer post-strike. *Relations Industrielles/Industrial Relations, 63*(2), pp. 223–245.

Clark, P. F., & Gray, L. S. (2008). Administrative practices in American unions: A longitudinal study. *Journal of Labour Research, 29*, pp. 42–55.

Cleveland, G., Gunderson, M., & Hyatt, D. (2003). Union effects in low-wage services: Evidence from Canadian childcare. *Industrial and Labor Relations Review, 56*, pp. 295–305.

Conference Board of Canada. (12 September 2002). *News release 02-30: Variable pay offers a bonus for unionized workplaces*. Retrieved 26 July 2006 from http://www.conferenceboard.ca/ press/2002/variable_pay.asp

Cooper-Hakim, A., & Viswesvaran, C. (2005). The construct of work commitment: Testing an integrative framework. *Psychological Bulletin, 131*, pp. 241–259.

Craig, A. W. J. (1988). Mainstream industrial relations in Canada. In G. Hebert, C. J. Jain & N. Meltz (Eds.), *The state of the art in industrial relations* (pp. 9–43). Kingston, ON: Industrial Relations Centre, Queen's University, and Centre for Industrial Relations, University of Toronto.

Deery, S., & Iverson, R. (2005). Labor–management cooperation: Antecedents and impact on organizational performance. *Industrial and Labor Relations Review, 58*, pp. 588–609.

Doucouliagos, C., & Laroche, P. (2003). What do unions do to productivity? A meta-analysis. *Industrial Relations, 42*, pp. 650–691.

Doucouliagos, C., & Laroche, P. (2008). Unions and profits: A meta-regression analysis. *Industrial Relations, 48*, pp. 146–184.

Doucouliagos, C., Laroche, P., & Stanley, T. (2005). Publication bias in union–productivity research? *Industrial Relations, 60*, pp. 320–346.

Dustmann, C., & Schönberg, U. (2009). Training and union wages. *Review of Economics & Statistics, 91*(2), pp. 363–376.

Eren, O. (2007). Measuring the union–nonunion wage gap using propensity score matching. *Industrial Relations, 46*(4), pp. 766–780.

Freeman, R. B., & Medoff, J. L. (1984). *What do unions do?* New York: Basic Books.

Friedman, B. A., Abraham, S. E., & Thomas, R. K. (2006). Factors related to employees' desire to join and leave unions. *Industrial Relations: A Journal of Economy and Society, 45*, pp. 102–110.

Godard, J. (2007). Unions, work practices, and wages under different institutional environments: The case of Canada and England. *Industrial & Labor Relations Review, 60*(4), pp. 457–476.

Gordon, M. E., & Denisi, A. S. (1995). A reexamination of the relationship between union membership and job satisfaction. *Industrial and Labor Relations Review, 48*, pp. 222–236.

Grant, E. K., Swidinsky, R., & Vanderkamp, J. (1987). Canadian union–nonunion wage differentials. *Industrial and Labor Relations Review, 41*, pp. 93–107.

Green, D. A., & Lemieux, T. (2001). The adult education and training survey: The impact of unionization on the incidence and financing of training in Canada. Hull, QC: Applied Research Branch, HRDC.

Hammer, T. H., & Avgar, A. (2005). The impact of unions on job satisfaction, organizational commitment, and turnover. *Journal of Labor Research, 26*, pp. 241–266.

Hart, S. M. (2002a). Norwegian workforce involvement in safety offshore: Regulatory framework and participants' perspectives. *Employee Relations, 24*, pp. 486–499.

Hart, S. M. (2002b). Unions and pay equity bargaining. *Relations industrielles, 57*, pp. 609–628.

Hart, S. (2010). Self-regulation, corporate social responsibility, and the business case: Do they work in achieving workplace equality and safety? *Journal of Business Ethics, 92*(4), pp. 585–600.

Hilyer, B., Leviton, L., Overman, L., & Mukherjee, S. (2000). Union-initiated safety training program leads to improved workplace safety. *Labor Studies Journal, 24*(4), pp. 53–66.

Hirsch, B. T. (2004). What do unions do for economic performance? *Journal of Labor Research, 25*, pp. 415–455.

Hirschmen, A. O. (1970). *Exit, voice and loyalty.* Cambridge, MA: Harvard University Press.

Hunt, G., & Rayside, D. (2000). Labor's response to diversity in Canada and the United States. *Industrial Relations, 39*, pp. 401–444.

James, P., & Walters, D. (2002). Worker representation in health and safety: Options for regulatory reform. *Industrial Relations, 33*, pp. 141–156.

Kaplan, R. S., & Norton, D. (1996). *The balanced scorecard: Translating strategy into action.* Boston: Harvard Business School Press.

Khan, S. (28 February, 2007). Repetitive strain. Retrieved 15 January 2011 from http://www.cbc.ca/news/background/health/rsi.html

Koch, M. J., & Hundley, G. (1997). The effects of unionism on recruitment and selection methods. *Industrial Relations, 36*, pp. 349–370.

Kuhn, P. (1998). Unions and the economy: What we know; what we should know. *Canadian Journal of Economics, 31*, pp. 1033–1056.

Kuruvilla, S., Gallagher, D. G., & Wetzel, K. (1993). The development of members' attitudes toward their unions: Sweden and Canada. *Industrial and Labor Relations Review, 46*, pp. 499–514.

Latham, G. P., & Pinder, C. C. (2005). Work motivation theory and research at the dawn of the twenty-first century. *Annual Review of Psychology, 56*, pp. 485–516.

Lewis, H. G. (1986). *Union relative wage effects: A survey.* Chicago: University of Chicago Press.

Livingstone, D. W., & Raykov, M. (2005). Union influence on worker education and training in Canada in tough times. *Just Labour, 5*, pp. 50–64.

Livingstone, D. W., & Raykov, M. (2008). Workers' power and intentional learning among nonmanagerial workers: A 2004 benchmark survey. *Relations Industrielles/Industrial Relations, 63*(1), pp. 30–56.

Locke, E. A. (1976). The nature and causes of job satisfaction. In M. D. Dunnette (Ed.), *Handbook of industrial and organizational psychology.* Chicago: Rand McNally pp. 1319–1328.

Long, R. J. (2006). *Compensation in Canada: Strategy, practice, and issues* (3rd edition). Toronto, ON: ITP Nelson Publishers.

Long, R. J., & Shields, J. L. (2009). Do unions affect pay methods of Canadian firms? A longitudinal study. *Relations Industrielles/Industrial Relations, 64*(3), pp. 442–465.

Luchak, A. A., & Gunderson, M. (2000). What do employees know about their pension plan? *Industrial Relations, 39*, pp. 646–670.

Markey, R., & Patmore, G. (2011). Employee participation in health and safety in the Australian steel industry, 1935–2006. *British Journal of Industrial Relations, 49*(1), pp. 144–167. DOI:10.1111/j.1467-8543.2009.00756.x

Martinello, F. (2009). Faculty salaries in Ontario: Compression, inversion, and the effects of alternative forms of representation. *Industrial & Labor Relations Review, 63*(1), pp. 128–145.

MFL Occupational Health Centre. (September 2003). *Repetitive strain injury (RSI)*. Retrieved 1 February 2011 from http://www.mflohc.mb.ca/fact_sheets_folder/repetitive_strain_injury.html

Mowday, R. T., Steers, R. M., & Porter, L. W. (1979). The measurement of organizational commitment. *Journal of Vocational Behavior, 14*, pp. 224–247.

Ng, I., & Maki, D. (1994). Trade union influence on human resource management practices. *Industrial Relations, 33*, pp. 121–135.

Parker, J., & Foley, J. (2010). Progress on women's equality within UK and Canadian trade unions: Do women's structures make a difference?. *Relations Industrielles/Industrial Relations, 65*(2), pp. 281–303.

Patterson, M. G., West, M. A., Shackleton, V. J., Dawson, J. F., Lawthom, R., Maitlis, S., Robinson, D. L., & Wallace, A. M. (2005). Validating the organizational climate measure: Links to managerial practices, productivity and innovation. *Journal of Organizational Behavior, 26*, pp. 379–408.

Pieroway, P., & Brown, T. C. (2006). Reactions to the introduction of a performance evaluation system in a unionized firm. Paper presented at the annual meeting of the Canadian Industrial Relations Association, York University, North York, ON.

Renaud, S. (1998). Unions, wages and total compensation in Canada: An empirical study. *Industrial Relations, 53*, pp. 710–729.

Renaud, S. (2002). Rethinking the union membership/job satisfaction relationship: Some empirical evidence in Canada. *International Journal of Manpower, 23*, pp. 137–150.

Rynes, S. L., Gerhart, B., & Parks, L. 2005. Personnel psychology: Performance evaluation and pay performance. *Annual Review of Psychology, 56*, pp. 571–600.

Saari, L. M., & Judge, T. A. (2004). Employee attitudes and job satisfaction. *Human Resource Management, 43*, pp. 395–407.

Singh, P., & Loncar, N. (2010). Pay satisfaction, job satisfaction and turnover intent. *Relations Industrielles/Industrial Relations, 65*, pp. 470–490.

Slichter, S., Healy, J., & Livernash, E. R. (1960). *The impact of collective bargaining on management*. Washington, DC: Brookings Institution.

Smith, P. C., Kendall, L. M., & Hulin, C. L. (1969). *The measurement of satisfaction in work and retirement.* Chicago: Rand-McNally.

Snape, E., Redman, T., & Chan, A. W. (2000). Commitment to the union: A survey of research and the implications for industrial relations and trade unions. *International Journal of Management Reviews, 2*, pp. 205–230.

Statistics Canada. (12 August 2003). Repetitive strain injury. *The Daily.* Retrieved 26 July 2005 from http://www.statcan.ca/Daily/English/030812/ d030812b.htm

Stringer, K., & Brown, T. C. (2008). A special kind of downsizing: An assessment of union member reaction to bumping. *Relations Industrielles/Industrial Relations, 63*(4), pp. 648–670.

Turnbull, P. (1991). Trade unions and productivity: Opening the Harvard "Black Boxes." *Journal of Labor Research, 12*, pp. 135–150.

UFCW (2011). *Health & safety.* Retrieved 2 February 2011 from http://www.ufcw.ca/index.php?option=com_content&view=article&id=32&Itemid=112&lang=en

Vakola, M., & Nikolaou, I. (2005). Attitudes towards organizational change: What is the role of employees' stress and commitment? *Employee Relations, 27*, pp. 160–174.

Verma, A. (2005). What do unions do to the workplace? Union effects on management and HRM policies. *Journal of Labor Research, 26*, pp. 415–449.

Verma, A., & Fang, T. (2002). Union wage premium. *Perspectives on Labor and Income 14*(4): 17–23.

Verma, A., & Fang, T. (2003). Workplace innovation and union status: synergy or strife? *Proceedings of 55th Annual Meeting, Industrial Relations Research Association,* January 2–5, 2003, Washington, DC (pp. 189–198). Retrieved April 11, 2011 from http://www.press.uillinois.edu/journals/irra/proceedings2003/verma.html

Waddoups, C. (2008). Unions and wages in Australia: Does employer size matter? *Industrial Relations, 47*(1), 136–144.

Wagar, T. H. (1997). Factors differentiating union and non-union organizations: Some evidence from Canada. *Labor Studies Journal, 22*(1), pp. 20–37.

Walsworth, S. (2010a). Unions and employment growth: The Canadian experience. *Industrial Relations, 49*(1), pp. 142–156.

Walsworth, S. (2010b). What do unions do to innovation? An empirical examination of the Canadian private sector. *Relations Industrielles/Industrial Relations, 65,* pp. 543–561.

Walters, D. (2004). Worker representation and health and safety in small enterprises in Europe. *Industrial Relations, 35,* pp. 169–186.

Wilson, T. (1996). *Diversity at work: The business case for equity.* Toronto: Wiley & Sons.

Zientara, P., & Kuczynsk, G. (2009). Employees' desire to join or leave a union: Evidence from Poland, *Industrial Relations, 48,* pp. 185–192.

CHAPTER 11

Public-Sector Issues

Learning Objectives

By the end of this chapter, you will be able to discuss

- why the public sector is a special industry;
- the factors accounting for public-sector union growth;
- theoretical differences between private and public sectors;
- bargaining power;
- essential services and special dispute resolution procedures; and
- management issues such as restructuring, privatization, and HR practice differences.

RECOGNITION OF HEALTHCARE PROFESSIONALS

It took 13 months of hard labour, 13 months of mobilization and demonstrations of all kinds, 13 months for the government of Quebec to agree with the arguments of the Federation [Fédération interprofessionnelle de la santé du Québec (FIQ)] and for an agreement in principle to be reached between the two parties. This agreement in principle finally recognizes the work, roles, duties and responsibilities of the healthcare professionals working in the Quebec public health network. The FIQ has, once again, demonstrated that it is the best organization to defend the healthcare professionals.

This agreement in principle is an historical moment for the Federation. For the very first time, the respiratory therapists, licensed practical nurses, perfusionists and nurses have brought a common project to negotiate one collective agreement for all the healthcare professionals. The challenge was considerable and the adversary tough, but the determination and patience of the Federation and its members enabled us to win.

When the FIQ left the bargaining table in June because the government was imposing what the other labour organizations had accepted, it took the decision to stand up to the government of Quebec, strong with its 58,000 members. The Federation was convinced that the specificities of the healthcare professionals had to be recognized for its true value. This recognition needed to be worthy of their responsibilities and their contribution in delivering quality care to the population of Quebec. The ensuing agreement in principle proved them right.

Every negotiation is difficult, and this one was no different from the others. However, for each gain torn from the government, it is a new step in the improvement of the working conditions of the members of the Federation. This agreement in principle will not resolve all the problems that healthcare professionals experience, but significant breakthroughs have been made. The many characteristics of the FIQ members have certainly been considered. The strength of diversity of the professionals making up the organization has been the leverage to come to this positive conclusion of the negotiations.

The gains obtained will help us get through the coming years with a little more serenity. However, the fight must go on in order that the situation of respiratory therapists, licensed practical nurses, perfusionists and nurses working in the public health network will continue to improve.

With this agreement, the FIQ can put its name in the history of battles for the improvement of the nursing and cardio-respiratory care professionals. Everyone can be proud of this agreement in principle and the extras it brings for the healthcare professionals.

Source: Régine Laurent (President), "The recognition of healthcare professionals: At last!," *FIQ en Action*, 23(14), retrieved 30 April 2011 from http://www.fiqsante.qc.ca/english/negotiations-working-conditions-2010.

Why Study Public-Sector Labour–Management Relations?

A Significant Industry

The public sector is an important component in Canada's labour force, representing 24.6 percent (3,509/14,258) of total employment in Canada (see Table 11.1).

Highly Unionized

Public-sector employees are more than four times likelier to be unionized than private-sector ones (71.2 percent union density as against 16 percent in the private sector). In addition, **collective bargaining coverage** is 74.8 and 17.5, respectively, in the public and private sectors (Table 11.1).

Important Part of the Labour Movement in Canada

From their growth in the 1960s, public-sector unions have emerged as the largest unions in Canada. Representing primarily employees at the municipal, provincial, and federal levels, the Canadian Union of Public Employees (CUPE), the National Union of Public and General Employees (NUPGE), and the Public Service Alliance of Canada (PSAC) rank first, second, and sixth in size in Canada, respectively (see Table 5.1). Public-sector unions are a vibrant part of the labour movement and are still showing some capacity for growth.

collective bargaining coverage

a statistic that represents all of the employees, both union and nonunion, covered by a collective agreement as a percentage of the labour force; it is always a larger number than union density, because union density excludes nonunion employees

Different Legislative Framework

Special laws govern labour–management relations in the public sector. For example, police officers and firefighters are deemed too essential to have

TABLE 11.1

Union Density: Public and Private Sectors, 2005–2010

Sector	2005			2010		
	Employees × 1000	Union Density	Coverage	Employees × 1,000	Union Density	Coverage
Public	3,131	71.3	75.2	3,509	71.2	74.8
Private	10,361	17.5	19.2	10,749	16	17.5

Source: Statistics Canada (2006 and 2010) "Union membership and coverage by selected characteristics," Perspectives on Labour and Income, 75-001-XIE2006108, 7(8), August 2006, and 75-001-XIE2010004, 22(4), December 2010.

the right to strike. The largest category of provincial and federal civil servants, however, is nonessential employees in clerical and administrative classifications.

Role of Government

An important difference between the sectors is the dual role of government. In public-sector bargaining, the government is both impartial umpire and employer. As employer, the government is a party to collective bargaining; as umpire, it is required to be a neutral to the bargaining process. In general, the government role has been changing in Canada from that of neutral third party to that of a party of direct interest (Swimmer & Thompson, 1995). Some argue that state intervention in collective bargaining (e.g., wage freezes and suspensions of collective bargaining) has resulted in a permanent dismantling of collective bargaining for public employees (Panitch & Swartz, 1993).

Gunderson (2005) points out that

> From 1991 to 1997, the federal government suspended collective bargaining for federal employees. Seven other provinces followed with wage freezes and mid-contract pay rollbacks for public sector employees. Numerous provincial governments imposed "social contracts" that mandated employees take a number of days off without pay. Larger proportions of public sector bargaining units were designated as "essential employees" who were denied the right to strike. Ad hoc back-to-work legislation has been increasingly imposed on public sector strikes.

Human Resources and Social Development Canada (2006) keeps a record of governmental orders suspending the right to strike or lock out for public employee unions. Alberta has exercised the suspension nine times; New Brunswick, five times; Newfoundland, once; Quebec, three times; and Saskatchewan, four times. Dachis and Hebdon (2010) show a sharp decline in back-to-work legislation from 1979 to 2009. Their research indicates that the probability of a freely negotiated settlement declines by two-thirds in the round of bargaining immediately after a back-to-work order or law. If the two sides of the agreement know the province will make the hard decisions for them, they have no reason to do so themselves. Back-to-work legislation may be appealing as a way to resume public services, but its long-term consequences for the collective bargaining process could be negative.

Imperfect Labour Market

Public services are often offered in noncompetitive markets. Services provided by teachers, nurses, firefighters, and police officers, for example, may be near monopolies; accordingly, these occupations may have monopoly powers. On the other hand, public employers may possess the power of a monopsony. Characteristics of monopsonistic markets include low wages and chronic labour shortages. Ashenfelter, Farber, and Ransom (2010) found evidence of monopsony in the labour market for teachers and nurses in the United States.

A justification for the monopolistic provision of some services is that they are **public goods**. Public goods might be inefficiently provided in a competitive market either because of abnormally high capital costs (e.g., a space program) or because individuals cannot be charged for the product (e.g., law enforcement). In the case of law enforcement, it would not be efficient or fair to charge only citizens who require police services.

One implication of the monopolistic provision of services of governments is that they are often essential to the health and safety of the public. This is the rationale used for denying these workers the right to strike. The International Labour Organization (ILO) rules allow governments to prevent strikes where services are essential as long as a reasonable substitute (such as arbitration) is made available.

public good

an item whose consumption does not reduce the amount available for others

Politics and Public Opinion

Politics plays a much greater role in public-sector collective bargaining than in the private sector. Some scholars argue that political power is a substitute for economic power (Swimmer & Thompson, 1995). Since governments actually gain revenue during a strike or lockout, the pressure is generated from the loss of services and the public perception of who is to blame for the job action. Increasingly, the battle for public opinion is important in determining collective bargaining outcomes (see IR Today 11.1).

IR Today 11.1

Strike Looms After School Bus Drivers Reject Contract Offer

HALIFAX—Parents of the 23,000 Halifax-area students who bus to school should start making plans to cope with a school bus strike.

Wednesday morning, 290 drivers, monitors and mechanics with Stock Transportation voted 98 per cent against the company's last offer. They could be on strike by Jan. 26, if no last-minute deal is reached.

Nearly half of the board's 52,000 students are bused to school.

Stock offered three per cent raises every year for three years. That would leave a bus driver with three years' experience making just over $14 an hour by the end of the contract, according to NSGEU president Joan Jessome.

The union wants $1 hourly raises each year, to $18 an hour by 2012 for drivers. "They're the lowest-paid bus drivers in the province," Jessome said. "There's no pension, no RSP's, very little medical, no dental. They're not bloated, by any stretch," he said, adding that one 19-year veteran driver makes less now than she did before privatization.

John Turney, regional vice-president for Stock, says the company can't afford to pay more than three per cent because it's locked into a five-year, $60 million contract with the Halifax Regional School Board until June 2011.

A strike is a "real possibility," Turney said. "The number one priority is to transport students safely. Without the drivers, mechanics and monitors, we don't feel we can do that," Turney said. "It would be prudent for parents to make alternate arrangements." Halifax Regional School Board spokesman Doug Hadley said the board can't bus kids to school without Stock.

Schools will stay open if there's a bus strike, he said. Parents who can't find another way to get their children to class can talk to principals and teachers to keep their children up to date on schoolwork.

The two sides have been negotiating since last February.

Source: Rachel Boomer, *Metro Halifax*, 7 January 2009. Reprinted with permission. Retrieved 30 April 2011 from http://www.metronews.ca/halifax/local/article/163441.

When politics and public opinion are involved, the parties will settle collective agreement outcomes that are less visible and more long-term (e.g., group benefits and pensions). Public opinion may also play a role in reducing strikes and lockouts.

The final issue involving politics is the line between policymaking in a democracy and the collective bargaining agenda of terms and conditions of employment. Generally, public employees cannot bargain over policy matters including such issues as staffing levels. Public-sector bargaining laws tend to restrict the scope of bargaining to conditions of employment.

History of Public-Sector Bargaining

After the craft and industrial waves, public-sector unions formed the third wave of unionization in the 1960s. Public-sector membership in Canada grew from only 40,000 in 1946 to 1.5 million by 1981 (Rose, 1995). Today there are about 3.5 million public-sector union members[1] in Canada (see Table 11.1).

Union Growth Factors

Several factors account for the rapid rise of public-sector unions in the 1960s.

Social Upheaval

The civil rights and antiwar movements of the 1960s provided a social context for the rise of public-sector unionism. A 1968 strike of black sanitation workers in Memphis, for example, attracted support from the civil rights movement, including from its leader, Dr. Martin Luther King, Jr. (IR Today 11.2). The main issues in this dispute were union recognition, unsafe working conditions, and the extremely low wages of the sanitation workers, most of whom qualified for social assistance despite working forty hours per week.

The Growth in Public Services

Public services grew rapidly in the 1960s and 1970s. The system of community colleges in Canada, for example, was established in this period in most provinces. As healthcare and education services grew, existing unions gained new members without the expense of organizing campaigns.

Dissatisfaction with Existing Employee Voice Mechanisms

Many public-sector workers belonged to staff associations in the 1950s and 1960s. These were civil service associations that were unaffiliated with organized labour and that generally shunned militant action. As public employees' demands for decent wages and working conditions increased, many of these weaker organizations were transformed or merged into unions. The motivation for change came from the rising expectations of public servants in the 1960s and 1970s and the inability of these associations to satisfy employee demands. In response to member pressure for

Memphis Sanitation Strike, 1968

Memphis, Spring 1968, marked the dramatic climax of the Civil Rights movement. . . . In the 1960s, Memphis's 1,300 sanitation workers formed the lowest caste of a deeply racist society, earning so little they qualified for welfare. In the film [*At the River I Stand*], retired workers recall their fear about taking on the entire white power structure when they struck for higher wages and union recognition.

But local civil rights leaders and the Black community soon realized the strike was part of the struggle for economic justice for all African Americans. The community mobilized behind the strikers, organizing mass demonstrations and an Easter boycott of downtown businesses. The national leadership of AFSCME put the international union's full resources behind the strike. One day, a placard appeared on the picket lines that in its radical simplicity summed up the meaning of the strike: "I am a man."

In March, Martin Luther King, Jr. came to Memphis as part of his Poor People's Campaign to expand the civil rights agenda to the economy . . . . [Dr. King led a rally and gave a speech, and] the next day, April 4, 1968, he was assassinated. Four days later, thousands from Memphis and around the country rallied to [pull off King's] nonviolent march. The city council crumbled and granted most of the strikers' demands. Those 1,300 sanitation workers had shown they could successfully challenge the entrenched economic structure of the South.

Source: "At the River I Stand: About the film," California Newsreel website. Reprinted with permission. Retrieved 30 April 2011 from http://www.newsreel.org/nav/title.asp?tc=CN0007&s=at%20 the%20river%20i%20stand.

full bargaining rights, for example, the Civil Service Association of Ontario gradually transformed itself into a full union, culminating with a name change to the Ontario Public Service Employees Union (OPSEU) in 1975 (Rapaport, 1999; Roberts, 1994). Today, OPSEU is the largest component of the National Union of Public and General Employees (NUPGE), Canada's second-largest union.

Union Mergers

Union mergers also played an important role in union growth in the 1960s and 1970s. CUPE, now Canada's largest union, was created out of a merger of two large municipal unions in the 1960s. The merger reduced interunion competition and increased resources for organizing new members. Similarly, NUPGE was created in the 1970s as a national federation of provincial government unions and associations across Canada.

Relative Absence of Employer Opposition

Governments at all levels—municipal, provincial, and federal—are reluctant to publicly oppose unions. U.S. research has shown that unions win representation election votes in over 70 percent of the certification applications in the public sector and less than 50 percent in the private sector (Bronfenbrenner & Juravich, 1995). Private-sector employees were also six times more likely to be fired for union organizing than their public-sector counterparts.

Removal of Legal Barriers

The passage of collective bargaining laws by the Canadian provinces and federal government in the 1960s and 1970s played an important role in facilitating future union organizing. These laws undoubtedly account for a significant component of union growth. Research shows that the passage of teacher bargaining laws in the United States was the most important factor in the growth of teacher unions (Saltzman, 1985).

An Economic Analysis of Union Power

In this section, we will analyze union power in the context of public-sector bargaining. That public-sector employees might have too much bargaining power was an early rationale used by those arguing against public-sector bargaining rights. According to some, collective bargaining would institutionalize the power of public employee unions so as to leave competing groups at a permanent and substantial disadvantage (Wellington & Winter, 1971). This greater union power, according to this argument, exists for three reasons:

- some services, if disrupted, present a danger to the health and safety of the public;
- demand is relatively inelastic; and
- public-sector strikes affect the public, who have the power to punish only one of the parties.

A theoretical examination of union power can be conducted using Marshall's conditions (1920), which we set out in Chapter 3. To review the four conditions that determine the inelasticity of demand for labour and the wage–employment tradeoff, unions are more powerful when

1. demand for the product or service is inelastic;
2. labour is not easily substituted;
3. supply of substitutes is inelastic (i.e., price of substitutes rises as more are demanded); and
4. labour is a small proportion of total costs.

Applying these factors to the public sector provides the following theoretical analysis. The first condition clearly gives more power to public-sector unions. Many public services have inelastic demand curves, because they are essential and would be demanded at almost any cost.

Similarly, for many services, it is difficult to substitute for labour. Public-safety jobs, for example, are highly skilled and cannot be easily outsourced or replaced with technology. In the case of some services, the public does have other options. For example, citizens can send information today through the post office or by fax, email, or courier. Other jobs can be contracted out to the private sector or replaced by cheaper part-time employees. As we will learn below, private-for-profit is a significant mode of service delivery in Canada.

Both factors 1 and 2 would appear to give public-sector unions more power.

Factor 3 is probably not important in explaining public–private differences in elasticities. The rising prices of substitutes will not likely be a major deterrent to replacing labour in either the public or private sectors.

Factor 4 serves to reduce union power in the public sector. Most public services are highly labour-intensive. In public safety, for example, labour costs can be as high as 70 to 80 percent of total costs.

In the end, we are left with an indeterminate outcome. Two factors (1 and 2) seem to increase union power; the third factor is neutral; and the last reduces union power. The inelasticity of demand for public-sector labour is therefore an empirical question. U.S. research shows that public-sector wages became more elastic over time and were roughly the same as private-sector ones by the 1980s (Lewin, Feuille, Kochan & Delaney, 1988). The wage elasticity of demand for public services undoubtedly increased in the 1970s and 1980s due to the surge in privatization of sanitation and other services in the 1970s.

Thus, the early forecasts that unions would have too much power in the public sector would appear to be unwarranted (Wellington & Winter, 1971).

Dispute Resolution in the Public Sector

Public-sector dispute resolution mechanisms were designed in the 1960s and 1970s to avoid strikes. It was believed that essential public employees could not be allowed to walk off their jobs because of the irreparable harm that might be done to the public and because union bargaining power would result in excessive wage gains in negotiations (Hebdon, 1996). These fears provided the rationale for extensive intrusions into the collective bargaining process in the public sector, in contrast to the voluntarism of private-sector dispute resolution.2 In Canada, each jurisdiction has had to fashion a policy with respect to the right to strike for various categories of public employees. Policies range from a ban on all strikes and lockouts to a private-sector model where all strikes are permitted. In the latter cases, there is almost always a requirement that essential services be provided. In Ontario, for example, public servants can strike, but only after the parties conclude an agreement that provides for essential services. Disputes over what is an essential service in Ontario are decided by the Ontario Labour Relations Board (Adell, Ponak & Grant, 2001). Where strikes are banned, Canadian collective bargaining laws provide for compulsory interest arbitration.

The result of the various strike policies is a legislative patchwork of conditional right to strike, interest arbitration, and in a few cases laws that give the union a choice of striking or arbitration. These three categories of final dispute resolution procedures are set out in Table 11.2 for each jurisdiction and for the following occupational groups: public servants, hospital employees, teachers, police officers, firefighters, and employees of Crown agencies.

TABLE 11.2

Collective Bargaining Dispute Resolution Process in the Public and Parapublic Sectors in Canada

	PUBLIC SERVANTS	HOSPITAL EMPLOYEES	PUBLIC SCHOOL TEACHERS/ COLLEGE AND UNIVERSITY PROFESSORS	POLICE OFFICERS	MUNICIPAL FIREFIGHTERS	EMPLOYEES OF CROWN CORPORATIONS
Federal	Union choice of a) arbitration, or b) conciliation/strike[1]	Union choice of a) arbitration, or b) conciliation/strike[1]	Strike/lockout permitted for schools run by band councils on Indian reserves	Royal Canadian Mounted Police officers not covered by a collective bargaining statue	Strike/lockout permitted[1] for airport firefighters (unless provided for municipally)	Strike/lockout permitted[1] for most Crown corporations
Alberta	Strike/lockout permitted[1]; Arbitration at the request of either party	Strike/lockout banned[2]; arbitration at the request of either or both parties, or the Minister[3]	P&S: Strike/lockout permitted[3] C: Compulsory binding arbitration[3] U: Negotiating procedures agreed to by the parties[3,4]	Strike/lockout banned; arbitration at the request of either or both parties	Strike/lockout banned; arbitration at the request of either or both parties or on Minister's own initiative	Same as for public servants
British Columbia	Mediation at the request of either party, strike/lockout permitted[1]	Strike/lockout permitted[1]	P&S: Strike/lockout permitted[1]; C&U: Strike/lockout permitted	At the request of either party, Minister may order arbitration if certain conditions are met	At the request of either party, Minister may order arbitration if certain conditions are met	Strike/lockout permitted[1]
Manitoba	Strike/lockout permitted[1]; Arbitration at the request of either party	Strike/lockout permitted[1], except for City of Winnipeg paramedics (arbitration at the request of either of both parites)	P&S: Strike/lockout banned; arbitration proceedings may be initiated by either party U: Strike/lockout permitted	M.P.: Strike/lockout permitted. Strike/lockout banned in Winnipeg; arbitration at the request of either or both parties.	Strike/lockout banned; arbitration at the request of either or both parties	Strike/lockout permitted[1]
New Brunswick	Strike/lockout permitted[1]	Strike/lockout permitted[1]	P&S: Strike/lockout permitted U: Strike/lockout permitted	Strike/lockout banned; arbitration at the request of either party	Strike/lockout banned; arbitration at the request of either party	Strike/lockout permitted[1]
Newfoundland and Labrador	Strike/lockout permitted[1,5]	Strike/lockout permitted[1,5] (rotating strike banned)	P&S: strike permitted; C&U: Strike/lockout permitted[1,5]	M.P.: strike/lockout permitted R.N.C.: Strike banned; arbitration at the request of either party	Strike/lockout permitted; St. John's: strike banned; arbitration at the request of either party	Strike/lockout permitted[1,5]

TABLE 11.2

Collective Bargaining Dispute Resolution Process in the Public and Parapublic Sectors in Canada (continued)

	PUBLIC SERVANTS	HOSPITAL EMPLOYEES	PUBLIC SCHOOL TEACHERS/ COLLEGE AND UNIVERSITY PROFESSORS	POLICE OFFICERS	MUNICIPAL FIREFIGHTERS	EMPLOYEES OF CROWN CORPORATIONS
Northwest Territories and Nunavut	Strike permitted[1]	Strike permitted[1]	P & S: Strike permitted	See Federal	Strike/lockout permitted	Strike permitted[1] (including the NWT Power Corporation)
Nova Scotia	Strike/lockout banned; arbitration at the request of either party	Strike/lockout permitted	C & provincial P&S: strike/lockout permitted P&S local school board; strike/lockout banned; arbitration at the request of either party U: Strike/lockout permitted	Strike/lockout banned; interest arbitration[6]	Strike/lockout banned; interest arbitration	Strike/lockout permitted
Ontario	Strike/lockout permitted[1]	Strike/lockout banned; arbitration Ambulance workers employed by municipalities: Strike/lockout permitted[1]	P&S, C, U: Strike/lockout permitted	M.P.: ban on withholding of services; arbitration at the request of either party O.P.P.: conciliation arbitration	Strike/lockout banned; arbitration	Strike/lockout permitted[1]
Prince Edward Island	Arbitration at the request of either party or on Attorney General's own initiative	Strike banned; mandatory arbitration	P&S: Arbitration at the request of either party or on Minister's own initiative U: Strike/lockout permitted after unsuccessful conciliation or mediation	Strike banned; mandatory arbitration	Strike banned; mandatory arbitration	Arbitration at the request of either party or on Attorney General's own initiative

TABLE 11.2

Collective Bargaining Dispute Resolution Process in the Public and Parapublic Sectors in Canada (continued)

	PUBLIC SERVANTS	HOSPITAL EMPLOYEES	PUBLIC SCHOOL TEACHERS/ COLLEGE AND UNIVERSITY PROFESSORS	POLICE OFFICERS	MUNICIPAL FIREFIGHTERS	EMPLOYEES OF CROWN CORPORATIONS
Quebec	Strike/lockout permitted[1] except for peace officers.[7] Union/employer committee must provide to the government an essential services list for approval by decree.	Strike permitted if will not endanger public health or safety, but prohibited for matters pertaining to clauses negotiated at the local or regional level or subject to local arrangements.[1] Lockouts always prohibited.	P&S, C: Strike/lockout permitted, but prohibited for matters pertaining to clauses negotiated at the local or regional level or subject to local arrangements U: Strike/lockout permitted	M.P. and S.Q.: Strike/lockout banned M.P.: Arbitration after receipt of a report of unsuccessful mediation or at the request of either party. S.Q.: Arbitration upon request of either or both parties; some policies on conditions of employment must be approved by the Treasury Board.	Strike/lockout banned; arbitration after receipt of a report of unsuccessful mediation or at the request of either party[3]	Strike/lockout permitted but prohibited for matters pertaining to clauses negotiated at the local or regional level or subject to local arrangements; some policies on conditions of employment (for Hydro Québec, liquor and lottery corporations, etc.) must be approved by the Treasury Board[1]
Saskatchewan	Strike/lockout permitted[1]	Strike/lockout permitted[1]	P&S: Union choice of arbitration at the request of either party or strike U: Strike/lockout permitted[1]	Strike/lockout permitted[1]	Strike/lockout permitted[1]; arbitration at the request of either party (binding if local union constitution prohibits strikes)	Strike/lockout permitted[1]
Yukon	Union choice of arbitration at the request of either party or strike[1]	Strike/lockout permitted[1]	P&S: Union choice of arbitration at the request of either party or strike	See Federal	Strike/lockout permitted	Union choice of arbitration at the request of either party or strike[1]

TABLE 11.2

Collective Bargaining Dispute Resolution Process in the Public and Parapublic Sectors in Canada (continued)

Labour Law Analysis; Strategic Policy, Analysis and Workplace Information
Labour Program; Human Resources and Skills Development Canada
February 1, 2010

Glossary:

P&S	Public Primary and Secondary Schools
C	Public Colleges
U	Universities
MP	Municipal Police
RNC	Royal Newfoundland Constabulary
OPP	Ontario Provincial Police
SQ	Sûreté du Québec

[1]Employees are prohibited from participating in a strike when they are required to provide essential services under the applicable labour relations legislation.

[2]As of April 1, 2009, ground ambulance service operators and their employees who are ambulance attendants will no longer be able to participate in work stoppages during labour disputes.

[3]The government may order emergency procedures and impose binding arbitration in circumstances involving damage to health or property or unreasonable hardship to persons who are not parties to the dispute.

[4]Compulsory binding arbitration to settle any collective bargaining dispute with a graduate students association, or with an academic staff association at a university established after March 18, 2004.

[5]If the House of Assembly resolves that a strike of employees is/would be injurious to public health, safety or security, it may declare a state of emergency and forbid the strike of all employees in a unit specified in the resolution, and may order the employees of the unit to return to work and that the dispute be resolved by binding adjudication.

[6]Only the following items may be considered in arbitration; Wages and salaries; Pay procedure on promotions, demotion, reclassification and increments; Hours of work; Overtime compensation; Premium allowances for work performed; Holidays; Vacations; Employee relocation expenses; Long Service Award; Leaves of absence other than for elective public office, political activity or education or training and development; Conditions of education leave; Conditions of sabbatical leave; Consolidated Health Plan; Layoff policy taking into account competency, merit and seniority of employees; Procedures for discipline and discharge for cause of employees; Grievance procedure; Mileage rate and allowance payable to employee for kilometers travelled when employee is required to use employee's own automobile on employer's business; Group life insurance; Long-term income–protection insurance; Duration of collective agreement; Interpretations and definitions of words and expressions used in collective agreement and not defined by collective agreement or applicable enactment.

[7]All employees who are peace officers and all employee groups of the general directorate responsible for civil protection within the Ministère de la Sécurité publique are forbidden to strike.

Sources: Collective bargaining dispute resolution process in the public and parapublic sectors in Canada. 2010. Reproduced with the permission of the Minister of Public Works and Government Services Canada, 2010. Collective bargaining dispute resolution process in the public and parapublic sectors in Canada. http://www.rhdcc–hrsdc.gc.ca/eng/labour/labour_law/ind_rel/pub.shtml. Human Resources and Skills Development Canada, 2011.

 11.1

Because there is such inconsistency across jurisdictions and occupations, it is difficult to identify patterns of dispute resolution in Canada. Nonetheless, police and firefighters tend to be restricted by laws that ban strikes and substitute interest arbitration. Nova Scotia is an exception; firefighters can legally strike there.

The difficult policy question involves the determination of what constitutes an essential service. Scholars have examined this question and noted the inconsistencies across Canada (Swan, 1985; Swimmer, 1989). In order to assess essential services policies across Canada, Adams (1981) ranks occupational sectors according to the degree of essentiality from the most critical (police and fire) to the least (teachers):

> As a general matter, however, there are at least seven principal sectors which are usually considered to have inordinate public interest because the interruption of service threatens one or more of life or limb; peace, order, and good government; or the basic sinews of the economy. These critical areas might be ranked in the following order:

> 1. Police and firefighters;
> 2. Hospitals and medical care;
> 3. Utilities;
> 4. Transportation;
> 5. Municipal services;
> 6. Civil servants;
> 7. Teachers and educational authorities. (pp. 139–140)

About Ontario's policy, Adams (1981) concludes:

> And like other jurisdictions, the uneven application of the process is as much a reflection of different interest group pressures as it is a discriminating concern for the public's welfare and the theoretical dictates of labour–management relations. (p. 140)

Returning to Table 11.2, we can see the inconsistency clearest perhaps in the variation of teacher dispute resolution across Canada. If we assume that the banning of strikes and lockouts is an indicator of the essentiality of services, then teachers are essential services in British Columbia,[3] Manitoba, and Prince Edward Island but not in the rest of Canada. The inconsistency of application of essentiality is also revealed *within* a province. Alberta, for example, provides a strike/lockout procedure for elementary and secondary teachers, binding arbitration for college teachers, and an arrangement for university faculty whereby they can set up their own procedures.

More Recent Developments in Dispute Resolution

Adell, Ponak, and Grant (2001) examine three models of dispute resolution in the public sector in Canada: the unfettered strike, the designation system, and interest arbitration.

Unfettered-Strike Model

The unfettered-strike model has been in effect for blue-collar workers at the local level of government in all provinces since World War II. It seems to work best when the services are not essential. When services are essential, unions may have too much bargaining power because they alone determine what services are to be provided in the event of a strike or lockout (Adell, Ponak & Grant, 2001). This model has the advantage of producing the most freely negotiated settlements. It is a positive attribute that is more important during a period of restructuring services, when the parties must resolve complex issues at the bargaining table. A negative attribute, however, is one without any procedure to determine essential services. The strike model invites back-to-work legislation.

R P C 11.2

Designation Model

In the designation model, the determining of what essential services are is negotiated by the parties either before bargaining starts (Ontario and British Columbia) or at the point of impasse (Quebec). Neutral tribunals are available to adjudicate disputes that arise from these negotiations.

The Quebec model began in 1982 with the establishment of the Essential Services Council, whose function is to determine essential services once impasse is reached. Adell, Ponak, and Grant (2001) conclude:

> As time has passed, both parties have become familiar with the policies and practices of the Quebec Essential Services Council in administering the designation system. This has permitted them to plan in advance for the conduct of strikes, and it has reduced the amount of bargaining and litigation needed with respect to essential services. These developments have given the Quebec public a sense of security which was lacking before the designation model was adopted.

The designation model is most common in Canada for nurses. It is found in Newfoundland, New Brunswick, Quebec, Manitoba, British Columbia, and the federal jurisdiction, and for psychiatric hospital nurses in Ontario (Adell, Ponak & Grant, 2001). The Quebec model for healthcare employees including nurses, however, has such high levels of "essential" designation (80 percent) in the legislation that it effectively removes the right to strike. As such, it is not really a designation model, where essential services determinations are made by independent tribunals.

No-Strike (or Interest Arbitration) Model

In this model, discussed more fully in Chapter 9, the right to strike is substituted with interest arbitration. It would appear that this category is declining in popularity in Canada. The Adell, Ponak, and Grant (2001) survey of practitioners concluded:

> Among our interviewees, the no-strike model, which substitutes compulsory interest arbitration for the right to strike, had few admirers outside Ontario health care. Almost no one who was operating under either the unfettered-strike model or the designation model advocated moving to the no-strike model.

Chilling Effect

Since arbitrators tend to split the difference between the last offers of management and labour at arbitration, the parties are reluctant to move closer to a settlement position in direct talks. This reluctance to negotiate is called the **chilling effect** of interest arbitration (Hebdon, 1996; Hebdon & Mazerolle, 2003; Olson, 1994).

If, for example, management offers 1 percent and the union demands 5 percent at arbitration, there is a good chance that an arbitrator would award a settlement somewhere between these extremes (possibly close to the midpoint of 3 percent). Therefore, if either management or the union were to modify its offer before arbitration, it would run the risk of adversely affecting its arbitration outcome.

chilling effect

the lack of bargaining flexibility caused by the parties' fear that a concession made in negotiations will reduce the arbitration outcome

Narcotic or Dependency Effect

As its name implies, the **narcotic or dependency effect** is a dependency that occurs because of high rates of arbitration usage. Over time, the parties may no longer being able to negotiate without third-party assistance (Olson, 1994).

A study of collective bargaining settlements in Ontario from 1984 to 1993 revealed a chilling and narcotic effect of interest arbitration:

narcotic or dependency effect

a result of frequent use of arbitration that may cause parties to lose the ability to freely negotiate settlements without third-party assistance

> A central finding is that bargaining units covered by legislation requiring compulsory interest arbitration arrive at impasse 8.7 to 21.7 percent more often than bargaining units in the right to strike sectors. Even after controlling for legislative jurisdiction, union, bargaining unit size, occupation, agreement length, time trend, and part-time status, strong evidence was found that compulsory arbitration has a chilling effect on the bargaining process. . . . It was also significant that this effect was greater the more the union operates in the arbitration sector as a proportion of total bargaining activity. This finding is supportive of a dependency effect whereby a union's high usage of arbitration fosters an inability to freely negotiate settlements. (Hebdon & Mazerolle, 2003)

On the other hand, teachers and school boards who respectively have the right to strike and lock out were able to freely negotiate settlements 97.4 percent of the time.

Final-offer arbitration, explained in Chapter 9, is a modification to interest arbitration designed to reduce these effects. If the problem is the split-the-difference arbitrator behaviour, this is prevented by constraining the arbitrator to select either the union's or management's last offer. Research shows that final-offer arbitration does produce more freely negotiated settlements in some jurisdictions in the United States (Hebdon, 1996). The procedure is not offered as a mandatory procedure in any Canadian jurisdiction.

Impact on Wage Outcomes

There is evidence that interest arbitration wage outcomes are higher than in jurisdictions where unions have the right to strike. Dachis and Hebdon (2010), for example, examined wage outcomes in the Canadian public sector from

TTC Work-to-Rule Pitch Fizzles

A work-to-rule campaign proposed by some TTC [Toronto Transit Commission] workers appears to have fizzled, but the city's transit union says its members remain frustrated at "having to work under the microscope."

"We've got 13- and 14-year-olds that feel that they have an entitlement to film our operators in the performance of their duties, and that's not acceptable," said Bob Kinnear, president of the Amalgamated Transit Union Local 113, which represents Toronto's transit workers.

Rumours of a TTC work-to-rule campaign started Sunday with posts made on a Facebook group after a stern memo from TTC management criticized the "culture of complacency and malaise" in the organization. The note to staff came after a slew of customer complaints related to lacklustre performance by TTC workers, sparked by a photo shot on a cellphone camera last month that showed a collector asleep in his booth at the McCowan subway station.

Adding to the beleaguered transit system's troubles, a bus driver was suspended indefinitely last week, pending an internal investigation, after a YouTube video shot by a frustrated rider showed the man taking a seven-minute coffee and washroom break while driving the 310 Blue Night bus south on Bathurst.

The TTC says it ran "problem-free" Monday morning, and there were no reports of any employees "working to rule." Kinnear said the call for working to rule was not initiated by the union, but by individual members who are frustrated by how they are being treated by TTC management and the public. He said he had not heard of any specific work-to-rule actions occurring Monday.

The Facebook group, "Toronto Transit Operators against public harassment," was formed to give TTC workers the opportunity to share "suggestions on how to fight back to the recent photo and video harassment from passengers just looking to make trouble for us," according to its description. It also encourages transit workers to post their own photos of passengers who break the rules.

"Reminder to work to rule on Monday. Check out ATU site," stated a post on the group's wall, according to media reports. The Amalgamated Transit Union's Toronto website had no information about any work-to-rule campaign, but parts of the site are restricted to members only.

The Facebook group was created after TTC chief general manager Gary Webster sent a terse memo to staff over the weekend, demanding that workers be held accountable when they demonstrate poor customer service. In a statement to all staff, Webster wrote that he is getting "increasingly tired of defending the reputation of the TTC; tired of explaining what is acceptable and what is not."

Webster goes on to express his frustration that, two weeks after management demanded better customer service from front-line workers, the organization is still under fire for photos and videos showing TTC workers slacking off. He says that expectations need to be clear and that customers deserve better for their fare. "We are in the customer service business, but some of the behaviour our customers have encountered recently would suggest otherwise," Webster wrote. "Our customers pay a fare and the city provides hundreds of millions of dollars every year to the TTC. This public transit agency belongs to the very people we serve.

"As chief general manager, I am ultimately accountable to our customers. As employees, you—and you alone—are accountable for your actions," he added.

"The culture of complacency and malaise that has seeped into our organization will end," Webster vowed. "I hold all of management responsible to make this happen. Reviews and plans are under way to address systemic issues regarding customer service, but real change starts with you.

Kinnear said Webster's memo makes it appear as if "he has given up." "He seems to be putting all the problems and all the ills of the TTC on the backs of the front-line employees, when that's just not reflective of what's going on out there," Kinnear said. He added that Webster has a responsibility to defend the TTC. "We do recognize that improvements have to be made, but for the (chief general manager) to simply put the onus on the front-line employees is irresponsible as far as we're concerned."

Kinnear said the union will be holding a news conference Tuesday morning, but he would not elaborate on the details.

Source: Brendan Kennedy and Adrian Morrow, *Toronto Star*, 8 February 2010, Used with permission of Torstar Syndication Services. Retrieved 15 June 2011 from http://www.thestar.com/ news/gta/ article/762105--ttc-work-to-rule-pitch-fizzles?bn=1.

1979 to 2007. They found that negotiated wage rates are about 1.2 percent higher under interest arbitration than where there is a right to strike. This confirmed an earlier result of Currie and McConnell (1991), who attributed higher settlements under arbitration to arbitrators' attaching greater weight to three factors: wage settlements previously agreed to by bargaining units in the same occupation (i.e., comparability); "catch-up" defined as compensation for prior real wage loss; and less attention to employer ability to pay.

Loss of Control

Finally, Adell, Ponak, and Grant (2001) found opposition to interest arbitration due to the loss of control over outcomes:

> For employers this means loss of budgetary control—the main reason for the Quebec government's rejection of interest arbitration. Union interviewees, for their part, expressed concern about the growing risk of government manipulation of the appointment of arbitrators and the criteria on which they base their awards.

In the context of the restructuring of the delivery of services, this loss of control takes on heightened importance. It is crucial that the parties take responsibility for their own solutions to complex problems rather than throwing them into the hands of a third-party arbitrator.

Innovations in Dispute Resolution

The fiscal pressures of the past two decades have created strains on existing collective bargaining processes. Paradoxically, the pressures have created a unique opportunity for labour and management to experiment with cooperative approaches to dispute resolution. For example, experiments with interest-based bargaining are plentiful at all levels of government in Canada (see Chapter 7).

Despite problems with arbitration, several jurisdictions have instituted a form that involves using the mediator as an arbitrator—called *mediation–arbitration* or simply *med-arb*. Med-arb has been used successfully to resolve grievances before the Grievance Settlement Board in Ontario (Telford, 2000). Also, several public-sector agencies across Canada have institutionalized new forms of mediation to resolve unfair labour practices and grievances.

The Four Generations of Public-Sector Bargaining

Public-sector collective bargaining may be divided into distinct periods or generations. The first generation represented the growth phase of employment and unions of the 1960s; the second was characterized by the retrenchment and citizen resistance of the 1970s; the third generation, in the 1980s, put a greater emphasis on the performance and productivity of public services (Lewin et al., 1988). In what may be described as a second period of hostility and retrenchment toward public-sector collective bargaining, the period from 1990 to current represents the fourth generation of public-sector collective bargaining. In this current fourth generation, public employees are increasingly under attack on the related fronts of collective bargaining and restructuring of services. Public-sector dispute resolution procedures are at the centre of the pressures on public-sector bargaining. The recent decision of the Supreme Court of Canada that constitutionalized collective bargaining will make it more difficult for governments to implement retrenchment policies by curbing union rights (discussed in Chapter 2).

Management Issues

As we indicated in the previous section, the current generation of collective bargaining has been marked by the restructuring of public services. In this section, we will examine the challenges facing management in this restraint period and the consequences for public-sector unions and employees. We begin by looking at the international context of public-sector restructuring.

Restructuring: An International Phenomenon

There is little doubt that public management has undergone profound changes over the past twenty years. Some claim that a new global paradigm has emerged. It puts greater emphasis on job performance and efficiency in the provision of public services (Osborne & Gaebler, 1992). A **new public management (NPM)** created in the developed world puts much greater emphasis on both private-sector practices and service provision (Hebdon & Kirkpatrick, 2005). But some question the extent to which NPM represents a coherent program of reform (Lynn, 1998). One problem is the appropriateness of exporting private-sector management values and practices into the public domain (Stewart & Walsh, 1992).

new public management (NPM)

a new approach to public administration in which public organizations are to become more decentralized, market-driven, and concerned with financial control, and managers more empowered and performance-oriented

Of the twenty-five countries in the OECD, twenty-three had a major human resources (HRM) initiative from 1989 to 1992. Of these twenty-three initiatives, nine had a policy to limit government and ten had a major privatization initiative (Swimmer, 2001). The twenty-three governments that implemented these NPM policies spanned the political spectrum from conservative to social democratic.

Evidence of the scope of restructuring can be seen in Table 11.3, with 75 percent of OECD countries planning to decrease the size of their public-sector workforce. Ireland, the Netherlands, Poland, and the United Kingdom all have downsizing initiatives in 2010. Estonia, Japan, and Slovenia all have ongoing workforce reduction programs in place. Finally, Canada, Denmark, and Finland have productivity programs that include such schemes as recruitment freezes and reduction of administrative employees.

Downsizing policies were pursued by strengthening the hands of provincial and federal finance ministries to impose spending limits, reducing transfer payments to lower levels of government, and cutting services and transferring responsibility to individuals and families (Ferrera & Hemerijck, 2003; Hebdon & Kirkpatrick, 2005). Although they were adopted in most OECD countries, these policies were taken furthest in liberal regimes such as the United States, New Zealand, and the United Kingdom.

TABLE 11.3

Restructuring the Workforce: Some Initiatives

RECENT DOWNSIZING INITIATIVES	ONGOING REDUCTION PROGRAMMES	PRODUCTIVITY PROGRAMMES
Ireland: 12% of civil service in the next 4 years	**Estonia:** 15.5% decrease between 2007 and 2010	**Canada:** Recruitment freeze and review of services
Netherlands: 15% in the next 4 years	**Japan:** Net reduction by 5% since 2005	**Denmark:** Reduction of administrative employees in favour of employees in people care
Poland: 10%	**Slovenia:** 1% reductions per year since 2004	**Finland:** Productivity programme
United Kingdom: 490,000 jobs as part of the spending reviews	**France:** General review of public policies (reduction of 100,000 staff since 2007)	

Note: Numbers and percentages about staff adjustment usually exclude some sectors, and apply to parts of the public service that differ across countries.

Source: OECD (2010), Getting It Right: Restructuring the government workforce. Public Employment and Management Working Party—annual meeting, Paris, 9 December 2010, from http://www.oecd.org/dataoecd/2/39/46898720.pdf.

Canadian Context

Driven by credit-rating downgrading in some provinces and increases in deficits and debt, public-sector managers struggled to cut costs. From 1988 to 1995, average provincial debt increased from 24 percent to 37 percent of gross domestic product (GDP) and federal debt increased from 50 percent to 70 percent of GDP (Swimmer, 2001). Associated with this process of cost cutting were attempts to reshape the management and organization of public services. One aspect of this was a movement across developed countries to privatize public services. The term *privatization* covers a range of actions that involve the private-for-profit sector. It may mean giving up responsibility for the service entirely by selling it to the private sector, or retaining control by hiring a private company to manage the service. The most common form of privatization in Canada is contracting out, whereby private firms run the service but the public sector retains ultimate responsibility through a contract for a specific term.

In examining the scope of contracting out, we cite a study of Canadian municipal managers in 2004 that summarizes how services are provided (public, private for profit, private not for profit, etc.) for sixty-seven defined services (Hebdon & Jalette, 2008). Since this study replicated an earlier one conducted in the United States in 2002–2003, we can compare Canadian and U.S. privatization rates.

Contrary to expectations, researchers found that the rate of private-for-profit services was significantly higher in Canadian cities and towns than in

TABLE 11.4

Comparison of Service Provision and Privatization by Service Category:*
American (2002–2003) and Canadian (2004) Cities and Towns (number of services in
parentheses—total 67)

	UNITED STATES		CANADA	
	% PROVIDED	% PRIVATE FOR PROFIT	% PROVIDED	% PRIVATE FOR PROFIT
Public works/transportation (20)	49.1	20.9	63.1	33.6
Public utilities (4)	31.4	22.4	22.7	31.6
Public safety (7)	65.3	15.5	58.8	16.8
Parks and recreation (3)	60.6	13	71.1	19.3
Health and human (15)	29.1	11.2	23.4	16.3
Culture and arts (3)	37.1	19.2	57.1	2.8
Support functions (15)	72	18.9	80.7	33.5
Weighted average	50.3	17.4	55.4	25.8

*The number of services for each municipal unit was totalled for the categories of "public employees only" and "private for profit." The totals
were then divided by total services provided for each city to produce a rate expressed as a percentage of total services.

U.S. ones. In addition, almost 64 percent of Canadian and 58 percent of U.S.
municipalities considered privatizing at least one service in the past five years.
Privatization is very much on the agenda of both Canadian and American city
managers.

To examine the breadth of cross-border service provision and privatization
differences, Table 11.4 provides a breakdown by the seven service categories
of public works/transportation; public utilities; public safety; parks and recreation; health and human; culture and arts; and support functions. It presents
the mean number of cities providing each of the seven service categories.

On average there were 5.1 percent more cities offering these services in
Canada than in the United States. Canadian municipalities provide more services in the categories of public works/transportation, parks and recreation,
culture and arts, and support functions. U.S. cities and towns, on the other
hand, provide more services in the categories of public utilities, public safety,
and health and human or social services.

Implications of Restructuring for
Union–Management Relations in Canada

Government Policies

Swimmer (2001) provides a summary of the restraint policy options available to Canadian governments given the high levels of unionization. These
restraint policies applied not only to direct employees of the government but
to services like schools, hospitals, and lower levels of government that depend
on funding from higher levels. Policies varied according to the managerial or
unionization status of the employees.

Management Employees

1. At the risk of lowering morale and losing experienced employees, governments were free to downsize and downgrade the conditions of managers.
2. Some governments offered special early retirement to managers.

Unionized Employees

1. Some governments demanded concessions from unionized employees using adversarial bargaining.
2. Others adopted a more cooperative approach by opening the books to reveal the bleak financial picture and working toward joint solutions.
3. Governments reduced compensation through legislation or through collective bargaining by threatening legislation if concessions were not made in negotiations.

The most common strategy for unionized employees was the third one—to reduce compensation either through legislation or the threat thereof (Hebdon & Warrian, 1999). Swimmer's research (2001) revealed that four jurisdictions in Canada relied exclusively on legislation (option 3) and another seven combined legislation with adversarial bargaining. Only four jurisdictions relied exclusively on bargaining (options 1 or 2).

The factors determining the option follow:

- political ideology—left-of-centre governments generally avoided legislation; Liberal and Conservative governments chose legislation in ten out of eleven cases;
- it was more difficult to take the adversarial bargaining option if interest arbitration was the dispute settlement mechanism—in four out of five cases, legislation was used where arbitration existed; and
- when the fiscal problem was more severe, legislation was more likely.

Management Issues

Innovation

socio-technical systems design

systems of new technology in which workers are complements to, not simply extensions of, technology; in which participation, communication, and collaboration are encouraged through an accommodative organizational structure; and in which individual workers achieve control through shared responsibility and minimal supervision

Innovative work practices (e.g., teamwork, job rotation, **socio-technical systems design**) may be more difficult in the public sector than in the private sector, for several reasons (Hebdon & Hyatt, 1996):

- *Higher unionization.* Unions may make the introduction of innovative programs more difficult but, once in, play a positive role in integrating them into the workplace (Meltz & Verma, 1995).
- *Crisis atmosphere.* Enhanced workplace participation and teamwork are less likely under threats of layoffs, privatization, and cost-cutting.
- *Civil service rules.* The civil service bureaucracy may act as a serious deterrent to implementing innovative employee involvement programs. For example, workplace reorganization that requires the elimination of several layers of supervisors may collide with civil service classification systems that thrive on a multiplicity of levels (Hebdon & Hyatt, 1996).

The conclusion of a case in the Ontario government involving the introduction of new technology combined with a location transfer of the work from Toronto to Thunder Bay is set out below (Hebdon & Hyatt, 1996):

> The case study revealed some insights into the potential benefits of worker involvement/socio-technical projects for management–labour relations. In the first place we found no evidence of a reduced role for the union after the reorganization. On the contrary, regular meetings between management and labour now take place at the local level. The Thunder Bay union local has been very active in pursuing its agenda of local issues.

> The effect of this STS [social technical system] is to enable workers to share in the benefits of the introduction of the new technology. This is manifest in two ways: higher productivity and more pay; and more meaningful jobs, although more research is needed to verify the latter effect. In a traditional collective bargaining sense, the result of the STS initiative can be characterized as "distributive," since it is reasonable to imagine that minimum conditions for agreement to STS would be higher pay, better jobs and a say in workplace design for union members and higher productivity and lower unit costs for the employer.

There is recent evidence that the human resources practices of public-sector managers are moving closer to those of their private-sector counterparts. Harel and Tzafrir (2002) examined public–private human resources practices in Israel. They looked at several key dimensions of a high-performance workplace and found that

> public sector management emphasizes HRM domains that deal with employee selection (probably because of the stricter Employment Equity regulations in governmental organizations) and grievance procedures because of the higher level of unionization. On the other hand, private sector management emphasizes employee growth and pay for performance. However, the authors also found evidence that the public sector is "moving" closer and closer to the private sector model by adopting "high performance work practices" in order to overcome the turbulent environment and public demand.

Union Issues

 11.3

Because privatization shifts jobs from the public to the private sector, we might expect a decline in public union membership to have resulted from the restructuring of the past decades. But the data in Table 11.1 do not support such a decline; in fact, membership has been increasing.

It is generally assumed in the academic literature that unions will oppose privatization because of the threat to jobs and compensation. Some recent research casts doubt on this assumption. A survey of union reactions to

TABLE 11.5

	Union Reaction to Privatization Consideration	
CHOICE	VARIABLE	FREQUENCY
Acquiescence	No reaction to the proposal	33
	Supported the proposal	3
Traditional collective bargaining	Strike, work slowdown, etc.	48
	Court challenge, arbitration	45
Proactive	Offered some alternatives to the proposal	37
	Sought to reduce adverse effects through negotiations	52

privatization at the municipal level of government in Canada in 2004 revealed that unions may have a range of responses (Jalette & Hebdon, forthcoming). In the survey, the respondents were asked to indicate whether "some private delivery was considered that affected jobs." Six possible union reactions to the private service delivery consideration were solicited. These reactions were not mutually exclusive categories; unions, for example, might strike and reduce adverse effects through negotiations. The range of reactions is set out in Table 11.5.

The summary shown in Table 11.5 divides the union responses into three categories: acquiescence, traditional collective bargaining, and proactive. The study's authors conclude that unions do make strategic choices in reacting to privatization proposals that affect their members.

ACQUIESCENCE   Acquiescence was the least popular category; nonetheless, the choices of support or no reaction were significant (36 cases).

TRADITIONAL COLLECTIVE BARGAINING   The most prevalent choices were the traditional collective bargaining ones of collective action (strikes, job actions, etc.) and legal opposition through the courts or arbitration (93 cases; see IR Notebook 11.1).

PROACTIVE   The most popular single choice was to try to reduce the worst effects of privatization through negotiations (52 cases). When combined with suggesting alternatives, this category was the second-largest (89 cases).

Research revealed that unionized cities attracted a greater number of new privatization proposals but that unions were successful in having them rejected. The most successful rejection strategy associated with these proposals was suggesting alternatives, while strikes and other industrial action, on the other hand, were not effective. Cities where multiple union strategies were employed had a lower long-term privatization rate. City managers also acted strategically by implementing adjustment policies that facilitated privatization. These results support a pragmatic view of union–management relations in which privatization was modified or mutually acceptable alternatives were found. Where, for example, the municipality created a strong set of adjustment policies (such as minimizing the effects on displaced employees, implementing privatization on a trial basis, or limiting the application of privatization to new or growing services), there were fewer industrial action responses (Jalette & Hebdon, forthcoming).

Summary

We have examined why public-sector labour–management relations play an important role in Canadian society today. You should understand the factors that gave rise to the growth of public-sector unionism and the theoretical differences between private and public sectors. You have applied economic analysis to union bargaining power and discovered that there is no a priori case for greater union power in the public sector.

The essential nature of many public services was discussed together with the special dispute resolution procedures developed to accommodate collective bargaining. In particular, the strengths and weaknesses of interest arbitration as a strike substitute were canvassed. We also studied the management problems of restructuring of public services, especially privatization, and some human resources differences between public and private sectors. Finally, we examined some recent evidence on the implications of restructuring for government, management, and labour.

Key Terms

chilling effect 358
collective bargaining coverage 345
narcotic or dependency effect 358

new public management (NPM) 361
public good 347
socio-technical systems design 364

Weblinks

Public Services International (International Public Sector Union):

http://www.world-psi.org

Recent changes in public-sector industrial relations legislation (click on "Public and Parapublic Sectors"):

http://www.hrsdc.gc.ca/eng/labour/labour_law/ind_rel/index.shtml

Record of suspension of the right to strike and lock out in Canada:

http://www.hrsdc.gc.ca/en/lp/spila/clli/irlc/10orders_suspending_right_to_strike_or_lock_out.shtml

Public-sector dispute resolution procedures in Canada:

http://www.hrsdc.gc.ca/en/lp/spila/clli/irlc/pub(e).pdf

Statutes governing collective bargaining for public servants:

http://www.hrsdc.gc.ca/en/lp/spila/clli/irlc/02Public_Servants.shtml

Statutes governing collective bargaining for hospital employees:

http://www.hrsdc.gc.ca/en/lp/spila/clli/irlc/03Hospital_Employees.shtml

Statutes governing collective bargaining for teachers:

http://www.hrsdc.gc.ca/en/lp/spila/clli/irlc/04Teachers.shtml

Statutes governing collective bargaining for police:

http://www.hrsdc.gc.ca/en/lp/spila/clli/irlc/05Police.shtml

Statutes governing collective bargaining for firefighters:

http://www.hrsdc.gc.ca/en/lp/spila/clli/irlc/06Firefighters.shtml

International Public Management Association for Human Resources:

http://www.ipma-hr.org

International Public Management Association—Canada:

http://www.ipma-aigp.ca

RPC Icons

11.1 Provides advice to clients on the establishment, continuation, and termination of bargaining rights

- government labour relationship acts

11.2 Collects and develops information required for good decision making throughout the bargaining process

- institutions and processes (both regulatory and nonregulatory) that govern the relationship between employers and employees
- the process of collective bargaining

11.3 Monitors applications of HR policies

- identification, assessment, development, implementation, maintenance, and monitoring processes of effective systems of managing HR information

Discussion Questions

1. Why study the public sector as a special topic?
2. What factors account for the growth of public-sector unions? What role has the passage of labour laws played?
3. Explain labour market imperfections for some public services.
4. Do public-sector unions have more power than their private-sector counterparts?

5. Are all public services essential? Based on your answer, what would be the most appropriate dispute resolution procedure for people in the following occupations: police, firefighting, hospital, maintenance, transit services, clerical and administrative, and teaching?
6. What are the pros and cons of interest arbitration?
7. What are the restraint policy options available to Canadian governments?
8. Define privatization and describe the range of union reactions to it.
9. How do HR practices differ between public and private sectors?

Using the Internet

1. Using the Internet links provided, find the law that covers firefighters in your province. Fully describe the firefighter dispute settlement procedures in the law.
2. Find two examples in Canada of a provincial order suspending the right to strike for public employees.
3. What are the aims and purposes of the International Public Management Association of Canada and Public Services International?
4. Find an example of a back-to-work order by a government in Canada after 2010? What were its effects on labour, management, and the public?

Exercises

1. Find a province that allows teachers to strike and one that bans teacher strikes. Outline the bargaining and dispute resolution procedures in the bargaining law. Why do you think these laws vary from province to province?
2. What has been the impact of public-sector restructuring on governments, management, and labour?

Case

The Case of the Ontario Office of the Registrar General

The Office of the Registrar General (ORG) is located within the Ontario Ministry of Consumer and Commercial Relations. Its mandate is to record, certify, and provide information (certified copies of registrations) on the province's vital statistics—live and still births, adoptions, marriages, changes of name, divorces, and deaths. In a typical year, the ORG handles about 360,000 registrations and 530,000 proofs of registration. Such revenue-generating services as the issuance of birth and death certificates and provision of certified copies of registration documents may be readily quantified. Unlike most public service, therefore, useful estimates of productivity are possible in this case.

Inciting a Crisis

Early in 1987, the provincial government in Ontario announced its intention to relocate some government functions to communities in northern Ontario. This initiative intended to promote both economic development and the establishment of a greater presence of the provincial government outside of the provincial capital, Toronto. The Northern Ontario Relocation Program included moving the Office of the Registrar General to Thunder Bay, a community of about 100,000 people located on the northwestern shore of Lake Superior, some 1,375 kilometres from Toronto. The Thunder Bay office was to be operational by April 1991.

The relocation to Thunder Bay was not popular with the Toronto staff, which numbered approximately 150 full-time equivalent (FTE), largely clerical, workers. Most of the Toronto staff members were women who had strong ties to Toronto. In fact, as it would turn out, only six of the Toronto staff would ultimately relocate to Thunder Bay.

The other managerial and clerical staff members chose to use the time between February 1987 and April 1991 to find employment in other areas of the provincial government or in the private sector in order to remain in Toronto. During this four-year period, 95 percent of the staff left the ORG and were replaced by contract staff until the move to Thunder Bay. The average experience level declined from fifteen years before the relocation announcement to less than one year just before the move to Thunder Bay.

Repercussions

The result of this staff turnover was predictable. Beginning in the first quarter of 1990, productivity levels began to decline and service delivery suffered enormously. Customers who sent requests for various records through the mail—7,000 per week, accounting for about 75 percent of requests (the other 25 percent of requests came through the walk-up counter service in Toronto)—waited, on average, one week for their requests to be processed in the 1988/89 fiscal year. By April 1990, the average turnaround time for mail requests had increased to slightly over three weeks and by August 1990, the wait was six weeks.

Other indicators provided evidence of the productivity problems facing the ORG. Many of the documents the ORG issues certified copies of are essential for proving status in order to obtain a passport, receive a health card (thus permitting access to medical services), registering in school and organized sporting activities, and settling legal claims. For many of these, time is of the essence to customers, and the slow turnaround time of the mail service incited customers to find ways of "jumping the queue." One was to use the walk-up counter in Toronto, which provided same-day service. The number of people using this service increased steadily from about 60,000 per year to 110,000 within the first year following relocation. The demand on this service began to stretch its limits, resulting in customers waiting at least three days for service. In addition, tens of thousands of Ontario citizens were requesting emergency assistance from their local members of provincial parliament (MPPs) to assist them with their requests. The ORG's response was to set up a special group to deal with these emergency requests. MPPs and their office staff readily determined that this was a more efficient process and began to ask for preferential services for nonemergency requests as well.

The growing demands for the walk-up counter and special MPP emergency service drained resources from the mail-in service. This, combined with lower productivity due to the high staff turnover, contributed to a growing backlog of document requests and vital statistics registrations.

Crisis? What Crisis?

Management's response to the growing backlog of requests was to hire more workers. By March 1991, the month prior to the move to Thunder Bay, the number of FTE staff had increased to 170, up from 137 four years earlier, and 25 FTEs more than the ORG's approved staff level. The small amount of training these workers received was applied to an antiquated technological infrastructure. Paper records of over 20 million documents contained in 40,000 volumes were stored in a 929-square-metre warehouse. Document retrieval required considerable expenditures of both time and physical effort.

The organizational structure of the ORG was also not conducive to the maintenance of productivity levels, let alone improvement. There were six layers of management between the director of the branch and the front-line staff. Twelve operational units, twenty-three job classifications, and forty-one separate job descriptions distinguished the 150 FTE staff. The result was that mail requests passed through six functional units before being issued, and communication between the units and management, and the units themselves, followed bureaucratic chains of command.

Between April 1987 and March 1990, productivity levels remained relatively constant—each FTE worker, on average, processed about 6,000 registration and proof of registration requests per year, at a cost of $4.40 per request. In the 1990/91 fiscal year, output per worker had fallen by 20 percent to 5,000 requests per FTE per year, at an average cost of $5.42 per request.

Superimposed over the declining productivity scenario, which was induced by the relocation notice and antiquated technology, was a looming economic recession and pressure for public-sector cost restraint through attrition and increased productivity. For the ORG, this meant a reduction in its approved staff complement of 147 FTEs in 1987 to 135 in 1989.

A Window of Opportunity

Although the immediate cause of the productivity woes experienced by ORG was the relocation announcement, the technological and organizational weaknesses were structural barriers to longer-term improvements in staff morale, service delivery, and productivity. The move to Thunder Bay was seen as an opportunity not only to resolve the move-induced productivity problems, but also to address the more fundamental structural problems.

The innovations envisioned for the new workplace were in the areas of

- employment equity;
- customer service;
- technology;
- organizational structure, participation, and flexibility; and

- forging new partnerships with the union, community, and the municipal and federal governments.

The exact policies for these innovations would follow the principles of socio-technical systems design (STS): workers are complements to, not simply extensions of, technology; job content is broad in scope and includes the attainment of new skills, which promote flexibility; participation, communication, and collaboration are encouraged through an accommodative organizational structure; and individual workers achieve control through shared responsibility and minimal supervision.

The Formula for Redesign

This section reviews the execution of the innovations and how the innovations were achieved.

a. Employment Equity

The Ontario government has established for itself employment equity goals. Women, racial minorities, Aboriginal peoples, the physically challenged, and francophones have been designated as groups that are underrepresented in provincial administration.

A concern raised by the Northern Ontario Relocation Program has been its potentially deleterious impact on meeting employment equity objectives. Reid, Foot, and Omar (1992) indicated that for the program as a whole (twelve groups consisting of 1,700 employees), only 12.9 percent of "designated group" employees relocated, compared to 30.9 percent of white, anglophone, able-bodied people. In addition, designated groups accounted for only 59.6 percent of new hires at the new location, compared to 62.6 percent in Toronto.

In order to address the employment equity objectives, the ORG organized a committee of designated group members to assist in recruitment. In addition, a management development program was established to train Native Canadian managers, and the workplace was designed with physical accessibility as a fundamental consideration.

The employment equity program was also expanded to include social assistance recipients and single parents. In conjunction with the federal government, the provincial government designed training programs to help in the development of life and job skills.

b. Customer Service

New technology provided opportunities to improve customer service. It is now possible for copies of birth, death, marriage, and other certificates to be produced immediately for those who go in person to the Toronto and Thunder Bay offices. The relevant scanned documents are called up onto a computer screen, verified, and printed within minutes. This has significantly reduced the inconvenience of what used to be a process of sorting through archived paper documents, which required a three-day waiting period and two visits to the office.

Other customer service improvements that were part of the broader initiative included extended hours of operation facilitated by the compressed-workweek policy; a more "customer-friendly" office design;

better information and instruction on the application process, such as better signs and instruction sheets with examples of how to complete any necessary forms, making it easier for customers to get what they want; and customer service training for all staff.

c.   Technology

Existing information storage and processing technology in place at the ORG before the move to Thunder Bay was capturing only about 5 percent of the information gathered by the branch. As a result, 10,000 square feet of space was required in downtown Toronto to store the paper records. In addition to the expense of the storage, there was the threat of time, fire, flood, or security problems that would jeopardize the physical existence of the documents and the pledge that these records would remain confidential.

The decision was made that the move to Thunder Bay would be accompanied by the purchase of an important technological innovation, namely auto imaging technology (AIT). AIT permits paper documents to be optically imaged and the data stored on optical platters. At the time the technology was purchased, it was believed that more than 50 percent of the branch's business information could be imaged and stored on platters. As will be discussed, the introduction of this technology led to better customer service. In addition, the technology resulted in better protection of the integrity of the records and a significant reduction in storage costs, and reduced the amount of labour necessary to manage the records by twenty-two non-bargaining-unit person-years.

The use of an STS approach required the integration of workers and their representatives with the new technology. To this end, it was necessary to establish the continuous involvement and support of OPSEU and the central human resources management agency concerning such administrative arrangements as flexible work time and sustaining community input on equity recruitment and training.

d.   Organizational Structure, Participation, and Flexibility

Human resources policies at the Thunder Bay office are based on the assumptions that employees are responsible, individuals are capable of making decisions, and groups can work effectively together with minimal supervision. These philosophies were implemented through organizational delayering, team management, generic job descriptions, pay-for-knowledge, alternative working hours, and workplace childcare.

Before the redesign, there were twelve functional units, each with a seven-level hierarchy between the level of registrar general and clerk. At the clerk level, there were eight more levels of positions. As mentioned earlier, this expansive breadth and depth of bureaucracy is reflected in the fact that in an organization of 150 staff members, there were forty-one different job descriptions and twenty-three different job classifications.

The twelve functional units were integrated into one multifunctional unit consisting of seven teams. The unit is directed by the deputy registrar general. Each team includes twelve team representatives and one team manager. Members of the team are capable of performing all of the necessary job functions. The net result is a reduction in the hierarchy of seven levels to three, including the removal of two levels of managerial (reporting) hierarchy. In addition, the eight layers within the clerical hierarchy have been replaced by one generic clerical position.

This innovation achieved three fundamental purposes: a flatter organizational structure that permits greater flexibility and encourages more independent lower-level decision making; fewer reporting, communication, and other protocol "seams"; and job enrichment as the forty-one job descriptions were replaced by three generic job descriptions—deputy registrar general, team manager, and team representative.

To encourage team representatives to acquire the skills necessary to perform all of the team's functions, a pay-for-knowledge plan was established. Beginning at an "introductory" or "entry" skill level, at which the worker has no direct experience and little knowledge of the work, workers progress through five knowledge levels for each job function in the team.

In order to better accommodate the widely divergent needs and work–family pressures of its employees, the ORG instituted work scheduling alternatives and a workplace childcare program. The work scheduling options include a compressed work week, a regular part-time night shift, regular part-time jobs for workers with disabilities, and flexible hours for single parents.

e. Forging New Partnerships

One of the most notable features of the ORG move to Thunder Bay was the emphasis placed on recasting and enriching old relationships and on establishing new partnerships within the Thunder Bay community.

COMMUNITY PARTNERSHIPS   As mentioned, the ORG established an Interagency Placement Committee, intended to encourage the recruitment of staff from the targeted employment equity community. The committee received over 450 referrals from race relations, Aboriginal, and disabled persons' organizations.

As a result of the assistance of this committee, 60 percent of the Thunder Bay ORG is staffed by members of groups that are generally underrepresented in the Ontario public service. The mosaic of the ORG includes 10 percent Aboriginal, 14 percent physically challenged, 5 percent francophone, and 6.3 percent visible minorities. Eighty-one percent of the work force is female.

Another interesting example of a broad community relationship nurtured as a result of the move was the public/private/nonprofit partnership formed between ORG, Arthur Anderson Consulting, and Goodwill Industries. Together, these organizations worked to scan 10 million paper documents for conversion to optical images. This was achieved by a staff that included eighty-six individuals drawn from the ranks of social assistance recipients, none of whom had any previous computer training. Goodwill Industries provided the training; Arthur Anderson provided technological support; and the ORG provided project management services. According to ORG officials, the project was completed ahead of schedule, and at a savings of $750,000 to the welfare system.

INTERGOVERNMENTAL PARTNERSHIPS   Some important intergovernmental partnerships were established through the ORG initiatives. The federal Canadian

Employment and Immigration Commission assisted with funding a strategy that trained some eighty workers from employment-equity-designated groups for employment in the Thunder Bay office of ORG.

A partnership was also formed between the provincial government and the municipal government of Thunder Bay. The Thunder Bay social services department assisted with recruiting and training of sole-support social assistance recipients.

UNION–MANAGEMENT PARTNERSHIPS   Last, but most certainly not least, the consultative relationship between the ORG and OPSEU was given an opportunity to be expanded. The ORG and OPSEU agreed to a number of initiatives to assist the overwhelming majority of workers not relocating to Thunder Bay to find employment within the Ontario public service or elsewhere. These measures included restricted job competitions for ORG staff, skills upgrading programs, job interview skills training, and psychological counselling.

An agreement between OPSEU and the ministry provided the framework for the implementation of the project. The pay of the clerical workers increased by as much as two pay grades; the number of workers has actually grown (partly due to an unexpected increase in demand for services); and there is little evidence of deskilling. There was reduced conflict over classification and promotion issues. The collapsing of job classes combined with job rotation has eliminated much interjob conflict through the formal grievance procedure. In addition, the open communications have resulted in workers becoming more active in workplace issues and, rather than threatening the worker–union relationship, enhancing the relationship.

Source: R. Hebdon and D. Hyatt, "Workplace innovation in the public sector: The case of the office of the Ontario Registrar General," *Journal of Collective Negotiations in the Public Sector, 25*(1) (1996), pp. 63–81. Used with permission of the publisher Baywood Publishing Co., Inc.

Question

Write a two- or three-page paper evaluating the labour–management relations effects of this innovation case at the Office of the Registrar General. Include in your essay a discussion of the strengths and weaknesses of the management and union actions and policies.

Endnotes

1. The 2.16 million is calculated by multiplying public-sector employment of 3.229 million by union density of 71.4.
2. Recall that in the private sector, third-party intervention was nearly always at the request of one or both parties.
3. The Government of British Columbia changed its teacher bargaining law in 2005 to ban all strikes.

References

Adams, G. (1981). The Ontario experience with interest arbitration. In J. Weiler (Ed.), *Interest arbitration*. Toronto: Carswell.

Adell, B., Ponak, A., & Grant, M. (2001). *Strikes in essential services*. Kingston, ON: Industrial Relations Centre Press, Queen's University.

Ashenfelter, Orley, Farber, Henry, & Ransom, Michael. (2010). Labor market monopsony. *Journal of Labor Economics, 28,*(2), pp. 203–210.

Bronfenbrenner, K., & Juravich, T. (1995). The impact of employer opposition on union certification win rates: A private/public sector comparison. Working paper no. 113. Washington, DC: Economic Policy Institute.

Currie, J., & McConnell, S. (1991). Collective bargaining in the public sector: The effect of legal structure on dispute costs and wages. *American Economic Review 81*(4), pp. 693–718.

Dachis, Benjamin, & Hebdon, Robert. (2010). *The laws of unintended consequences: The effect of labour legislation on wages and strikes*. C. D. Howe Institute.

Ferrera, M., & Hemerijck, A. (2003). Recalibrating Europe's welfare regimes. In J. Zeltin & D. M. Trubek (Eds.), *Governing work and welfare in a new economy*. Oxford: Oxford University Press, pp. 88–128.

Gunderson, M. (2005). Two faces of union voice in the public sector. *Labor Research Journal, 26*(3), pp. 393–413.

Harel, G., & Tzafrir, S. (2002). HRM practices in the public and private sectors: Differences and similarities. *Public Administration Quarterly, 25*, pp. 316–355.

Hebdon, R. (1996). Public sector dispute resolution in transition. In D. Belman, M. Gunderson & D. Hyatt (Eds.), *Public sector employment in a time of transition* (pp. 85–125). Madison, WI: Industrial Relations Research Association.

Hebdon, R., & Hyatt, D. (1996). Workplace innovation in the public sector: The case of the office of the Ontario Registrar General, *Journal of Collective Negotiations in the Public Sector, 25*(1), pp. 63–81.

Hebdon, Robert, & Jalette, Patrice. (2008). The restructuring of municipal services: A Canada–United States comparison. *Journal of Environment and Planning, C–Local Government and Policy, 26*, pp. 144–58.

Hebdon, R., & Kirkpatrick, I. (2005). Changes in the organisation of public services and their effects on employment relations. In S. Ackroyd, R. Batt, P. Thompson & P. Tolbert (Eds.), *Oxford handbook of work and organization*. Oxford: University Press, pp. 531–553.

Hebdon, R., & Mazerolle, M. (2003). Regulating conflict in public sector labour relations: The Ontario experience (1984–1993). *Relations industrielles, 58*(4), pp. 667–686.

Hebdon, R., & Warrian, P. (1999). Coercive bargaining: Public sector restructuring under the Ontario Social Contract 1993–96. *Industrial and Labor Relations Review, 52*(2), (January), pp. 196–212.

Human Resources and Social Development Canada. (2006). Orders suspending right to strike or lock out. Retrieved 15 April 2011 from http://www.hrsdc.gc.ca/eng/lp/spila/clli/irlc/10orders_suspending_right_to_strike_or_lock_out.shtml

Jalette, P., & Hebdon, R. (Forthcoming). Unions and privatization: Opening the "black box." *Industrial and Labor Relations Review*.

Lewin, D., Feuille, P., Kochan, T. A., & Delaney, J. T. (1988). *Public sector labor relations: Analysis and readings* (3rd edition). Lexington, MA: D. C. Heath.

Lynn, L. (1998). The new public management as an international phenomenon: A sceptical viewpoint. In L. Jones & K. Schedler (Eds.), *International perspectives on the new public management*. Greenwich, CT: JAI Press, pp. 105–122

Marshall, A. (1920). *Principles of economics* (8th edition). London: Macmillan and Co., Ltd.

Meltz, N. M., & Verma, A. (1995). Developments in industrial relations and human resource practices in Canada: An update from the 1980s. In T. A. Kochan, R. P. Locke & M. J. Piore (Eds.), *Employment relations in a changing world economy* (pp. 91–130). Cambridge, MA: MIT Press.

Olson, C. (1994). Final offer versus conventional arbitration revisited: Preliminary results from the lab. Paper presented at the 4th Bargaining Group Conference. Toronto: Centre for Industrial Relations.

Osborne, D., & Gaebler, T. (1992). *Reinventing government: How the entrepreneurial spirit is transforming the public sector*. Reading, MA: Addison Wesley.

Panitch, L., & Swartz, D. (1993). *The assault on trade union freedoms*. Toronto: Garamond Press.

Rapaport, D. (1999). *No justice, no peace: The 1996 OPSEU strike against the Harris government in Ontario*. Kingston, ON: McGill–Queen's University Press.

Reid, F., Foot, D., & Omar, A. (1992). Decentralization of provincial government activities: Implications for employment equity. In T. Kuttner (Ed.), *The industrial relations system*. Proceedings of the Canadian Industrial Relations Association Annual Conference (pp. 345–354). Charlottetown, PE: CIRA.

Roberts, W. (1994). *Don't call me servant: Government work and unions in Ontario 1911–1984*. Toronto: Ontario Public Service Employees Union.

Rose, J. B. (1995). The evolution of public sector unionism. In G. Swimmer & M. Thompson (Eds.), *Public sector collective bargaining in Canada* (pp. 2–52). Kingston, ON: IRC Press.

Saltzman, G. M. (1985). Bargaining laws as a cause and consequence of the growth of teacher unionism. *Industrial and Labor Relations Review, 38*(3), pp. 335–352.

Stewart, J., & Walsh, K. (1992). Change in the management of public services. *Public Administration, 70*, pp. 499–518.

Swan, K. P. (1985). Differences among provinces in public sector dispute resolution. In D. W. Conklin, T. J. Courchene & W. A. Jones (Eds.), *Public sector compensation*. Toronto: Ontario Economic Council.

Swimmer, G. (1989). Critical issues in public sector industrial relations. In A. S. Sethi, (Ed.), *Collective bargaining in Canada*. Scarborough, ON: Nelson.

Swimmer, G. (2001). *Public sector labour relations in an era of restraint and restructuring*. Don Mills, ON: Oxford University Press.

Swimmer, G., & Thompson, M. (1995). *Public sector collective bargaining in Canada*. Kingston, ON: IRC Press.

Telford, M. (2000). *Med-Arb: A viable dispute resolution alternative*. Kingston, ON: Queen's University, IRC Press.

Wellington, H., & Winter, R. K. (1971). *The unions and the cities*. Washington, DC: Brookings Institution.

CHAPTER 12

Globalization of Labour Markets

Learning Objectives

By the end of this chapter, you will be able to discuss

- labour's ongoing role in the areas of social and economy policy;
- labour's current and ongoing role in advocating human rights and equality;
- the definition and theories of globalization;
- the implications of globalization for unions, women and children, collective bargaining, and labour policy;
- union responses to globalization;
- union revitalization; and
- the future of industrial relations, including a new role for the International Labour Organization and the human rights approach to labour regulation.

Tracy Chen and Max Kowlowski are sitting in the coffee shop enjoying a well-deserved break after their final exam in labour relations. Tracy sits back and smiles. "It is so good to have all my exams completed. Now I can relax and enjoy the Christmas break."

"Easy for you to say," replies Max. "I still have to get all of my holiday shopping done before I head east for Christmas."

Tracy looks up from her coffee. "I know we promised not to talk about the exam, Max, but I have to ask, how did you reply to Professor Smith's question regarding the role of labour in today's economy?"

Max smiles. "Okay. But I'm only going to give you a quick answer—this is a 'school-free' coffee discussion, remember? I basically said that there would always be a role for labour. History has shown that the labour movement has often been the catalyst for legislation and social change and that it will continue to be. I also added that just as the union movement adapted from a craft-based economy to an industrial-based economy, we would see labour adjust to the new global and more service-based economy. How about you?"

Tracy looks at him in astonishment. "I said the exact opposite. I said that historically the labour movement has always followed that of the States. Given the rapid state of decline in the American labour movement, Canada would follow to the point where it would be nonexistent in all but public-sector workplaces. After all, we have seen extensive pressure from the private sector since the 1980s to minimize the role of unions; in the public sector, collective bargaining has been replaced by legislation; and labour has made few inroads in the emerging sectors of the economy. I also added that the movement to more progressive HRM practices has made unions all but obsolete."

Max takes a sip of coffee. "I can't believe that we have such different answers. I wonder what Smith was looking for."

"Who knows," replies Tracy. "She always says that there are no right or wrong answers in labour relations; it just depends on how you argue your view."

Max guzzles down the last of his coffee. "Well, I guess we'll find out in a few days. In the meantime, I have to shop for five nephews and a niece before my flight at 7 a.m. tomorrow. Any ideas?"

Tracy just laughs as they walk out of the coffee shop. "Me, I'm lazy. I just buy gift certificates. There's a bookstore next door. Just think—all your shopping done in one place."

Max shakes his head as he walks in the other direction. "Yeah, Tracy, I can see that it really is the thought that counts for you. See you after the break."

As the preceding vignette points out, there are differing views of labour's role in today's economy. As we reflect upon what we have learned from this text, we will turn our focus toward globalization of labour markets and the role of labour.

Advocate for Rights and Freedoms

As we discussed in Chapter 4, the labour movement has often been the catalyst for advocating for rights and freedoms. Whether we look at labour's push for a nine-hour workday in the 1890s, its recognition of employees' ability to freely quit jobs, or its ongoing drive to ensure a "fair" minimum wage rate, labour has often been at the forefront of advancing the rights and freedoms of workers (both unionized and nonunionized).

Social and Economic Policy Issues

You may recall from Chapter 4 that the Canadian Labour Congress (CLC) was formed in 1956 with a mandate to assist with the creation of a national health-care scheme, improve unemployment insurance, develop a national pension plan, and increase minimum wages at the federal and provincial levels. These issues were important to all working people, both unionized and not unionized. Today, these issues remain core to the CLC (see IR Notebook 12.1).

Equity Programs

As we discussed in Chapters 4, 5, and 11, we have seen significant changes in the makeup of the labour movement over the years. If we think back to the days of craft unions, most union members (and workers) were male. Later, we saw the influential role that the female phone operators played in the 1911 Winnipeg General Strike. In the 1960s, women became increasingly involved in paid employment activities, and legislation was passed allowing public-sector employees, many of whom are women, to unionize. In fact, the labour force participation rate of women between the ages of twenty-five and sixty-four increased from less than 50 percent in the mid-1970s to 70 percent by the late 1980s. This 70 percent rate remained constant through the 1990s (Beaudry & Lemieux, 1999). Moreover, the unionization rate of women (30.9 percent) in 2010 was higher than that of men (28.2 percent) (Statistics Canada, 2010). Given the rise of female participants in the work force, it should not be surprising that labour has been active in equity issues related to women and other groups. In this section, we will present an overview of labour's current efforts in the equity arena.

From an advocacy perspective, the federations of labour have been active in equity issues. For example, the CLC's homepage has a link to its human rights and equality issues page (Canadian Labour Congress, 2009). Topics that the CLC includes in its discussion of human rights and equality are

- Aboriginal workers
- Pride
- Women

Excerpts from the Action Plan of the Canadian Labour Congress

Among the many programs and policies adopted by delegates to the 2008 convention, key priorities for immediate action include:

Building and Renewing the Labour Movement

- Establish a Working Committee on Organizing, identify training needs, financial resources, and assist affiliates in developing long term organizing strategies that are responsive to changing demographics, increasing urbanization and the changing nature of the economy. Our goal is to increase union density in Canada.
- Prioritize organizing women, young workers, aboriginal workers and workers of colour; fight for secure jobs, decent wages and contracting in provisions in collective agreements.
- Work with affiliates, federations and labour councils for key labour law changes such as anti-scab laws, automatic certification and sectoral bargaining and promote labour rights as basic human rights.

The Growing Gap and Women's Economic Equality

- Work with anti-poverty and community groups to increase minimum wages, fight for improvements to EI, universal social programs and improved pensions.
- Campaign for federal pro-active pay equity legislation to address the gender pay gap.
- Take concrete action to end violence against women.
- Demand a comprehensive non-profit pan Canadian child care program;

Defending and Expanding Quality Public Services

- Fight privatization, deregulation and public private partnerships in all their forms and fight to expand needed education, social and community services.

- Renew our fight to halt privatization of public health care.

Decent Jobs and a Strong and Sustainable Canadian Economy

- Further develop our vision of a strong, democratic and independent Canadian economy based on re-regulation and expansion of public ownership in the oil industry.
- Demand the abrogation of NAFTA and continue to oppose the FTAA, SPP, TILMA, Atlantica, and proposed trade agreements such as those being negotiated with South Korea and Colombia.
- Push for domestic procurement programs and infrastructure programs, with a major focus on building community and city support.
- Strict enforcement of health and safety legislation; recognize workplace stress as a compensable condition; recognize the right to refuse for psychological reasons; improve working alone protection; press for provincial and territorial compensation boards to expand the range of occupational diseases which are compensable and implement fair policies; promote occupational death and disease registry.

Peace, Development and International Solidarity

- Demand that Parliament take immediate steps to end the military occupation of Afghanistan and bring Canadian troops home. Work with affiliates and social justice groups to oppose the military intervention and build solidarity with Afghani workers.
- Promote sustainable development and pressure the government to live up to 0.7% of GDP to Official Development Assistance (ODA).

Source: Canadian Labour Congress, "Action plan," 2008, Used with permission. Retrieved 3 May 2011 from http://www.canadianlabour.ca/convention/2008-convention/action-plan.

- Workers of colour
- Workers with disabilities
- Young workers

Labour has been active in the equality movement not only at all levels of government as a lobbyist, but also at the union level in terms of collective bargaining issues. For example, an entire section of the journal *Just Labour: A Canadian Journal of Work and Society* (entitled "Advancing the Equity Agenda Inside Unions and at the Bargaining Table"), edited by Stinson, Warskett, and Bickerton (2006), was dedicated to examining the role of unions in advancing equity issues—in particular, women's issues—at the collective bargaining table. Over the past decade, other scholars have examined how issues of pay equity (Hart, 2002) and freedom from discrimination based on sexual orientation (Hunt, 1997) have been negotiated by Canadian unions, as well as the extent to which Canadian collective agreements have included provisions for various equality issues (e.g., disabilities, sexual orientation, employment equity, sexual harassment, and equal pay) (Brown, 2003). However, these gains are not always easy for labour to achieve. As discussed by Swinton (1996), unions and collective bargaining can play an important role in promoting equity for disadvantaged groups; however, unions can also face challenges as they attempt to balance seniority rights with equality rights. Remember that unions are required to represent all workers equally given their duty of fair representation. They can sometimes have a difficult time, though, "fairly" representing the interests of long-time (and often male) members while simultaneously representing those of emerging (and often less senior) disadvantaged members.

As is shown in Chapter 5, labour takes political action on social issues at all levels of government, through the CLC, provincial labour federations, and local labour councils. Collective bargaining is also used to enshrine new rights into collective agreements. Let's take a look at the most recent human rights issue, namely, sexual orientation, by examining how issues of discrimination based on sexual orientation and same-sex benefits have been addressed in the labour movement.

Ⓡ Ⓟ Ⓒ 12.1

IR Today 12.1

Equality in Action: Issues of Sexual Orientation

Over the last decade or so, there has been an increased movement toward protecting workers from discrimination based on sexual orientation. However, the issue continues to emerge, with issues such as same-sex marriage still being debated in legislatures. In fact, while the Human Rights Commission recommended that sexual orientation be included as a prohibited grounds of discrimination in 1979 (and a second equality-for-all committee recommended the same in 1985), it was not until 1996 (shortly after a Supreme

Court ruling) that Parliament formally included sexual orientation as a prohibited grounds of discrimination under the *Canadian Human Rights Act*.

Yet the labour movement was active in this area long before 1996. In general, the labour movement has focused on two issues: freedom from discrimination based on sexual orientation and same-sex benefits. As is documented in several industrial relations papers, the labour movement at the CLC and provincial federation levels were actively involved in this area well before the mid-1990s. The CLC passed resolutions calling for nondiscrimination based on sexual orientation in the 1980s, and in 1990 passed a resolution stating that same-sex benefits were a bargaining priority. At the national level, both CUPE and the CAW unions devoted considerable resources to the issue. These activities included special committees dedicated to the sexual orientation issue. At the collective bargaining level, these unions (and others) also took action. For example, while the CAW had very few same-sex benefits clauses in 1996, by the late 1990s, it had become a bargaining priority. By 2002, 44 percent of CAW agreements had such provisions. Also, at the local level, labour relations literature has shown grievances and arbitrations concerning sexual orientation issues dating back to the mid-1990s. Overall, we can see that labour—at all levels—has been very active in this emerging area of equality.

Sources: T. C. Brown, "Sexual orientation and the labour movement: A comparison of the Canadian and American response to the issues of gays and lesbians," Canadian Industrial Relations Association 35th Annual Conference, University of Ottawa, June 12–14, 1998; T. C. Brown, "Sexual orientation provisions in Canadian collective agreements," Industrial Relations, 58(4) (2003), pp. 644–666; T. Bonoguore, "House votes not to reopen same-sex marriage issue," The Globe and Mail, 7 December 2006, retrieved 13 December 2006 from http://www.theglobeandmail.com/servlet/story/RTGAM.20061207.wsamesex07/BNStory/National; J. Eaton and A. Verma, "Does 'fighting back' make a difference? The case of the Canadian Auto Workers Union," Journal of Labor Research, 27 (Spring 2006), pp. 187–212; G. Hunt, "Sexual orientation and the Canadian labour movement," Relations industrielles, 52(4) (1997), pp. 787–811; G. Hunt and D. Rayside, "The geo-politics of sexual diversity: Measuring progress in the U.S., Canada and the Netherlands," New Labor Forum, 8 (Spring/Summer 2001), pp. 37–47; M. C. Hurley, Sexual orientation and legal rights (Ottawa: Government of Canada, Law and Government Division, 2005); personal collective bargaining experience of the authors.

Having looked some of the activities and challenges facing labour today, the story would not be complete without a thorough look at globalization and its impacts.

What Is Globalization?

Globalization is the international movement over the past twenty years to integrate world economies by removing barriers to the trade of goods and services as well as by enhancing capital and labour mobility. As the International Monetary Fund (IMF) explains,

> Economic "globalization" is a historical process, the result of human innovation and technological progress. It refers to the increasing integration of economies around the world, particularly through trade and financial flows. The term sometimes also refers to the movement of people (labour) and knowledge (technology) across international borders. There are also broader cultural, political and environmental dimensions of globalization that are not covered here (2008).

At its most basic, there is nothing mysterious about globalization. The term has come into common usage since the 1980s, reflecting technological advances that have made it easier and quicker to complete international transactions—both trade and financial flows. It refers to an extension beyond national borders of the same market forces that have operated for centuries at all levels of human economic activity—village markets, urban industries, or financial centres.

Markets promote efficiency through competition and the division of labour—the specialization that allows people and economies to focus on what they do best. Global markets offer greater opportunity for people to tap into more and larger markets around the world. It means that they can have access to more capital flows, technology, cheaper imports, and larger export markets. But markets do not necessarily ensure that the benefits of increased efficiency are shared by all.

International institutions such as the World Bank and the IMF acknowledge the continuing problem of the equitable distribution of globalization's increased worldwide production. The implication is that markets do not automatically allocate benefits equitably either within nations or between rich and poor ones (Krugman, 2008). A central policy question for our purposes, therefore, is the extent to which the labour market should be regulated under globalization and what should be the role of collective bargaining (see also Chaykowski & Abbott, 2001).

Globalization: A New Political Economy?

For some, globalization has created a new political economy, which has resulted from a combination of new or reinvented institutions (World Trade Organization [WTO], IMF and World Bank); an internationalization of corporations from multinational to **transnational corporations (TNCs)** (e.g., worldwide commodity chains); and a globalization of business strategies (Fairbrother & Hammer, 2005). According to this school of thought, a new model of capitalism has emerged that requires new modes of labour market regulation. The contours of the new modes are taking shape, but it is too early to give them precise definition. Nonetheless, we will gaze into the crystal ball and predict labour's regulatory future in the last section of this chapter. But before we do that, we must review theories of globalization and examine their effects on industrial relations.

transnational corporations (TNCs)

global corporations that may integrate product chains horizontally; for example, parts of the final product might be made in a dozen countries spanning five continents

Theories of Globalization[1]

Free Market Globalization

The free market globalization theory asserts that competitive pressures of the marketplace will force corporations and governments to submit to international norms and standards. That is, markets will dictate labour conditions and constrain government regulation. In the absence of regulation (e.g., minimum wage laws), wages and conditions will be pushed into a race to the bottom. Under free market globalization, there is little space for such industrial relations institutions as collective bargaining. This theory also predicts that, under competitive pressures, national systems of industrial relations will converge over time.

Institutional Globalization

The institutional globalization theory differs from free market globalization in the role played by national institutions, which perform an important mediating function between market pressures and society. International differences between employment systems over such terms as poverty rates, a stabilizing middle class, and human right and equality issues may be partially explained by the existence of such vigorous institutions as collective bargaining, human rights commissions, and employment standards agencies.

Integration of Free Market and Institutional Globalization

In the integration theory, market forces, the decline of the service sector, and institutional factors combine to define a unique employment relations system. Globalization was found to create convergent pressures on governments, management, and labour. However, the evidence from several Organization for Economic Co-operation and Development (OECD) economies including Canada does not support convergence (Bamber, Lansbury & Wailes, 2004; Traxler, 1996). Nonetheless, several common elements of globalization were identified:

1. *Decentralization of bargaining.* In North America, pattern bargaining broke down in several industries (e.g., meatpacking, pulp and paper, and construction).
2. *Greater management power.* Most countries saw a trend to more management and less union power (Bamber, Lansbury & Wailes, 2004). Although collective bargaining remained an important institution, the focus had shifted to the workplace or enterprise level.
3. *Decrease in strikes.* There were fewer strikes in most countries including Canada (see Chapter 9).
4. *Impact on corporations.* Production systems tend to become globalized. The Canadian auto industry, for example, has adopted some Japanese and Swedish production methods and practices. The internal labour market model is disappearing and is being replaced by the core–periphery model, in which workers on the periphery have less training, higher turnover, and lower commitment (Chaykowski & Gunderson, 2001).

Impact of Globalization on Industrial Relations in Canada

Employment

North American Free Trade Agreement (NAFTA)
a free trade agreement between Canada, the United States, and Mexico that was signed in 1994 and included a labour side agreement, the North American Agreement on Labor Cooperation

gross national product
the value of all goods and services produced by a country in a year

In Canada, globalization has affected employment through the **North American Free Trade Agreement (NAFTA)**, which caused a decrease in full-time employment and a corresponding increase in part-time employees (mostly women) and self-employed people (mostly men) (Chaykowski & Abbott, 2001). Like all other developed countries, Canada has been affected by the structural shift from manufactured goods to services. In Canada, this has meant a steady decline in manufacturing as a proportion of **gross national product** (GNP). During boom periods, however, both Canada and the United States see unemployment decreases. The structural changes have shifted employment risks in terms of job security and compensation to individuals. The general population has widespread job fears due to outsourcing (see IR Today 12.2).

The CEO Poll: The Trouble with Outsourcing

Controversy has surrounded Foxconn International Holdings, the giant electronics manufacturer with facilities in China, for its labour practices and the suicide rate among its workers. Apple Inc., which contracts manufacturing to Foxconn, has also come under media scrutiny for its relationship to the company. Canadian business leaders, in a poll conducted by COMPAS Inc., are divided on whether Apple is likely to suffer damage to its reputation, and whether North American companies should insist on better standards when outsourcing.

Slightly more than a third of respondents said Apple is likely to experience any damage to its image, and fewer still expected the issue to affect the company's share price.

Foxconn, meanwhile, has responded to the issue by hiking employee pay by 30%, which the CEOs see as both an appropriate response to the company's mistreatment of its workers, and a sign of further wage pressures in China. "We must expect more than moderate cost increases during the next year or two," according to one respondent.

The panel was divided, however, on the issue of North American companies imposing management standards on foreign suppliers. "We don't have the right to tell China how to run its economy," wrote one respondent. "We have the choice to buy, or not to buy."

Others echoed this belief. "I don't think that one can enforce North American management standards in a foreign country," wrote another respondent. "However, due diligence and continued monitoring should be done to ensure that employees are fairly paid."

In their comments, many of the CEOs suggested a shift in manufacturing back to North America is the only way to truly ensure fair treatment. "Bring manufacturing home," wrote one. But North Americans' reliance on inexpensive labour and products makes that an unlikely prospect, according to others: "Until our insatiable desire for cheap goods begins to wane, we will learn of more Foxconn situations," said another respondent.

Source: Joe Castaldo, "The CEO Poll: The trouble with outsourcing," July 17, 2010, Reprinted with permission of Canadian Business. Retrieved from http://www.canadianbusiness.com/managing/ceo-poll/article.jsp?content= 20100617_170825_1712.

Unions and Collective Bargaining

The primary focus of Canadian and American unions is collective bargaining. If success is defined by the capacity to take wages out of competition, then globalization has reduced union success (Chaykowski & Abbott, 2001). Union decline in the United States and to a lesser extent in the private sector in Canada has reduced union power, and plant closure is now more than ever a believable threat. An important question is the extent to which freedom of association and collective bargaining will be protected under globalization.

Labour Policy

Chaykowski and Abbott (2001) echo the previous theme that free markets will not necessarily provide the optimum allocation of resources in society. Research shows that market deregulation may not be the only or the best policy option (Kim & Sakamoto, 2010; Warnecke & De Ruyter, 2010). For example, Quebec has a decree system, more common in Europe, whereby wages negotiated in the unionized sector are applied by policy to the nonunion sector. A study in the building services sector in Canada concluded:

> The comparative institutional advantages of the decree system help employers to secure greater labour market stability and low-inflation wage settlements, which accounts for the relatively good economic performance of the sector. (Jalette, 2006)

Globalization has created social policy disequilibrium, and new systems must be created. A particular concern is for such equity-based policies as pay and employment equity and antidiscrimination and human rights laws. Another problem is that foreign governments are increasing pressure to reduce taxes and regulations to compete for investment. The competition may come from neighbouring American states or more likely China or India (see IR Today 12.2).

Research also shows that globalization has increased wage inequality within higher-wage countries (e.g., Canada and the U.S.) (Chaykowski & Gunderson, 2001; Krugman, 2008; OECD, 2009). However, in Canada, the evidence shows that stronger employment laws and unions have mitigated this effect somewhat.

Chaykowski and Gunderson (2001) argue that Canadian governments should act strategically to adopt policies that prepare our work force for global pressures. To maintain our high wages, for example, we must increase investments in human capital (training and education) and generally adopt policies that improve the productivity and skills of the work force. In this process, there is a problem covering workers who are in the periphery since they often do not qualify for the benefits of social policies. Education and training subsidies, for example, may not apply to part-time or casual employees if there are strict eligibility requirements such as a minimum number of hours that must be worked.

Women and Children

Concerns have been expressed that globalization may have a negative impact on women and children. More specifically, if gender-based analysis is not applied to international trade agreements, women and children may be affected by cutbacks in social programs (Neil & Laidlaw-Sly, 2001). Transnational corporations, it is feared, will be able to evade such labour standards as employment security, hours of work, child labour, and minimum wages (International Labour Organization, 2010). Canada is in competition with corporations that employ workers worldwide. Some workers may be employed under sweatshop conditions and some may be child labourers. Poor women in developing countries are particularly vulnerable (Neil & Laidlaw-Sly, 2001).

 The National Council of Women of Canada (NCWC), a lobby group founded in 1983, supports equitable distribution of resources, universal health care, education, social services, sustainable environmental standards, and fair labour practices. The NCWC points out that women's work is not included in GNP and is, therefore, not taken into account in calculating the benefits and costs of social programs. It is also concerned that Canada's social programs will be seen as unfair subsidies under such free trade rules as Chapter 11 in NAFTA, which allows foreign corporations to sue the Canadian government.

Unions

As discussed above, globalization has enhanced corporate power, constrained governments' ability to protect workers, and eroded the *Wagner Act* model of unionism. Capital is no longer bound by the traditional social compromise, and in many countries, the power of the state to defend social rights has declined. Thus, labour needs to look beyond the state and the traditional social contract models of the postwar period for strategies to defend labour rights (Ashby & Hawking, 2009; Riisgaard, 2005).

Globalization and Canadian Unions

Union Density and Coverage

Globalization has had similar effects, as shown in cross-country comparisons. Several patterns are evident from the data shown in Table 12.1. Union density has fallen over the ten-year period 1999–2008 in 22 of the 23 countries.

To stop or reverse the private-sector union decline in most countries, unions will have to find ways to organize workers in nonstandard work arrangements. Some scholars argue that Canada's ability to maintain overall union density in the face of globalization is dependent on the labour movement's ability to reach out to women members (Yates, 2006).

Of note in Table 12.1 is the wide gap in some countries between density and coverage. Recall that coverage is union density plus those employees who are directly affected by the collective bargaining settlement but who are not union members. In North America, there is very little difference between density and coverage. But in many other countries (e.g., those in Europe and Australia), coverage rates are much higher than union density and are more reflective of union power and influence than union density rates. The United States appears an outlier when coverage is examined, with a rate of 13.1 percent and 13 out of the 23 countries showing a coverage rates over 50 percent of the labour force.

To complete the analysis, the decline in union density shown in Table 12.1 has not been matched by a similar decline in coverage. Over a shorter four-year period, 11 of the 23 countries in the table show an increase in union coverage and presumably union power despite the influences of globalization.

Canadian Labour Challenges

After a thorough investigation of the internal and external pressures facing unions from globalization, Kumar and Schenk (2006, pp. 50–55) describe several challenges facing Canadian labour. They note that union density in Canada has declined from 40 percent in the mid-1980s to 30.6 percent in 2004

TABLE 12.1

Union Density and Coverage in 23 Countries*

	UNION DENSITY										DENSITY CHANGE 1999–2008	2000 COVERAGE	2004 COVERAGE	COLLECTIVE BARGAINING COVERAGE CHANGE 2000–2004
	1999	2000	2001	2002	2003	2004	2005	2006	2007	2008				
Austria	37.4	36.6	35.9	35.8	34.7	34.4	33.6	32.5	30.8	28.9	−8.5	95.1	98.1	3.0
Italy	35.4	34.8	34.2	33.8	33.7	34.1	33.6	33.2	33.5	33.4	−2.0	79.9	90.4	10.5
Sweden	80.6	79.1	78.0	78.0	78.0	78.1	76.5	75.1	70.8	68.3	−12.3	90.0	90.1	0.1
Finland	76.3	75.0	74.5	73.5	72.9	73.3	72.4	71.7	70.3	67.5	−8.8	88.8	89.2	0.4
Belgium	50.9	49.5	49.6	50.9	51.9	53.1	52.9	54.1	52.9	51.9	1.0	83.9	88.3	4.4
Spain	16.0	16.7	15.9	16.0	15.8	15.5	15.0	14.6	14.2	14.3	−1.7	82.8	80.4	−2.5
Australia	25.2	24.7	24.4	23.0	22.8	22.0	22.1	20.1	18.5	18.6	−6.6	80.2	79.3	−0.9
Netherlands	24.6	22.9	21.9	21.7	21.2	21.3	21.0	20.4	19.3	18.9	−5.7	79.8	79.0	−0.8
Denmark	74.9	74.2	73.8	73.2	72.4	71.7	71.7	69.4	69.1	67.6	−7.3	79.9	78.3	−1.6
Norway	54.8	54.4	53.9	54.5	55.1	55.0	54.9	54.9	53.7	53.3	−1.5	70.1	75.0	4.9
Germany	25.3	24.6	23.7	23.5	23.0	22.2	21.6	20.7	19.9	19.1	−6.2	67.6	71.5	3.9
Portugal	22.4	21.6	21.1	20.7	21.4	21.4	21.2	20.8	20.8	20.4	−2.0	78.1	69.9	−8.2
Greece	26.8	26.5	25.8	25.5	25.3	24.5	24.6	24.7	24.5	24.0	−2.8	60.5	56.6	−4.0
Ireland	39.0	38.4	38.2	36.4	37.8	35.9	34.1	33.3	32.4	32.3	−6.7	44.6	44.9	0.3
Poland	26.0	24.2	22.5	23.5	23.7	19.7	18.3	16.8	15.2	15.6	−10.4	49.5	40.5	−9.0
Hungary	24.5	21.7	20.0	17.4	17.9	16.9	17.5	17.0	16.9	16.8	−7.7	31.7	39.9	8.2
United Kingdom	30.1	30.2	29.6	29.3	29.6	29.4	28.4	28.1	27.9	27.1	−3.0	29.0	39.1	10.1
Switzerland	21.0	20.8	20.5	20.4	20.1	19.6	19.4	19.0	18.7	18.3	−2.7	41.4	37.8	−3.6
Slovak Republic	34.2	32.3	29.1	27.4	26.1	23.6	22.8	20.6	18.8	16.8	−17.4	46.3	34.0	−12.3
Canada	28.1	28.3	28.4	28.4	28.5	27.8	27.7	27.4	27.3	27.1	−1.0	32.2	29.9	−2.3
Japan	22.2	21.5	20.9	20.3	19.7	19.3	18.8	18.3	18.3	18.2	−4.0	15.0	23.6	8.6
New Zealand	21.6	22.3	22.2	22.3	21.2	20.9	21.0	21.4	21.5	20.8	−0.8	24.6	23.6	−1.0
United States	13.4	12.8	12.8	12.6	12.4	12.0	12.0	11.5	11.6	11.9	−1.5	14.0	13.3	−0.7

*Union density 1999–2008 and collective bargaining coverage 2000 and 2004, selected OECD countries (from highest to lowest coverage in 2004).

Source: OECD, Trade Union Density, Labour (database), OECD. Stat Extracts, http://stats.oecd.org (Accessed data 29 Jan 2011)

and that unless "decisive steps are taken by unions to change their internal and external environments, the union density rate is likely to continue to slip further."

Democratization

Unions must take steps internally to enhance democracy in terms of engaging their members and developing their capacities. Studies show that internal democracy can play an important role in a union's ability to cope with the pressures of globalization (Ashby & Hawking, 2009; Levesque & Murray, 2005).

Leadership and Alternative Vision

As is discussed in Chapter 5, most unions in the Canadian Labour Congress (CLC) and the Confederation of National Trade Unions (CNTU) support a social unionism vision. This means they usually support universal health-care and education, women's and minorities' rights, full employment policies, and so on. Union tactics and strategies for growth depend on their success in developing a common vision for the rank-and-file members and union leaders. According to Kumar and Schenk (2006), in a democratic setting, leadership is the ability to engage members in wide-ranging discussions and problem solving, and generally to act on their union's vision.

Organizing

"The U.S. experience suggests that organizing new members is closely related to effective bargaining, a capacity to mobilize workers through political action and community alliances, and developing a participatory union culture" (Kumar & Schenk, 2006, p. 53). Also, given the growth in employment in small workplaces (<20 employees), more centralized bargaining structures should be encouraged to reduce servicing costs.

Contingent Workers

About one-third of the work force in Canada are in jobs that are nonstandard (i.e., neither permanent nor full-time). The jobs are also nonpermanent or precarious (e.g., irregular part-time, casual, contract, temporary, or self-employed) (Kumar & Schenk, 2006). These jobs have low security, poor wages, often no benefits, and are almost always nonunion. As discussed above, the *Wagner Act* model is ill equipped to offer viable collective bargaining for such workers.

Organizational Innovation

A significant number of unions in Canada are actively involved in a critical reassessment of goals, strategies, and ways of operating (Kumar & Schenk, 2006). "Organizational structures, for example, are undergoing modification so as to encompass women, workers of colour, youth, people with disabilities, and aboriginals to reflect both changing demographics and the necessary inclusiveness for union solidarity" (Kumar & Schenk, 2006, p. 54). Thus, a key challenge for unions is to embrace recent immigrants from Asia and Africa, particularly in Canada's major cities: Toronto, Montreal, and Vancouver.

Union Education

Many unions have yet to develop a comprehensive educational program for their members. According to Taylor (2001), unions need

> new approaches that meet the needs of labour organizations for trained and critically engaged workplace representatives, that provide union members a thorough understanding of the labour movement and its agenda, and that allow trade unionists to gain access to a range of educational opportunities from basic skills to university-level courses.

RPC 12.2

Union Responses to Globalization

Creating Global Unions

As a first step to the creation of global unions, unions have been actively joining with partners in other countries to mount cross-border campaigns (Bronfenbrenner, 2007).

In an effort to enhance their bargaining power, the United Steelworkers merged with a union in the United Kingdom to create the world's first global union (see IR Today 12.3). A primary purpose of the merger is to coordinate negotiations with multinational corporations.

Corporate Codes of Conduct in the 1970s

Corporate codes of conduct are nonbinding standards that may apply to such matters as labour (child labour, freedom of association, collective bargaining, and forced labour) and environmental protection. As early as the 1970s, unions started to work through the International Confederation of Free Trade Unions (ICFTU)[2] and international secretariats of their unions to pressure corporations to adopt labour codes of conduct. At the same time, unions worked through the ILO and the OECD, which were promoting such codes (Fairbrother & Hammer, 2005). The pressure continued through the 1990s with support from nongovernmental organizations and the newly created global union federations (GUFs). Global union federations are international organizations made up of such occupational unions as teachers, textile workers, transport workers, metalworkers, and public employees.

Studies show that corporate codes have serious weaknesses in terms of lack of access to information, failure to address collective bargaining and freedom of association issues, and inadequate monitoring or enforcement mechanisms (Fairbrother & Hammer, 2005). A 1998 ILO investigation of 215 codes found that only around 15 percent refer to freedom of association or the right to collective bargaining. In addition, a 1999 OECD investigation revealed that only

IR Today 12.3

Workers Uniting

Workers Uniting is the name of the new international union created by Unite—the biggest union in the UK and Republic of Ireland and the United Steelworkers (USW), North America's largest private sector union. Go to http://www.workersuniting.org/PDF/Job%202102%20 Workers%20uniting%20A5%20.pdf to download a leaflet containing information on the new union.

WHYPERLINK "http://www.workersuniting.org/PDF/ Job%202102%20Workers%20uniting%20A5%20.pdf" click here to download a leaflet with further information.

Workers Uniting will draw on the energies of the two unions, more than three million active and retired workers from the United States, Canada, Great Britain and the Republic of Ireland who work in virtually every sector of the global economy, including manufacturing, service, mining and transportation.

"This union is crucial for challenging the growing power of global capital," said USW President Leo W. Gerard. "Globalization has given financiers license to exploit workers in developing countries at the expense of our members in the developed world. Only global solidarity among workers can overcome this sort of global exploitation wherever it occurs."

"In addition to empowering the interests of our unions' members, said Derek Simpson, General Secretary of Unite's Amicus section, "our mission is to advance the interests of millions of workers throughout the world who are being shamefully exploited."

In a video broadcast at the USW's convention, Tony Woodley, General Secretary of Unite's T&GU section said, "The creation of our new union is only the beginning. We're laying the foundations of an even larger and stronger global union yet to come."

The new global union's founding Constitution calls on its combined membership to "build global union activism, recognizing that uniting as workers across international boundaries is the only way to challenge the injustices of globalization."

Consistent with this calling, Workers Uniting will "match our words with action and resources, utilizing our collective expertise and knowledge through collective bargaining, organizing, global political action and international solidarity."

During the past year while discussions about the creation of a new global union have been ongoing, the two unions have been actively engaged in joint efforts to advance global union activism, including:

- Extensive discussions about strategies that each of the unions has adopted for saving manufacturing capacity in their respective countries.
- Joint collective bargaining efforts with common employers in the paper, chemical and titanium industries.
- International solidarity projects, such as efforts to protect the rights and safety of trade unionists in Colombia and Mexico.
- Participation by rank and file delegations of activists in each other's education, rapid response, health and safety, civil rights and women's conferences.
- Exposure to the political processes in each other's countries, including Democratic Party primaries and Labour Party conference.

Source: From Workers Uniting website: http://www.workersuniting .org/default.aspx?page=1 Reprinted with permission.

---

20 percent of 182 codes referred explicitly to the ILO conventions on freedom of association and the right to collective bargaining (Riisgaard, 2005).

In addition, developing countries tend to oppose corporate codes as a form of rich nation protectionism. Nonetheless, Canadian consumers will pay 10 to 20 percent more for ethically made goods, and it is argued that corporate codes if universally applied can be a useful first step in moving toward international labour standards (Verma, 2001).

Labour Rights Campaigns

Labour shifted its focus from corporate codes to campaigns for labour rights due to the new political economy defined by the World Bank, the IMF, and the WTO in 1995, together with a shift from multinational corporations to transnational corporations with their global commodity chains and internationalization of business strategies (Fairbrother & Hammer, 2005). Through the 1990s and into the 2000s, the ICFTU and GUFs pressured the World Bank, the IMF, and the WTO to adopt the following core labour standards:

- elimination of forced labour;
- freedom of association and collective bargaining (ILO Conventions 87 and 98);
- equal pay and freedom from discrimination; and
- elimination of child labour.

When the WTO failed to include labour standards in 2001, the ICFTU shifted its focus to international framework agreements with transnational corporations (TNCs) (Bourque, 2008; Fairbrother & Hammer, 2005).

International Framework Agreements (IFAs)

Some argue that international framework agreements are important instruments for unions to (1) defend and advance workers, rights through trade union cooperation, (2) create new organizing opportunities, (3) expand collective bargaining to the international level, and (4) enhance social dialogue within TNCs (Bourque, 2008; Riisgaard, 2005). However, these goals need to be enhanced by international trade union structures with more resources and responsibilities than the GUFs currently have (Bourque, 2008, p. 45).

New international allies in the negotiation of IFAs are nongovernmental organizations (NGOs). These organizations embrace such issues as women's rights, the environment, and human rights—areas that have overlapping interests with the labour movement (Bronfenbrenner, 2007; Riisgaard, 2005).

There are some signs that IFAs are expanding into new areas and having positive results for labour. As an International Labour Organization study found,

> Twelve of the 70 companies that have signed IFAs are now from non-European countries. Eight of these have signed agreements since 2006. This is an encouraging trend in itself, especially since this group now includes a British, a Canadian (Quebecor), and a Japanese company. Resistance to IFAs in those countries has been strong and these modest developments are worth noting. (Stevis, 2010)

By February 2011, the GUFs had negotiated some 80 IFAs. For example, the International Metalworkers' Federation (IMF) has signed 19 IFAs. These agreements are negotiated globally but achieve rank-and-file support through local implementation. Unlike codes of conduct, they often include a commitment to core labour standards, health and safety, and union involvement, and have a procedure for dealing with agreement violations. As is shown in Table 12.2, IFAs also provide a strong basis for a union role in the affairs of transnational

TABLE 12.2

Comparison of Codes of Conduct and IFAs

CODES OF CONDUCT	INTERNATIONAL FRAMEWORK AGREEMENTS
Unilateral initiatives	Negotiated between labour and corporate management
May recognize all core labour standards	Recognize all core labour standards
Rarely cover suppliers	Usually cover suppliers
Monitoring, if any, controlled by management	Unions involved in implementation
Weak basis for labour–management dialogue	Strong basis for union–management dialogue

Source: P. Fairbrother and N. Hammer, "Global unions: Past efforts and future prospects," *Relations industrielles, 60*(3), pp. 405–431.

corporations in terms of application to suppliers, negotiations with corporate management, and implementation involvement. As an example, the Daimler IFA has been used to solve disputes in Brazil and Turkey (Stevis, 2009).

In summary, the arrival of a new political economy, together with a union renewal process, has resulted in the possibility of new forms of international unionism built around multi-union international framework agreements and single-union global agreements.

The Future of Industrial Relations Under Globalization

While Canadian labour law has continuously been updated through countless amendments since the *Wagner Act* was adopted in Canada after World War II, the model remains more or less intact. But, as we have shown throughout this book, the world of work has changed dramatically since the passage of the *Wagner Act* model in Canada. This raises the question of the relevance of the current model to today's economic environment. Globalization has increased the pressures on corporations to be internationally competitive, and at the same time has reduced their ability to agree to compensation and work rules that are out of step with international norms. State labour laws and standards have become less relevant in this global trade environment.

The New Role of the ILO

With these liberalization trends has come a general shift in attention toward international standards and norms. In the labour market, for example, there is much greater interest in and attention to the labour standards that have been established by the ILO. The ILO, a tripartite (management, labour, and government) agency of the United Nations, has established standards on such human rights issues as child labour, forced labour, freedom of association, and the right to collective bargaining. These fundamental principles were affirmed unanimously by 182 countries (including Canada) in 2008 (see IR Notebook 12.2). It is also worth noting that the preamble to the *Canada Labour Code* contains an important reference to Canada's commitment to Convention 87 of the ILO (collective bargaining and the right to organize).[3]

FIGURE 12.1

International Labour Organization Structure

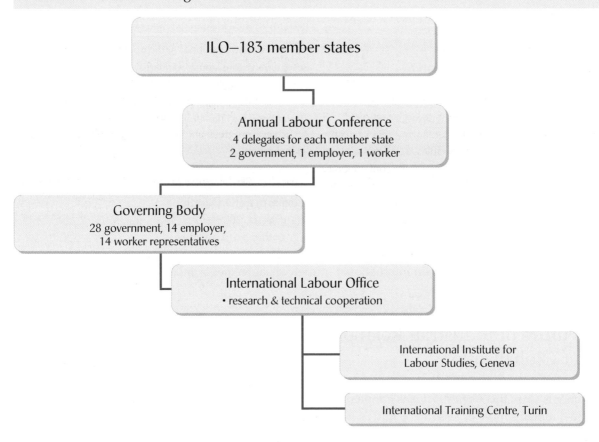

At any moment in time, the ILO will be working with forty or fifty countries on a wide array of labour market regulation and social policy issues that have been voted into ILO conventions (Swepston, 2003). They include

- dedicating governments to full, productive, and freely chosen employment;
- the importance of an efficient system of labour administration including the establishment of statistical data on unemployment, injuries, union membership, etc.; and
- the need for labour inspectorates.

Other labour standards include

- employment laws and policies;
- wages;
- conditions of work (e.g., weekly hours, night work);
- occupational health and safety;
- social security (e.g., medical, sickness, employment insurance, family and maternity leaves);

IR Notebook 12.2

ILO Declaration on Social Justice for a Fair Globalization

The International Labour Organization unanimously adopted the ILO Declaration on Social Justice for a Fair Globalization on 10 June 2008. This is the third major statement of principles and policies adopted by the International Labour Conference since the ILO's Constitution of 1919. It builds on the Philadelphia Declaration of 1944 and the Declaration on Fundamental Principles and Rights at Work of 1998. The 2008 Declaration expresses the contemporary vision of the ILO's mandate in the era of globalization. This landmark Declaration is a powerful reaffirmation of ILO values. It is the outcome of tripartite consultations that started in the wake of the Report of the World Commission on the Social Dimension of Globalization. By adopting this text, the representatives of governments, employers' and workers' organizations from 182 member States emphasize the key role of our tripartite Organization in helping to achieve progress and social justice in the context of globalization.

Source: ILO Director General, International Labour Organization website, Used with permission. Retrieved 2 May 2011 from http://www.ilo.org/global/ topics/economic-and-social-development/globalization/ WCMS_099766/lang–en/index.htm

- industrial relations procedures (e.g., conciliation and arbitration, cooperative bargaining, grievances);
- equal pay for work of equal value;
- migrant workers' rights; and
- special conditions for those employed as fishermen, dockers, or agricultural workers.

Implementation of ILO Standards

RPC 12.3

A criticism of the ILO is that its conventions cannot be imposed on nation states; that is, there is no legal mechanism of enforcement. Nonetheless, the ILO has developed an elaborate enforcement system that has three elements.

Standards Obligations

The ILO constitution requires member states to submit all conventions and recommendations to their competent authorities (normally legislature) within eighteen months of adoption for implementation or ratification (in the case of conventions) (Rogers, Lee, Swepston & Daele, 2009; Swepston, 2003). All states under Article 22 of the ILO constitution must report on conventions that have been ratified, and these reports must be copied to national employer and worker organizations. (For ratification of ILO Convention 87 by country, visit the ILO's website.)

Supervisory System for Ratified Conventions

To monitor and rule on noncompliance, the ILO has established two committees:

THE COMMITTEE OF EXPERTS This committee is composed of twenty jurist members appointed by the governing body of the ILO. Its mandate is to investigate, rule on, and report unratified conventions of member states.

CONFERENCE COMMITTEE   The conference committee mandate is to rule on the application of labour standards by member states. It is tripartite in nature and has the power to request governments to appear before it to discuss cases of noncompliance (Swepston, 2003).

Special Procedures on Freedom of Association

In 1950 the United Nations created a special body for the protection of trade union rights: the Fact-Finding and Conciliation Commission on Freedom of Association. But because its procedures applied only to ratified conventions, and freedom of association issues usually involved questions of fact, not law, the ILO created a special committee: the **Committee on Freedom of Association (CFA)** in 1951 (Swepston, 2003).

From 1951 to 2001, the CFA examined over 2,000 cases and developed jurisprudence. The CFA consists of nine members and an independent chair appointed by the governing body; it meets three times per year in Geneva. Complaints may be lodged only by governments or by employers' and workers' organizations. The subject matters of complaints include collective bargaining, legislation, strikes, and unfair practices that affect unions (anti-union measures). In most cases, governments cooperate with the CFA to provide explanations and facts. CFA decisions have resulted in the release of unionists from prison or return from exile.

Committee on Freedom of Association (CFA)

a special committee established by the ILO in 1951 to examine cases of labour rights violations

---

IR Today 12.4

Canada and the ILO–The Good and "Not So Good"

We start with an example of the positive role that Canada is playing by partnering with the ILO.

ISLAMABAD–The Government is committed to reducing gender inequality and to promote employment opportunities for women in Pakistan, stated by the Federal Secretary of Labour and Manpower, Mr Tariq Iqbal Puri. He was addressing the Signing Ceremony of Canadian $8 million national project titled "Promoting Gender Equality for Decent Work" 2010–2015. He appreciated the generous financial support of the Government of Canada and the technical support of ILO to help women for decent employment opportunities. He expressed his confidence that ILO is known in public for implementing successful projects.

While speaking on the occasion, the Canadian High Commissioner, Mr Randolph Mank highlighted Canada's support to Pakistan for the socio-economic develop-

ment of people, particularly women and their economic empowerment. He mentioned that CIDA had a good experience of working with ILO on a similar project during 2005–2009 and the new project would surely add value to the successes made in this regard.

Canada, on the other hand, has not ratified several of the ILO conventions, failed to implement several others, and has been frequently condemned by the Freedom of Association Committee for violations.

According to a labour group consisting of two of Canada's largest unions, the United Food and Commercial Workers and the National Union of Public and General Employees, Canada's record at the ILO has been deficient:

- Since 1982, Canada's record with respect to the number of complaints submitted to the ILO's Freedom of Association Committee is the worst of any of the International Labour Organization's

An Alternative Approach? Freedom of Association as a Human Right

But how are the ILO's core labour standards relevant to today's Canadian workplaces? We offer this "human rights approach" as a window into a possible future direction of collective bargaining.[4] As collective bargaining becomes more globalized, international norms and standards are bound to play an ever-increasing role. Evidence of the expanding reliance on these international principles can be found in a 2001 decision of the Supreme Court of Canada, discussed in Chapter 2 as the *Dunmore* decision (summarized in IR Today 12.5).[5]

Dunmore and the ILO

Prior to *Dunmore*, the Supreme Court of Canada had been reluctant to interfere with the sovereignty of federal and provincial legislatures (Adams, 2003). The *Canadian Charter of Rights and Freedoms* guarantees that all workers have the right to organize and to advance employment interests without fear of reprisals. *Dunmore* imposes a duty on Canadian governments to provide legislation to ensure that the right to organize can be freely exercised. The *Dunmore* decision also extended associational rights to both individuals and collectivities. Finally, providing evidence of the shift to a greater reliance on international norms, the Supreme Court repeatedly cited ILO standards, as the following excerpt from *Dunmore* on the application to the collective illustrates:

> The collective dimension of s. 2(d) is also consistent with developments in international human rights law, as indicated by the jurisprudence of the Committee of Experts on the Application of Conventions and Recommendations and the ILO Committee on Freedom of Association (see, e.g., International Labour Office, *Freedom of Association: Digest of decisions and principles of the Freedom*

of *Association Committee of the Governing Body of the ILO* [4th (revised) ed. 1996]). Not only does this jurisprudence illustrate the range of activities that may be exercised by a collectivity of employees, but the International Labour Organization has repeatedly interpreted the right to organize as a collective right (see International Labour Office, Voices for Freedom of Association, *Labour Education* 1998/3, No. 112: "freedom is not only a human right; it is also, in the present circumstances, a collective right, a public right of organization" (per Léon Jouhaux, workers' delegate). (*Dunmore v. Ontario*, 2001, para. 16)

An International Consensus

It is important to note that, internationally, freedom of association includes the right to collective bargaining (e.g., the ILO views freedom of association as a fundamental human right that includes collective bargaining). The term *collective bargaining* is broadly interpreted to include such nonunion forms of representation as autonomous employee associations, mandatory joint health and safety committees, and various wage consultation employee associations.

The strength of the human rights approach rests on the broad consensus developed in the 1990s between international institutions, governments, management, and labour around freedom of association as a human right. The organizations endorsing and supporting freedom of association were the

---

IR Today 12.5

Dunmore v. Ontario

In 1994, the NDP government in Ontario enacted the *Agricultural Labour Relations Act* (ALRA). The act gave collective bargaining rights to Ontario agricultural workers for the first time in 1995. The Harris Conservative government repealed the ALRA, returning agricultural workers to their previous status and nullifying collective agreements negotiated under the new act and union certifications.

The United Food and Commercial Workers International Union and Tom Dunmore, an agricultural worker, applied to the Ontario courts, challenging the repeal of the ALRA and the exclusion of agricultural workers from the provisions of the *Labour Relations Act*. Dunmore and the union argued that the government's action infringed the rights of agricultural workers to freedom of associa-

tion and equality under sections 2(d) and 15(1) of the *Canadian Charter of Rights and Freedoms*.

In an 8–1 ruling, the Supreme Court of Canada declared that the exclusion of agricultural workers from the provisions of Ontario's *Labour Relations Act* violates the workers' right to freedom of association guaranteed by s. 2(d) of the *Charter*.

In the end, the Court declared s. 3(b) of the *Ontario Labour Relations Act* unconstitutional and declared the *Labour Relations and Employment Statute Law Amendment Act* unconstitutional to the extent that it gave effect to the exclusion of agricultural workers in s. 3(b) of Ontario's *Labour Relations Act*.

Source: Lancaster House, "Dunmore," *Supreme Court Decision Summaries*, 2001.

OECD, the WTO, the ILO, the UN (e.g., the Global Compact), the International Chamber of Commerce, the International Organization of Employers, fifty major TNCs, and the U.S. Council for International Business (Adams, 2002).

Moreover, the unanimous declaration set out in IR Notebook 12.2 means that all nations endorse the principle "that human rights and fundamental freedoms are the birthright of all human beings and their protection and promotion is the first responsibility of governments." Further, the international consensus also holds that "all human rights are universal, indivisible, interdependent, and interrelated" (Adams, 2002).

Implications for Labour Policy

Treating freedom of association (including collective bargaining) as a fundamental human right has profound implications for labour policy. Current policy is founded on the notion that workers have the right to choose collective bargaining and that employers have a say in that decision. Under this policy, the government's role is to ensure that workers are free to choose a union without fear or intimidation from employers or unions. Typically, the reform debate is about how best to protect this free choice. But imagine workers being given a choice over any of the other fundamental rights—forced labour, discrimination, or child labour. These are all equal birthright human rights: inviolate, indivisible, and absolute.

The more accepted international labour policy is built on the idea that government's role is much more proactive. It must not just give workers the right to choose but also provide whatever mechanisms are necessary to give all working people the human right to be consulted in their working conditions (i.e., to give workers a voice) (Adams, 2002). Evidence from the United States shows that the government has failed to protect workers' right to choose a union due to unchecked interference from employers (Compa, 2000). Even managers may be subject to discipline if they do not vigorously oppose union organizers.

In a provocative book, Adams (2006) identifies a new high road to freedom of association bolstered by international law, such institutions as the UN and ILO, and the Canadian constitution. In 1948, the United Nations universally declared that freedom of association was a fundamental human right. Key implications of the universal declaration are that there is no hierarchy of rights and human rights cannot be entrusted to the vagaries of the political process of nation states. In North America, however, labour policy is typically seen as a balancing act between employer and worker interests—a process that has seen a gradual erosion of human rights. According to Adams, the human rights entrenched in these doctrines highlight the archaic practices of labour–management relations in Canada today. These practices are out of step with international norms and the *Canadian Charter of Rights and Freedoms* as interpreted by the Supreme Court of Canada in 2001 (*Dunmore v. Ontario*). There is strong evidence that the unrepresented, given the choice, would prefer to have some form of collective organization (union, association, or other) deal with management (Freeman & Rogers, 1993).

Systemic Denial of Rights?

Governments have repeatedly committed themselves to supporting freedom of association as a human right but practised a labour relations policy that effectively denies representation to millions of workers. This human rights denial—similar to the concept of systemic discrimination—is unintentional.

Adams (2006) canvassed union opinions on the new human rights approach to representation. It ranged from support, through study and consideration, to scepticism. Many unions, it seems, embrace the human rights approach but are not prepared to risk creating substitute organizations. However, the human rights approach has attracted two important Canadian unions to the fold: the National Union of Public and General Employees, Canada's second-largest union, primarily representing employees of provincial governments, and the United Food and Commercial Workers Union, a large private-sector union in the front line of organizing new types of workers in Canada (e.g., Walmart, agricultural workers in Ontario, and more recently migrant workers in Manitoba and Quebec). But these large and powerful unions do not speak for the labour movement in Canada. While the Canadian Labour Congress unanimously passed a motion supporting labour rights as human rights, it does not appear to have unanimity on support for nonstatutory forms of representation.

A New Social Movement?

Globalization has unquestionably increased pressures on unions. But there may be an opportunity under globalization for an international revival of labour rights. The human rights approach may provide the intellectual foundation of a new social movement.

Summary

Globalization does not mean the end of regulation of the labour market, especially if labour in rich and developing countries is to share in the increased wealth. Without government intervention, it is unlikely that women and children will benefit from increased trade in goods and services. Such labour market institutions as collective bargaining are adapting to meet the needs of management and labour. The focus of bargaining is shifting to the firm, reflecting the flexibility required by global competition. To survive and grow, unions need to adapt to the changing environment.

Union revitalization will depend on such factors as democratization, leadership, organizing, contingent workers, organizational innovation, and union education. Globalization has caused the labour movement to take new approaches to the representation of union members. Unions are increasingly turning to their global federations to negotiate international framework agreements to gain recognition and improve conditions in transnational corporations. Other unions are taking direct action by negotiating global agreements. Only time will tell whether these new institutional arrangements will become the norm under globalization.

We took another look into the future in examining the new human rights approach to freedom of association and collective bargaining. This approach challenges some of the foundations of the *Wagner Act* model of collective bargaining. To satisfy the requirement of freedom of association, unions may not be the only representational form, and employees (and employers) may not get to choose this freedom. The state may be obligated to provide some form of freedom of association for all workers, the same as it does for other human rights.

Finally, it seems clear that the International Labour Organization will play an important regulatory function in this new world.

Key Terms

Committee on Freedom of Association (CFA) 398

gross national product 386

North American Free Trade Agreement (NAFTA) 386

transnational corporations (TNCs) 385

Weblinks

CLC social and economic policies:

http://canadianlabour.ca/index.php/economic_issues

CLC human rights and equality policies:

http://www.canadianlabour.ca/human-rights-equality

International Monetary Fund and globalization:

http://www.imf.org/external/np/exr/ib/2000/041200.htm#II

National Council of Women of Canada:

http://www.ncwc.ca

Union discussion of issues pertaining to youth:

- CUPE Alberta:

    http://www.alberta.cupe.ca/young-workers

- Ontario Federation of Labour youth page:

    http://www.ofl.ca/youth

- Saskatchewan Federation of Labour youth page:

    http://www.sfl.sk.ca/youth.php

Workers Uniting: The Global Union

www.workersuniting.org

International Trade Union Confederation:

http://www.ituc-csi.org

Affiliates of the ITUC:

http://www.ituc-csi.org/article1577.html

International Labour Organization:

http://www.ilo.org/public/english/index.htm

ILO databases:

http://www.ilo.org/public/english/support/lib/dblist.htm

Global union federations:

http://www.global-unions.org

International framework agreements:

http://www.global-unions.org/framework-agreements.html

Ratification of ILO conventions by country:

http://www.ilo.org/ilolex/english/convdisp1.htm

Government of Canada labour and globalization:

http://www.hrsdc.gc.ca/eng/labour/labour_globalization/index.shtml

Federal government's commitment to the ILO's core labour standards:

http://www.canadianlabour.ca/issues/social-and-economic-issues

RPC Icons

12.1 Provides advice to clients on the establishment, continuation, and termination of bargaining rights

- institutions and processes (both regulatory and nonregulatory) that govern the relationship between employers and employees

12.2 Provides advice to clients on the establishment, continuation, and termination of bargaining rights

- organizing tactics of unions
- collective bargaining processes and issues

12.3 Monitors applications of HR policies
- context and content of policy
- relevant legislation (e.g., human rights, employment equity, pay equity)
- the identification, assessment, development, implementation, maintenance, and monitoring processes of effective systems of managing HR information

Discussion Questions

1. Based on the information covered in this text and your own views, what do you see as the largest challenges facing the labour movement this decade?

2. The opening vignette presented two different views of the future of labour in Canada. Max presents a view that the labour movement will continue to play an important role in the twenty-first century. In contrast, Tracy argues that the labour movement will become obsolete. Who do you think is right? Why?

3. Define globalization. Describe three theories of globalization and explain how they differ.

4. Describe three effects of globalization on industrial relations in Canada.

5. What is the difference between union density and coverage? What steps will Canadian unions have to take to avoid further decline of private-sector members?

6. Describe three union responses to globalization. What were the strengths and weaknesses of each approach?

7. Compare the effectiveness of codes of conduct and international framework agreements in providing labour rights.

8. What is the ILO? What are the core labour standards as defined by ILO conventions?

9. How does the ILO enforce its policies?

10. What is the human rights approach to freedom of association and collective bargaining?

11. What are the implications of the human rights approach for North American labour policy?

Using the Internet

1. Many unions are increasing their focus on youth. Look at the websites of a few unions and see what actions they are taking geared toward youth. Alternatively, conduct an Internet search using the terms *union*, *labour*, and *youth*, and see what you find.

2. Equality issues have often been core to the labour movement. Using the Negotech website (**http://negotech.labour.gc.ca/cgi-bin/search/ negotech/search-eng.aspx**), run searches to see the frequency and types of clauses that unions have negotiated concerning equality.

3. What is the subject matter of ILO Conventions 87 and 98?

4. What ILO conventions deal with child labour?

5. What is a global union federation? Find one and outline the contents of an agreement made between the GUF and a global corporation.

Exercises

1. Look at recent media (i.e., TV, newspaper, websites, etc.) stories concerning labour negotiations and/or strikes. To what extent do you see issues of job security, equality, diversity, or globalization covered?
2. Many campuses have unions on-site. Look at the publications and/or websites for the university and unions. To what extent do you see the public-sector changes mentioned in the text (i.e., budget cuts, downsizing, job security, and privatization)?
3. Interview three to five of your friends who are not in this course. Ask them what they see as the role of unions in today's economy and whether they feel there is still a need for labour unions. To what extent do their views reflect the topics discussed in this chapter?
4. Many universities and colleges across Canada are unionized. Make contact with one of the on-campus unions and/or a university's labour relations department and request an interview. What do they see as the biggest challenges facing labour relations on your campus over the coming five to ten years?
5. Find an international framework agreement. Analyze how the ILO's core labour standards are protected (or not) in the agreement.
6. At the home site of a global union federation, find the Canadian unions or federations that belong to it.
7. Go to the ILO website and determine if Canada and the United States have ratified Conventions 87 and 98 pertaining to freedom of association and collective bargaining.

Case

World Works Council Established at PSA Peugeot Citroën

FRANCE—The framework agreement signed by the International Metalworkers' Federation (IMF), the European Metalworkers' Federation (EMF) and PSA Peugeot Citroën in 2006 provided that the parties would "meet every three years to review the measures taken and plan adjustments as needed through riders to the agreement" to take into account the global changes in the corporation's business.

The new agreement signed on May 20, 2010 in Paris strengthens PSA Peugeot Citroën's commitments to the international core labour standards and stresses the extension of the Group's requirements to its business partners. In addition it incorporates new commitments to environmental protection and sustainable development. The main improvements to the agreement are:

- Strengthening the provisions on occupational health and safety;
- The application of the principle of equal pay for work of equal value, regardless of the contractual arrangement under which workers are employed;

- The promotion of environmental protection and commitments to reduce greenhouse gas emissions;
- The involvement of trade unions in the audits carried out as part of the monitoring process; and
- The setting up of a World Works Council to follow up the agreement implementation.

In addition to the members of the EWC, union representatives from PSA subsidiaries in Brazil and Argentina will sit on this Council which will meet for the first time in the second part of June 2010.

IMF General Secretary Jyrki Raina welcomed the improvements to the 2006 agreement and in particular the creation of a World Works Council, in view of the Group's international development. He added, "This new agreement is an essential tool for promoting sustainable industrial relations and decent working conditions in PSA Peugeot Citroën, its suppliers and subcontractors."

Present in 160 countries, the PSA Peugeot Citroën Group is focusing its international development on China, Latin America and Russia. In April 2010 the Group launched a new car assembly plant in Kaluga, Russia. The plant 70 per cent owned by PSA Peugeot Citroën and 30 per cent by Mitsubishi Motors is expected to employ some 3,000 workers in 2012 when the plant becomes fully operational. In China, PSA Peugeot Citroën has a joint-venture with Dongfeng and just signed a letter of intent with China Chang'an Automobile Group for the creation of another joint venture. PSA Peugeot Citroën employs about 187,000 people throughout the world.

The renewal of this framework agreement is in line with the IMF Action Programme 2009–2013 which calls on the IMF to "identify opportunities to strengthen existing agreements, and the options and means that are optimal for pursuing improvements of their content."

Source: International Metalworkers' Federation (IMF), "World Works Council established at PSA Peugeot Citroën," retrieved 3 May 2011 from http://www.imfmetal.org/index.cfm?c=23122.

Questions

1. Find the agreement on the Internet.
2. Briefly describe the scope of coverage of the agreement.
3. How does this agreement protect workers' rights?
4. How does it differ from any Canadian collective agreement?
5. Find an international framework agreement with a Canadian company and compare it to the IFA with the PSA Peugeot Citroën Group.

Endnotes

1. This section draws on the work of Bamber, Lansbury, and Wailes (2004).
2. In 2006 the ICFTU was replaced by a new federation called the International Trade Union Confederation (UTUC).
3. Note also the federal government's commitment to the ILO's core labour standards by looking under "International Affairs" at the HRSD website (http://www.hrsdc.gc.ca/eng/labour/labour_globalization/ila/index.shtml).

4. For more on this approach, see Adams (2002), Gross (2003, 2010), Gross and Compa (2009), and Compa (2000).
5. Dunmore v. Ontario (Attorney General). 2001 SCC 94. File No. 27216.

References

Adams, R. (2002). Choice or voice? Rethinking American labor policy in light of the international human rights consensus. *Employee Rights and Employment Policy Journal, 5,* pp. 521–548.

Adams, R. (2003). The revolutionary potential of *Dunmore. Canadian Labour and Employment Law Journal, 10,* pp. 83–116.

Adams, R. (2006). *Labour left out.* Ottawa: Canadian Centre for Policy Alternatives.

Ashby, Stephen, & Hawking, C. J. (2009). *Staley: The fight for a new American labor movement.* Champlain: University of Illinois Press.

Bamber, G. J., Lansbury, R. D., & Wailes, N. (Eds.). (2004). *International and comparative employ-ment relations* (4th edition). London: Sage.

Beaudry, P., & Lemieux, T. (1999). Evolution of the female labour force participation rate in Canada, 1976–1994: A cohort analysis. *Canadian Business Economics,* Summer, pp. 1–14.

Bourque, Reynauld. (2008). International framework agreements and the future of collective bar-gaining in multinational companies. *Just Labour, 12,* pp. 30–47.

Bronfenbrenner, Kate. (2007). *Global unions: Challenging trans-national capital through cross-border campaign.* Ithaca, NY: Cornell Press.

Brown, T. C. (2003). Sexual orientation provisions in Canadian collective agreements. *Industrial Relations, 58,* pp. 644–666.

Canadian Labour Congress. (2009). "Human rights and equality," retrieved 3 May 2011 from http://www.canadianlabour.ca/human-rights-equality

Chaykowski, R., & Abbott, M. (2001). The challenge of globalization to Canadian economic and social well-being. In Richard P. Chaykowski (Ed.), *Globalization and the Canadian economy: The implications for labour markets, society and the state* (pp. 1–26). Kingston, ON: School of Policy Studies, Queens University.

Chaykowski, R., & Gunderson, M. (2001). The implications of globalization for labour and labour markets. In Richard P. Chaykowski (Ed.), *Globalization and the Canadian economy: The impli-cations for labour markets, society and the state* (pp. 27–60). Kingston, ON: School of Policy Studies, Queens University.

Compa, Lance. (2000). *Unfair advantage: Workers' freedom of association in the United States under human rights standards.* New York: Human Rights Watch.

Dunmore v. Ontario (Attorney General). (2001). SCC 94. File No. 27216.

Fairbrother, P., & Hammer, N. (2005). Global unions: Past efforts and future prospects. *Relations industrielles, 60*(3), pp. 405–431.

Freeman, R. B., & Rogers, J. (1993). Who speaks for us? Employee representation in a nonunion labor market. In B.E. Kaufman and M.M. Kleiner, eds., *Employee representation* (pp. 13–79). Madison, WI: Industrial Relations Research Association.

Gross, J. (2003). A long overdue beginning: The promotion and protection of workers' rights as human rights. In J. Gross (Ed.), *Workers' rights as human rights,* pp. 1–22. Ithaca, NY: Cornell University.

Gross, J. (2010). *A shameful business: The case for human rights in the American workplace.* New York: Cornell University.

Gross, J., & Compa, Lance. (2009). *Human rights in labor and employment relations: International and domestic perspectives.* Ithaca, NY: Cornell University Press.

Hart, S. M. (2002). Unions and pay equity bargaining in Canada. *Relations industrielles, 57*(4), pp. 609–629.

Hunt, G. (1997). Sexual orientation and the Canadian labour movement. *Relations industrielles, 52,* pp. 787–811.

International Labour Organization. (2010). *Accelerating action against child labour: ILO Global Report on child labour.* Retrieved from http://www.ilo.org/ipecinfo/product/viewProduct. do?productId=13853

International Monetary Fund. (2008). "Globalization: A Brief Overview" retrieved August 3, 2011 from http://www.imf.org/external/np/exr/ib/2008/053008.htm

Jalette, P. (2006). When labour relations deregulation is not an option: The alternative logic of building service employers in Quebec. *International Journal of Comparative Labour Law and Industrial Relations, 22*(3), pp. 329–346.

Kim, ChangHwan, & Sakamoto, Arthur. (2010). Assessing the consequences of declining unionization and public-sector employment: A density-function decomposition of rising inequality from 1983–2005. *Work and Occupations, 37*(2), pp. 119–136.

Krugman, Paul. (2008). Inequality and redistribution. In Serra Narcís & Joseph Stiglitz (Eds.), *The Washington consensus reconsidered towards a new global governance,* pp. 31–41. Oxford: University Press.

Kumar, P., & Schenk, C. (2006). *Paths to union renewal: Canadian experiences.* Toronto: Broadview Press.

Levesque, C., & Murray, G. (2005). Union involvement in workplace change: A comparative study of local unions in Canada and Mexico. *British Journal of Industrial Relations, 43*(3), p. 489.

Neil, M., & Laidlaw-Sly, C. (2001). Globalization and women's human rights: The implications for labor markets, society and the state. Ottawa: Canadian Workplace Research Network, pp. 190–204.

OECD (Organisation for Economic Co-operation and Development). (2009). Tipping back the balance. *The OECD Observer, 270/271* (December 2008–January 2009), p. 8.

Riisgaard, L. (2005). International framework agreements: A new model for securing workers' rights? *Industrial Relations, 44*(4), pp. 707–737.

Rogers, G., Lee, E., Swepston, L., & Daele, J. (2009). *The ILO and the quest for social justice.* Ithaca, NY: Cornell Press.

Statistics Canada. (2010). Unionization. *Perspectives on Labour and Income,* October.

Stevis, Dimitris. (2009). International framework agreements and global social dialogue: The Daimler case. Employment Working Paper No. 46. Geneva: Multinational Enterprises Programme, International Labour Organization.

Stevis, Dimitris. (2010). International framework agreements and global social dialogue: Parameters and prospects. Employment Working Paper No. 47. Geneva: International Labour Organization.

Stinson, J., Warskett, R., & Bickerton, G. (Eds.). (2006). Advancing the equity agenda inside unions and at the bargaining table. *Just Labour: A Canadian Journal of Work and Society, 8,* pp. 50–114.

Swepston, L. (2003). Closing the gap between international law and U.S. labor law. In J. Gross (Ed.), *Workers' rights as human rights,* pp. 23–52. Ithaca, NY: Cornell Press.

Swinton, K. (1996). Accommodating equality in the unionized workplace. *Osgoode Law Journal, 33,* pp. 703–747.

Taylor, J. (2001). *Union learning: Canadian labour education in the twentieth century.* Toronto: Thompson Publishing House.

Traxler, F. (1996). Collective bargaining and industrial change: A case of disorganization? A comparative analysis of eighteen OECD countries. *European Sociological Review, 12*(3), pp. 271–287.

Verma, A. (2001). *Beyond corporate codes of conduct: What governments can do to strengthen labour standards within the context of free trade.* Ottawa: Canadian Workplace Research Network, pp. 211–217.

Warnecke, Tonia, & De Ruyter, Alex. (2010). Positive economic freedom: An enabling role for international labor standards in developing countries? *Journal of Economic Issues, 44*(2), pp. 385–393.

Yates, C. (2006). Women are key to union renewal: Lessons from the Canadian labour movement. In P. Kumar & C. Schenk (Eds.), *Paths to union renewal: Canadian experiences,* pp. 103–22. Toronto: Broadview Press.

Appendix A

Arbitration: The Case of Bradley Ennis

Instructions

Your instructor will assign the case to groups or individuals. Once it has been assigned, you will take on the role of management or union (as per your instructor's direction). You will then write an argument appropriate for your assigned role. You may also be required to present your arguments in class on a date designated by your instructor. A key part of this assignment will be the application of arbitral principles of "just cause" for discipline and discharge. This assignment is based on (1) independent research of arbitration jurisprudence; (2) lecture material; (3) the assigned text; and (4) the attached case.

To understand the principles involved in the case, it will be necessary to review relevant arbitral jurisprudence. The texts *Canadian Labour Arbitration* by Brown and Beatty and *Collective Agreement Arbitration in Canada* by Palmer and Palmer offer excellent summaries. Both are probably available at your library. It will also be helpful to review cases reported in the series Labour Arbitration Cases (LACs), which should also be available at the library.

The completed assignment should require a *maximum* of seven typewritten, double-spaced pages (excluding references and cover sheet). To do well on this assignment, you will need to

1. demonstrate a sound knowledge of the elements of just cause;
2. clearly present arguments appropriate for your assigned role of management or union;
3. cite relevant jurisprudence (LACs) to support your argument;
4. present your ideas in a clear manner (correct grammar, punctuation, style, etc.); and
5. ensure that your reasoning is *concise and logically consistent*.

The Case of Bradley Ennis (Version 1)[1]

The Facts

The facts of the case are not in dispute. Bradley Ennis was a registered nurse employed in the trauma unit of All Saints' Hospital. Ennis is now 45 years old and was hired by All Saints' Hospital on May 1, 1992. His performance record until 2008 was acceptable. The hospital has a three-point performance rating system: (1) needs improvement; (2) satisfactory performance; and (3) superior performance. Over the years Ennis's performance ratings were "satisfactory" for most years and "superior" for his last three years.

In his role as trauma nurse, Ennis was responsible for monitoring patient care, administering potentially lethal drugs (e.g., narcotics), monitoring patient regimes, and counselling patients and their families concerning care options. Accordingly, nurses on this unit were required to maintain certification as "trauma specialists." Ennis received this certification in 1995 and had maintained it ever since.

Ennis was verbally counselled and received two written warnings for absenteeism on January 27, 2008, July 23, 2008, and October 15, 2008, respectively. He was terminated on December 3, 2008, following a three-day leave of absence without permission. The letter of discharge states that he was terminated for failing to call in sick as well as for excessive absenteeism (17.5 percent as against a hospital average of 7 percent). A union representative was present during each of the meetings where warnings were presented to Ennis. Also, on October 15, 2008, Ms. Gupta (his manager) reminded Ennis about the hospital's confidential Employee Assistance Plan (EAP). Gupta advised Ennis that he could call the EAP about anything, including drug and alcohol addiction or the recent death of his daughter, that might be affecting his attendance.

Before his discharge, Ennis sought treatment for a drug (prescribed sedatives—sleeping pills) and alcohol addiction. He has been in and out of counselling since March 2009. Between the initial treatment in March 2009 and the time of the arbitration hearing (February 25, 2010), he had three major relapses in which he stopped attending his counselling sessions (dates May 20, 2008, November 21, 2008, and October 25, 2009). He has been drug- and alcohol-free since November 11, 2009. At the time of dismissal, management was unaware that he was being treated for his addiction.

Ennis's addiction counsellor, Dr. Cooper, believes that he has an 80 percent chance of remaining chemical-free over the next few years. In Dr. Cooper's opinion, it was the unexpected death of Ennis's five-year-old daughter, who died at the ER of the hospital where he worked in December 2007, that caused the subsequent addiction. Specifically, Ennis was unable to sleep and was prescribed sleeping pills shortly after his daughter's death. The medication was never stolen from the hospital; it was purchased elsewhere. Now that his client has recovered from this shock, Dr. Bradley believes that Ennis can maintain an acceptable attendance and performance record as a trauma nurse in the future.

Regarding other employees, Ms. Gupta states that only one other trauma nurse, out of a staff of 45, had an absenteeism rate greater than 10 percent (13 percent). That nurse was never given a warning of any kind.

Key Dates

May 1, 1992	Ennis hired
January 27, 2008	Verbal counselling
July 23, 2008	Written warning
October 15, 2008	Second written warning
December 3, 2008	Termination
March 2009	Ennis first seeks treatment
February 25, 2010	Arbitration

Relevant Collective Agreement Clause

ARTICLE 32—CORRECTIVE ACTION AND DISCIPLINE

32.1. Employees can be disciplined only for just cause. Such discipline must be reasonable and commensurate with the seriousness of the violation.

32.2. Both the union and the hospital believe in the concept of progressive discipline. Accordingly, they agree that a verbal counselling should

take place prior to any disciplinary action. Should an employee's conduct or performance not improve after this counselling, the normal progression of discipline will be as follows:

- Step 1: Written warning
- Step 2: Second written warning
- Step 3: Suspension without pay
- Step 4: Termination

32.3 Notwithstanding clause 32.2, it is understood that certain offences are sufficiently serious to warrant immediate discharge and/or a faster progression through the process outlined in 32.2.

32.4 Employees have the right to have a union representative present during any of the steps outlined in clause 32.2.

The Case of Bradley Ennis (Version 2)[2]

The Facts

The facts of the case are not in dispute. Bradley Ennis was a registered nurse employed in the trauma unit of All Saints' Hospital. Ennis is now 45 years old and was hired by All Saints' Hospital on May 1, 1992. His performance was commendable. The hospital has a three-point performance rating system: (1) needs improvement; (2) satisfactory performance; and (3) superior performance. Each year between (and including) 1992 and 2007, Ennis received the highest rating of "superior performance."

In his role as trauma nurse, Ennis was responsible for monitoring patient care, administering potentially lethal drugs (e.g., narcotics), monitoring patient regimes, and counselling patients and their families concerning trauma care options. Accordingly, nurses on this unit were required to maintain certification as "trauma specialists." Ennis received this certification prior to being hired and had maintained it ever since.

Ennis was verbally counselled and received two written warnings for absenteeism on January 27, 2008, July 23, 2008, and October 15, 2008, respectively. He was terminated on December 3, 2008, following a three-day leave of absence without permission. The letter of discharge states that he was terminated for failing to call in sick as well as for excessive absenteeism (15 percent as against a hospital average of

7 percent). A union representative was present during each of the meetings where warnings were presented to Ennis. At no point during these meetings was Ennis reminded of the hospital's confidential Employee Assistance Plan (EAP).

Subsequent to the discharge, Ennis sought treatment for a drug (narcotics) and alcohol addiction. He has been in and out of counselling since March 2009. Between the initial treatment in March 2009 and the time of the arbitration hearing (February 25, 2010), he had three major relapses in which he stopped attending his counselling sessions (dates May 20, 2009, July 2, 2009, and October 25, 2009). He has been drug- and alcohol-free since November 11, 2009.

Ennis's addiction counsellor, Dr. Cooper, believes that he has a 65 percent chance of remaining chemical-free over the next few years. In Dr. Cooper's opinion, it was the unexpected death of Ennis's five-year-old daughter, who died at the ER of the hospital where he worked in December 2007, that caused the subsequent addiction. Specifically, Ennis was unable to sleep and started to use narcotics as a sleep aid. The narcotics were never stolen from the hospital; they were purchased elsewhere. Now that his client has recovered from this shock, Dr. Cooper believes that Ennis can maintain an acceptable attendance and performance record as a trauma nurse in the future.

Key Dates

May 1, 1992	Ennis hired
January 27, 2008	Verbal counselling
July 23, 2008	Written warning
October 15, 2008	Second written warning
December 3, 2008	Termination
March 2009	Ennis first seeks treatment
February 25, 2010	Arbitration

Regarding other employees, Ms. Gupta (his manager) states that only one other trauma nurse, out of a staff of 30, had an absenteeism rate greater than 10 percent (11 percent). That nurse was given a written warning. Since this warning, her attendance has been satisfactory. Hence, further discipline was not necessary in that case.

Relevant Collective Agreement Clause

ARTICLE 32—CORRECTIVE ACTION AND DISCIPLINE

32.1 Employees can be disciplined only for just cause. Such discipline must be reasonable and commensurate with the seriousness of the violation.

32.2 Both the union and the hospital believe in the concept of progressive discipline. Accordingly, they agree that a verbal counselling should take place prior to any disciplinary action. Should an employee's conduct or performance not improve after this counselling, the normal progression of discipline will be as follows:

- Step 1: Written warning
- Step 2: Second written warning
- Step 3: Suspension without pay
- Step 4: Termination

32.3 Notwithstanding clause 32.2, it is understood that certain offences are sufficiently serious to warrant immediate discharge and/or a faster progression through the process outlined in 32.2.

32.4 Employees have the right to have a union representative present during any of the steps outlined in clause 32.2.

The Case of Bradley Ennis (Version 3)[3]

The Facts

The facts of the case are not in dispute. Bradley Ennis was a registered nurse employed in the trauma unit of All Saints' Hospital. Ennis is now 45 years old and was hired by All Saints' Hospital on May 1, 1992. His performance record until 2008 was satisfactory. The hospital has a three-point performance rating system: (1) needs improvement; (2) satisfactory performance; and (3) superior performance. Each year between (and including) 1992 and 2007, Ennis received a performance rating of "satisfactory."

In his role as trauma nurse, Ennis was responsible for monitoring patient care, administering potentially lethal drugs (e.g., narcotics), monitoring patient regimes, and counselling patients and their families concerning trauma care options. Accordingly, nurses on this unit were required to maintain certification as "trauma specialists." Ennis received this certification in 1995 and had maintained it ever since.

Ennis was verbally counselled and received two written warnings for absenteeism on January 27, 2008, July 23, 2008, and October 15, 2008, respectively. He was terminated on December 3, 2008, following a three-day leave of absence without permission. A union representative was present during each of these meetings. At no point was Ennis reminded about the Employee Assistance Plan (EAP) in place at the hospital. On November 26, 2008, management found four containers of narcotics in his locker. This was the exact amount of morphine that Ennis had signed as being "contaminated and destroyed" on November 19, 2008. The letter of discharge states that he was terminated for failing to call in sick, excessive absenteeism (15 percent as against a hospital average of 7 percent), and theft of narcotics from the hospital.

Subsequent to the discharge, Ennis sought treatment for a drug (narcotics) and alcohol addiction. He has been in and out of counselling since March of 2009. Between the initial treatment of March 2009 and the time of the arbitration hearing (Feb 25, 2010), he had three major relapses in which he stopped attending his counselling sessions (dates May 20, 2009, July 2, 2009, and October 25, 2009). He has been drug- and alcohol-free since November 11, 2009.

Ennis's addiction counsellor, Dr. Cooper, believes that he has a 60 percent chance of remaining chemical-free over the next few years. In Dr. Cooper's opinion, it was the unexpected death of Ennis's five-year-old daughter, who died at the ER of the hospital where he worked in December 2007, that caused the subsequent addiction. Specifically, Ennis had started to take the medications to help him "de-stress" after this daughter's death. Now that his client has recovered from this shock, Dr. Bradley believes that Ennis can maintain an acceptable attendance and performance record as a trauma nurse in the future.

In terms of other employees, Ms. Gupta (his manager) states that only one other trauma nurse, out of a staff of 45, had an absenteeism rate greater than 10 percent (13 percent). She was given a written warning. Since that warning, her attendance has been satisfactory. Hence, further discipline was not necessary in her case.

Key Dates

May 1, 1992	Ennis hired
January 27, 2008	Verbal counselling
July 23, 2008	Written warning
October 15, 2008	Second written warning
December 3, 2008	Termination
March 2009	Ennis first seeks treatment
February 25, 2010	Arbitration

Relevant Collective Agreement Clause

ARTICLE 32—CORRECTIVE ACTION AND DISCIPLINE

32.1 Employees can be disciplined only for just cause. Such discipline must be reasonable and commensurate with the seriousness of the violation.

32.2 Both the union and the hospital believe in the concept of progressive discipline. Accordingly, they agree that a verbal counselling should take place prior to any disciplinary action. Should an employee's conduct or performance not improve after this counselling, the normal progression of discipline will be as follows:

- Step 1: Written warning
- Step 2: Second written warning
- Step 3: Suspension without pay
- Step 4: Termination

32.3 Notwithstanding clause 32.2, it is understood that certain offences are sufficiently serious to warrant immediate discharge and/or a faster progression through the process outlined in 32.2.

32.4 Employees have the right to have a union representative present during any of the steps outlined in clause 32.2.

Endnotes

1 This case is pure fiction and is not an actual arbitration. It was created for educational purposes by the second author.

2 This case is pure fiction and is not an actual arbitration. It was created for educational purposes by the second author.

3 This case is pure fiction and is not an actual arbitration. It was created for educational purposes by the second author.

Appendix B

Collective Bargaining Simulation: Consolidated Metals Ltd. (CML)[1]

Instructions

Below you will find all of the information you need to conduct a collective bargaining simulation, including

- the background of the organization (CML);
- the current collective agreement;
- a comparison of CML's employment package with those of its competitors; and
- a memorandum of agreement to record the settlement.

Your instructor will assign you to either the management or union team. Before beginning the collective bargaining exercise, each team should do the following:

1. Read the case materials.
2. Develop your bargaining goals and strategies.
3. Prepare the initial set of proposals that you will share with the other team. (Remember, this may not be your final bargaining goals—these are your opening positions.)

Your instructor will provide you with information about

- the length of the bargaining simulation;
- whether interest arbitration is available if you cannot reach a settlement in the time provided; and
- any report/assignment requirement. He or she may chose to use the assignment that follows at the end of this Appendix.

Remember, just as in the real world, your provincial labour relations act requires that you bargain in good faith and make every effort to negotiate a collective agreement.

The Consolidated Metals Ltd. (CML) Case[2]

Consolidated Metals Ltd. (CML) has been in operation for more than forty years and unionized since it was founded in 1971. It has always operated out of a facility on Main Street in St. John's, Newfoundland, because of that location's access to the harbourfront. Access to the harbourfront is critical for CML, which has traditionally manufactured steel and metal parts for fishing boats and vessels making transatlantic voyages. To capitalize on the traditional fishing and trading routes, CML acquired a second (nonunion) plant in 1985, which is located in Gloucester, Massachusetts.

The relationship between the management group of CML and the United Metal Workers of Canada (UMW) has generally been strong. Wages, benefits, and working conditions have usually been better than those the competition. In particular, the firm has tried to pay slightly above the going market rate. To date, there has been only one strike. It took place in 1990 and was largely centred on the issue of job security given the poor economic conditions of that period. At that time, the fishery was in a crisis due to the collapse of the cod fishery. Given the dramatic decrease in demand for its marine-related metal products, the company laid off about one-quarter of its staff and froze all wages for three years.

Fortunately, the development of several offshore oil fields in the area created a new market for CML. No longer exclusively focused on the fishing industry, CML now gets approximately 40 percent of its yearly revenues from the fabrication of metal products for the offshore oil companies and their suppliers. This new market has resulted in the firm hiring about 130 new employees over the past three years. As the parties prepare to enter a new round of bargaining, several key events are taking place.

For the union, the last contract (signed two years ago) was ratified by only 55 percent of the membership. Given the 1990 job cuts and wage freezes, many members felt that the new offshore contracts should have resulted in greater gains at the bargaining table. In fact, the membership voted in a whole new slate of union leaders to form this year's collective bargaining team. Word in the plant is that the membership wanted a more militant negotiations team that would take a firm stand on issues related to job security, increased wages, and improved vacations and pensions. It is also clear the union faces a challenge meeting the needs of a diverse membership. While the typical union member is 45 years old, with about 17 years of service, the current negotiations team will need to balance the needs of its newer members as well as those of the "old guard."

Management has just received notice that it is at risk of losing its largest offshore oil contract. Given the problems meeting the offshore production quotas, the management team has been informed that the present contract may not be renewed. Moreover, there is a rumour that a new firm may get the contract (Plant 2 in the attached comparison). This firm has the advantage of brand-new equipment. It currently runs three eight-hour shifts a day, seven days a week. Hence, it is in a better position to meet the needs of the offshore oil industry. Thus, CML management is currently examining the possibility of a substantial reorganization to better meet the needs of the offshore industry. This could include raising production quotas and replacing present equipment with new, up-to-date labour-saving machines in the St. John's plant (cost = $2 million). The new machinery would result in layoffs of about one-third of the staff and the contracting-out to cheaper labour sources in times of high product demand. Two alternative strategies have been openly discussed. First, purchase the new equipment (cost = $2 million) and move to a three-eight-hour-shift (i.e., twenty-four hours per day, seven days per week) operation. This option could occur without hiring any new employees or laying off any current staff; however, the firm's total payroll costs could not increase. Second, close the St. John's plant and move all production to the sister plant contract (Plant 4 in the attached comparison) located in Gloucester, Massachusetts, a cheaper location. This location would still permit shipping of the products to the offshore oil fields. The management negotiations team has been given a clear message that the collective agreement must facilitate the renewal of the key offshore contract and total payroll costs cannot increase.

Other Information

As is shown in Table 1, CML provides a competitive compensation and benefits package. The average wage in CML is $16.75 per hour. This compares to an average of $19.11 for the other metal manufacturers.

The benefits are co-paid (80 percent company, 20 percent employee). The benefits include dental plan, vision plan, life insurance coverage of two times base salary, medical insurance for hospitalization and prescription drugs, and a sick benefit plan (coverage up to 75 percent of earnings for any absence due to illness, maximum fifty-two weeks). Current cost of the benefit plan to the employee is $400 per year; the company share is $1,600 per employee per year.

In addition, CML contributes an amount equivalent to 7.5 percent of each employee's earnings into a retirement fund that can be used by the employee in retirement.

Costing Information for Any Proposed Changes

- *Overtime.* Each employee currently works an average of 5.0 hours of overtime per week. Overtime cost is time and a half. At present, employees have to volunteer for overtime.
- *Wages.* Present average is $16.75.
- *Vacation.* The current entitlement to vacation is as set out below (see next table). Any changes to the vacation plan would be costed using the following formula: Average hourly wage × 40 hours × Number of employees impacted.
- *Shift premiums.* Most employees (i.e., 60 percent) work day shift (8 a.m. to 4 p.m.). Forty percent of employees are permanently assigned to evening (i.e., second) shift (4 p.m. to 12 midnight). The shift premium is currently $1 per hour. There is no night (i.e., third) shift (12 midnight to 8 a.m.). If production is needed in the night shift, it is voluntary and paid at overtime rates.

Years of Service	Weeks	No. of Employees
Less than 1	1 day/month of service to a maximum of 2 weeks	30
More than 1 but less than 3	2	100
More than 3 but less than 5	2	10
More than 5 but less than 10	3	30
More than 10 but less than 15	4	40
More than 15 but less than 20	4	50
More than 20 but less than 25	5	100
More than 25 but less than 30	5	110
More than 30	5	30
Total		500

- *Retirement fund.* Currently 7.5 percent of regular wages are placed by CML into a retirement fund for the employee. Any changes should be calculated as follows: Average hourly wage × 40 hours per week × 52 weeks × % invested by the company.

COLLECTIVE BARGAINING AGREEMENT
Between
Consolidated Metals Ltd.
(hereinafter referred to as the Company)
and
The United Metalworkers of Canada
(hereinafter referred to as the Union)

ARTICLE 1. Recognition

Section 1.1 The Company recognizes the Union as the sole and exclusive bargaining agent for all employees at the plant located at 44 Main Street West, St. John's, save and except office employees, human resources management staff, security guards, and production supervisors.

ARTICLE II. Management Rights

Section 2.1 The Union recognizes that the Company has the exclusive right to manage the business and to exercise such right without restriction, save and except such prerogatives of management as may be specifically modified by the terms and conditions of this Agreement.

Section 2.2 The Union recognizes that the Company has the right to discipline and discharge employees for just cause.

ARTICLE III. Hours of Work

Section 3.1 The normal work hours for all employees shall be eight (8) hours per day and forty (40) hours per week, Monday to Friday.

Section 3.2 All time worked by an employee in excess of eight (8) hours per day or forty (40) hours per week, and all time worked on weekends, shall be paid for at an overtime rate of one and one-half times the normal hourly rate. All overtime is voluntary.

Section 3.3 Employees who work the second shift will receive a shift premium of $1.00 per hour worked.

ARTICLE IV. Seniority, Layoffs, Etc.

Section 4.1 An employee's seniority rights shall be measured on a plant-wide basis, starting from the first day or hour worked.

Section 4.2 In the event of a layoff, employees with the least plant-wide seniority will be laid off first, and employees with the most seniority will be retained, subject to their ability to perform the available work without being trained.

Section 4.3 In the event of layoff, the Company will provide a severance payment equal to four (4) weeks' base pay plus an additional one (1) week's pay per year of service.

ARTICLE V. Vacancies, New Jobs, Promotions, Etc.

Section 5.1 The Company shall post vacancies or new job openings on designated bulletin boards. Such postings shall include a statement of the required job qualifications, wage rate, and any other pertinent information. Interested applicants shall submit written bids to the Company's Human Resources Department. Any such jobs shall be awarded on the basis of seniority when the qualifications of applicants are approximately equal.

ARTICLE VI. Joint Committee

Section 6.1 The parties agree to the establishment of a Joint Labour/Management Committee composed of an equal number of representatives of the Company and the Union. The purpose of this Committee will be to provide a means of communication over any matter affecting the interests of either party to this Agreement. The Company may follow the recommendations of the Joint Committee. However, the final decision rests with management.

ARTICLE VII. Wages

Section 7.1 The following rates of pay will be operative for the duration of this agreement:

Job Grade	Job Titles	Hourly Rate Range
Grade 10	Janitor, Tool Keeper	$10.50–$11.50
Grade 20	Shipper, Receiver, Forklift Operator	$11.50–$12.50
Grade 30	Materials Handler, Order Processor	$12.50–$14.50
Grade 40	Machine Operator, Tin Cutter, Drill Press Operator	$13.50–$15.50
Grade 50	Quality Inspector, Smelter Operator	$14.50–$16.50
Grade 60	Trades (e.g., Welder, Electrician)	$16.50–$18.50

Section 7.2 All employees shall receive pay increases of $0.50 per hour six months after employment in their job grade, and every six months thereafter, until they reach the maximum rate of pay for their job grade.

ARTICLE VIII. Health and Welfare Plan

Section 8.1 The parties agree to the creation of a Health and Welfare Plan covering absence due to illness, dental care, eye care, life insurance, and supplementary healthcare needs (i.e., hospitalization and prescription drugs).

Section 8.2 The Company agrees to reimburse employees eighty percent (80%) of all costs incurred in respect of Section 8.1 above.

ARTICLE IX. Retirement Fund

Section 9.1 The Company agrees to place 7.5% of each employee's base annual salary, excluding any overtime or shift premiums, into a retirement fund for that employee. This cost is incurred solely by the Company. In addition, the employee can opt to place up to 7.5% of his/her salary in the fund.

Section 9.2 When the employee retires, (s)he will receive the entire amount invested per Section 9.1 on his/her behalf.

ARTICLE X. Vacation

Section 10.1 Each employee who has been with the Company for a full year will receive paid vacation as follows:

Years of Service	Weeks of Vacation
More than 1 but less than 5	2 weeks
More than 5 but less than 10	3 weeks
More than 10 but less than 20	4 weeks
Greater than 20	5 weeks

Section 10.1 Employees with less than one (1) year of service will receive one (1) day of vacation per month of service, to a maximum of ten (10) days.

ARTICLE XI. Grievance

Section 11.1 It is understood that employees (with or without the assistance of the shop steward) may bring a complaint to their immediate supervisor in an attempt to settle the issue at any time without filing a formal grievance.

Section 11.2 The formal grievance process will be as follows:

Step 1: The employee will (with his/her shop steward) present a written grievance to his/her supervisor. The supervisor will have ten (10) workdays to investigate the situation and respond. If the grievance is not satisfactorily resolved, it moves to Step 2.

Step 2: The grievance is presented to the department manager by the chief shop steward. The department manager will have ten (10) workdays to respond to the grievance. If the grievance is not satisfactorily resolved, it moves to Step 3.

Step 3: The grievance is presented to the plant manager and Union local president. The plant manager will have ten (10) workdays to respond to the grievance. If the grievance is not satisfactorily resolved, it moves to Step 4.

Step 4: The grievance is presented to the Vice-President of Industrial Relations by the President of the National Union (or delegate). The Vice-President will have ten (10) workdays to respond to the grievance. If the grievance is not satisfactorily resolved, it moves to arbitration and follows the current process outlined in the *Newfoundland and Labrador Labour Relations Act*.

ARTICLE XII. Progressive Discipline

Section 12.1 The Company and the Union believe in the practice of progressive discipline. Prior to formal progressive disciplinary action taking place, the employee may receive a verbal counselling from his/her supervisor. This will take place in the presence of the shop steward. The only documentation of this meeting will be the time, date, and nature of the discussion. This will be placed in the supervisor's file and will be moved to the employee's human resources file only if progressive discipline steps are taken within twenty-four (24) months of this counselling.

Section 12.2 The normal progression of progressive discipline shall be as follows:

Step 1: Written Warning
Step 2: Suspension
Step 3: Discharge

Section 12.3 It is understood that certain offences will result in a faster progression through the progressive discipline process outlined in Section 12.2.

Section 12.4 Copies of all written warnings, suspensions, and discharges must be given to the employee (in the presence of his/her shop steward). Copies will also be placed in the employee's human resources file. All documentation concerning progressive discipline must be removed from the employee's file after a period of twenty-four (24) months if no other disciplinary action occurs.

ARTICLE XIII. Duration

Section 13.1 This agreement shall be effective October 31, 2009, and will remain in force until October 31, 2011; thereafter, it shall be automatically renewed from time to time for further periods of one year unless either party, at least sixty (60) days prior to October 31, 2011, or any subsequent expiration date, serves on the other party written notice of its desire to terminate or amend the Agreement.

IN WITNESS THEREOF, the parties have caused this Agreement to be executed by their duly authorized representatives on this 31st day of October, 2009.

For the Company

John Smith _____

Samantha Chen _____

Hector O'Kane _____

For the Union

Rajeev Singh _____

Rita Knight _____

Glen Brown _____

MEMORANDUM OF SETTLEMENT
Between
Consolidated Metals Ltd.
and
The United Metalworkers of Canada

The parties agree as follows (use additional pages if necessary):

ARTICLE I. Recognition

ARTICLE II. Management Rights

ARTICLE III. Hours of Work

ARTICLE IV. Seniority, Layoffs, Etc.

ARTICLE V. Vacancies, New Jobs, Promotions, Etc.

ARTICLE VI. Joint Committee

ARTICLE VII. Wages

ARTICLE VIII. Health and Welfare Plan

ARTICLE IX. Retirement

ARTICLE X. Vacation

ARTICLE XI. Grievance

ARTICLE XII. Progressive Discipline

ARTICLE XIII. Duration

Signatures:

COMPANY	**UNION**
_____	_____
_____	_____
_____	_____
_____	_____

TABLE 1

Comparison of Working Terms and Conditions of Similar Firms in the Area

	Plant 1	Plant 2	Plant 3	Plant 4	Plant 5	Plant 6	Average
No. of employees	500	600	675	525	675	400	562.50
Unionized?	Yes	No	Yes	No	Yes	Yes	
Contract duration	2 years	N/A	3 years	N/A	3 years	2 Years	2.50
Average wage	$16.75	$16.50	$17.00	$15.20	$15.80	$15.40	$16.11
Year 1 wage increase	2.50%	3.00%	2.75%	1.50%	2.00%	1.75%	2.25%
Year 2 wage increase	2.00%	2.00%	2%	1.50%	2.00%	1.75%	1.88%
Overtime							
Voluntary?	Yes	Yes. But will assign in reverse order of seniority if insufficient volunteers.	No. Management can assign.	Yes	Yes. But will assign in reverse order of seniority if insufficient volunteers.	No	
Overtime rate	1.5	1.5	2	1.5	2	2	1.75
Vacation							
2 weeks at __ years	1	1	1	1	1	1	1.0
3 weeks at __ years	5	3	3	5	3	4	3.83
4 weeks at __ years	10	10	10	15	5	9	9.83
5 weeks at __ years	20	15	15	20	10	15	15.83
6 weeks at __ years		25	20		15		20.00
Shift							
Regular 2nd shift	Yes	Yes	Yes	Yes	Yes	Yes	
Regular 3rd shift	No	Yes	Yes	No	No	Yes	
Shift premium							
Regular 2nd shift	$1.00	$1.00	$1.50	$0.75	$1.00	$1.00	$1.04
Regular 3rd shift		$1.50	$1.50			$2.00	$1.67
Retirement/pension as % of wage rate	7.50%	8.00%	7.00%	N/A	7.50%	5.00%	7.00%
Contracting-out	No language	Only if no one on layoff can perform the work.	Only if no one on layoff can perform the work.	No restrictions	Yes. But only for jobs of <6 months.	No restrictions	
Layoff/severance pay	4 weeks plus 1 week per year of service	2 weeks per year of service	2 weeks plus 1 week per year of service	<5 years' service = 8 weeks >5 years' service = 15 weeks	2 weeks plus 2 weeks per year of service; maximum of 30 weeks	2 weeks per year of service; maximum of 26 weeks	

(handwritten note next to Plant 5 / Plant 6 "Voluntary?" row: "what does this mean?")

Negotiation Assignment

The negotiation assignment and simulation exercise requires each union and management team to participate in a negotiation simulation and to submit an assignment that critically examines the process and outcomes of this experience.

Using information provided in class, your textbook and the case assigned by your instructor, please answer the following two questions. The first question focuses largely on issues related to bargaining strategy; the second focuses on the collective agreement that resulted from your collective bargaining simulation. Note that the final assignment must not exceed ten pages of double-spaced text.

1. *Bargaining strategy*. Please answer the following:
   a. What bargaining strategy did your team plan to use in the present round of negotiations? Justify this choice.
   b. What bargaining strategy did you expect the other team to initially adopt? Why?
   c. What bargaining strategy did your team actually use in bargaining? Justify this answer and provide examples of tactics used during bargaining that are consistent with your answer. Explain why your team was, or was not, successful in implementing the strategy you had intended to use (see your answer to part (a) above).
   d. What effect, if any, did the bargaining strategies used by both teams have on your team's satisfaction with
      i. the outcomes of the negotiation process, and
      ii. the quality of the relationship developed with the other team?
   e. Do you think the other team was more, less, or equally satisfied with the outcomes and the quality of the relationship developed during negotiations? Why?
   f. Based on your experience from this round of bargaining, what bargaining strategy do you think your team and the other team would adopt if you entered a second round of negotiations? Why?

2. *Collective agreement outcomes*. Please answer the following:
   a. What were your team's priorities (maximum of 5 priorities)? Please rank these hoped-for changes in order of importance to your team (1= most important, 5 = least important). Justify your ranking.
   b. Discuss how your five priorities would affect the underlying interests of both your team and the other team.
   c. Were any of these priorities strike or lockout issues for your team? Please justify.
   d. Was your team successful in negotiating these priorities into the new collective agreement? Why or why not?
   e. What effect, if any, did the relative power of the parties have on the outcomes of this round of bargaining? Why? How could power affect the next round? Why?

Endnotes

1 The collective agreement and the assignment used in this case were both adapted from a version created by Andrew Luchak. Used with permission

2 This case was created solely for educational purposes by the second author. It is not based on any true company, union, or event.

Appendix C

Collective Bargaining Simulation: Wally's Janitorial Services[1]

Simulation Instructions and Background Information

Introduction

In this simulation, you will play a member either of the management bargaining team representing Wally's Janitorial Services Incorporated (WJS) or of the union bargaining team representing the employees of WJS. You will deal with a complex mix of bargaining issues, and you will be subjected to a variety of pressures during negotiations.

Advance Preparation

Before the bargaining session, you should read two sets of information:

1. The "Background Information," presented in this document under that heading. This is information that both management and union teams have access to.
2. The private team information. This information is not to be shared with your bargaining opponents. It will be provided by your instructor once he/she assigns you to a management or union team.

Specific Bargaining Instructions

- *Confidentiality of negotiations.* It is *not* necessary to conduct the negotiations in confidence. You are free to discuss your negotiations with other students in the class; however, negotiating may only be conducted during the allotted class time.
- *Bargaining issues.* Teams may only propose changes with respect to the issues provided in the case instructions. As members of bargaining teams, students may not manipulate any costs other than janitor salary costs. In addition, students cannot manipulate the level of firm revenue. They may only negotiate the four issues specified in the case.

- *Legal environment.* The legal framework for this simulation will be the *Employment* (or *Labour*) *Standards Act* and the *Labour Relations Act* of your province. Citing legislation is not appropriate for this simulation.
- *Role profiles.* Students may adopt specific roles as indicated in the text, but no detailed role profiles will be given.
- *Duration of agreement.* The agreement shall be effective for one full year (i.e., the teams are negotiating a one-year contract). Teams may not negotiate an agreement longer than one year.
- *Bargaining in good faith.* Teams are expected to bargain in good faith. In particular, they are required to meet and to bargain with the intention of reaching an agreement. Furthermore, once an item has been agreed upon by both teams, it is not appropriate to reopen negotiation of that item except by mutual agreement of the teams.

Background Information

Wally's Janitorial Services Incorporated (WJS) was founded in 1980 by three competitors who had been working separately as independent janitors in large office settings. As independent providers of janitorial services, these three men would bid on jobs to clean office or retail space for large companies who owned their own facilities or for landlords who included maintenance as part of their rental fee. Compared to an in-house janitorial department, the independent contractors could provide a lower cost option (because they were always bidding against each other) and superior quality (because they were held accountable for their services because their contracts could be terminated).

As a result of this fierce competition, the three independent janitors found they could only make a profit by staying in one location per shift. Generally, an office/retail space was cleaned twice a week. This meant that ideally a contractor would have only three clients at one time (each client is cleaned twice a week for six days of work per week). For an independent contractor to keep himself and his small crew busy for an entire shift (8 p.m. to 4 a.m.), he would require very large clients. Having a number of smaller clients meant additional costs in terms of vehicles and time to transport equipment and labour from one client's site to another. At the time there were only a few large office/retail spaces in Saskatoon, so the independent contractors would fight over these few profitable clients and then fill the remainder of their work week with non-profitable smaller clients as a means of keeping their labour employed. One particularly bleak February evening, the most junior of these men, Wally Wentworth, approached his two main competitors and pitched his idea to consolidate their efforts and form a new firm. The other two agreed to accept minority ownership and employment as executives in the new firm.

Since its inception in 1980, Wally's Janitorial Services Incorporated (WJS) has been growing along with the city of Saskatoon. It has retained market domination and continues to focus on large clients. WJS presently employs 95 people. Of this total 15 are nonunionized employees and work as clerical staff, managers, or executives. The remaining 80 employees are all unionized and are classified into 11 categories of janitors based on seniority. In Table 1 the total number of janitors in each classification and their yearly income is presented. Notice that after 10 years of service an employee is in the 10th classification and earns $50,000 a year. For these employees there is no further classification advancement or pay increase in subsequent years.

TABLE 1

Wally's Janitorial Service, Salary Schedule for Janitors

Salary Scale	Annual Income in $	2009 Number of Janitors	2009 Janitor Salary Cost in $	Current Number of Janitors	Estimated* 2010 Cost in $
0	24,000	4	96,000	4	96,000
1	25,000	6	150,000	4	100,000
2	26,000	4	104,000	6	156,000
3	28,000	8	224,000	3	84,000
4	30,000	0	0	7	210,000
5	32,000	6	192,000	0	0
6	36,500	5	182,500	6	219,000
7	40,000	3	120,000	5	200,000
8	44,000	4	176,000	3	132,000
9	50,000	5	250,000	4	200,000
10	56,000	35	1,960,000	38	2,128,000
Totals		**80**	**3,454,500**	**80**	**3,525,000**

*The estimated 2010 cost multiplies the 2009 incomes by the current number of janitors.

WALLY'S JANITORIAL SERVI3CE BUDGET INFORMATION

Current Year (November 2010–November 2011) Projected Budget

Total Revenue (net of taxes)		**$21,222,320**
Expenditures		
Administration:		
Professional salaries	$1,137,500	
Clerical/secretarial salaries	$ 281,250	
Other	$ 250,000	
Subtotal		$1,668,750

Capital and Other Business Functions:		
Equipment and vehicles	$ 6,558,100	
Marketing and sales	$ 1,420,000	
Aides	$ 1,187,600	
Materials/supplies	$ 943,750	
Subtotal		$10,109,450
Janitorial staff:		
Salaries	$3,525,000	
Training and certification	$ 975,000	
Insurance and safety	$ 258,750	
Subtotal		$4,278,750
Fixed charges:		
Retirement	$ 1,176,450	
Other	$ 425,700	
Subtotal		$1,602,150
Debt servicing		$1,026,000
Transportation:		
Salaries	$ 400,000	
Other	$ 395,000	
Subtotal		$795,000
Total expenditures		**$19,960,100**
Budget surplus (shortfall)		**$1,262,220**

WALLY'S JANITORIAL SERVICE
Previous Year Budget Information for 2009
(November 2009–November 2010)

Total Revenue (net of taxes)		**$22,099,897**
Expenditures		
Administration:		
Professional salaries	$ 1,137,248	
Clerical/secretarial salaries	$ 281,067	
Other	$ 261,129	
Subtotal		$1,679,444
Capital and Other Business Functions:		
Equipment and vehicles	$7,748,000	
Marketing and sales	$1,394,643	
Aides	$ 1,183,275	
Materials/supplies	$ 842,633	
Subtotal		$11,168,551

Janitorial Staff:		
Salaries	$3,454,500	
Training and certification	$ 812,268	
Insurance and safety	$ 225,198	
Subtotal		$4,011,966
Fixed charges:		
Retirement	$ 1,120,428	
Other	$ 324, 774	
Subtotal		$1,445,201
Debt servicing		$900,260
Transportation:		
Salaries	$ 399,698	
Other	$ 301,527	
Subtotal		$701,225
Total expenditures		**$20,386,647**
Budget surplus (shortfall)		**$1,713,250**

The ownership and management team is particularly proud of the work culture at WJS, which is considered a key to the firm's success. Most of the people who work for WJS have had trouble fitting into traditional jobs. Some of them have criminal records, while others are recovering alcoholics and/or drug addicts. Partly because of the difficulty in recruiting night workers who perform routine and sometimes distasteful work, the hiring philosophy at WJS has been much more inclusive than at other firms. An applicant's past is considered less important than an honest handshake and a promise from applicants to do their best and conduct themselves with integrity. This approach has worked very well. With few exceptions the employees are grateful for the opportunity and work very hard. The City of Saskatoon and the Saskatoon Police Services have recognized WJS efforts to successfully reintegrate felons into society with several Corporate Citizenship Awards.

In the late 1990s the city of Saskatoon suffered from an economic downturn. Several of WJS's clients went out of business or left the city. The downturn also created a second problem for WJS. A surplus of office/retail space caused rent levels to fall dramatically. With falling rent prices, the landlords who include janitorial services as part of their rental fee turned to WJS to renegotiate cheaper or reduced services (and sometimes both). The WJS leadership reacted by increasing the pace of work, freezing wages, and replacing any workers who were not willing to accept the "new economic reality." This led to widespread discontent among the janitors and the successful certification of a trade union. In January of 1999, the janitors of WJS formed Local 45 of the Canadian Union of Service Employees (CUSE). After negotiations a first collective agreement was constructed that provided some basic protections for workers. Since then the collective agreement has been successfully renegotiated several times without a strike or lockout.

It is now November 16, 2010. The contract between WJS and CUSE expired on June 30, 2010. Since then the WJS bargaining team and the CUSE bargaining team have met on several occasions in an attempt to finalize the contract, but these attempts have not been successful. There are several remaining bargaining issues, and while both sides are adamant that they wish to avert a work stoppage, they are facing tremendous pressure.

Despite the strong Saskatchewan economy, profits have fallen below acceptable levels. Out-of-province competitors from eastern Canada, fleeing contracting economies, have established a foothold in Saskatoon. Increased competition has forced WJS to lower their fees and reduced revenue. The WJS bargaining team believes that without concessions that allow management to reduce costs and improve productivity, the company is not likely to avoid massive layoffs.

For the members of CUSE, the strong Saskatchewan economy has meant the cost of living has dramatically increased. The workers feel they are entitled to a cost-of-living adjustment to reflect rising costs of housing, food, transportation, etc., in the city of Saskatoon. They also believe management should stick to their original instincts to trust the employees to do their best. They are resentful of policies that either monitor their work or speed it up.

Since the expiration of the collective agreement, there has been more and more talk among the membership of CUSE about the possibility of calling a strike if the contract is not finalized by the end of the fall. However, the executive of the union agreed that, in the interest of demonstrating their willingness to work with the WJS bargaining team, their members would continue with their normal duties, without a contract, on a day-to-day basis.

The union and the leadership team at WJS wish to reach a settlement and avert a strike; however, the union is adamantly committed to improving the conditions of its membership, and the management is just as committed to keeping its costs as low as possible so that it can reposition itself in the new, more competitive market. Nevertheless, each side feels it has room to negotiate on certain issues.

Final Settlement Form for the Four Outstanding Issues Between Wally's Janitorial Services and CUSE Local 45
(Hand in one form once negotiations are complete.)

1. Reduction in Staff

_____

_____

_____

_____

2. Salary

_____

_____

_____

_____

_____

3. Benefits

_____

_____

_____

_____

_____

4. Performance Evaluation

_____

_____

_____

_____

_____

| Management Names and Signatures | Union Names and Signatures |

Endnote

1   The authors gratefully acknowledge, and thank, Scott Walsworth (creator of this case) for allowing us to use it in the textbook.

Glossary

alternative dispute resolution (ADR) resolving disputes without going to court (p. 299)

apprenticeship a process in which trainees learn a trade under the supervision of a senior tradesperson (p. 108)

arbitration a quasi-judicial process whereby a neutral third party makes a final and binding determination on all outstanding issues in dispute (p. 45)

article a section of a collective agreement (p. 245)

attitudinal structuring the difficult process of building the mutual respect and trust necessary for an enduring and positive collective bargaining relationship (p. 211)

back-to-work legislation legislation requiring that strike action cease and employees return to work (p. 124)

balanced scorecard using multiple measures to assess a firm's effectiveness (p. 329)

bargaining unit the group of employees in an organization that are eligible to be represented by a union (p. 35)

base pay the part of pay that is solely based on time worked (p. 317)

bottom line the minimum position necessary in negotiations to avoid a strike or lockout; it represents for the union the best possible outcome short of strike (p. 212)

bumping a process whereby senior employees pass on their layoff to more junior employees (p. 259)

business unionism (or pure-and-simple unionism) unionism that focuses on improving wages and the working conditions of its members (p. 111)

certification recognition of a union by a labour board after completion of the procedures under the labour act (p. 32)

chilling effect the lack of bargaining flexibility caused by the parties' fear that a concession made in negotiations will reduce the arbitration outcome (p. 358)

clause a specific section of an article (p. 245)

closed shop a form of union security in which membership in the union is a condition of employment (p. 158)

collective agreement a written document outlining the terms and conditions of employment in a unionized workplace (p. 3)

collective bargaining the process by which management and labour negotiate the terms and conditions of employment in a unionized workplace (p. 4)

collective bargaining coverage a statistic that represents all of the employees, both union and nonunion, covered by a collective agreement as a percentage of the labour force; it is always a larger number than union density, because union density excludes nonunion employees (p. 345)

collective voice the ability of a group or union to express concerns (p. 313)

Committee on Freedom of Association (CFA) a special committee established by the ILO in 1951 to examine cases of labour rights violations (p. 398)

company union a union that a company helped create (p. 139)

conciliation see *mediation*

contract zone exists if each side's bottom line overlaps; in other words, to avoid a strike or lockout, management will offer more and the union will accept less than the point where their negotiating positions intersect (p. 215)

conventional interest arbitration interest arbitration where the arbitrator can choose among the proposals or fashion one of his or her own (p. 298)

conversion mechanisms the processes used to convert inputs into outputs of the industrial relations system (p. 13)

corrective action a warning process designed to improve employee performance or behaviour (p. 259)

craft or occupational unionism unions that typically allow into membership only trades or occupations that are in the same family of skills (p. 140)

Crown corporations corporations owned by the government (p. 124)

culpable at fault, guilty (p. 292)

defined benefit a type of pension plan that guarantees a specific payout (p. 322)

deregulation a policy designed to create more competition in an industry by allowing prices to be determined by market forces (p. 78)

disposable income income after taxes and benefits from social programs (e.g., unemployment insurance payments) (p. 91)

distributive bargaining a form of negotiations in which two parties compete over the distribution of some fixed resource (p. 210)

distributive justice employees' perception of fairness in the outcomes of workplace decisions (p. 179)

dues check-off a process whereby union dues are deducted automatically from pay (p. 118)

duty of fair representation a legal obligation on the union's part to represent all employees equally and in a nondiscriminatory manner (p. 37)

elasticity of supply (demand) the labour responsiveness of supply (demand) caused by a change in the wage rate; for example, if a small increase in wages causes a large increase in the supply of labour, the supply curve is said to be elastic (p. 80)

Employee Assistance Program (EAP) a counselling service available to employees (p. 321)

employee relations the study of the employment relationship between employers and individual employees, usually in nonunion settings (p. 4)

employee value chain a belief that organizational effectiveness is based on employee effectiveness (p. 329)

employment equity equity in employment levels and opportunities between targeted community groups (women, visible minorities, Aboriginals, and disabled employees) and major employers (p. 58)

employment relations the study of employment relationships and issues in union and nonunion workplaces (p. 4)

exchange rate the value of one country's currency relative to another country's currency (p. 11)

exclusive jurisdiction what exists when a single union represents all workers of a trade or occupational grouping (p. 111)

exclusivity principle the idea that a union is granted the sole right to represent all employees in the defined bargaining unit (p. 32)

explicit reference equity clause in collective agreements that specifies which groups are covered (p. 249)

feedback loop the mechanism by which outputs of the industrial relations system flow back to the external environment (p. 9)

final-offer arbitration interest arbitration in which the arbitrator must choose one of the parties' proposals (p. 298)

first agreement (or first contract) arbitration arbitration that determines the first collective agreement (p. 298)

gain sharing a group performance pay that is based on firm productivity gains (p. 321)

goal that which a person seeks to obtain or achieve (p. 12)

good faith bargaining an obligation on union and management to make a serious attempt to reach a settlement (p. 38)

Great Depression a period of significant economic downturn resulting from the stock market crash of 1929 (p. 116)

"great recession" a serious downturn in the economy around late 2008 characterized by very low or negative growth and high unemployment triggered by the financial collapse in 2007, the worst since the Great Depression of the 1930s (p. 78)

grievance a formal complaint that a specific clause in the collective agreement has been violated (p. 284)

grievance mediation a voluntary nonbinding process whereby a neutral third party examines the grievance (p. 299)

gross national product the value of all goods and services produced by a country in a year (p. 386)

high-performance work practices comprehensive human resources strategies designed to improve the effectiveness of the organization (p. 188)

hiring hall a union-run centre that refers union labour to job sites as requested by firms (p. 86)

human relations a managerial view that believes that effective management practices can minimize the conflict between managers and employees (p. 177)

human resources the study of the employment relationship between employers and individual employees (p. 4)

indirect pay (or benefits) anything that an employer pays for, to the benefit of the employee, that is not part of base or performance pay (p. 317)

industrial dispute a disagreement arising from entering into, renewing, or revising a collective agreement (p. 271)

industrial relations the study of employment relationships and issues, often in unionized workplaces (p. 3)

industrial unionism a type of inclusive unionism that represents a broad range of skills and occupations (p. 142)

industrial unions unions that organize all workers of an industry/workplace regardless of trade (p. 117)

inflation the increase in prices over time (p. 11)

institutionalists those subscribing to the theory that the operation of labour markets requires a knowledge and understanding of such social organizations as unions, nongovernmental community organizations, and international institutions (p. 137)

integrative bargaining a form of bargaining in which there is potential for a solution that produces a mutual gain; also called win-win bargaining, principled negotiations, and interest-based bargaining (p. 211)

intention to quit a survey measure that assesses the likelihood that an employee will quit (p. 329)

interest arbitration an arbitration that determines terms and conditions of the collective agreement while it's being negotiated (p. 297)

interest-based bargaining (IBB) a cooperative form of bargaining in which the parties focus more on the interests of the parties and not the exaggerated positions; also called *principled, integrative, cooperative, positive-sum,* or *collaborative negotiations* (p. 225)

interest rate the rate a bank charges for borrowing money (p. 11)

International Labour Organization a tripartite (government, management, and labour) agency of the United Nations with the mandate to establish and enforce global labour standards (p. 138)

intra-team (or intra-organizational) bargaining bargaining within union and management teams during the collective bargaining process; individual union team members, for example, may represent a group with particular interests, such as shift workers (p. 211)

job analysis a process whereby the key competencies for a job are identified (p. 317)

job evaluation a process whereby the firm determines the value of a job (p. 317)

job satisfaction an employee's assessment of his or her job experience (p. 329)

jurisprudence past decisions (usually in a legal context) (p. 291)

labour relations the study of employment relationships and issues between groups of employees (usually in unions) and management; also known as *union–management relations* (p. 3)

legislative reference equity clause in collective agreements that references legislation (p. 249)

letter of understanding letter between the parties, usually placed at the end of an agreement and describing a specific practice they have agreed to follow (p. 245)

lockout a work stoppage invoked by management (p. 272)

macroeconomic policy a policy that applies to economy-wide goals, such as inflation, unemployment, and growth (p. 78)

mandatory retirement a requirement that employees retire at age 65 (p. 12)

master–servant relationship the essence of the common-law employment relationship pertaining to nonunion workplaces; employment relationships in which employees have few rights (p. 107)

mediation a dispute-resolution process in which a neutral third party acts as a facilitator (p. 38)

meta-analysis a statistical technique that looks for trends across many studies (p. 325)

mitigation factors factors argued by the union for a reduction in a sanction (p. 293)

monopoly effect the union's ability to raise wages above nonunion rates (p. 317)

monopsony occurs when a firm is the sole market buyer of a good, service, or labour (p. 84)

multi-skill training training to provide employees with a variety of skills, some of which may not normally be part of their job (p. 254)

narcotic or dependency effect a result of frequent use of arbitration that may cause parties to lose the ability to freely negotiate settlements without third-party assistance (p. 358)

neoclassical economics view a view of industrial relations grounded in economics that sees unions as an artificial barrier to the free market (p. 16)

new model unionism the movement to trade (or craft) unions (p. 108)

new public management (NPM) a new approach to public administration in which public organizations are to become more decentralized, market-driven, and concerned with financial control, and managers more empowered and performance-oriented (p. 361)

nonstandard work arrangements work arrangements that differ from the norm in terms of employment term, location, schedule, hours of work, or pay (p. 194)

nonunion representation occurs when a group of nonunion employees meets with management regarding employment terms and conditions (p. 192)

North American Free Trade Agreement (NAFTA) a free trade agreement between Canada, the United States, and Mexico that was signed in 1994 and included a labour side agreement, the North American Agreement on Labor Cooperation (p. 78)

organizational commitment an employee's commitment to the organization (p. 331)

organizational justice employees' perception of fair treatment at work (p. 178)

participative management processes that ensure employee participation in workplace decisions (p. 190)

pay equity women and men being paid relatively equally for work of equal value (p. 58)

P.C. 1003 the Canadian government imported the *Wagner Act* model in 1944; under the *War Measures Act,* it was introduced by the Privy Council as P.C. 1003 (p. 31)

performance pay the part of pay that is based on output or performance (p. 317)

pluralist and institutional view a view of industrial relations stressing the importance of institutions and multiple actors (including labour) in the employment relationship (p. 16)

political economy a view of industrial relations grounded in socialism and Marxism that stresses the role of inherent conflict between labour and management (p. 17)

political nonpartisanship a belief that unions should not be aligned with any political party (p. 111)

power the ability to make someone agree to your terms (p. 13)

prima facie case union establishes, at arbitration, that the collective agreement was in place and that the grievor was employed, covered by that agreement, and disciplined. (p. 291)

privatization the transfer or contracting out of services to the private sector (p. 78)

probationary period a short period of time after an employee is hired in which he or she is not fully protected by a union (p. 314)

procedural justice employees' perception of fairness in workplace procedures (p. 179)

profit sharing a group performance pay that is based on firm profits (p. 321)

public good an item whose consumption does not reduce the amount available for others (p. 347)

public-sector or social justice unionism unions of public-sector employees at all three levels of government: local, provincial, and federal; typically advocates of a philosophy of social justice (p. 143)

pyramiding compounding of premiums or benefits (p. 256)

Rand Formula a union security provision in which employees do not have to join the union but all employees must pay dues (p. 158)

ratification the process by which each party approves the settlement reached at the bargaining tables by the management and union teams (p. 223)

recall the process by which a laid-off employee gets rehired (p. 314)

recruitment techniques designed to make potential employees aware of job openings (p. 314)

red-circling protecting employees' pay at a level higher than the normal rate of their current job (p. 250)

residual rights a principle whereby management retains all rights it held before unionization except those changed by the agreement (p. 248)

rights (or grievance) arbitration arbitration concerning alleged violations of the collective agreement (p. 290)

same-sex benefits same-sex partners receiving the same benefits as opposite-sex partners (p. 249)

scientific management the application of engineering principles to define specific tasks in the production process thereby removing the autonomy of skilled craft workers (associated with Frederick Taylor) (p. 29)

seniority the length of time a person has been a member of the union (p. 15)

shock effect occurs when increased costs and protection shock management into stricter management practices (p. 313)

Snider **Case** a landmark court case in 1925 that determined that labour matters fell under the purview of the provinces under the British *North America Act* (p. 30)

socialist unionism unionism that challenges capitalism and seeks equity for union and nonunion members (p. 111)

socio-technical systems design systems of new technology in which workers are complements to, not simply extensions of, technology; in which participation, communication, and collaboration are encouraged through an accommodative organizational structure; and in which individual workers achieve control through shared responsibility and minimal supervision (p. 364)

spillover effect a belief that increases in union wages result in decreases in nonunion wages (p. 320)

strategic choice framework a view that emphasizes the role of management and strategies in the industrial relations system (p. 180)

strategies processes developed and implemented to achieve goals (p. 13)

strike an action by workers in which they cease to perform duties and do not report to work (p. 4); a work stoppage invoked by a union (p. 272)

super seniority the status of union representatives who, while in office, have highest seniority in the bargaining unit (p. 260)

threat effect a belief that nonunion employers increase wages to avoid unionization (p. 320)

total compensation the total base pay, performance pay, and indirect pay that an employee receives (p. 317)

trade union unions that organize all workers of a trade regardless of their industry or workplace (p. 109)

transnational corporations (TNCs) global corporations that may integrate product chains horizontally; for example, parts of the final product might be made in a dozen countries spanning five continents (p. 385)

tripartite a tripartite board has three stakeholders: management, labour, and government (p. 32)

unfair labour practice an alleged violation of the labour relations act (p. 35)

union a group of workers recognized by law who collectively bargain terms and conditions of employment with their employer (p. 3)

union acceptance management's seeing unionization as a democratic right, and accepting that part, if not all, of its operations will be unionized (p. 185)

union commitment an employee's commitment to his or her union (p. 322)

union coverage a broader measure than union density; includes nonmembers covered by the collective agreement (p. 158)

union density a fraction that expresses union members as a percentage of the nonagricultural labour force (p. 157)

union removal a management strategy designed to remove the union from the workplace (p. 186)

union resistance a management policy seeking to limit the spread of unions in the firm (p. 185)

union satisfaction an employee's assessment of his or her union experience (p. 322)

union security the method by which unions are able to maintain membership and dues collection in a bargaining unit (p. 158)

union shop a form of union security in which new employees must join the union but only after a probation period (p. 158)

union substitution a management strategy designed to give nonunion employees all the advantages of unionization (p. 186)

utility function the sum of individual preferences for such measurable items as wages and benefits (p. 155)

values a set of standards or principles (p. 12)

voluntarism the notion that collective bargaining is a private matter between the parties and that government intervention should be kept to a minimum (p. 38)

wage differential the difference in wages earned by two groups of workers (p. 320)

Wagner Act named after the bill's sponsor, Senator Robert F. Wagner of New York, and more formally known as the *National Labor Relations Act* of the United States (p. 29)

wildcat strike an illegal strike during the term of the collective agreement (p. 272)

work to rule the strategy of employees who perform only to the minimum standard required (p. 272)

Index

Major components - CBA Simulation

1) Prep + Research
→ ⊠ Pg 415 → Consolidated mtlabs
→ complete "Preparation documents" 2 work on today kirst class.
+ Research → Literature Review from peer reviewed journals

2) Simulation -
→ out of class,
- after Nov 5/ before Nov 12 class   Chapter 7

3) Report → each mgmt/union group separately submitting report
→ ~~summary~~ executive summary / prep. documents/research/
methodology (chapter 7) → supplied by case concepts
& rationale → supplied by case concepts
→ new collective agreement (new activities)

4) Presentation   (Nov. 25)
10-mins (combined union/mgmt)
(focus on Pg. 422 of text Q1 + Q2)
↓
"Research" section
of Rubin + cause concept.

May 5 – IR – Complete
May 6 – T&D
May 7 – T&D
8 – T&D
9 – R&S
10 – R&S
11 – R&S
12 – R&S
13 – Comp.
14 – Comp
15 – Comp
16 – Plan
17 – Plan
18 – Plan
19 – Plan
20 – Plan IR
21 – IR
22 – IR
23 – OHS
24 – OHS
25 – OHS
26 – OB
27 – OB
28 – T&D
29 – T&D/Comp
30 – Comp
31 – Comp
1 – R&S/OHS
2 – Plan
3 – IR/

OHS
Comp
T&D
R&S
IR

3am

weekday 5pm to 10pm } 8hrs
3am to 6am }

4 chapters

weekend { 3am – 9:00am
9:30am – 5:30am
5:30am – 10 am

Enotes.

...it Ans - Smart
- A newspaper case
- 1st Par - 5
- 15

Read our the Chapter
Focus on the notes

~~6 Pages~~
10 Pages
5 Pages

Mon 18th Nov — Ch-7
Tues 19th Nov — ToD — 1st chapter
Wed 20 — ch-8 - 1R
Thur 21 — Ch-2 - ToD
Fri 22 — Ch-9 - 1R
Sat 23 — Ch-5 - ToD
Sun 24 — Ch-10 - 1R
Mon 25 — Ch-11 - IR
Tues 26 — Ch-12 - IR
Wed 27 — Ch-4 - ToD
Thur 28 — Ch-5 - T×D
Fri 29
Sat 30
Sun 1
Monday 2

White coat
Removable gloves
removable fur
Purse
velvet jacket
shirt
shirt - checkered
hanging sweater
navy jacket